FLOCKS © L. NICHOLS 2018
FIRST EDITION

PRINTED IN CHINA

ISBN-13: 978-0-9991935-2-5
ISBN-10: 0-9991935-2-X

SA 035

LIBRARY OF CONGRESS CONTROL NUMBER — 2017958131

PUBLISHED BY SECRET ACRES
200 PARK AVENUE SOUTH, 8TH FL.
NEW YORK, NY 10003

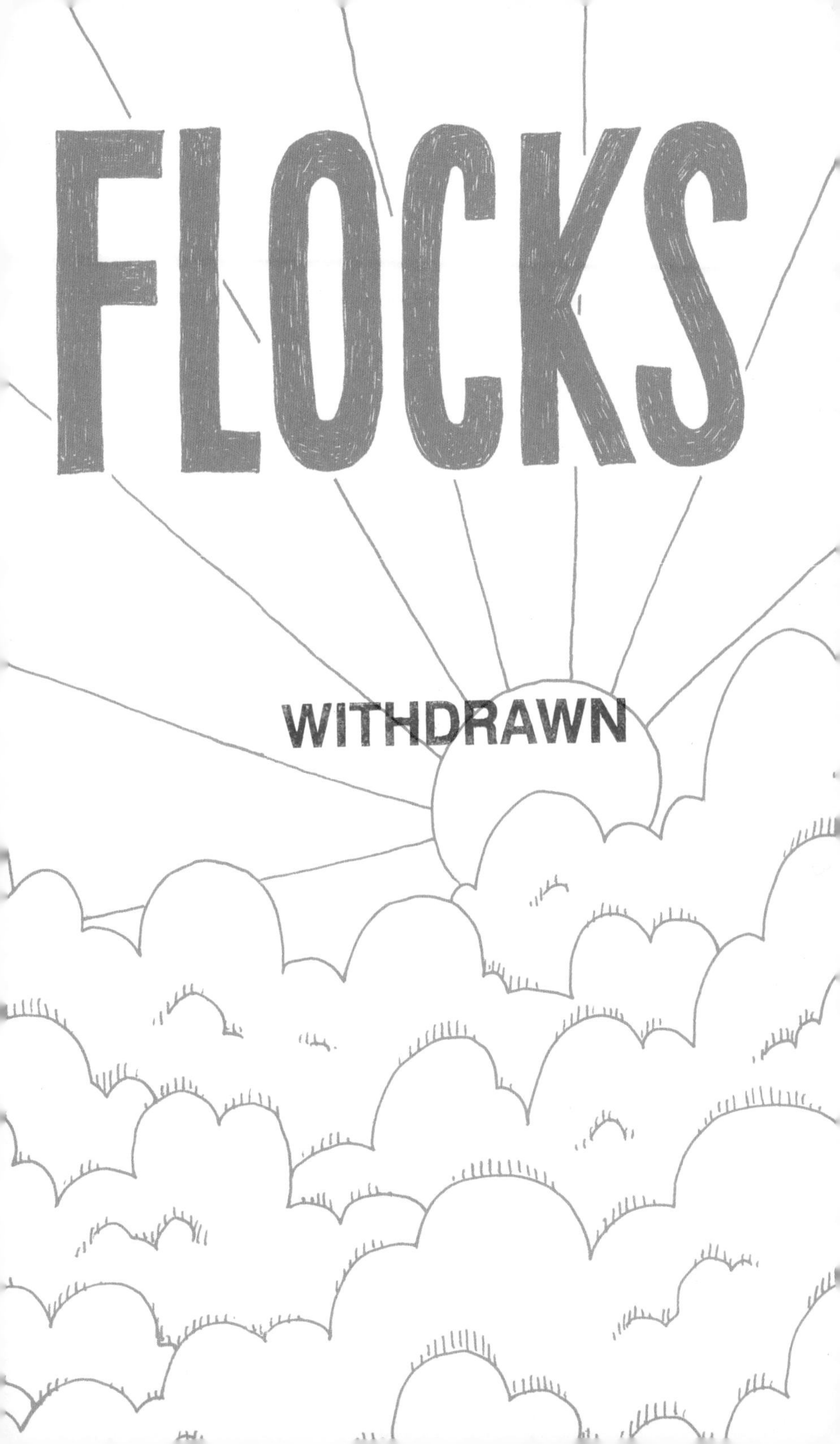
FLOCKS

FOR ALL THE PEOPLE IN BETWEEN
♡ I HOPE YOU FIND A HOME ♡

CHAPTER ONE

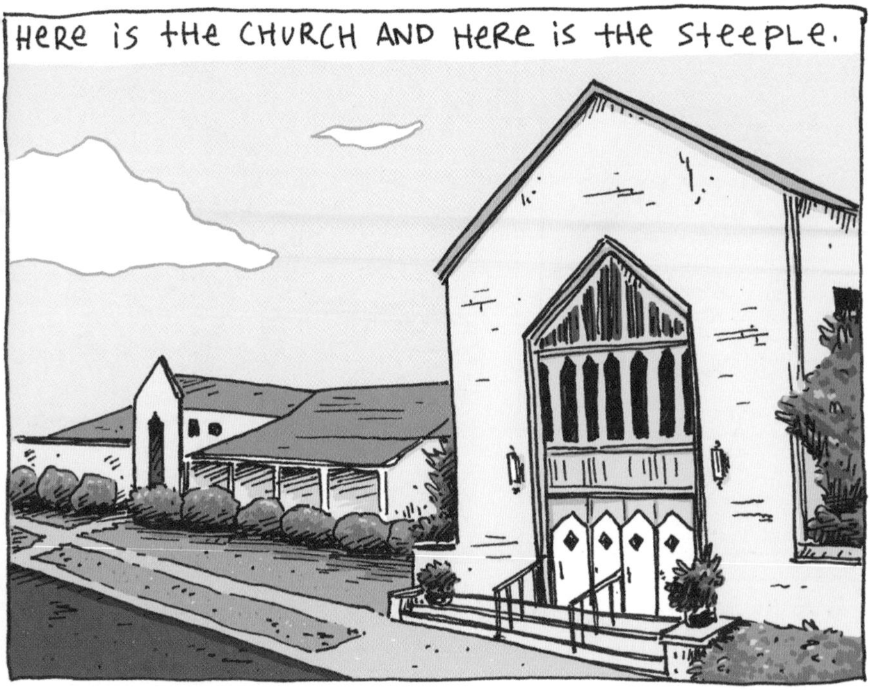
Here is the church and here is the steeple.

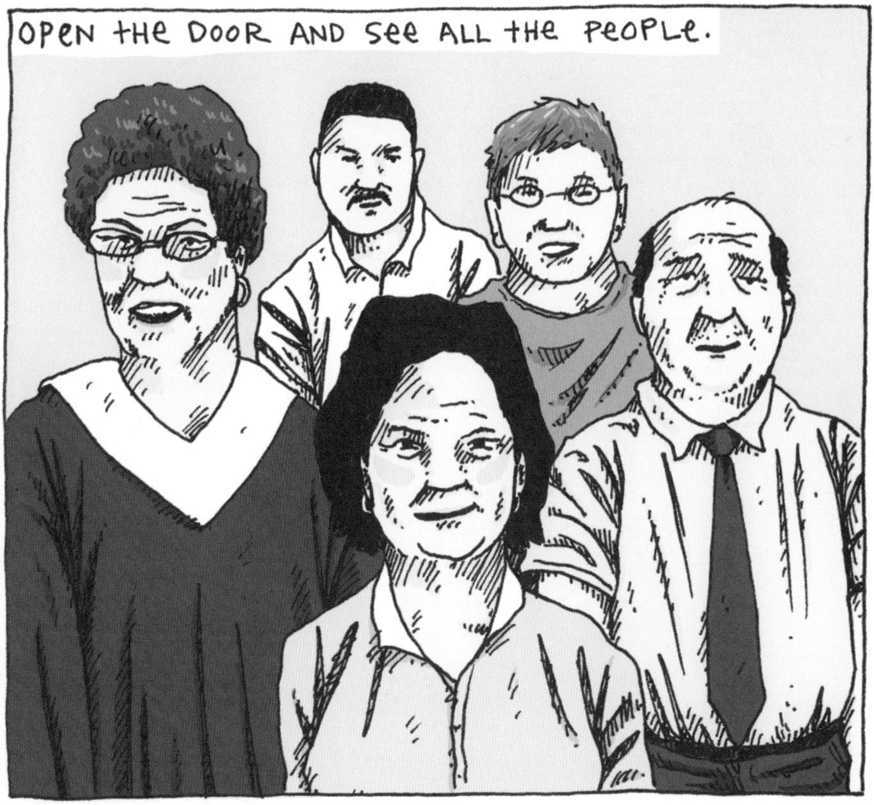
Open the door and see all the people.

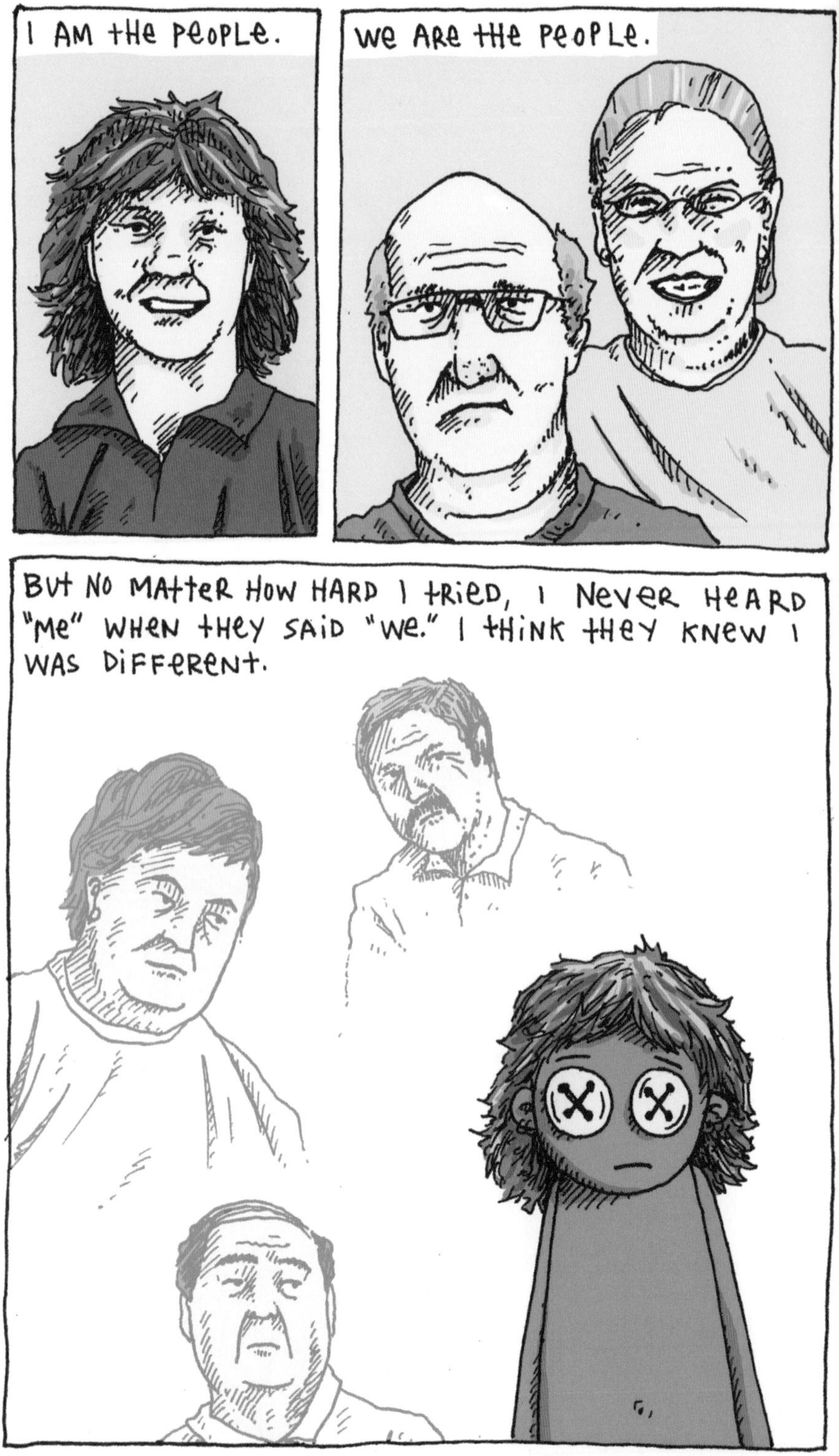
I AM THE PEOPLE.
WE ARE THE PEOPLE.
BUT NO MATTER HOW HARD I TRIED, I NEVER HEARD "ME" WHEN THEY SAID "WE." I THINK THEY KNEW I WAS DIFFERENT.

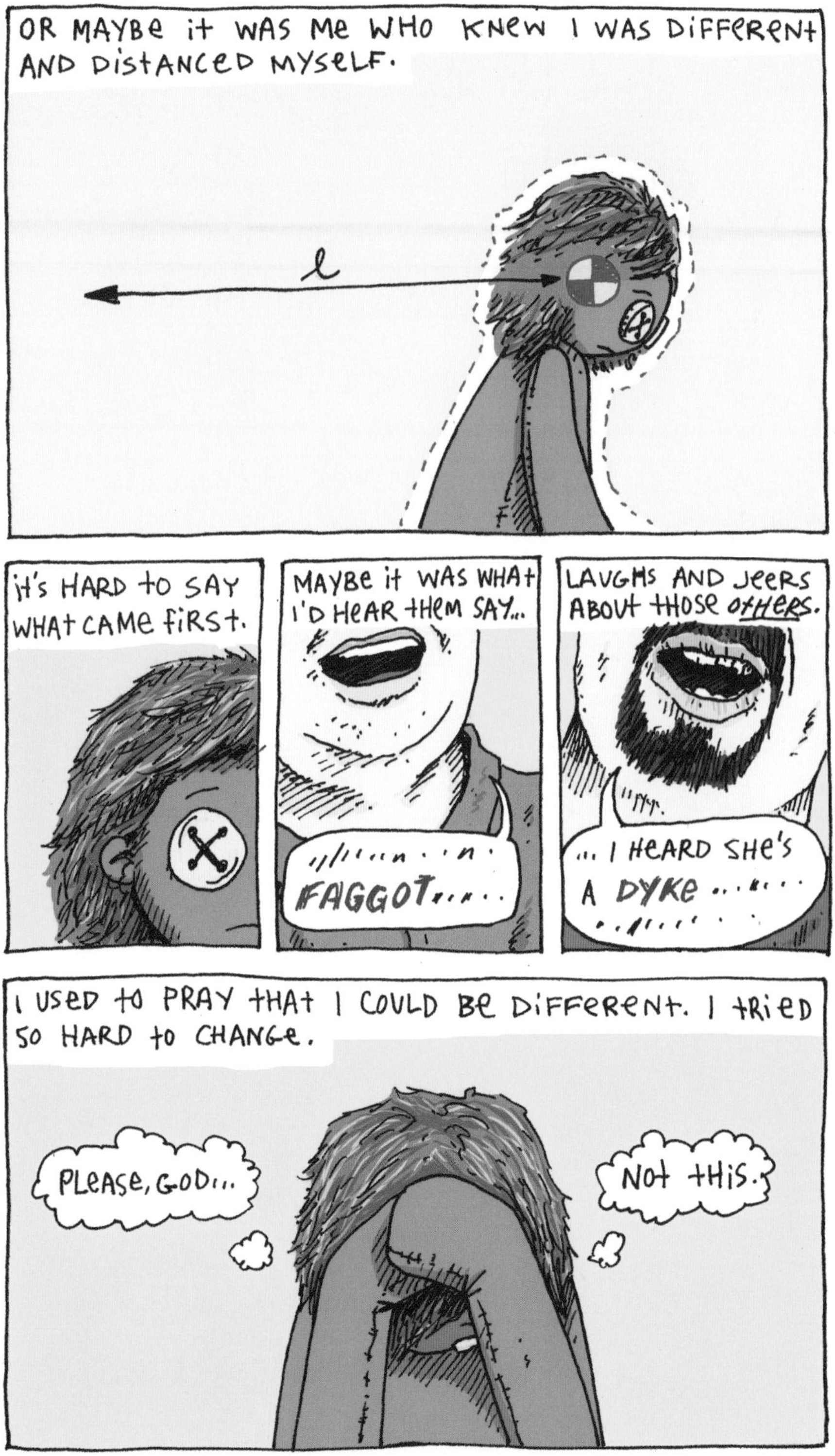
OR MAYBE IT WAS ME WHO KNEW I WAS DIFFERENT AND DISTANCED MYSELF.
IT'S HARD TO SAY WHAT CAME FIRST.
MAYBE IT WAS WHAT I'D HEAR THEM SAY...
FAGGOT...
LAUGHS AND JEERS ABOUT THOSE OTHERS.
...I HEARD SHE'S A DYKE...
I USED TO PRAY THAT I COULD BE DIFFERENT. I TRIED SO HARD TO CHANGE.
PLEASE, GOD...
NOT THIS.

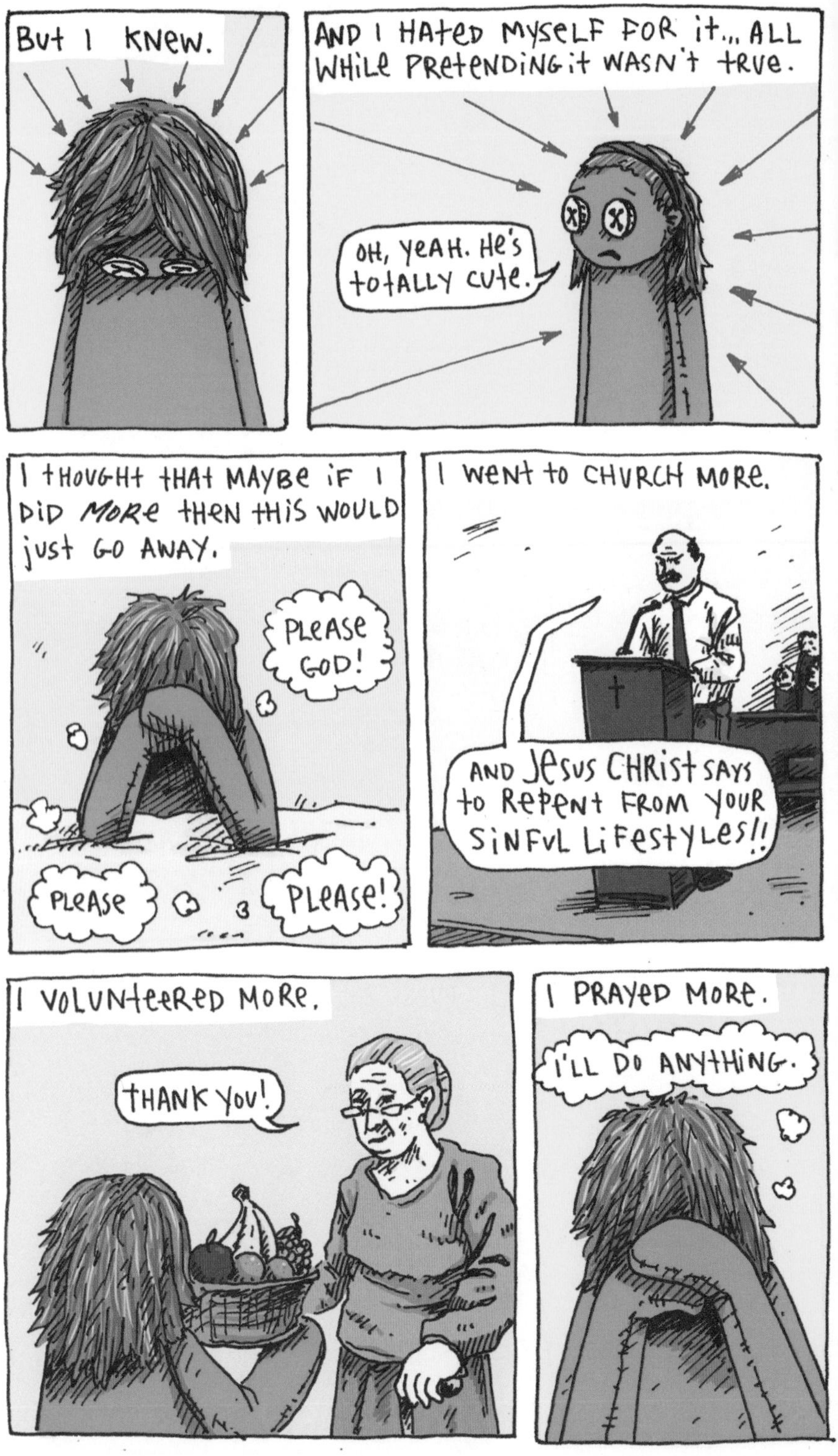
But I KNEW.
AND I HATED MYSELF FOR it... ALL WHILE PRETENDING it WASN'T TRUE.
OH, YEAH. He's totally cute.
I THOUGHT THAT MAYBE IF I DID MORE THEN THIS WOULD just GO AWAY.
PLEASE GOD!
PLEASE
PLEASE!
I WENT to CHURCH MORE.
AND JESUS CHRIST SAYS to REPENT FROM YOUR SINFUL LIFESTYLES!!
I VOLUNTEERED MORE.
THANK YOU!
I PRAYED MORE.
I'LL DO ANYTHING.

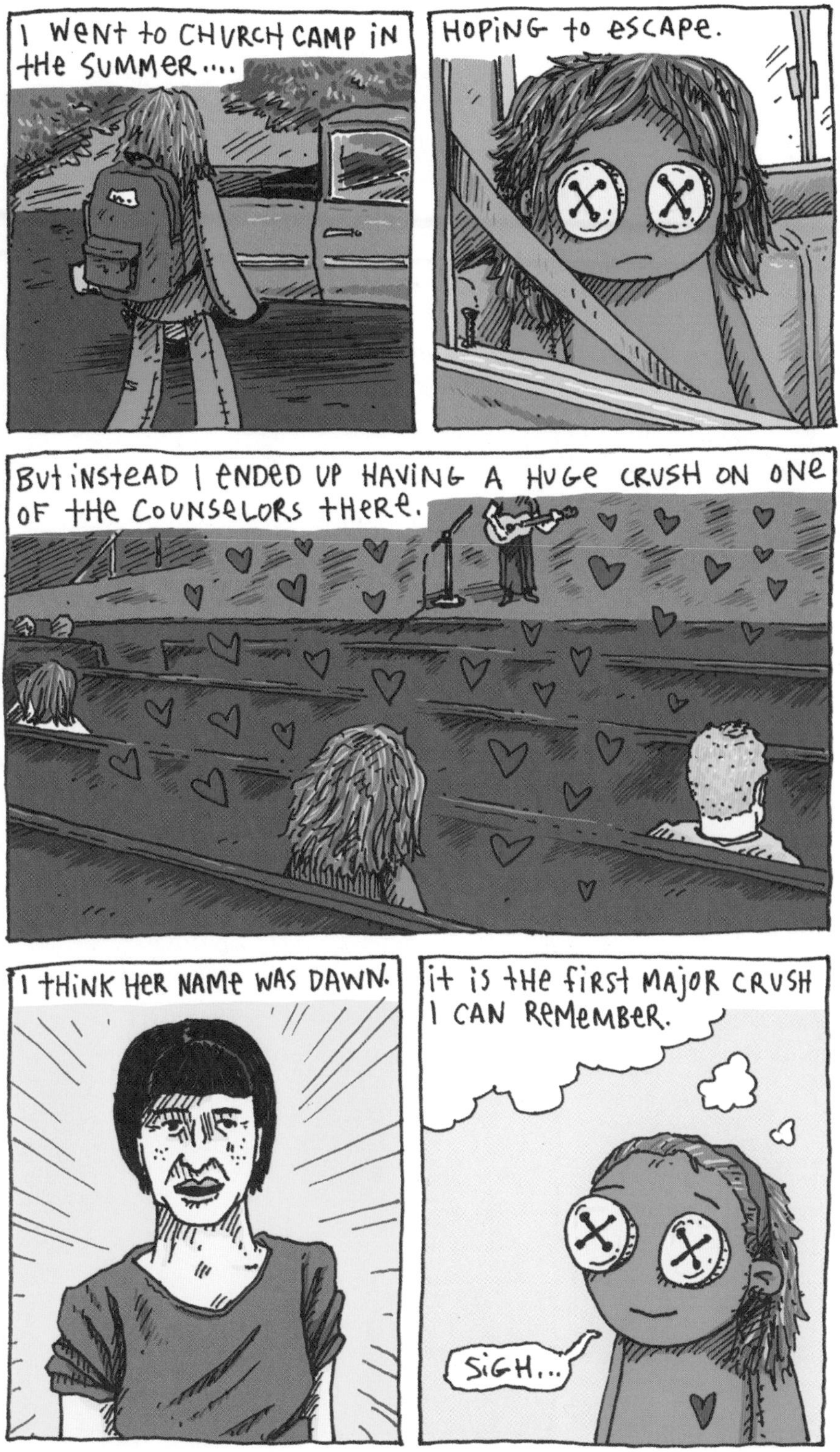
I WENT to CHURCH CAMP IN tHE SUMMER....
HOPING to escape.
But iNStEAD I ENDED UP HAVING A HUGE CRUSH ON ONE OF tHE COUNSELORS tHERE.
I tHINK HER NAME WAS DAWN.
it is tHE first MAJOR CRUSH I CAN REMEMBER.
SiGH...

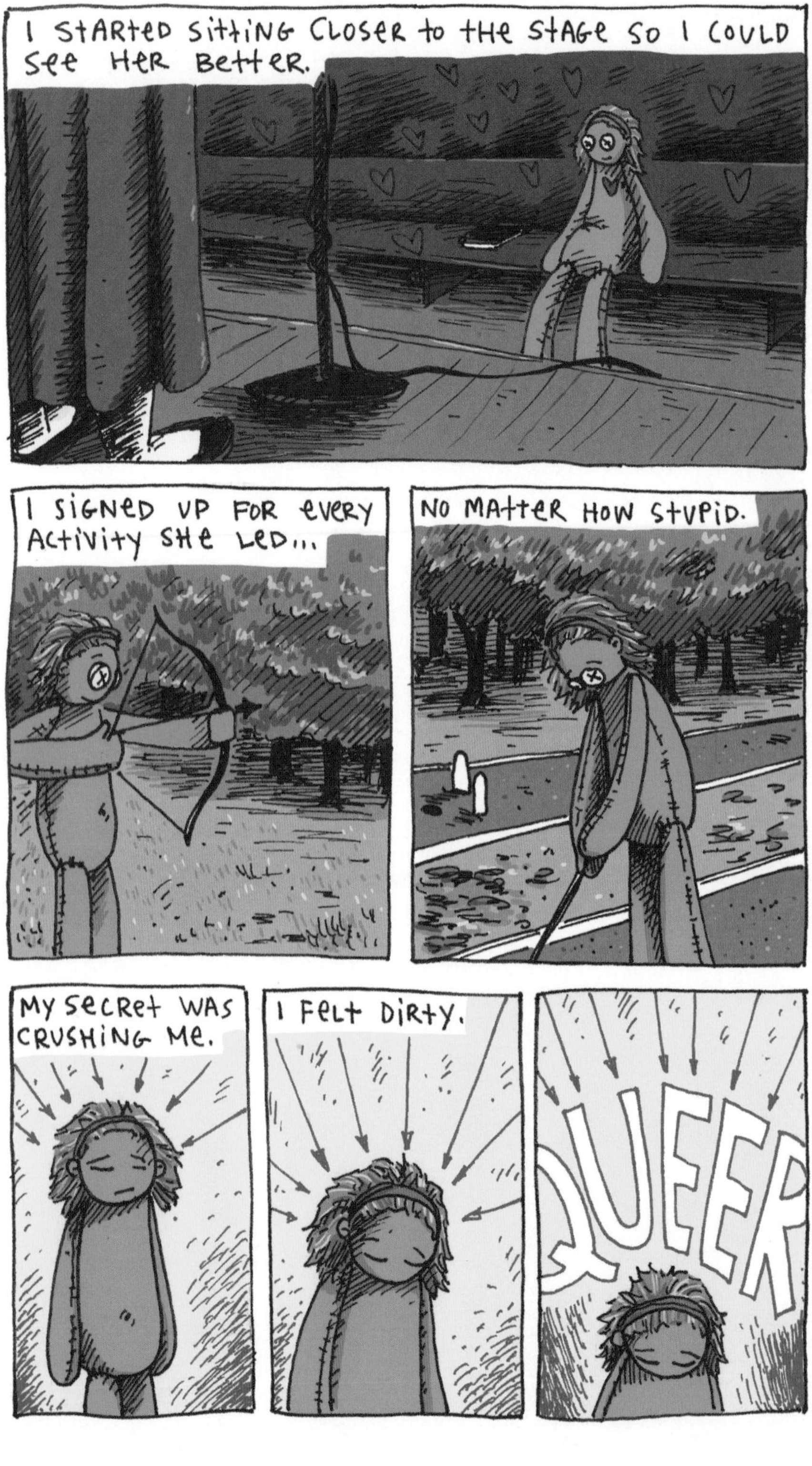
I STARTED SITTING CLOSER TO THE STAGE SO I COULD SEE HER BETTER.
I SIGNED UP FOR EVERY ACTIVITY SHE LED...
NO MATTER HOW STUPID.
MY SECRET WAS CRUSHING ME.
I FELT DIRTY.
QUEER

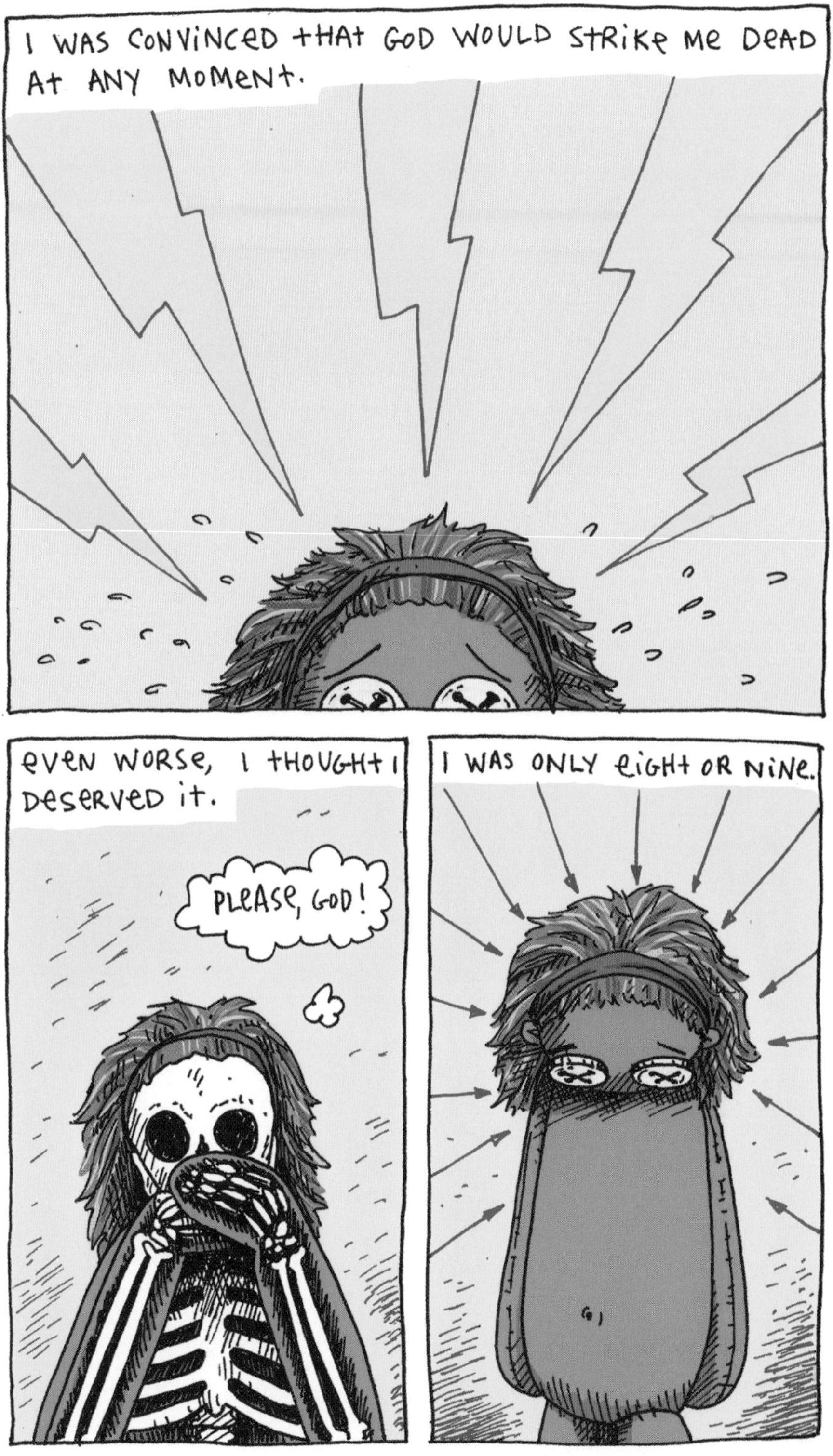
I WAS CONVINCED THAT GOD WOULD STRIKE ME DEAD AT ANY MOMENT.
EVEN WORSE, I THOUGHT I DESERVED IT.
PLEASE, GOD!
I WAS ONLY EIGHT OR NINE.

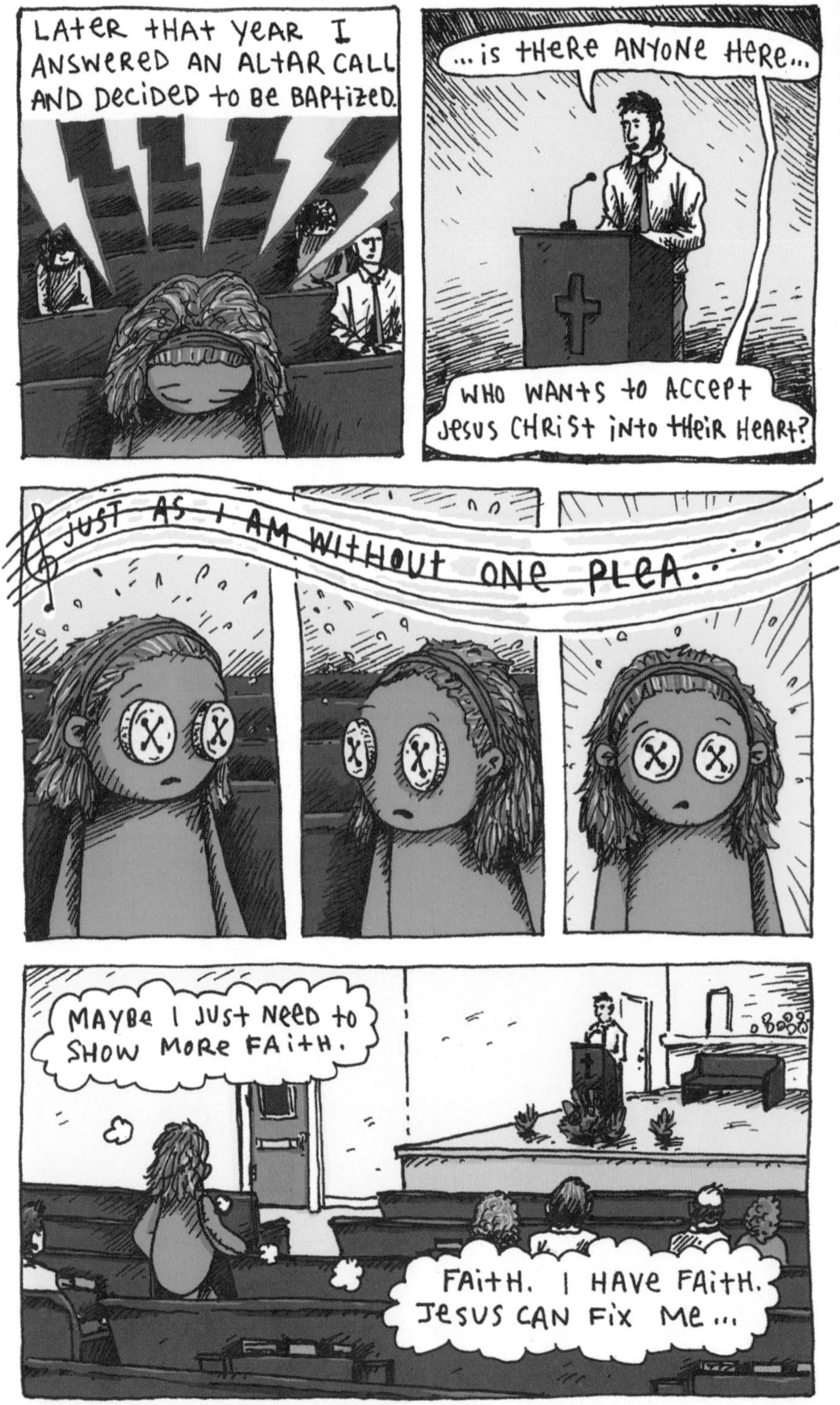
LATER THAT YEAR I ANSWERED AN ALTAR CALL AND DECIDED TO BE BAPTIZED.
...IS THERE ANYONE HERE...
WHO WANTS TO ACCEPT JESUS CHRIST INTO THEIR HEART?
JUST AS I AM WITHOUT ONE PLEA...
MAYBE I JUST NEED TO SHOW MORE FAITH.
FAITH. I HAVE FAITH. JESUS CAN FIX ME...

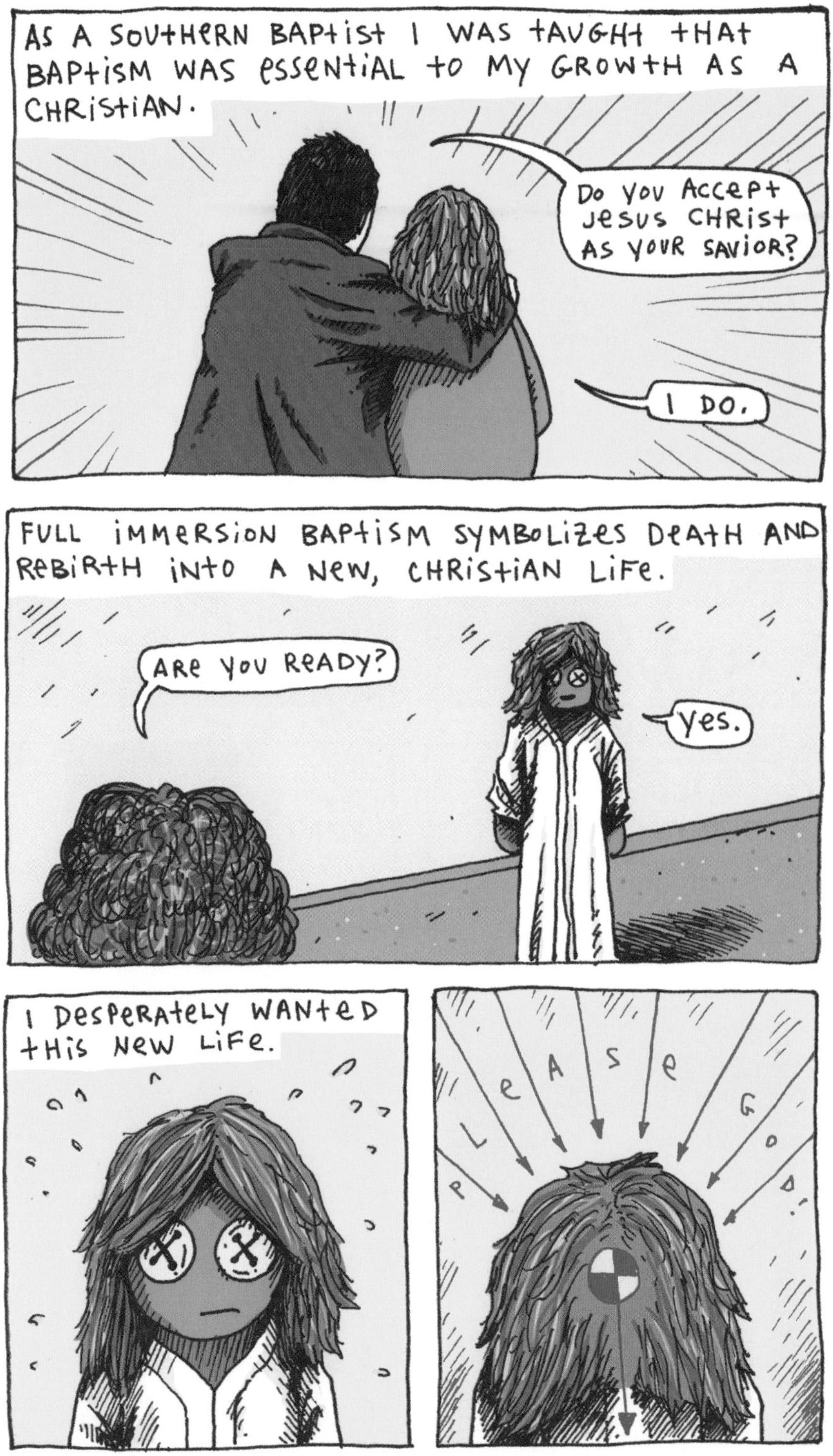
AS A SOUTHERN BAPTIST I WAS TAUGHT THAT BAPTISM WAS ESSENTIAL TO MY GROWTH AS A CHRISTIAN.
DO YOU ACCEPT JESUS CHRIST AS YOUR SAVIOR?
I DO.
FULL IMMERSION BAPTISM SYMBOLIZES DEATH AND REBIRTH INTO A NEW, CHRISTIAN LIFE.
ARE YOU READY?
YES.
I DESPERATELY WANTED THIS NEW LIFE.
PLEASE GOD.

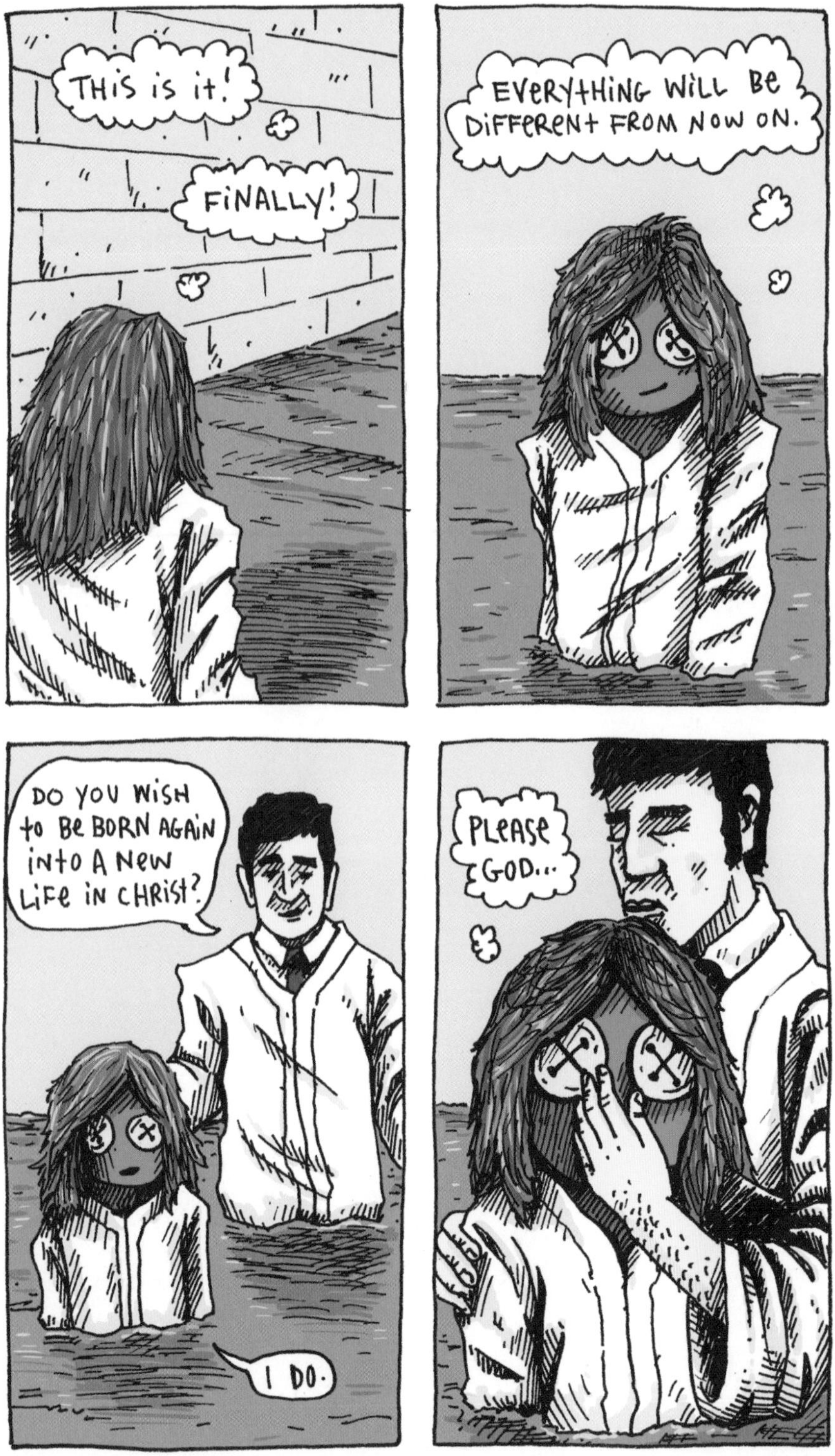
THIS is it!
FINALLY!
EVERYTHING WILL BE DIFFERENT FROM NOW ON.
DO YOU WISH to BE BORN AGAIN into A NEW LIFE in CHRIST?
I DO.
PLEASE GOD...

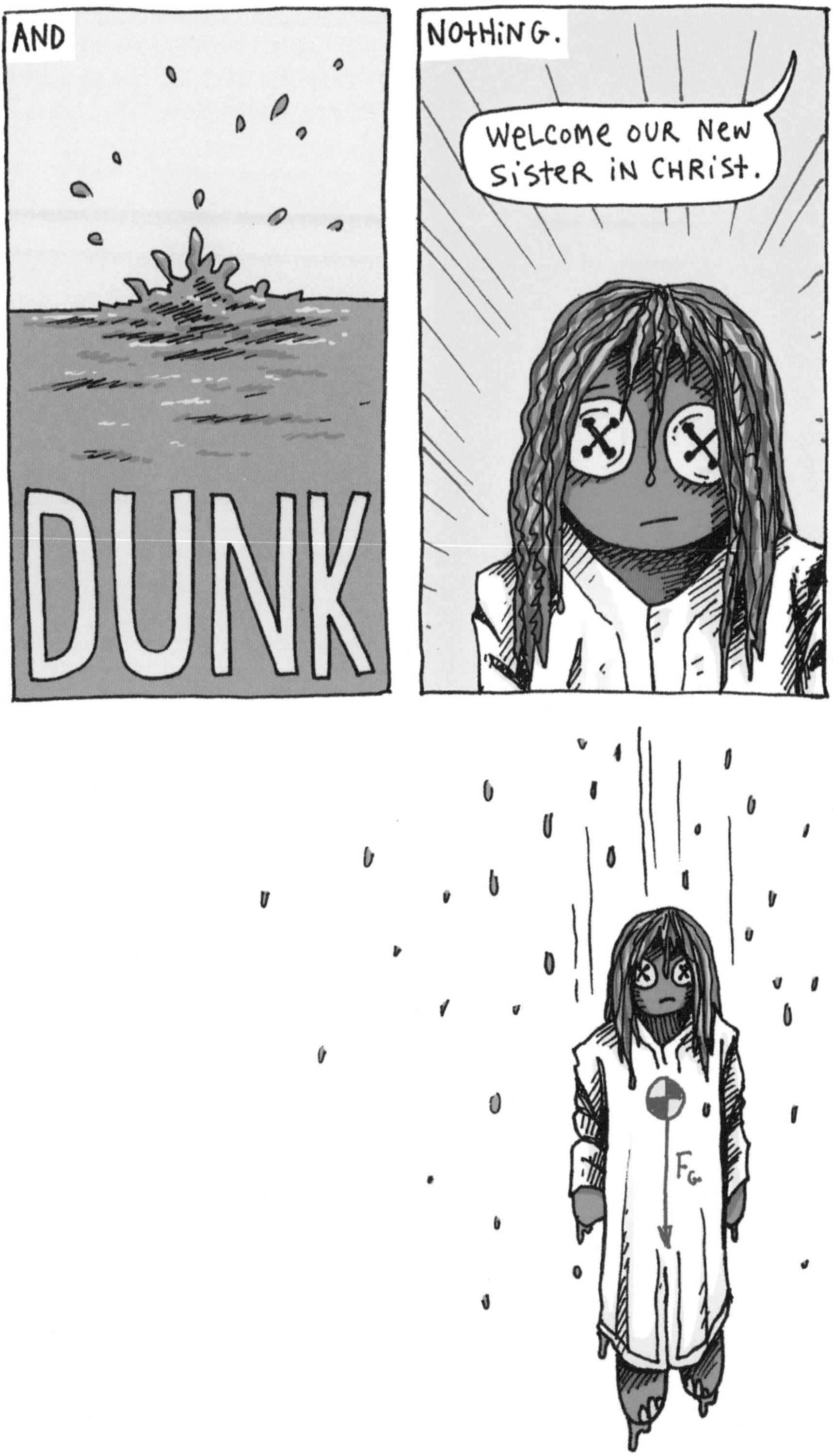
AND
DUNK
NOTHING.
WELCOME OUR NEW SISTER IN CHRIST.
FG

I BLAMED MYSELF FOR THIS.

INSTEAD OF QUESTIONING THE CHURCH'S TEACHINGS, I THREW MYSELF EVEN FURTHER IN.

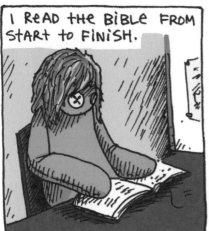

I READ THE BIBLE FROM START TO FINISH.

I WENT TO SUNDAY SCHOOL.

I SANG IN THE CHURCH CHOIR.

I WENT TO THE SUNDAY EVENING SERVICE...

AND ALSO TO THE WEDNESDAY EVENING ONE.

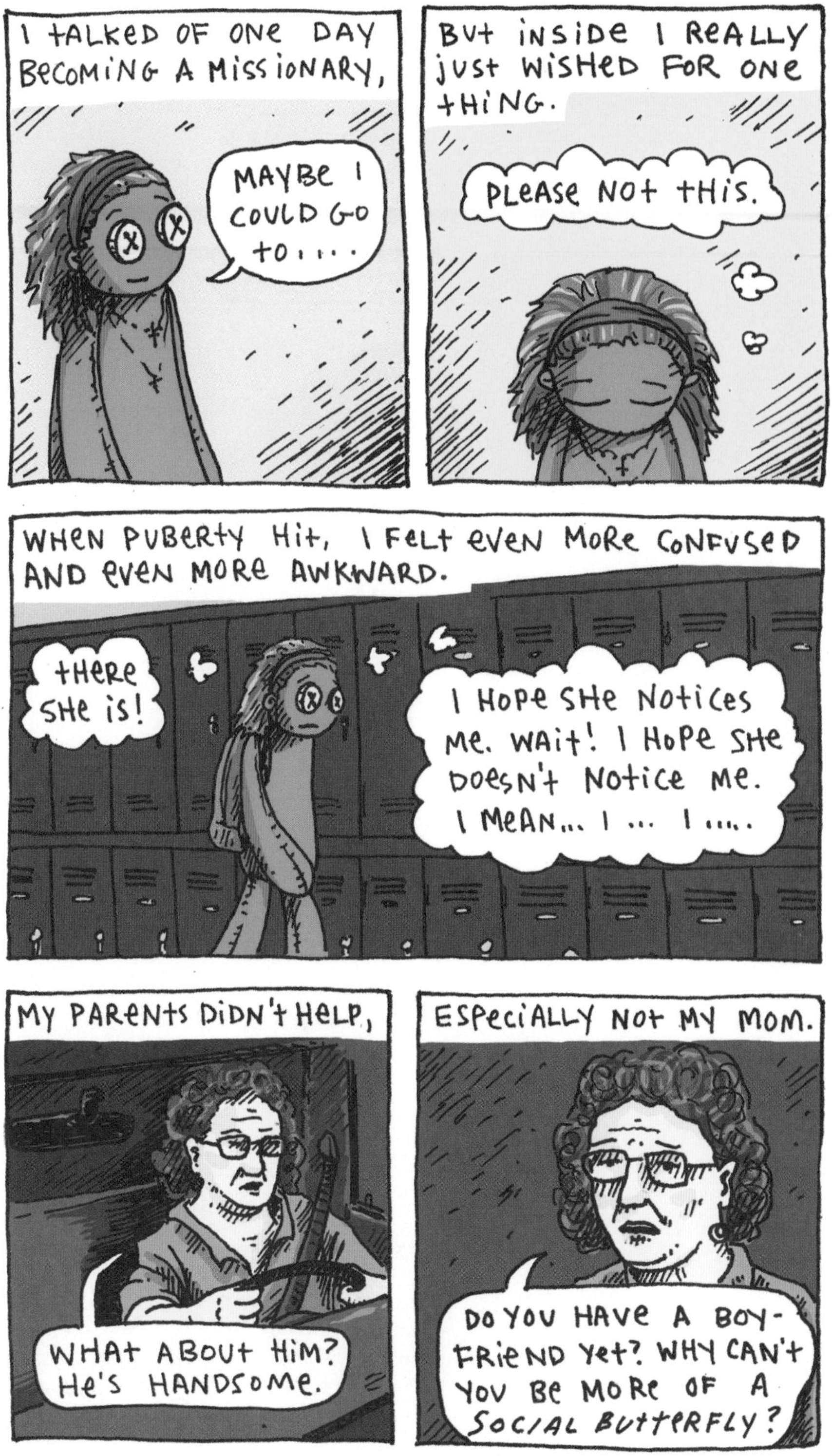
I TALKED OF ONE DAY BECOMING A MISSIONARY,
MAYBE I COULD GO TO....
BUT INSIDE I REALLY JUST WISHED FOR ONE THING.
PLEASE NOT THIS.
WHEN PUBERTY HIT, I FELT EVEN MORE CONFUSED AND EVEN MORE AWKWARD.
THERE SHE IS!
I HOPE SHE NOTICES ME. WAIT! I HOPE SHE DOESN'T NOTICE ME. I MEAN... I ... I.....
MY PARENTS DIDN'T HELP,
WHAT ABOUT HIM? HE'S HANDSOME.
ESPECIALLY NOT MY MOM.
DO YOU HAVE A BOY-FRIEND YET? WHY CAN'T YOU BE MORE OF A *SOCIAL BUTTERFLY*?

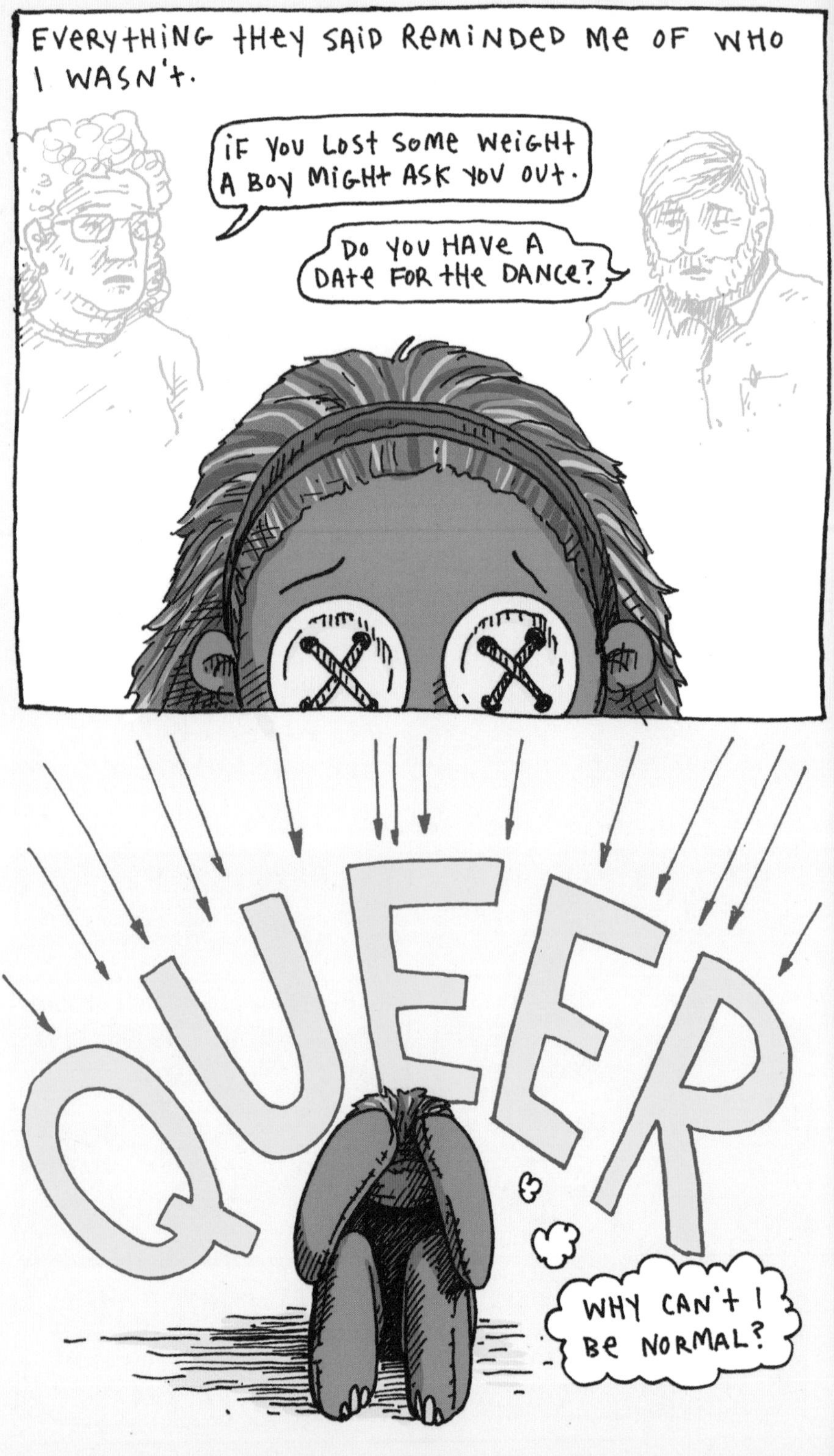
EVERYTHING THEY SAID REMINDED ME OF WHO I WASN'T.
IF YOU LOST SOME WEIGHT A BOY MIGHT ASK YOU OUT.
DO YOU HAVE A DATE FOR THE DANCE?
QUEER
WHY CAN'T I BE NORMAL?

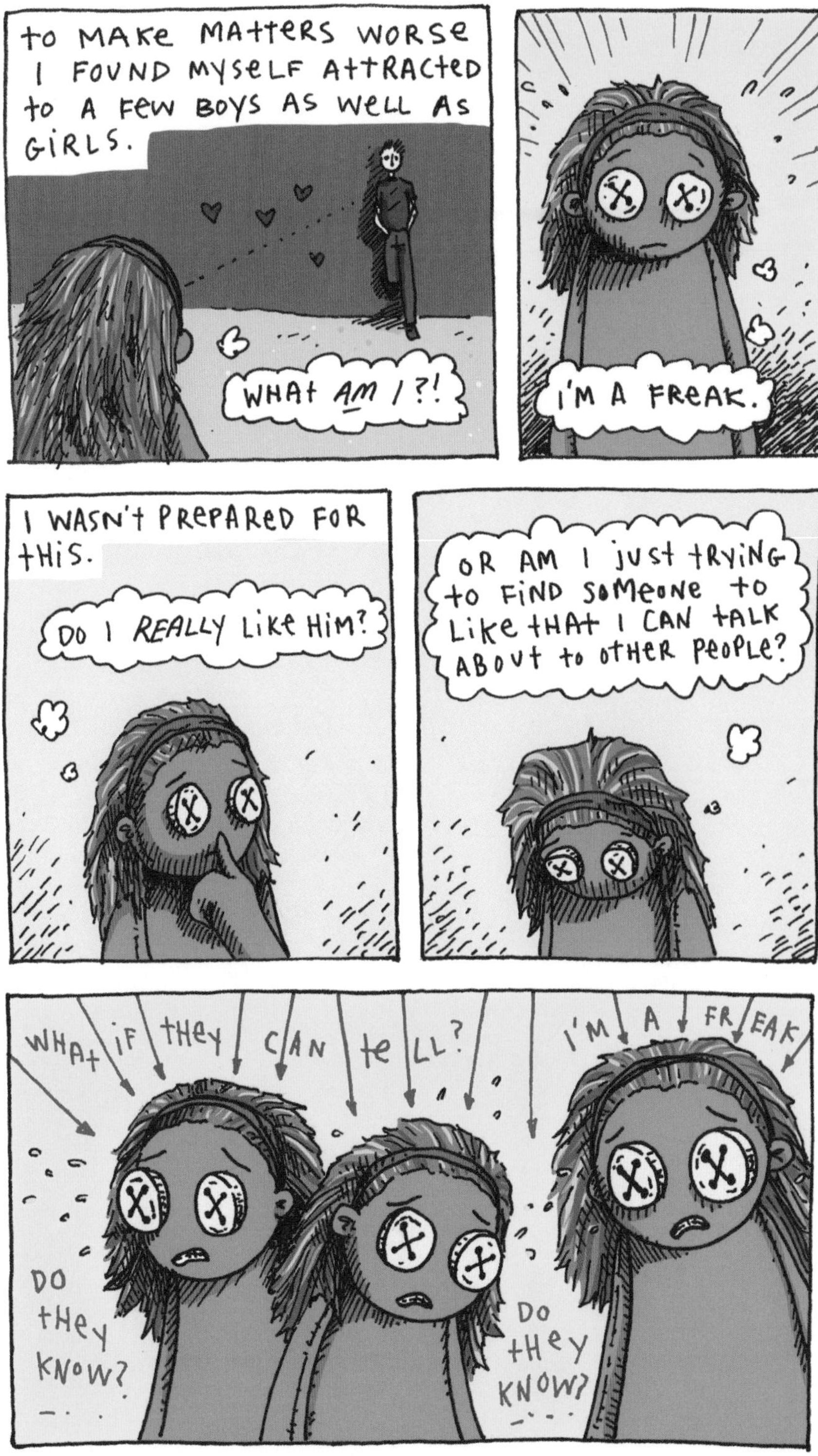
TO MAKE MATTERS WORSE I FOUND MYSELF ATTRACTED TO A FEW BOYS AS WELL AS GIRLS.
WHAT AM I?!
I'M A FREAK.
I WASN'T PREPARED FOR THIS.
DO I REALLY LIKE HIM?
OR AM I JUST TRYING TO FIND SOMEONE TO LIKE THAT I CAN TALK ABOUT TO OTHER PEOPLE?
WHAT IF THEY CAN TELL?
I'M A FREAK
DO THEY KNOW?
DO THEY KNOW?

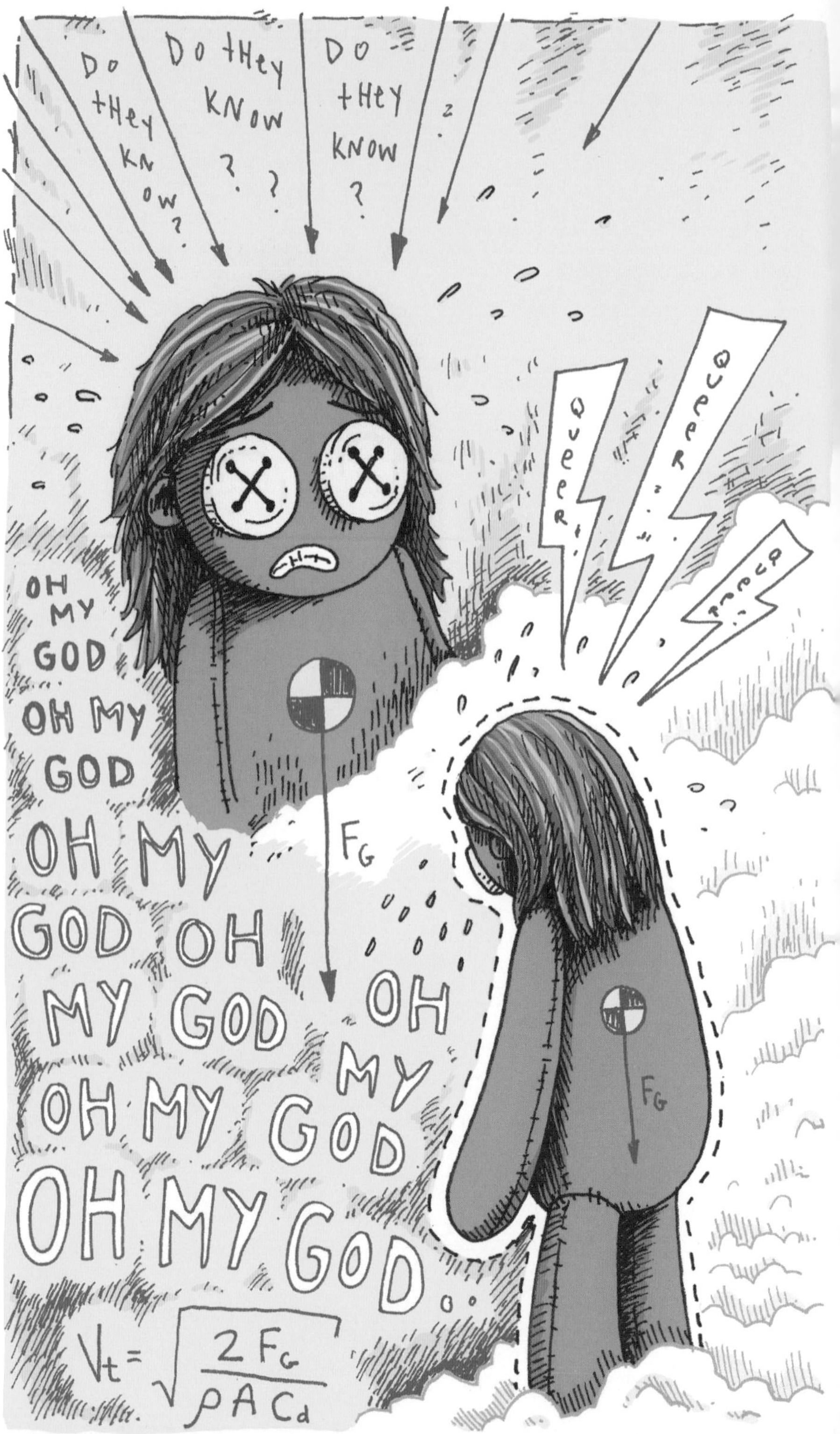

Do tHey KNow?
Do tHey KNow?
Do tHey KNow?
QUEER!
QUEER
QUEER
OH MY GOD
OH MY GOD
OH MY GOD OH MY GOD OH MY
OH MY GOD
OH MY GOD..
F_G
F_G
$V_t = \sqrt{\frac{2F_G}{\rho A C_d}}$

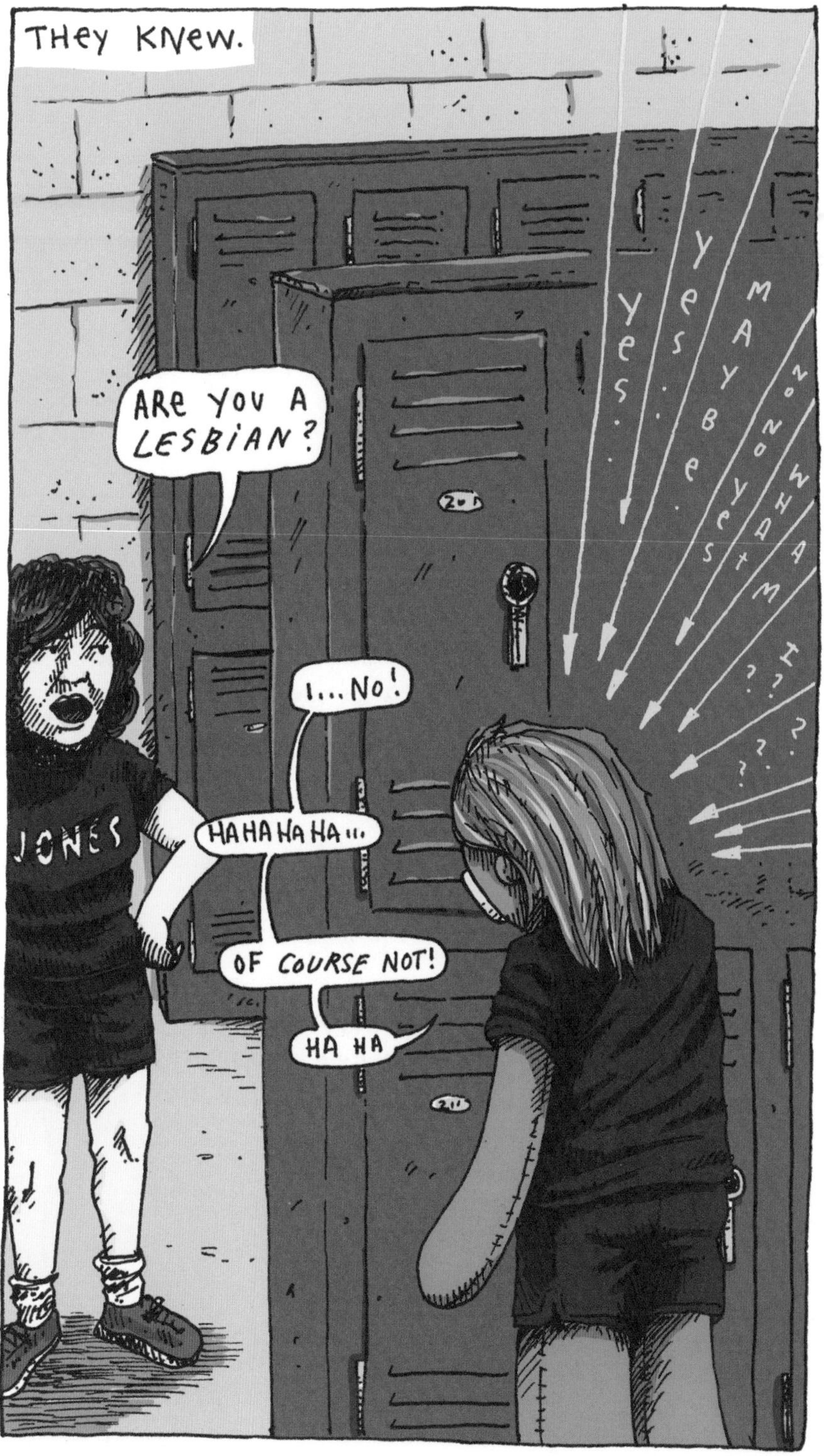
THEY KNEW.
ARE YOU A LESBIAN?
I... NO!
HAHAHAHA...
OF COURSE NOT!
HA HA
yes.
yes.
MAYBE.

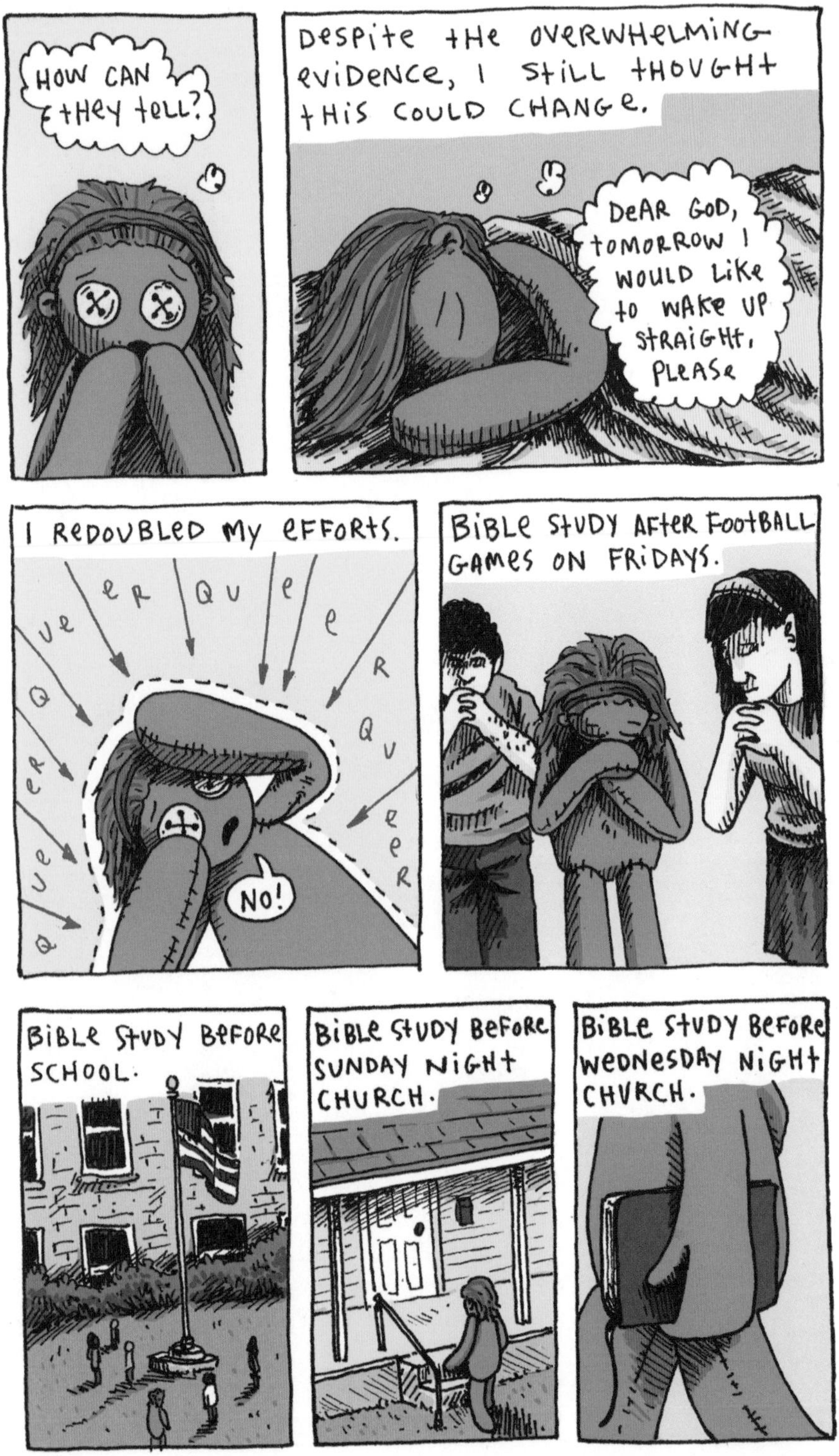
HOW CAN they tell?
DESPITE THE OVERWHELMING EVIDENCE, I STILL THOUGHT THIS COULD CHANGE.
DEAR GOD, TOMORROW I WOULD LIKE TO WAKE UP STRAIGHT, PLEASE
I REDOUBLED MY EFFORTS.
QUEER
QUEER
QUEER
QUEER
NO!
BIBLE STUDY AFTER FOOTBALL GAMES ON FRIDAYS.
BIBLE STUDY BEFORE SCHOOL.
BIBLE STUDY BEFORE SUNDAY NIGHT CHURCH.
BIBLE STUDY BEFORE WEDNESDAY NIGHT CHURCH.

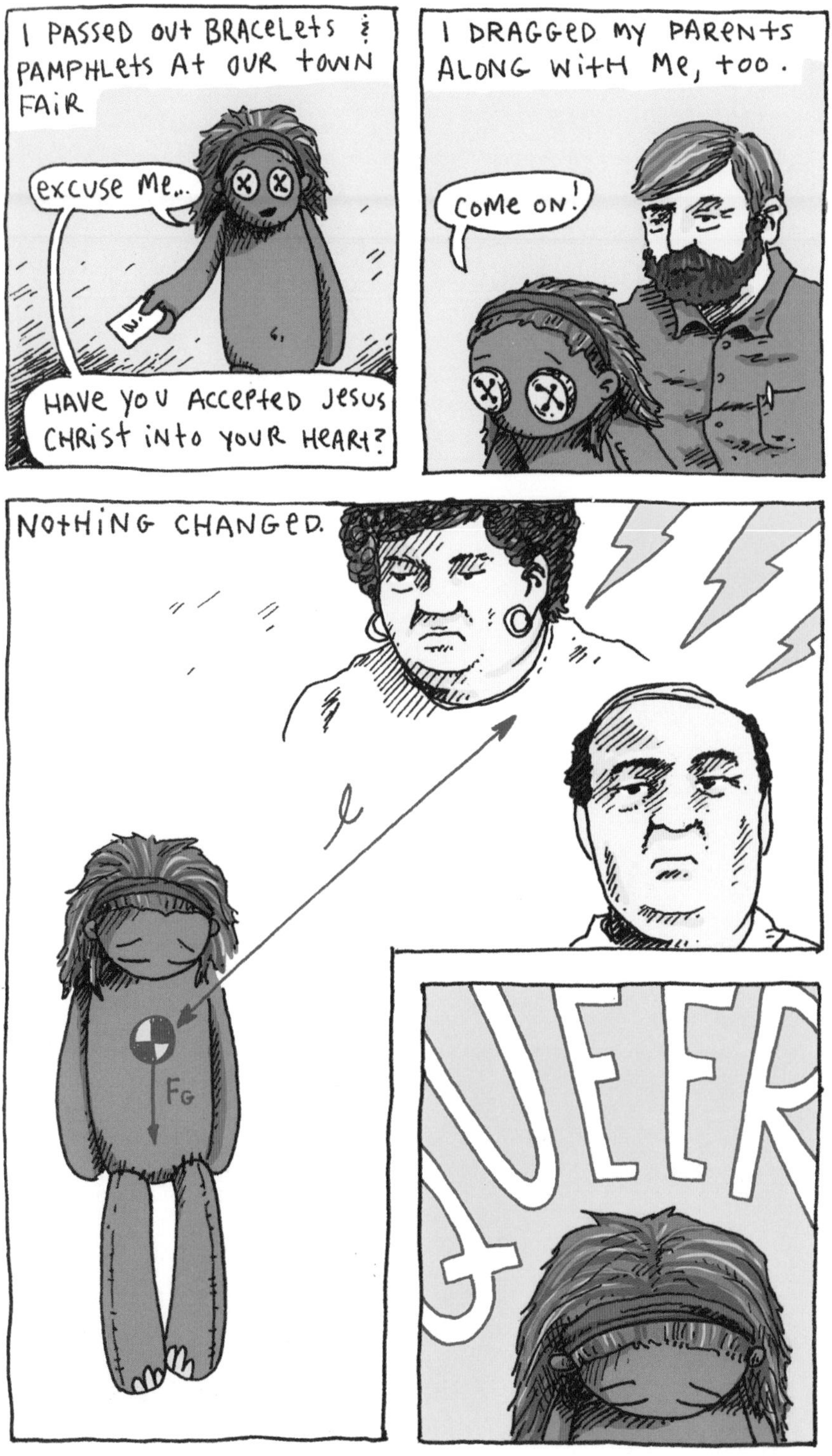
I PASSED OUT BRACELETS & PAMPHLETS AT OUR TOWN FAIR
excuse me...
HAVE YOU ACCEPTED JESUS CHRIST INTO YOUR HEART?
I DRAGGED MY PARENTS ALONG WITH ME, TOO.
COME ON!
NOTHING CHANGED.
ℓ
F_G
QUEER

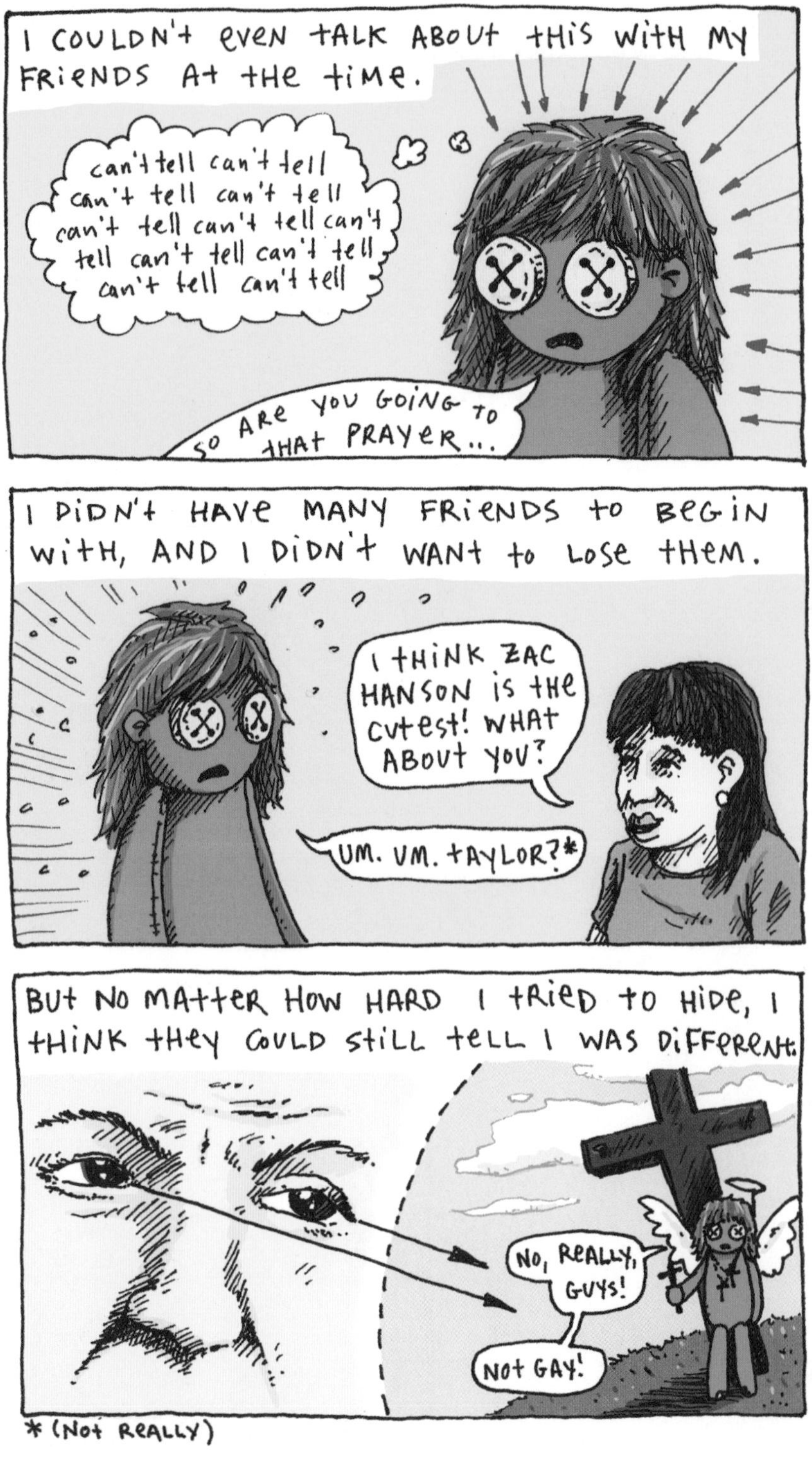
I COULDN'T EVEN TALK ABOUT THIS WITH MY FRIENDS AT THE TIME.
can't tell can't tell can't tell can't tell can't tell can't tell can't tell can't tell can't tell can't tell can't tell
SO ARE YOU GOING TO THAT PRAYER...
I DIDN'T HAVE MANY FRIENDS TO BEGIN WITH, AND I DIDN'T WANT TO LOSE THEM.
I THINK ZAC HANSON IS THE CUTEST! WHAT ABOUT YOU?
UM. UM. TAYLOR?*
BUT NO MATTER HOW HARD I TRIED TO HIDE, I THINK THEY COULD STILL TELL I WAS DIFFERENT.
NO, REALLY, GUYS!
NOT GAY!

* (NOT REALLY)

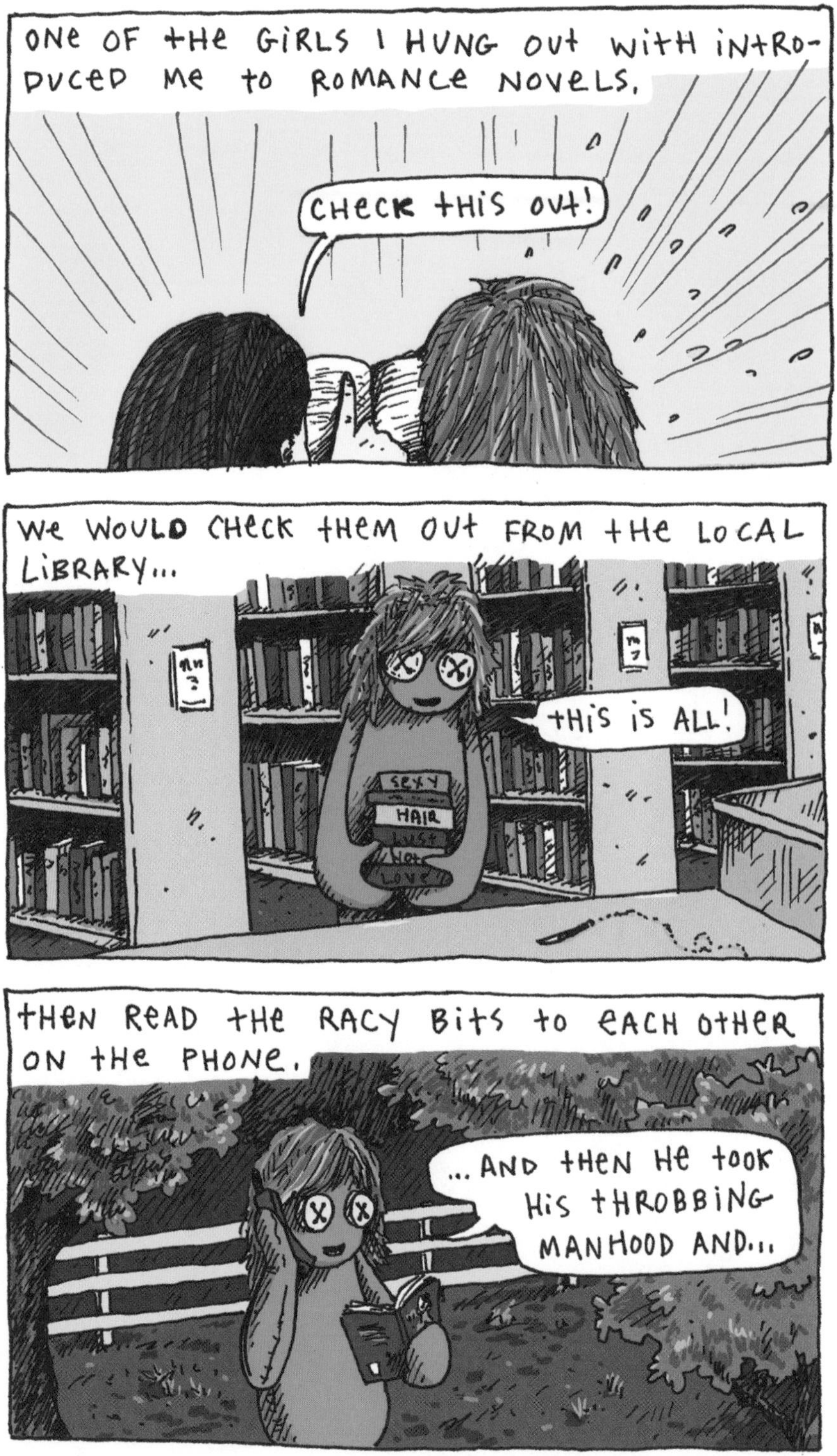

ONE OF THE GIRLS I HUNG OUT WITH INTRODUCED ME TO ROMANCE NOVELS.
CHECK THIS OUT!
WE WOULD CHECK THEM OUT FROM THE LOCAL LIBRARY...
THIS IS ALL!
THEN READ THE RACY BITS TO EACH OTHER ON THE PHONE.
...AND THEN HE TOOK HIS THROBBING MANHOOD AND...

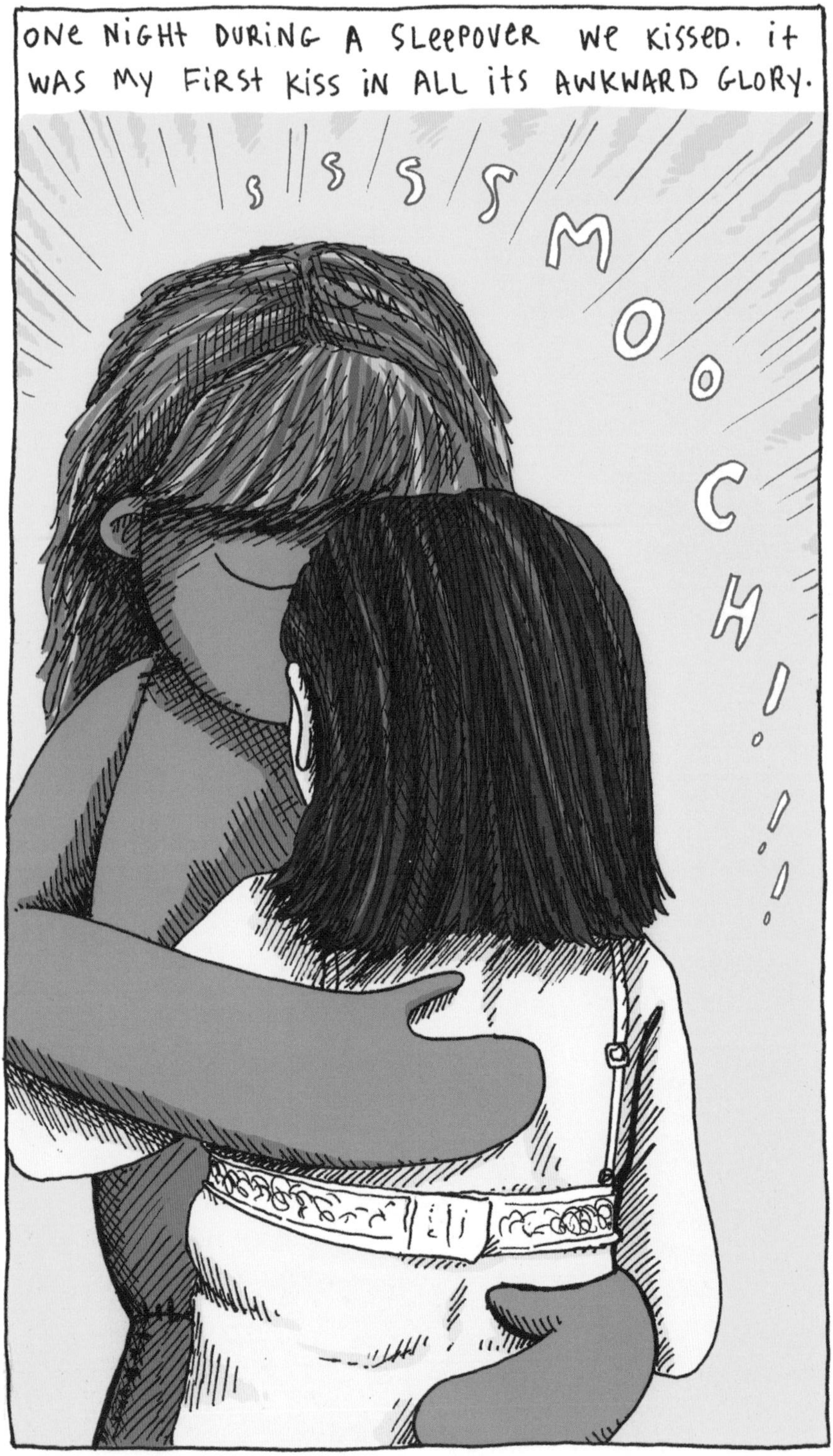
ONE NIGHT DURING A SLEEPOVER WE KISSED. IT WAS MY FIRST KISS IN ALL ITS AWKWARD GLORY.
SSSSMOOCH!!!

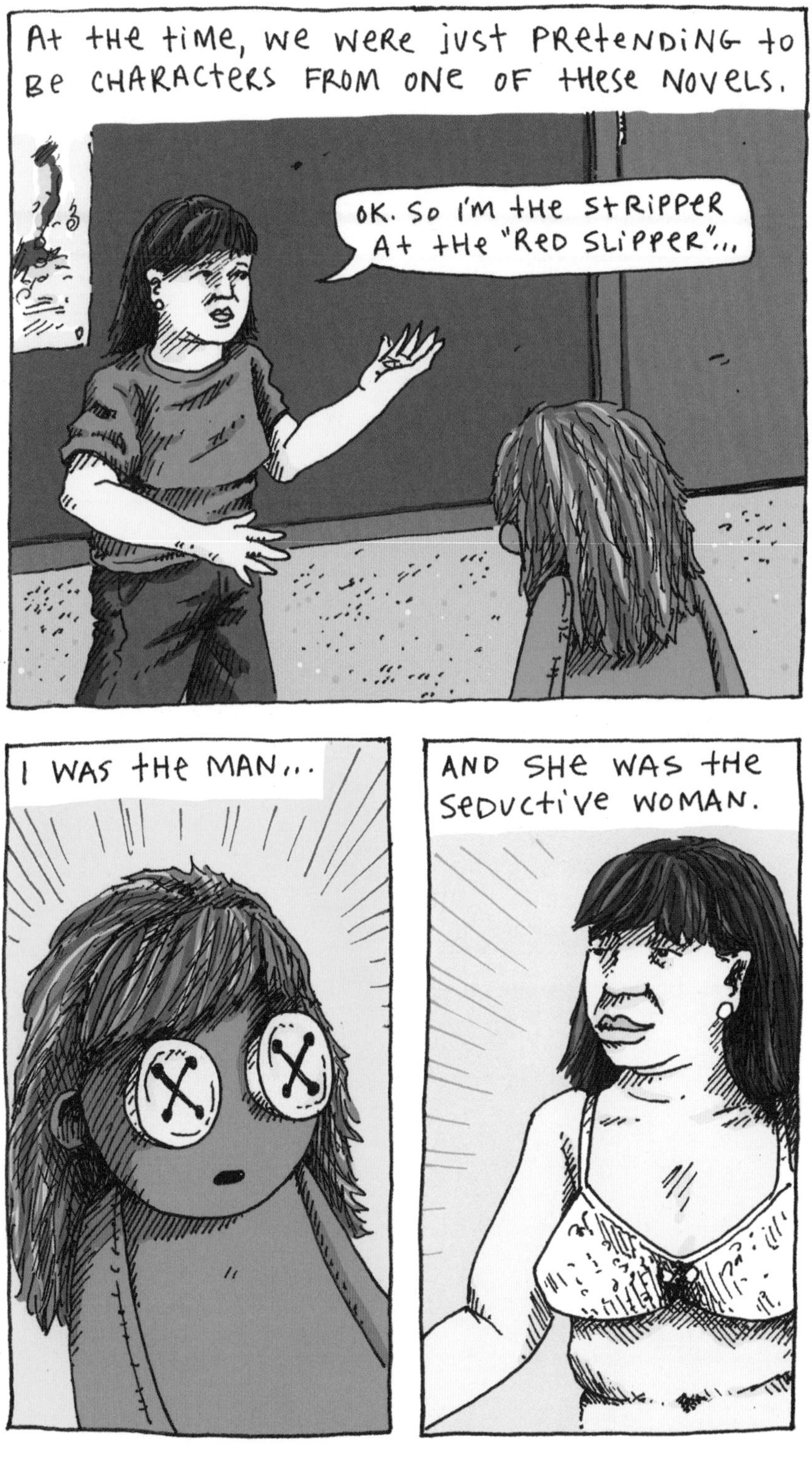
At the time, we were just pretending to be characters from one of these novels.
OK. So I'm the stripper at the "Red Slipper"...
I was the man...
And she was the seductive woman.

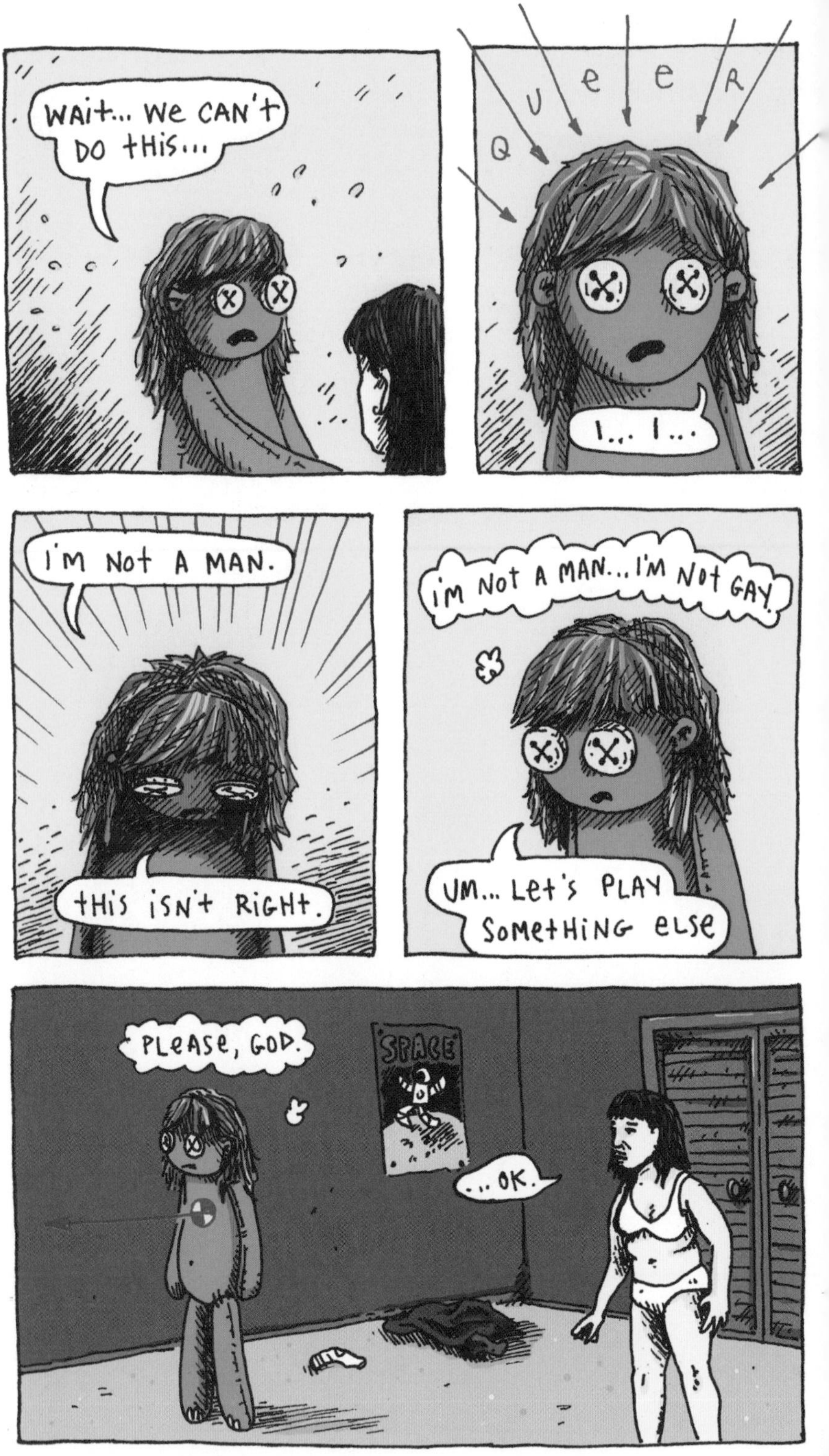
WAIT... WE CAN'T DO THIS...
Q U E E R
I... I...
I'M NOT A MAN.
THIS ISN'T RIGHT.
I'M NOT A MAN... I'M NOT GAY.
UM... LET'S PLAY SOMETHING ELSE
PLEASE, GOD.
SPACE
...OK.

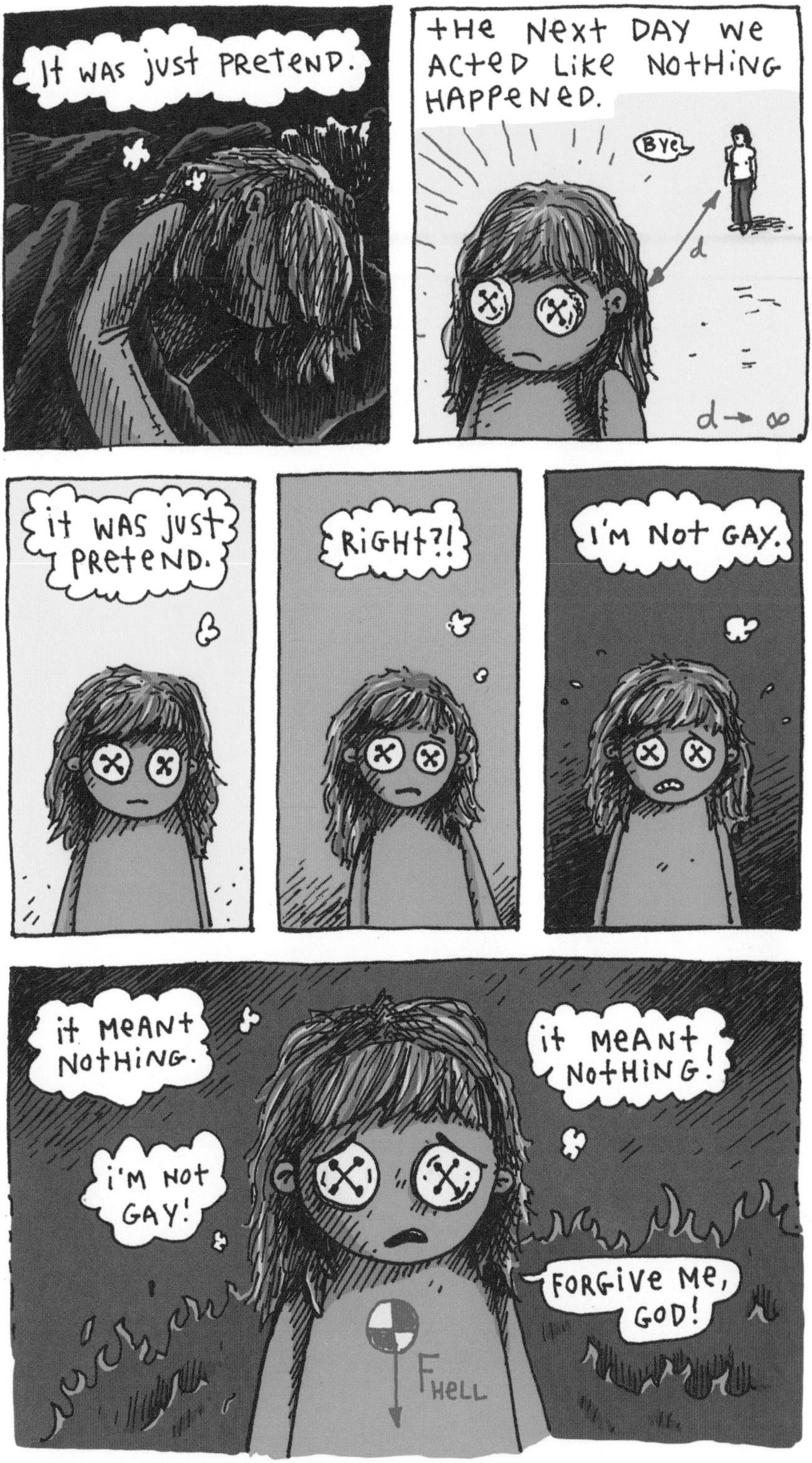
It was just pretend.
the next day we acted like nothing happened.
Bye!
d
d → ∞
it was just pretend.
Right?!
I'm not gay.
it meant nothing.
it meant nothing!
i'm not gay!
Forgive me, God!
F HELL

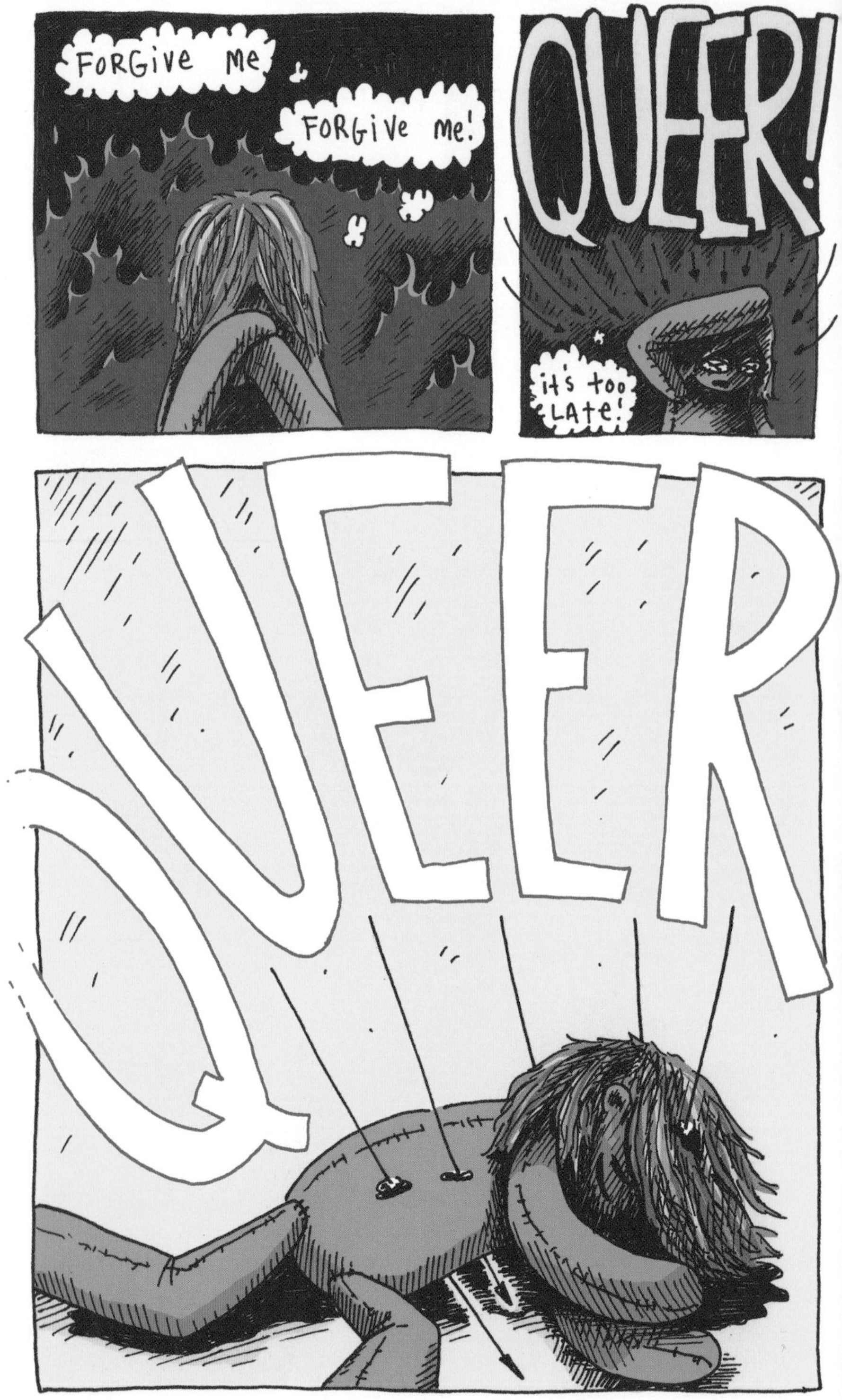
FORGIVE ME
FORGIVE ME!
QUEER!
it's too LATE!
QUEER

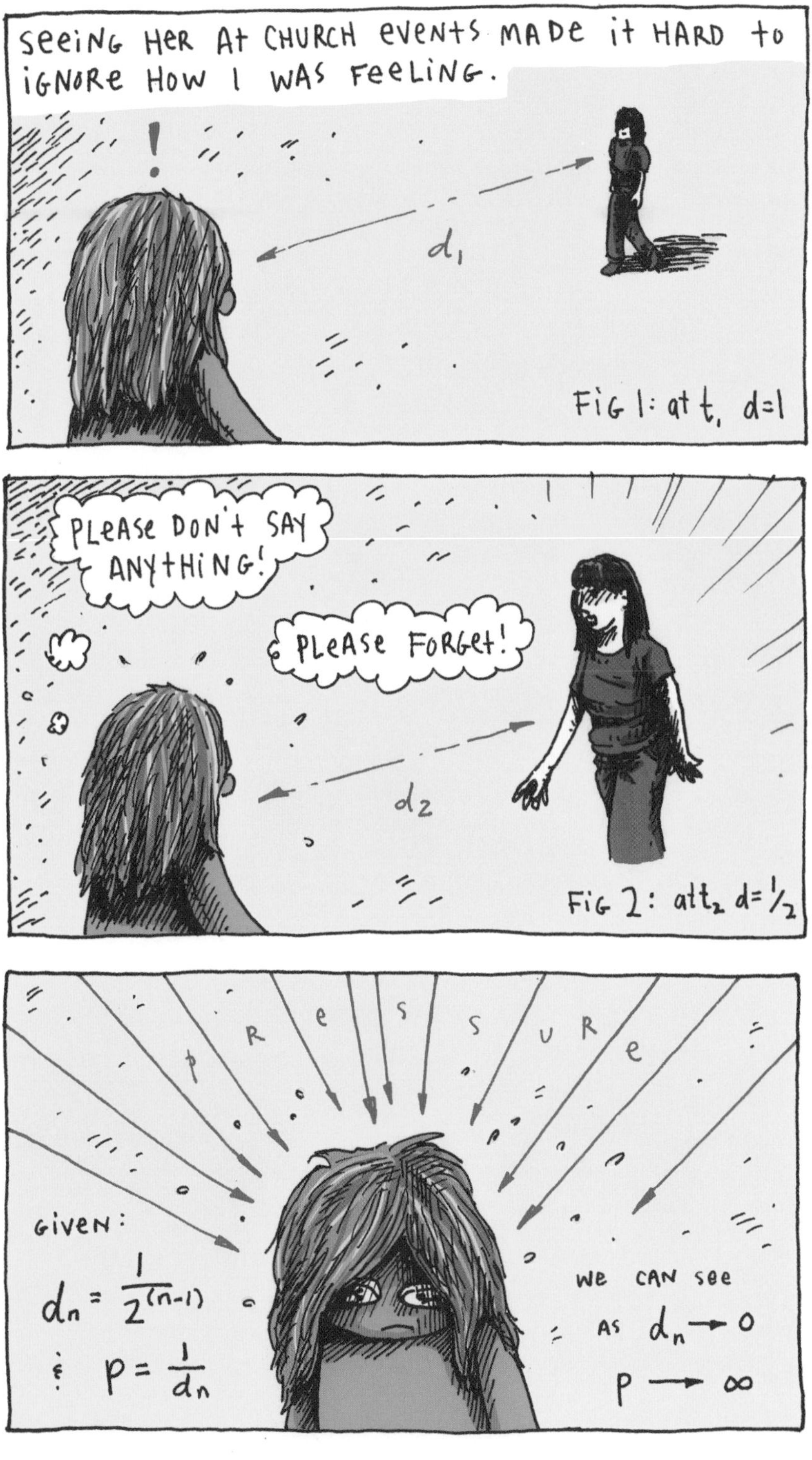
SEEING HER AT CHURCH EVENTS MADE IT HARD TO IGNORE HOW I WAS FEELING.
!
d_1
FIG 1: at t_1 $d=1$
PLEASE DON'T SAY ANYTHING!
PLEASE FORGET!
d_2
FIG 2: at t_2 $d=\frac{1}{2}$
P R E S S U R E
GIVEN:
$d_n = \frac{1}{2^{(n-1)}}$
& $p = \frac{1}{d_n}$
WE CAN SEE
AS $d_n \to 0$
$p \to \infty$

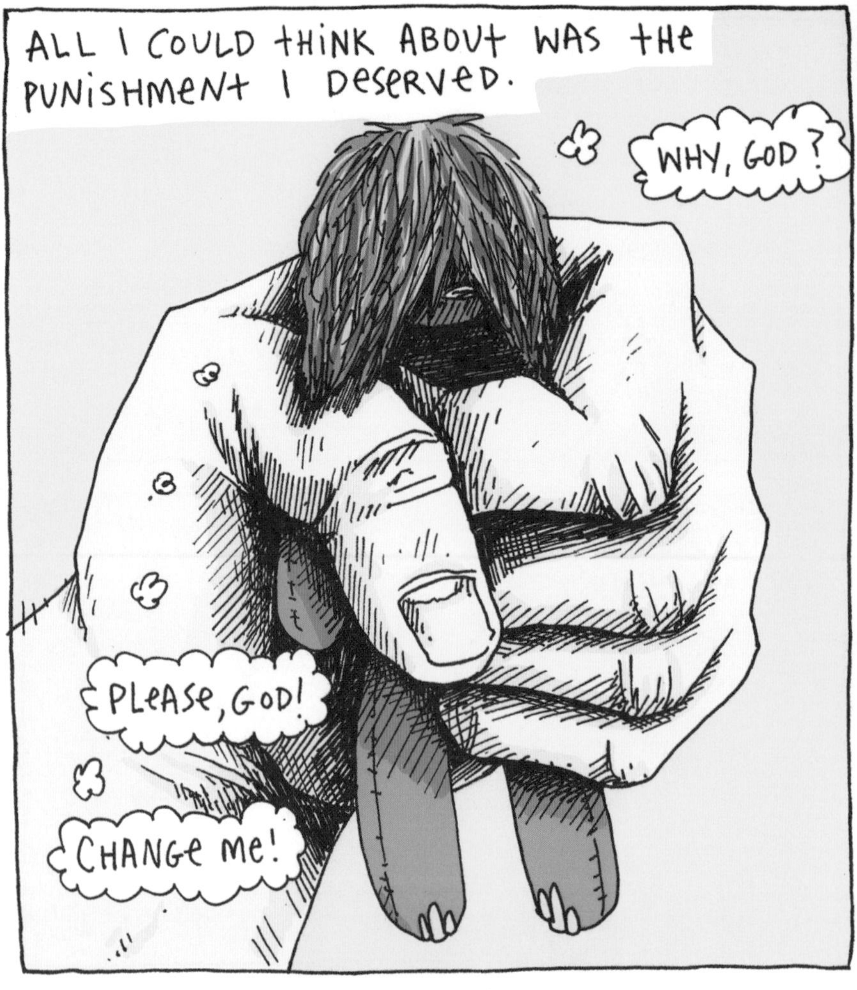
ALL I COULD THINK ABOUT WAS THE PUNISHMENT I DESERVED.
WHY, GOD?
PLEASE, GOD!
CHANGE ME!

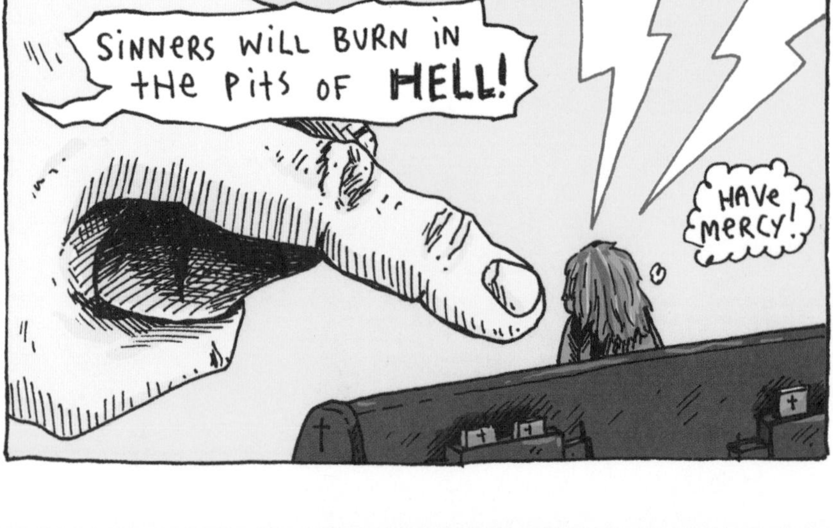
SINNERS WILL BURN IN THE PITS OF HELL!
HAVE MERCY!

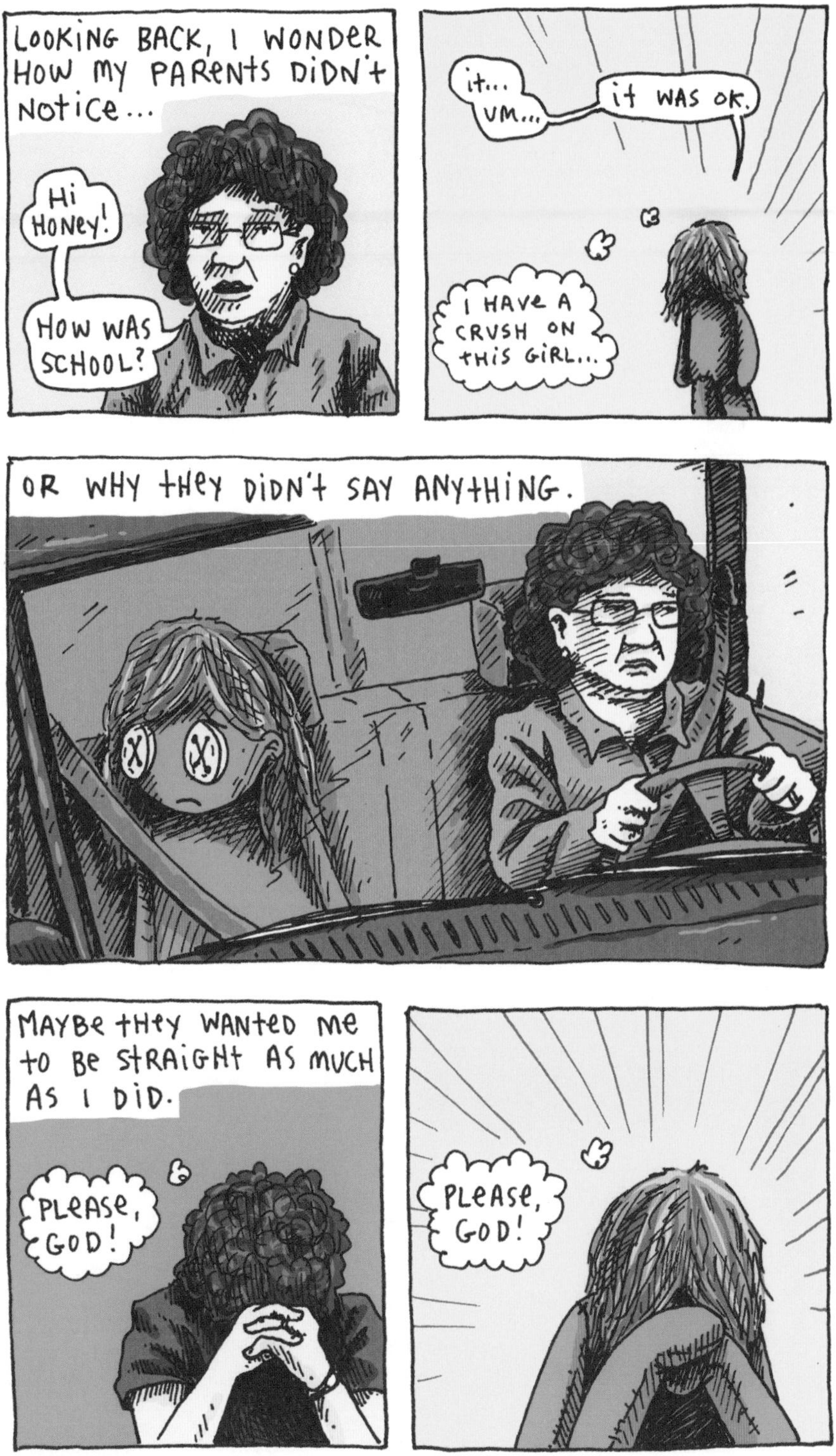
LOOKING BACK, I WONDER HOW MY PARENTS DIDN'T NOTICE...
HI HONEY!
HOW WAS SCHOOL?
IT... UM...
IT WAS OK.
I HAVE A CRUSH ON THIS GIRL...
OR WHY THEY DIDN'T SAY ANYTHING.
MAYBE THEY WANTED ME TO BE STRAIGHT AS MUCH AS I DID.
PLEASE, GOD!
PLEASE, GOD!

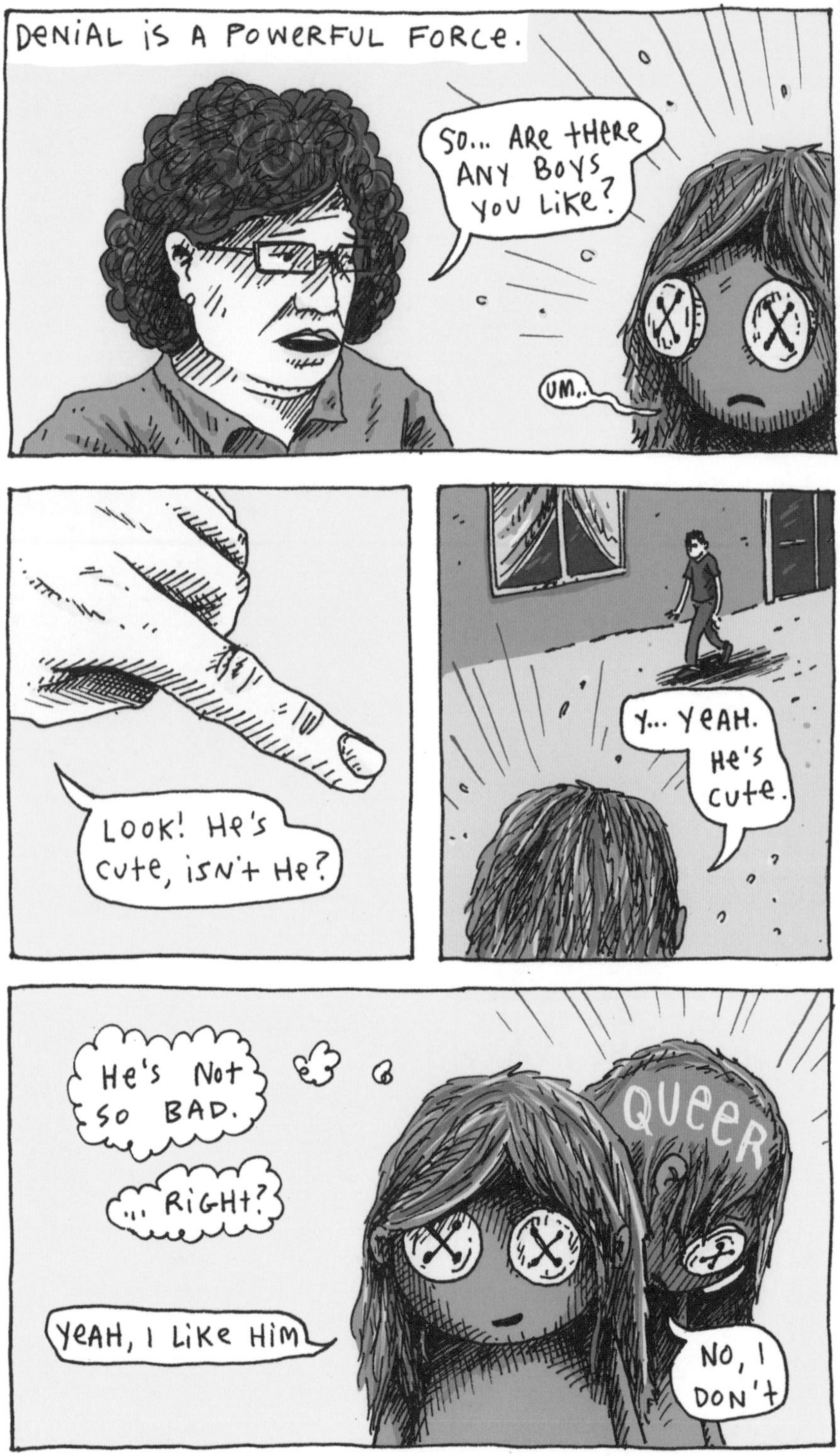
DENIAL IS A POWERFUL FORCE.
SO... ARE THERE ANY BOYS YOU LIKE?
UM..
LOOK! HE'S CUTE, ISN'T HE?
Y... YEAH. HE'S CUTE.
HE'S NOT SO BAD.
... RIGHT?
YEAH, I LIKE HIM
QUEER
NO, I DON'T

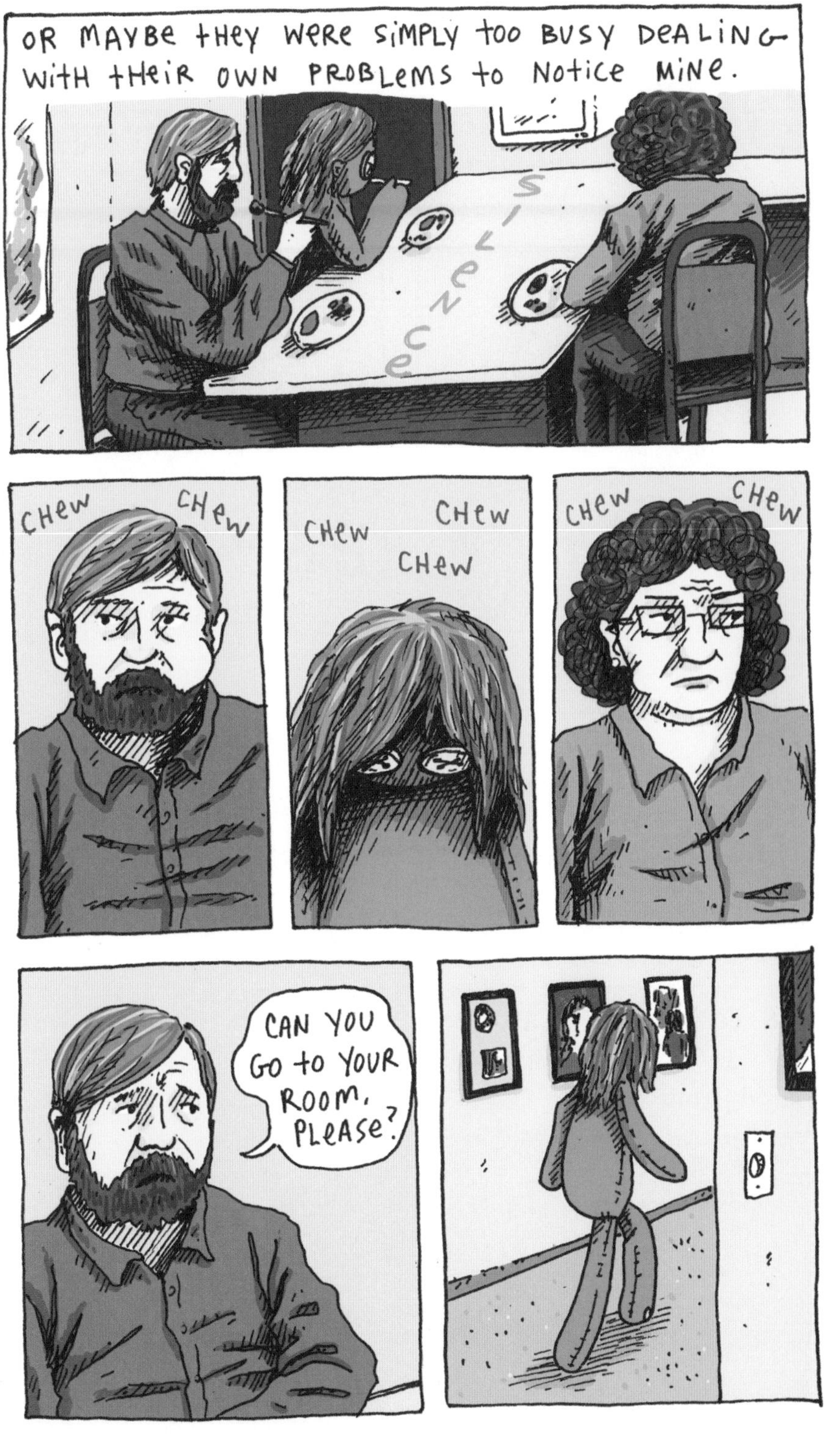
OR MAYBE THEY WERE SIMPLY TOO BUSY DEALING WITH THEIR OWN PROBLEMS TO NOTICE MINE.
SILENCE
CHEW CHEW
CHEW CHEW CHEW
CHEW CHEW
CAN YOU GO TO YOUR ROOM, PLEASE?

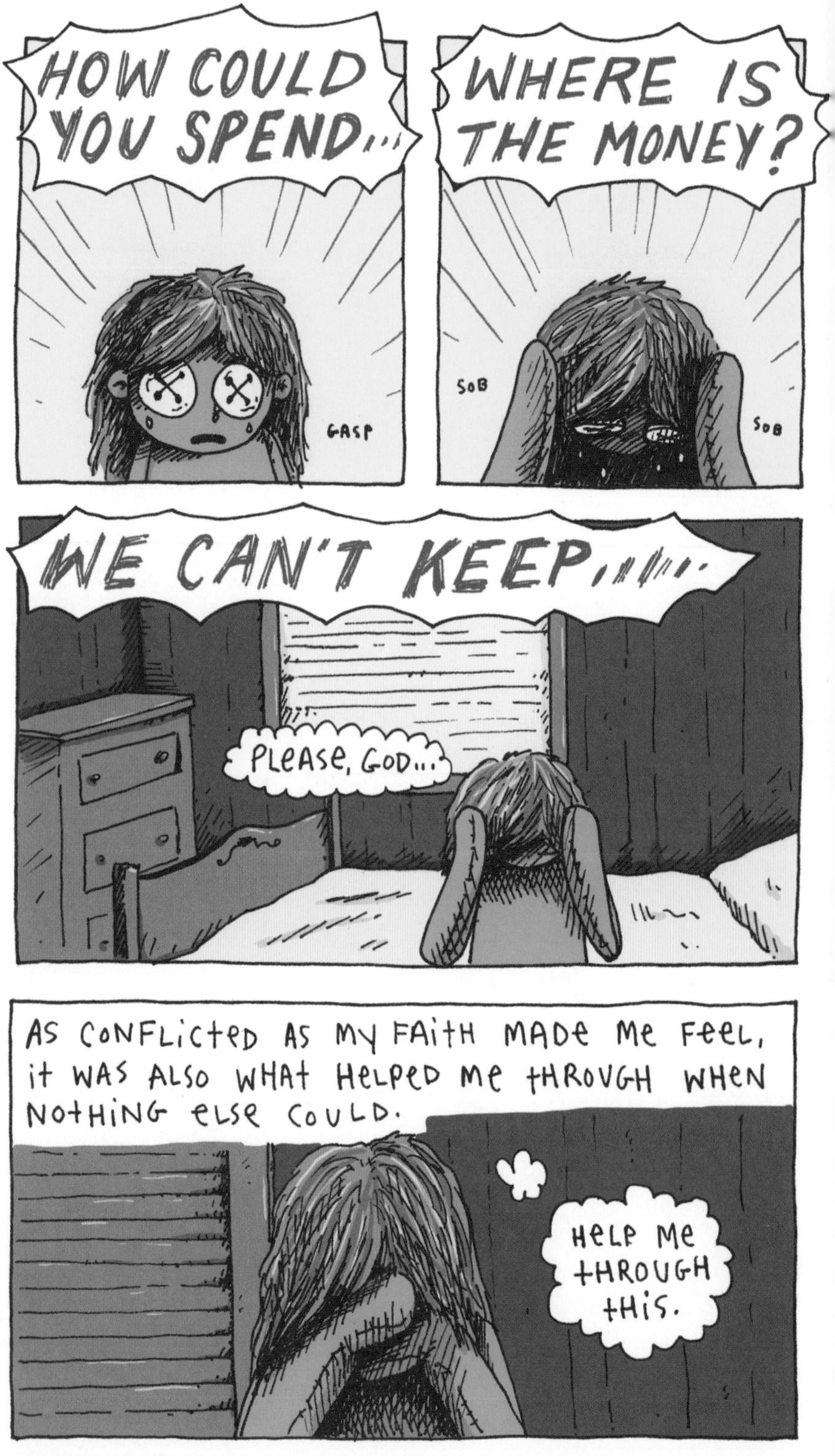
HOW COULD YOU SPEND...
GASP
WHERE IS THE MONEY?
SOB
SOB
WE CAN'T KEEP...
PLEASE, GOD...
AS CONFLICTED AS MY FAITH MADE ME FEEL, IT WAS ALSO WHAT HELPED ME THROUGH WHEN NOTHING ELSE COULD.
HELP ME THROUGH THIS.

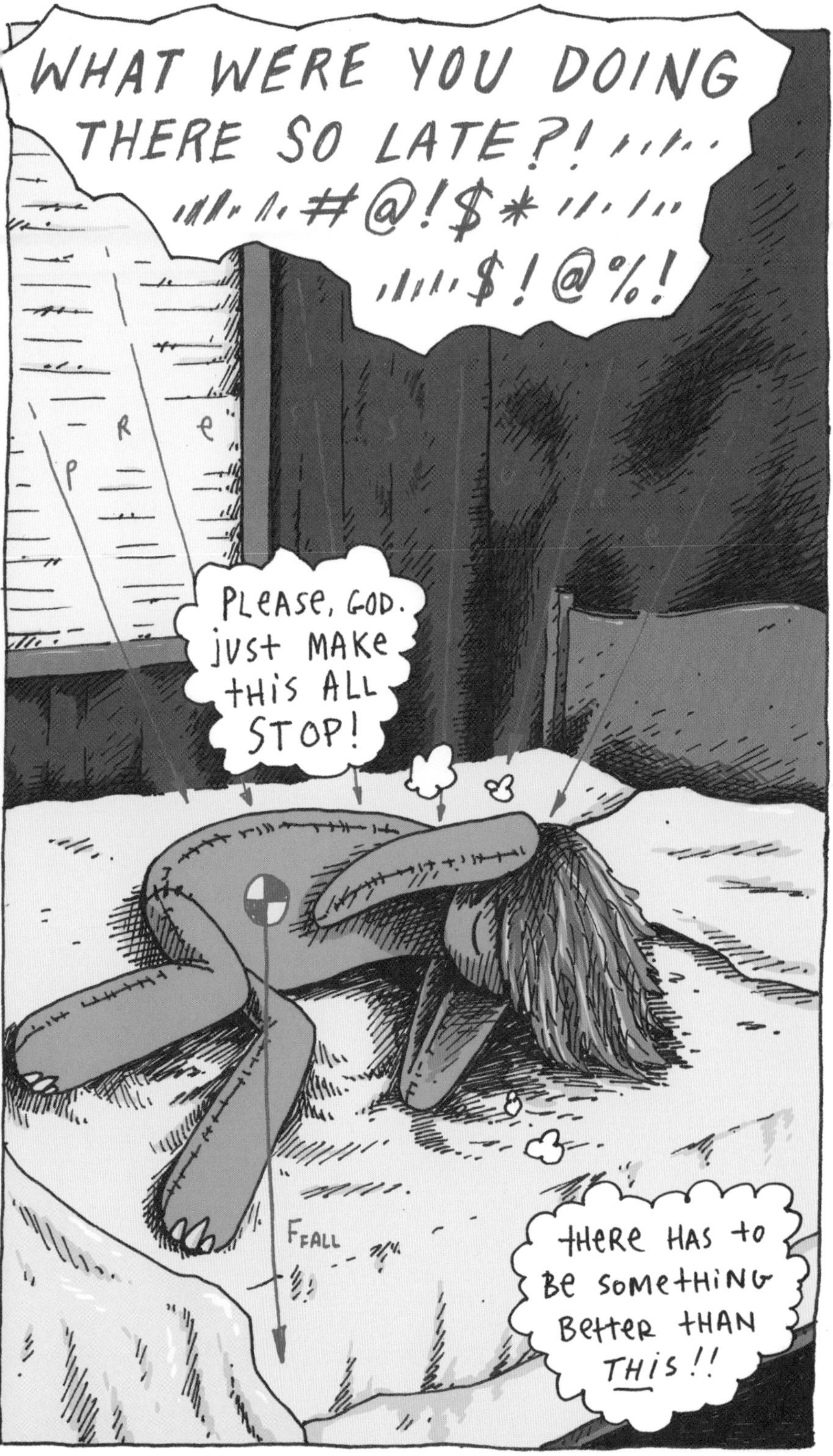
WHAT WERE YOU DOING THERE SO LATE?! #@!$* $!@%!
PLEASE, GOD. JUST MAKE THIS ALL STOP!
FFALL
THERE HAS TO BE SOMETHING BETTER THAN THIS!!

CHAPTER TWO

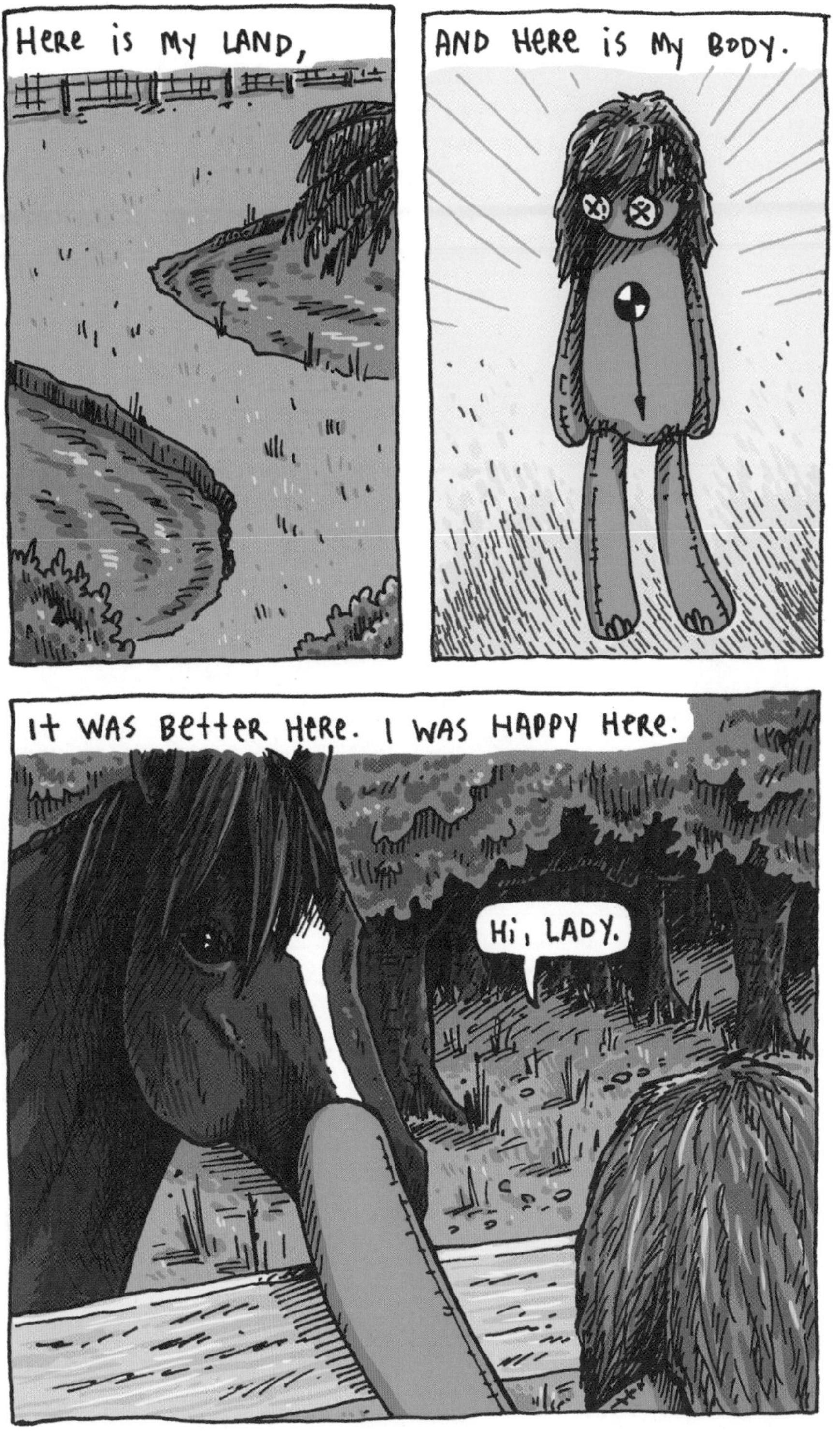
Here is my LAND,
AND Here is my BODY.
It WAS Better Here. I WAS HAPPY Here.
Hi, LADY.

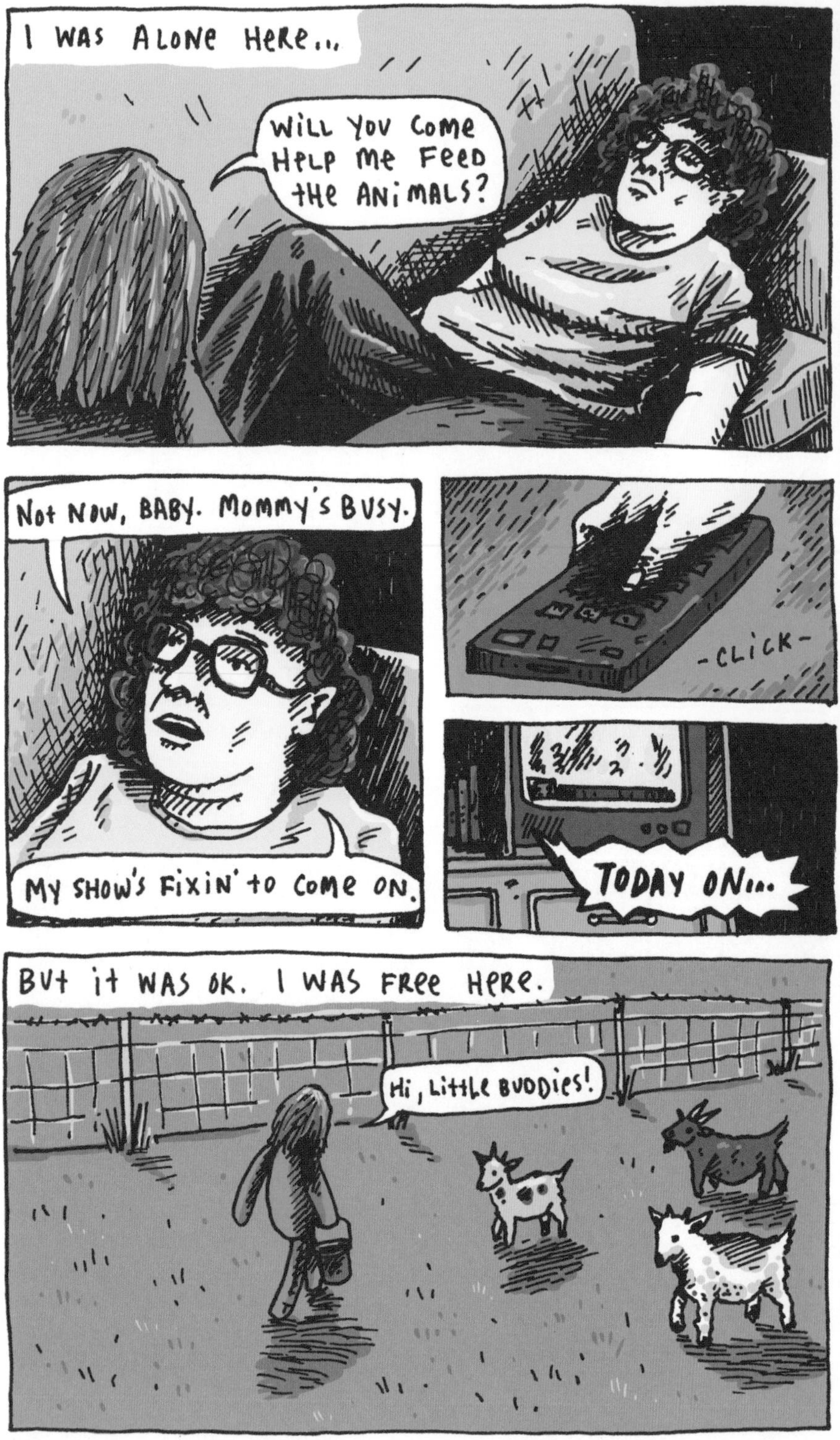
I WAS ALONE HERE...
WILL YOU COME HELP ME FEED THE ANIMALS?
NOT NOW, BABY. MOMMY'S BUSY.
MY SHOW'S FIXIN' TO COME ON.
-CLICK-
TODAY ON...
BUT IT WAS OK. I WAS FREE HERE.
HI, LITTLE BUDDIES!

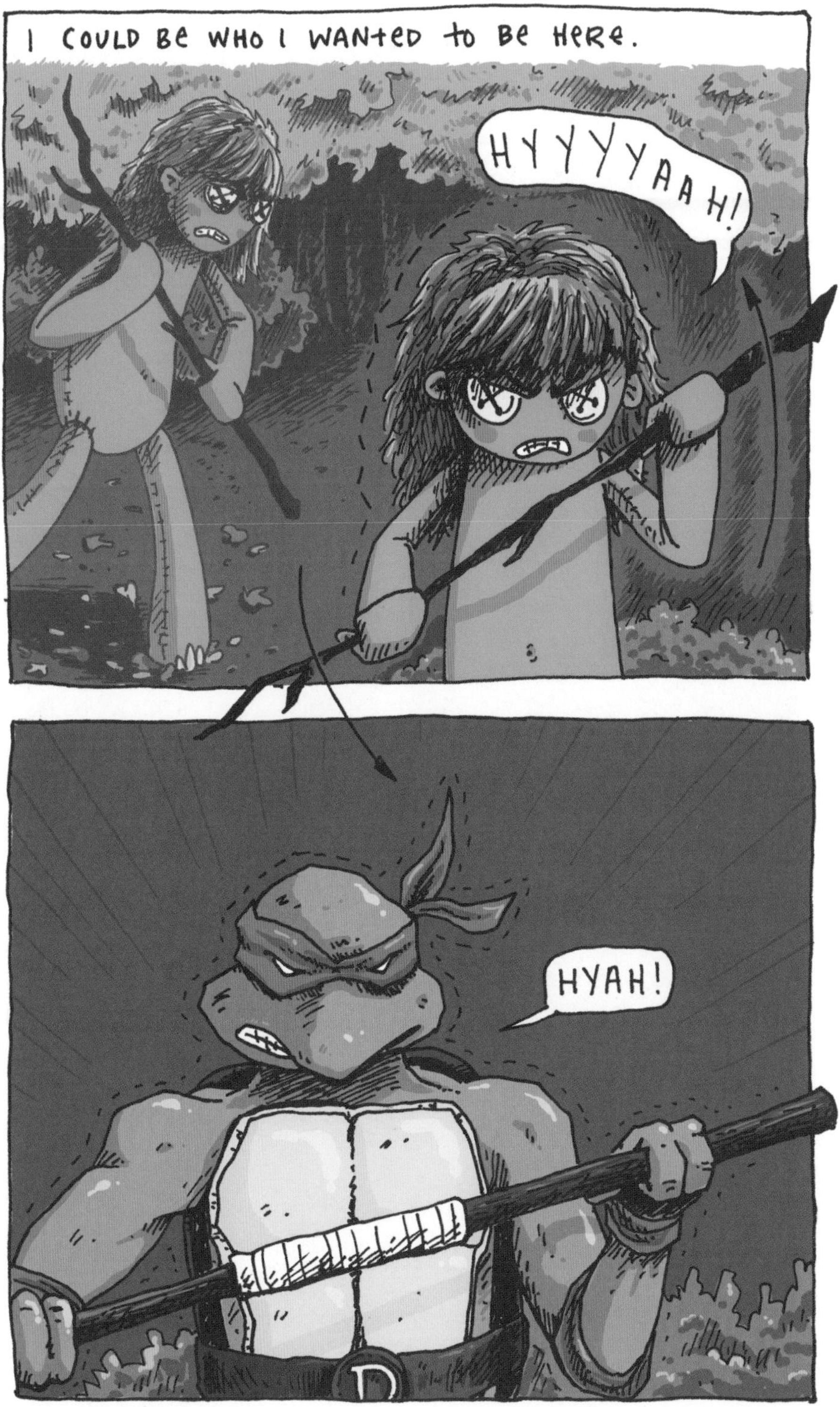
I COULD BE WHO I WANTED TO BE HERE.
HYYYYAAH!
HYAH!

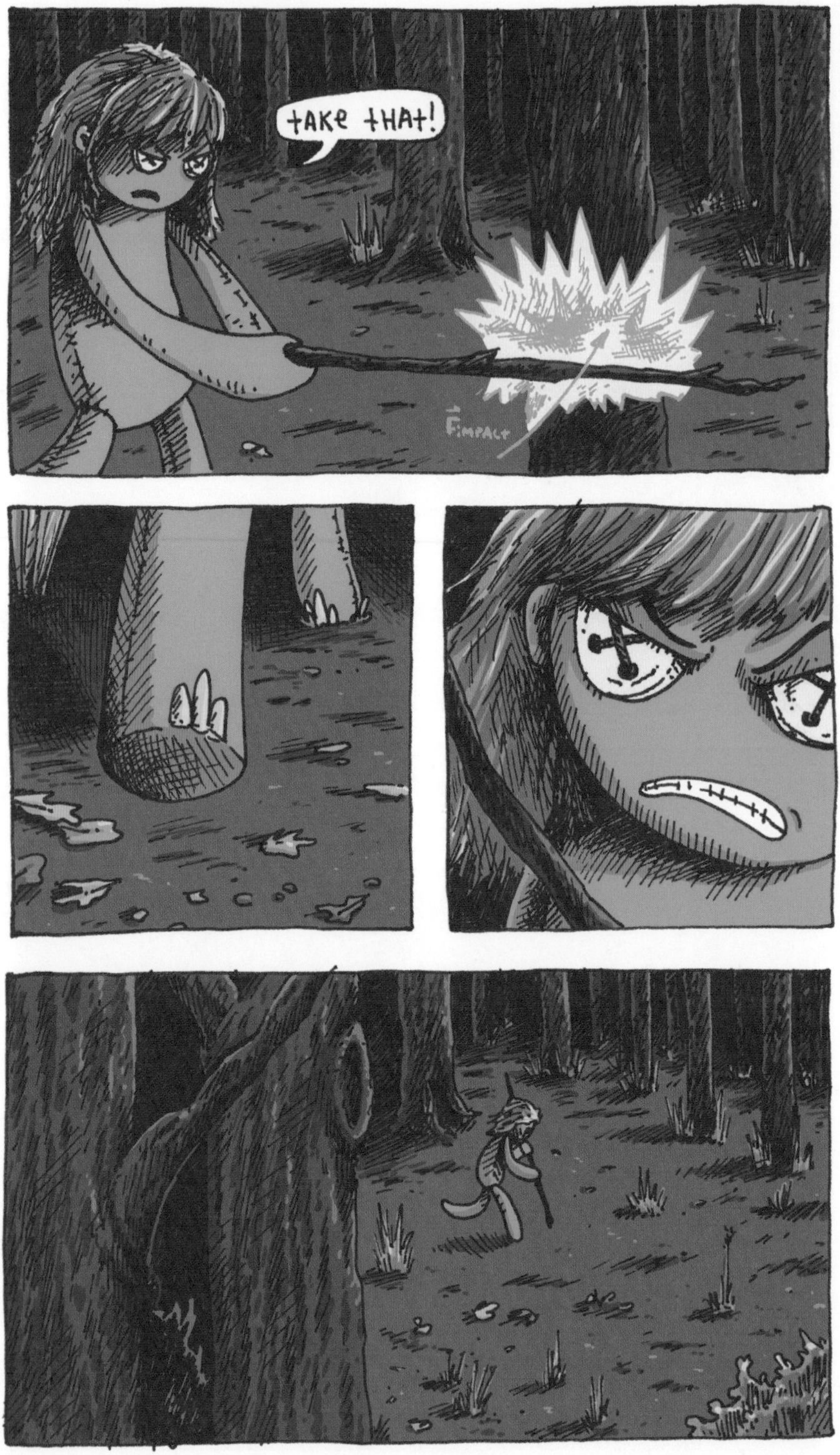
take that!
IMPACT

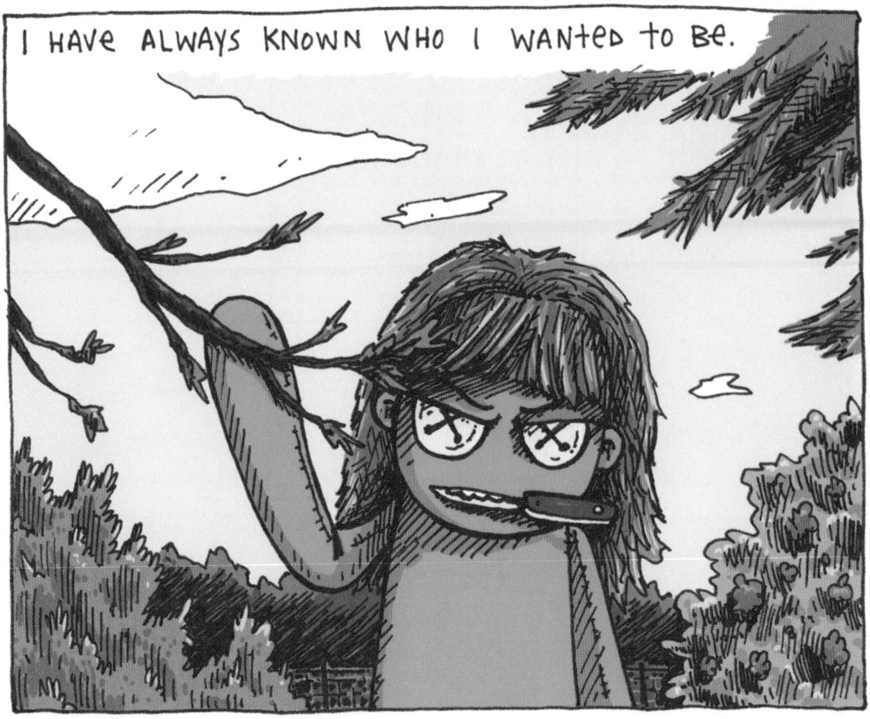
I HAVE ALWAYS KNOWN WHO I WANTED TO BE.

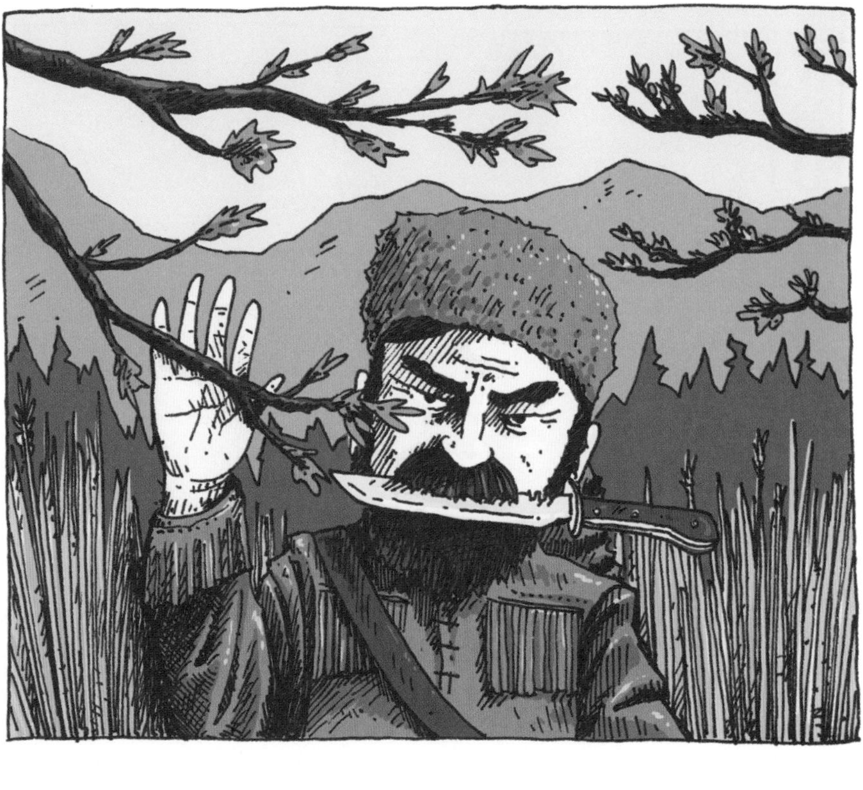

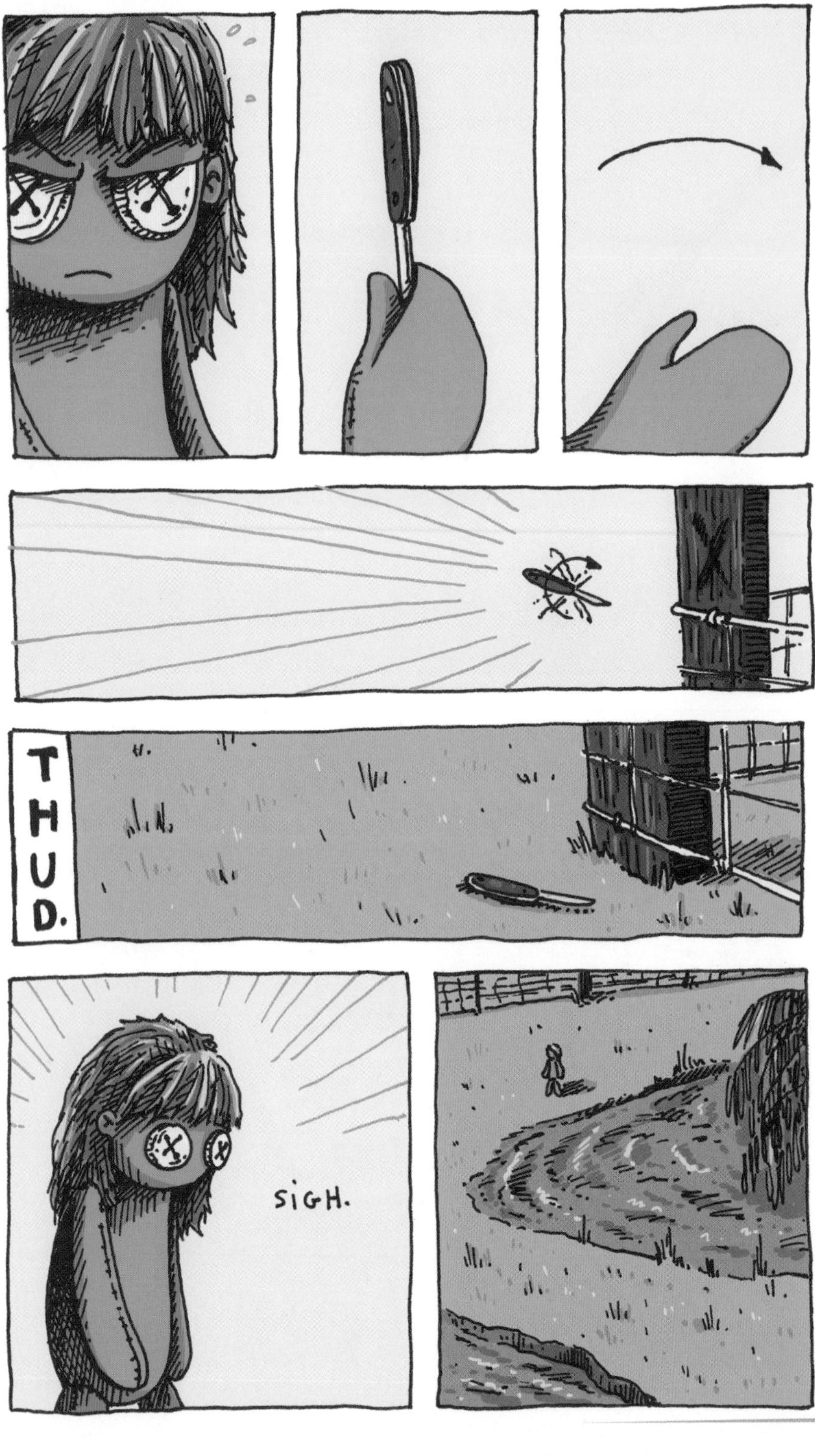
THUD.
SIGH.

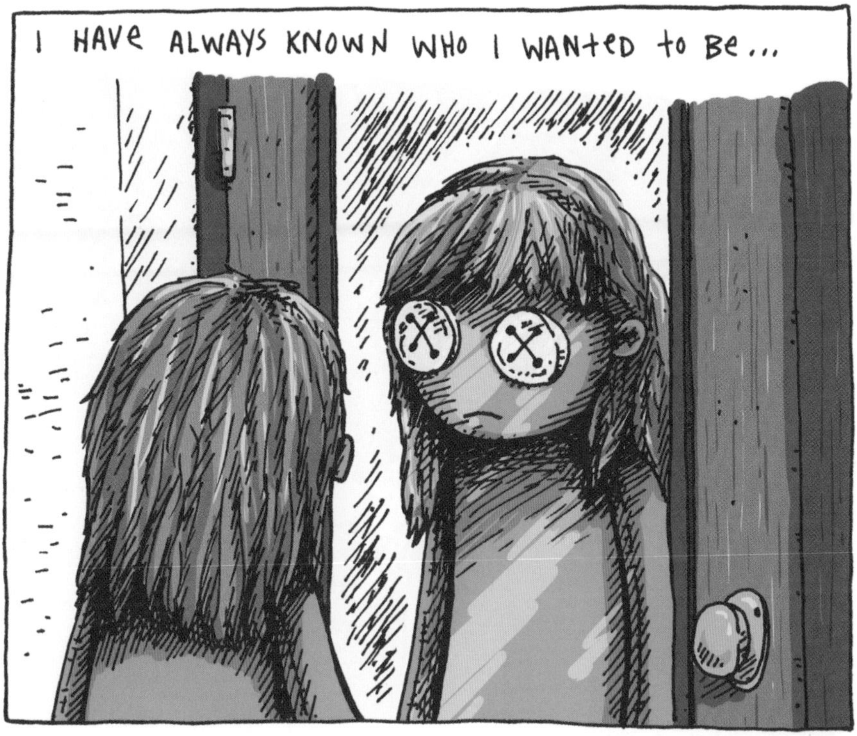
I HAVE ALWAYS KNOWN WHO I WANTED TO BE...

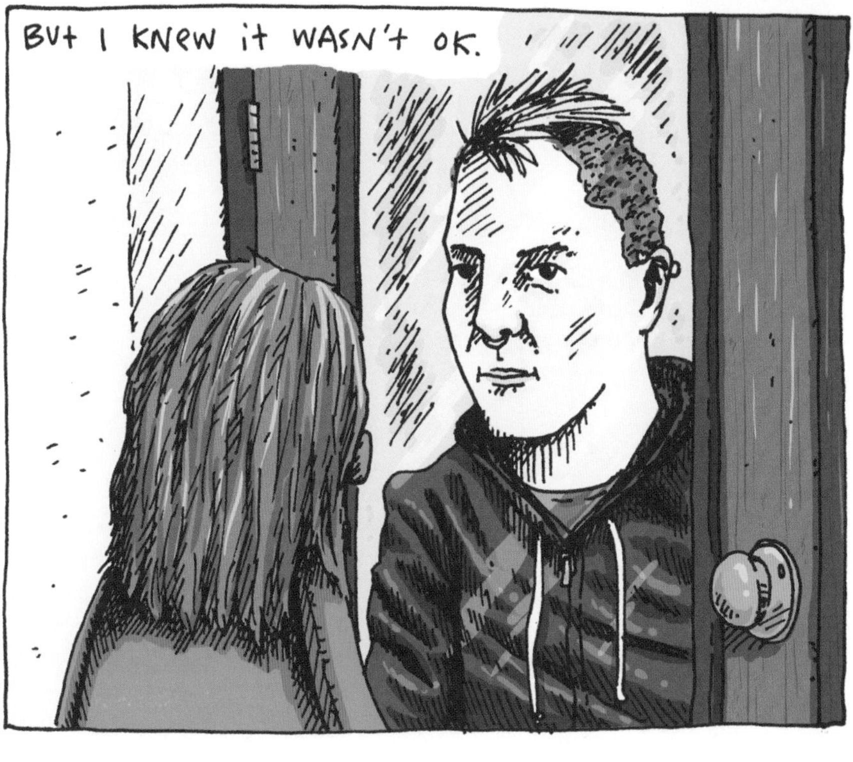
BUT I KNEW IT WASN'T OK.

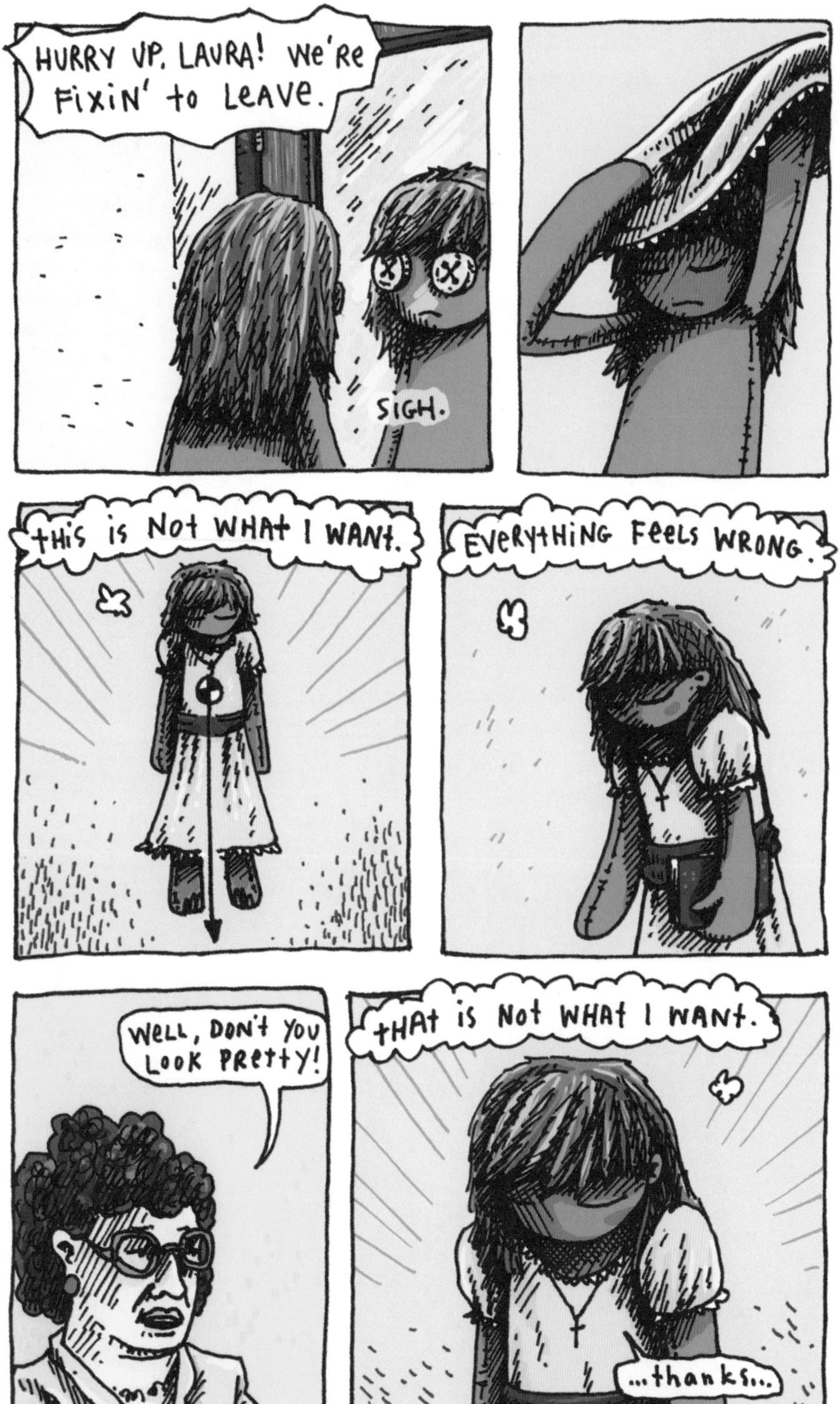
HURRY UP, LAURA! We're FixiN' to Leave.
SIGH.
this is Not WHAT I WANT.
EVERYTHING Feels WRONG.
WeLL, DON'T YOU LOOK PRETTY!
THAT is Not WHAT I WANT.
...thanks...

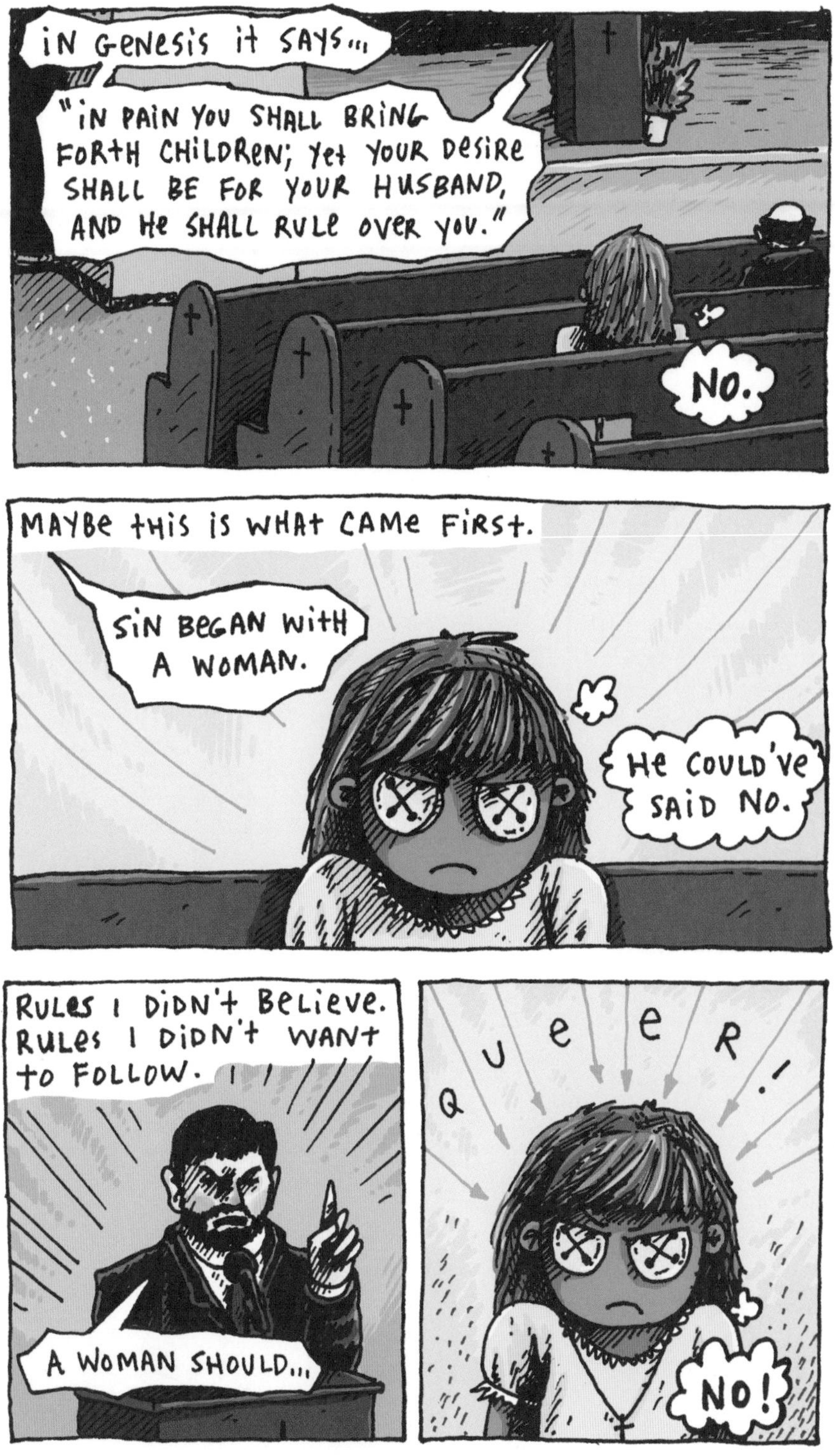
in Genesis it says...
"in PAIN YOU SHALL BRING FORTH CHILDREN; Yet YOUR DeSiRe SHALL BE FOR YOUR HUSBAND, AND He SHALL RULe OVER YOU."
NO.
MAYBE THIS IS WHAT CAME FIRST.
SIN BEGAN WITH A WOMAN.
He COULD've SAID NO.
RULES I DIDN'T BELIEVE. RULES I DIDN'T WANT TO FOLLOW.
A WOMAN SHOULD...
QUEER!
NO!

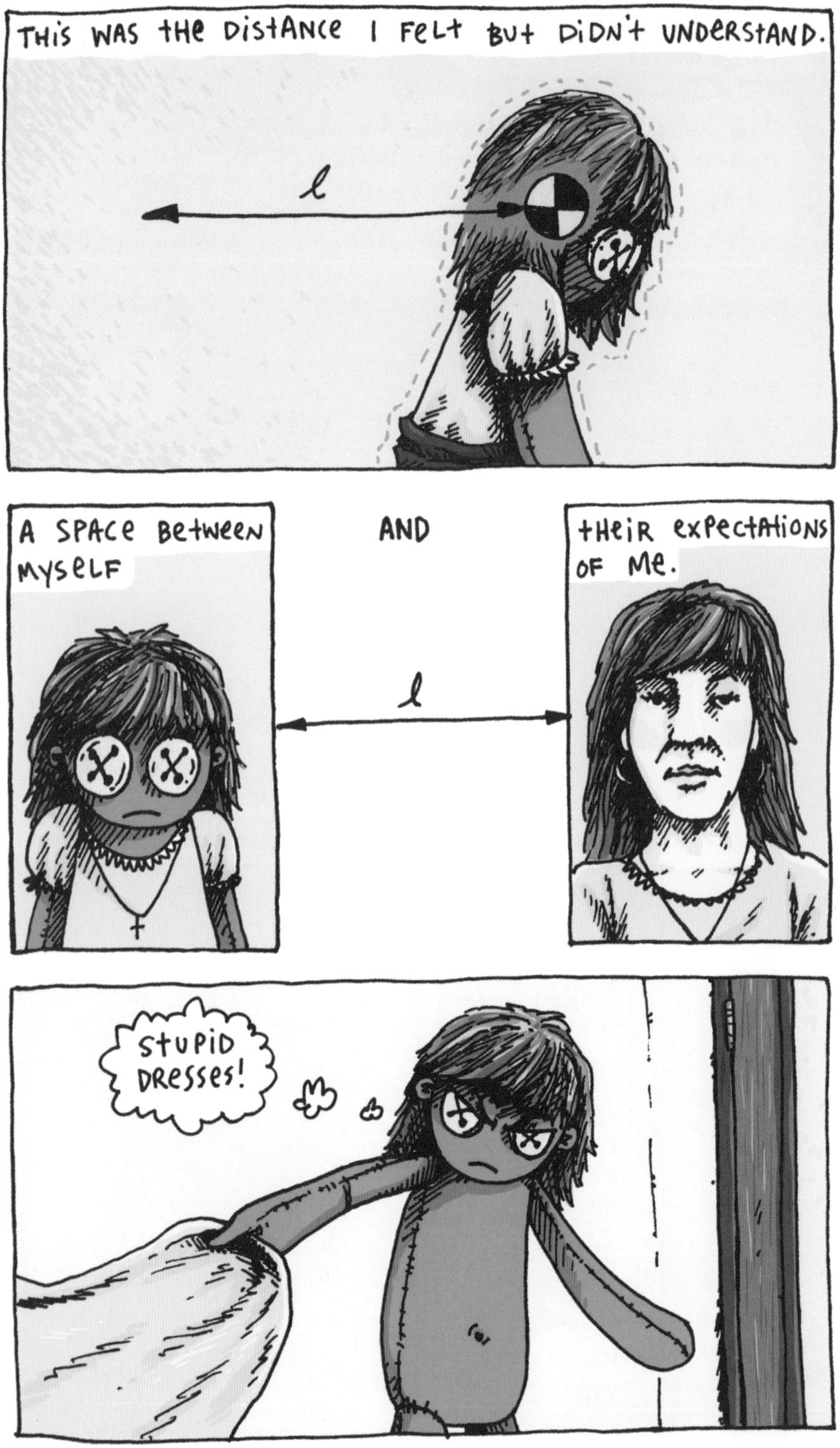
THIS WAS THE DISTANCE I FELT BUT DIDN'T UNDERSTAND.
ℓ
A SPACE BETWEEN MYSELF
AND
THEIR EXPECTATIONS OF ME.
ℓ
STUPID DRESSES!

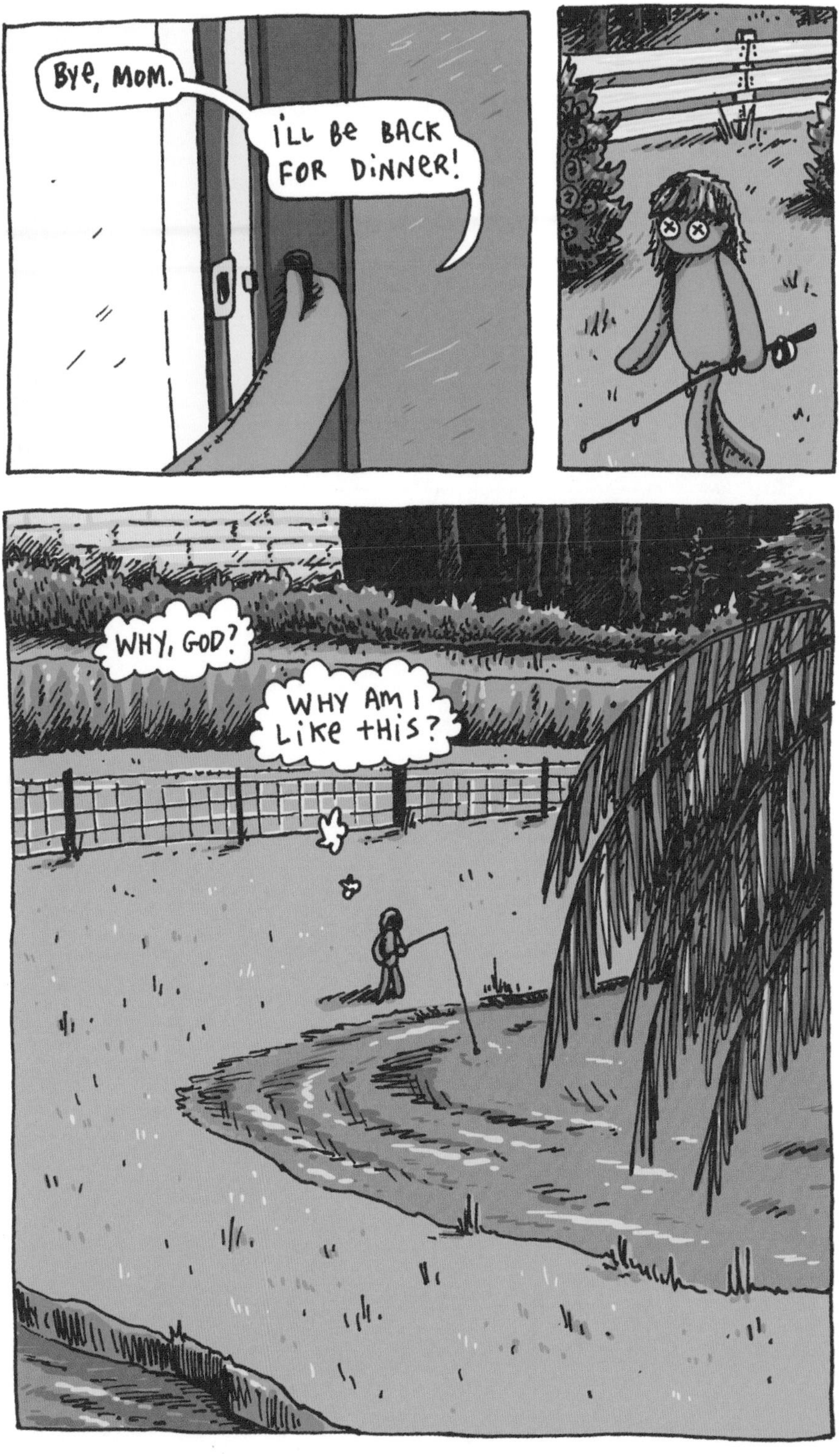
Bye, MOM.
I'LL Be BACK FOR DiNNeR!
WHY, GOD?
WHY AM I LiKe tHiS?

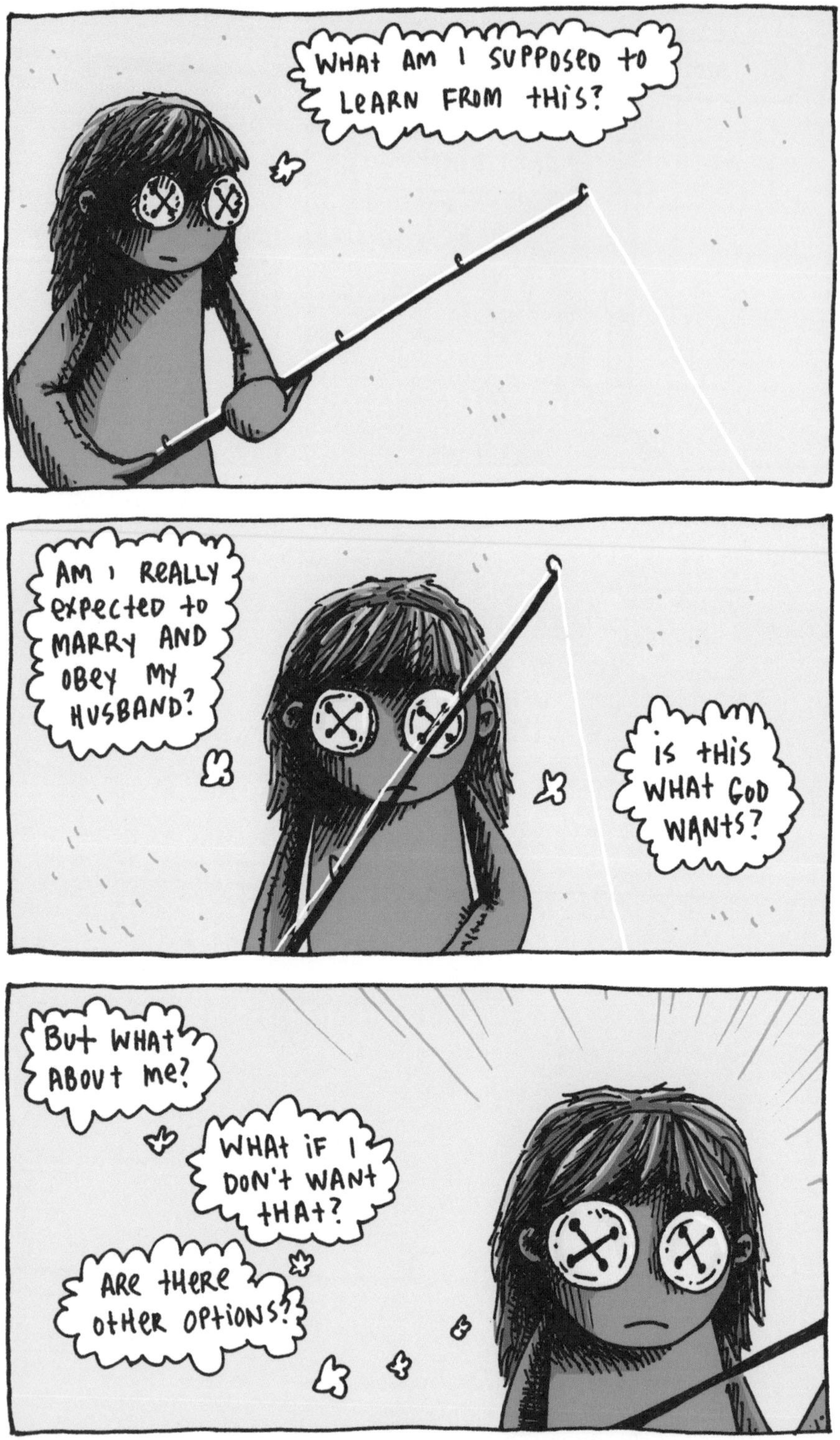
WHAT AM I SUPPOSED TO LEARN FROM THIS?
AM I REALLY EXPECTED TO MARRY AND OBEY MY HUSBAND?
IS THIS WHAT GOD WANTS?
BUT WHAT ABOUT ME?
WHAT IF I DON'T WANT THAT?
ARE THERE OTHER OPTIONS?

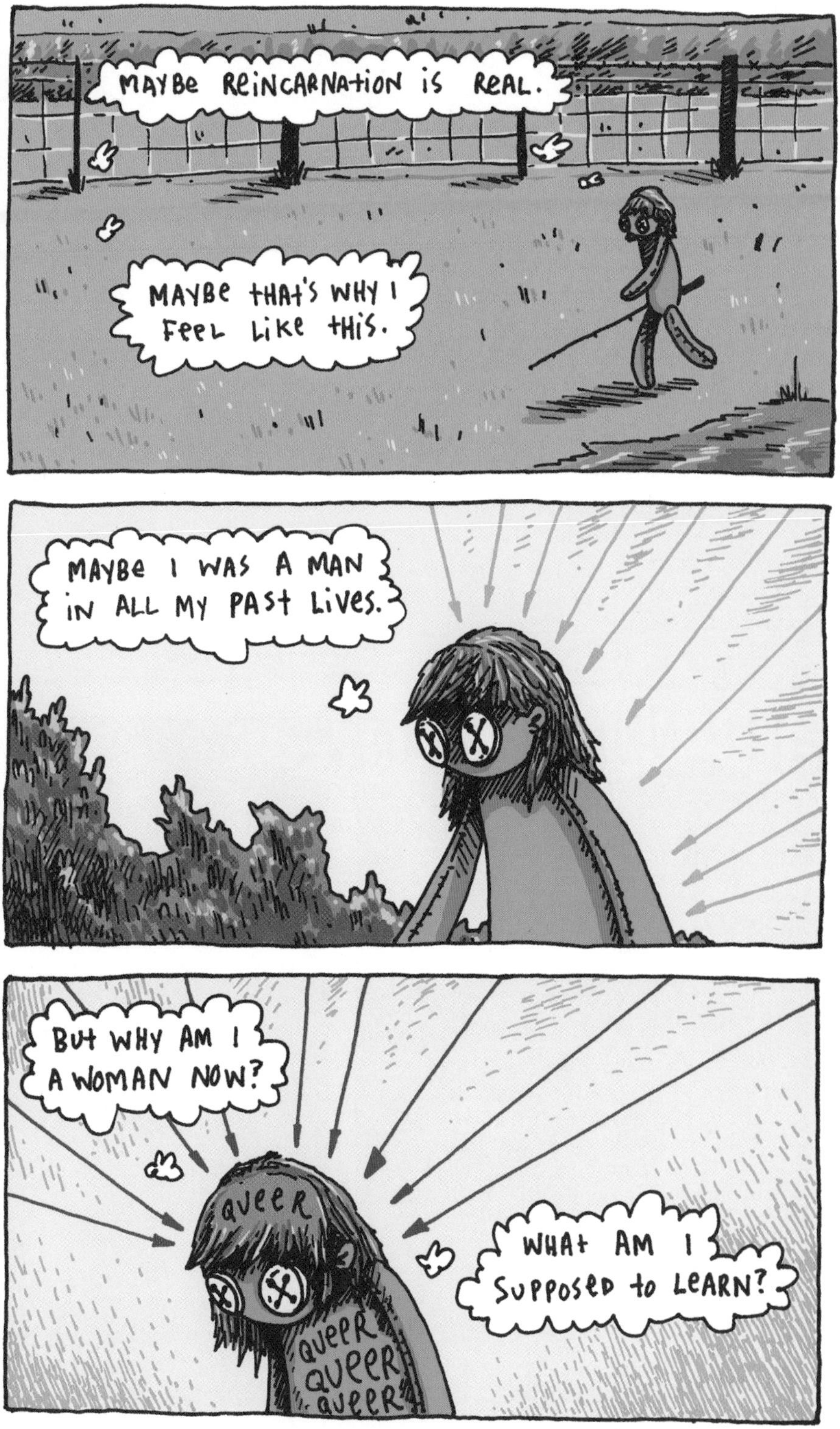
MAYBE REINCARNATION IS REAL.
MAYBE THAT'S WHY I FEEL LIKE THIS.
MAYBE I WAS A MAN IN ALL MY PAST LIVES.
BUT WHY AM I A WOMAN NOW?
QUEER
WHAT AM I SUPPOSED TO LEARN?
QUEER QUEER QUEER

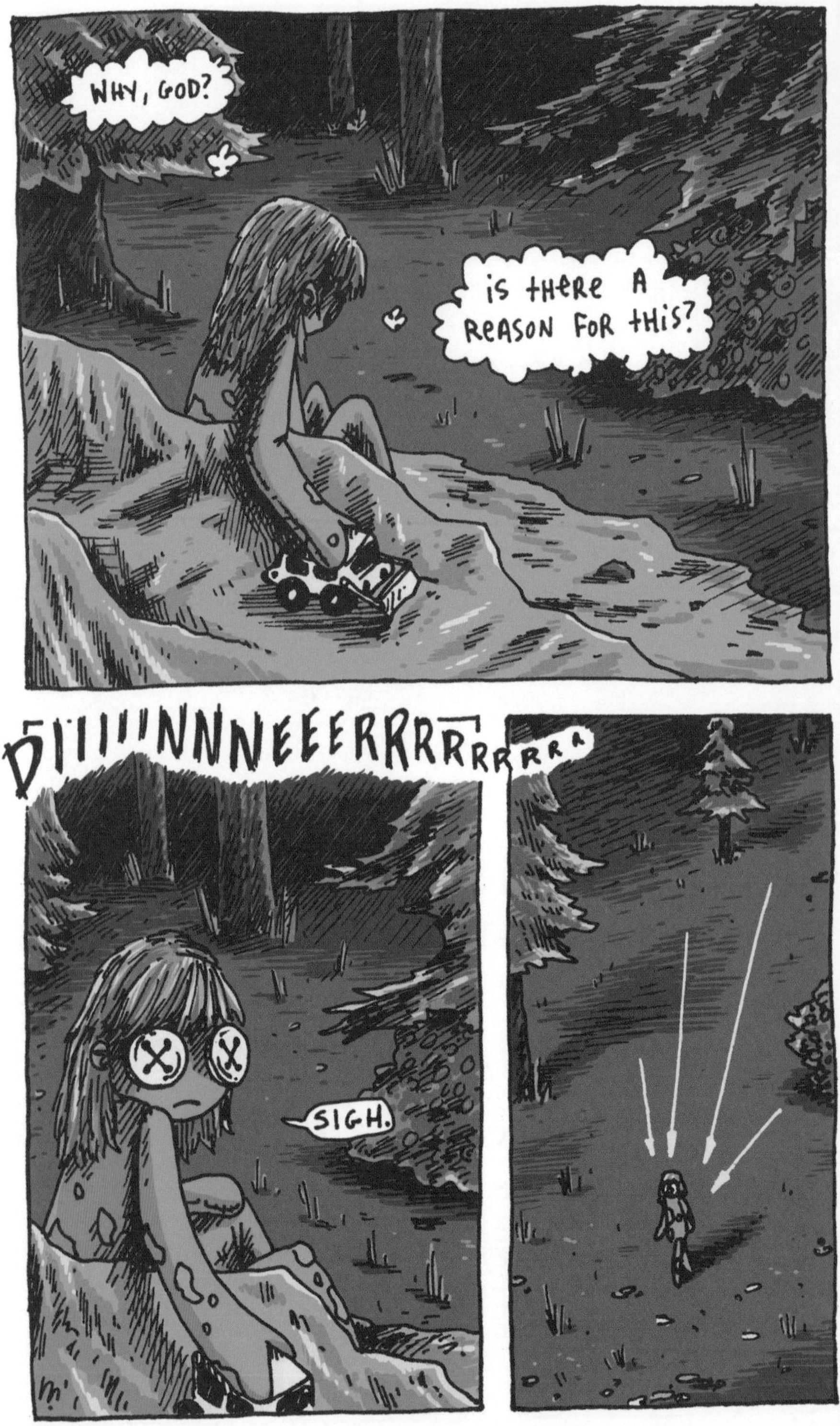
WHY, GOD?
is there A REASON FOR this?
DIIIIINNNEEERRRRRRRRA
SIGH.

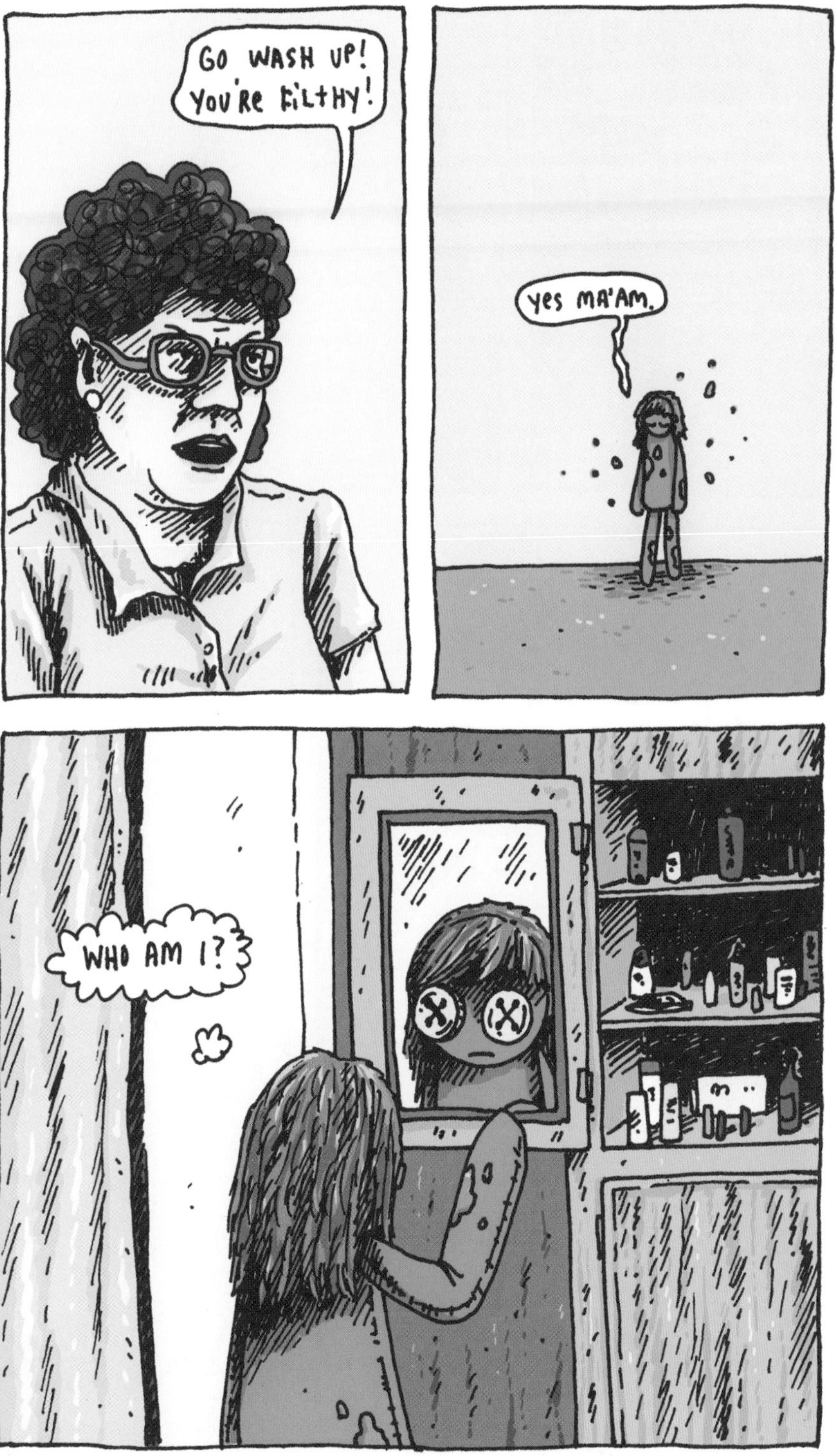
GO WASH UP! YOU'RE FILTHY!
YES MA'AM.
WHO AM I?

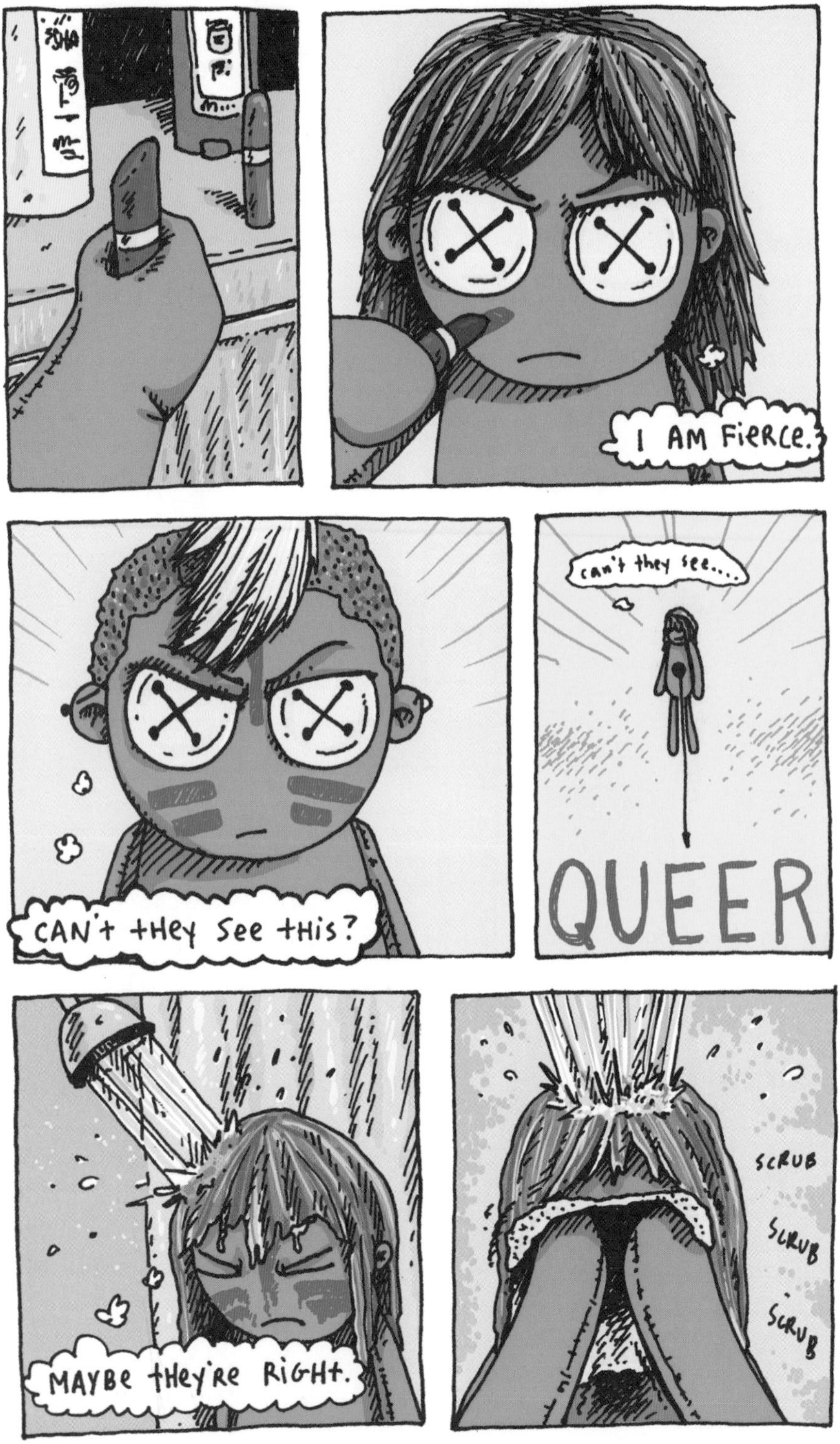
I AM FIERCE.
CAN'T THEY SEE THIS?
CAN'T THEY SEE...
QUEER
MAYBE THEY'RE RIGHT.
SCRUB
SCRUB
SCRUB

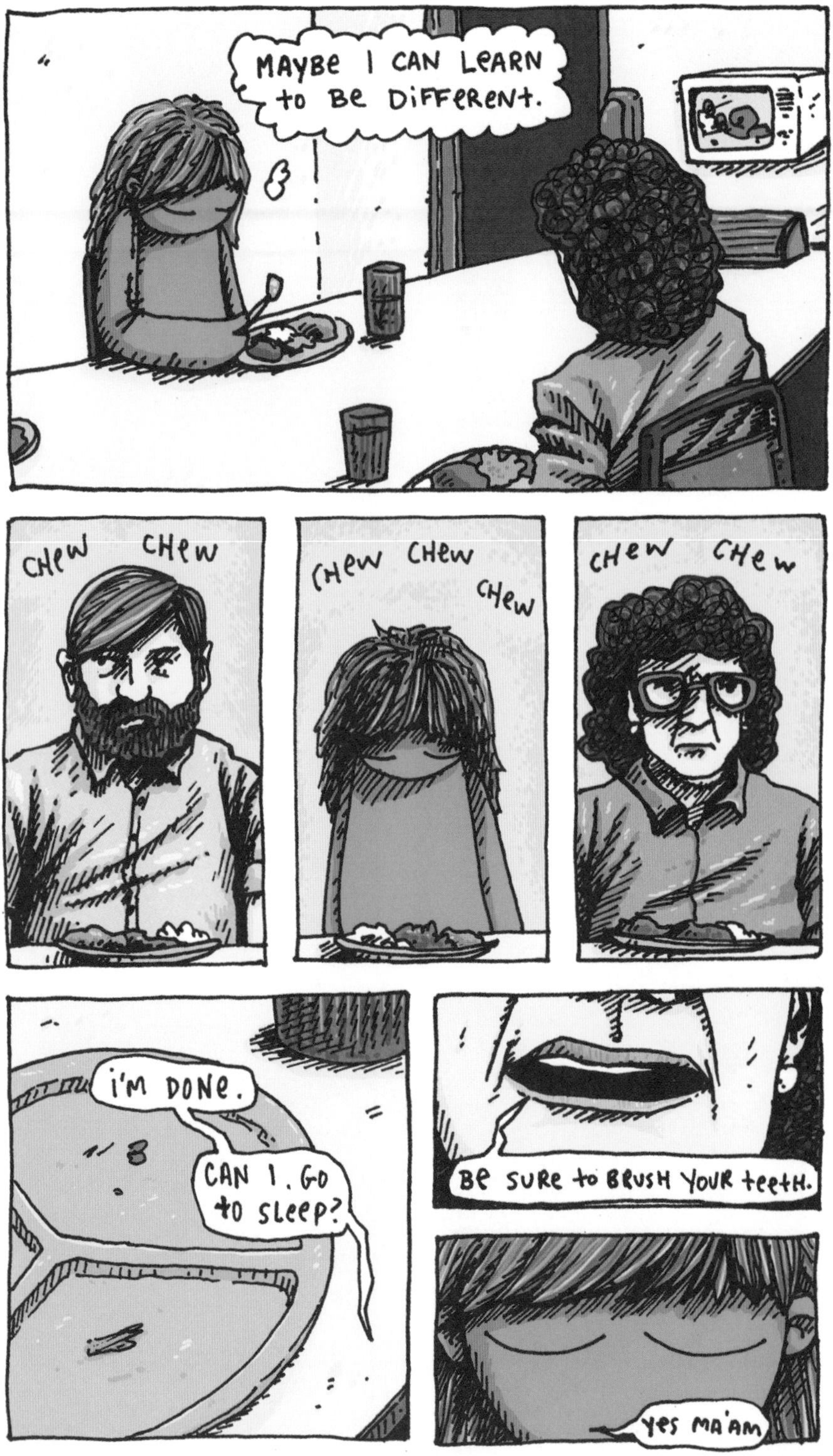
MAYBE I CAN LEARN to BE DIFFERENT.
CHEW CHEW
CHEW CHEW CHEW
CHEW CHEW
I'M DONE.
CAN I. GO to SLEEP?
BE SURE to BRUSH YOUR teeth.
yes MA'AM

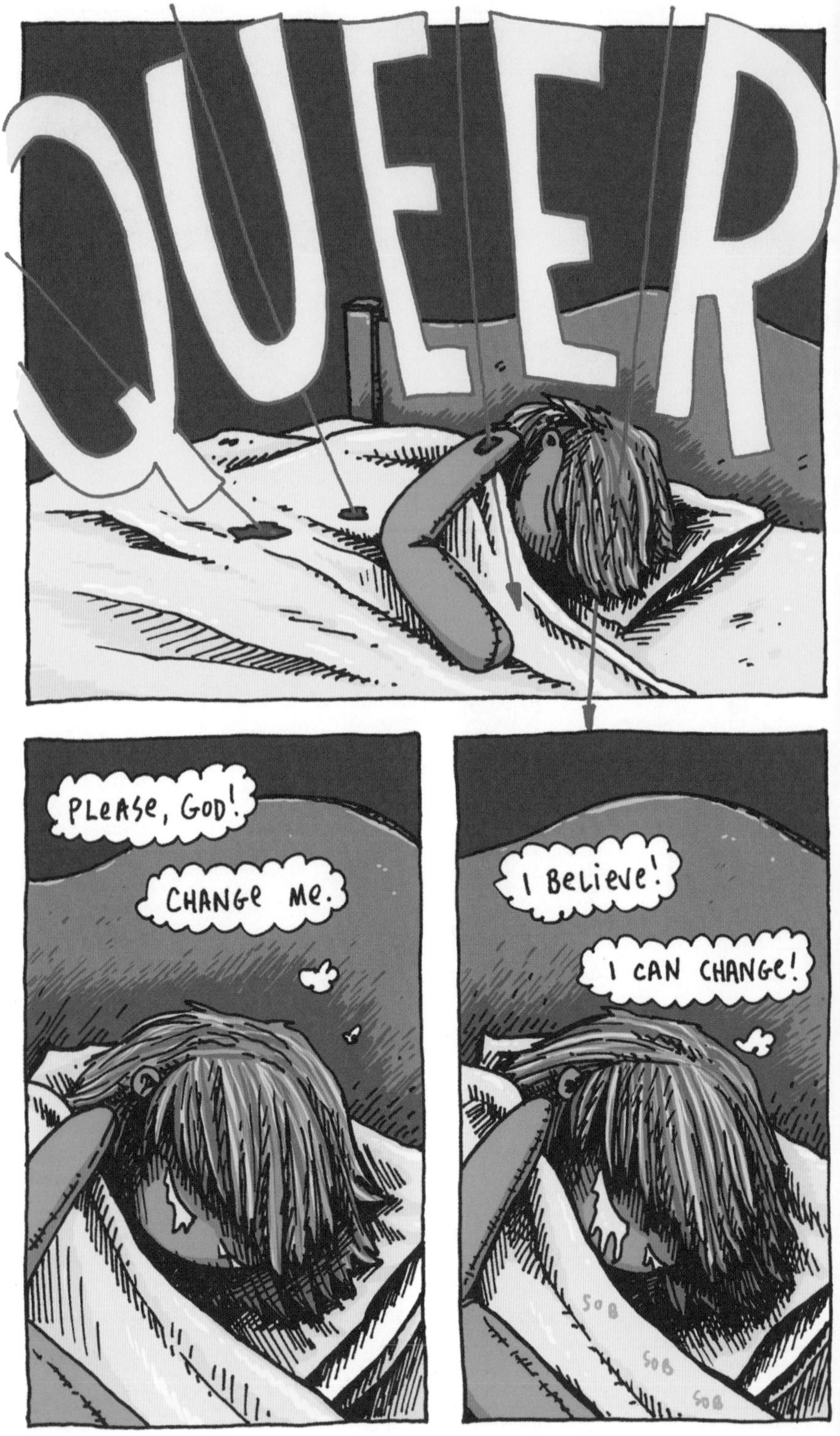
QUEER
PLEASE, GOD!
CHANGE ME.
I BELIEVE!
I CAN CHANGE!
SOB
SOB
SOB

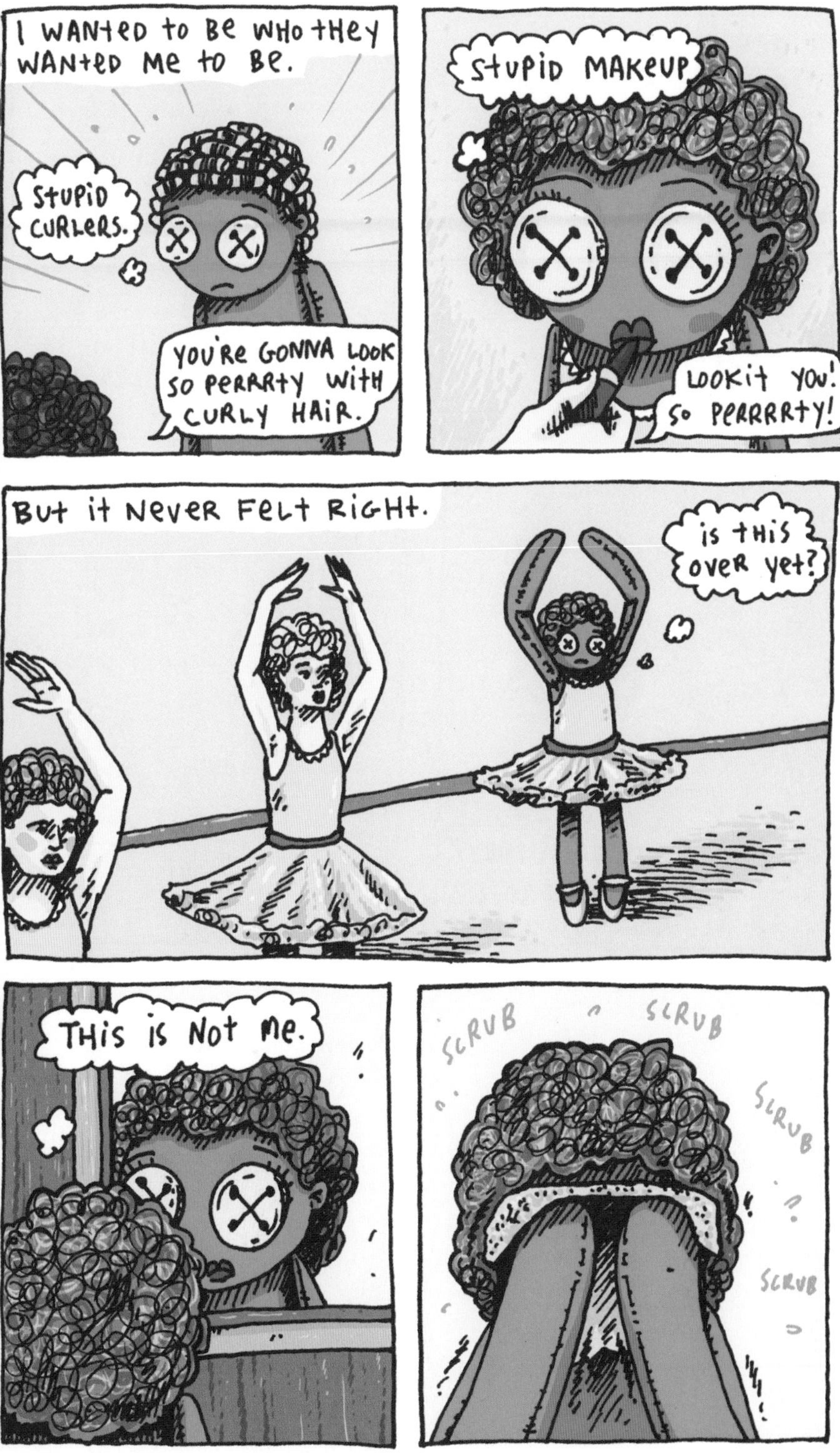
I WANTED TO BE WHO THEY WANTED ME TO BE.
STUPID CURLERS.
YOU'RE GONNA LOOK SO PERRRTY WITH CURLY HAIR.
STUPID MAKEUP
LOOKIT YOU! SO PERRRRRTY!
BUT IT NEVER FELT RIGHT.
IS THIS OVER YET?
THIS IS NOT ME.
SCRUB
SCRUB
SCRUB
SCRUB

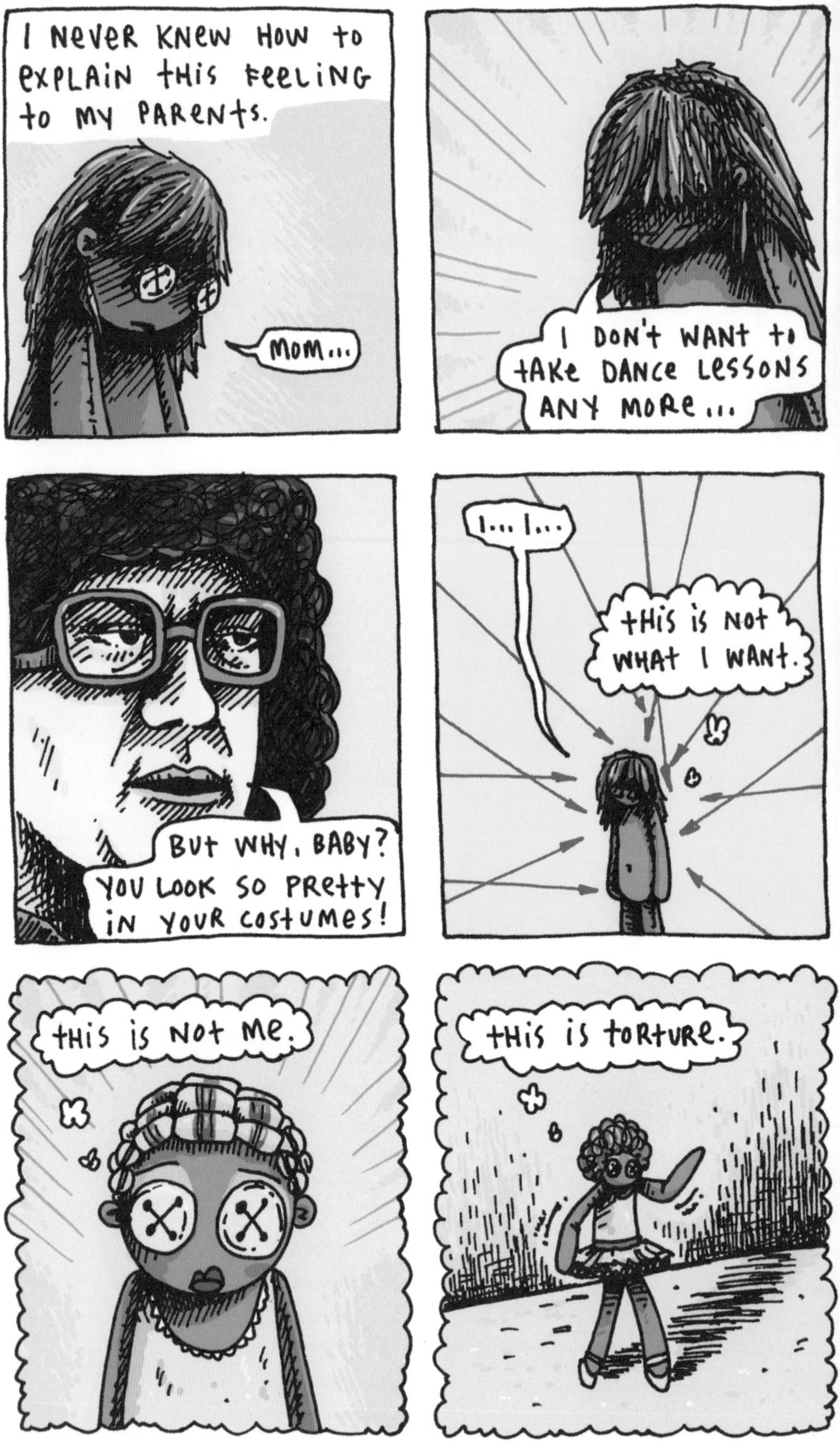
I NEVER KNEW HOW TO EXPLAIN THIS FEELING TO MY PARENTS.
MOM...
I DON'T WANT TO TAKE DANCE LESSONS ANY MORE...
BUT WHY, BABY? YOU LOOK SO PRETTY IN YOUR COSTUMES!
I... I...
THIS IS NOT WHAT I WANT.
THIS IS NOT ME.
THIS IS TORTURE.

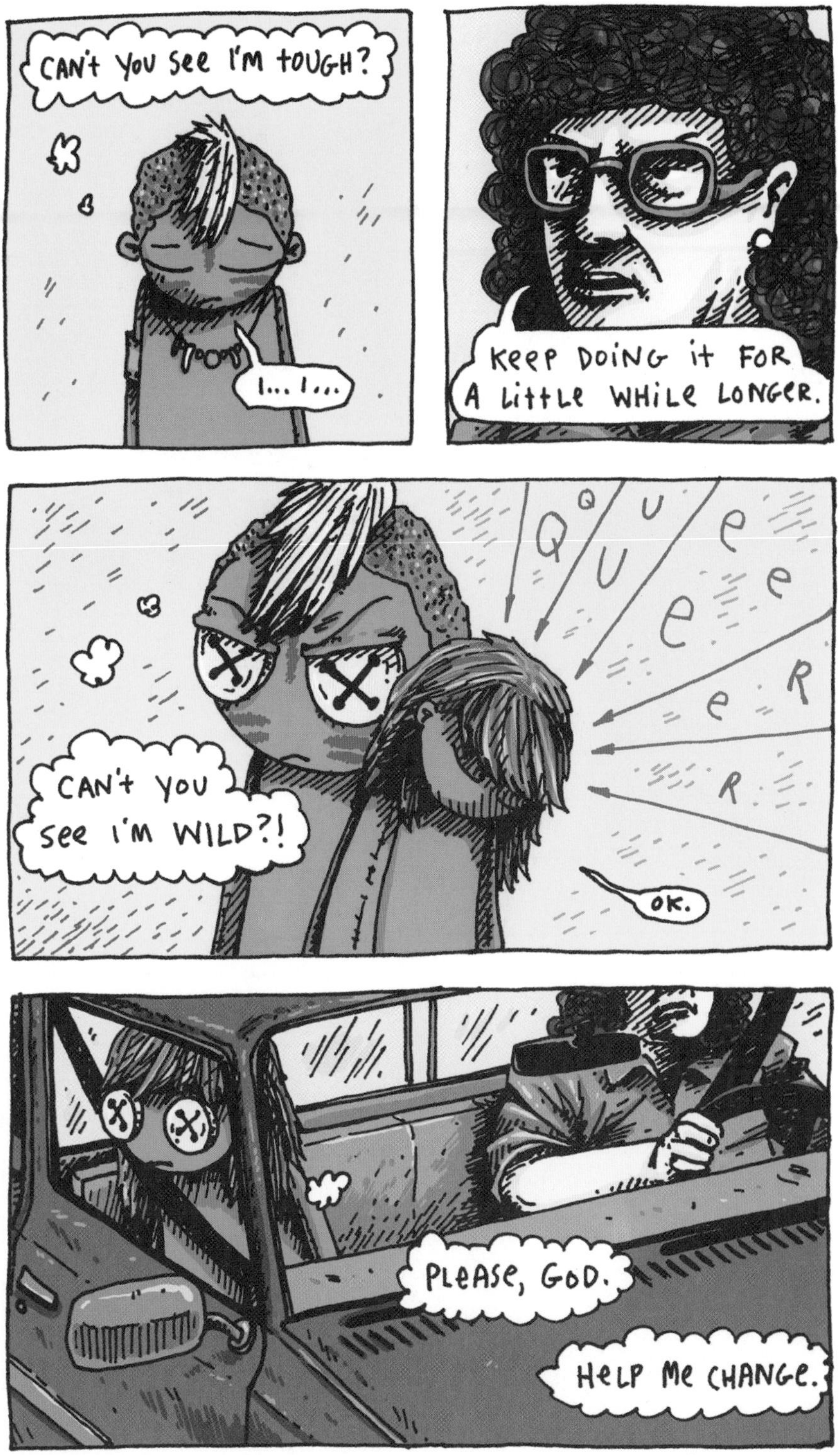
CAN'T YOU SEE I'M TOUGH?
I... I...
KEEP DOING IT FOR A LITTLE WHILE LONGER.
Q U E E R
Q U e e e R
CAN'T YOU SEE I'M WILD?!
OK.
PLEASE, GOD.
HELP ME CHANGE.

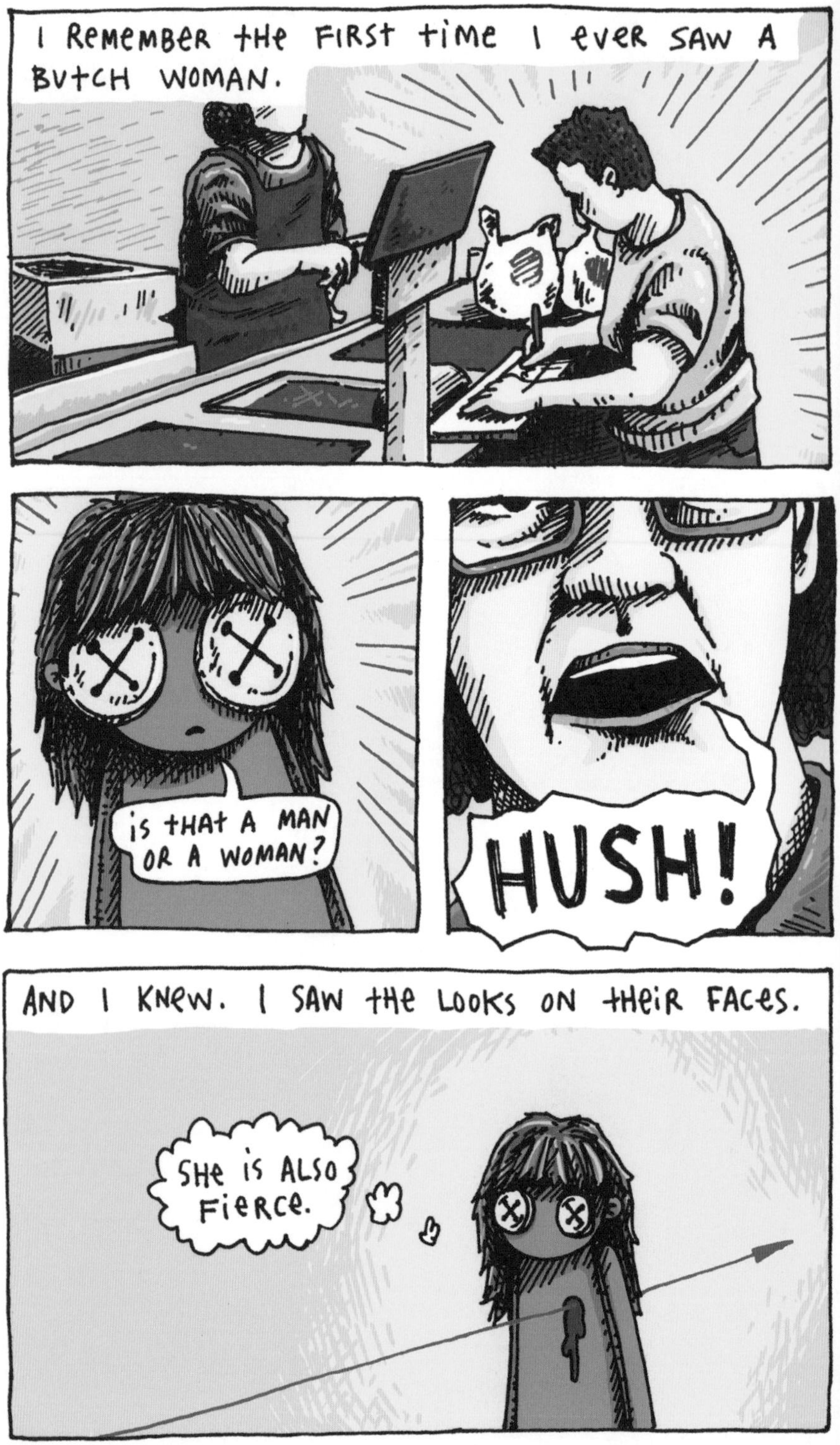
I REMEMBER THE FIRST TIME I EVER SAW A BUTCH WOMAN.
IS THAT A MAN OR A WOMAN?
HUSH!
AND I KNEW. I SAW THE LOOKS ON THEIR FACES.
SHE IS ALSO FIERCE.

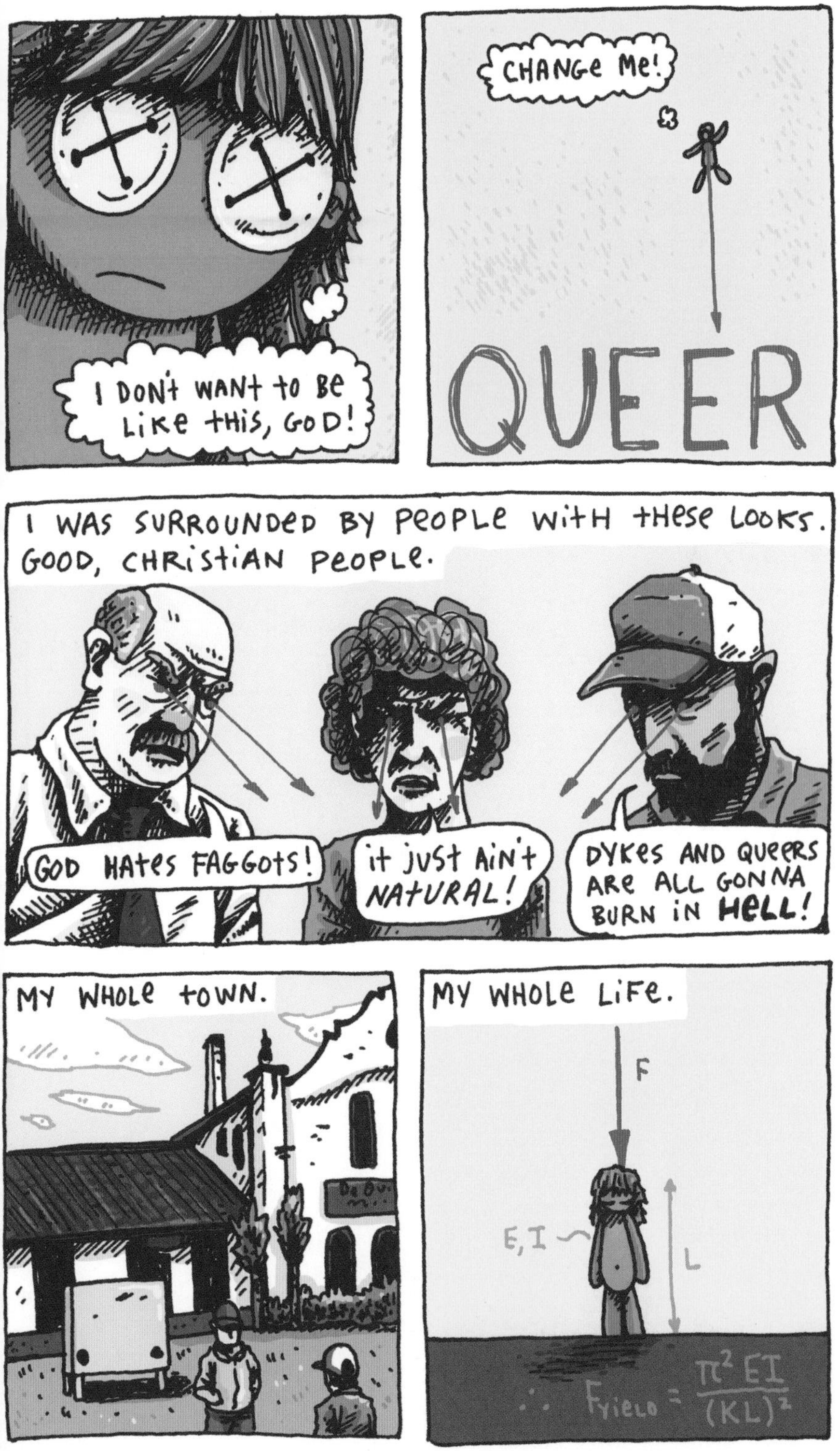

I DON'T WANT TO BE LIKE THIS, GOD!
CHANGE ME!
QUEER
I WAS SURROUNDED BY PEOPLE WITH THESE LOOKS. GOOD, CHRISTIAN PEOPLE.
GOD HATES FAGGOTS!
IT JUST AIN'T NATURAL!
DYKES AND QUEERS ARE ALL GONNA BURN IN HELL!
MY WHOLE TOWN.
MY WHOLE LIFE.
F
E, I
L
$\therefore F_{yield} = \frac{\pi^2 EI}{(KL)^2}$

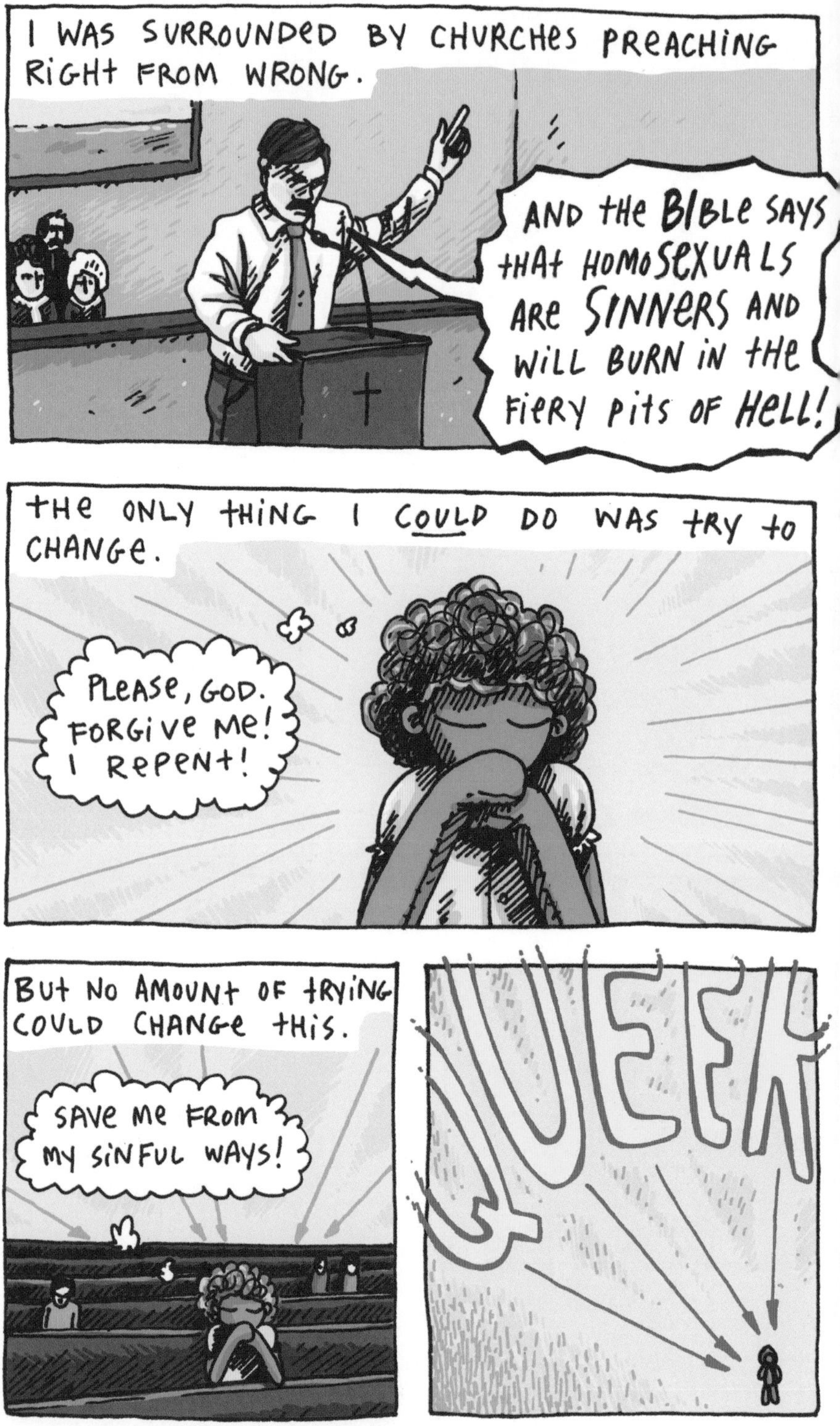
I WAS SURROUNDED BY CHURCHES PREACHING RIGHT FROM WRONG.
AND THE BIBLE SAYS THAT HOMOSEXUALS ARE SINNERS AND WILL BURN IN THE FIERY PITS OF HELL!
THE ONLY THING I COULD DO WAS TRY TO CHANGE.
PLEASE, GOD. FORGIVE ME! I REPENT!
BUT NO AMOUNT OF TRYING COULD CHANGE THIS.
SAVE ME FROM MY SINFUL WAYS!
QUEER

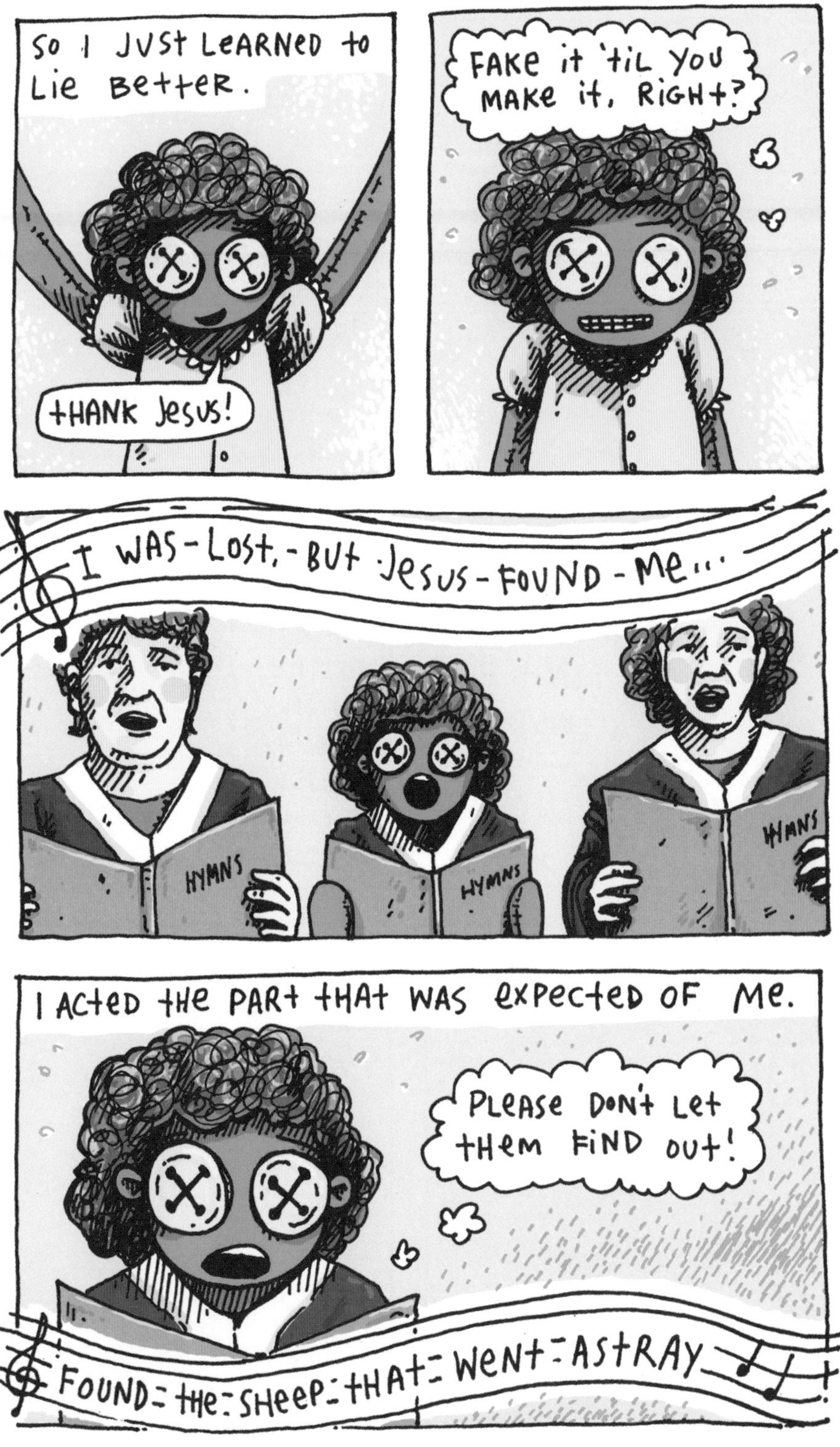

SO I JUST LEARNED TO LIE BETTER.
THANK JESUS!
FAKE IT 'TIL YOU MAKE IT, RIGHT?
I WAS-LOST,-BUT JESUS-FOUND-ME...
HYMNS
HYMNS
HYMNS
I ACTED THE PART THAT WAS EXPECTED OF ME.
PLEASE DON'T LET THEM FIND OUT!
FOUND-THE-SHEEP-THAT-WENT-ASTRAY

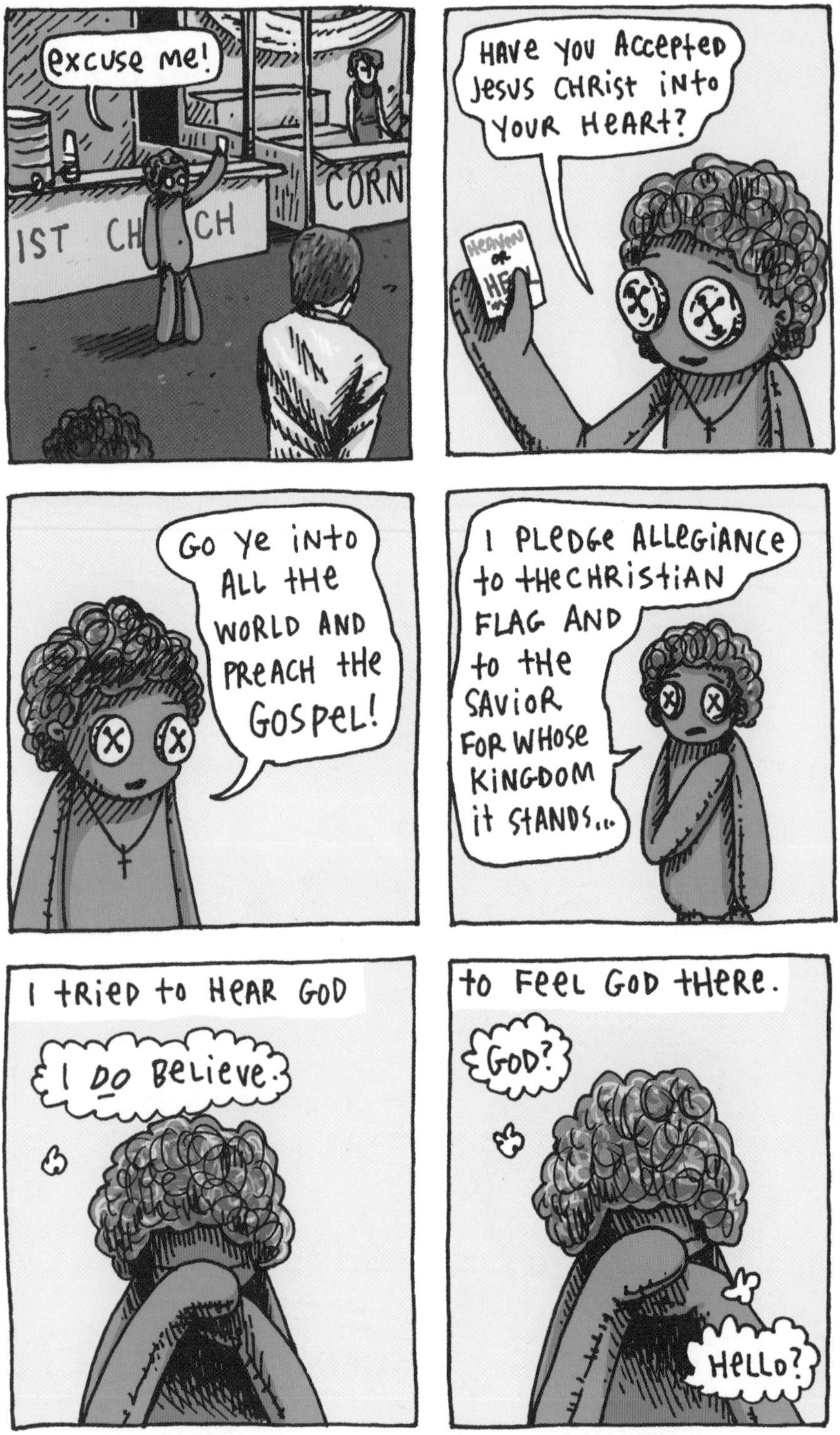
excuse me!
IST CH CH
CORN
HAVE YOU ACCEPTED JESUS CHRIST INTO YOUR HEART?
HEAVEN OR HELL
GO YE INTO ALL THE WORLD AND PREACH THE GOSPEL!
I PLEDGE ALLEGIANCE TO THE CHRISTIAN FLAG AND TO THE SAVIOR FOR WHOSE KINGDOM IT STANDS...
I TRIED TO HEAR GOD
I DO BELIEVE.
TO FEEL GOD THERE.
GOD?
HELLO?

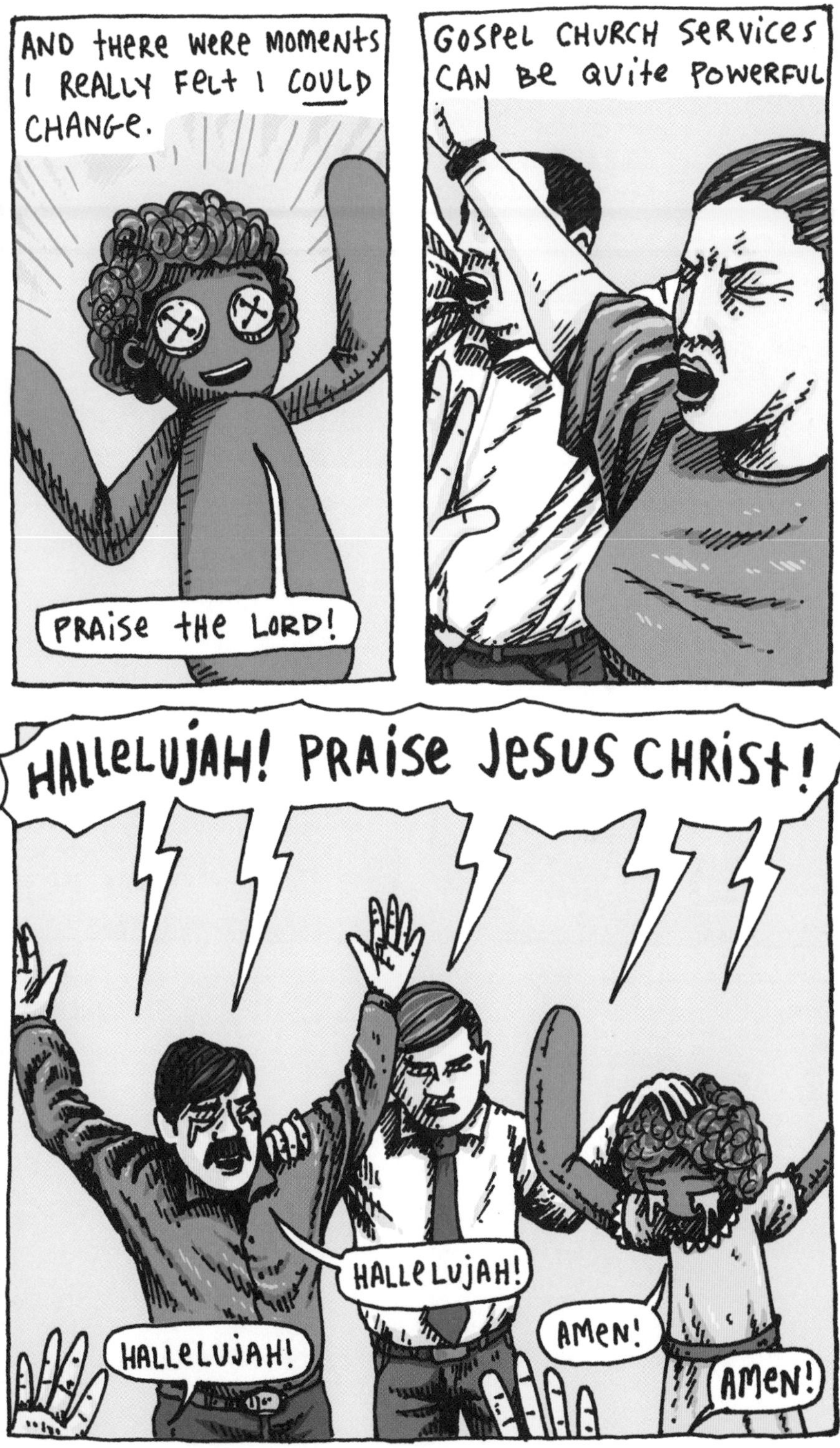
AND THERE WERE MOMENTS I REALLY FELT I COULD CHANGE.
PRAISE THE LORD!
GOSPEL CHURCH SERVICES CAN BE QUITE POWERFUL
HALLELUJAH! PRAISE JESUS CHRIST!
HALLELUJAH!
HALLELUJAH!
AMEN!
AMEN!

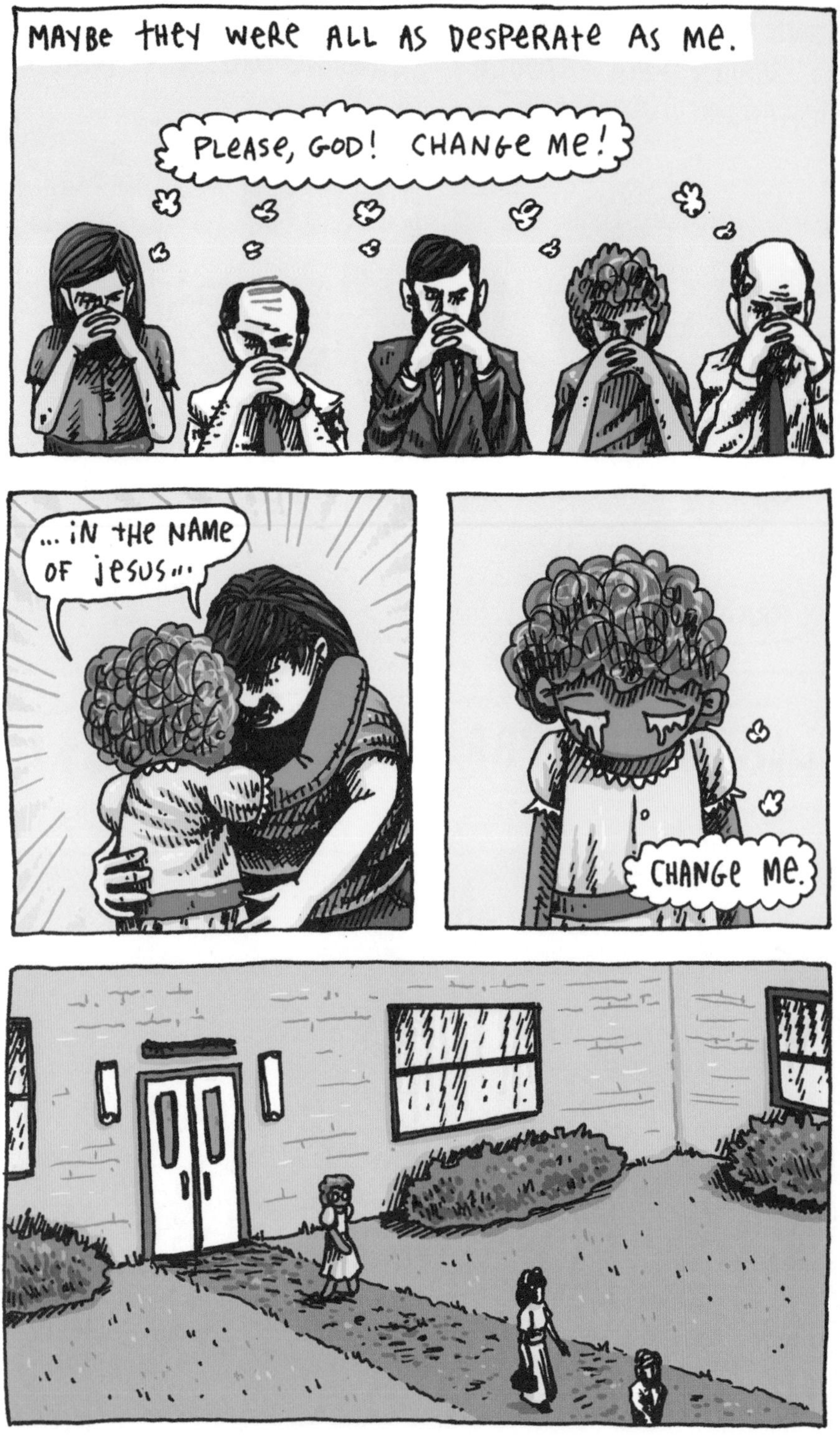
MAYBE THEY WERE ALL AS DESPERATE AS ME.
PLEASE, GOD! CHANGE ME!
...IN THE NAME OF JESUS...
CHANGE ME.

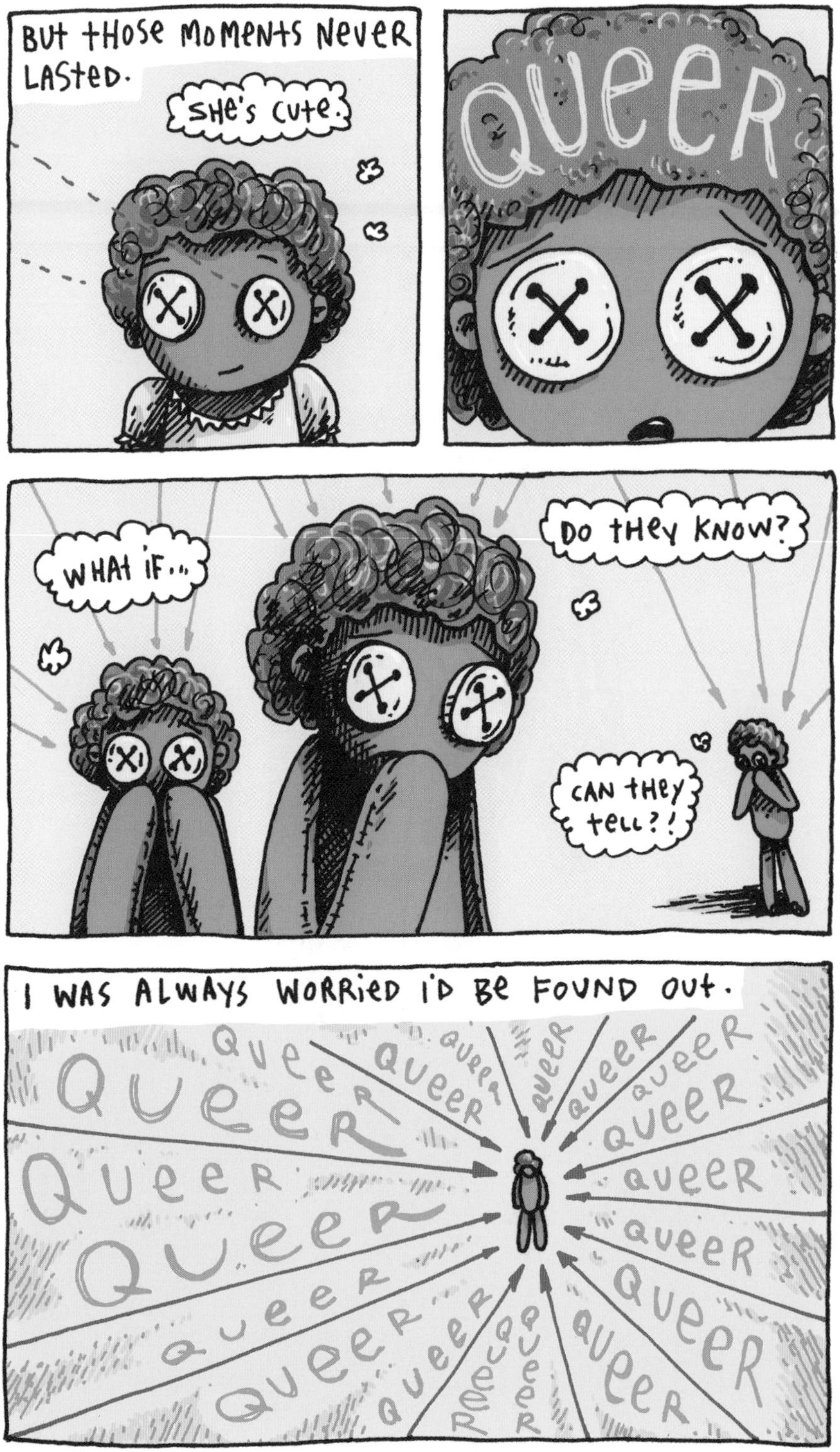
But those moments never lasted.
She's cute.
QUEER
What if...
Do they know?
Can they tell?!
I was always worried I'd be found out.

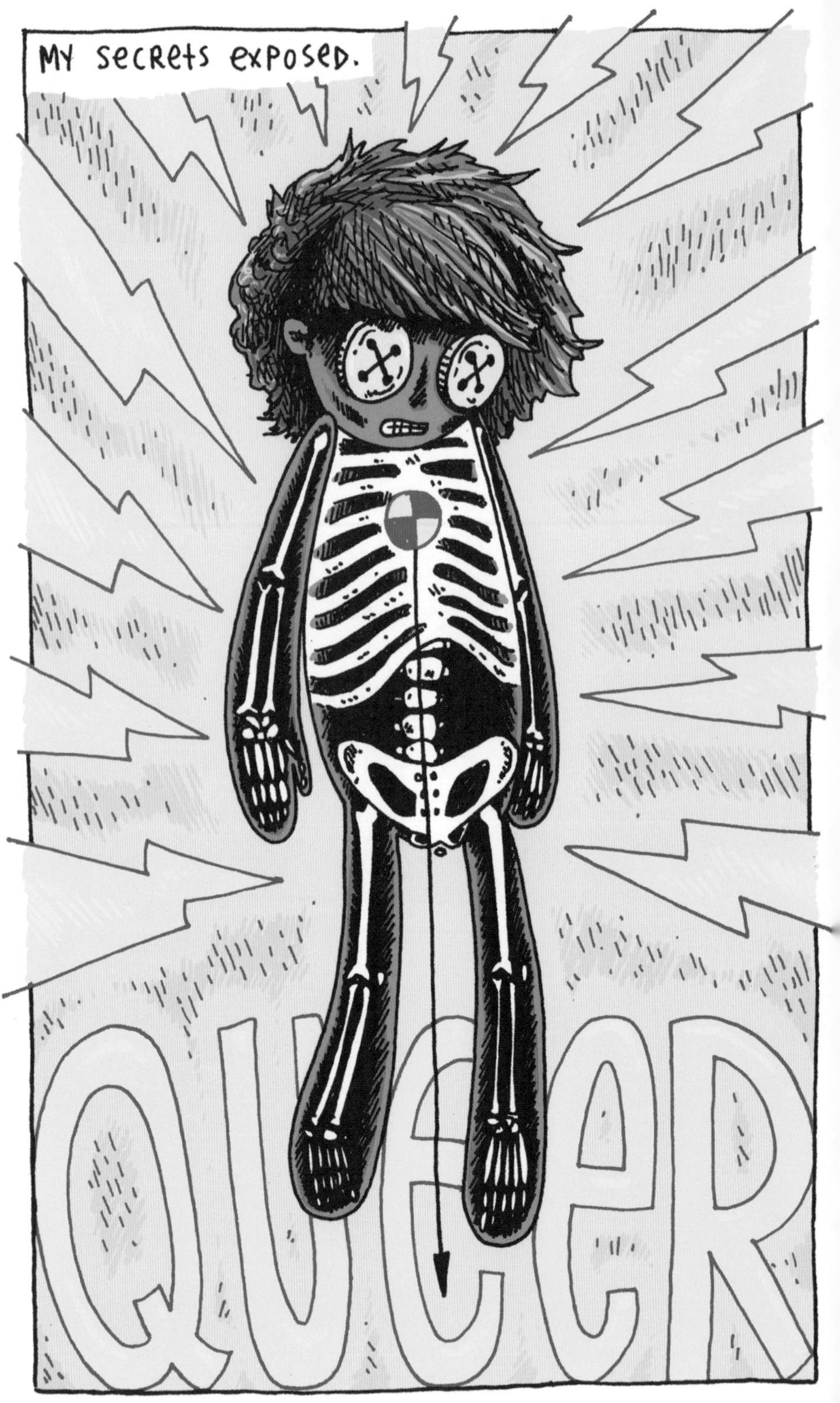
My secrets exposed.
QUEER

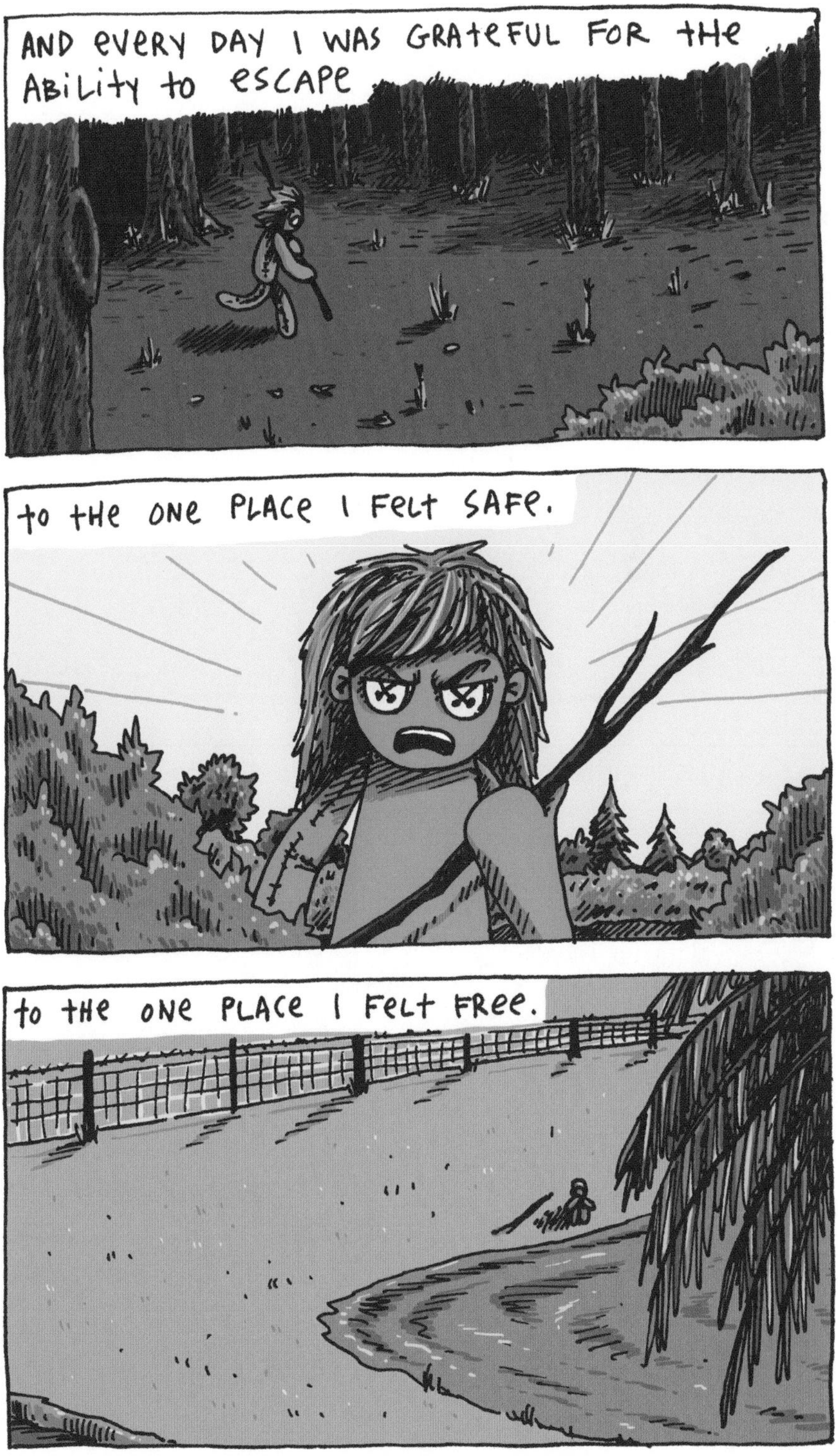
AND EVERY DAY I WAS GRATEFUL FOR THE ABILITY TO ESCAPE
TO THE ONE PLACE I FELT SAFE.
TO THE ONE PLACE I FELT FREE.

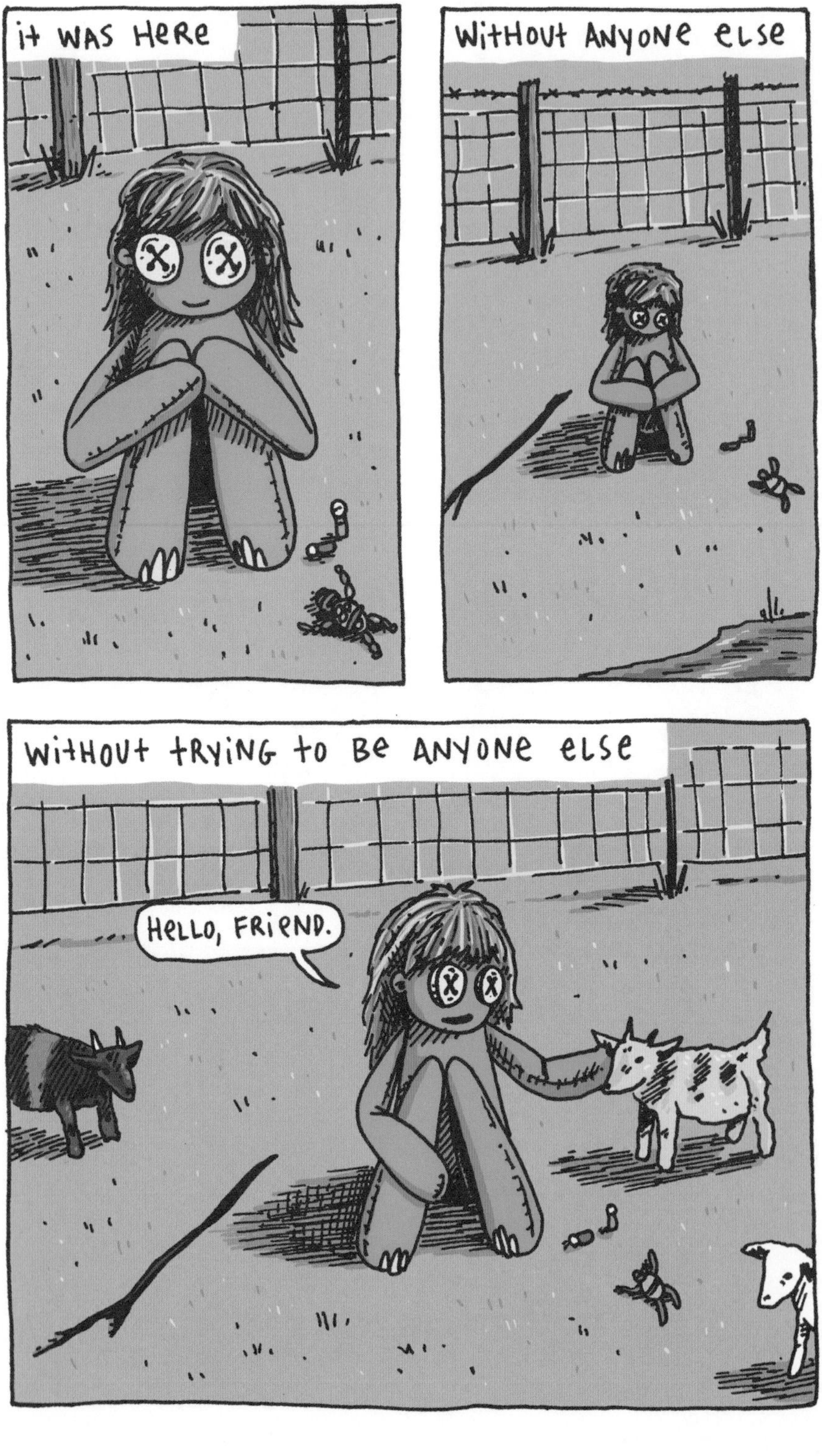
it WAS Here
WithOut ANyONe eLse
WithOut tRyiNG to Be ANyONe eLse
HeLLo, FRieND.

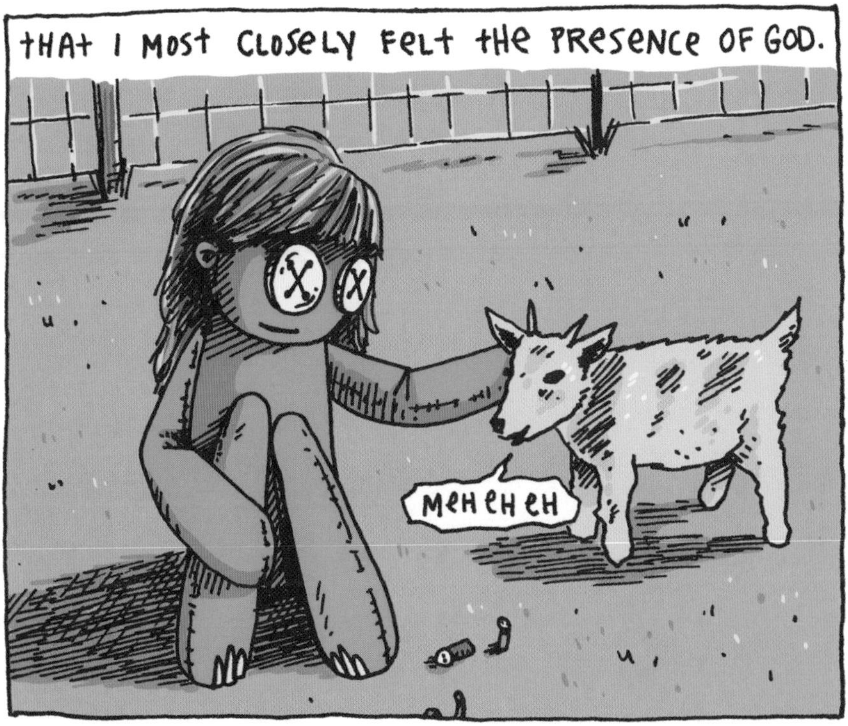
THAT I MOST CLOSELY FELT THE PRESENCE OF GOD.
MEHEHEH

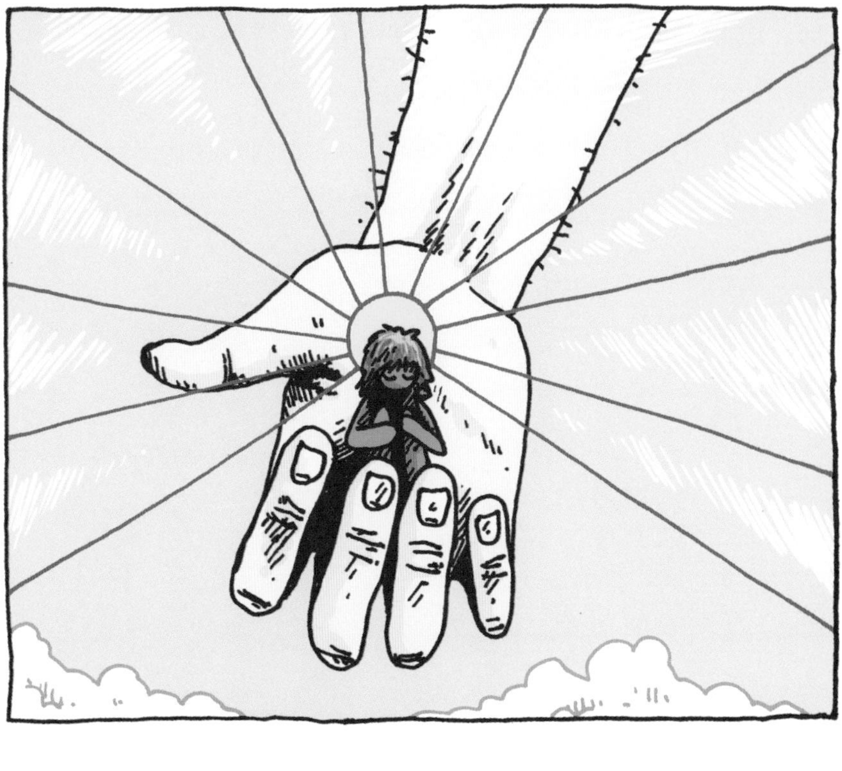

CHAPTER THREE

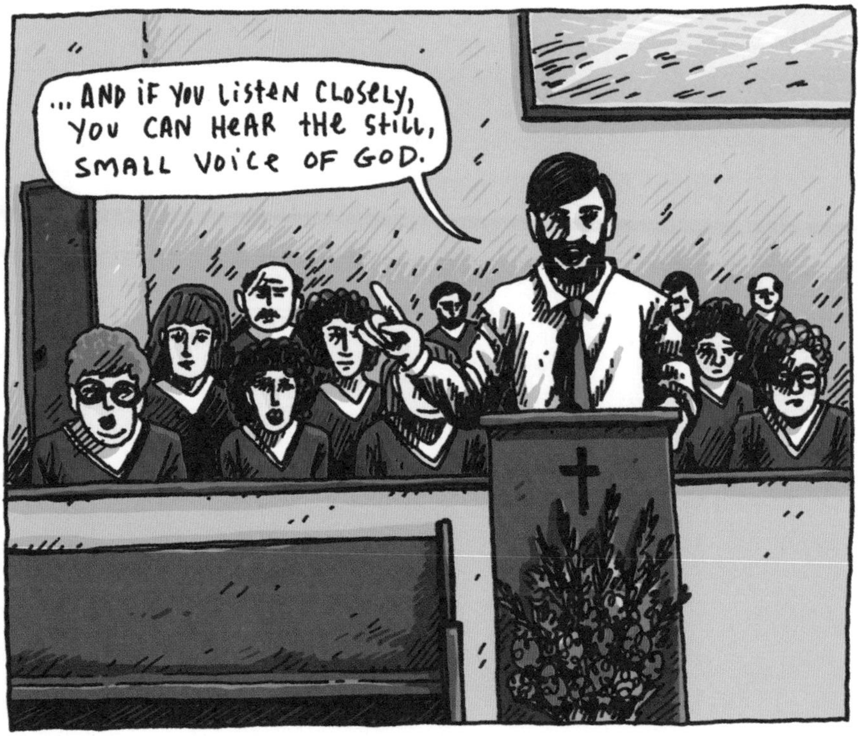
...AND IF YOU LISTEN CLOSELY, YOU CAN HEAR THE STILL, SMALL VOICE OF GOD.

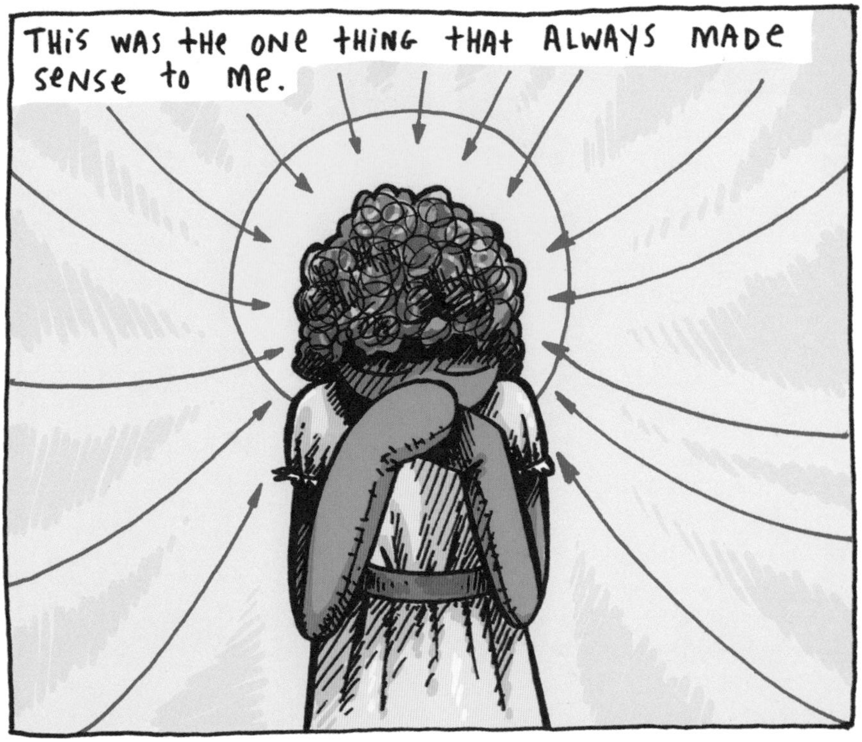
THIS WAS THE ONE THING THAT ALWAYS MADE SENSE TO ME.

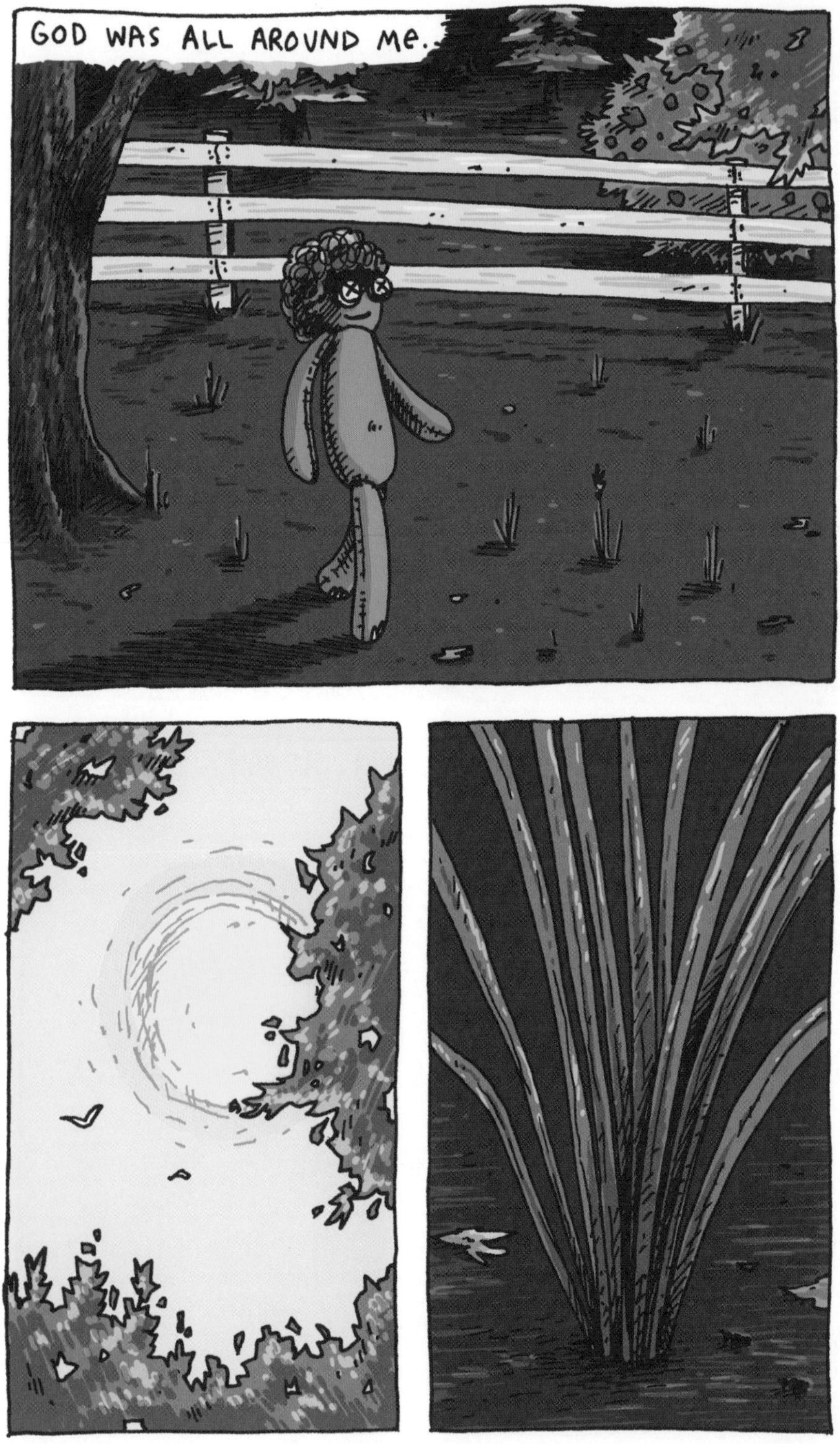
GOD WAS ALL AROUND ME.

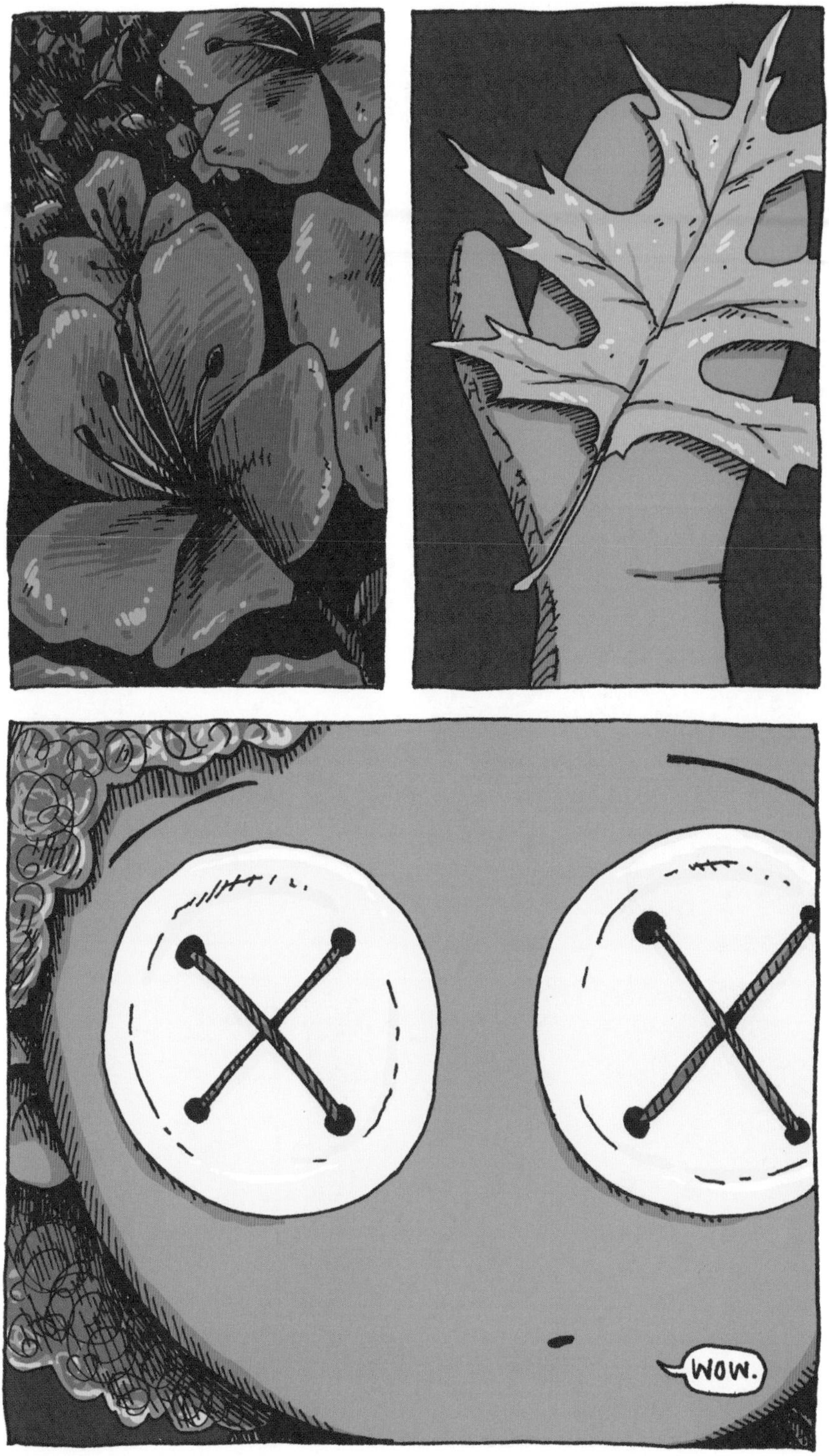
WOW.

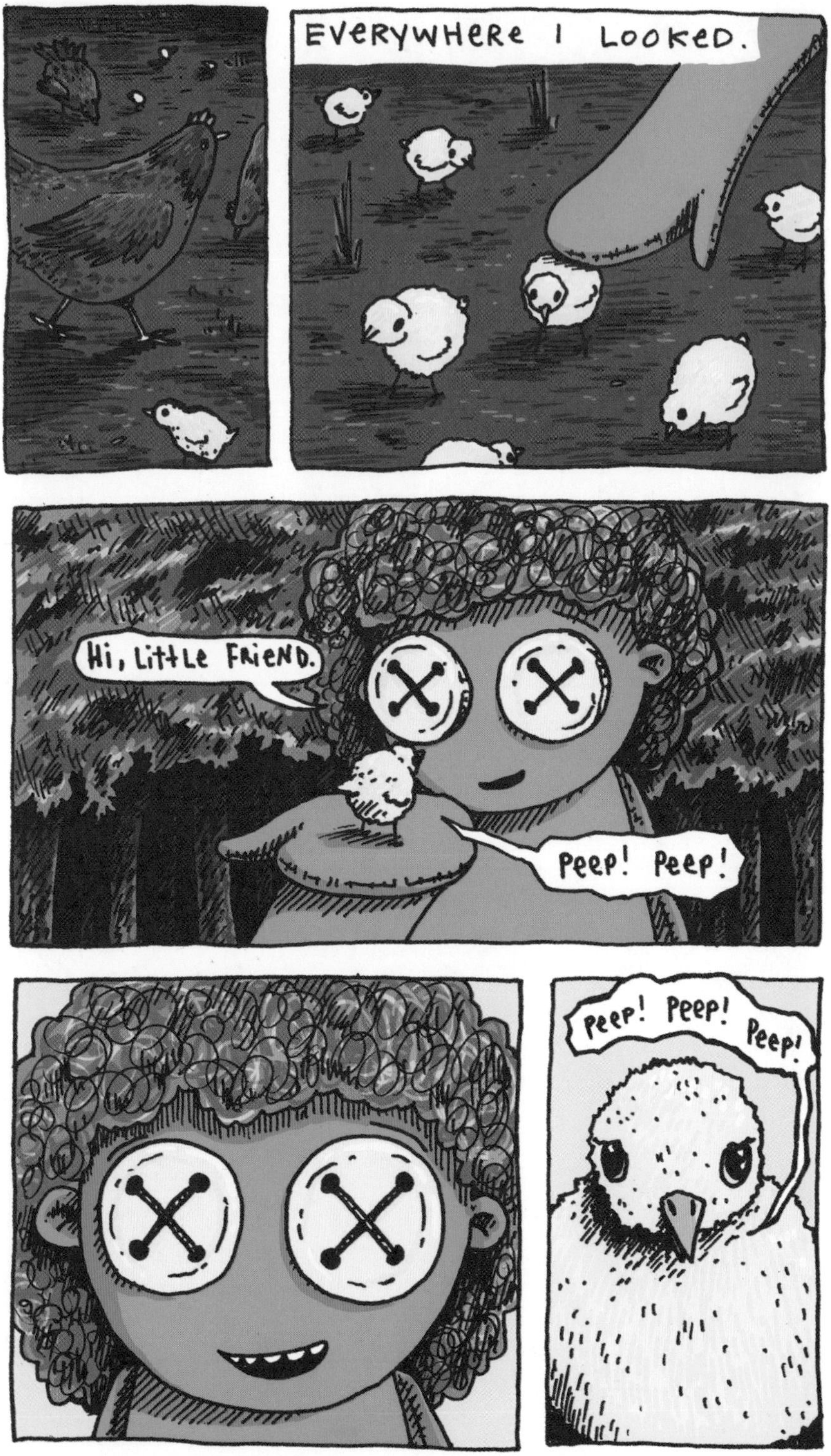
EVERYWHERE I LOOKED.
Hi, LiTTLE FRIEND.
Peep! Peep!
Peep! Peep! Peep!

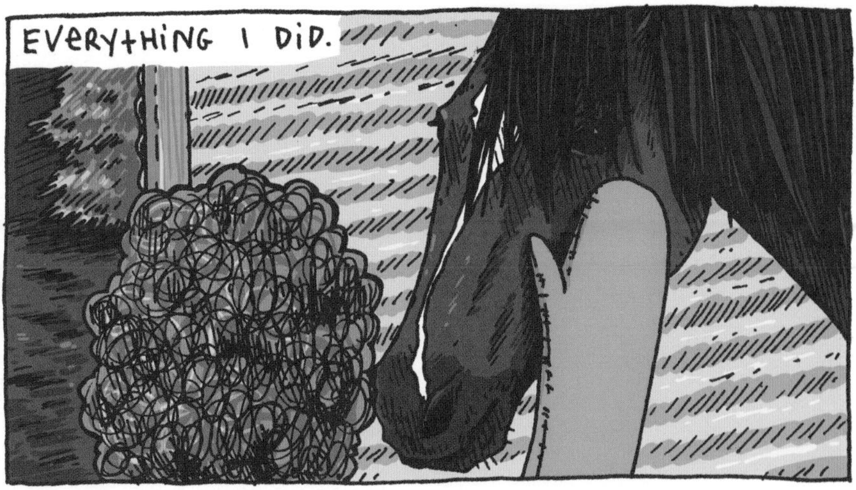
EVERYTHING I DID.

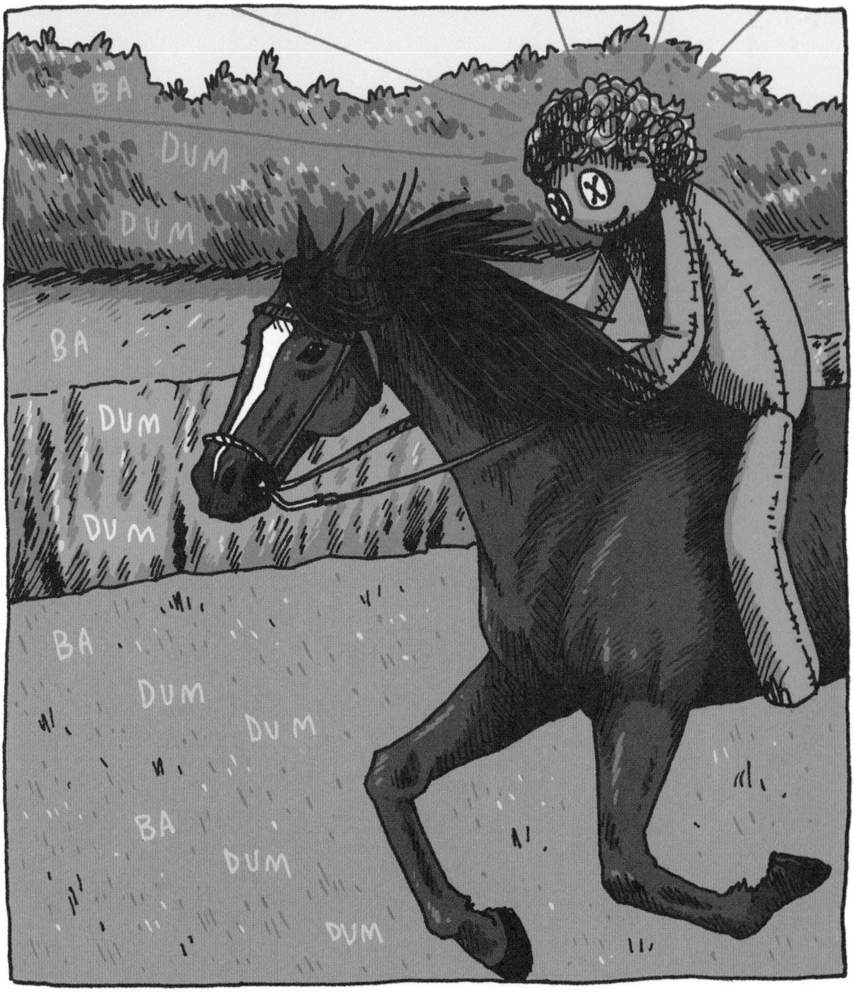
BA
DUM
DUM
BA
DUM
DUM
BA
DUM
DUM
BA
DUM
DUM

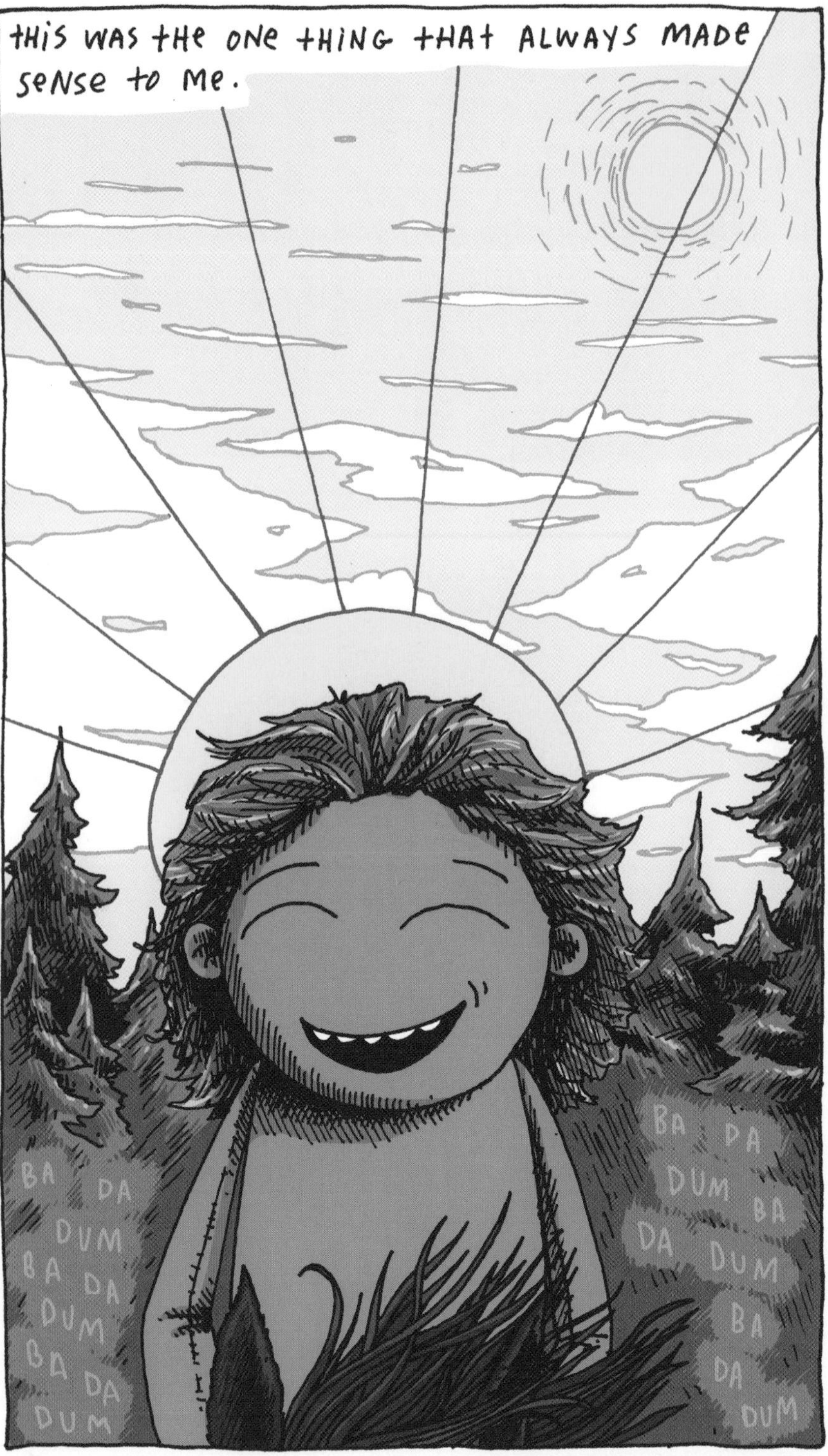
this was the one thing that always made sense to me.
BA DA DUM BA DA DUM BA DA DUM
BA DA DUM BA DA DUM BA DA DUM

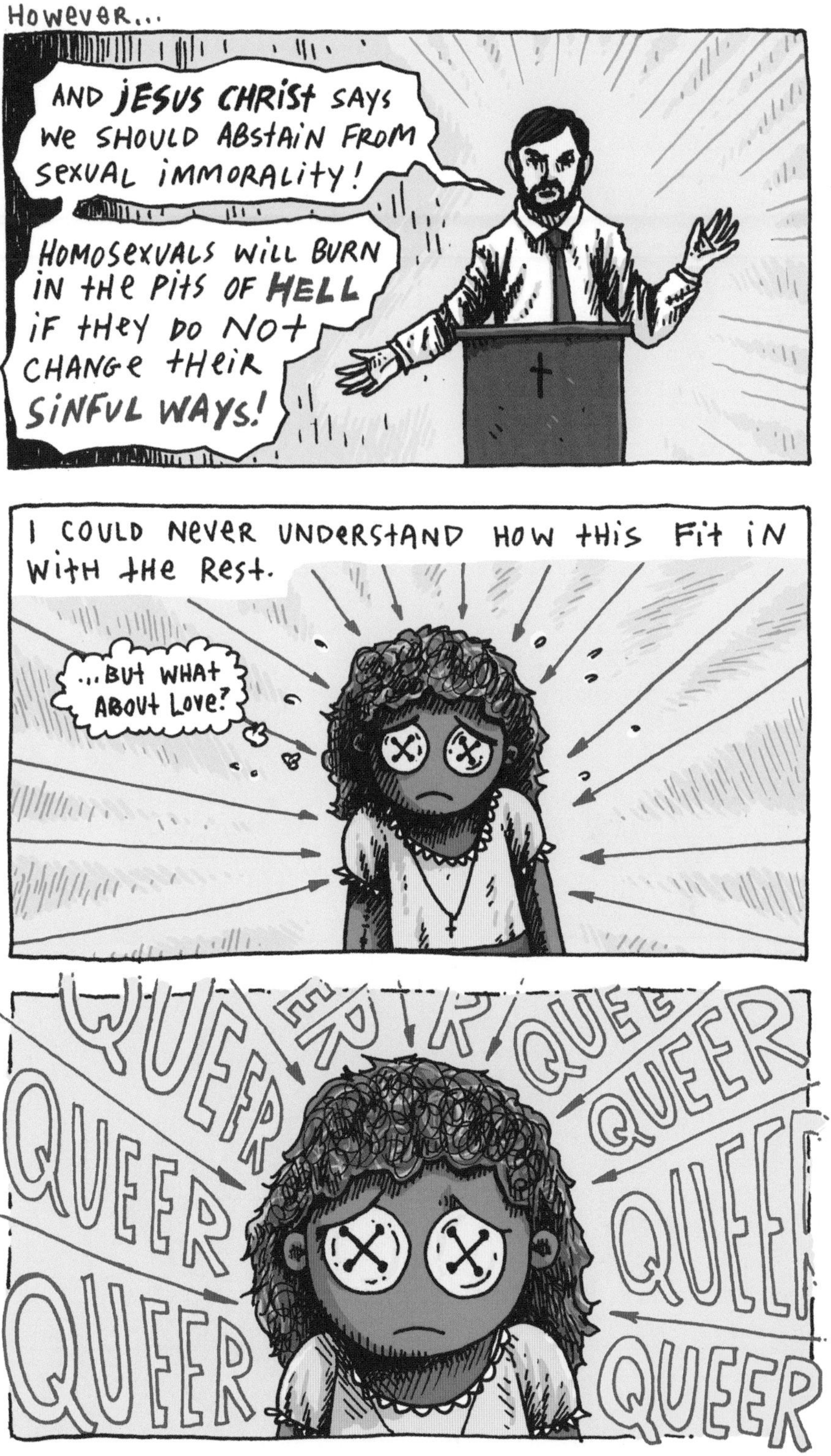
However...
AND JESUS CHRIST SAYS WE SHOULD ABSTAIN FROM SEXUAL IMMORALITY!
HOMOSEXUALS WILL BURN IN THE PITS OF HELL IF THEY DO NOT CHANGE THEIR SINFUL WAYS!
I COULD NEVER UNDERSTAND HOW THIS FIT IN WITH THE REST.
...BUT WHAT ABOUT LOVE?
QUEER
QUEER
QUEER
QUEER
QUEER
QUEER
QUEER

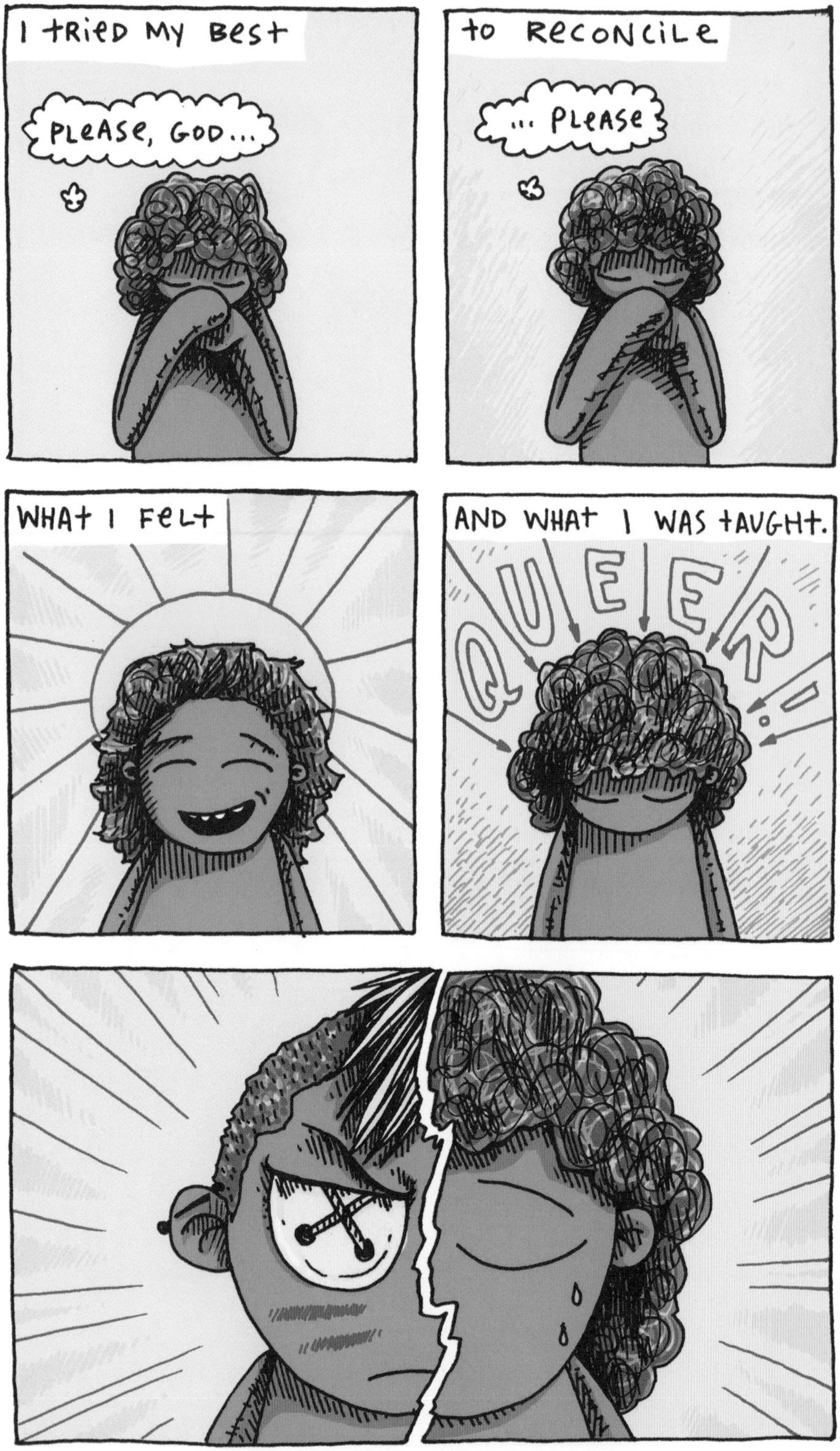
I tried my best
Please, God...
to reconcile
... Please
What I felt
And what I was taught.
QUEER!

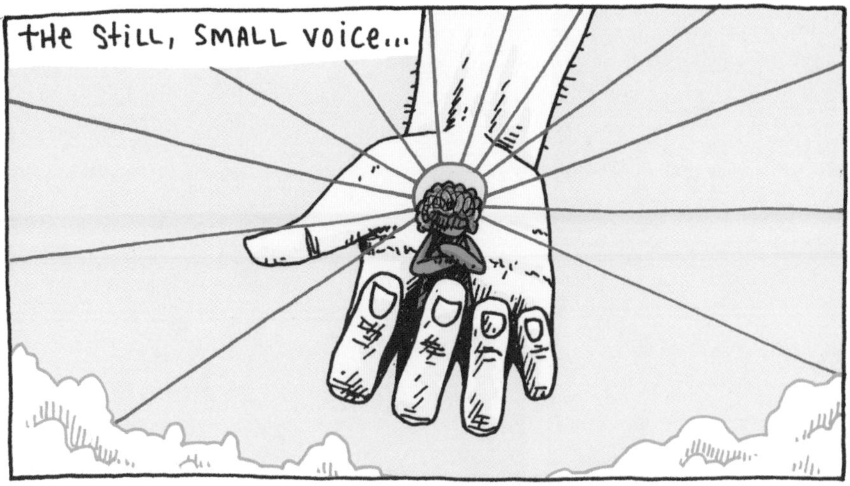
tHe Still, SMALL voice...

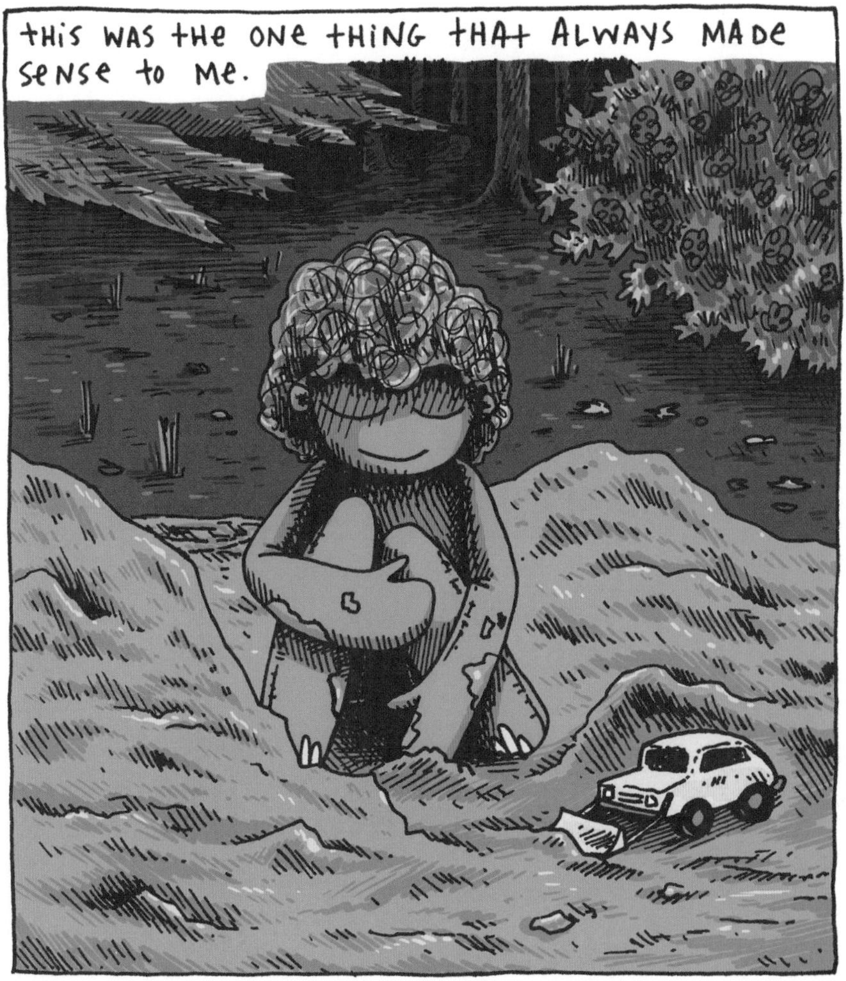
tHis WAS tHe ONe tHING tHAt ALWAYS MADe sense to Me.

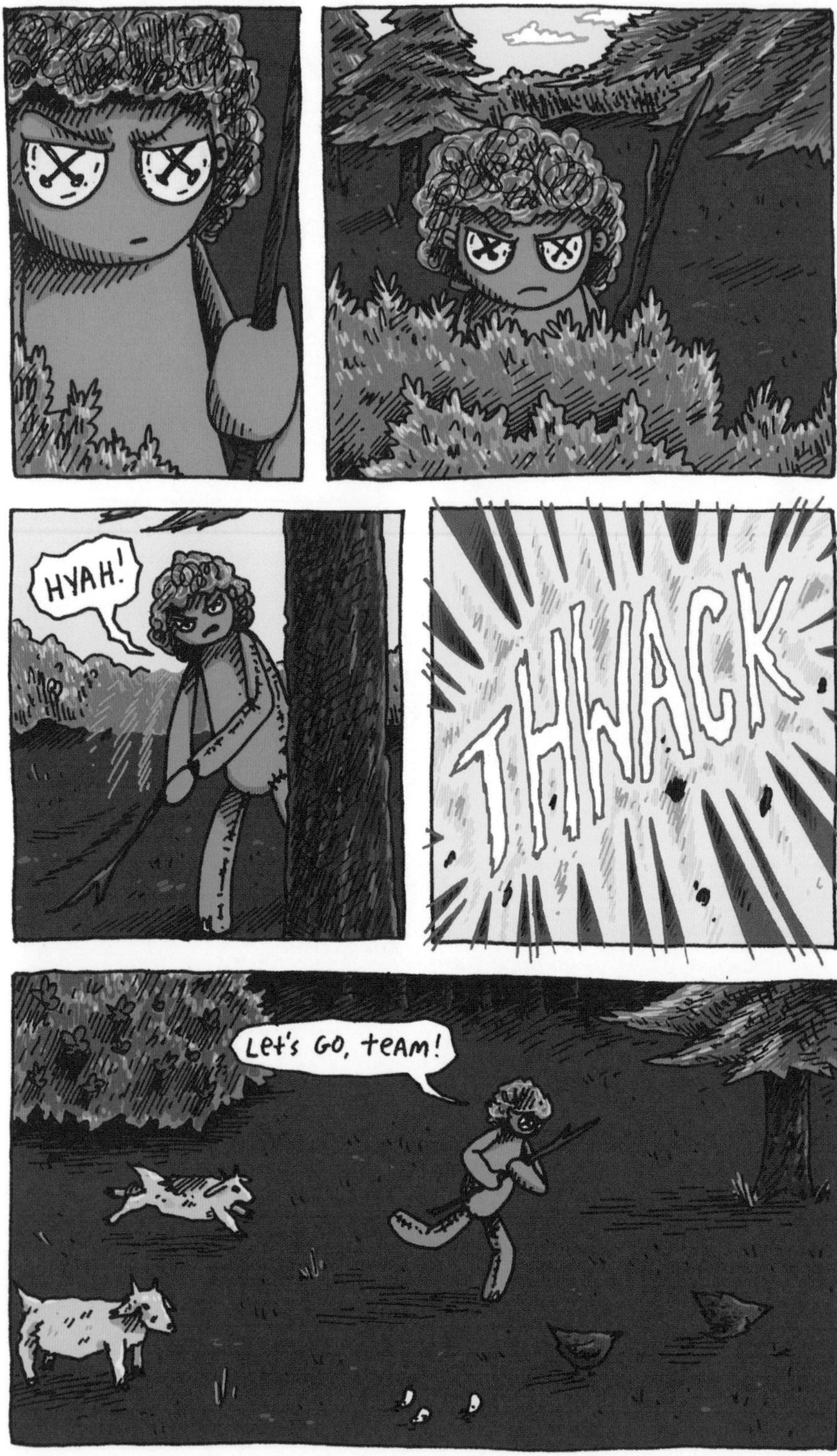
HYAH!
THWACK
Let's GO, team!

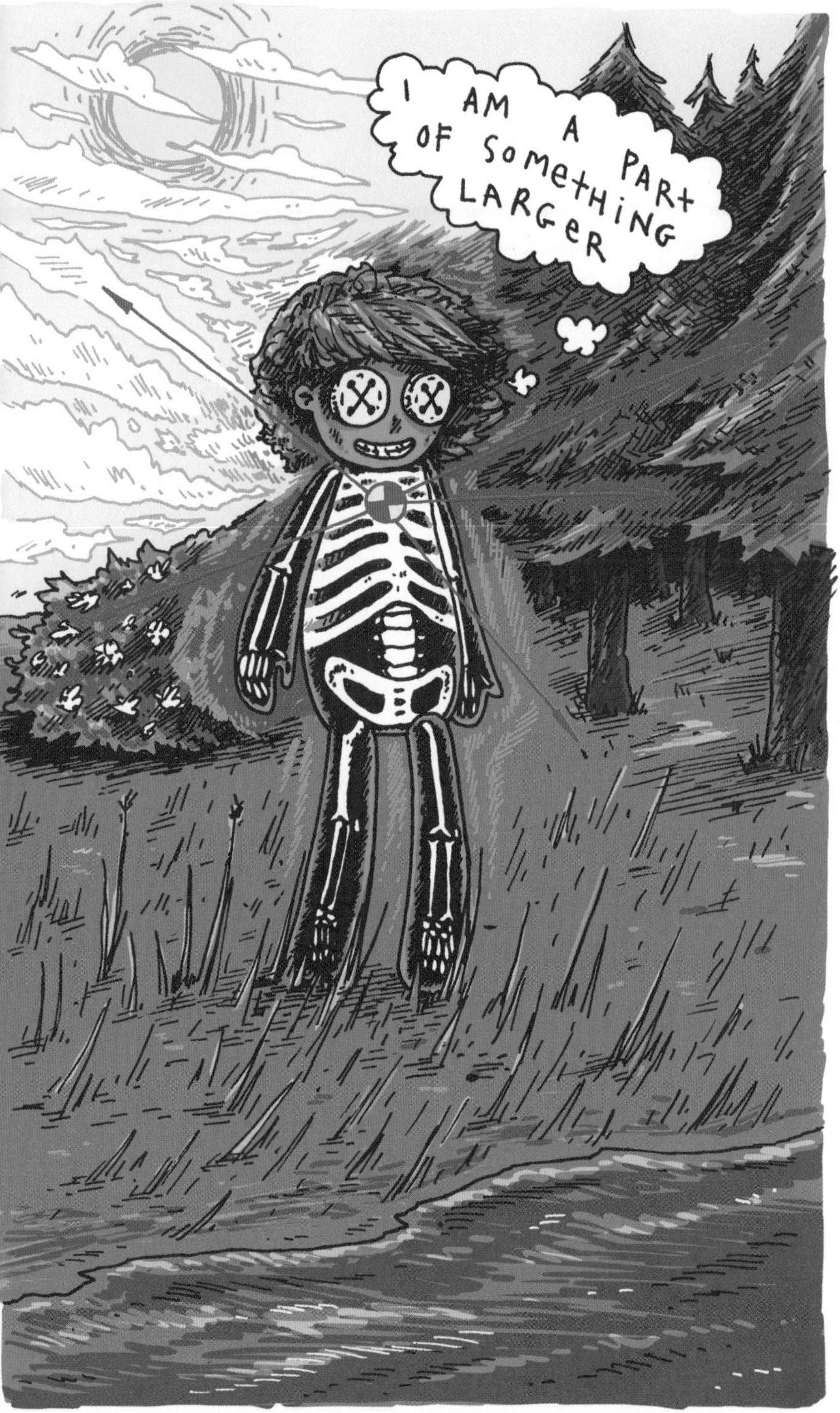
I AM A PART OF SOMETHING LARGER

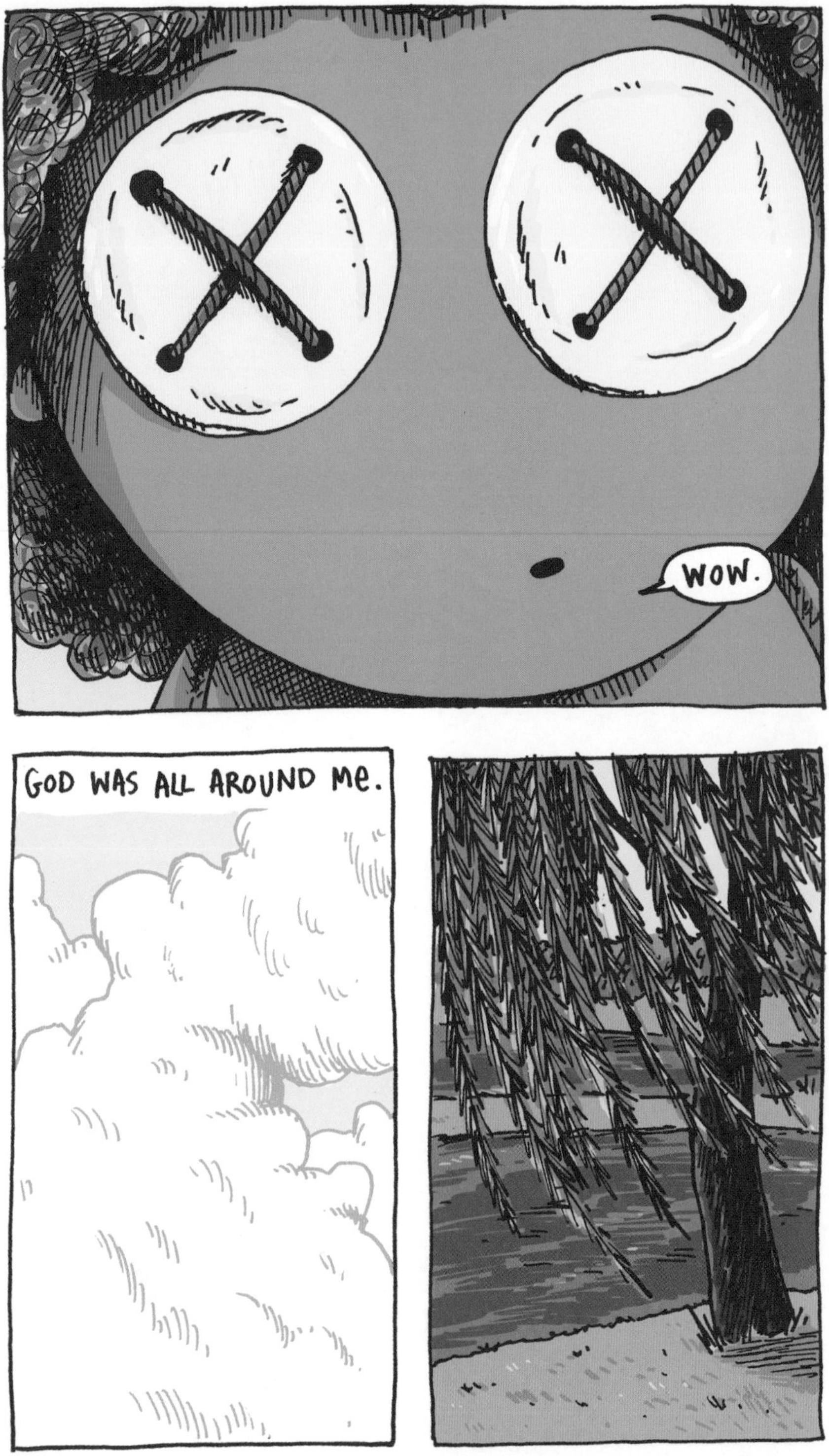
WOW.
GOD WAS ALL AROUND ME.

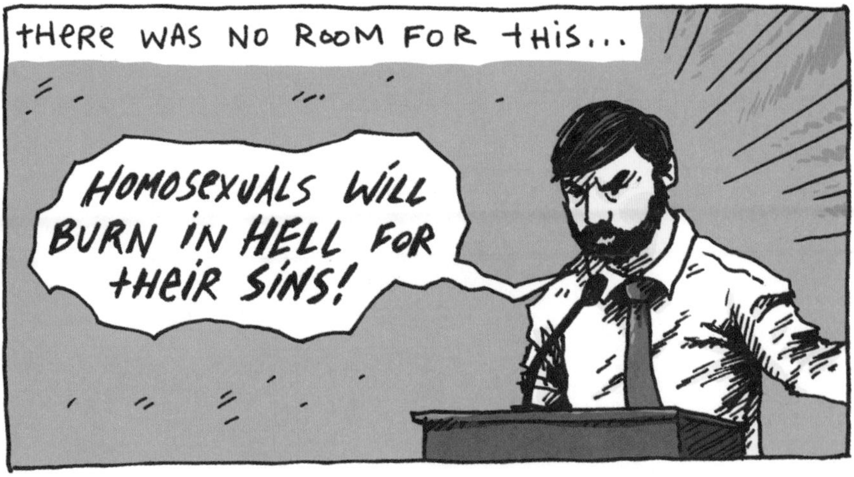
THERE WAS NO ROOM FOR THIS...
HOMOSEXUALS WILL BURN IN HELL FOR THEIR SINS!

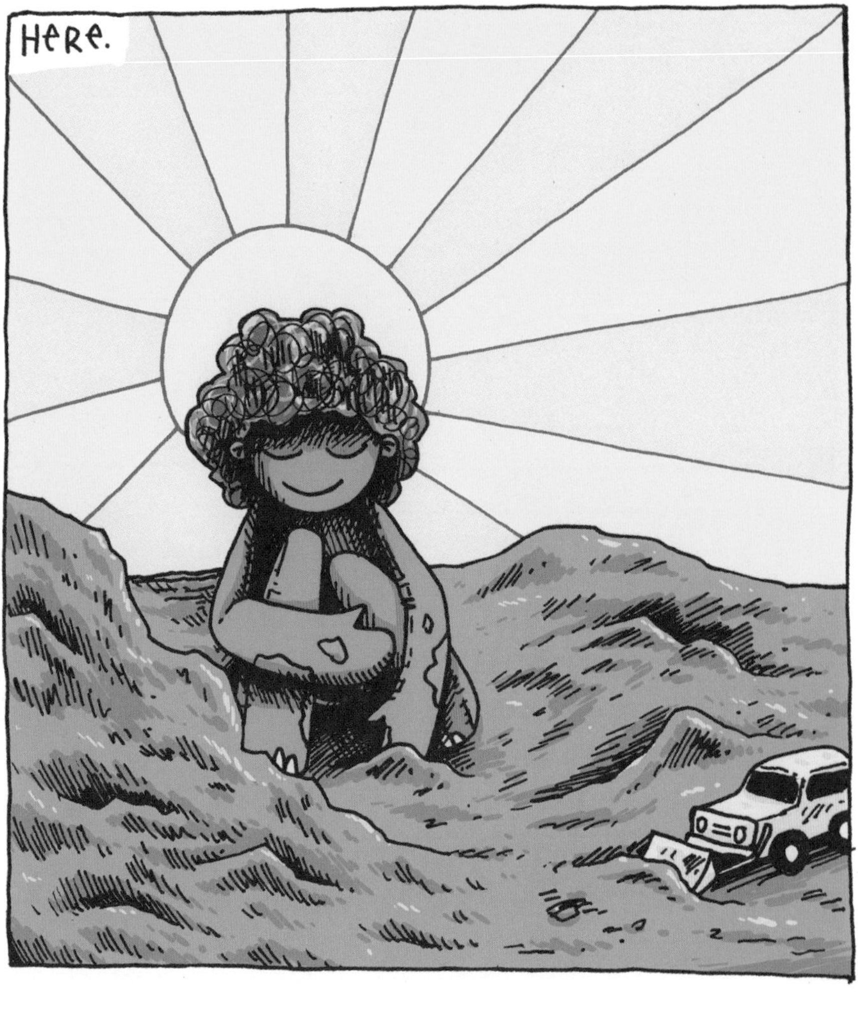
HERE.

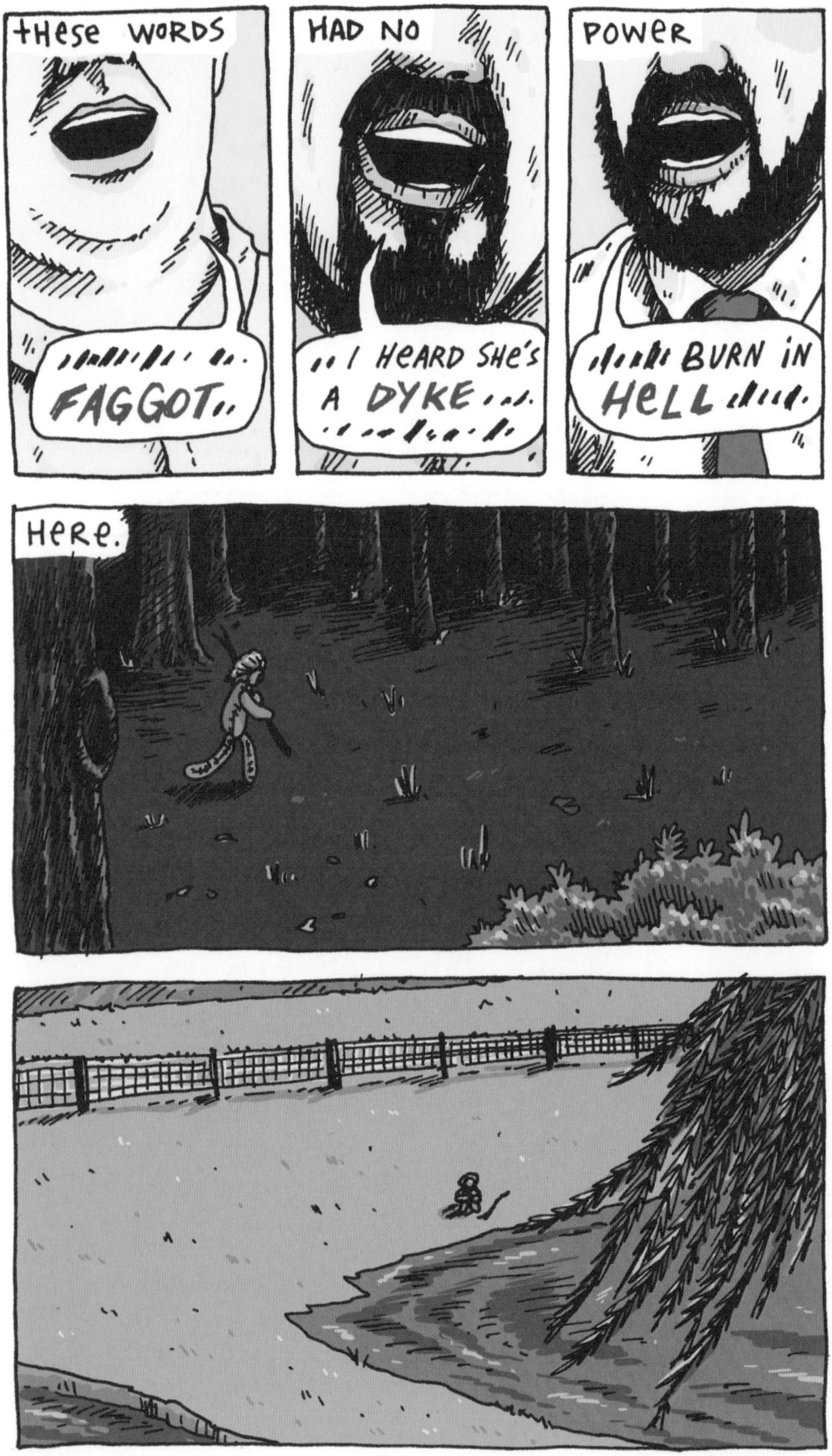
these WORDS
FAGGOT
HAD NO
I HEARD SHE'S A DYKE
POWER
BURN IN HELL
Here.

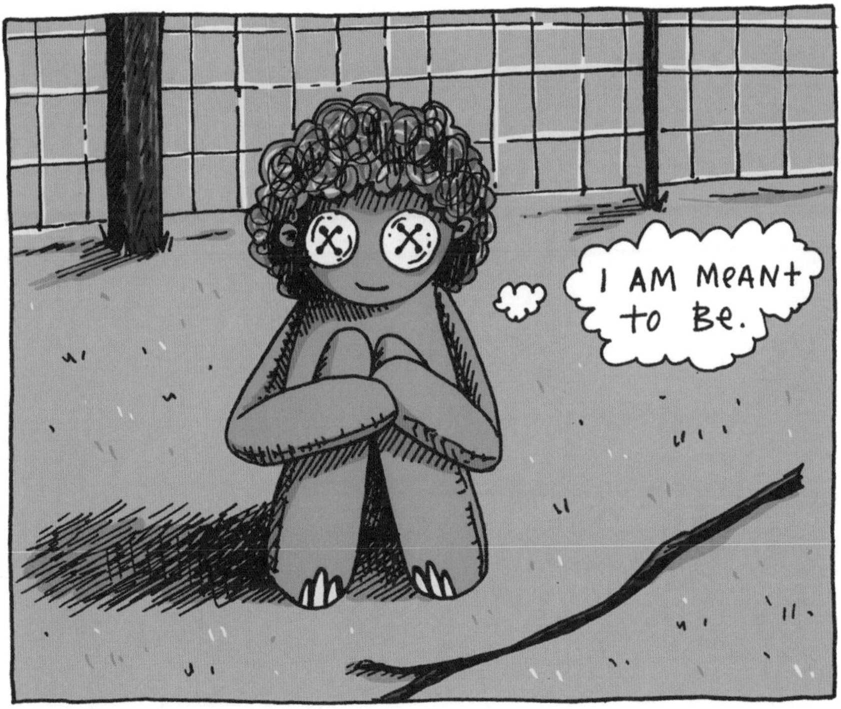
I AM MEANT TO BE.

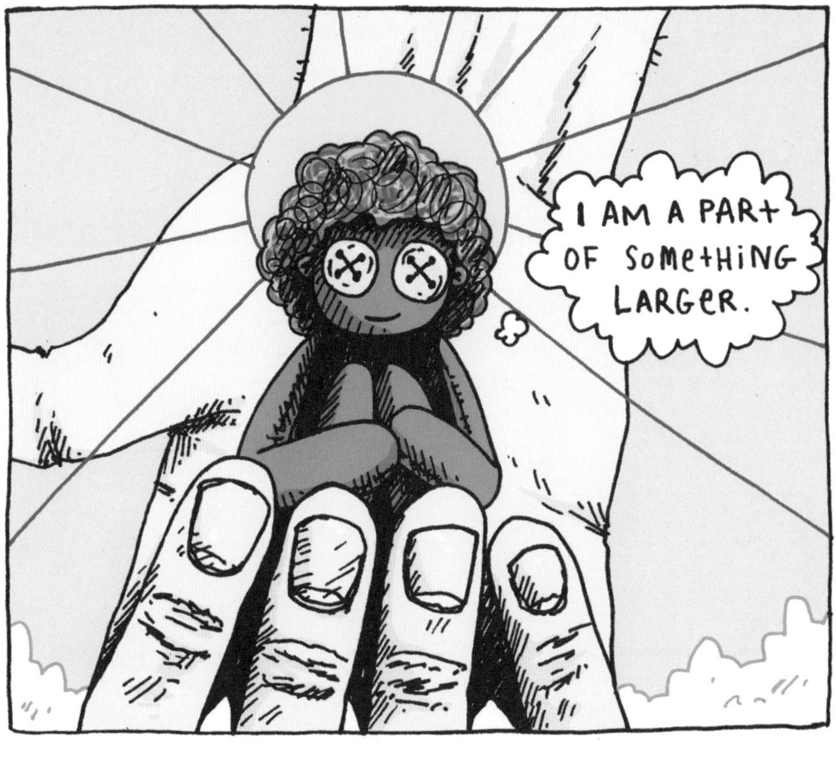
I AM A PART OF SOMETHING LARGER.

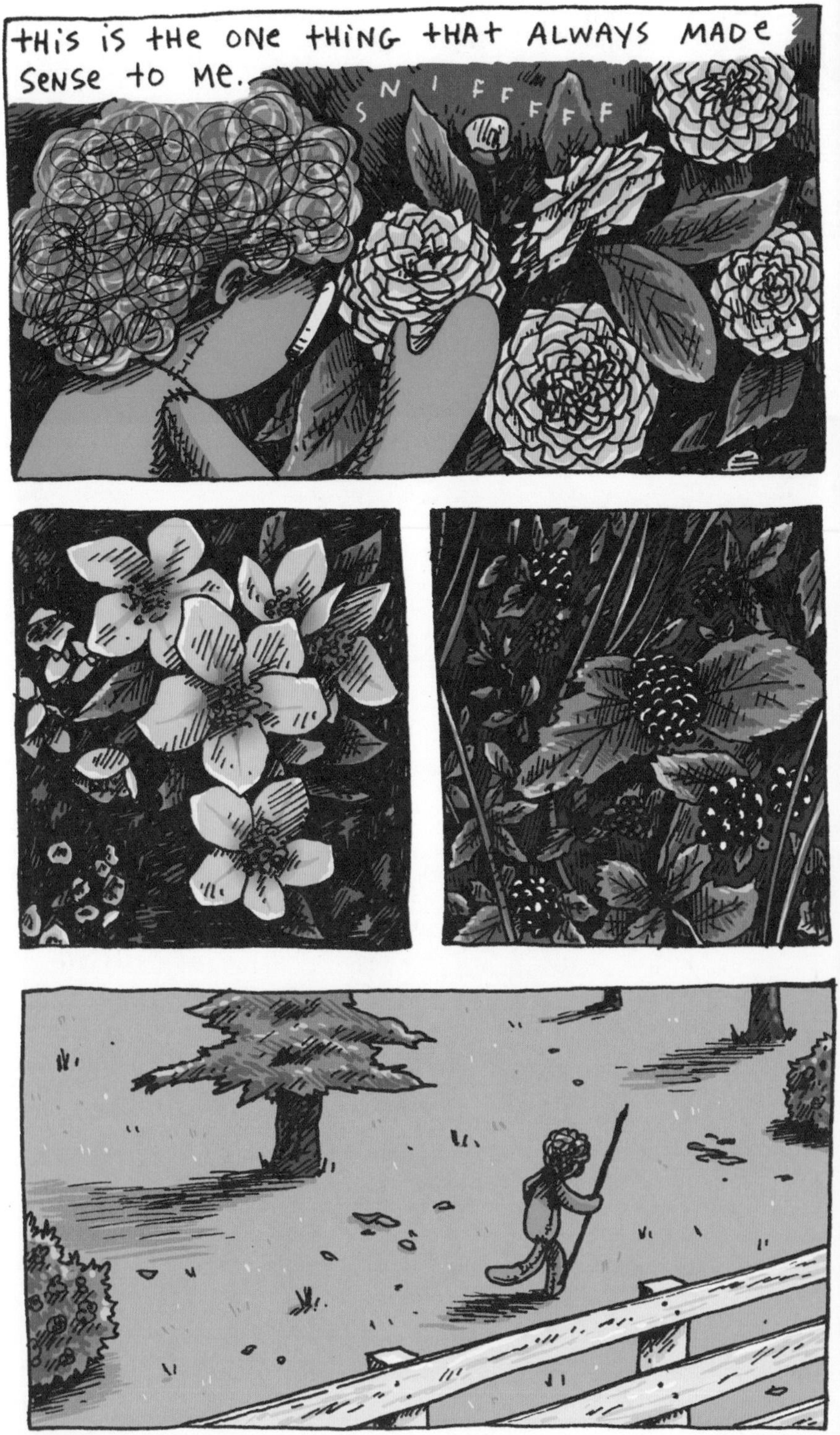
this is the one thing that always made sense to me.
SNIFFFFFF

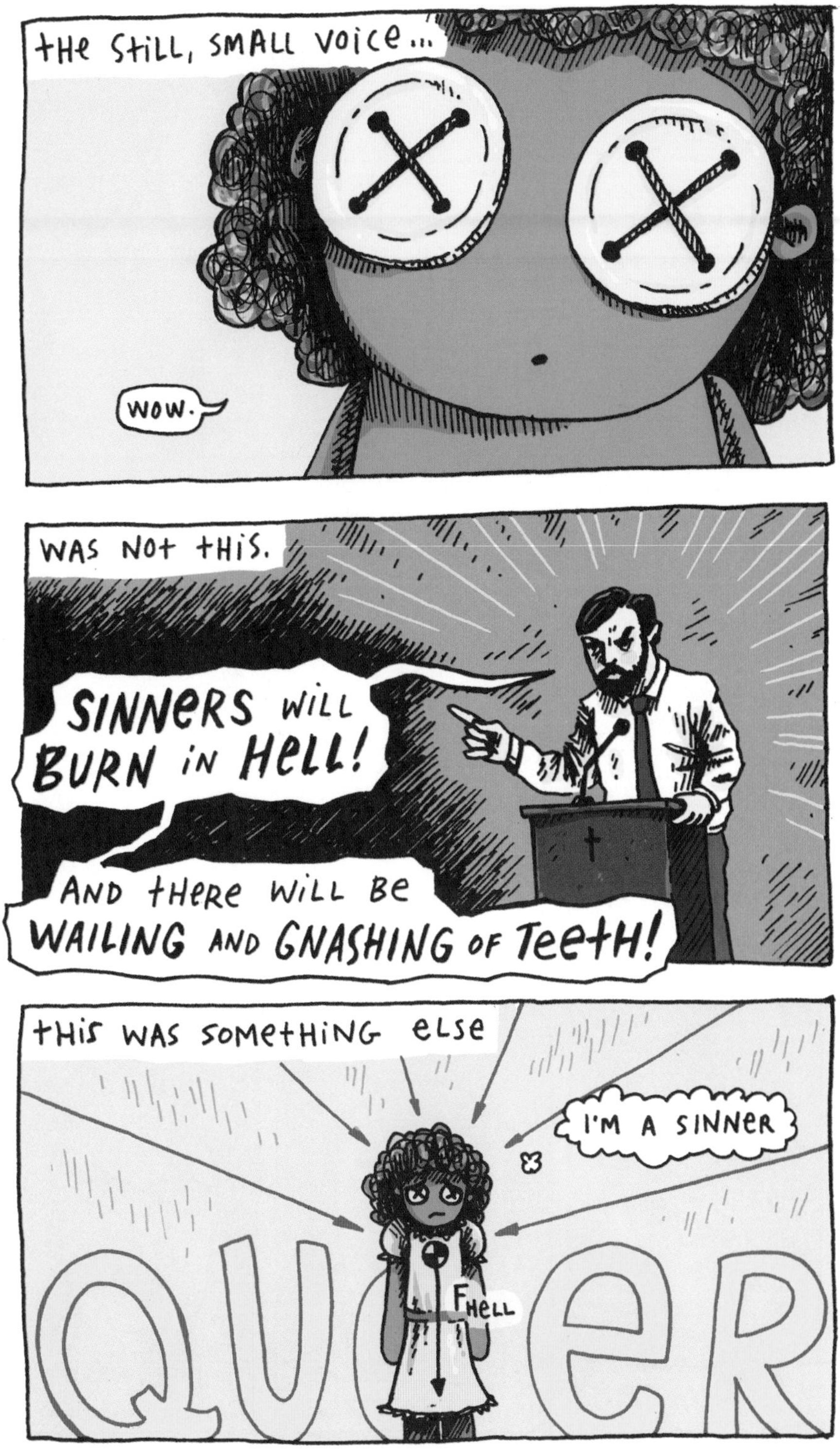

the still, small voice...
WOW.
was not this.
SINNERS WILL BURN IN HELL!
AND THERE WILL BE WAILING AND GNASHING OF TEETH!
this was something else
I'M A SINNER
QUEER
HELL

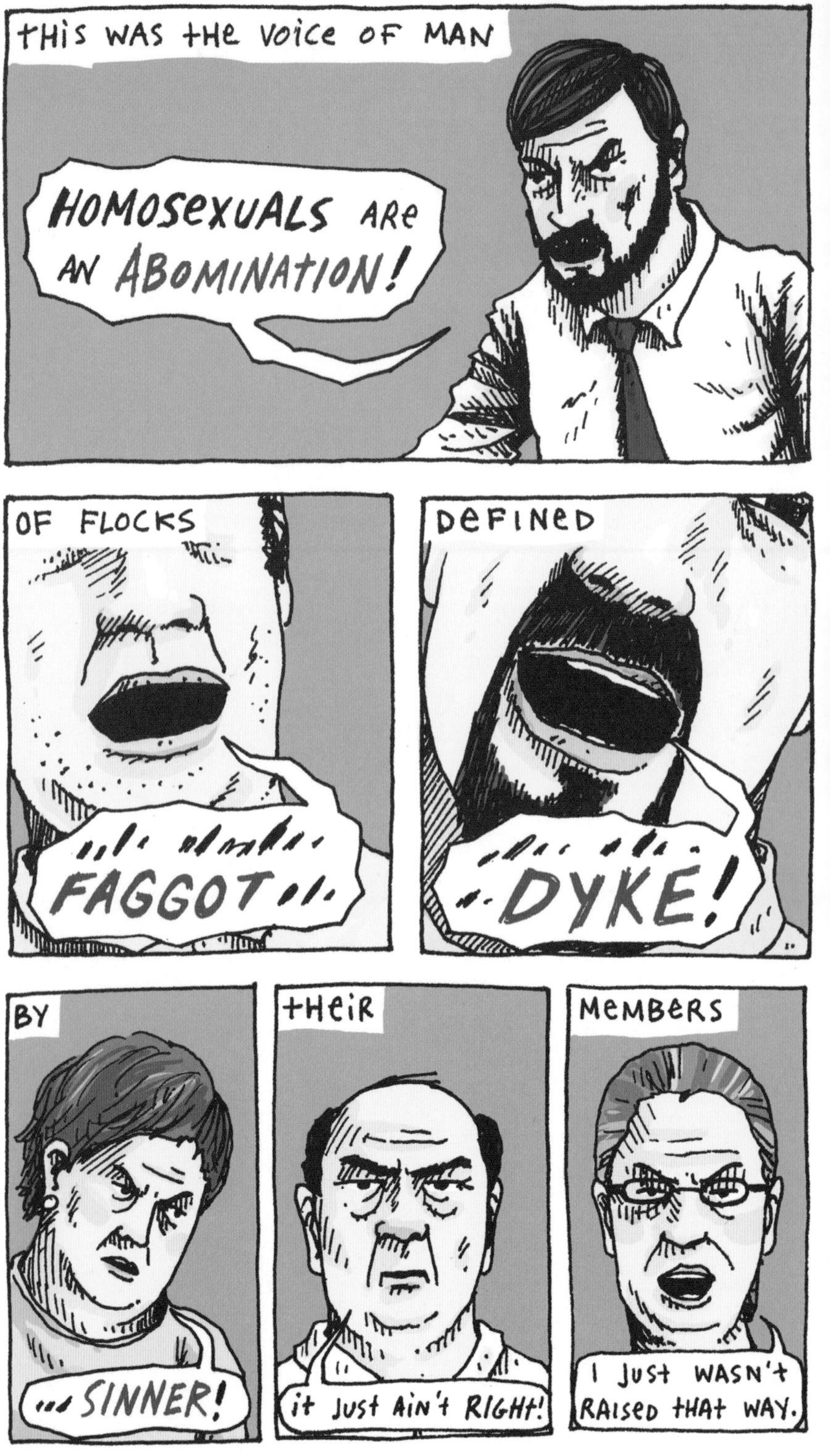
THIS WAS THE VOICE OF MAN
HOMOSEXUALS ARE AN ABOMINATION!
OF FLOCKS
FAGGOT
DEFINED
DYKE!
BY
SINNER!
THEIR
IT JUST AIN'T RIGHT!
MEMBERS
I JUST WASN'T RAISED THAT WAY.

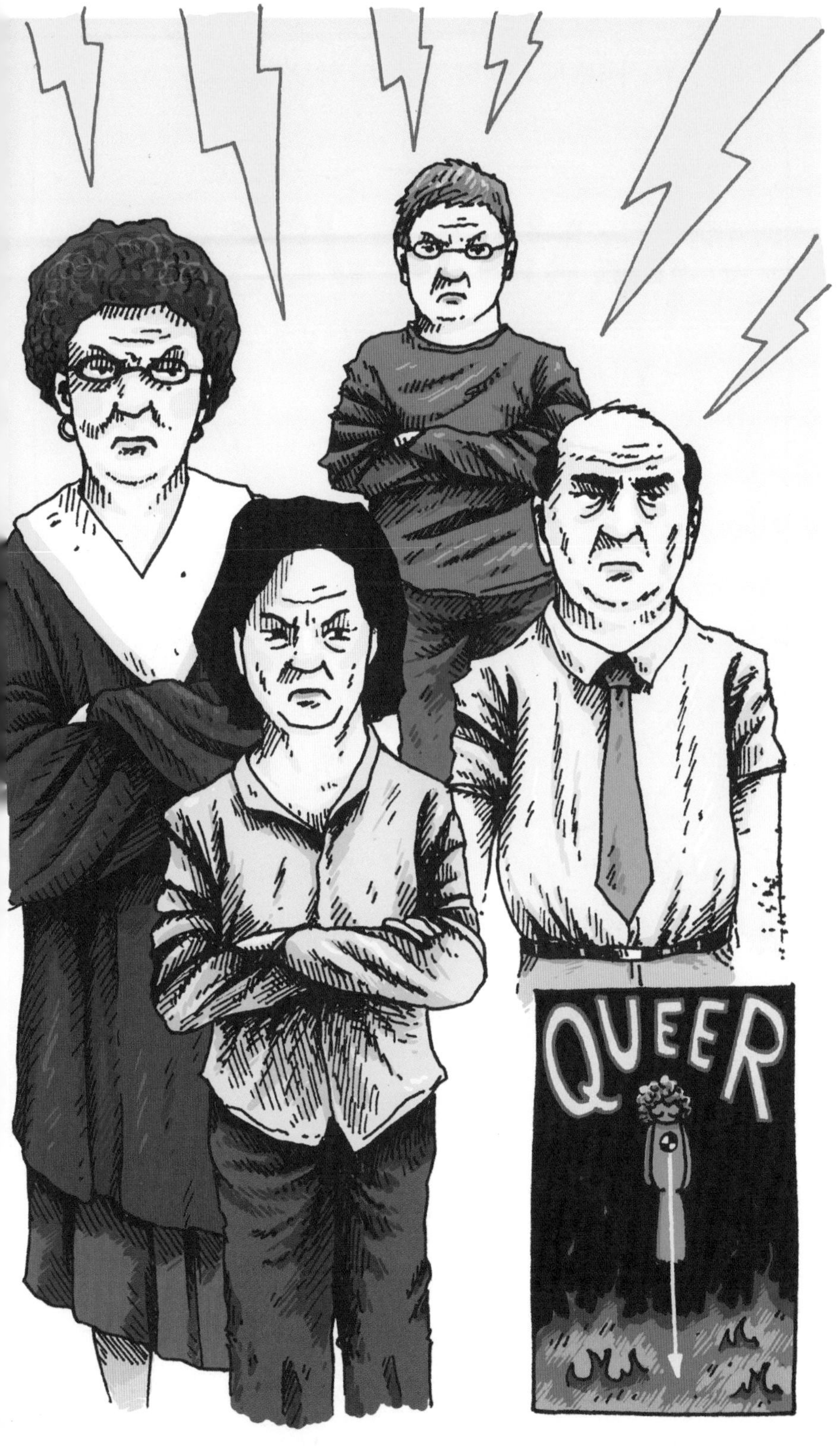
QUEER

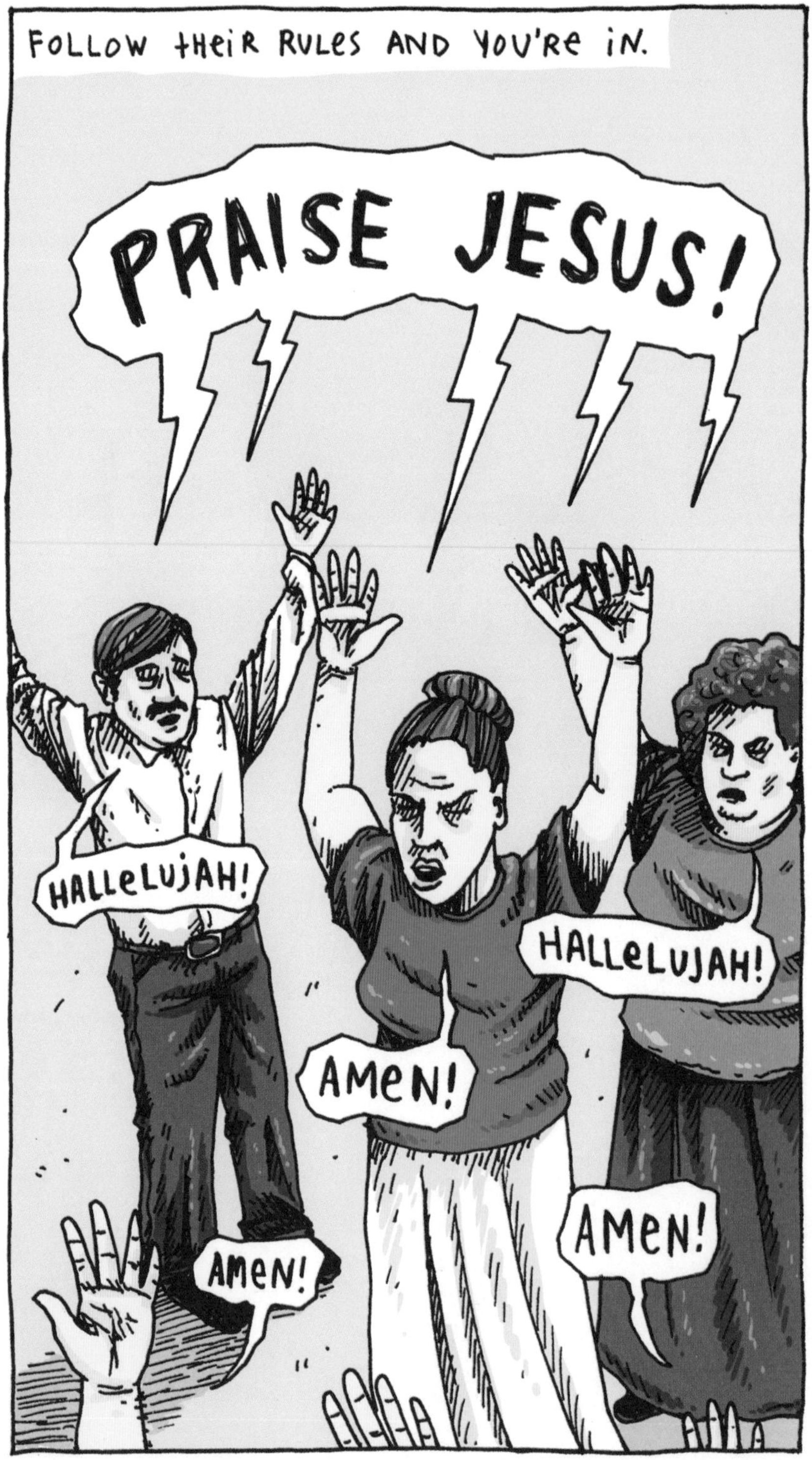
FOLLOW THEIR RULES AND YOU'RE IN.
PRAISE JESUS!
HALLELUJAH!
HALLELUJAH!
AMEN!
AMEN!
AMEN!

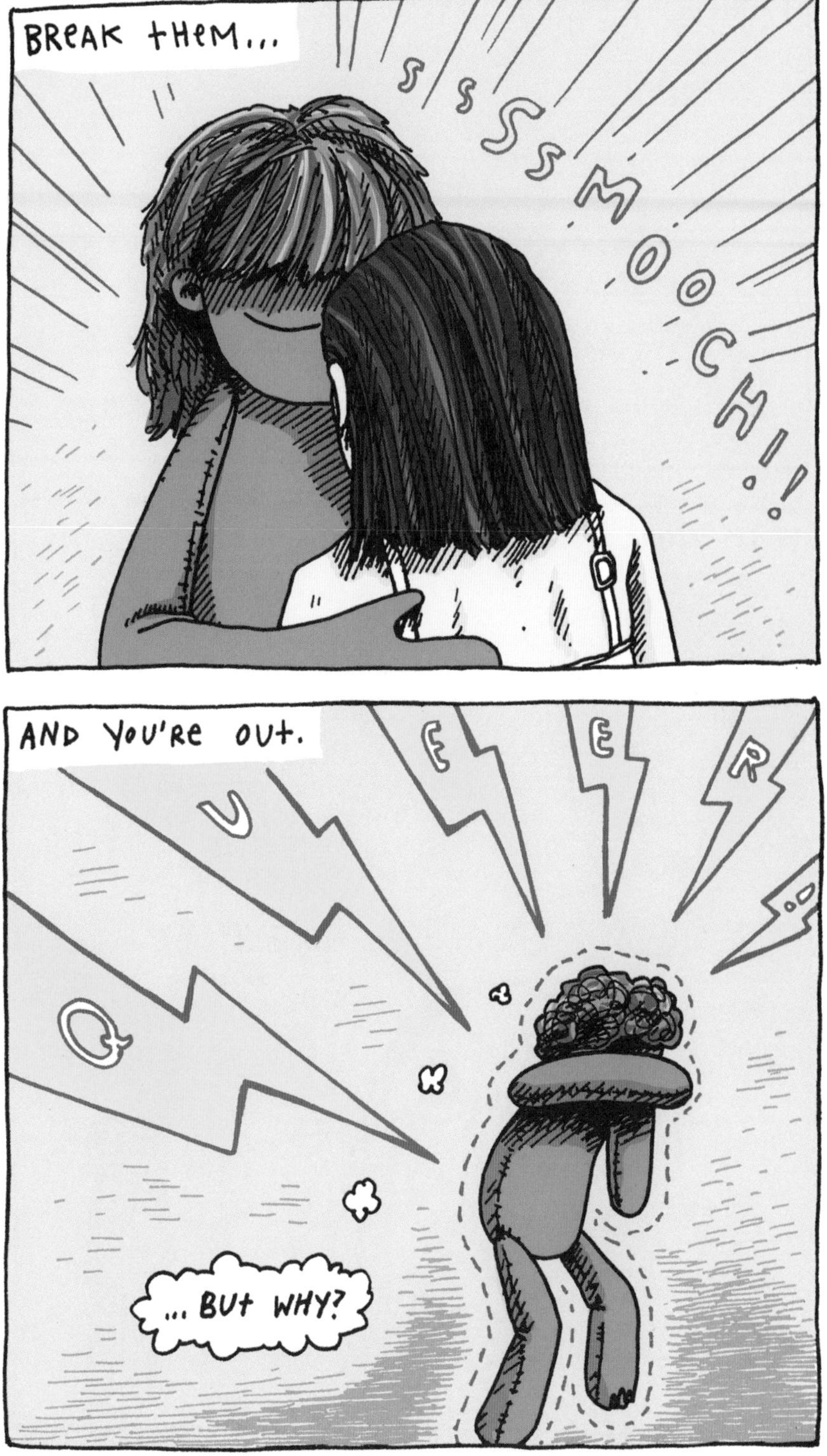
BREAK THEM...
SSSSMOOOCH!!
AND YOU'RE OUT.
QUEER!
...BUT WHY?

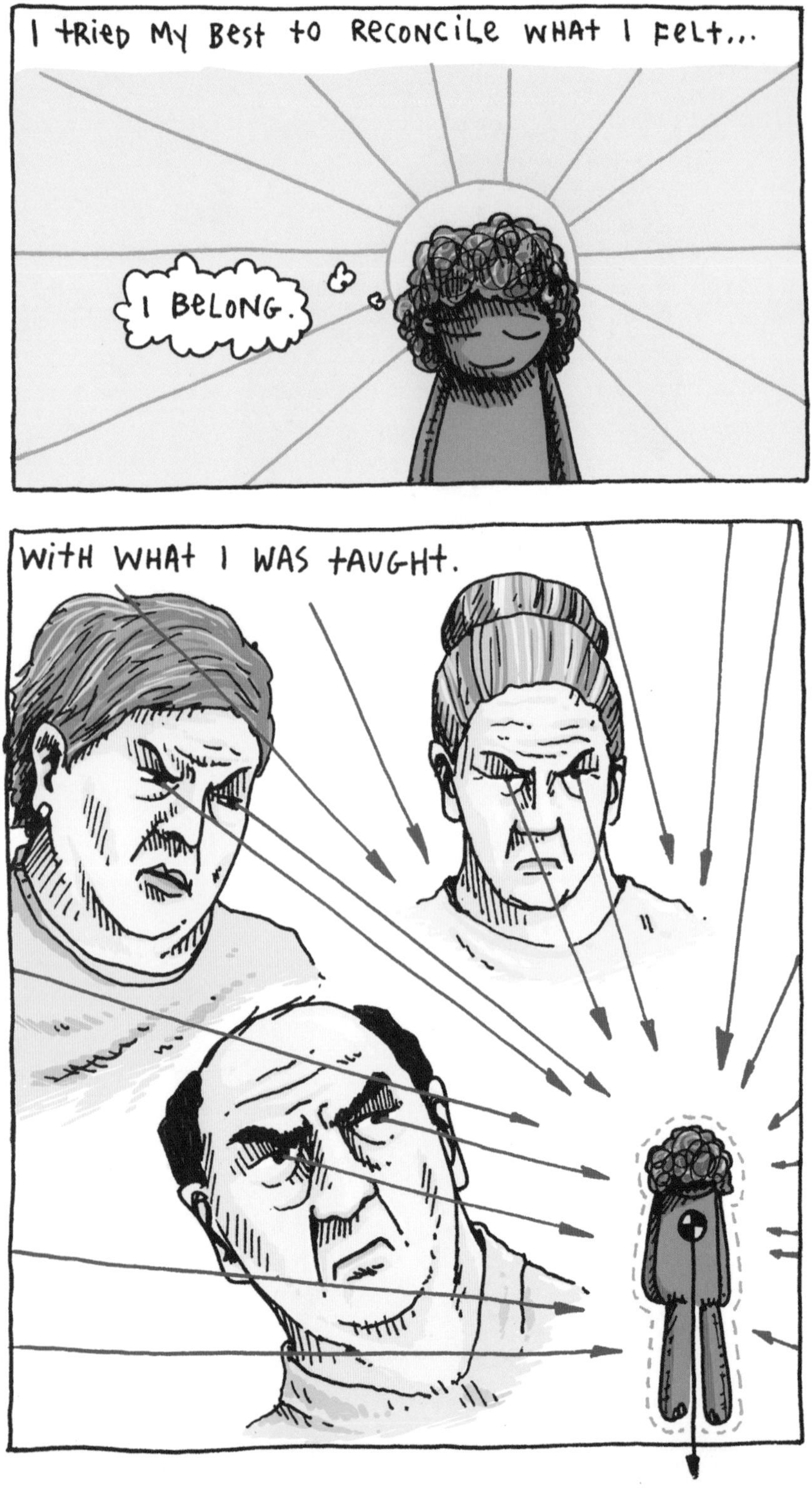
I tried my best to reconcile what I felt...
I belong.
with what I was taught.

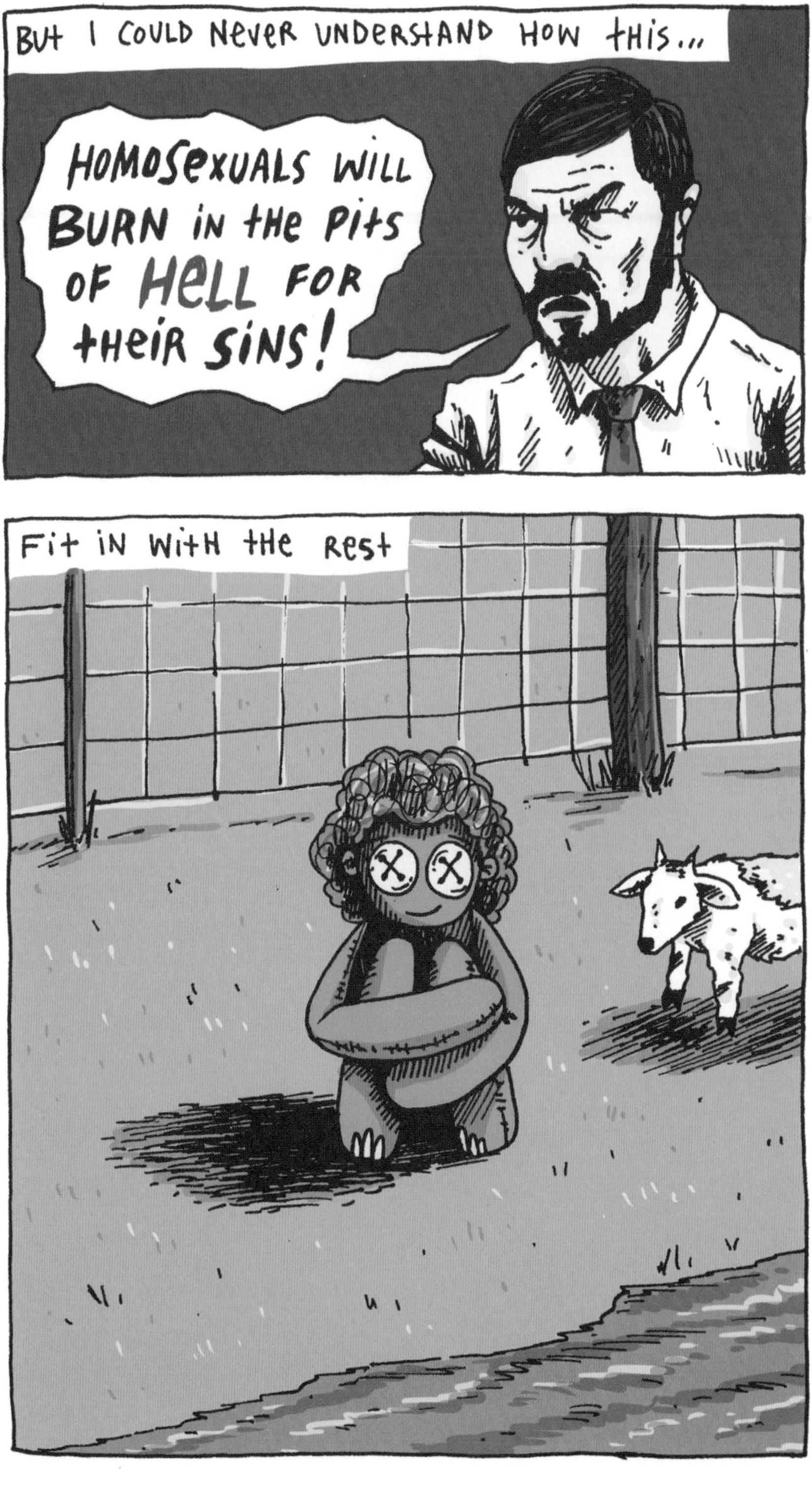
BUT I COULD NEVER UNDERSTAND HOW THIS...
HOMOSEXUALS WILL BURN IN THE PITS OF HELL FOR THEIR SINS!
FIT IN WITH THE REST

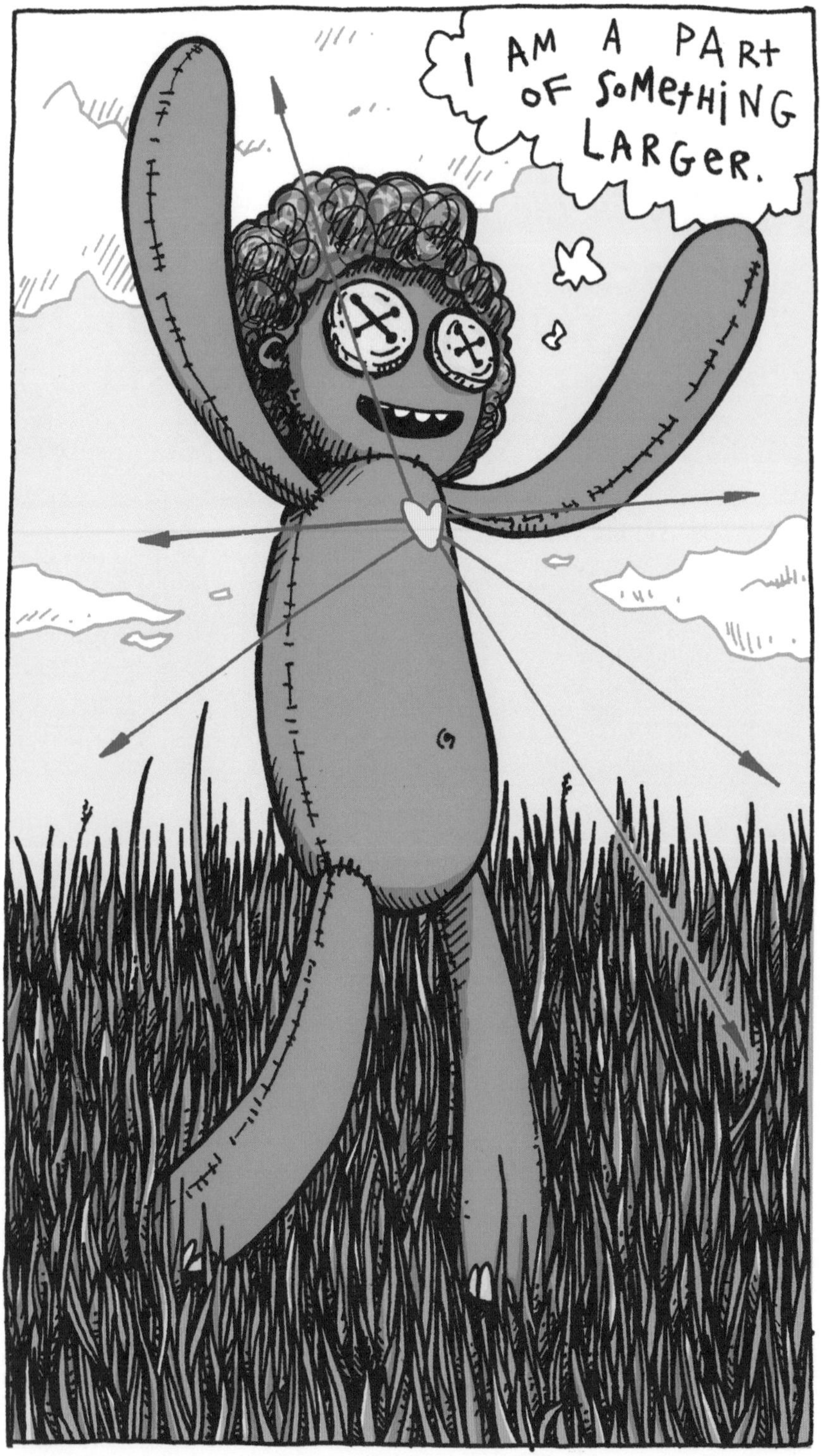
I AM A PARt OF SoMEtHiNG LARGeR.

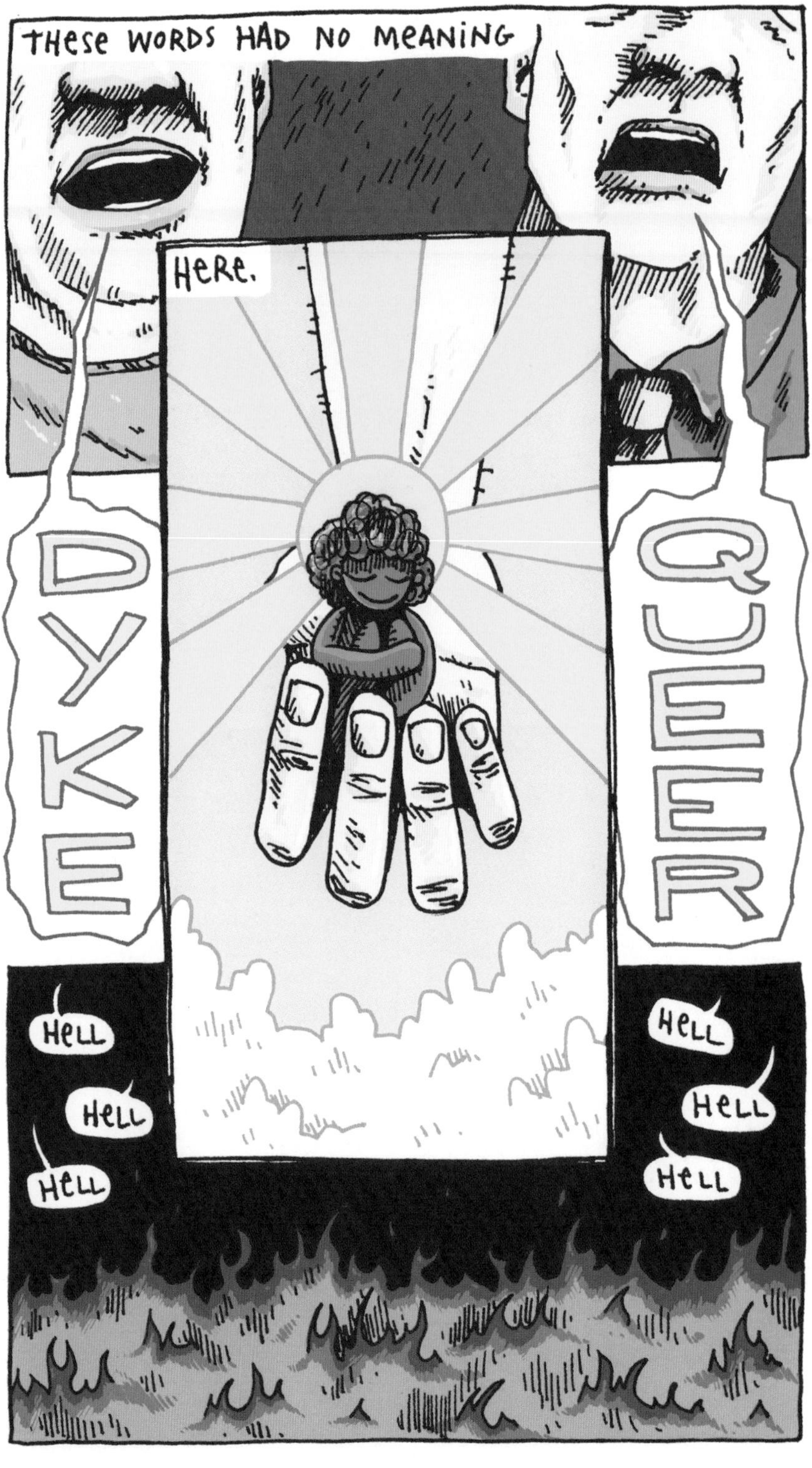
THESE WORDS HAD NO MEANING
HERE.
DYKE
QUEER
HELL
HELL
HELL
HELL
HELL
HELL

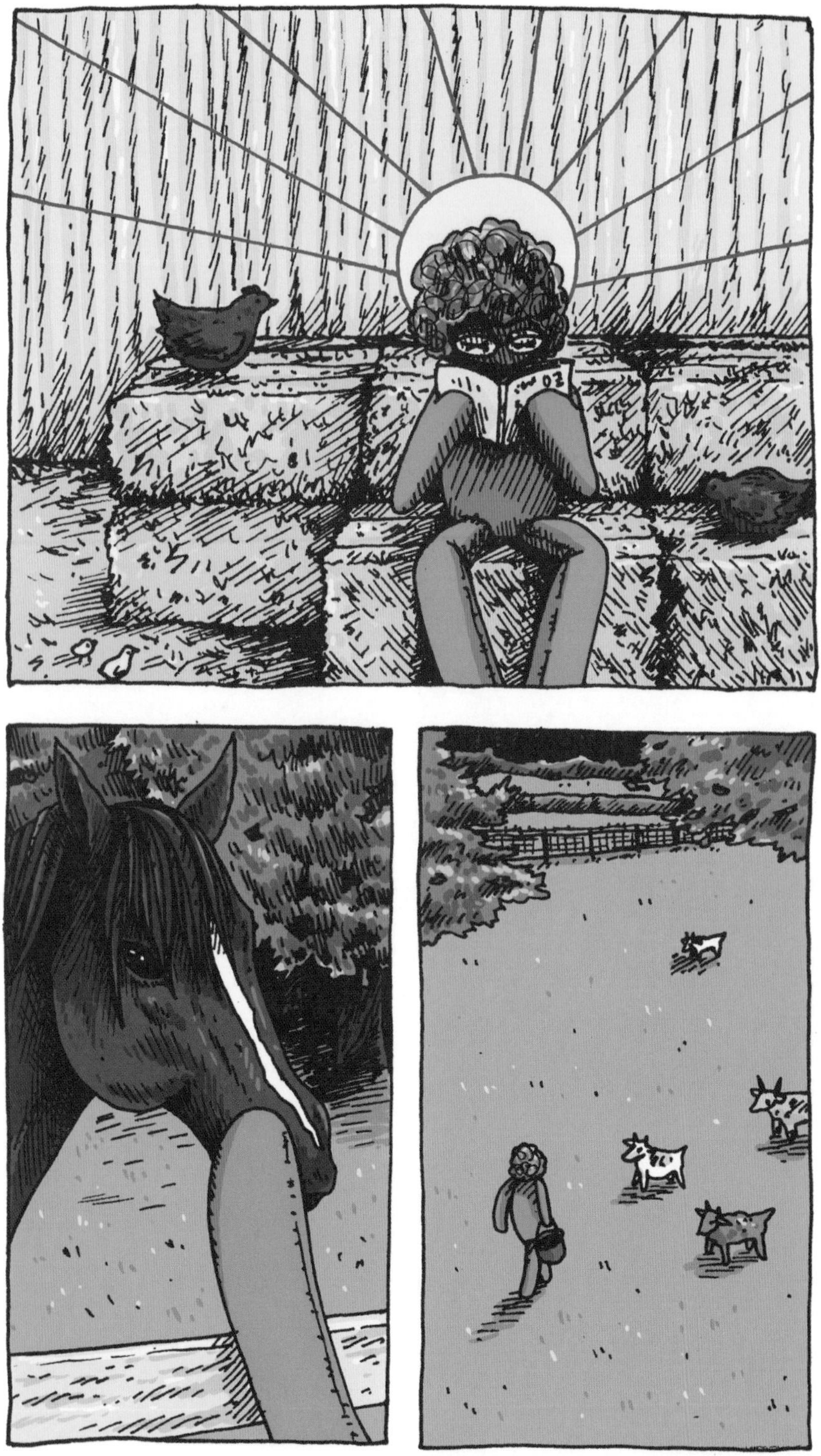
OZ

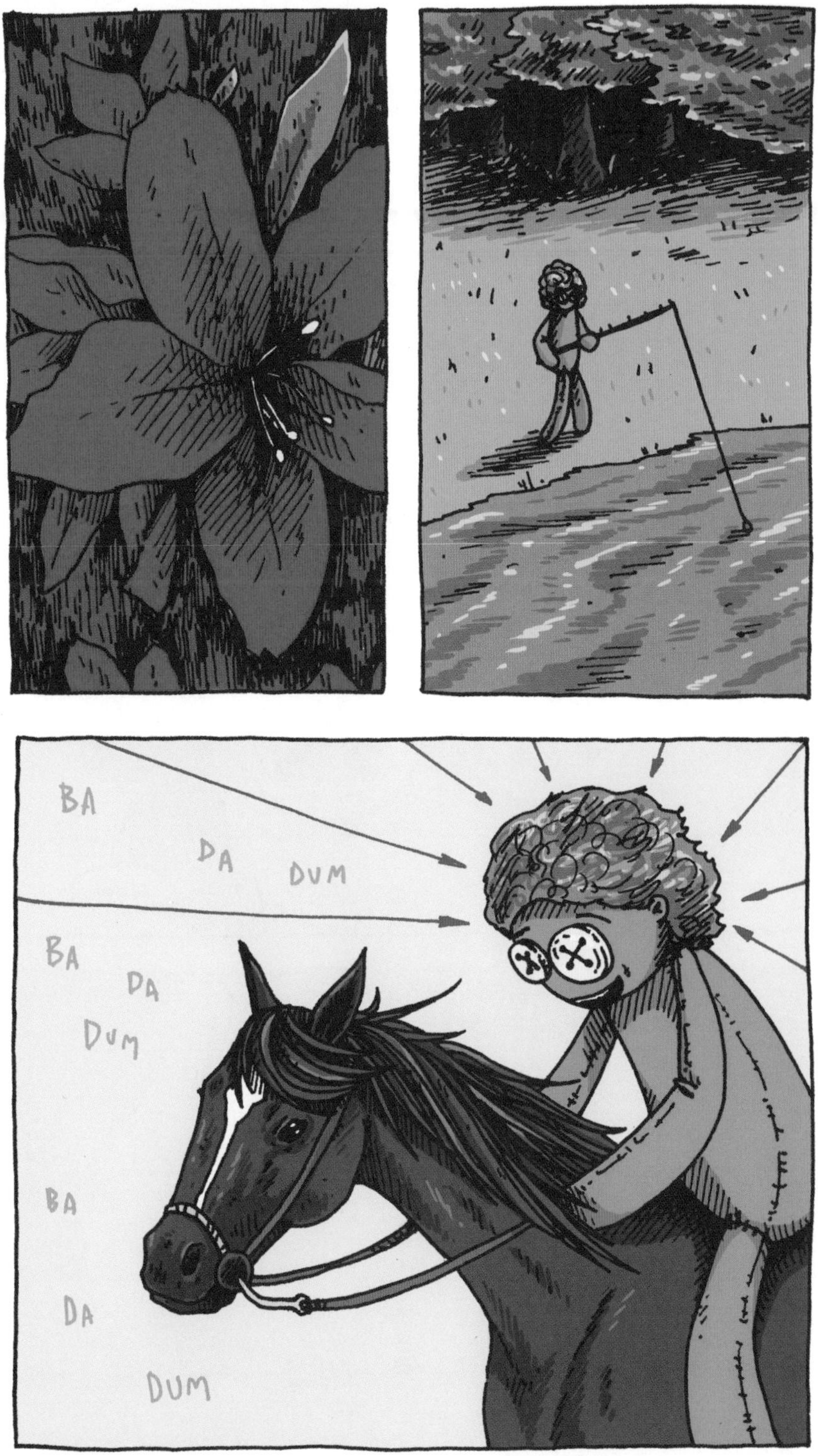
BA
DA
DUM
BA
DA
DUM
BA
DA
DUM

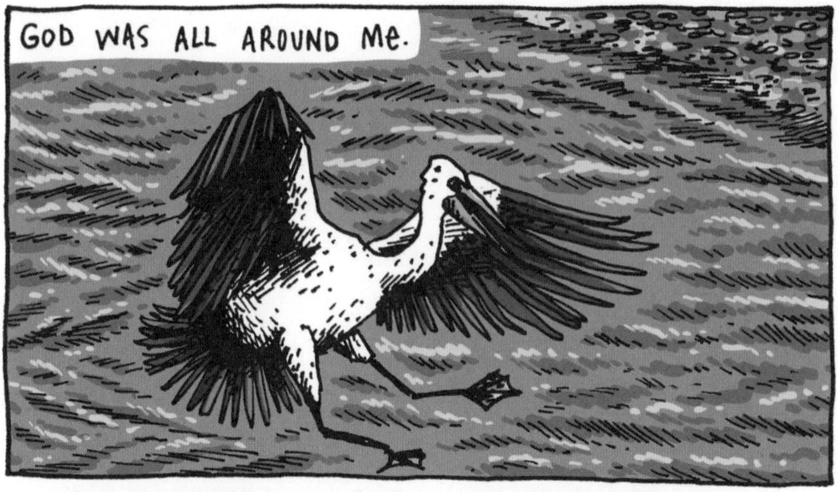
GOD WAS ALL AROUND ME.

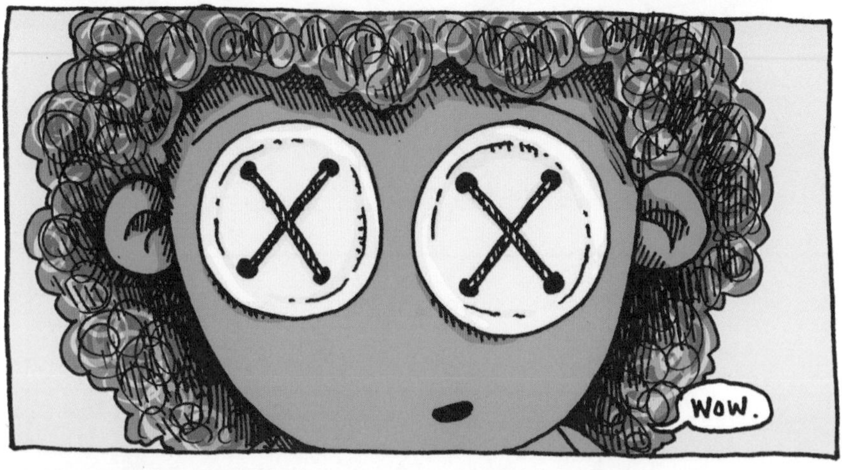
WOW.

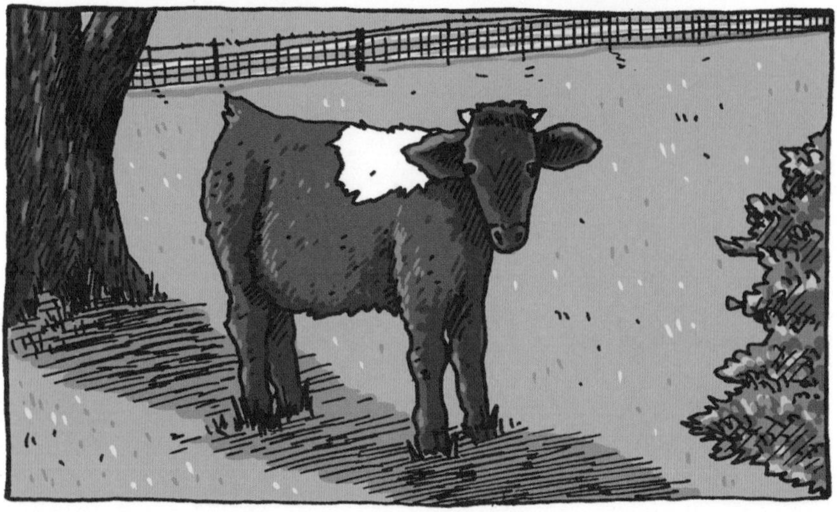

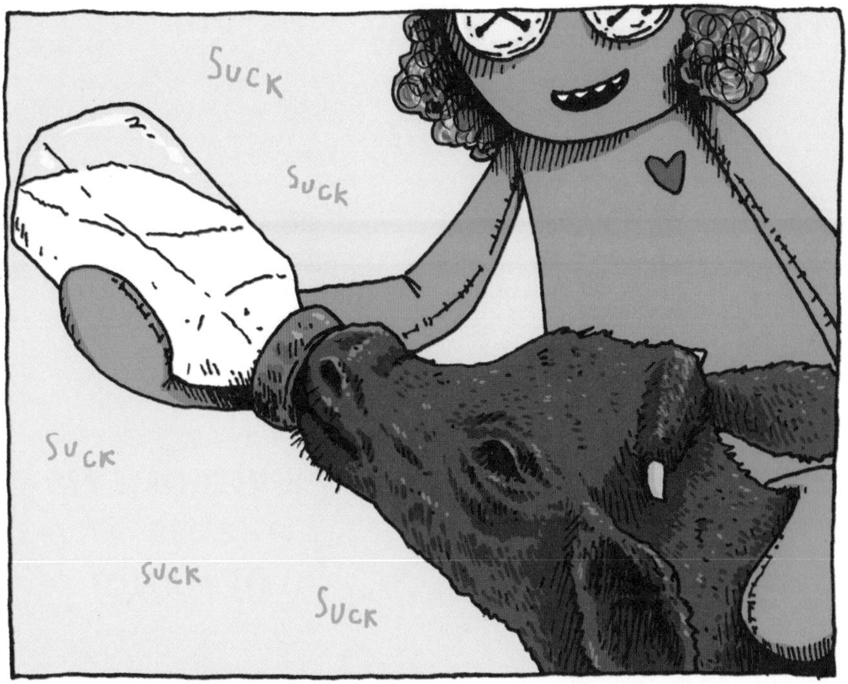
SUCK
SUCK
SUCK
SUCK
SUCK

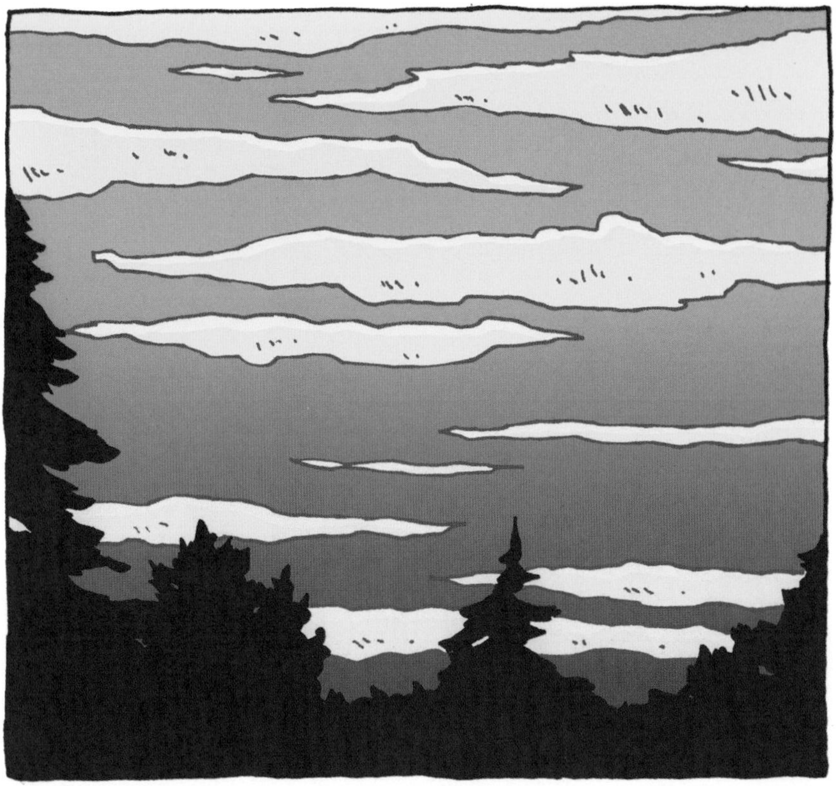

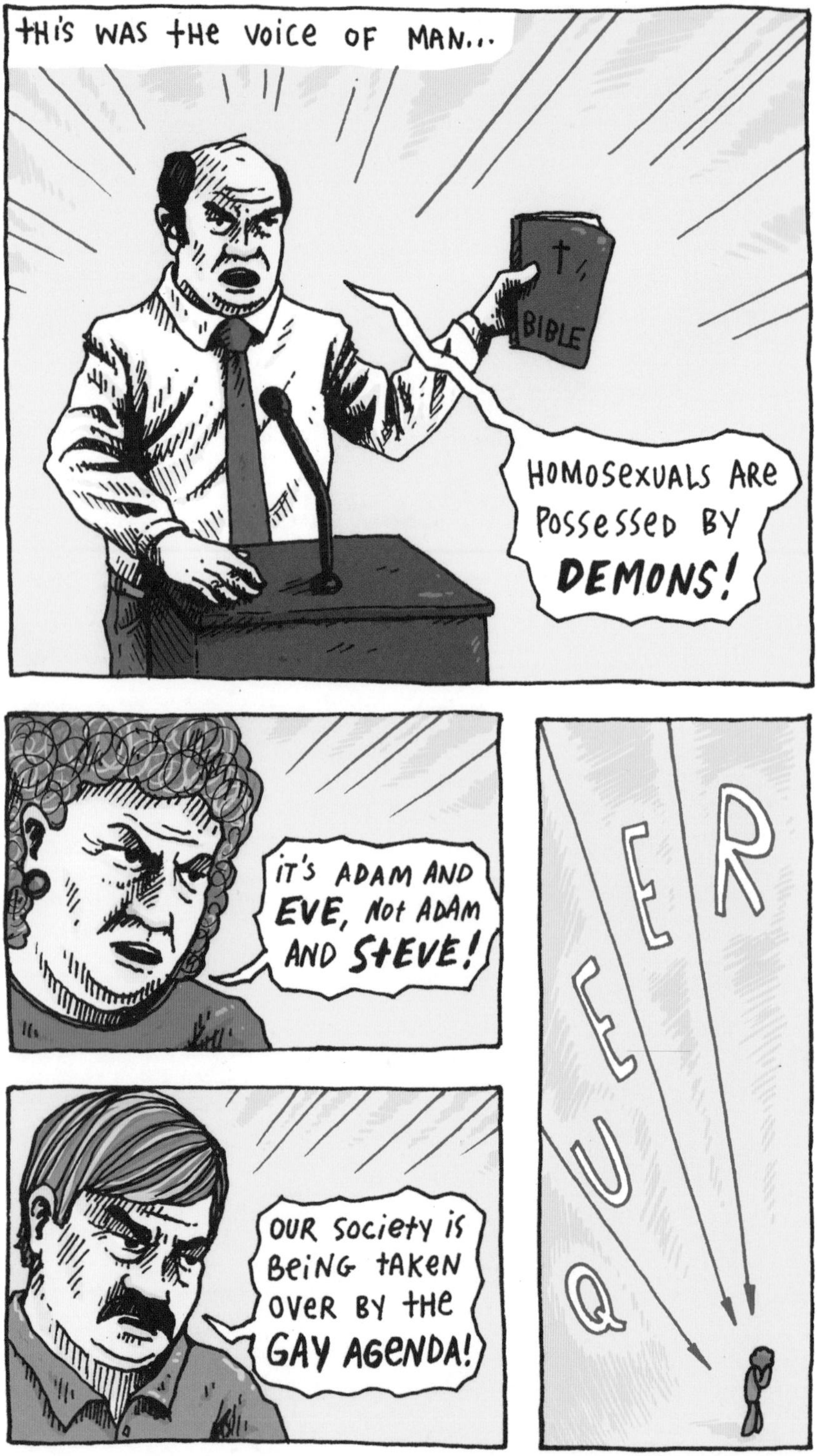
this was the voice of man...
BIBLE
HOMOSEXUALS ARE POSSESSED BY DEMONS!
IT'S ADAM AND EVE, NOT ADAM AND STEVE!
OUR SOCIETY IS BEING TAKEN OVER BY THE GAY AGENDA!
QUEER

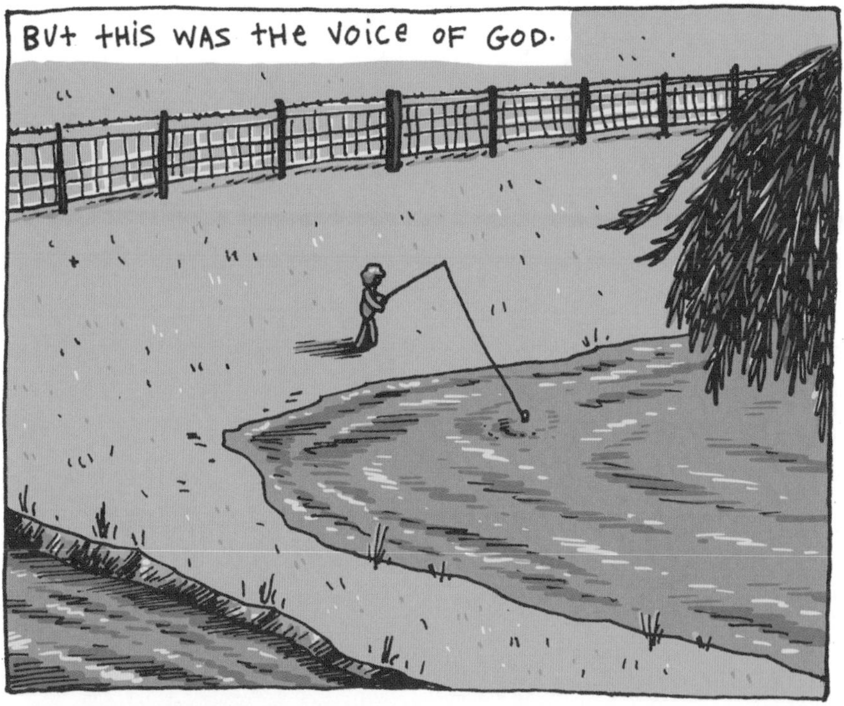
BUT THIS WAS THE VOICE OF GOD.

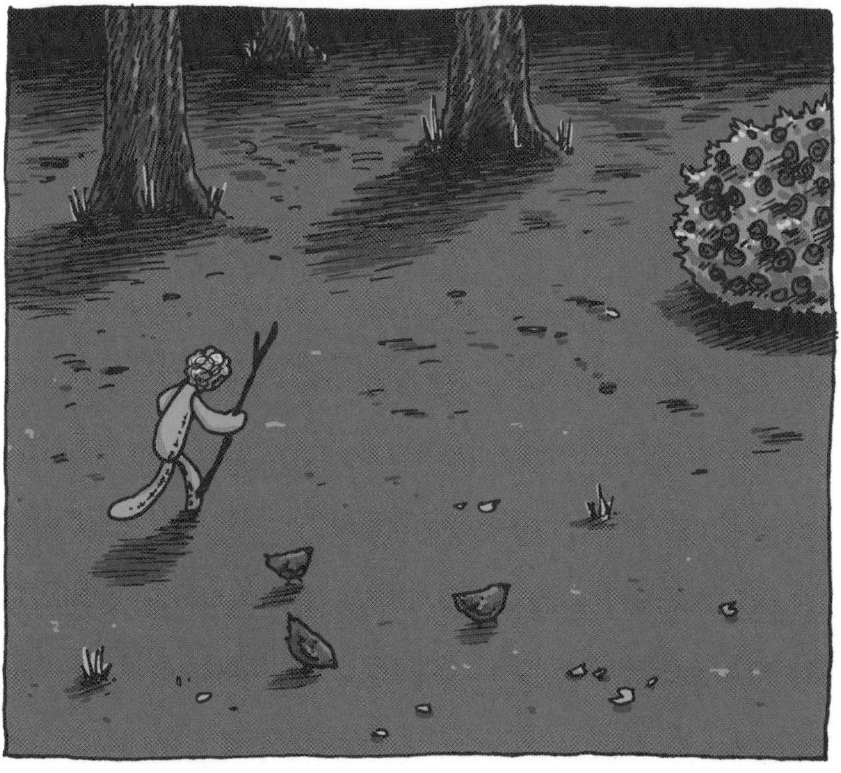

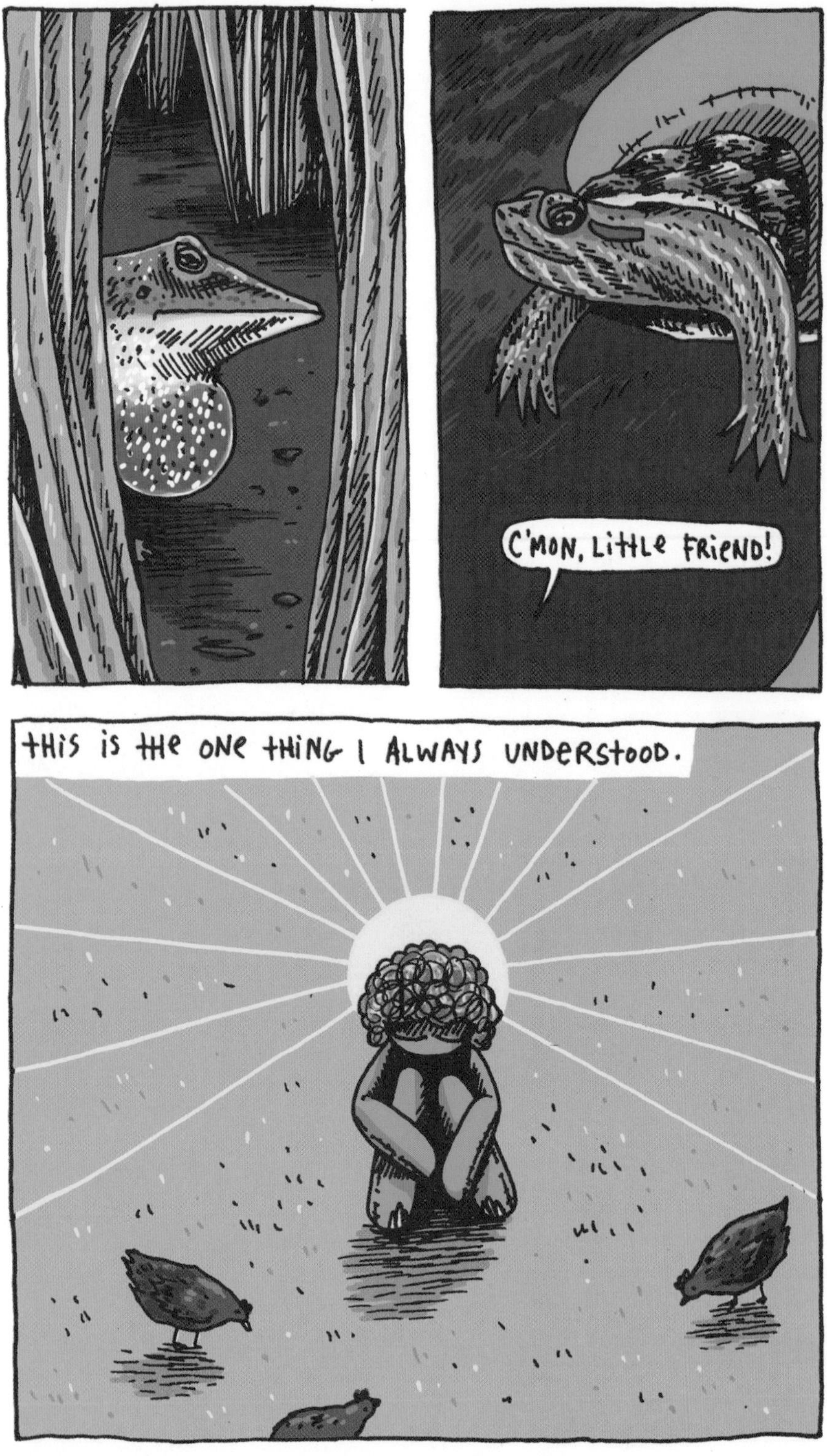
C'MON, LITTLE FRIEND!
THIS IS THE ONE THING I ALWAYS UNDERSTOOD.

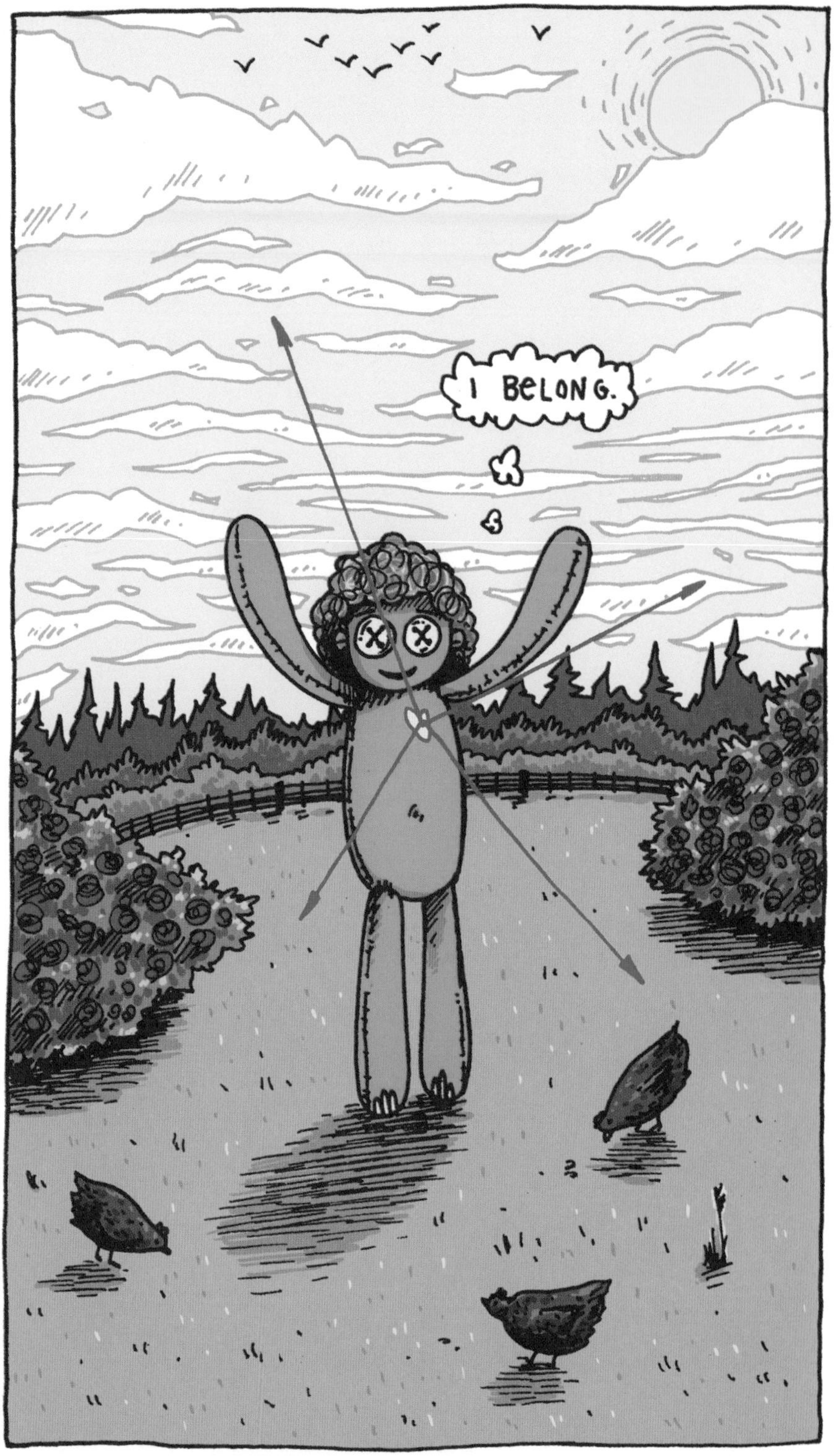
I BELONG.

CHAPTER FOUR

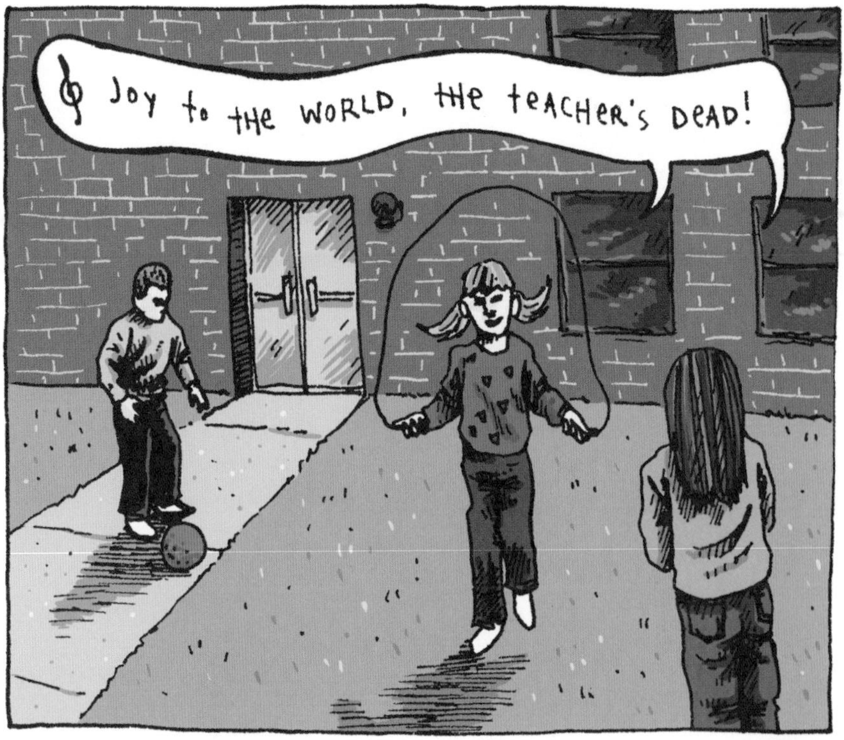
Joy to the WORLD, the teacher's DEAD!

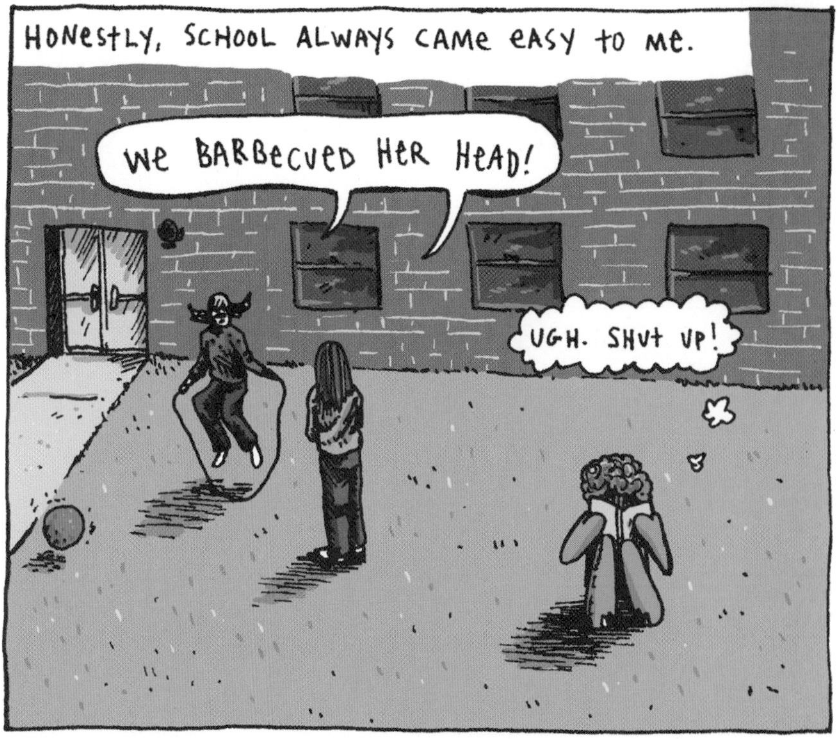
HONESTLY, SCHOOL ALWAYS CAME EASY TO ME.
WE BARBECUED HER HEAD!
UGH. SHUT UP!

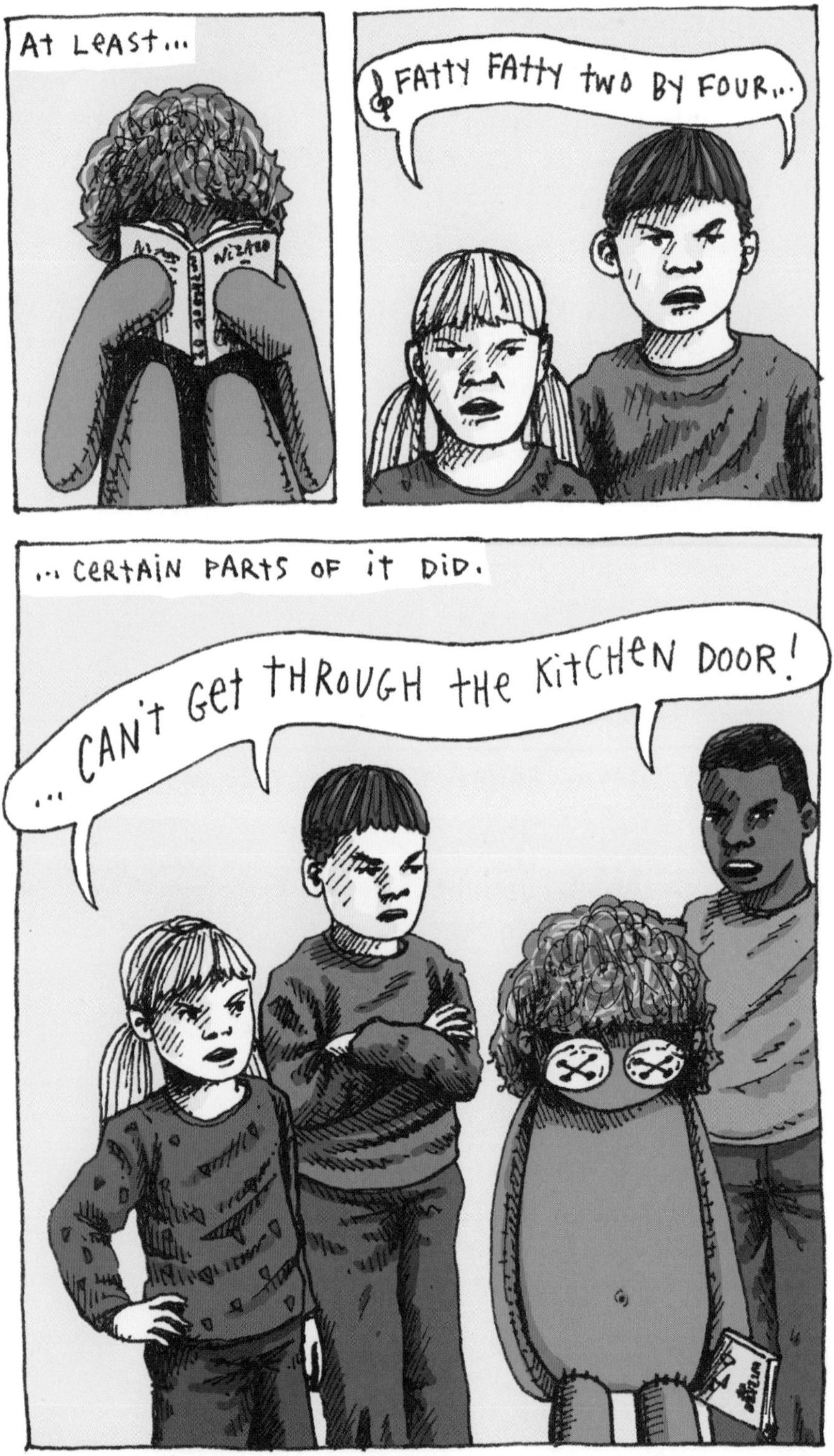
At least...
Fatty Fatty two by four...
...certain parts of it did.
...Can't get through the kitchen door!

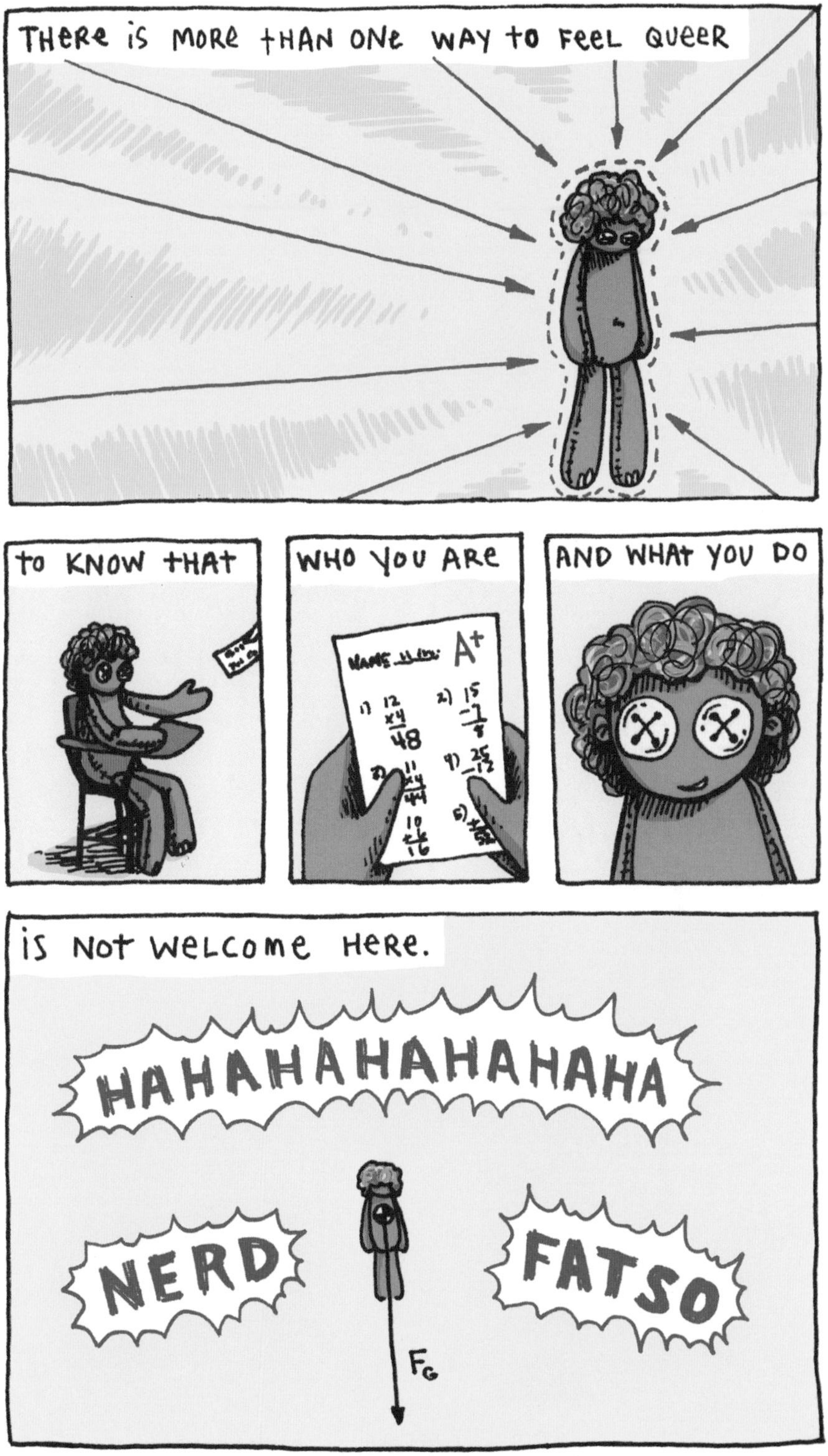
THERE IS MORE THAN ONE WAY TO FEEL QUEER
TO KNOW THAT
WHO YOU ARE
A+
AND WHAT YOU DO
IS NOT WELCOME HERE.
HAHAHAHAHAHAHA
NERD
FATSO
F_G

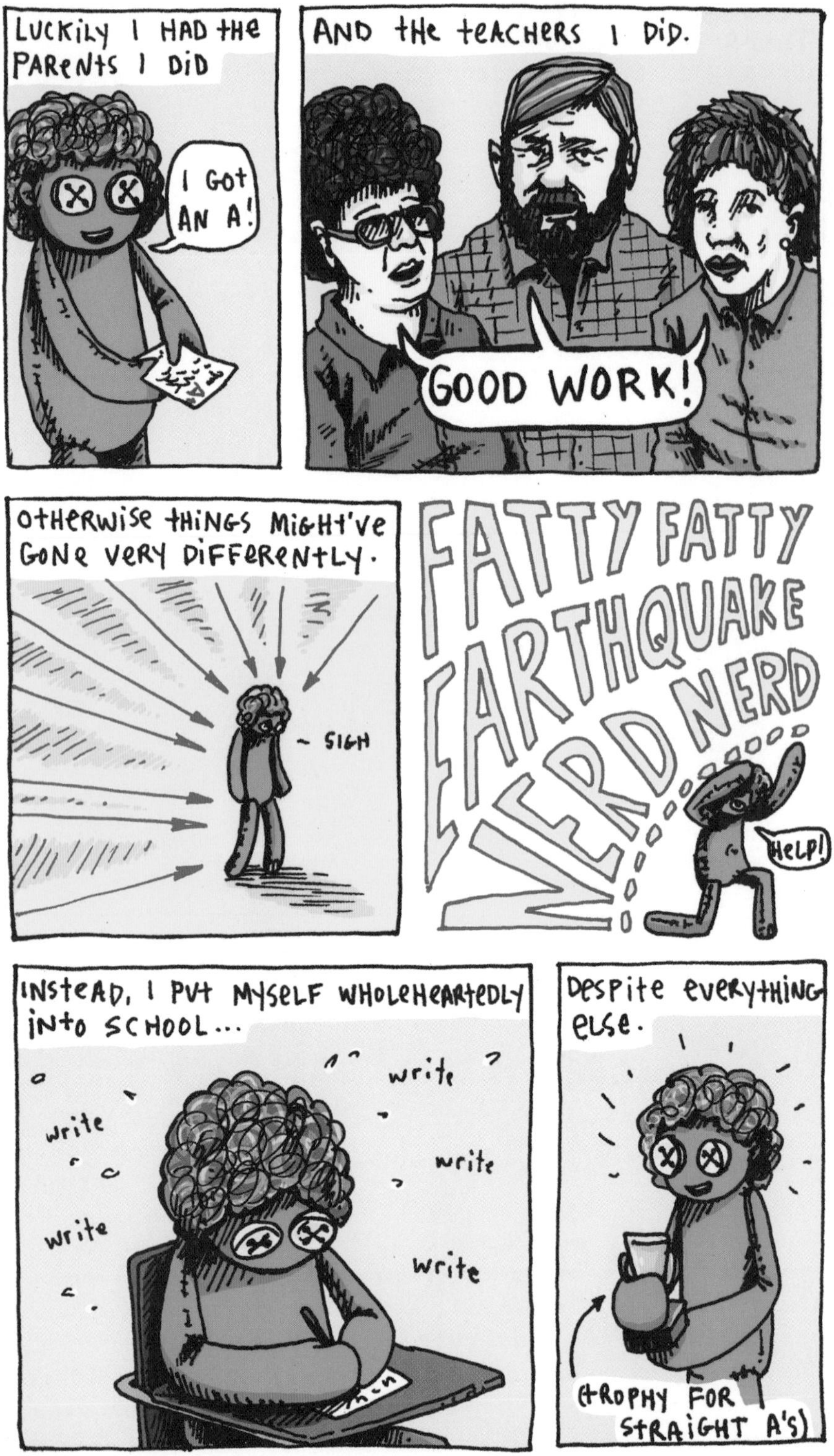
LUCKILY I HAD THE PARENTS I DID
I GOT AN A!
AND THE TEACHERS I DID.
GOOD WORK!
OTHERWISE THINGS MIGHT'VE GONE VERY DIFFERENTLY.
~ SIGH
FATTY FATTY
EARTHQUAKE
NERD NERD
NERD
HELP!
INSTEAD, I PUT MYSELF WHOLEHEARTEDLY INTO SCHOOL...
write
write
write
write
write
DESPITE EVERYTHING ELSE.
(TROPHY FOR STRAIGHT A'S)

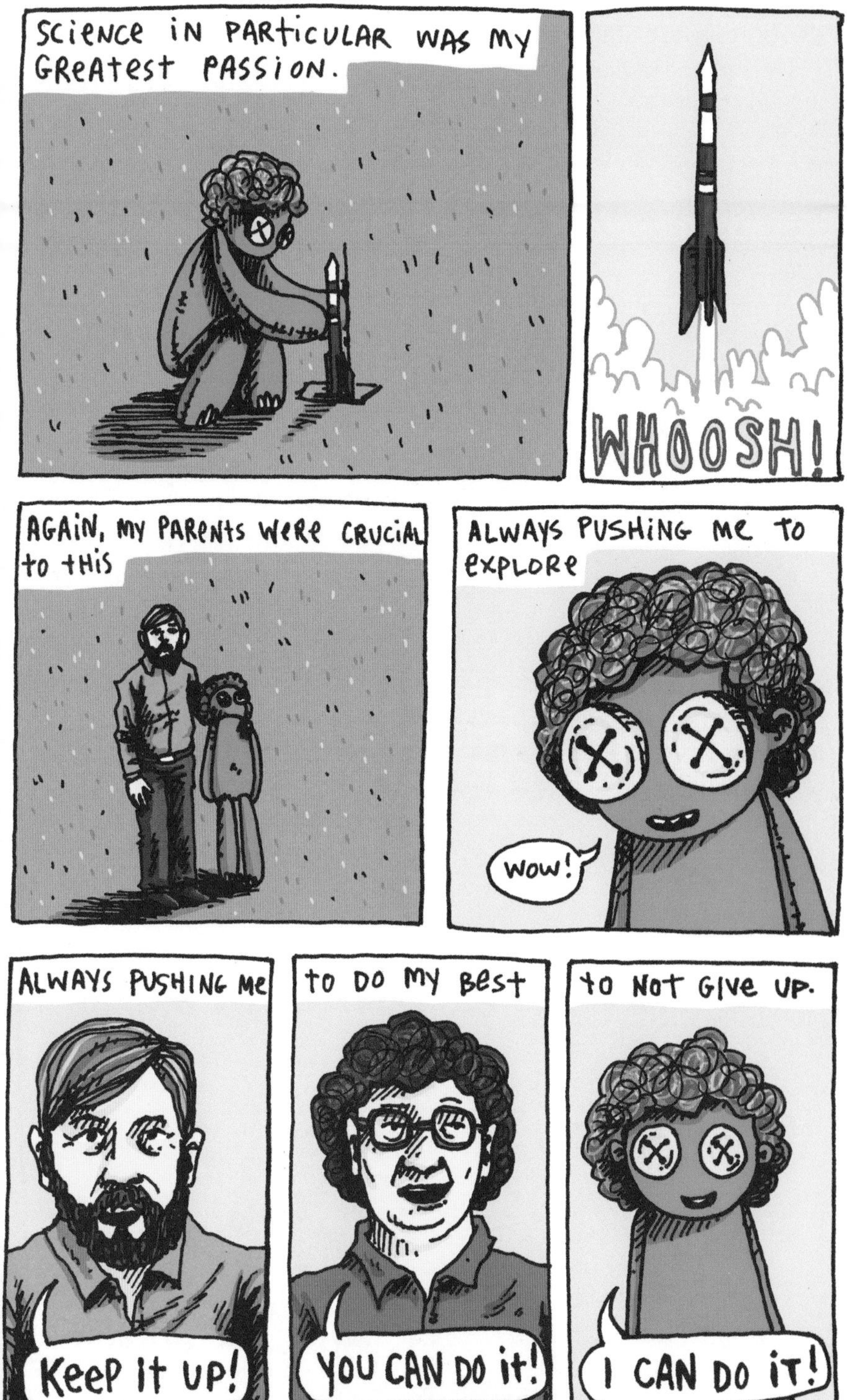
SCIENCE IN PARTICULAR WAS MY GREATEST PASSION.
WHOOSH!
AGAIN, MY PARENTS WERE CRUCIAL TO THIS
ALWAYS PUSHING ME TO EXPLORE
WOW!
ALWAYS PUSHING ME
KEEP IT UP!
TO DO MY BEST
YOU CAN DO IT!
TO NOT GIVE UP.
I CAN DO IT!

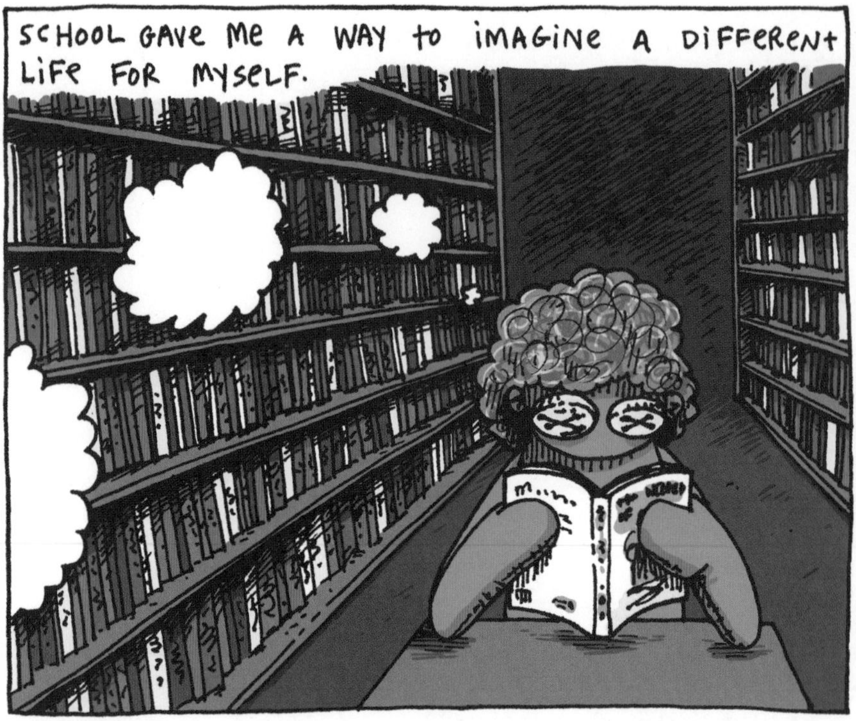
SCHOOL GAVE ME A WAY TO IMAGINE A DIFFERENT LIFE FOR MYSELF.

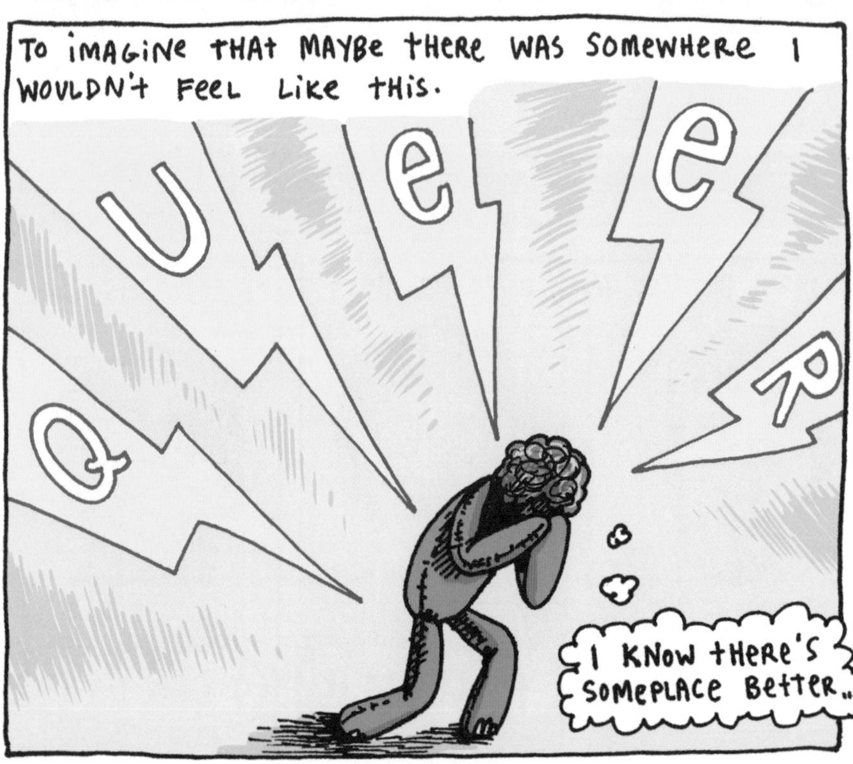
TO IMAGINE THAT MAYBE THERE WAS SOMEWHERE I WOULDN'T FEEL LIKE THIS.
QUEER
I KNOW THERE'S SOMEPLACE BETTER...

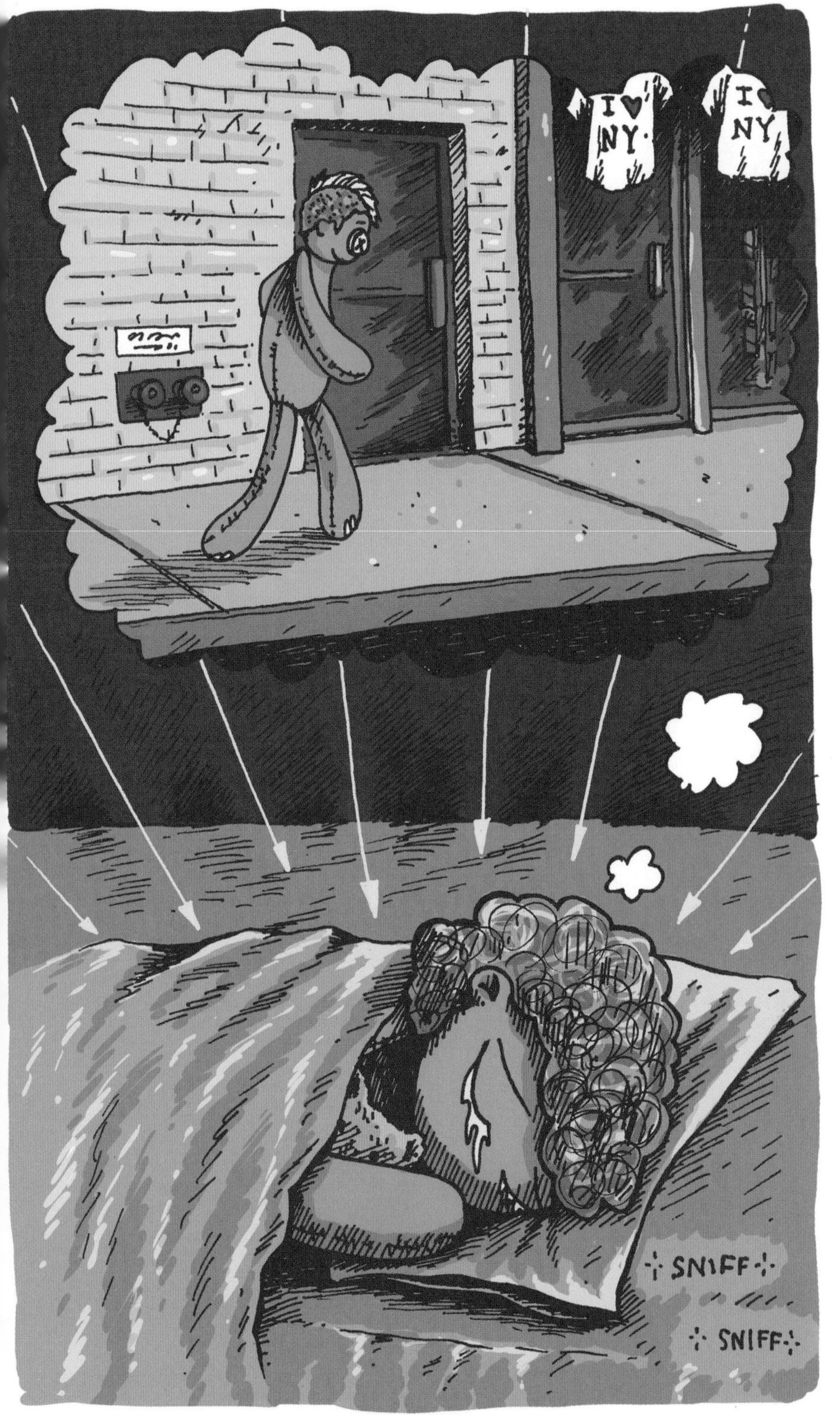

I ♥ NY
I NY
SNIFF
SNIFF

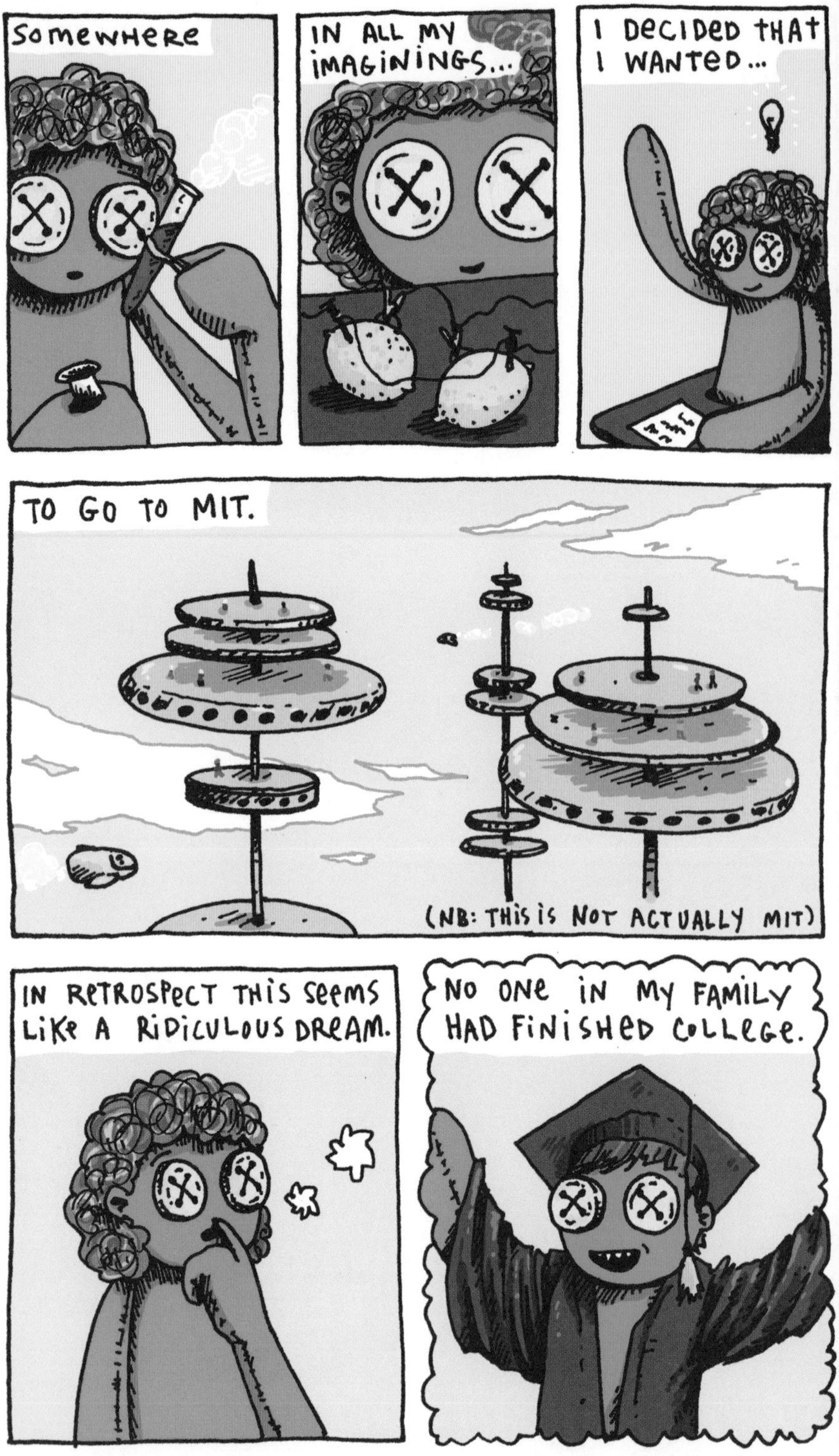
SOMEWHERE
IN ALL MY IMAGININGS...
I DECIDED THAT I WANTED...
TO GO TO MIT.
(NB: THIS IS NOT ACTUALLY MIT)
IN RETROSPECT THIS SEEMS LIKE A RIDICULOUS DREAM.
NO ONE IN MY FAMILY HAD FINISHED COLLEGE.

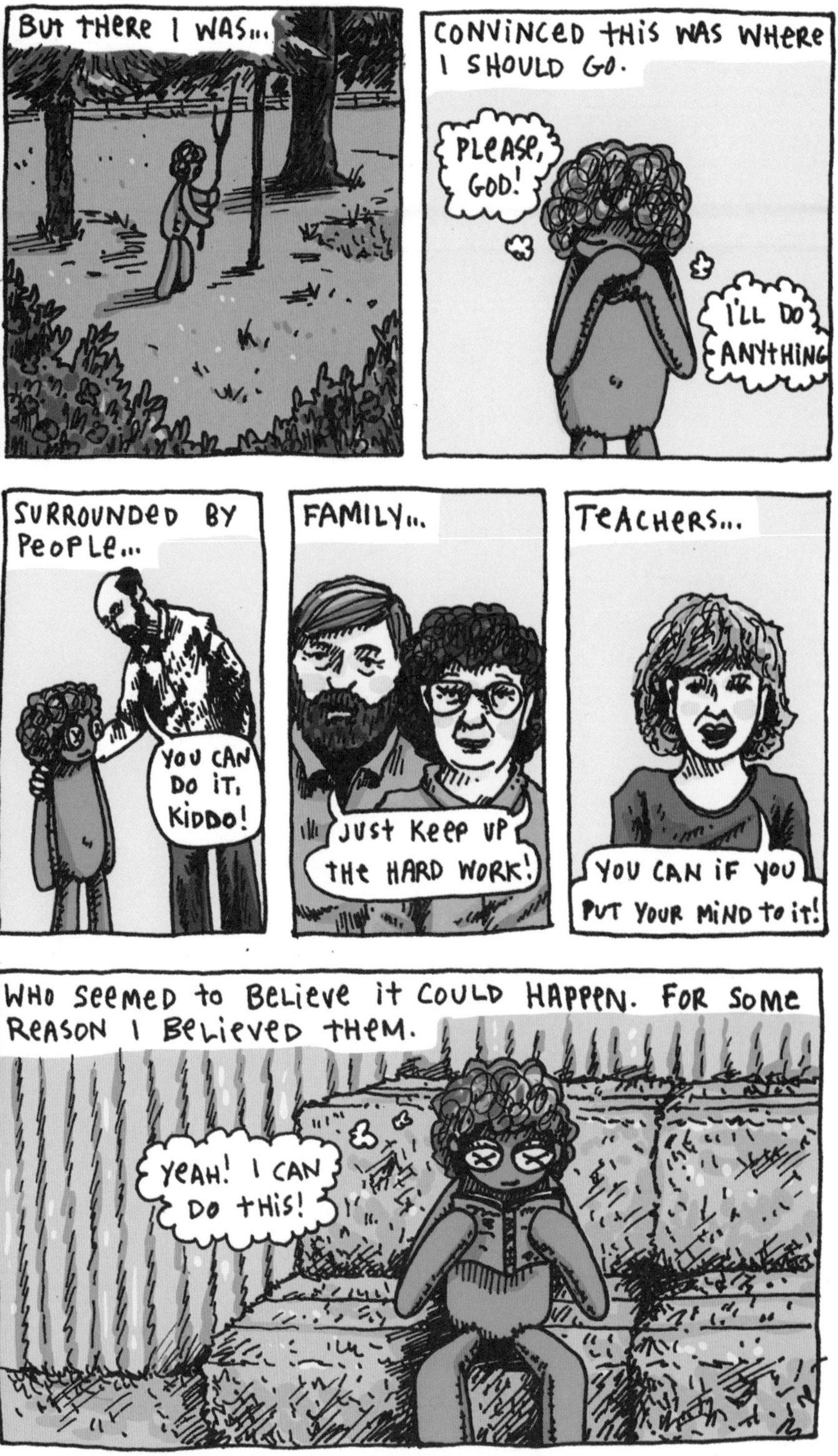
BUT THERE I WAS...
CONVINCED THIS WAS WHERE I SHOULD GO.
PLEASE, GOD!
I'LL DO ANYTHING
SURROUNDED BY PEOPLE...
YOU CAN DO IT, KIDDO!
FAMILY...
JUST KEEP UP THE HARD WORK!
TEACHERS...
YOU CAN IF YOU PUT YOUR MIND TO IT!
WHO SEEMED TO BELIEVE IT COULD HAPPEN. FOR SOME REASON I BELIEVED THEM.
YEAH! I CAN DO THIS!

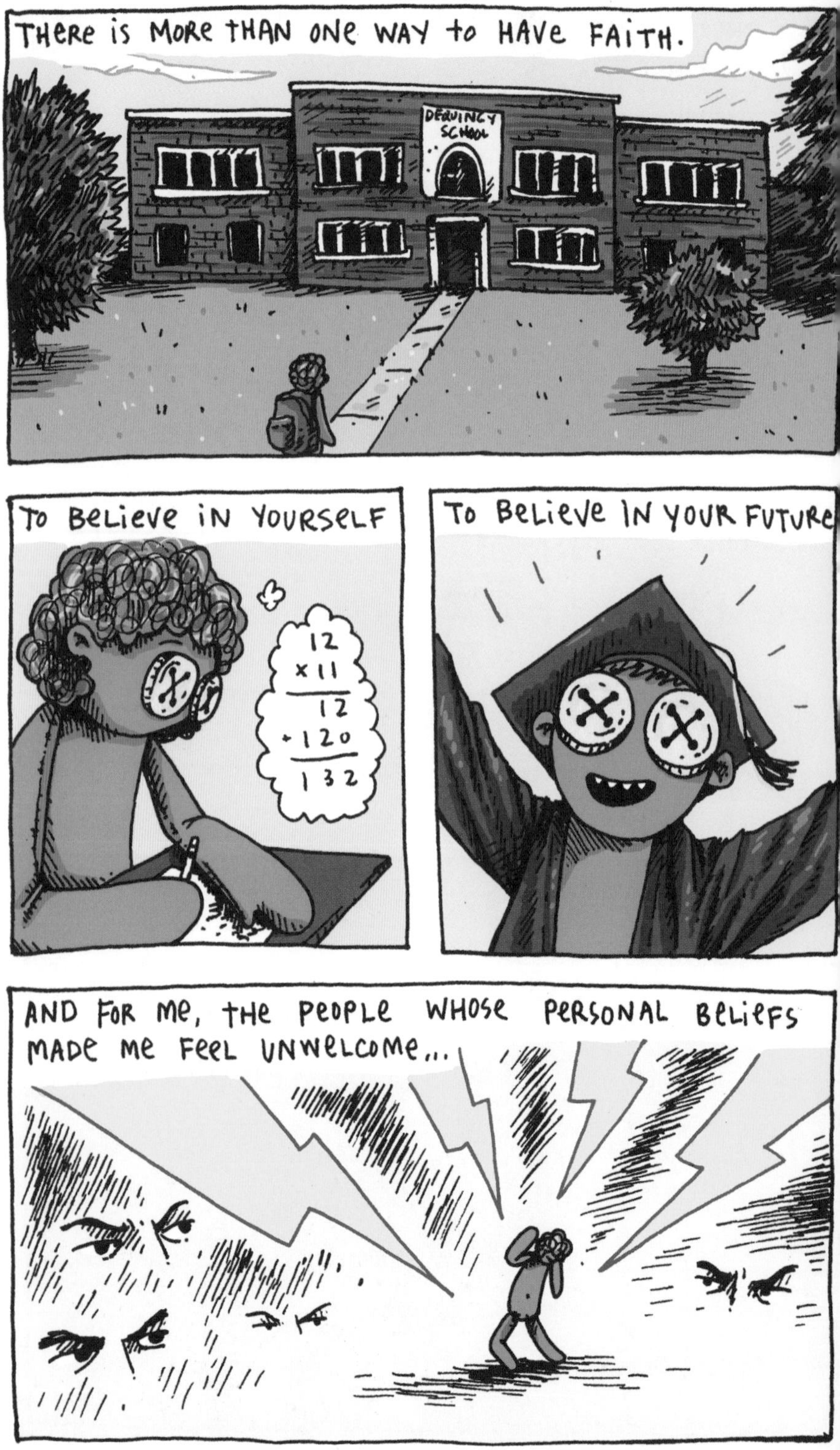
THERE IS MORE THAN ONE WAY TO HAVE FAITH.
DEQUINCY SCHOOL
TO BELIEVE IN YOURSELF
12
x 11
12
+ 120
132
TO BELIEVE IN YOUR FUTURE
AND FOR ME, THE PEOPLE WHOSE PERSONAL BELIEFS MADE ME FEEL UNWELCOME...

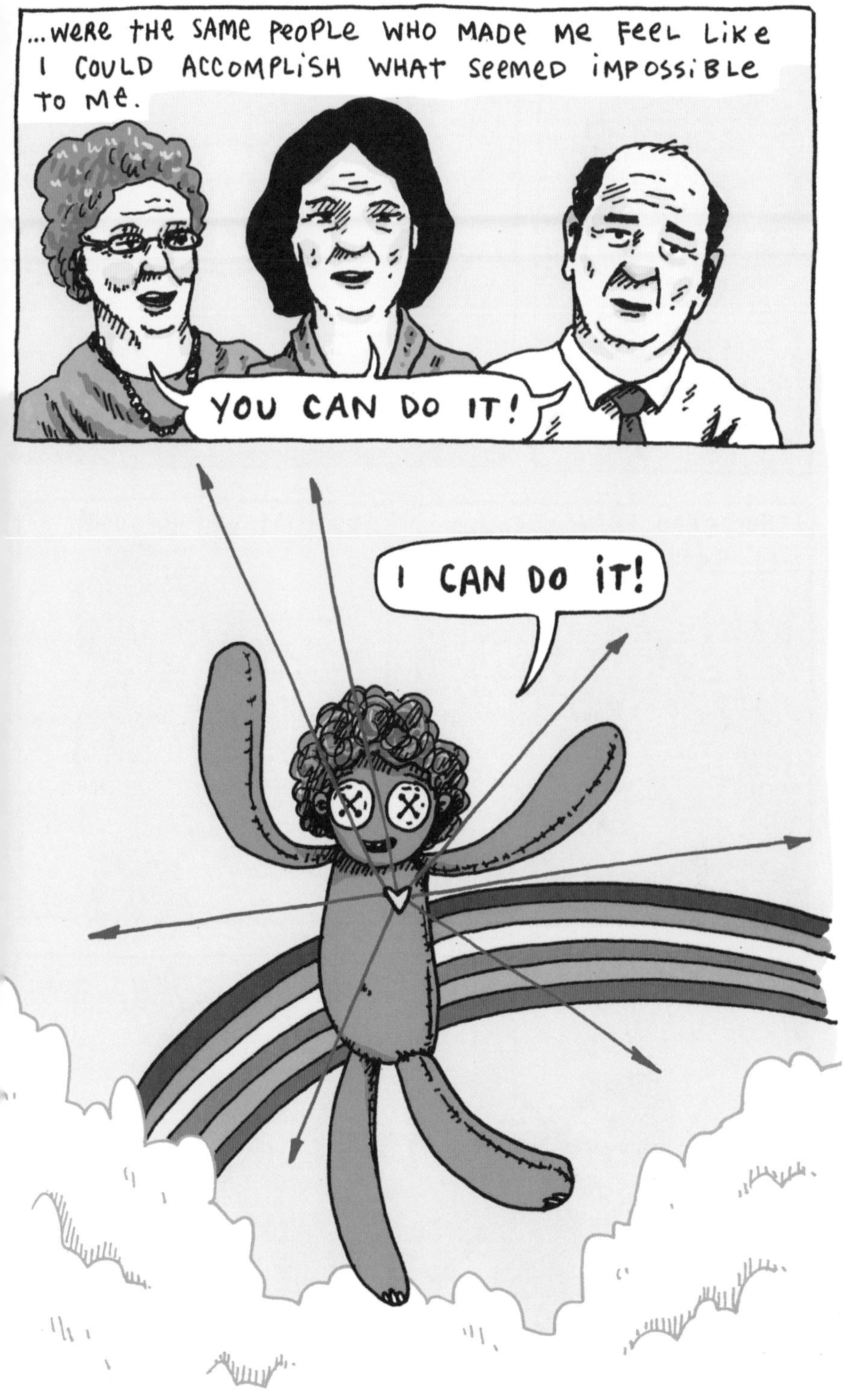
...WERE THE SAME PEOPLE WHO MADE ME FEEL LIKE I COULD ACCOMPLISH WHAT SEEMED IMPOSSIBLE TO ME.
YOU CAN DO IT!
I CAN DO IT!

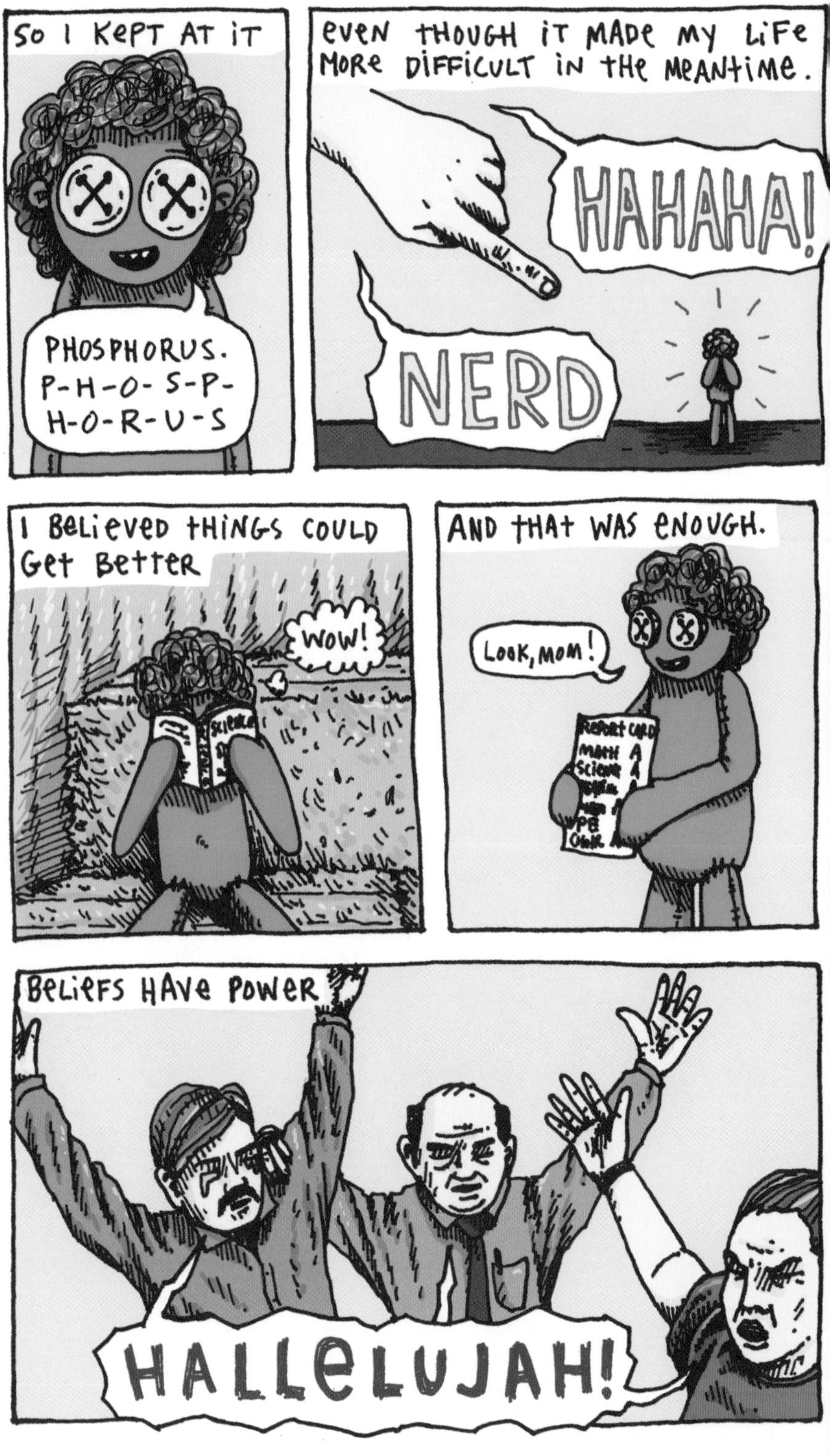
SO I KEPT AT IT
PHOSPHORUS. P-H-O-S-P-H-O-R-U-S
EVEN THOUGH IT MADE MY LIFE MORE DIFFICULT IN THE MEANTIME.
HAHAHA!
NERD
I BELIEVED THINGS COULD GET BETTER
WOW!
SCIENCE
AND THAT WAS ENOUGH.
LOOK, MOM!
REPORT CARD
MATH A
SCIENCE A
PE
BELIEFS HAVE POWER
HALLELUJAH!

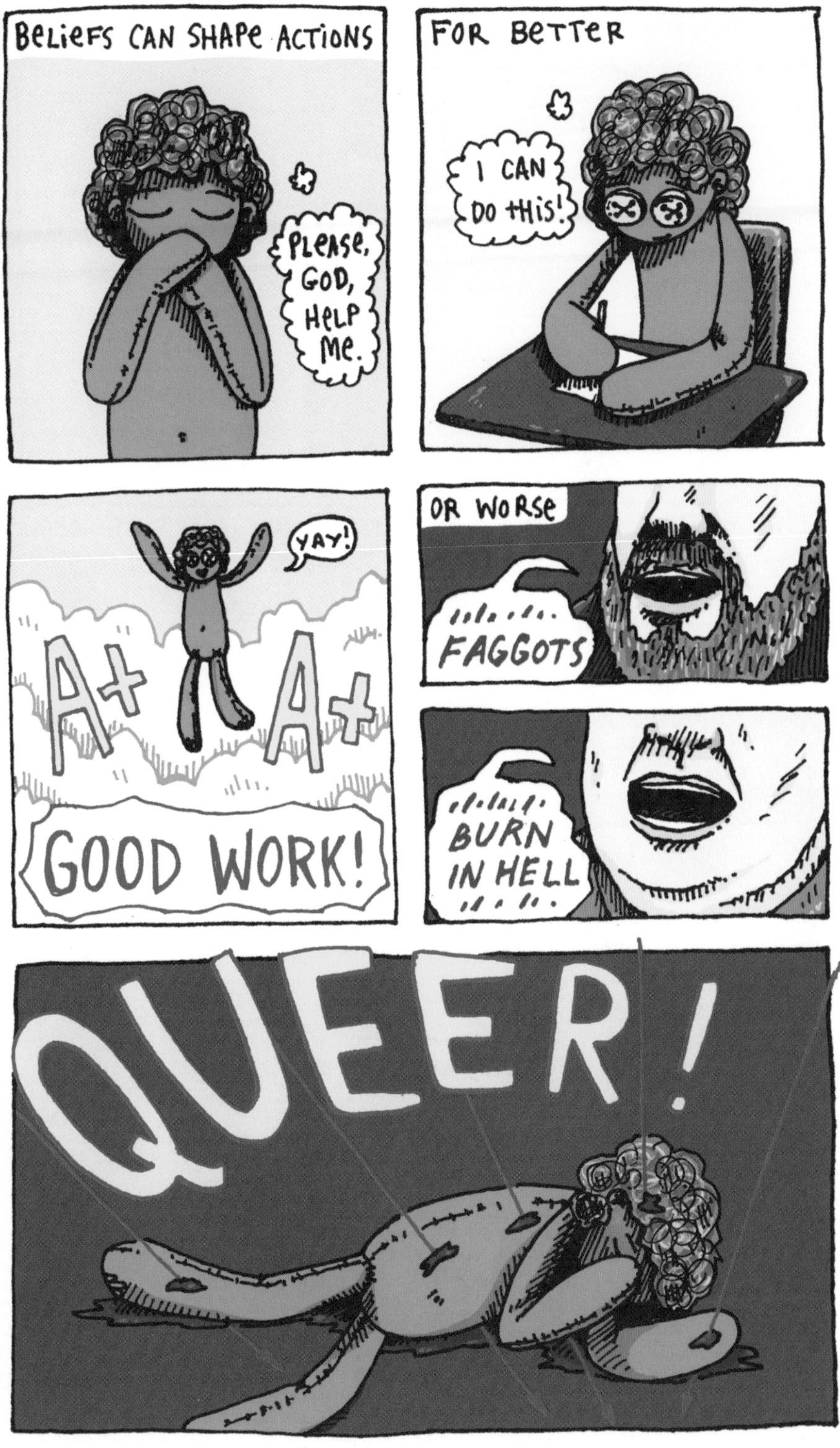
BELIEFS CAN SHAPE ACTIONS
PLEASE, GOD, HELP ME.
FOR BETTER
I CAN DO THIS!
YAY!
A+ A+
GOOD WORK!
OR WORSE
FAGGOTS
BURN IN HELL
QUEER!

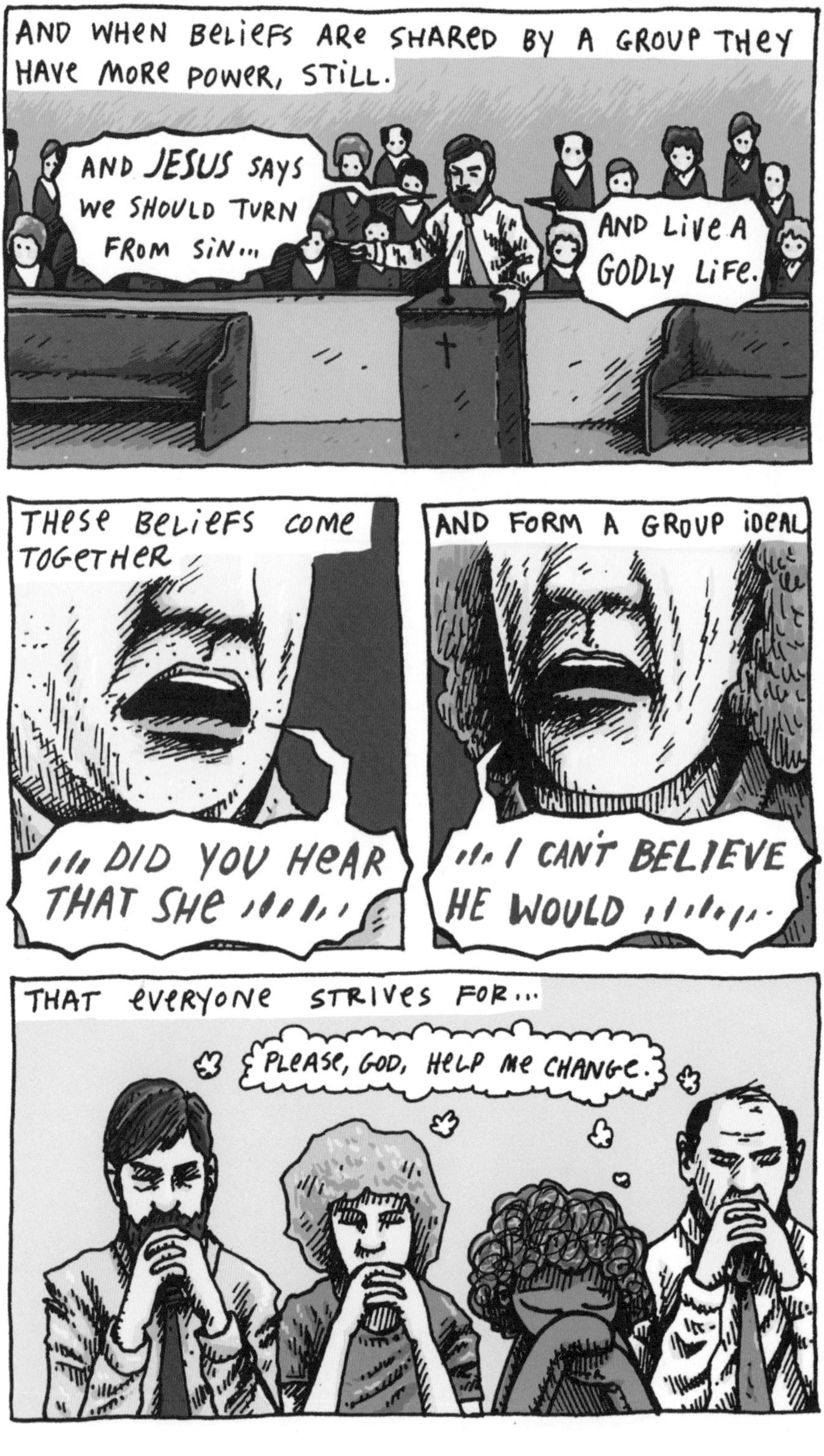
AND WHEN BELIEFS ARE SHARED BY A GROUP THEY HAVE MORE POWER, STILL.
AND JESUS SAYS WE SHOULD TURN FROM SIN...
AND LIVE A GODLY LIFE.
THESE BELIEFS COME TOGETHER
... DID YOU HEAR THAT SHE ......
AND FORM A GROUP IDEAL
... I CAN'T BELIEVE HE WOULD ......
THAT EVERYONE STRIVES FOR...
PLEASE, GOD, HELP ME CHANGE.

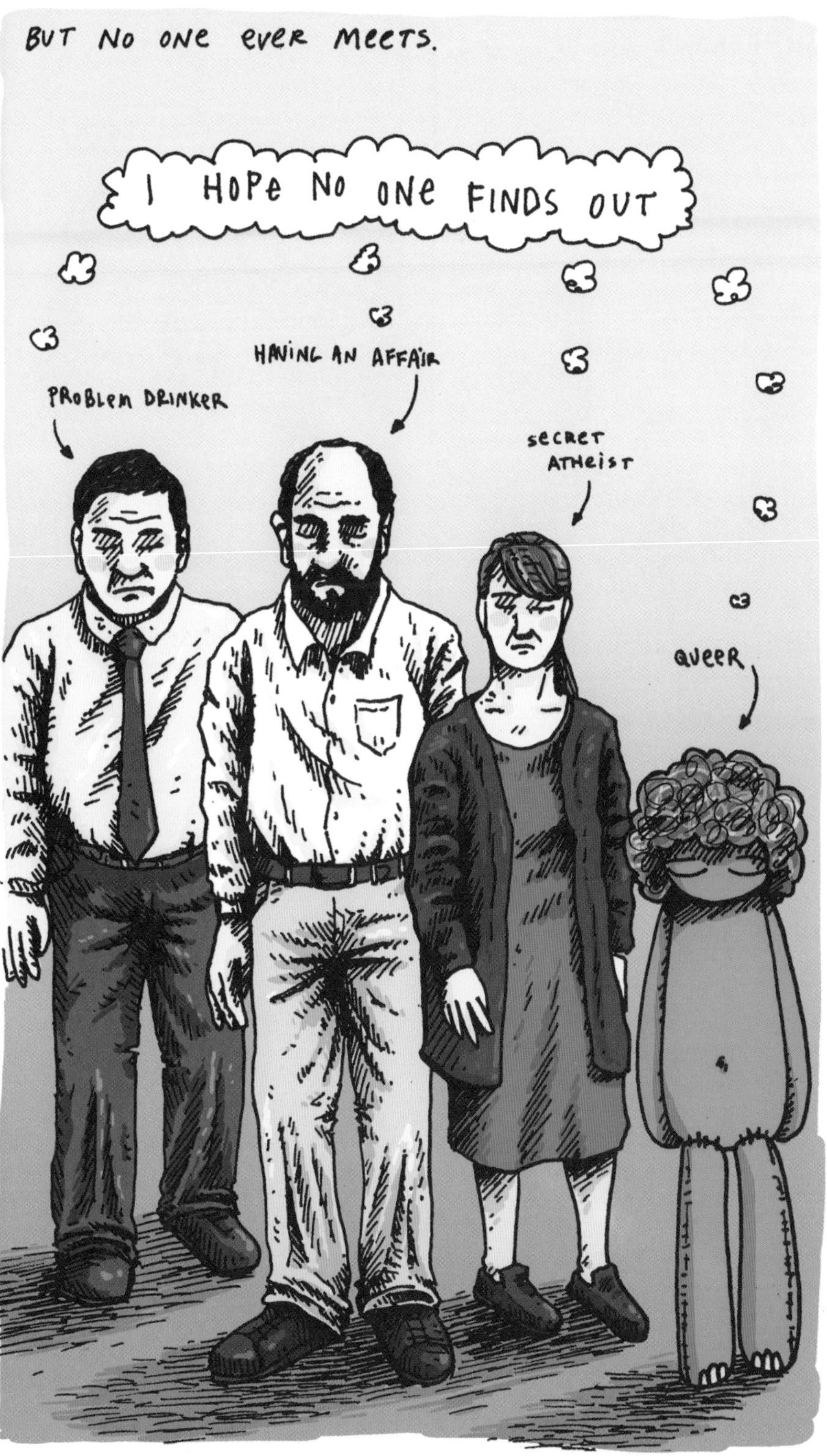
BUT NO ONE EVER MEETS.
I HOPE NO ONE FINDS OUT
PROBLEM DRINKER
HAVING AN AFFAIR
SECRET ATHEIST
QUEER

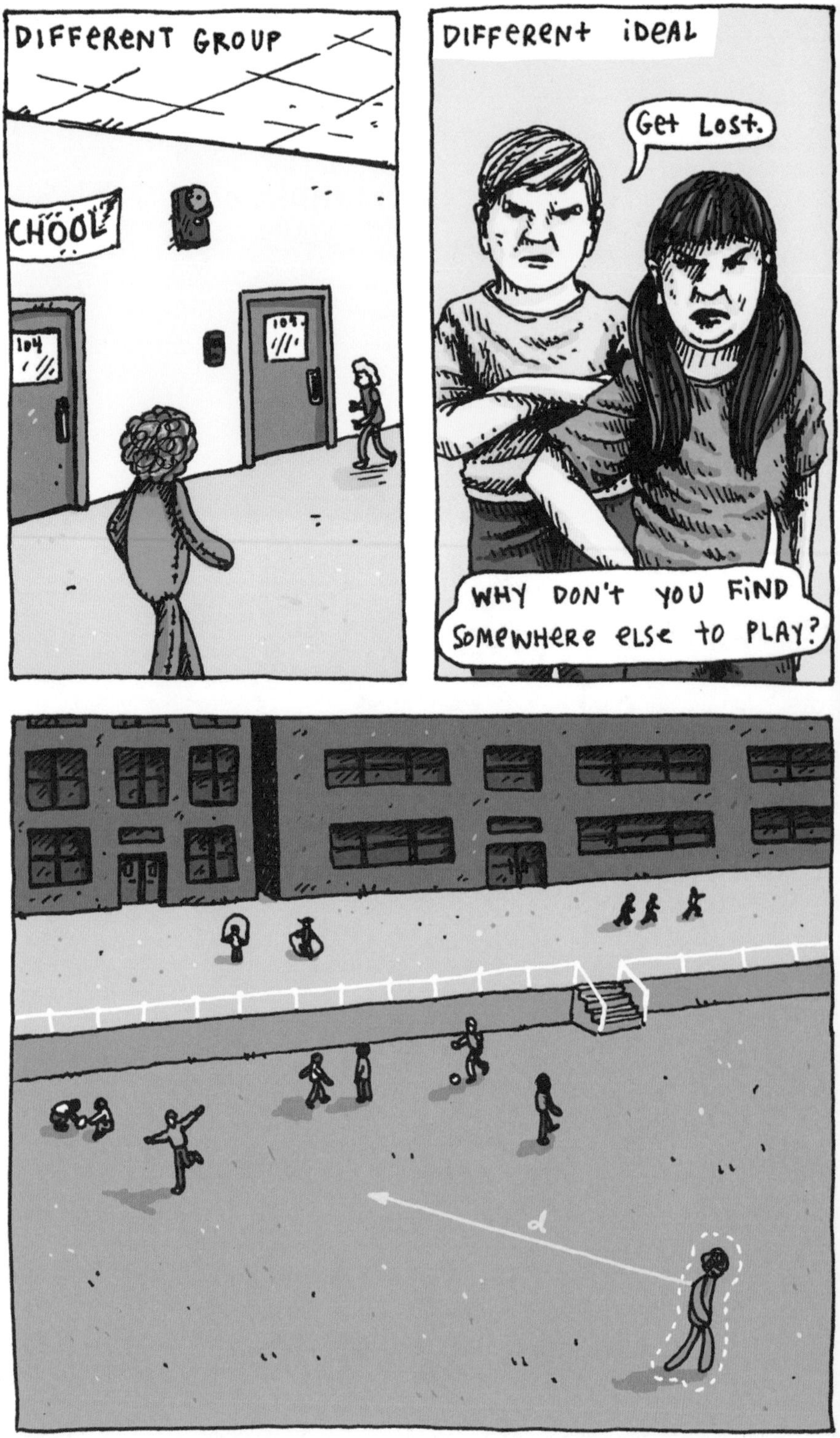
DIFFERENT GROUP
CHOOL
104
103
DIFFERENT IDEAL
Get Lost.
WHY DON'T YOU FIND SOMEWHERE ELSE TO PLAY?
d

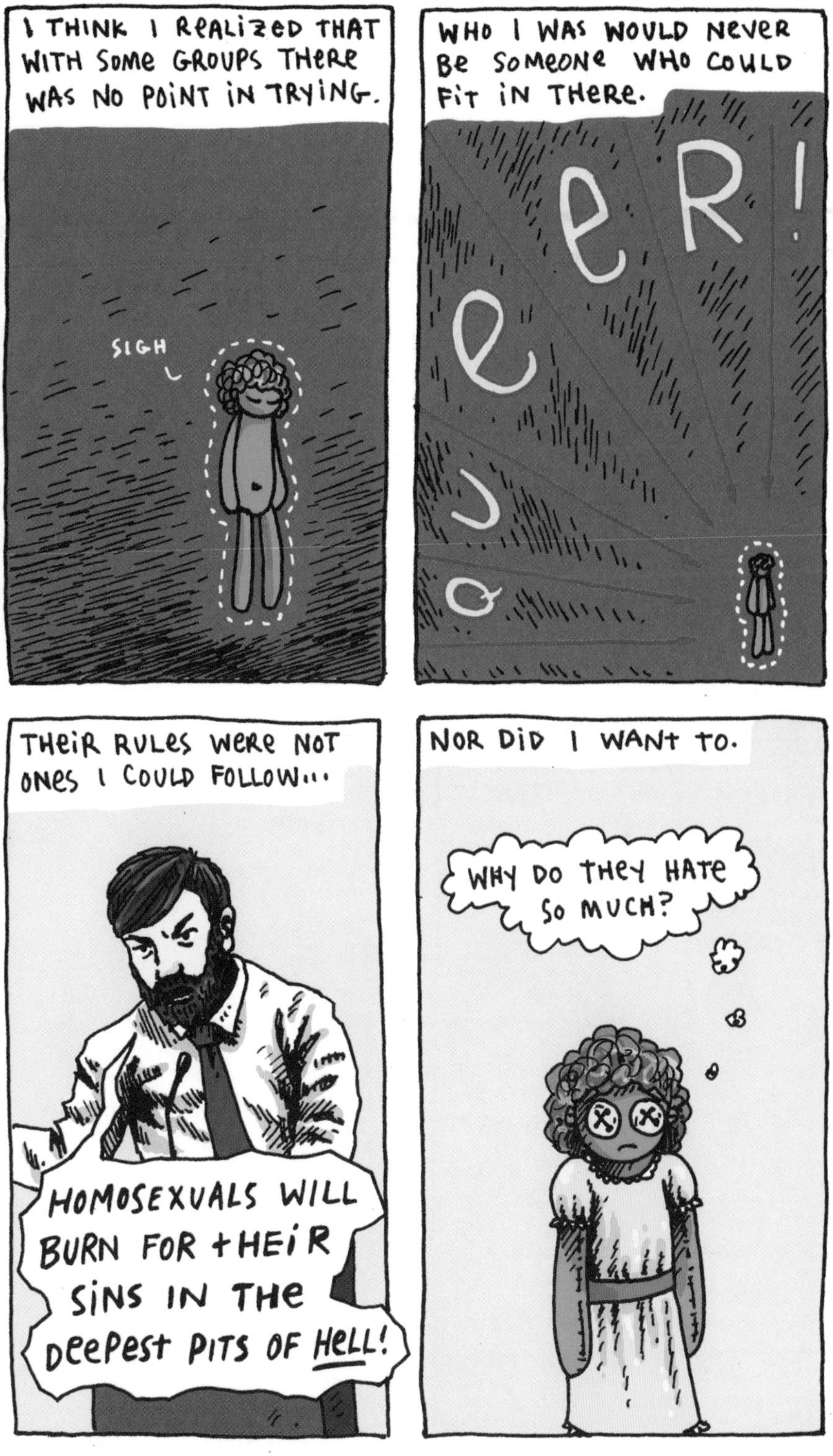
I THINK I REALIZED THAT WITH SOME GROUPS THERE WAS NO POINT IN TRYING.
SIGH
WHO I WAS WOULD NEVER BE SOMEONE WHO COULD FIT IN THERE.
QUEER!
THEIR RULES WERE NOT ONES I COULD FOLLOW...
HOMOSEXUALS WILL BURN FOR THEIR SINS IN THE DEEPEST PITS OF HELL!
NOR DID I WANT TO.
WHY DO THEY HATE SO MUCH?

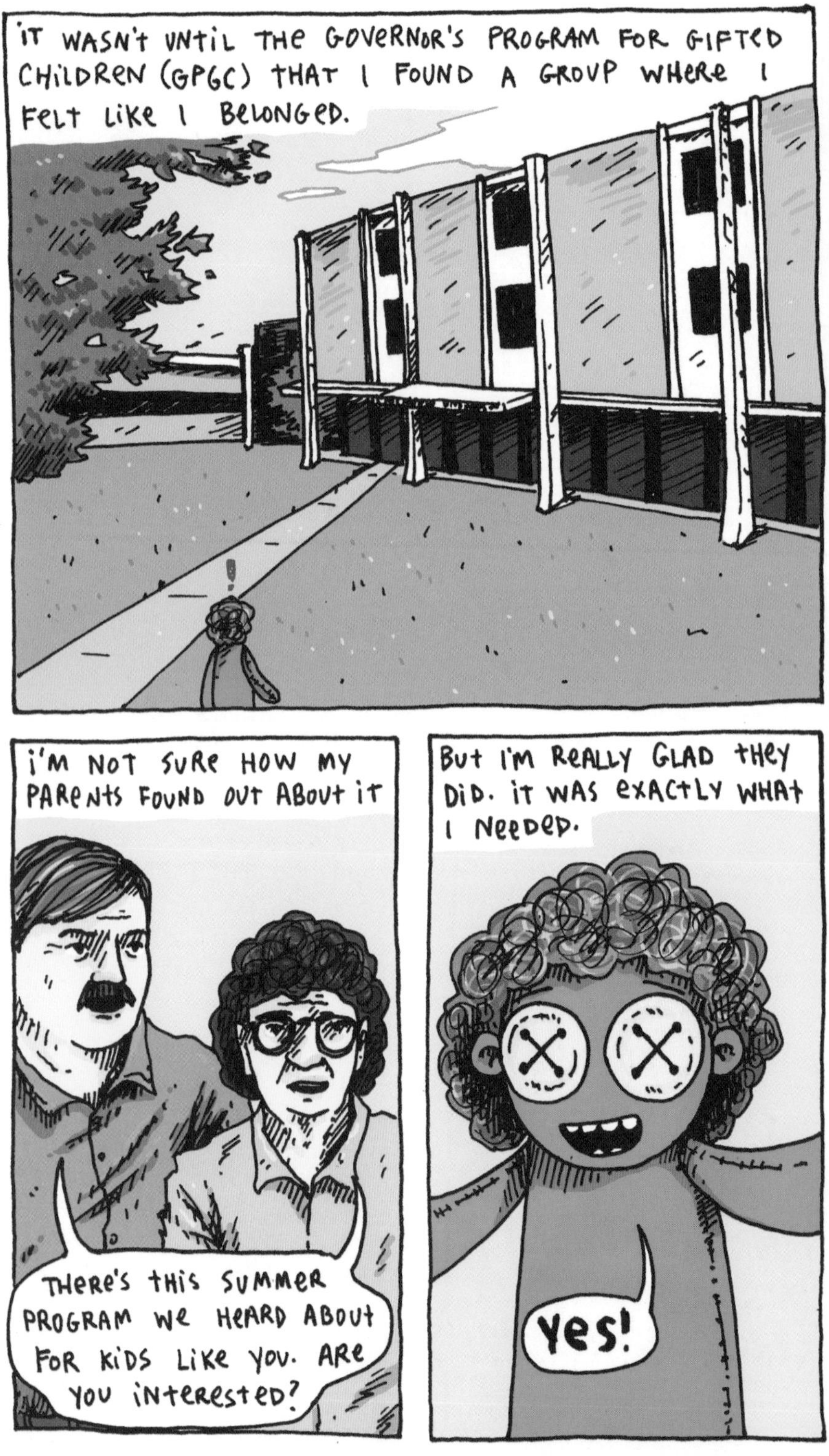
IT WASN'T UNTIL THE GOVERNOR'S PROGRAM FOR GIFTED CHILDREN (GPGC) THAT I FOUND A GROUP WHERE I FELT LIKE I BELONGED.
I'M NOT SURE HOW MY PARENTS FOUND OUT ABOUT IT
THERE'S THIS SUMMER PROGRAM WE HEARD ABOUT FOR KIDS LIKE YOU. ARE YOU INTERESTED?
BUT I'M REALLY GLAD THEY DID. IT WAS EXACTLY WHAT I NEEDED.
YES!

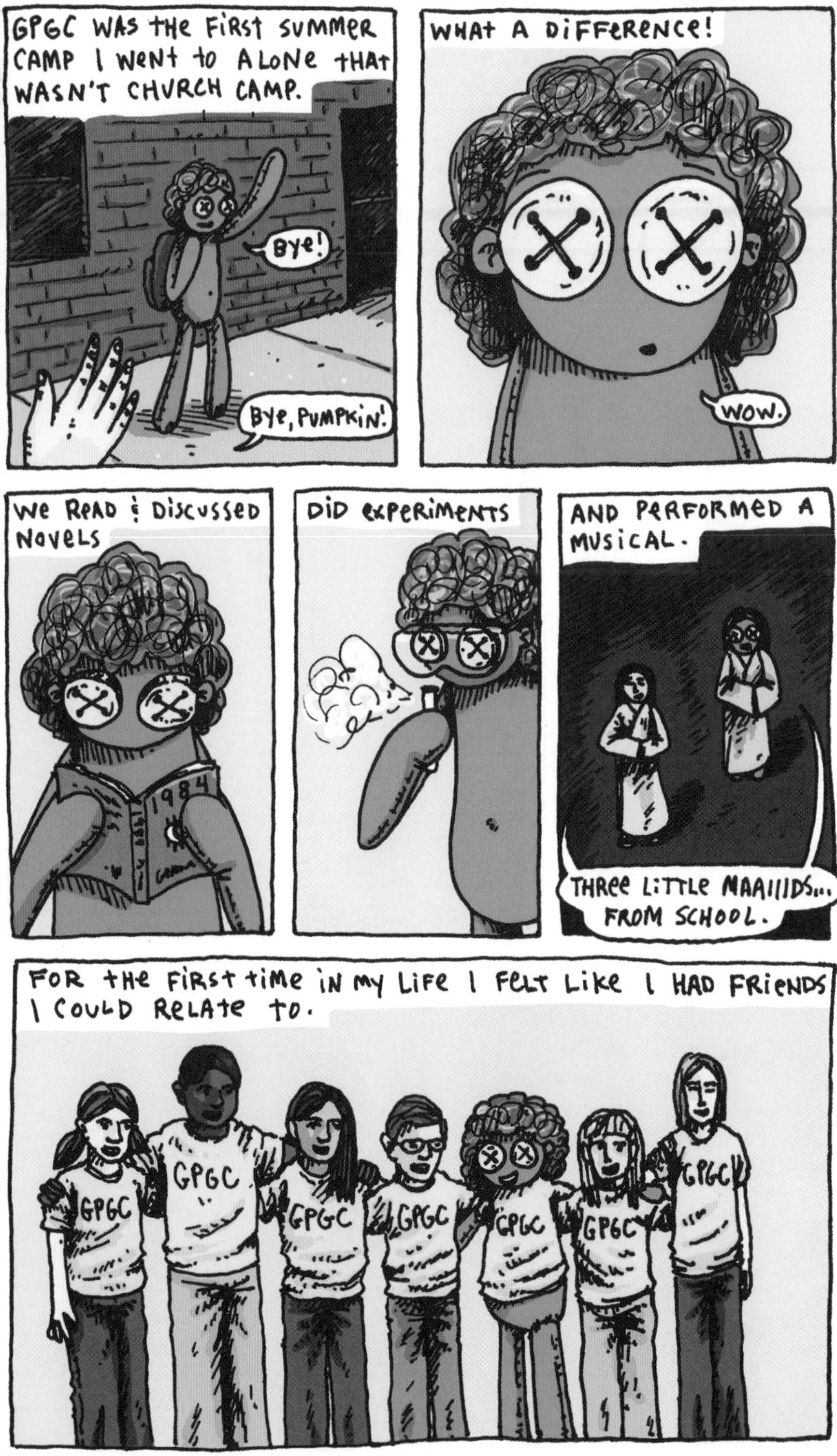
GPGC WAS THE FIRST SUMMER CAMP I WENT TO ALONE THAT WASN'T CHURCH CAMP.
BYE!
BYE, PUMPKIN!
WHAT A DIFFERENCE!
WOW.
WE READ & DISCUSSED NOVELS
1984
DID EXPERIMENTS
AND PERFORMED A MUSICAL.
THREE LITTLE MAAIIIDS... FROM SCHOOL.
FOR THE FIRST TIME IN MY LIFE I FELT LIKE I HAD FRIENDS I COULD RELATE TO.
GPGC
GPGC
GPGC
GPGC
GPGC
GPGC
GPGC

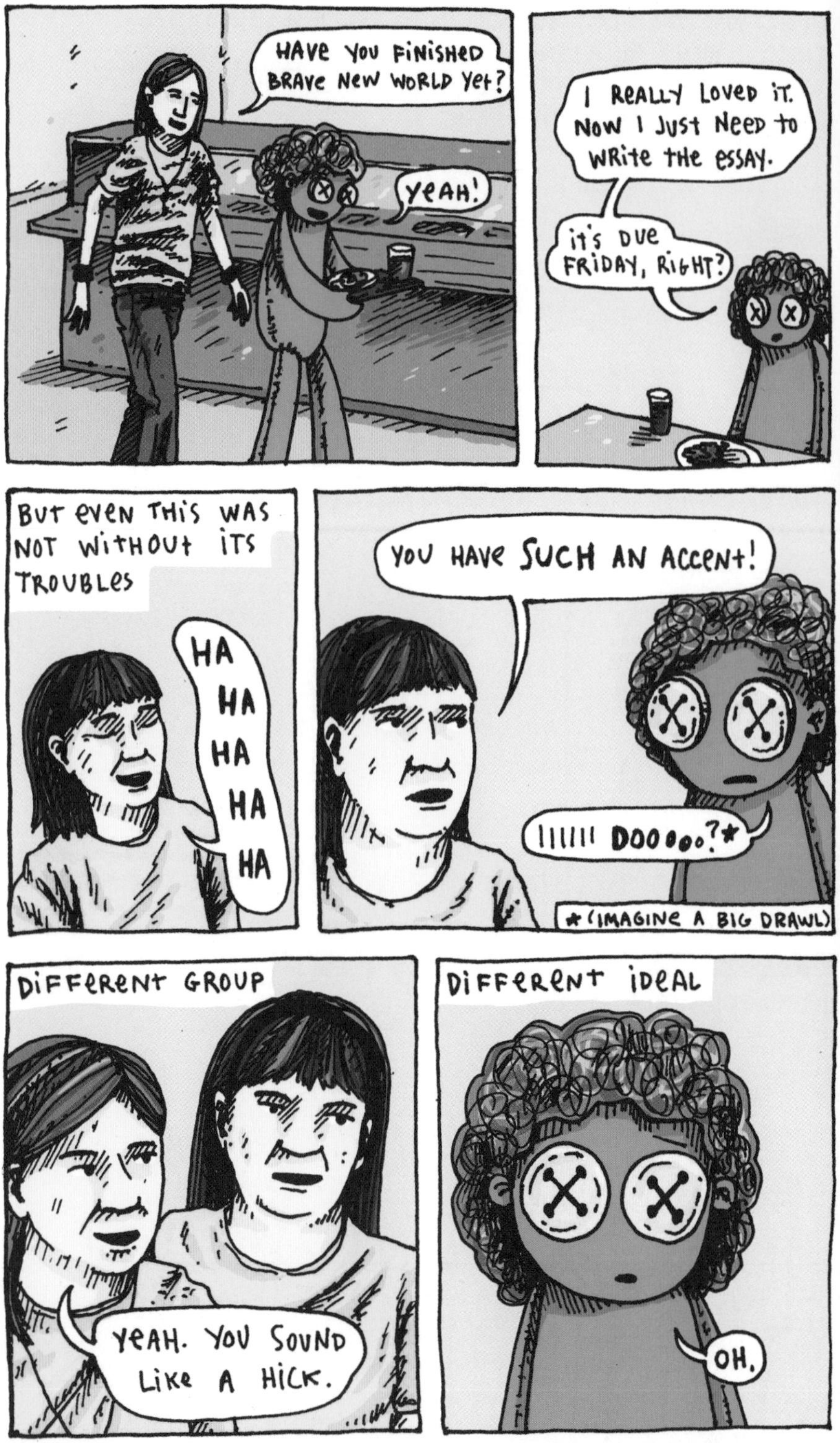
HAVE YOU FINISHED BRAVE NEW WORLD YET?
YEAH!
I REALLY LOVED IT. NOW I JUST NEED TO WRITE THE ESSAY.
IT'S DUE FRIDAY, RIGHT?
BUT EVEN THIS WAS NOT WITHOUT ITS TROUBLES
HA HA HA HA HA
YOU HAVE SUCH AN ACCENT!
IIIIII DOOooo?*
* (IMAGINE A BIG DRAWL)
DIFFERENT GROUP
YEAH. YOU SOUND LIKE A HICK.
DIFFERENT IDEAL
OH.

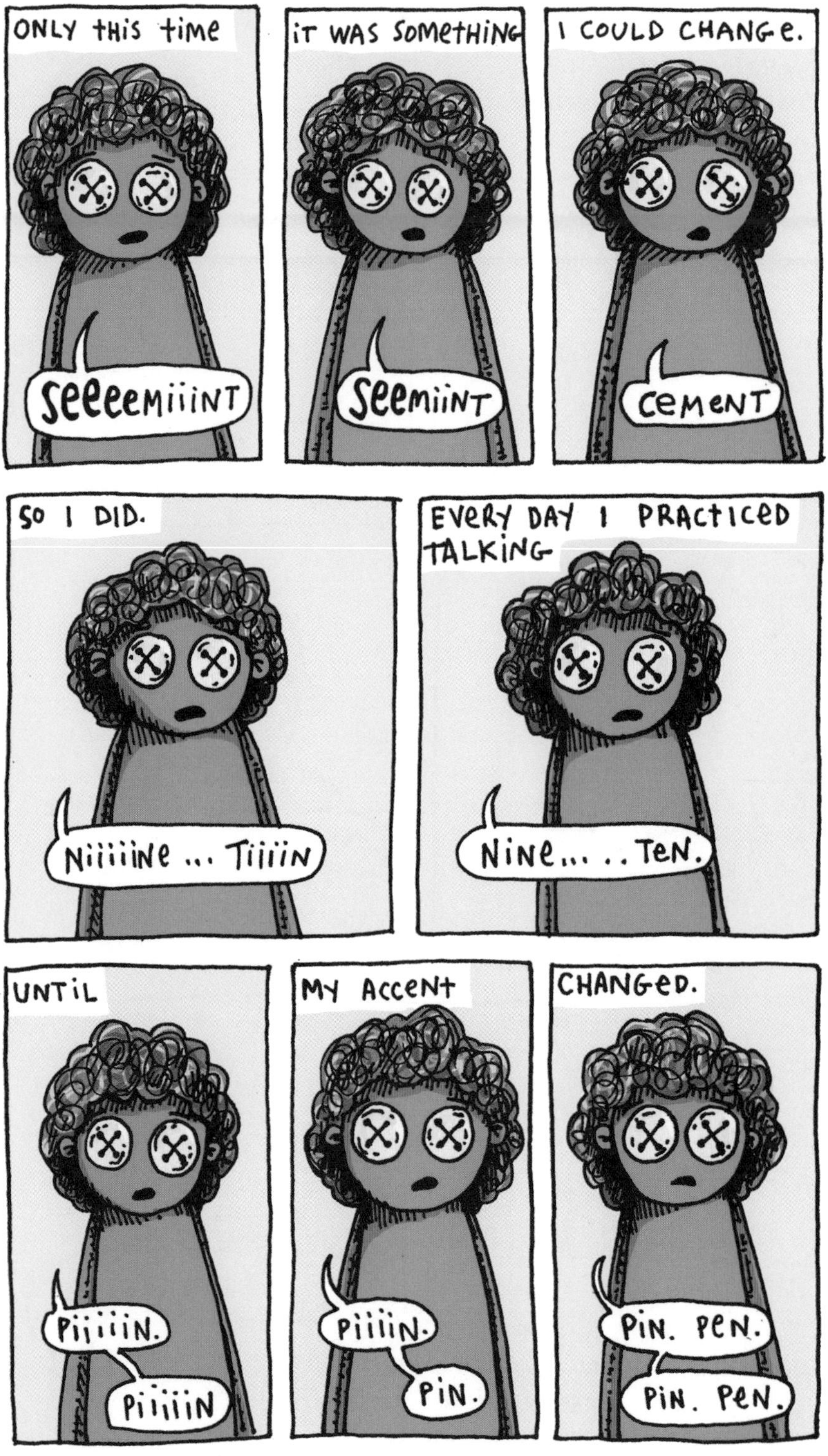
ONLY THIS TIME
SEEEEMIIINT
IT WAS SOMETHING
SEEMIINT
I COULD CHANGE.
CEMENT
SO I DID.
NIIIIINE ... TIIIIN
EVERY DAY I PRACTICED TALKING
NINE... ..TEN.
UNTIL
PIIIIIN.
PIIIIIN
MY ACCENT
PIIIIN.
PIN.
CHANGED.
PIN. PEN.
PIN. PEN.

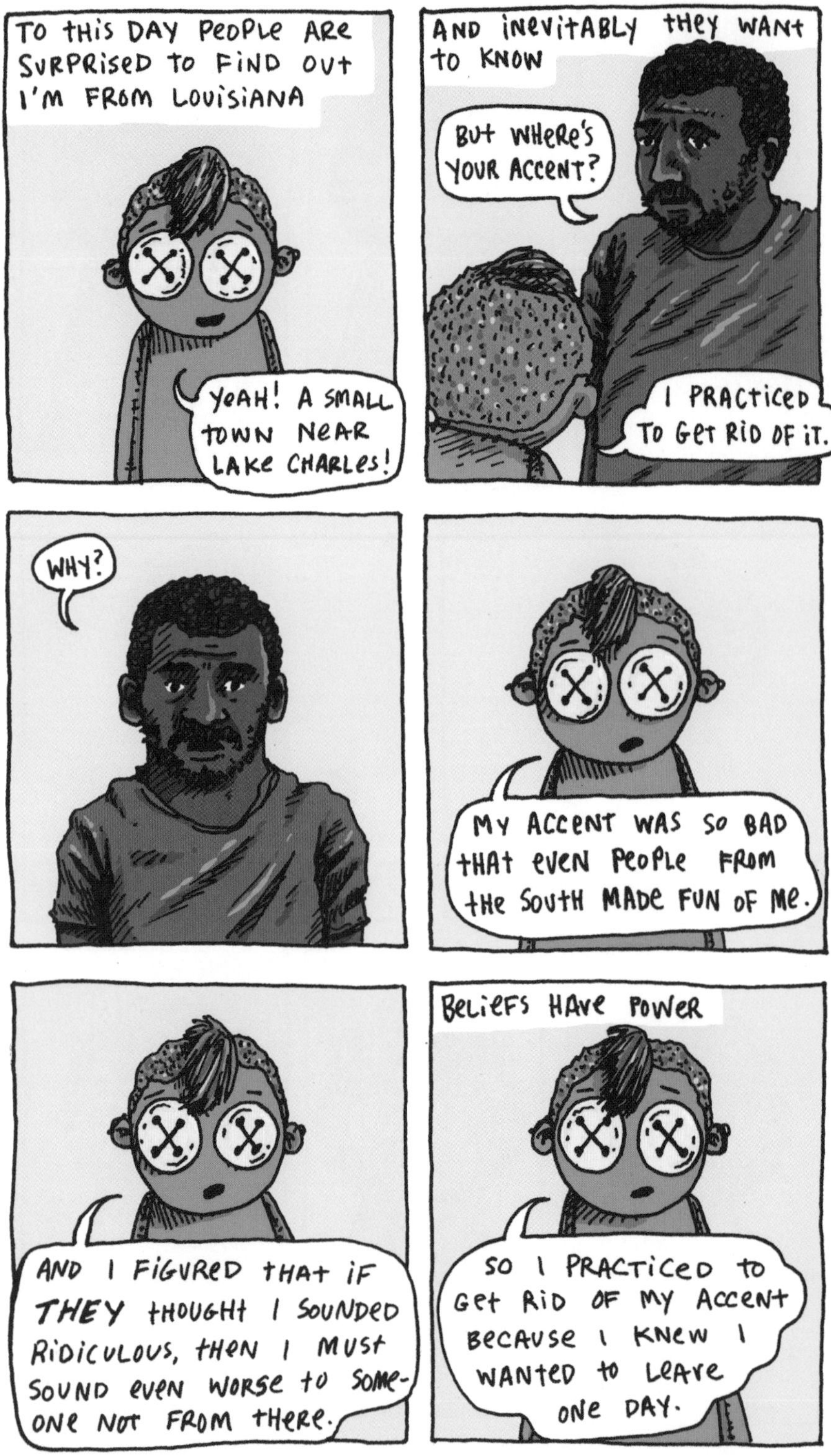
TO THIS DAY PEOPLE ARE SURPRISED TO FIND OUT I'M FROM LOUISIANA
YEAH! A SMALL TOWN NEAR LAKE CHARLES!
AND INEVITABLY THEY WANT TO KNOW
BUT WHERE'S YOUR ACCENT?
I PRACTICED TO GET RID OF IT.
WHY?
MY ACCENT WAS SO BAD THAT EVEN PEOPLE FROM THE SOUTH MADE FUN OF ME.
AND I FIGURED THAT IF THEY THOUGHT I SOUNDED RIDICULOUS, THEN I MUST SOUND EVEN WORSE TO SOME-ONE NOT FROM THERE.
BELIEFS HAVE POWER
SO I PRACTICED TO GET RID OF MY ACCENT BECAUSE I KNEW I WANTED TO LEAVE ONE DAY.

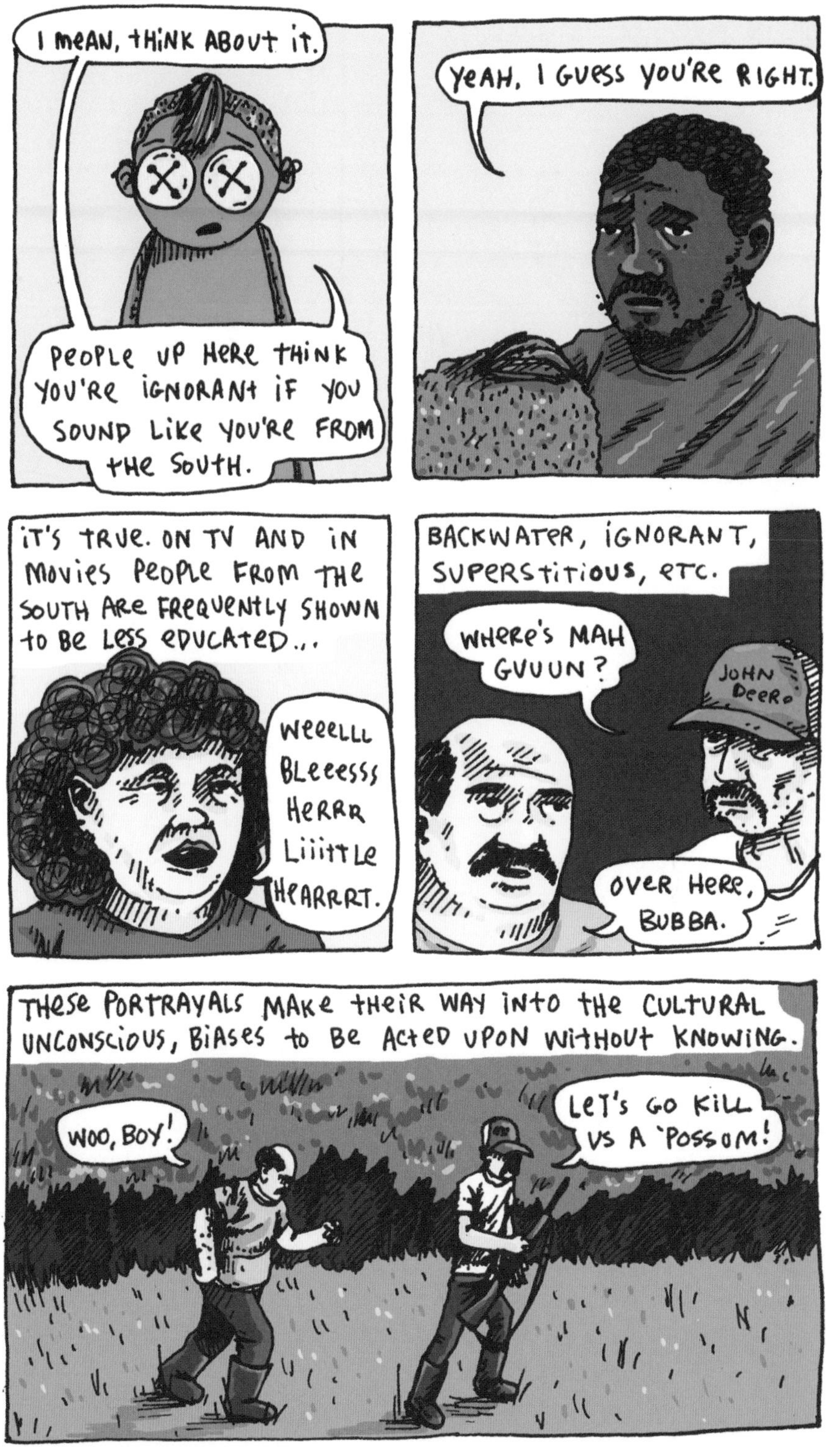

I MEAN, THINK ABOUT IT.
PEOPLE UP HERE THINK YOU'RE IGNORANT IF YOU SOUND LIKE YOU'RE FROM THE SOUTH.
YEAH, I GUESS YOU'RE RIGHT.
IT'S TRUE. ON TV AND IN MOVIES PEOPLE FROM THE SOUTH ARE FREQUENTLY SHOWN TO BE LESS EDUCATED...
WEEELLL BLEEESSS HERRR LIIITTLE HEARRRT.
BACKWATER, IGNORANT, SUPERSTITIOUS, ETC.
WHERE'S MAH GUUUN?
JOHN DEERO
OVER HERE, BUBBA.
THESE PORTRAYALS MAKE THEIR WAY INTO THE CULTURAL UNCONSCIOUS, BIASES TO BE ACTED UPON WITHOUT KNOWING.
WOO, BOY!
LET'S GO KILL US A 'POSSOM!

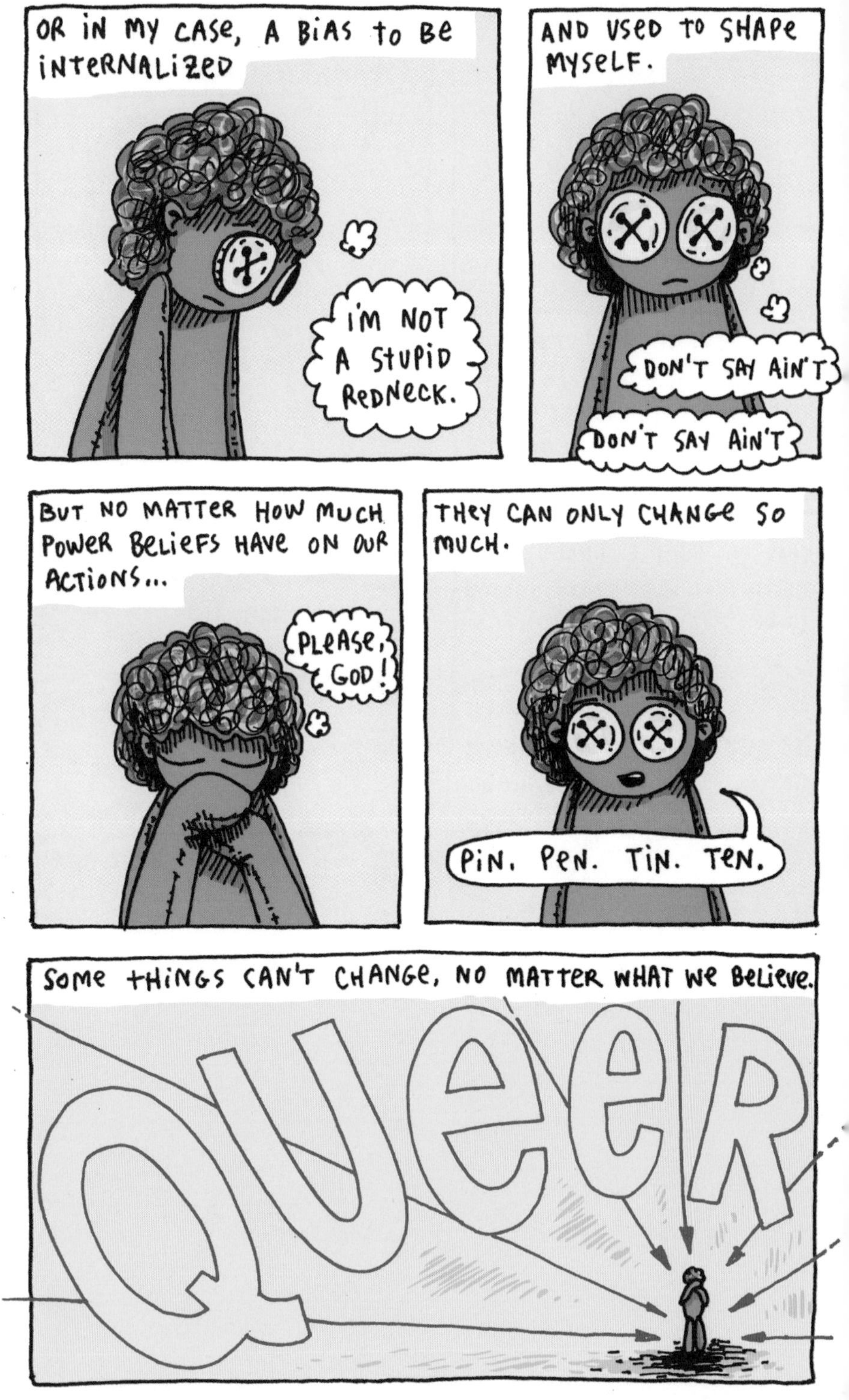
OR IN MY CASE, A BIAS TO BE INTERNALIZED
I'M NOT A STUPID REDNECK.
AND USED TO SHAPE MYSELF.
DON'T SAY AIN'T
DON'T SAY AIN'T
BUT NO MATTER HOW MUCH POWER BELIEFS HAVE ON OUR ACTIONS...
PLEASE, GOD!
THEY CAN ONLY CHANGE SO MUCH.
PIN. PEN. TIN. TEN.
SOME THINGS CAN'T CHANGE, NO MATTER WHAT WE BELIEVE.
QUEER

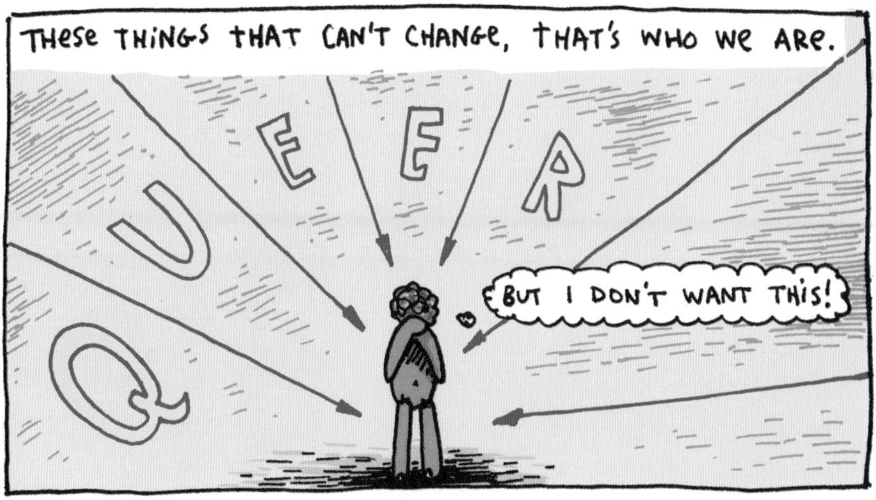
THESE THINGS THAT CAN'T CHANGE, THAT'S WHO WE ARE.
QUEER
BUT I DON'T WANT THIS!

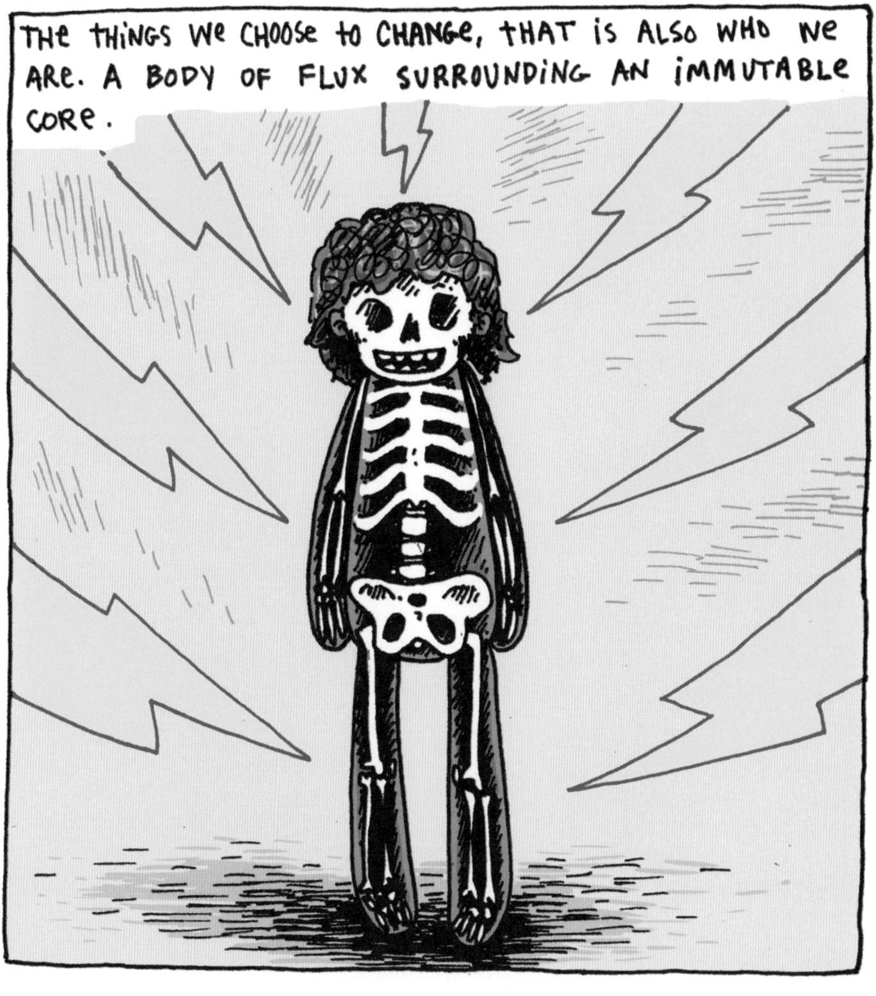
THE THINGS WE CHOOSE TO CHANGE, THAT IS ALSO WHO WE ARE. A BODY OF FLUX SURROUNDING AN IMMUTABLE CORE.

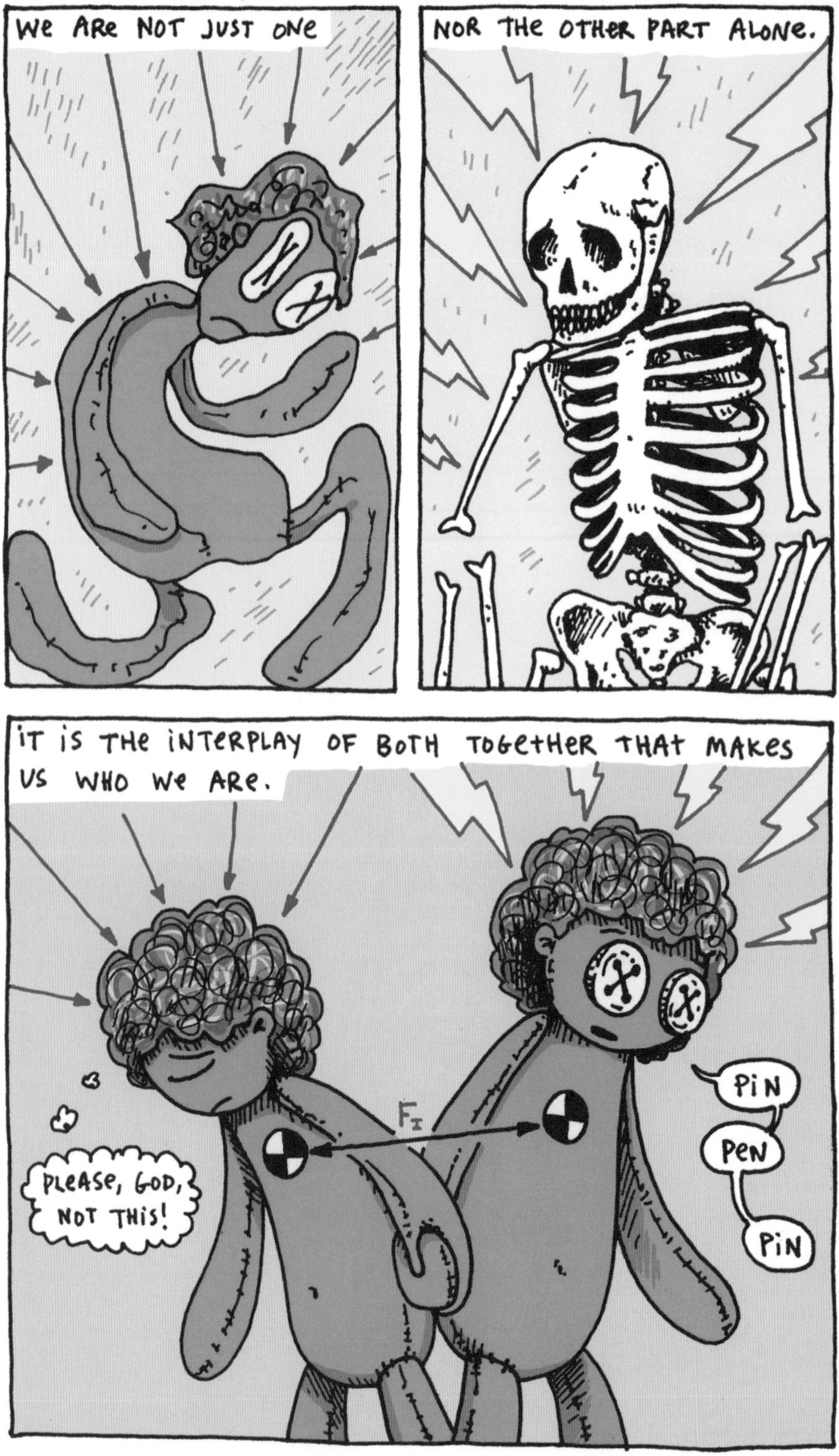
WE ARE NOT JUST ONE
NOR THE OTHER PART ALONE.
IT IS THE INTERPLAY OF BOTH TOGETHER THAT MAKES US WHO WE ARE.
PLEASE, GOD, NOT THIS!
FI
PIN
PEN
PIN

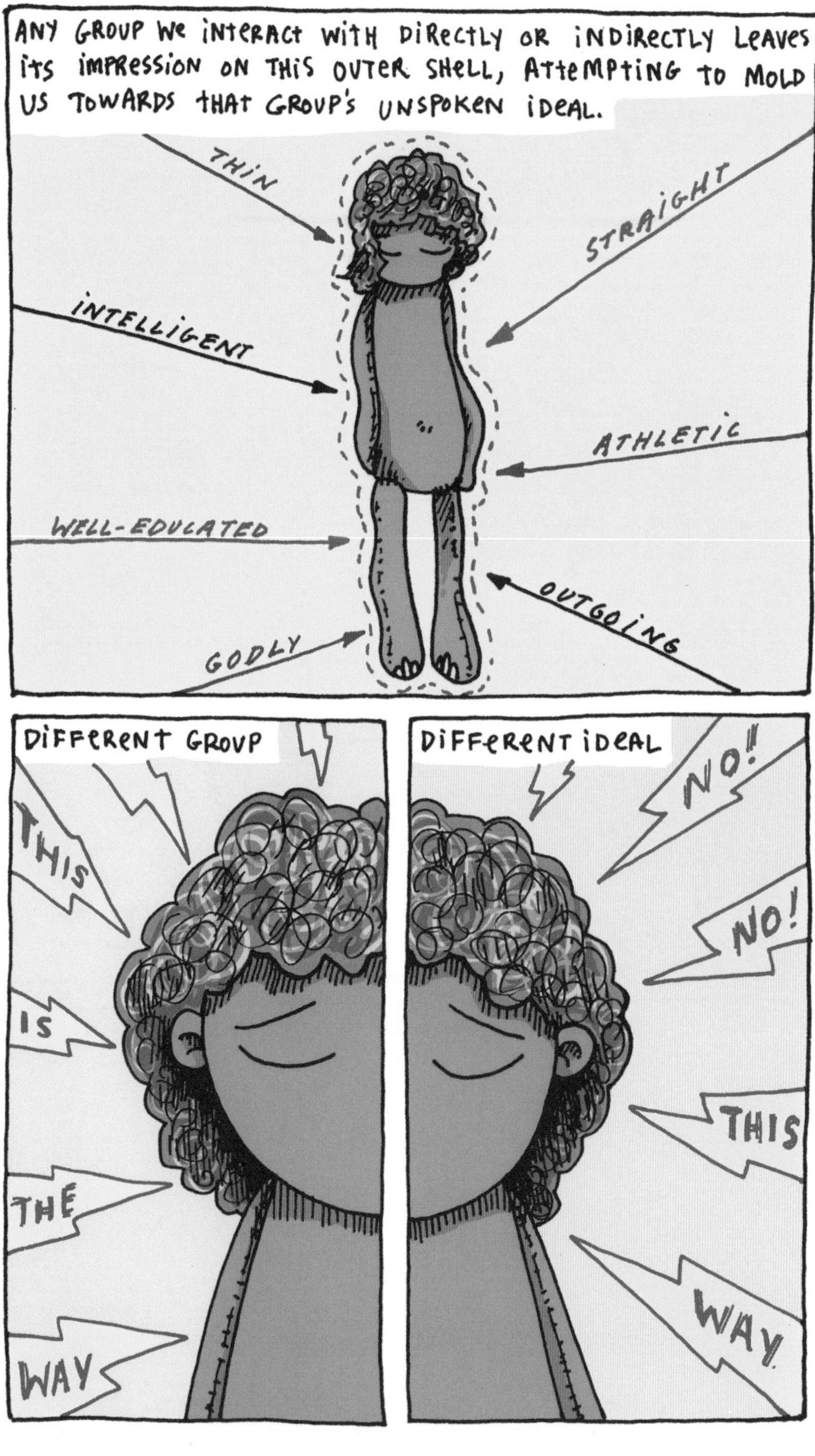
ANY GROUP WE INTERACT WITH DIRECTLY OR INDIRECTLY LEAVES ITS IMPRESSION ON THIS OUTER SHELL, ATTEMPTING TO MOLD US TOWARDS THAT GROUP'S UNSPOKEN IDEAL.
THIN
STRAIGHT
INTELLIGENT
ATHLETIC
WELL-EDUCATED
OUTGOING
GODLY
DIFFERENT GROUP
THIS
IS
THE
WAY
DIFFERENT IDEAL
NO!!
NO!
THIS
WAY

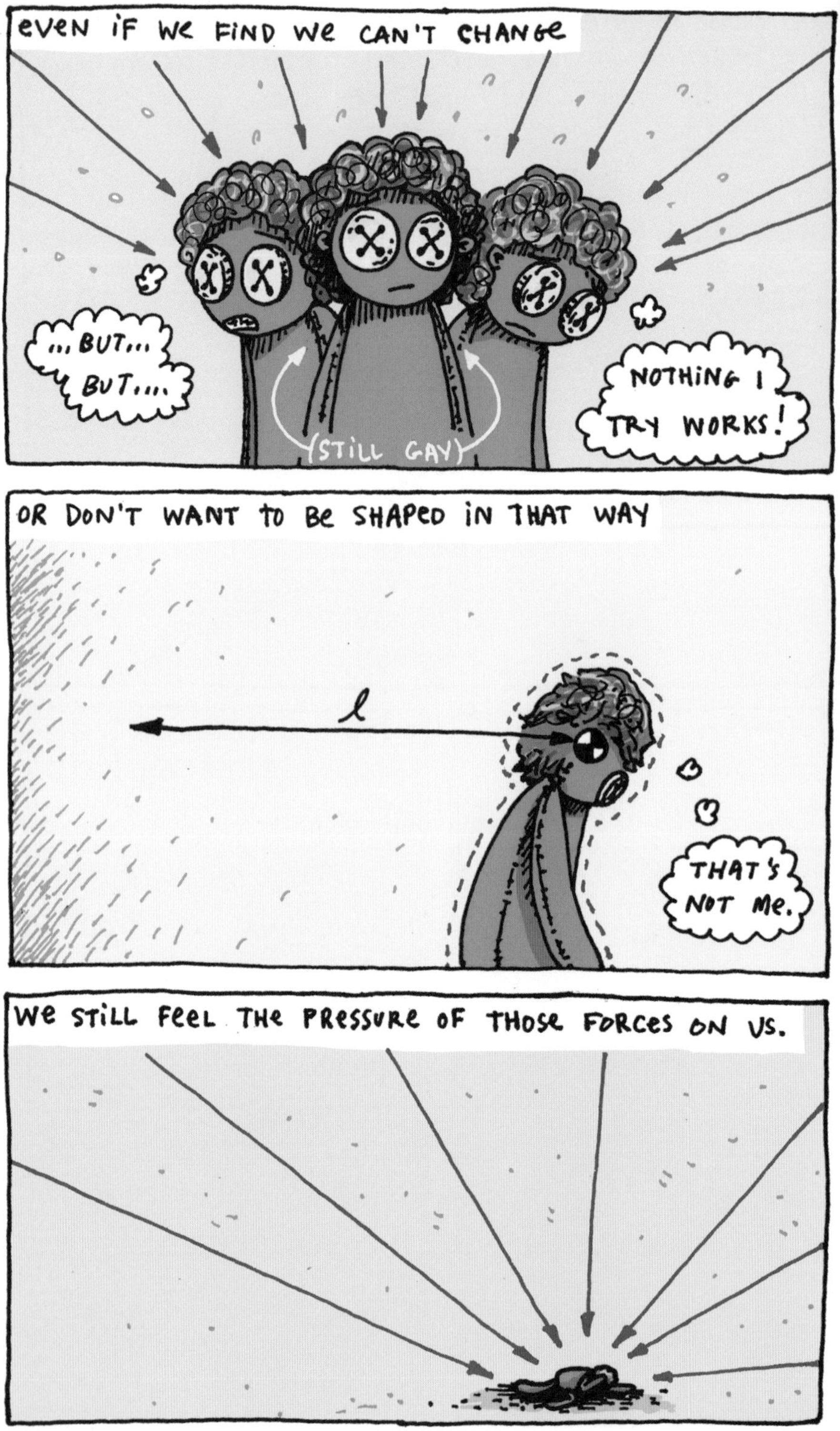
even if we find we can't change
...BUT... BUT....
(STILL GAY)
NOTHING I TRY WORKS!
OR DON'T WANT TO BE SHAPED IN THAT WAY
THAT'S NOT ME.
we still feel the pressure of those forces on us.

AND IF WE'RE LUCKY THE PRESSURES OF THE GROUPS WILL BALANCE OUT, LEAVING US ROOM TO GROW.

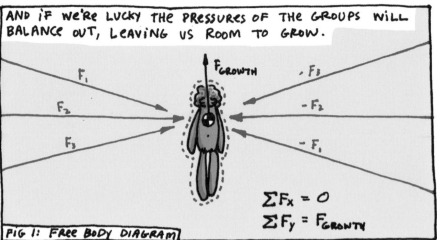

$$\sum F_x = 0$$
$$\sum F_y = F_{GROWTH}$$

FIG 1: FREE BODY DIAGRAM

BECAUSE IF YOU THINK ABOUT IT, THE INVERSE OF PRESSURE TO CHANGE

FAGGOT.

IS ENCOURAGEMENT TO STAY STRONG...

WAY TO GO, KIDDO!

BUT ONLY IN THE WAYS

KEEP UP THE GOOD GRADES!

THE GROUPS

HOW'S MY ACCENT NOW?

BETTER!

AGREE WITH.

YOU CAN DO IT!

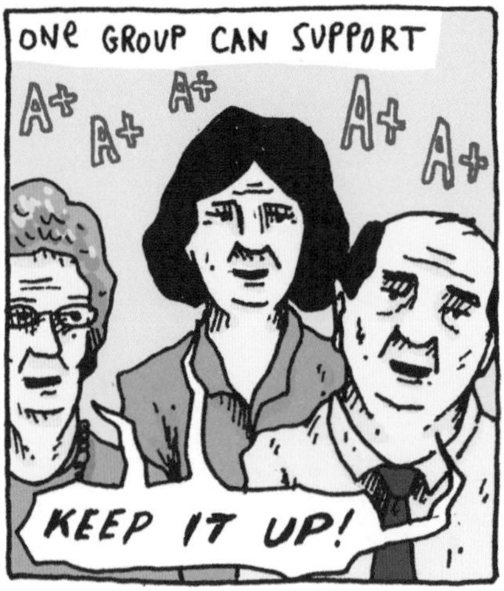
ONE GROUP CAN SUPPORT
A+ A+ A+ A+ A+
KEEP IT UP!

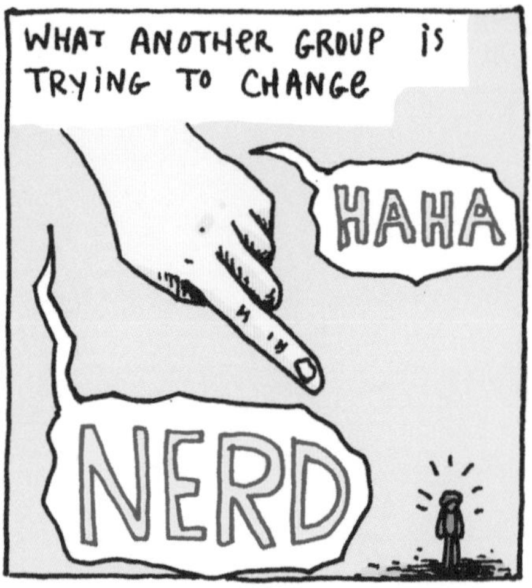
WHAT ANOTHER GROUP IS TRYING TO CHANGE
HAHA
NERD

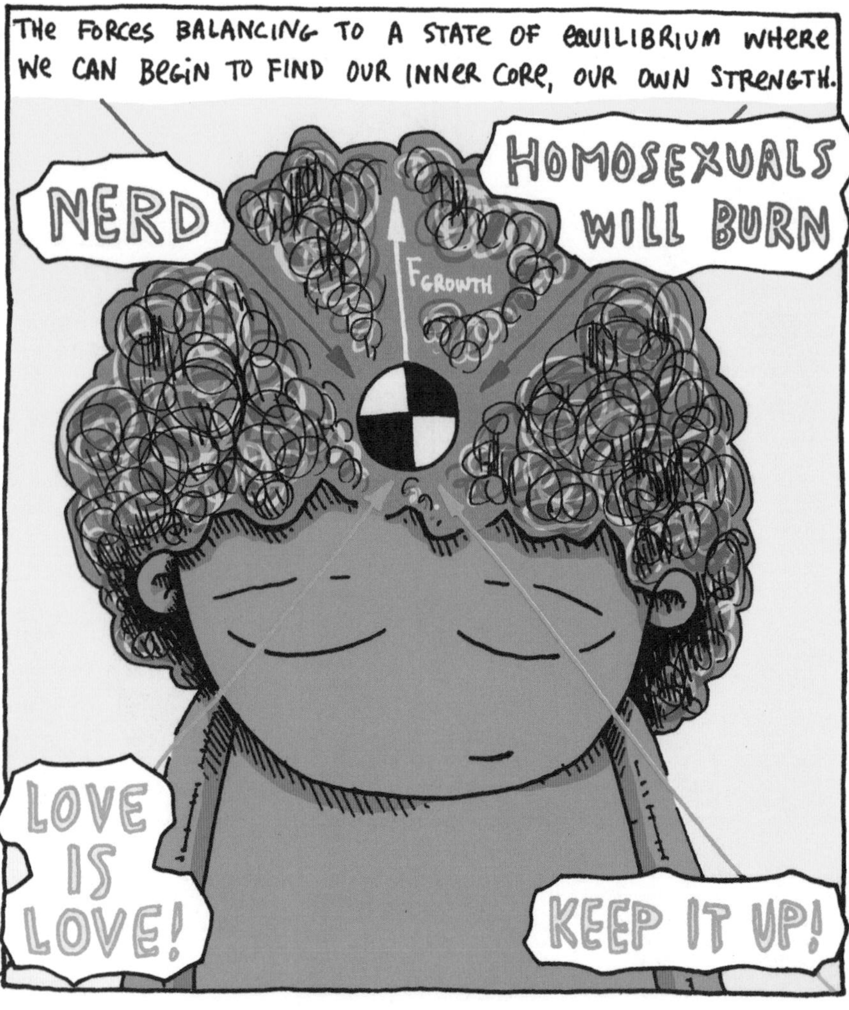
THE FORCES BALANCING TO A STATE OF EQUILIBRIUM WHERE WE CAN BEGIN TO FIND OUR INNER CORE, OUR OWN STRENGTH.
NERD
HOMOSEXUALS WILL BURN
F GROWTH
LOVE IS LOVE!
KEEP IT UP!

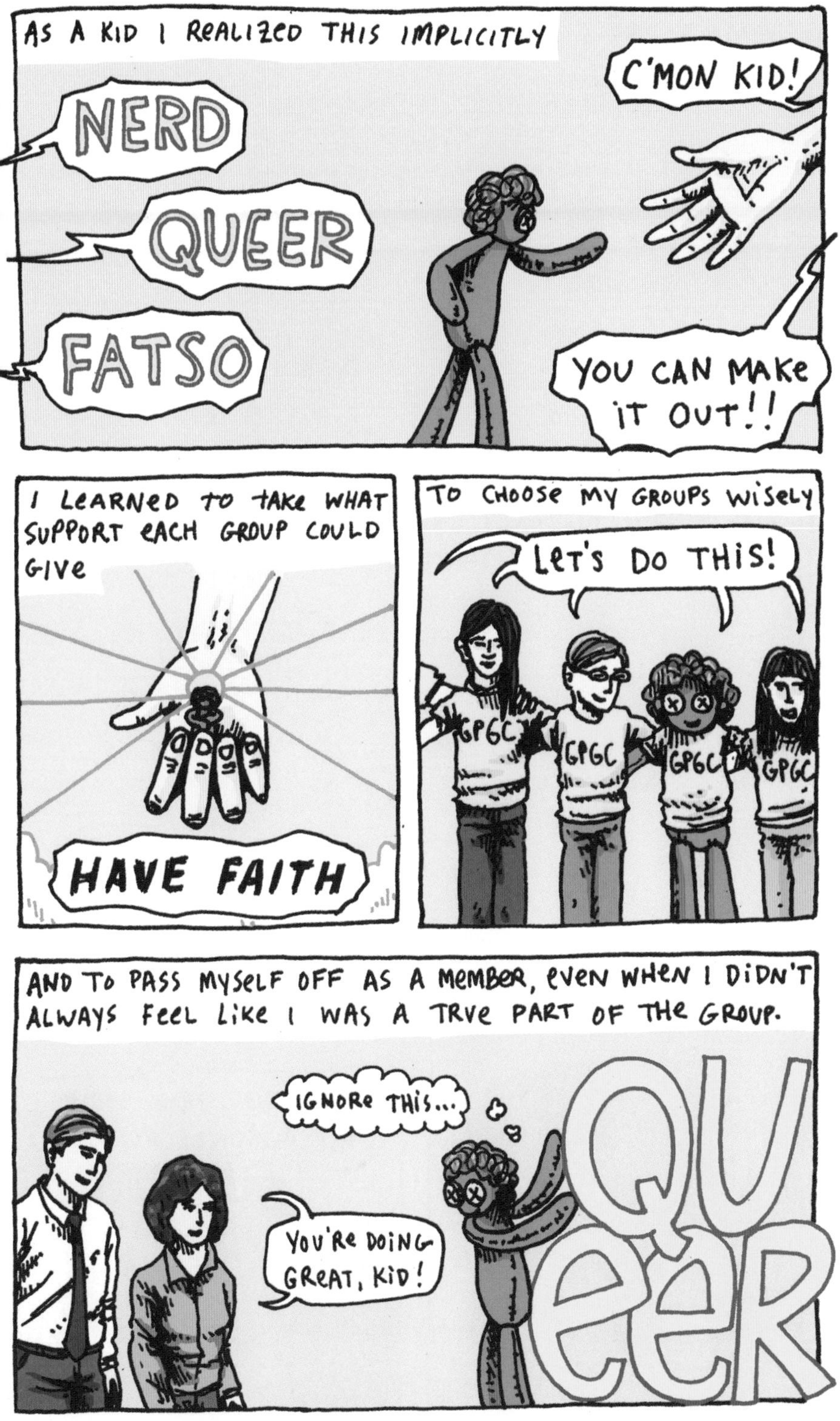
AS A KID I REALIZED THIS IMPLICITLY
NERD
QUEER
FATSO
C'MON KID!
YOU CAN MAKE IT OUT!!
I LEARNED TO TAKE WHAT SUPPORT EACH GROUP COULD GIVE
HAVE FAITH
TO CHOOSE MY GROUPS WISELY
LET'S DO THIS!
GPGC
GPGC
GPGC
GPGC
AND TO PASS MYSELF OFF AS A MEMBER, EVEN WHEN I DIDN'T ALWAYS FEEL LIKE I WAS A TRUE PART OF THE GROUP.
IGNORE THIS...
YOU'RE DOING GREAT, KID!
QUEER

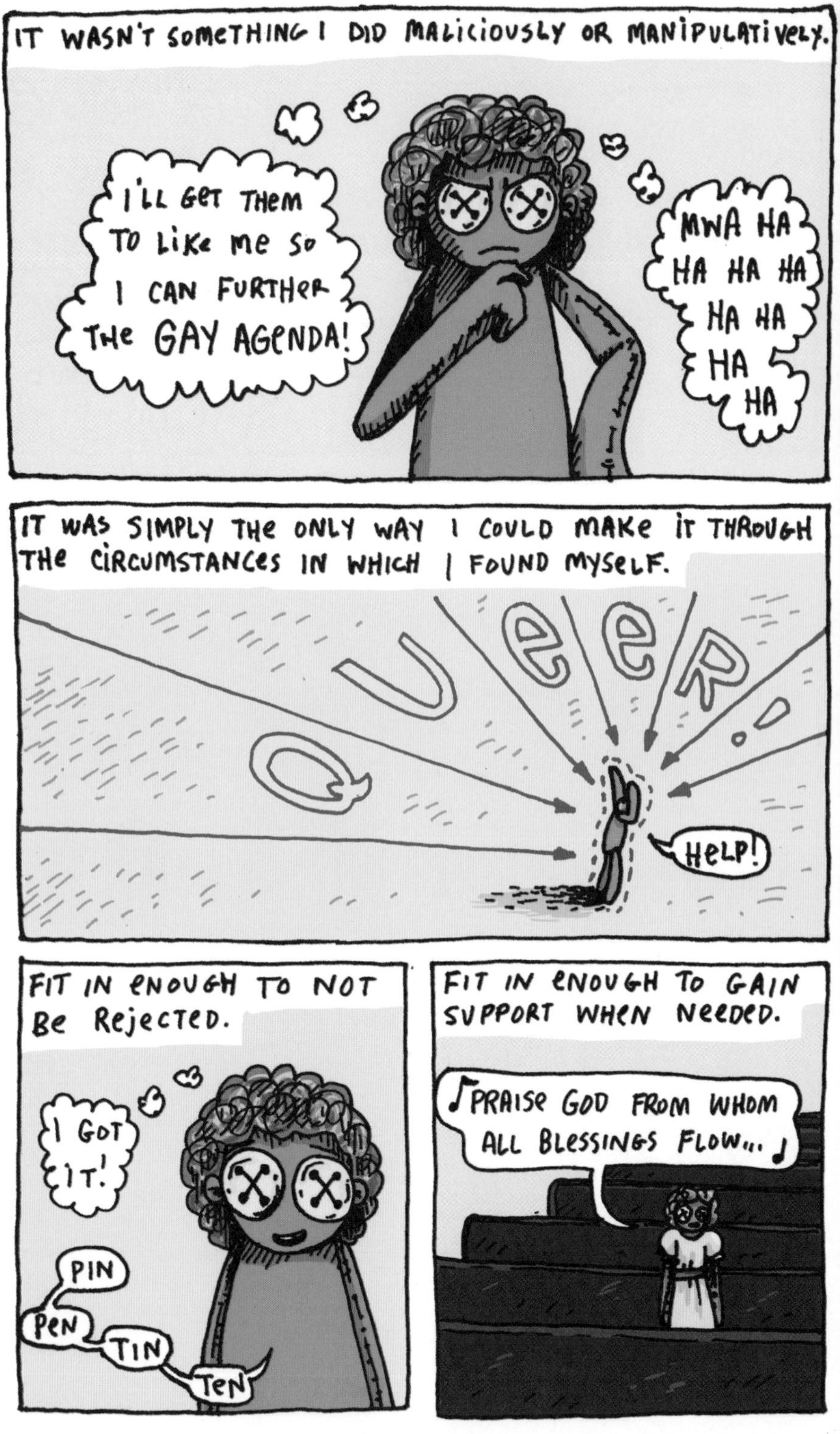
IT WASN'T SOMETHING I DID MALICIOUSLY OR MANIPULATIVELY.
I'LL GET THEM TO LIKE ME SO I CAN FURTHER THE GAY AGENDA!
MWA HA HA HA HA HA HA HA HA
IT WAS SIMPLY THE ONLY WAY I COULD MAKE IT THROUGH THE CIRCUMSTANCES IN WHICH I FOUND MYSELF.
QUEER!
HELP!
FIT IN ENOUGH TO NOT BE REJECTED.
I GOT IT!
PIN
PEN
TIN
TEN
FIT IN ENOUGH TO GAIN SUPPORT WHEN NEEDED.
♪PRAISE GOD FROM WHOM ALL BLESSINGS FLOW...♪

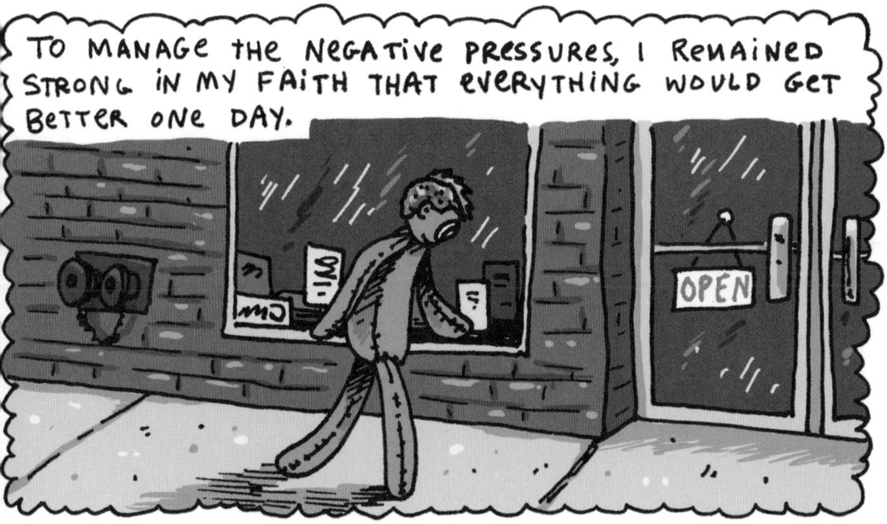
TO MANAGE THE NEGATIVE PRESSURES, I REMAINED STRONG IN MY FAITH THAT EVERYTHING WOULD GET BETTER ONE DAY.
OPEN

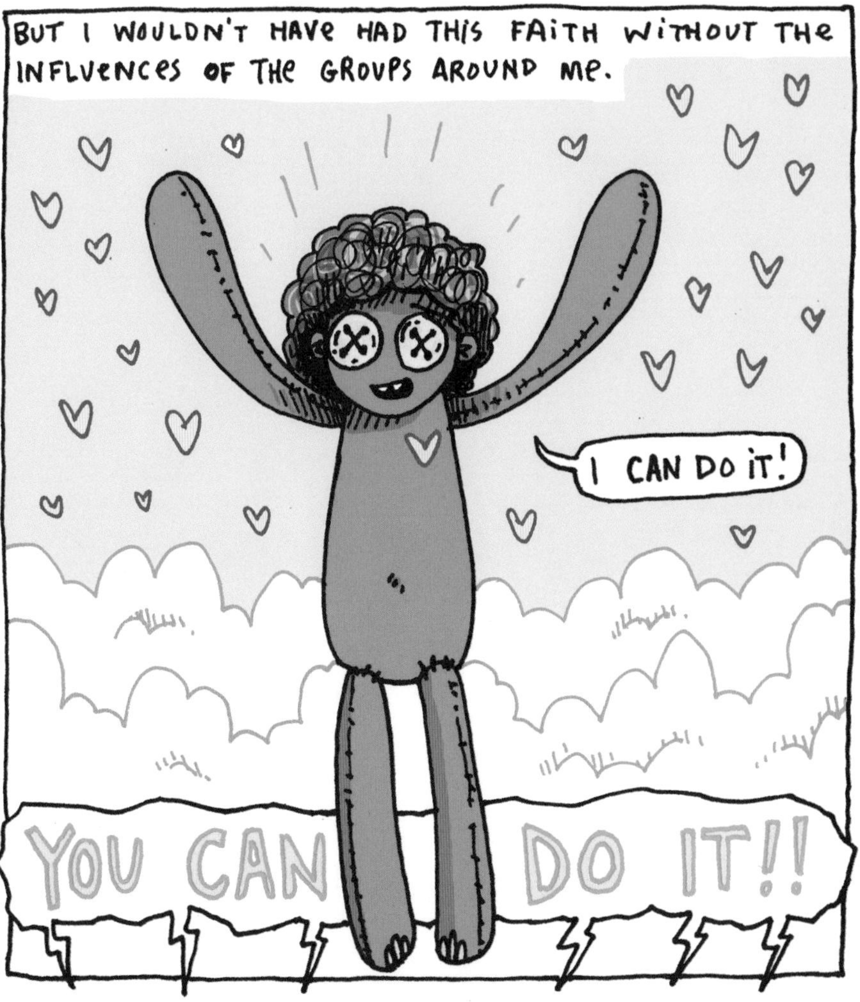
BUT I WOULDN'T HAVE HAD THIS FAITH WITHOUT THE INFLUENCES OF THE GROUPS AROUND ME.
I CAN DO IT!
YOU CAN DO IT!!

CHAPTER FIVE

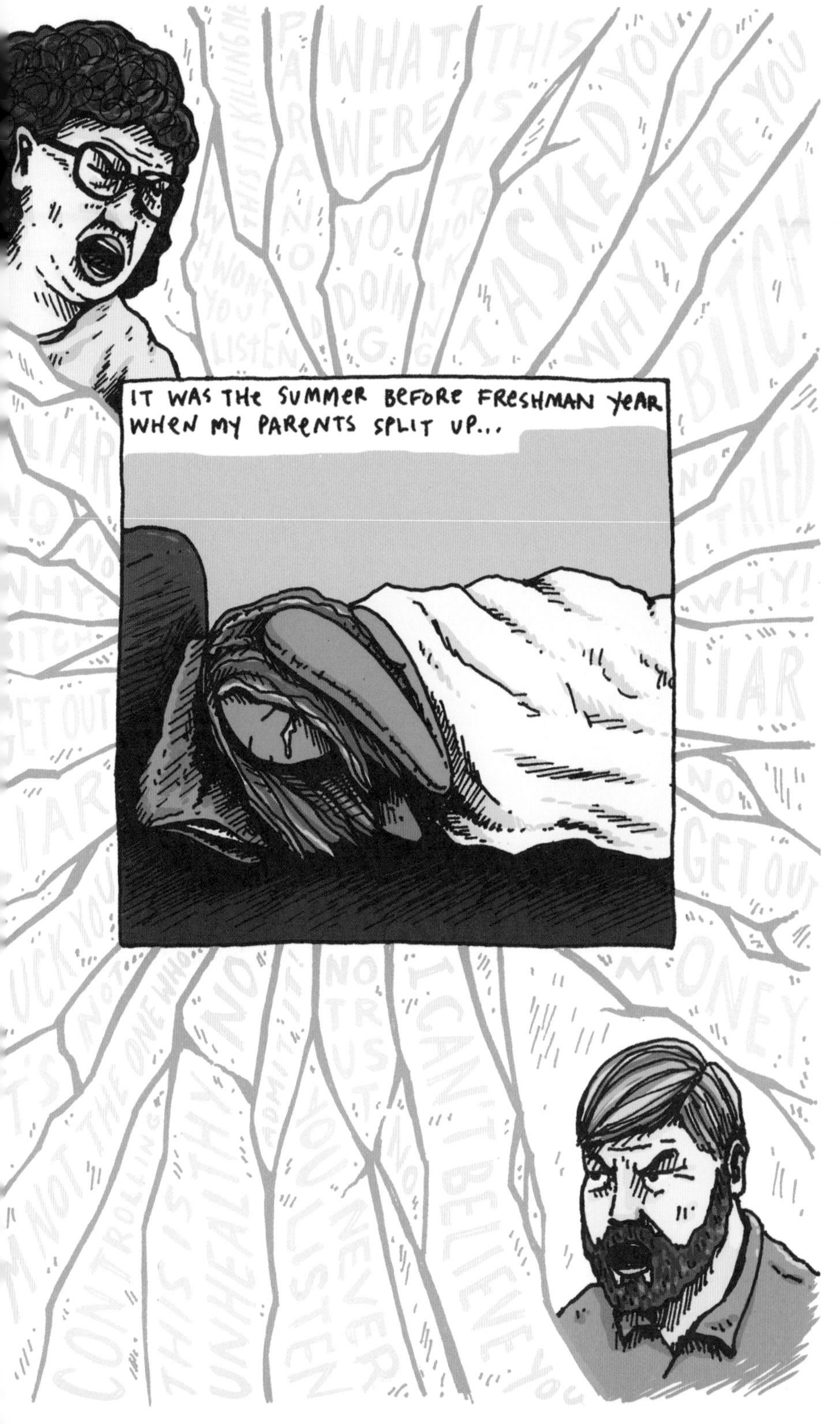
IT WAS THE SUMMER BEFORE FRESHMAN YEAR WHEN MY PARENTS SPLIT UP...

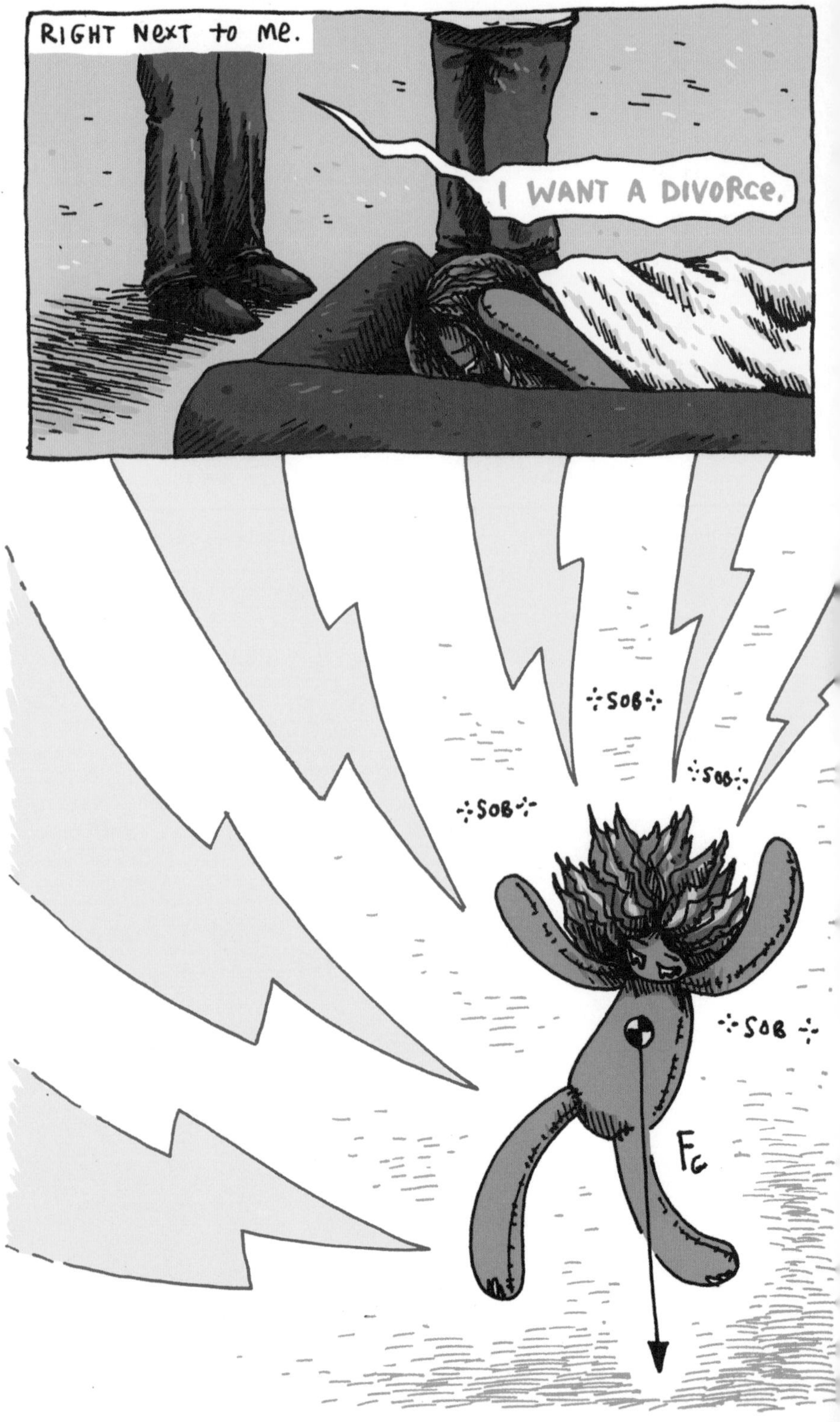
RIGHT NEXT TO ME.
I WANT A DIVORCE.
SOB
SOB
SOB
SOB
FG

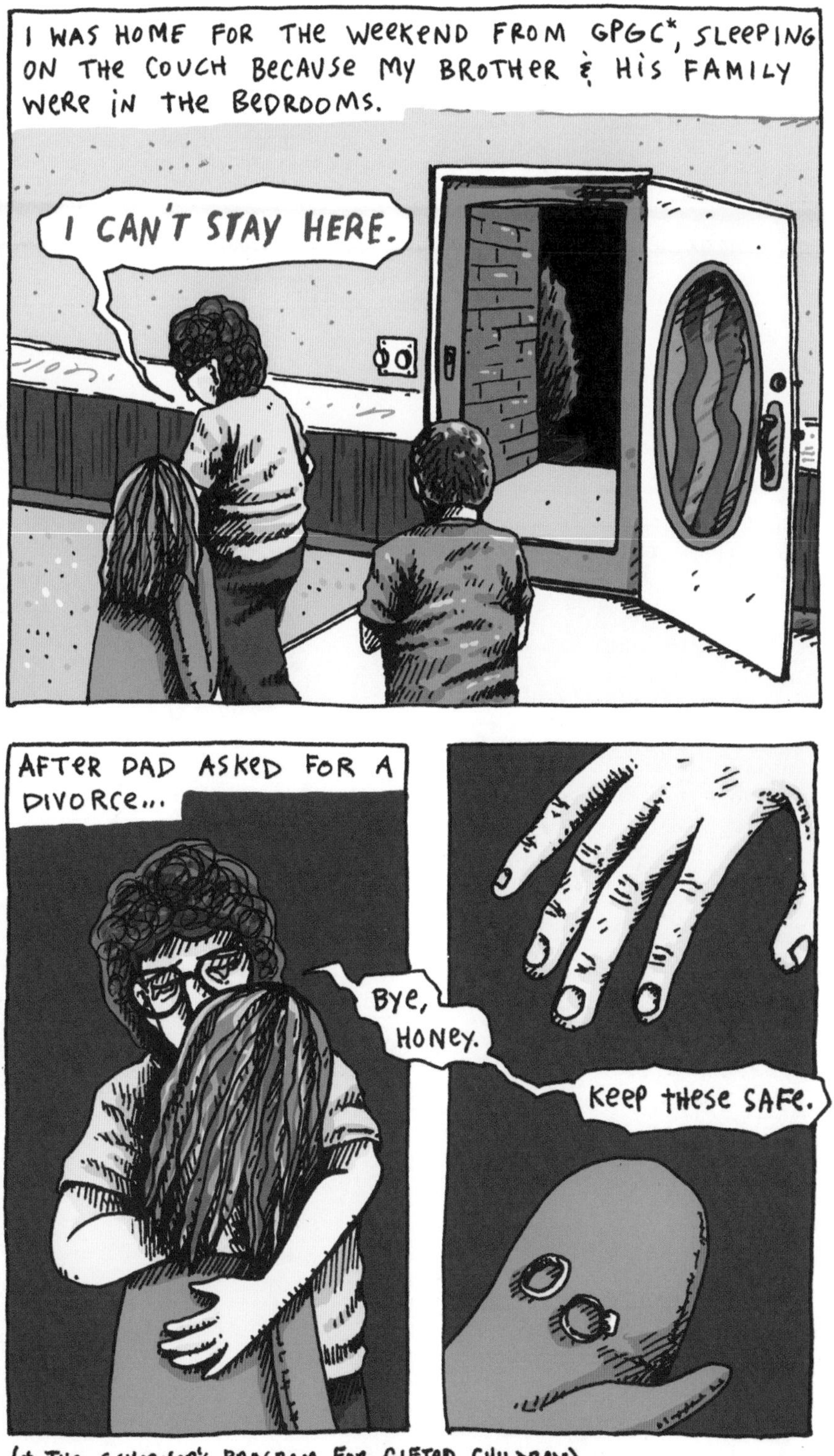
I WAS HOME FOR THE WEEKEND FROM GPGC*, SLEEPING ON THE COUCH BECAUSE MY BROTHER & HIS FAMILY WERE IN THE BEDROOMS.
I CAN'T STAY HERE.
AFTER DAD ASKED FOR A DIVORCE...
BYE, HONEY.
KEEP THESE SAFE.

(* THE GOVERNOR'S PROGRAM FOR GIFTED CHILDREN)

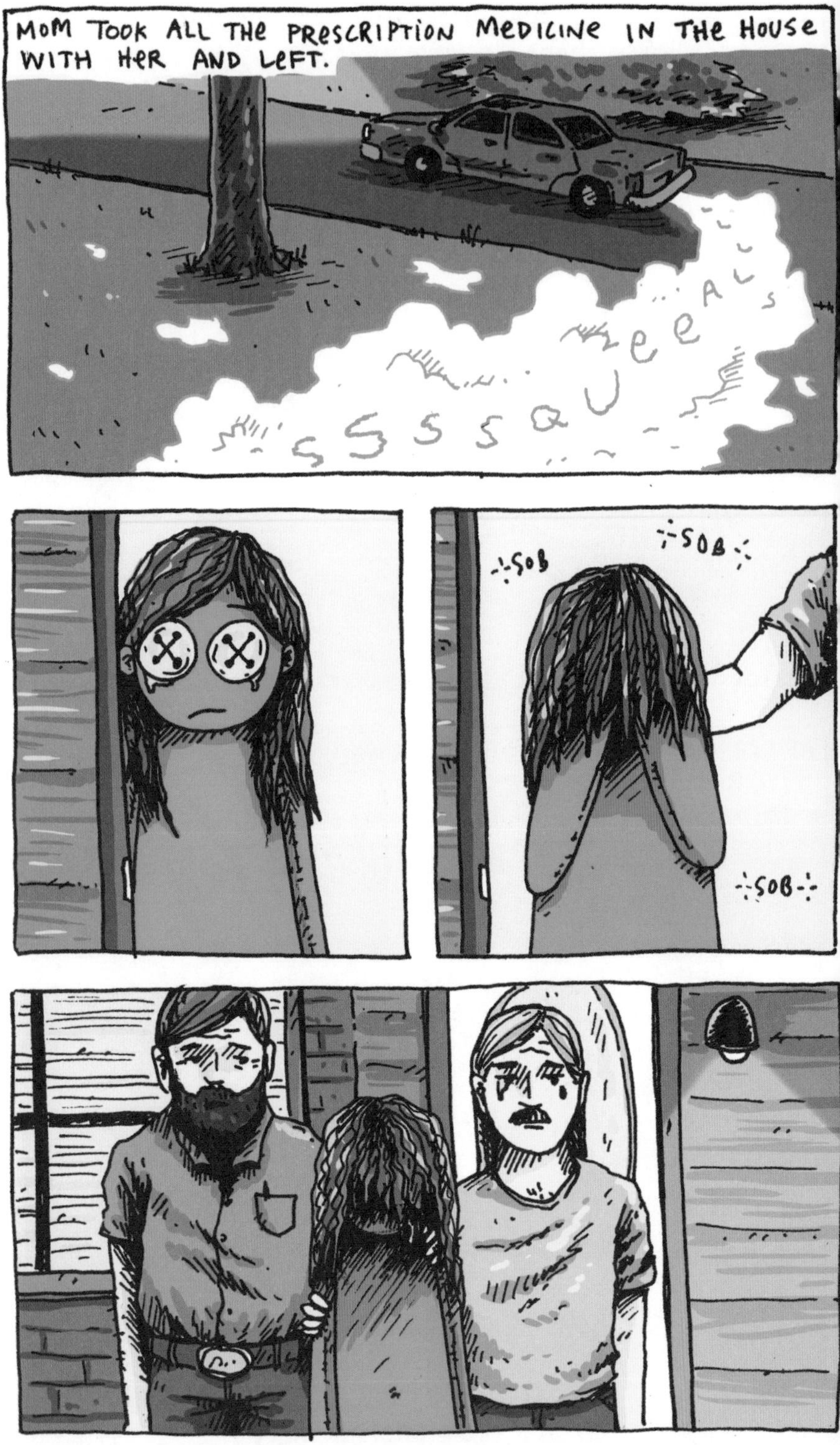
MOM TOOK ALL THE PRESCRIPTION MEDICINE IN THE HOUSE WITH HER AND LEFT.
SSSSQUEEALS
SOB
SOB
SOB

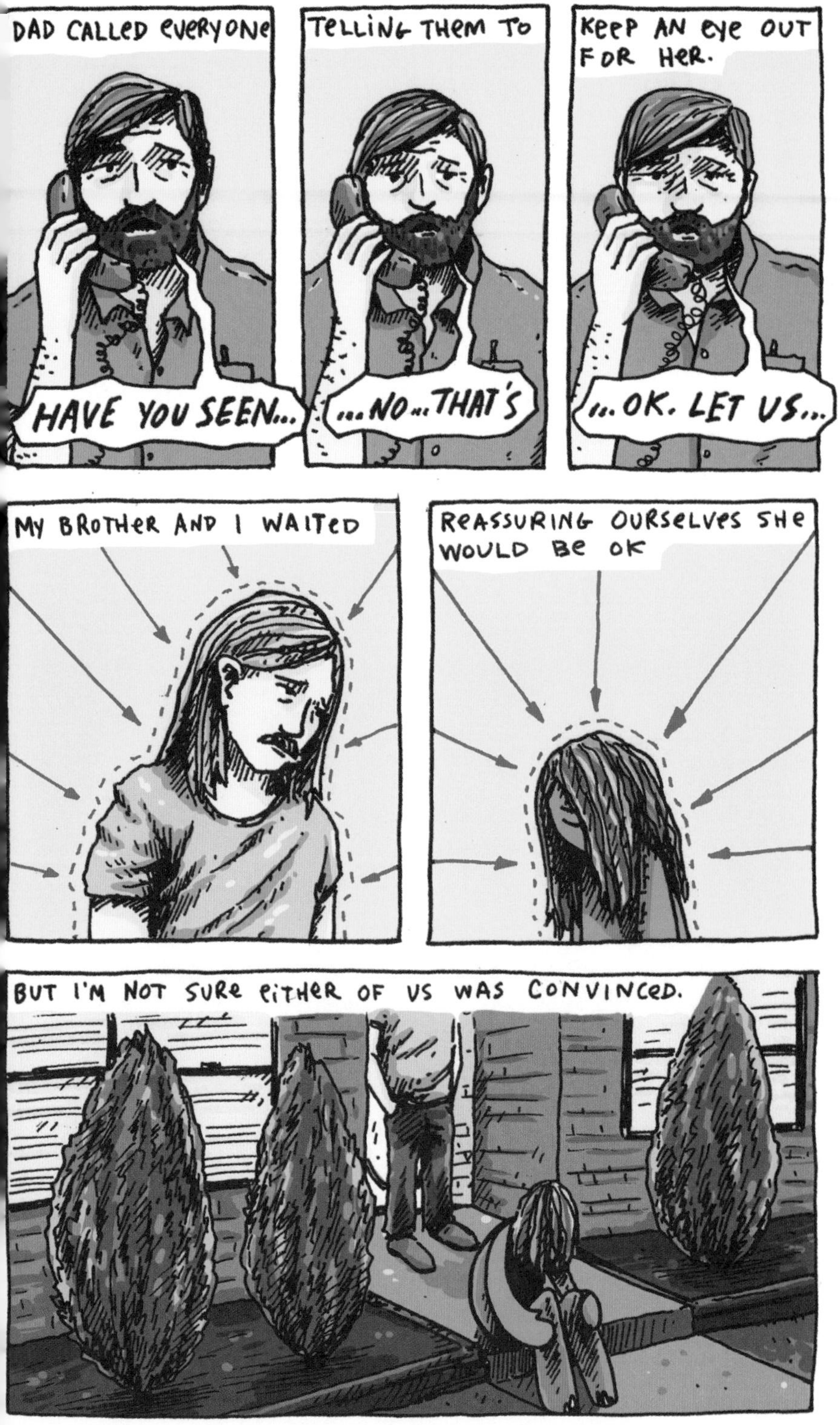
DAD CALLED EVERYONE
HAVE YOU SEEN...
TELLING THEM TO
...NO...THAT'S
KEEP AN EYE OUT FOR HER.
...OK. LET US...
MY BROTHER AND I WAITED
REASSURING OURSELVES SHE WOULD BE OK
BUT I'M NOT SURE EITHER OF US WAS CONVINCED.

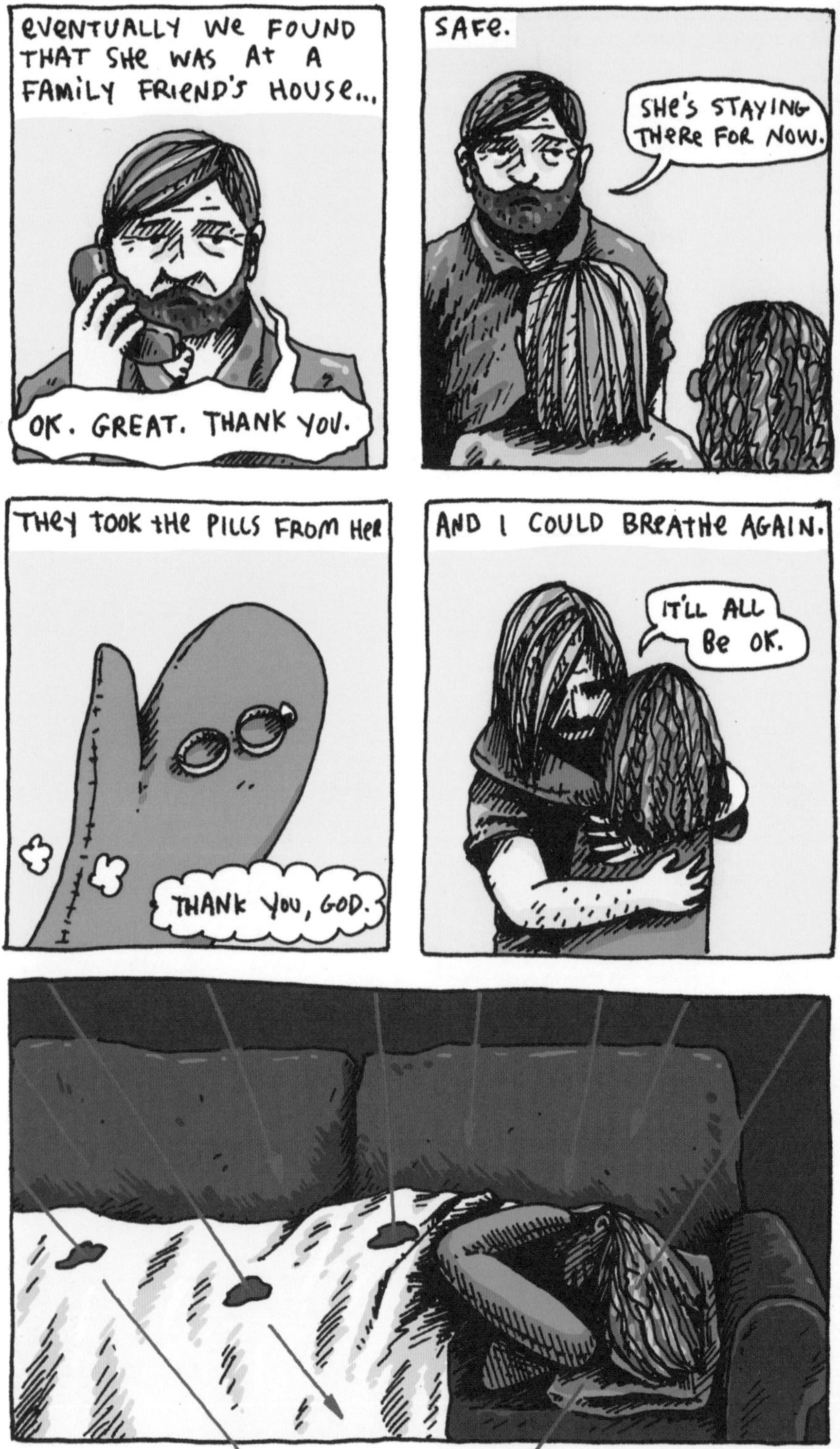
EVENTUALLY WE FOUND THAT SHE WAS AT A FAMILY FRIEND'S HOUSE...
OK. GREAT. THANK YOU.
SAFE.
SHE'S STAYING THERE FOR NOW.
THEY TOOK THE PILLS FROM HER
THANK YOU, GOD.
AND I COULD BREATHE AGAIN.
IT'LL ALL BE OK.

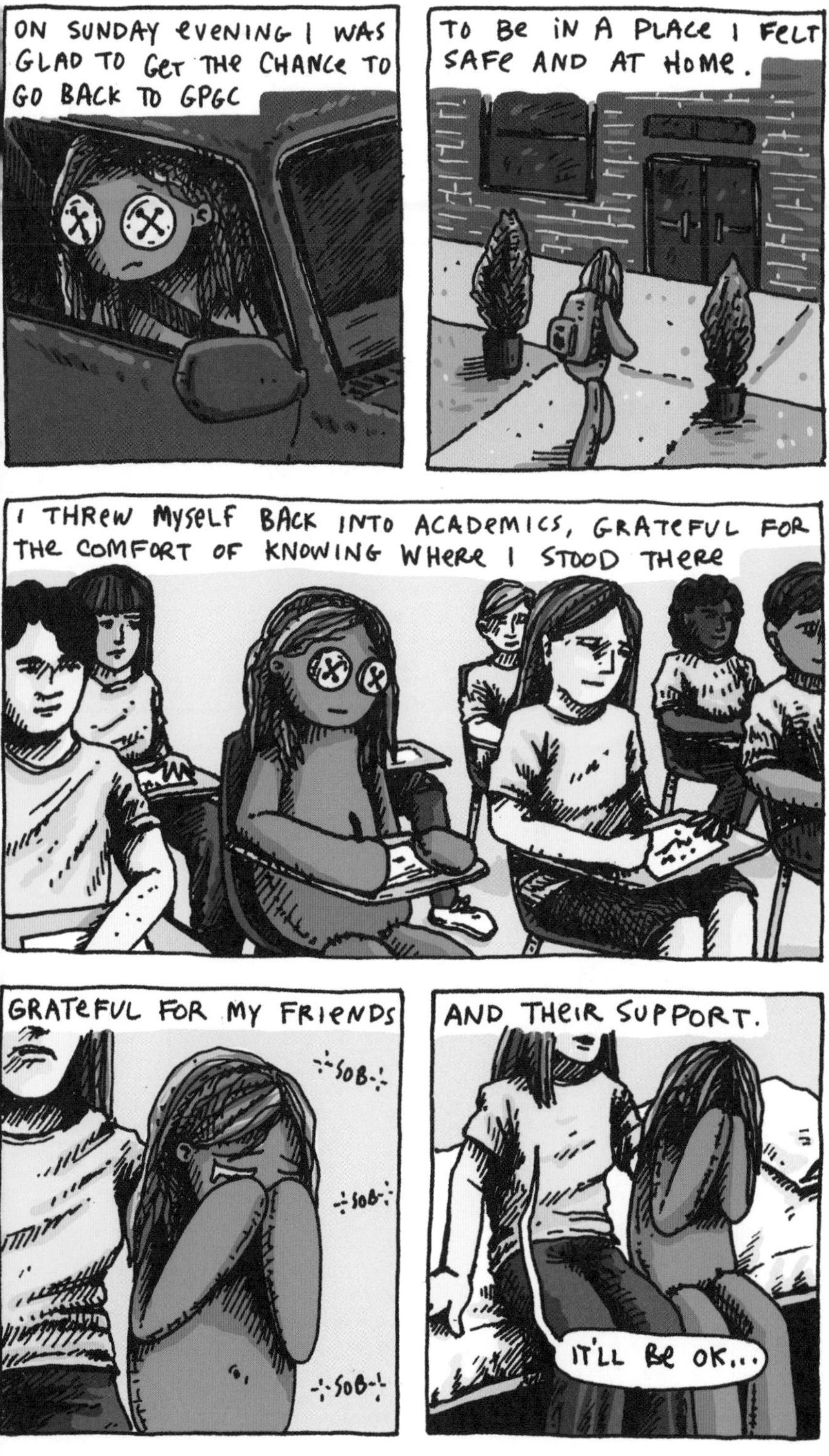
ON SUNDAY EVENING I WAS GLAD TO GET THE CHANCE TO GO BACK TO GPGC
TO BE IN A PLACE I FELT SAFE AND AT HOME.
I THREW MYSELF BACK INTO ACADEMICS, GRATEFUL FOR THE COMFORT OF KNOWING WHERE I STOOD THERE
GRATEFUL FOR MY FRIENDS
SOB
SOB
SOB
AND THEIR SUPPORT.
IT'LL BE OK...

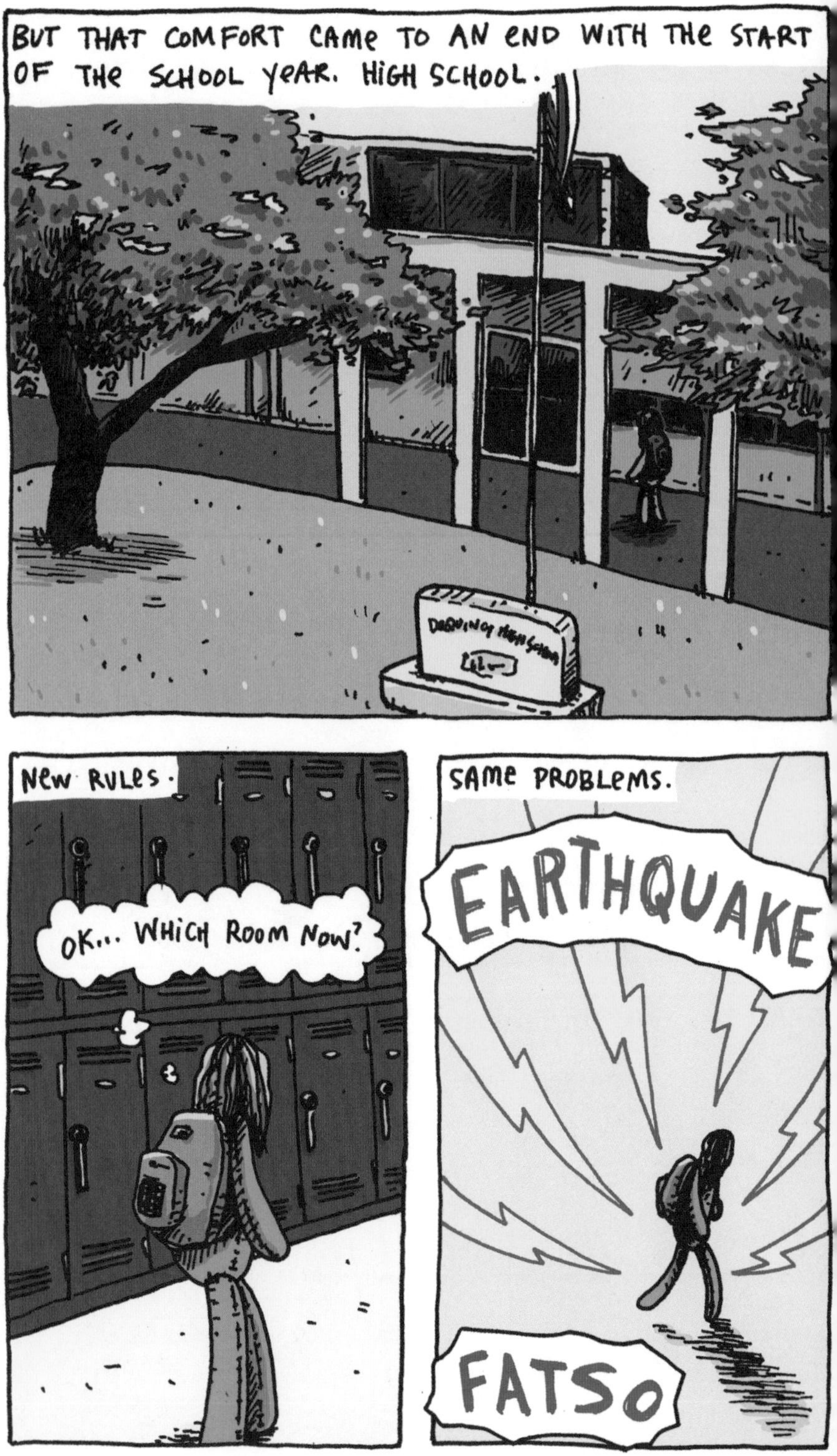
BUT THAT COMFORT CAME TO AN END WITH THE START OF THE SCHOOL YEAR. HIGH SCHOOL.
NEW RULES.
OK... WHICH ROOM NOW?
SAME PROBLEMS.
EARTHQUAKE
FATSO

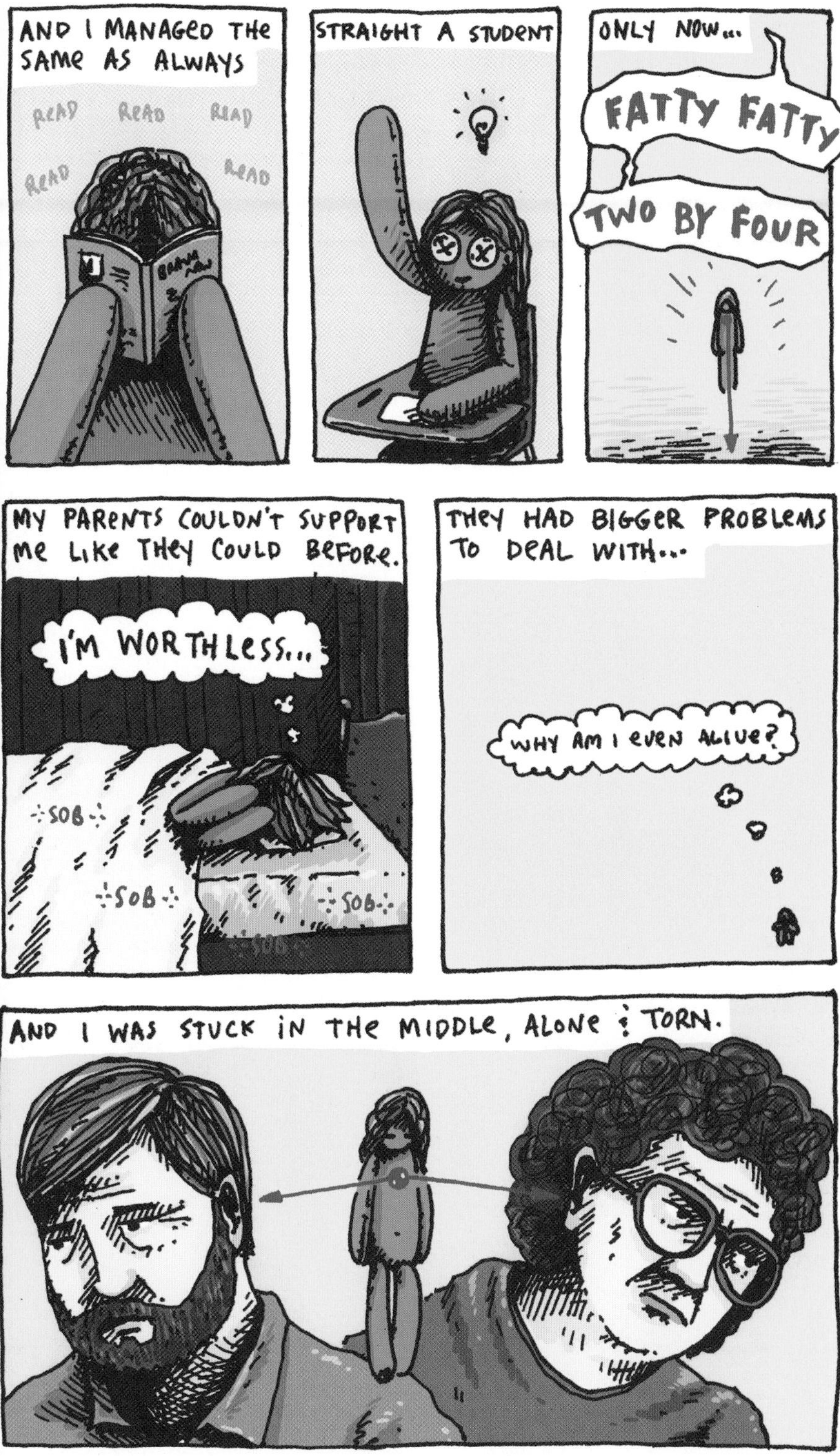

AND I MANAGED THE SAME AS ALWAYS
READ READ READ
READ READ
STRAIGHT A STUDENT
ONLY NOW...
FATTY FATTY
TWO BY FOUR
MY PARENTS COULDN'T SUPPORT ME LIKE THEY COULD BEFORE.
I'M WORTHLESS...
SOB
SOB
SOB
SOB
THEY HAD BIGGER PROBLEMS TO DEAL WITH...
WHY AM I EVEN ALIVE?
AND I WAS STUCK IN THE MIDDLE, ALONE & TORN.

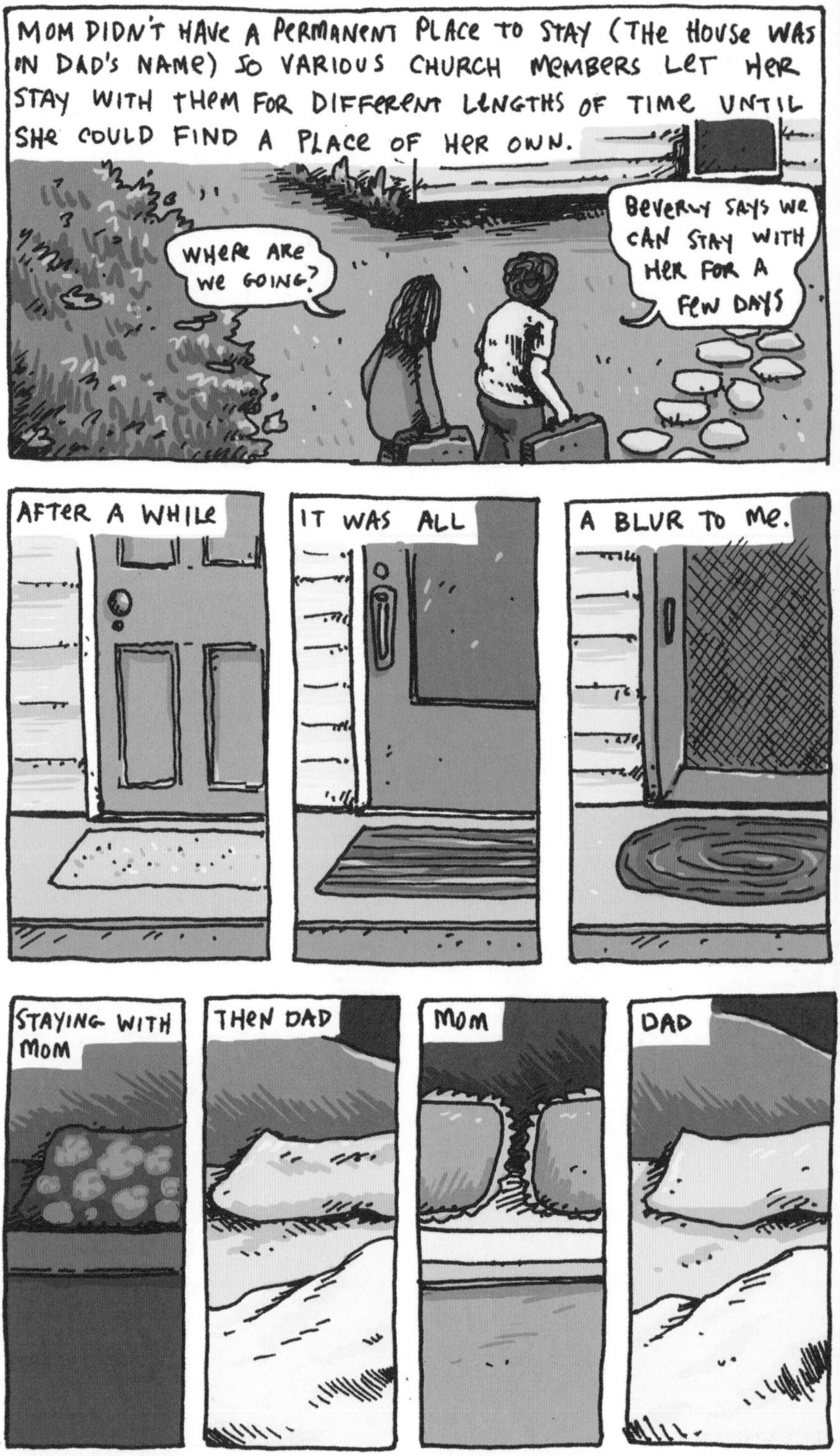
MOM DIDN'T HAVE A PERMANENT PLACE TO STAY (THE HOUSE WAS IN DAD'S NAME) SO VARIOUS CHURCH MEMBERS LET HER STAY WITH THEM FOR DIFFERENT LENGTHS OF TIME UNTIL SHE COULD FIND A PLACE OF HER OWN.
WHERE ARE WE GOING?
BEVERLY SAYS WE CAN STAY WITH HER FOR A FEW DAYS
AFTER A WHILE
IT WAS ALL
A BLUR TO ME.
STAYING WITH MOM
THEN DAD
MOM
DAD

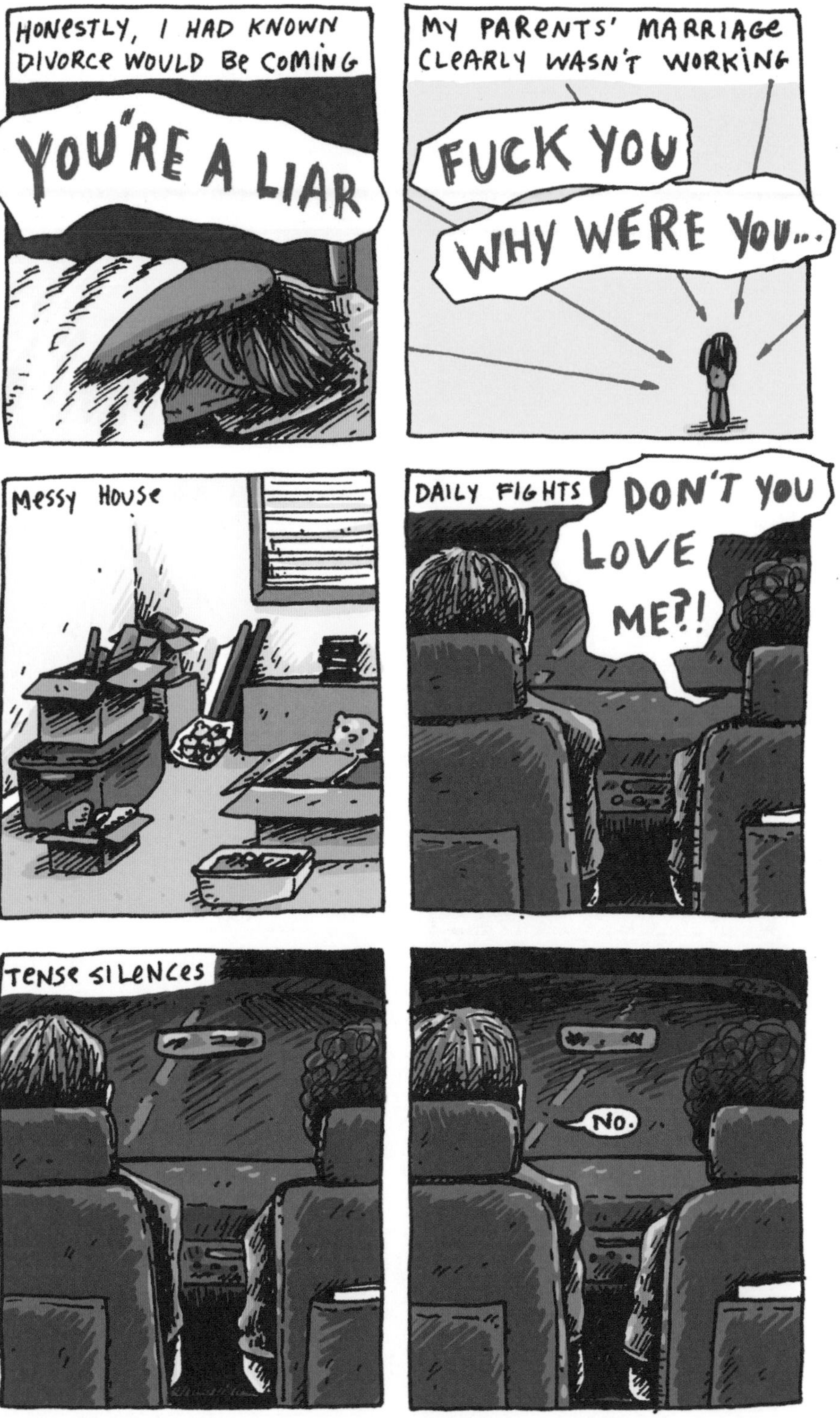
HONESTLY, I HAD KNOWN DIVORCE WOULD BE COMING
YOU'RE A LIAR
MY PARENTS' MARRIAGE CLEARLY WASN'T WORKING
FUCK YOU
WHY WERE YOU...
MESSY HOUSE
DAILY FIGHTS
DON'T YOU LOVE ME?!
TENSE SILENCES
NO.

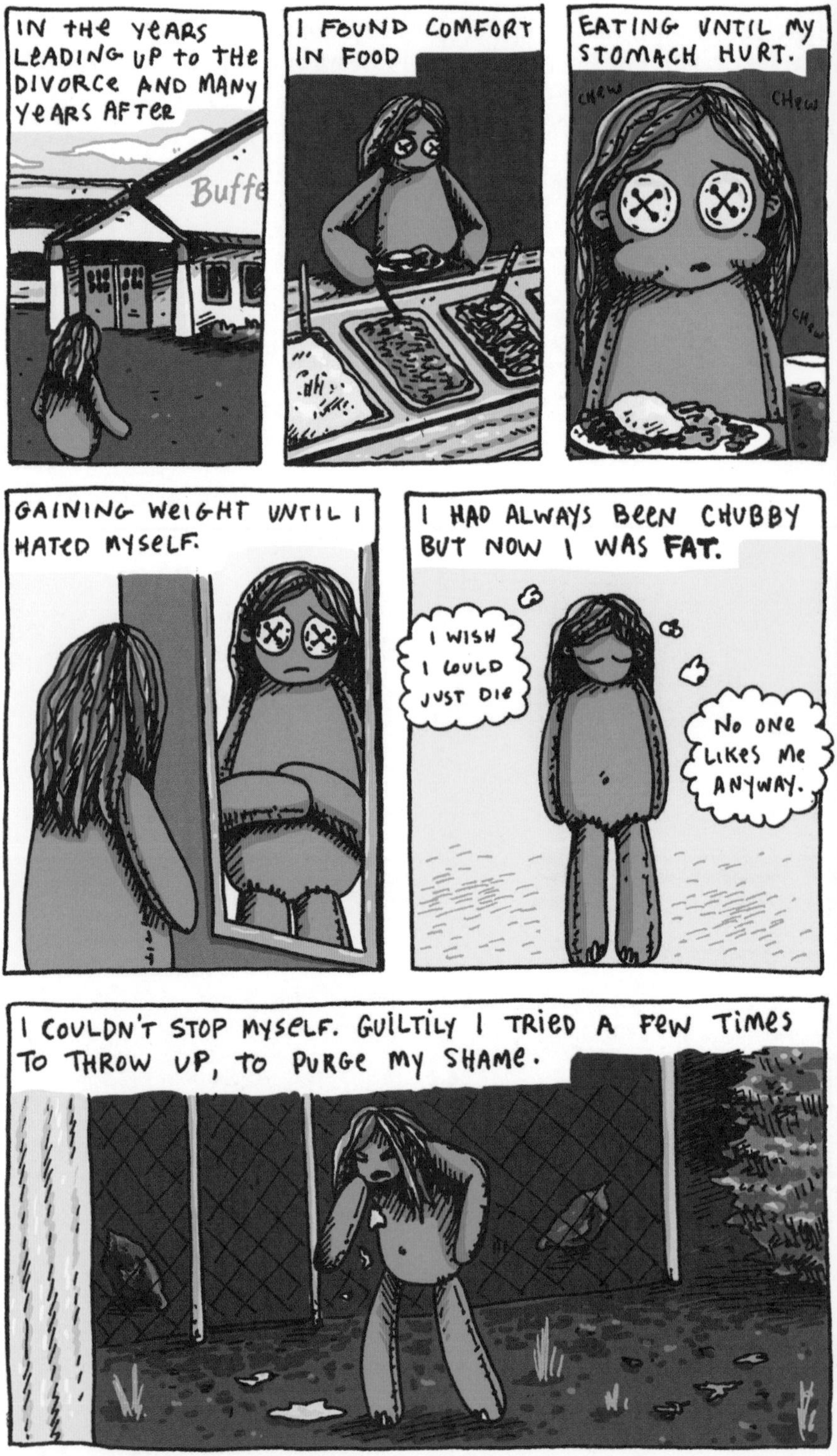
IN THE YEARS LEADING UP TO THE DIVORCE AND MANY YEARS AFTER
Buffe
I FOUND COMFORT IN FOOD
EATING UNTIL MY STOMACH HURT.
CHEW
CHEW
CHEW
GAINING WEIGHT UNTIL I HATED MYSELF.
I HAD ALWAYS BEEN CHUBBY BUT NOW I WAS FAT.
I WISH I COULD JUST DIE
NO ONE LIKES ME ANYWAY.
I COULDN'T STOP MYSELF. GUILTILY I TRIED A FEW TIMES TO THROW UP, TO PURGE MY SHAME.

BUT THAT DIDN'T WORK FOR ME

I WAS STUCK WITH MYSELF

$F_g = mg$

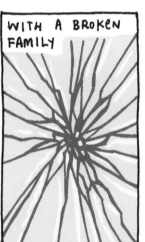

WITH A BROKEN FAMILY

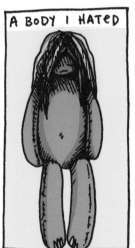

A BODY I HATED

AND SECRETS TO HIDE.

QUEER

AT NIGHT I WOULD LIE AWAKE CRYING, WISHING I COULD DIE AND START AGAIN.

I'M WORTHLESS

GOD, PLEASE LET THIS ALL END.

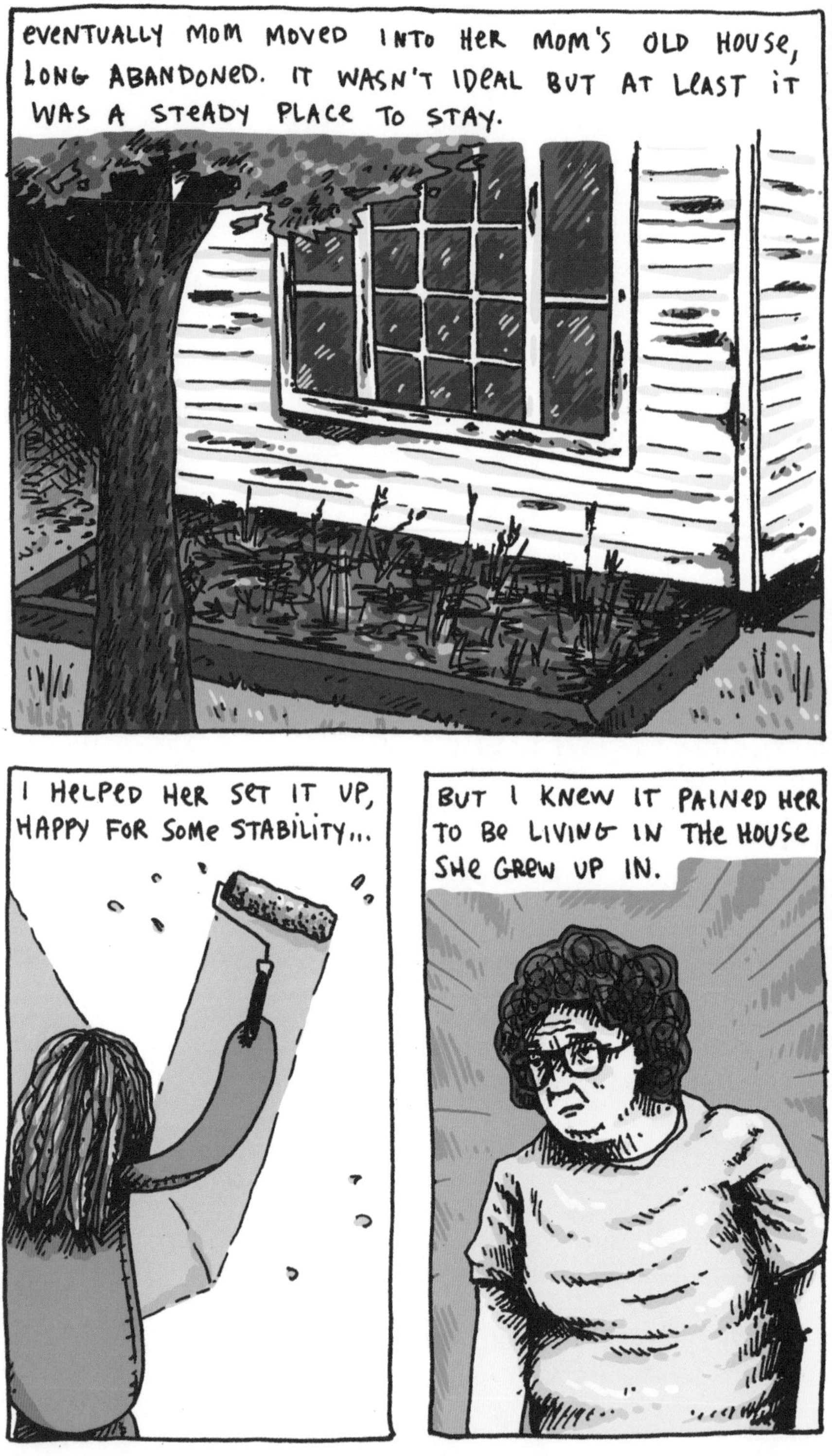
EVENTUALLY MOM MOVED INTO HER MOM'S OLD HOUSE, LONG ABANDONED. IT WASN'T IDEAL BUT AT LEAST IT WAS A STEADY PLACE TO STAY.
I HELPED HER SET IT UP, HAPPY FOR SOME STABILITY...
BUT I KNEW IT PAINED HER TO BE LIVING IN THE HOUSE SHE GREW UP IN.

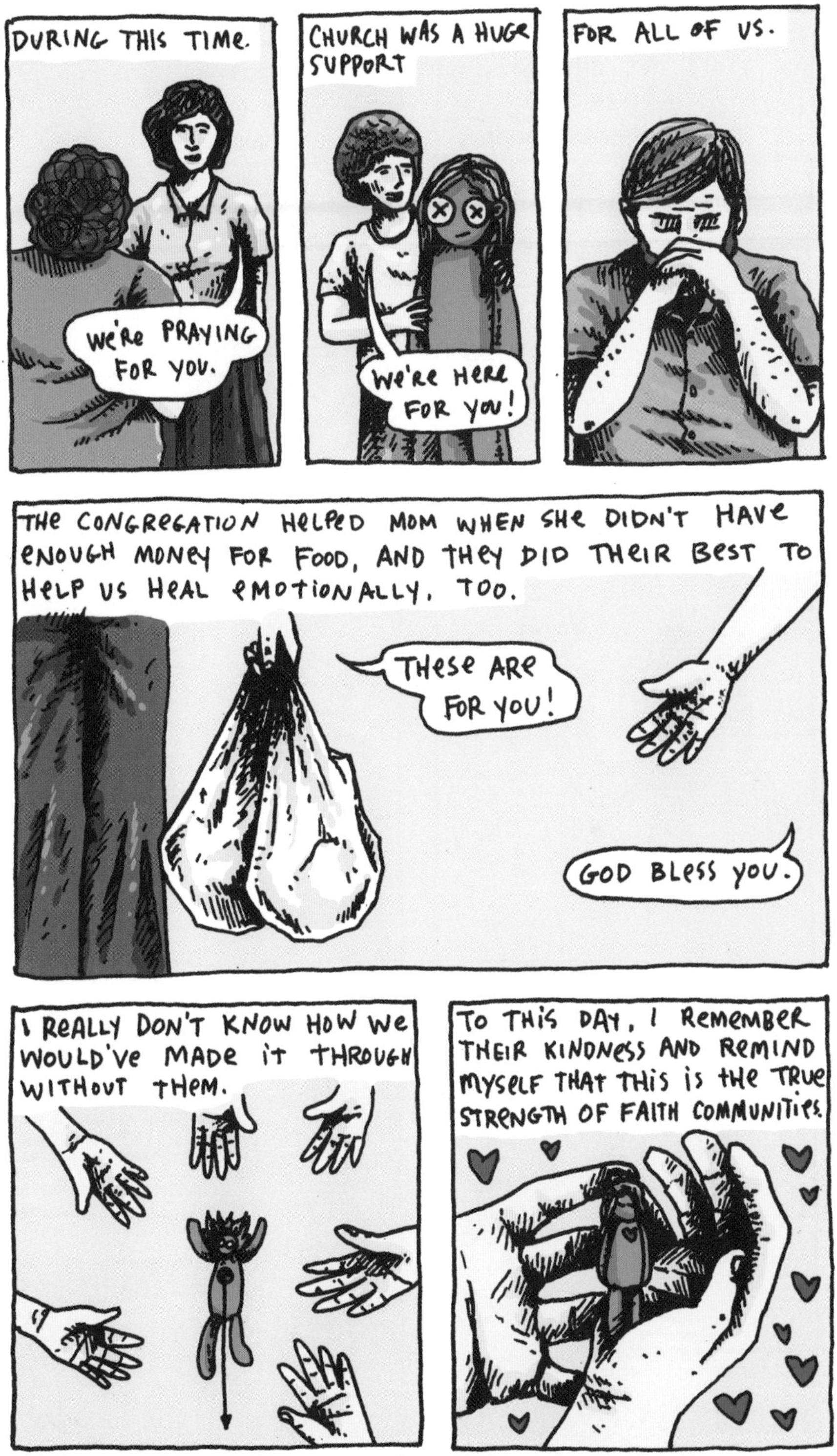

DURING THIS TIME.
We're PRAYING FOR YOU.
CHURCH WAS A HUGE SUPPORT
We're HERE FOR YOU!
FOR ALL OF US.
THE CONGREGATION HELPED MOM WHEN SHE DIDN'T HAVE ENOUGH MONEY FOR FOOD, AND THEY DID THEIR BEST TO HELP US HEAL EMOTIONALLY, TOO.
THESE ARE FOR YOU!
GOD BLESS YOU.
I REALLY DON'T KNOW HOW WE WOULD'VE MADE IT THROUGH WITHOUT THEM.
TO THIS DAY, I REMEMBER THEIR KINDNESS AND REMIND MYSELF THAT THIS IS THE TRUE STRENGTH OF FAITH COMMUNITIES.

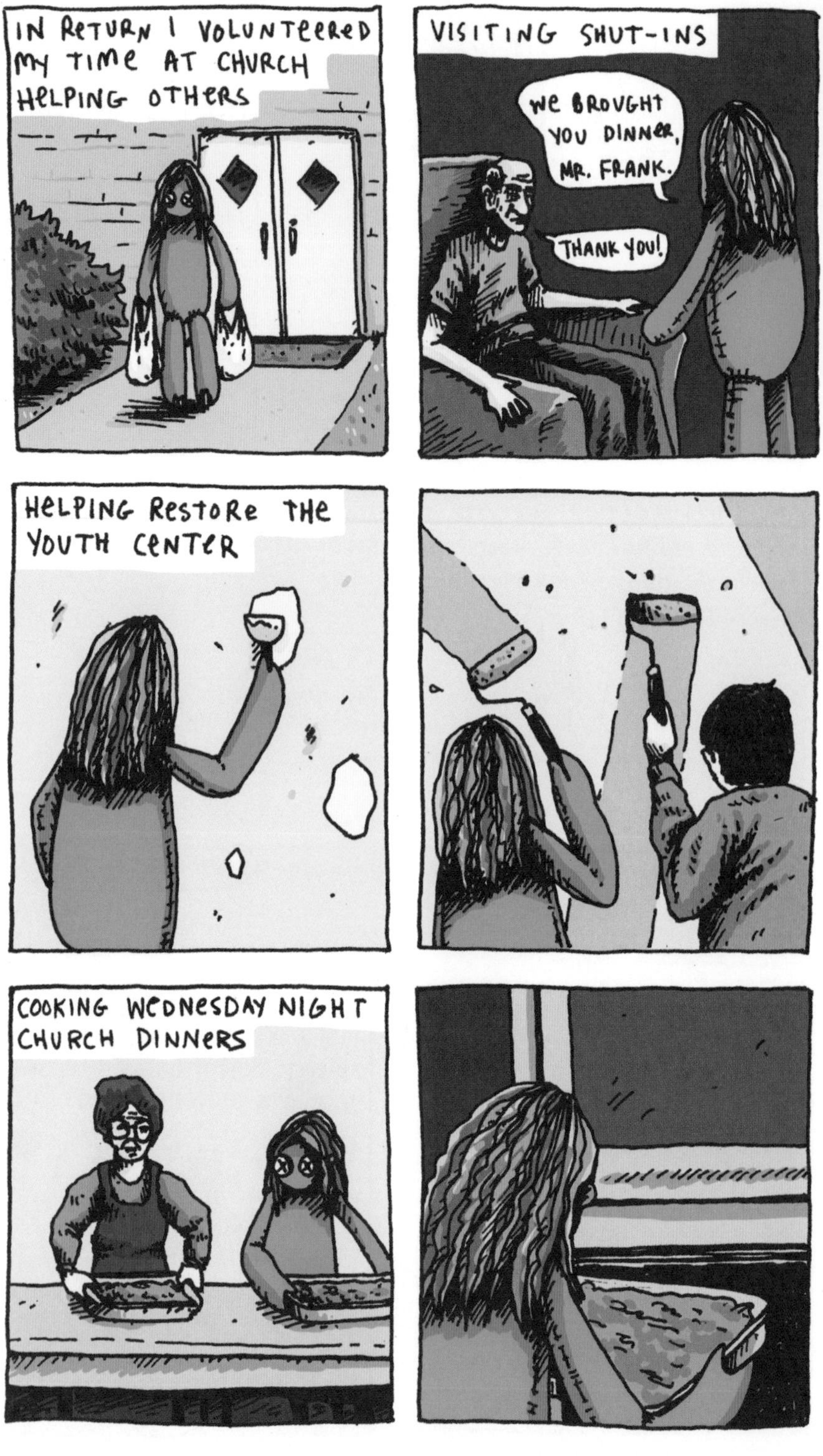
IN RETURN I VOLUNTEERED MY TIME AT CHURCH HELPING OTHERS
VISITING SHUT-INS
WE BROUGHT YOU DINNER, MR. FRANK.
THANK YOU!
HELPING RESTORE THE YOUTH CENTER
COOKING WEDNESDAY NIGHT CHURCH DINNERS

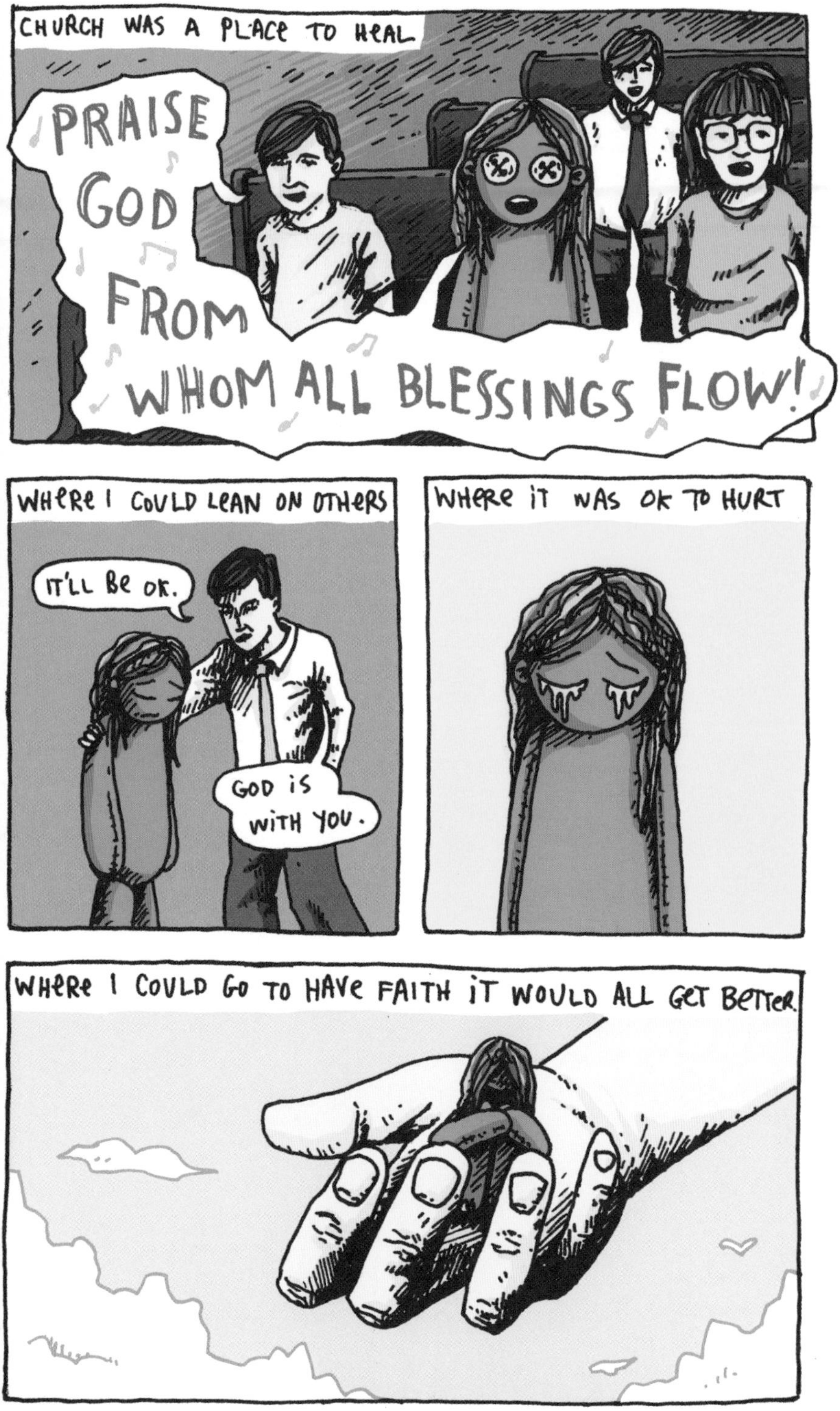
CHURCH WAS A PLACE TO HEAL
PRAISE GOD FROM WHOM ALL BLESSINGS FLOW!
WHERE I COULD LEAN ON OTHERS
IT'LL BE OK.
GOD IS WITH YOU.
WHERE IT WAS OK TO HURT
WHERE I COULD GO TO HAVE FAITH IT WOULD ALL GET BETTER.

ONCE MY MOM SETTLED IN, I SPENT MY TIME DIVIDED BETWEEN THERE...

AND DAD'S

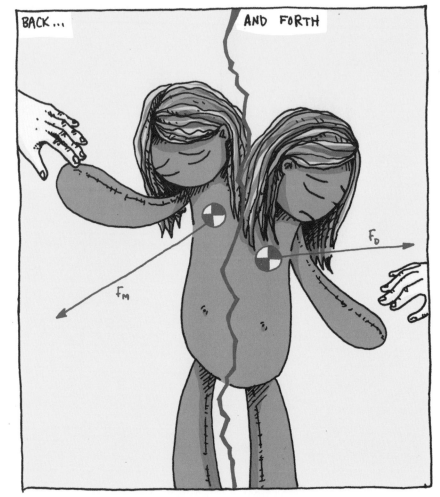

BACK...

AND FORTH

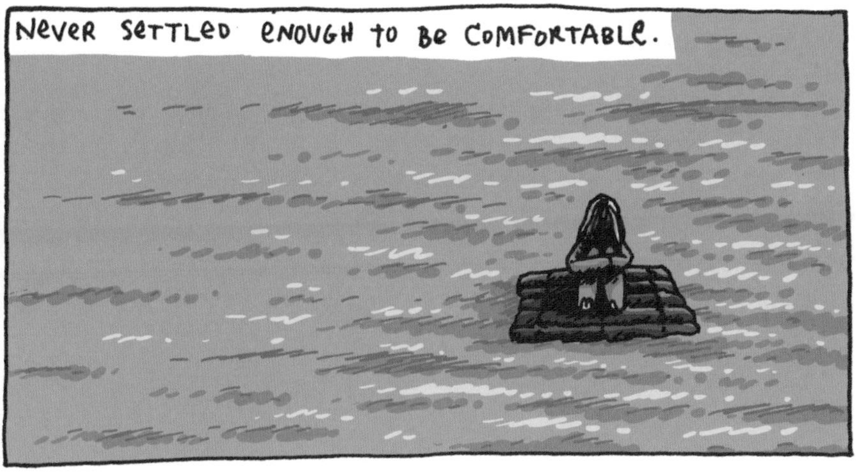
NEVER SETTLED ENOUGH TO BE COMFORTABLE.

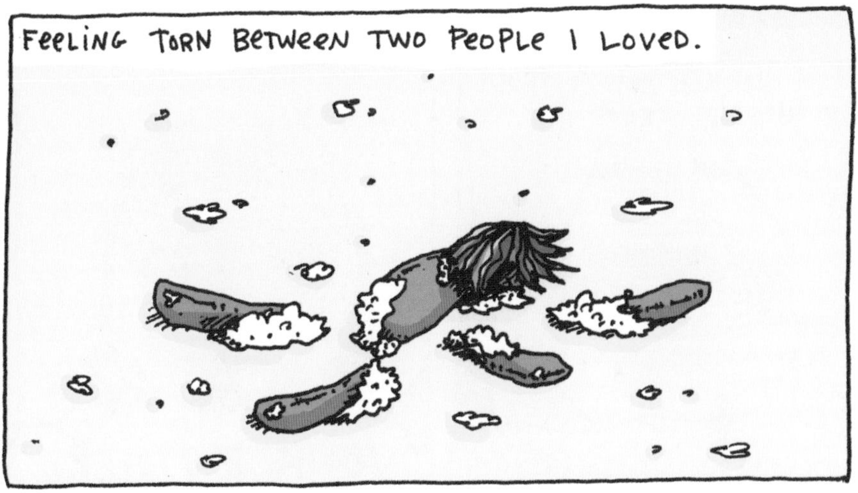
FEELING TORN BETWEEN TWO PEOPLE I LOVED.

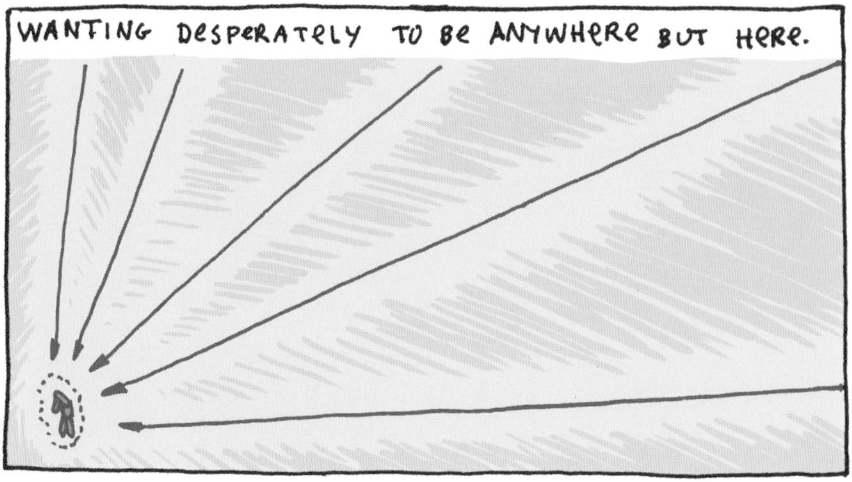
WANTING DESPERATELY TO BE ANYWHERE BUT HERE.

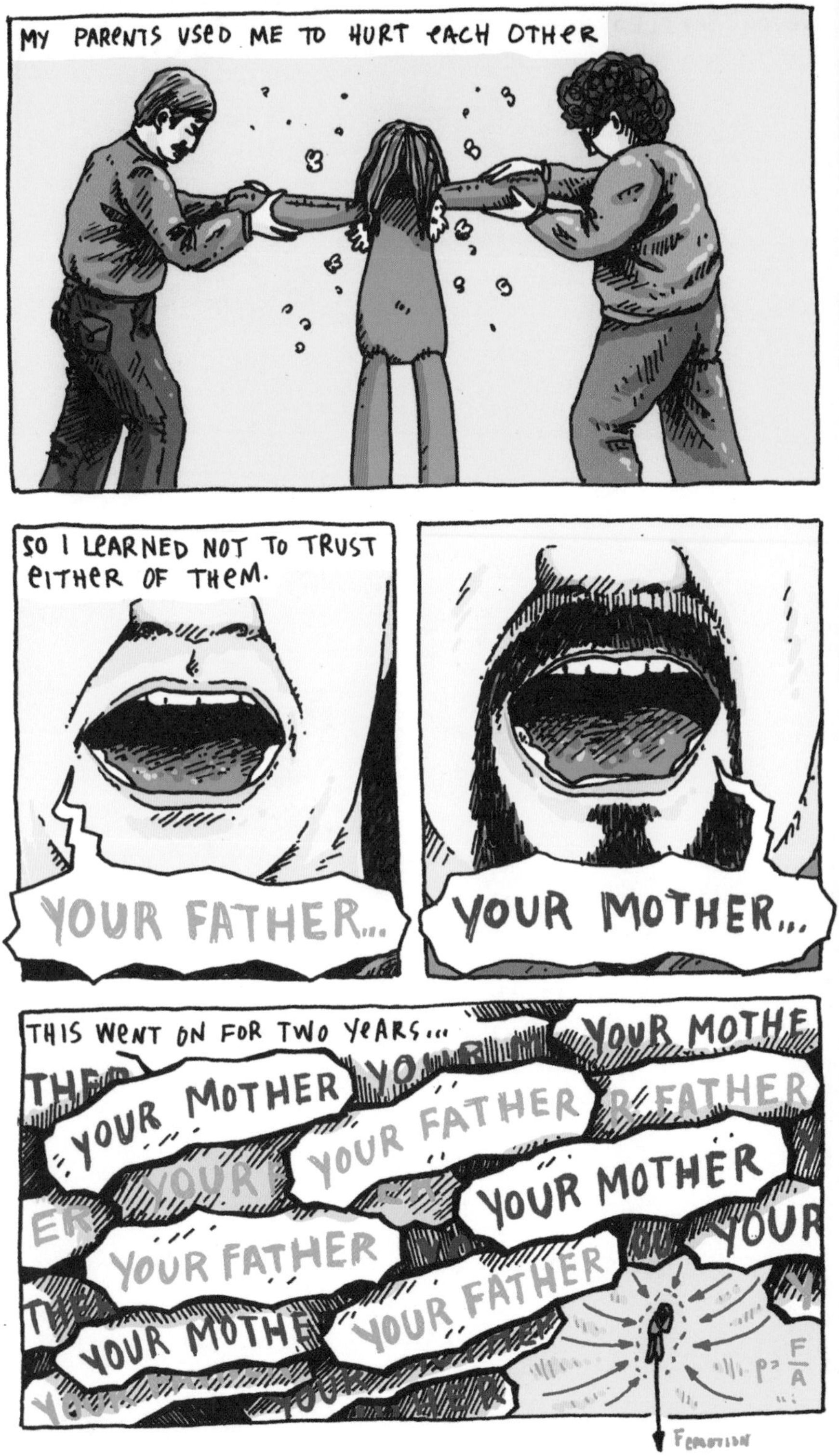
MY PARENTS USED ME TO HURT EACH OTHER
SO I LEARNED NOT TO TRUST EITHER OF THEM.
YOUR FATHER...
YOUR MOTHER...
THIS WENT ON FOR TWO YEARS...
YOUR MOTHE
YOUR MOTHER
YOUR FATHER
YOUR MOTHER
YOUR FATHER
YOUR FATHER
YOUR MOTHE
P = F/A
Femotion

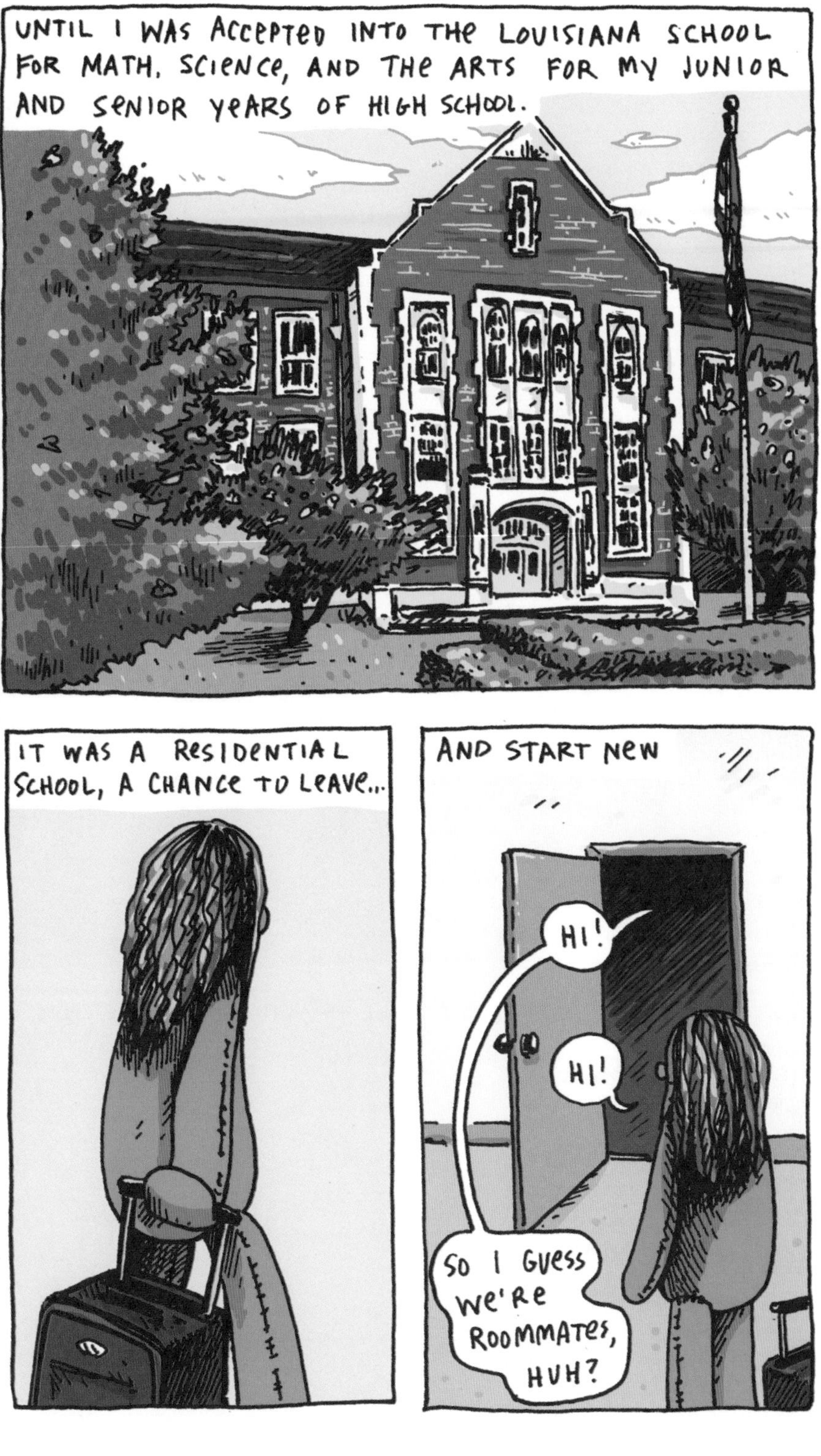
UNTIL I WAS ACCEPTED INTO THE LOUISIANA SCHOOL FOR MATH, SCIENCE, AND THE ARTS FOR MY JUNIOR AND SENIOR YEARS OF HIGH SCHOOL.
IT WAS A RESIDENTIAL SCHOOL, A CHANCE TO LEAVE...
AND START NEW
HI!
HI!
SO I GUESS WE'RE ROOMMATES, HUH?

THERE I WAS JUST ONE SMART KID AMONGST MANY
DO YOU KNOW WHERE THE ANNEX IS?
I'M ALMOST LATE FOR MATH CLASS.
AN ENTIRE SCHOOL THAT FELT LIKE GPGC TO ME
WHICH WHEEL OF TIME BOOK ARE YOU ON?
THE THIRD.
AND SINCE IT WAS RESIDENTIAL, I COULD ESCAPE THE MESS BACK HOME..
YOUR MOTHE
YOUR FAT
YOUR MOT
FATHER
YOUR MOTHE

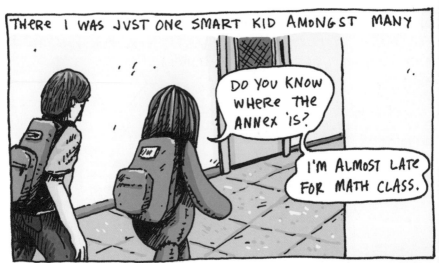

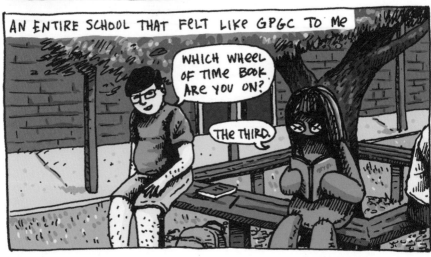

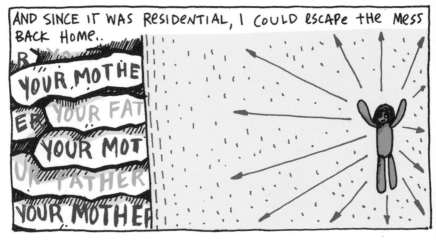

I STARTED WITH SUMMER SCHOOL BEFORE JUNIOR YEAR

HI EVERYONE! I'M MZ. GLEASON. MZ. WITH A "Z" BECAUSE IT'S A COMPLEX NUMBER, LIKE ME.

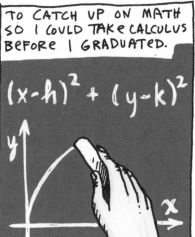

TO CATCH UP ON MATH SO I COULD TAKE CALCULUS BEFORE I GRADUATED.

$$(x-h)^2 + (y-k)^2$$

DEQUINCY WASN'T THE BEST PREPARATION, BUT I WORKED HARD, EXCELLED...

AND EVEN MADE FRIENDS.

HA HA HA HA HA HA HA HA

A SUMMER OF JOY FOR THE FIRST TIME IN RECENT MEMORY

WHEN THE SCHOOL YEAR STARTED, I WAS READY TO DIVE IN

TRIG

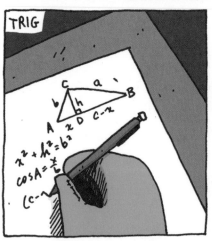

PRE-CALCULUS

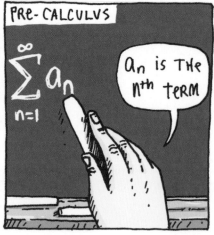

aₙ is THE nᵗʰ term

ANATOMY

DIFFERENTIAL CALCULUS

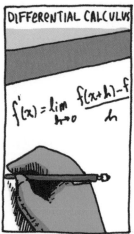

CHEMISTRY

GERMAN
VOR DEM GESETZ STEHT EIN TÜRHÜTER.
INTEGRAL CALCULUS
$\int x \cos x \, dx = x \sin x - \int 1(\sin x)dx$
PHYSICS
F_F
M
F_N
$\vec{v}$
h
α
F_G
$F_F = \mu$
y
x
$\sum F_x = F_G \sin \alpha$
MULTIVARIABLE CALCULUS
$\iint xy^2 \, dA$
y
1
2
x
COMPARATIVE ANATOMY
HUMERUS
RADIUS
ULNA
INTRO TO POINT-SET TOPOLOGY
a
b
c
The only open sets are
$X, \phi, \{a, b\}$
ALL TAKEN WITH ONE GOAL IN MIND... COLLEGE AND MY FUTURE LIFE.

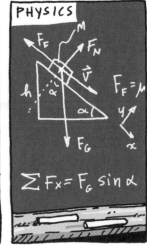

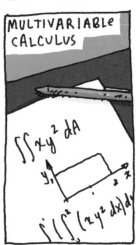

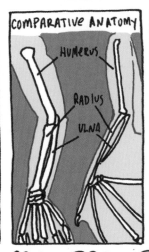

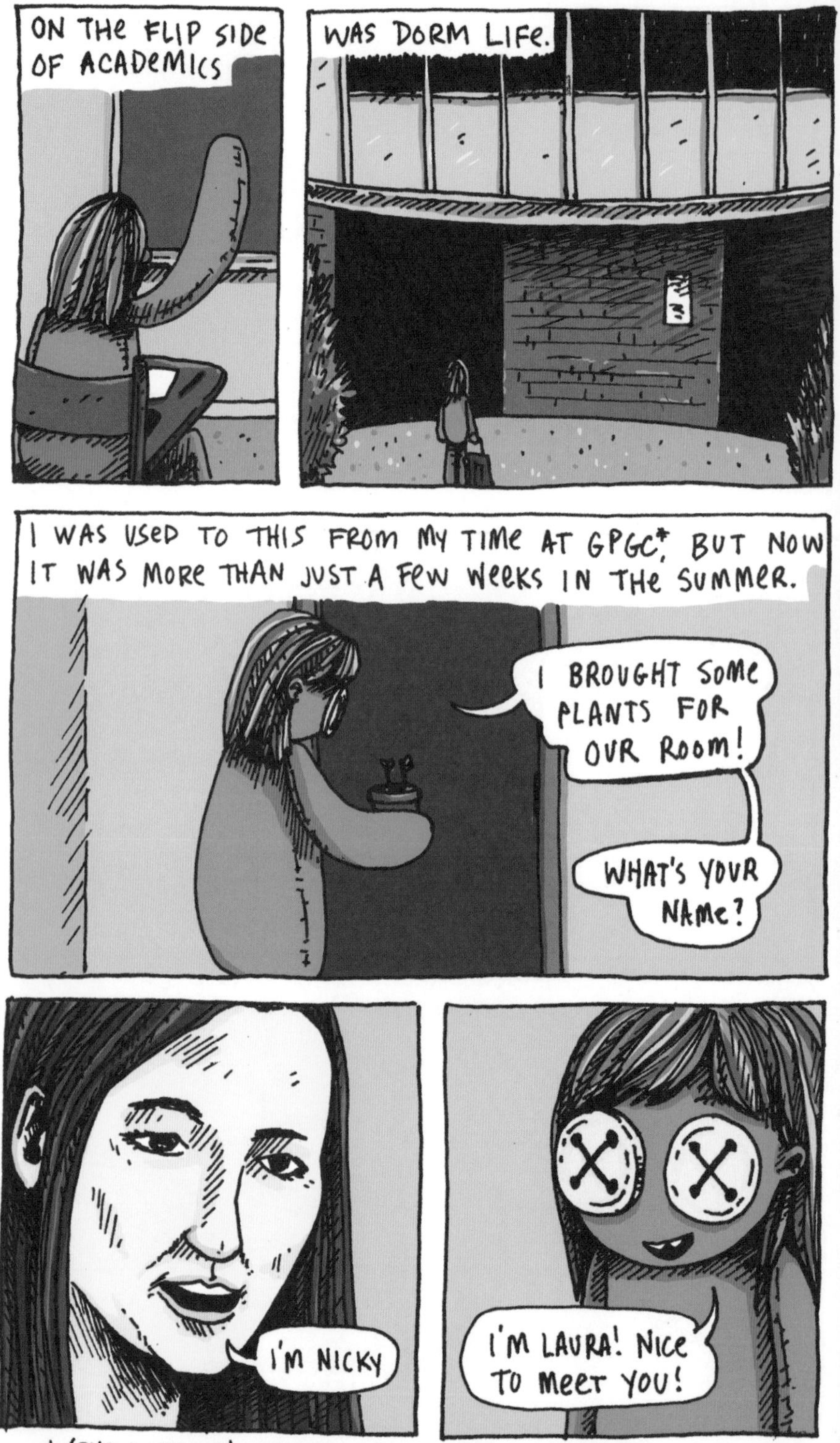
ON THE FLIP SIDE OF ACADEMICS
WAS DORM LIFE.
I WAS USED TO THIS FROM MY TIME AT GPGC*, BUT NOW IT WAS MORE THAN JUST A FEW WEEKS IN THE SUMMER.
I BROUGHT SOME PLANTS FOR OUR ROOM!
WHAT'S YOUR NAME?
I'M NICKY
I'M LAURA! NICE TO MEET YOU!
*(THE GOVERNOR'S PROGRAM FOR GIFTED CHILDREN)

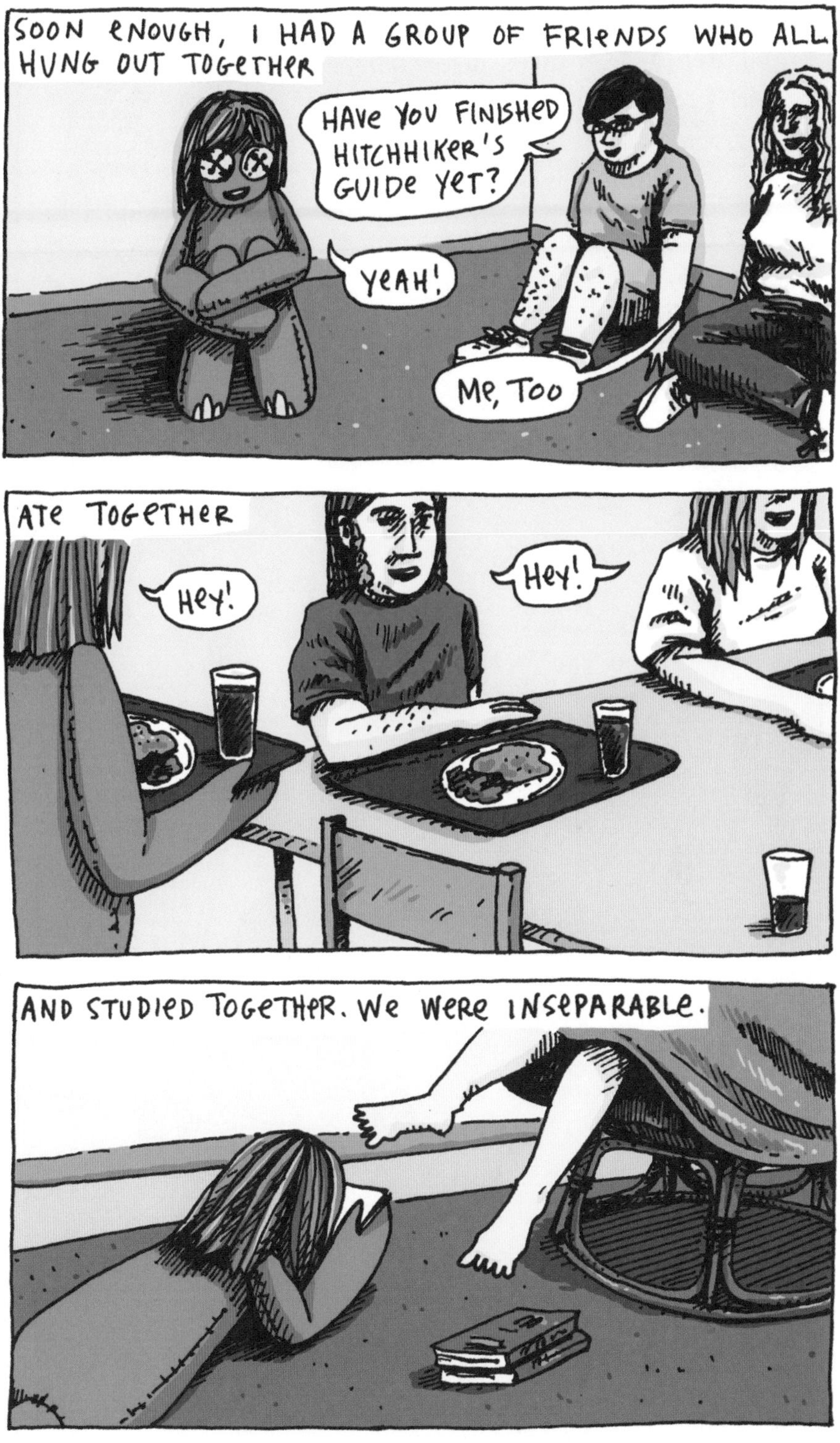
SOON ENOUGH, I HAD A GROUP OF FRIENDS WHO ALL HUNG OUT TOGETHER
HAVE YOU FINISHED HITCHHIKER'S GUIDE YET?
YEAH!
ME, TOO
ATE TOGETHER
HEY!
HEY!
AND STUDIED TOGETHER. WE WERE INSEPARABLE.

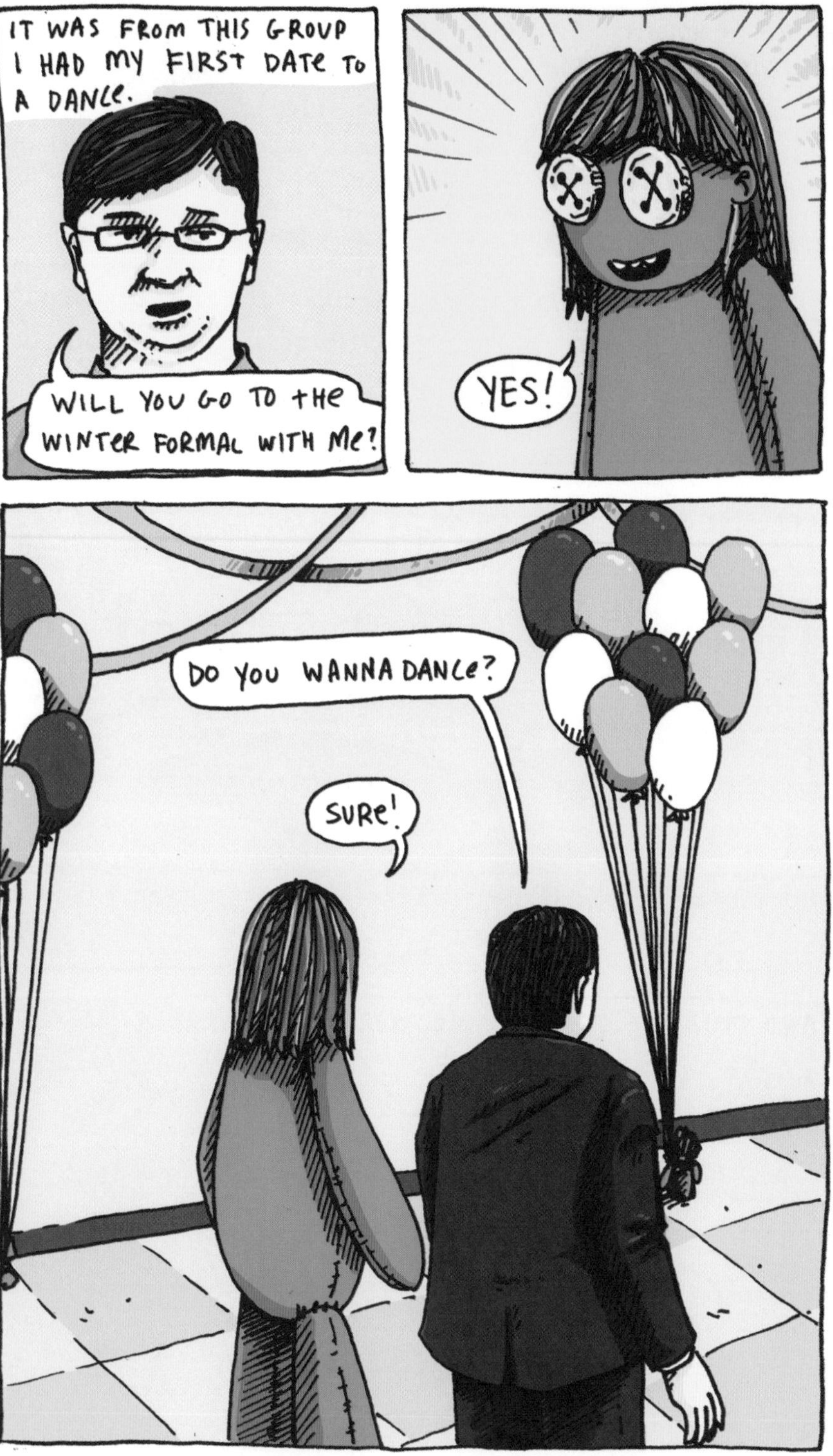
IT WAS FROM THIS GROUP I HAD MY FIRST DATE TO A DANCE.
WILL YOU GO TO THE WINTER FORMAL WITH ME?
YES!
DO YOU WANNA DANCE?
SURE!

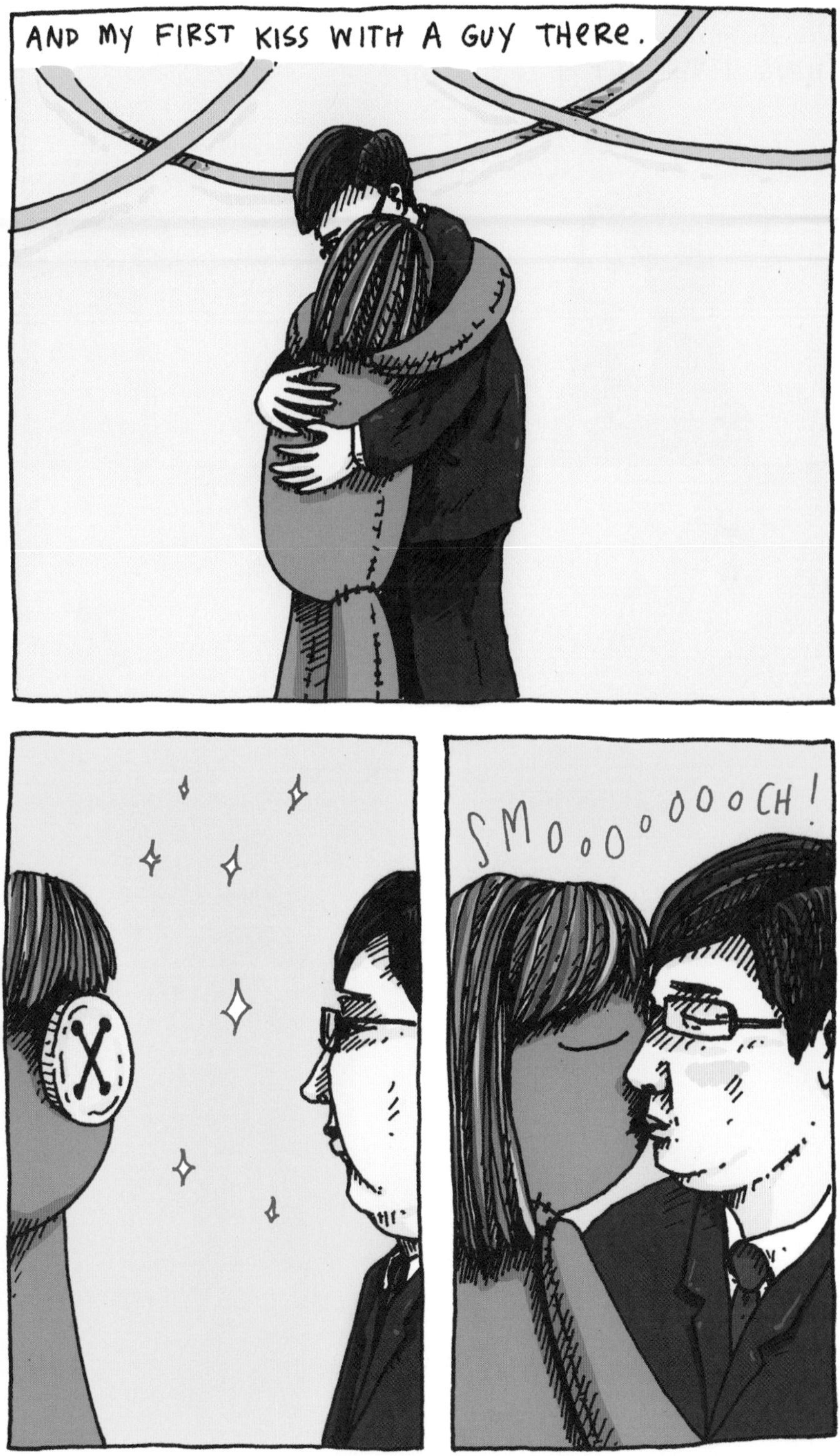
AND MY FIRST KISS WITH A GUY THERE.
SMOoOoOOOOCH!

AND IT WAS THIS GROUP THAT FIRST SAID OUT LOUD THE THING I THOUGHT I COULD HIDE.
ADMIT IT.
YOU LIKE GIRLS.
Q
U
E
E
R
F HELL

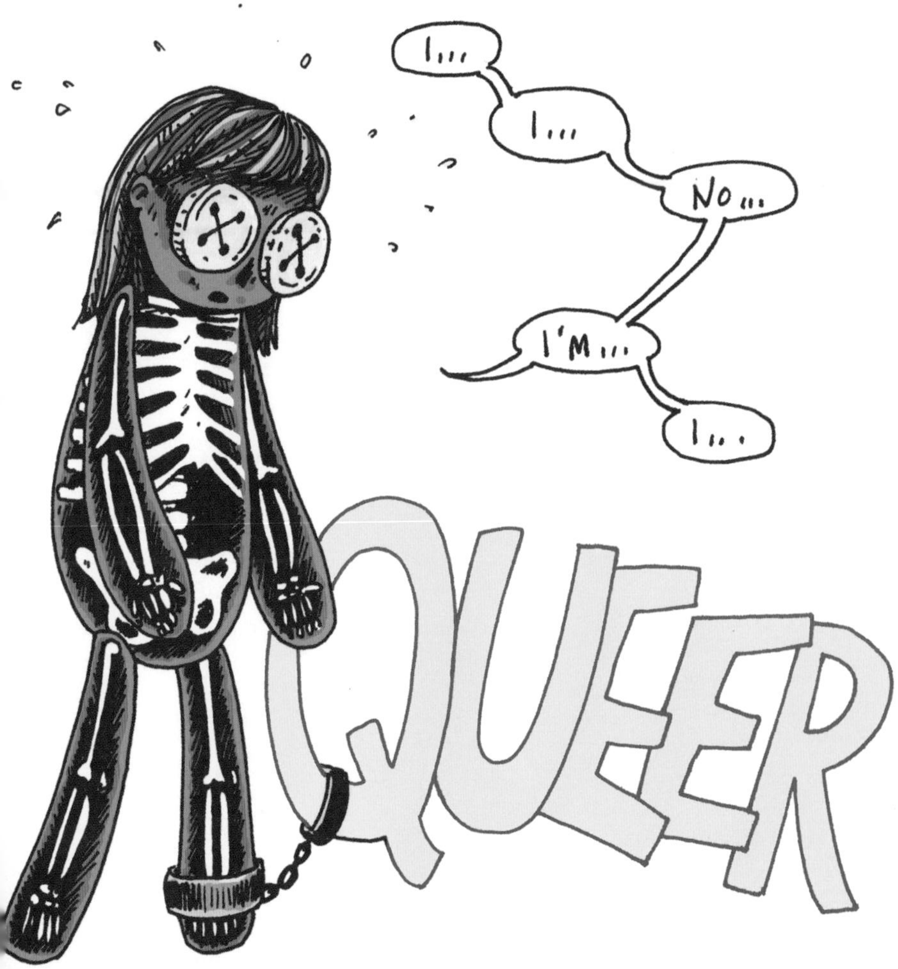
I...
I...
NO...
I'M...
I...
QUEER

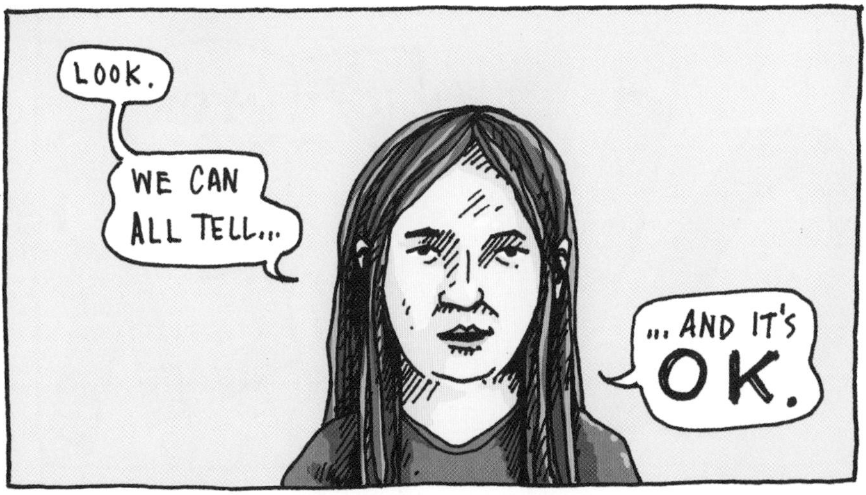
LOOK.
WE CAN ALL TELL...
...AND IT'S OK.

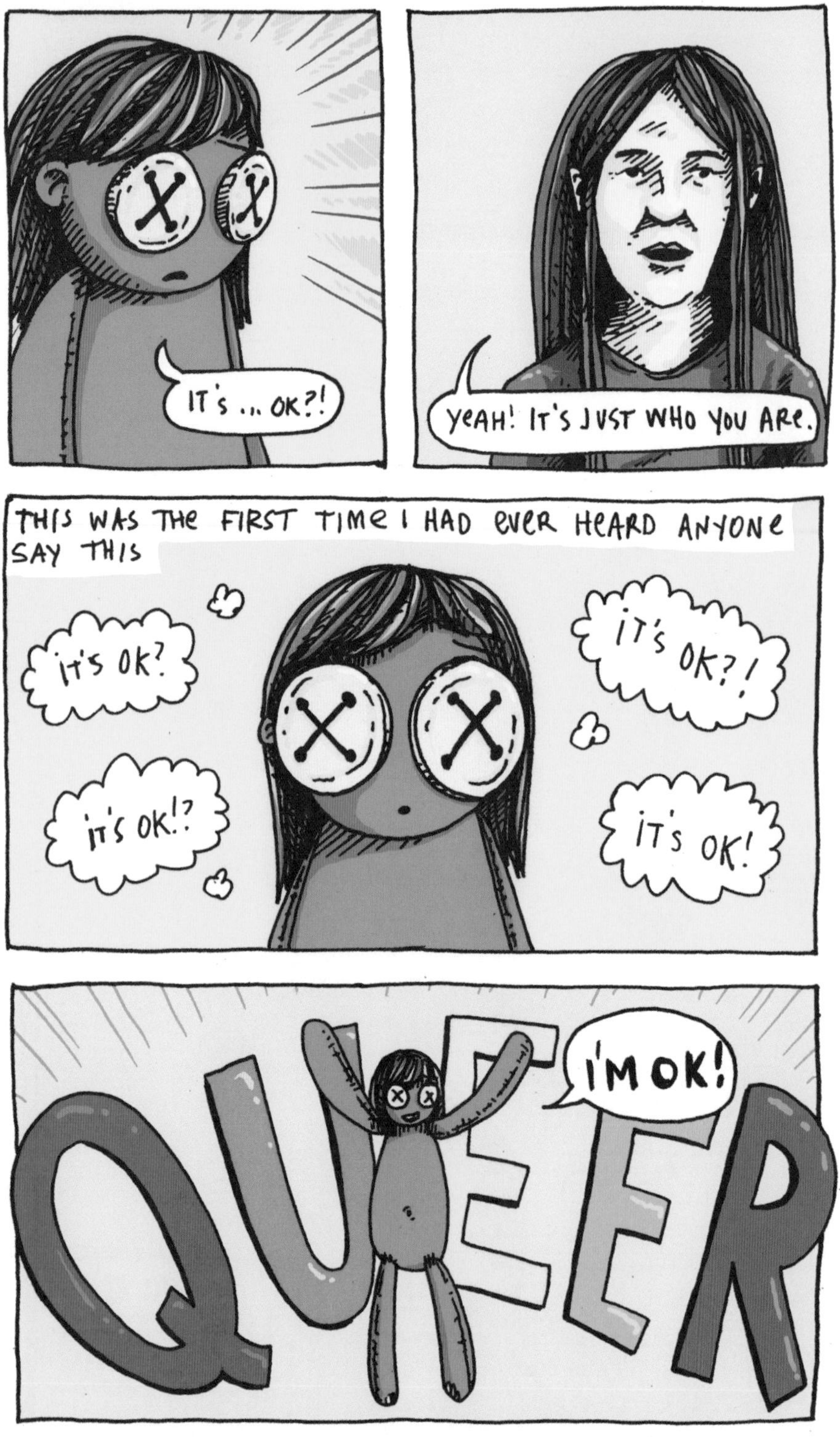
IT'S ... OK?!
YEAH! IT'S JUST WHO YOU ARE.
THIS WAS THE FIRST TIME I HAD EVER HEARD ANYONE SAY THIS
IT'S OK?
IT'S OK?!
IT'S OK!?
IT'S OK!
QUEER
I'M OK!

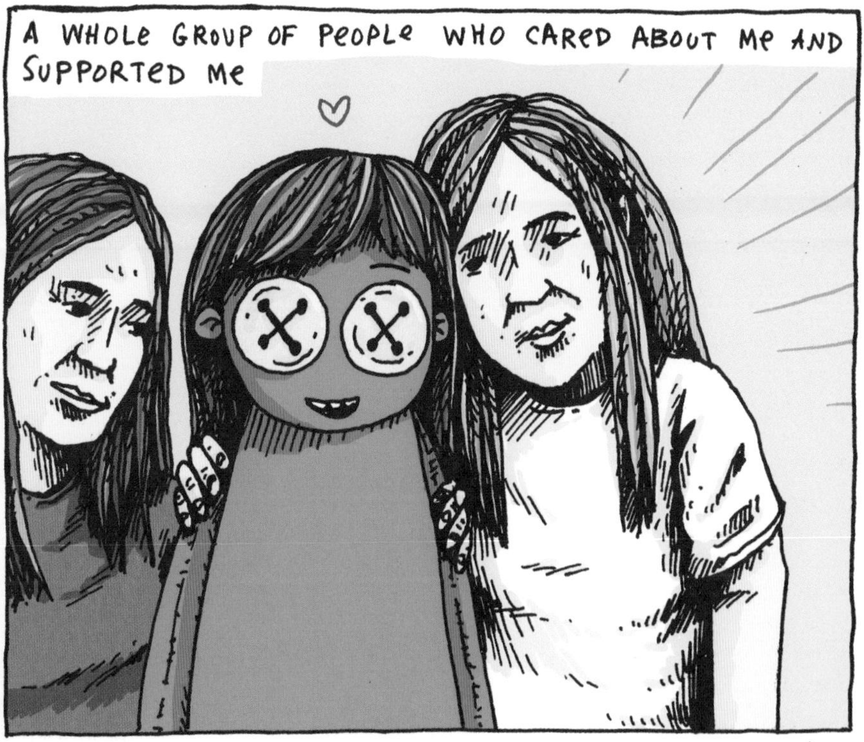
A WHOLE GROUP OF PEOPLE WHO CARED ABOUT ME AND SUPPORTED ME

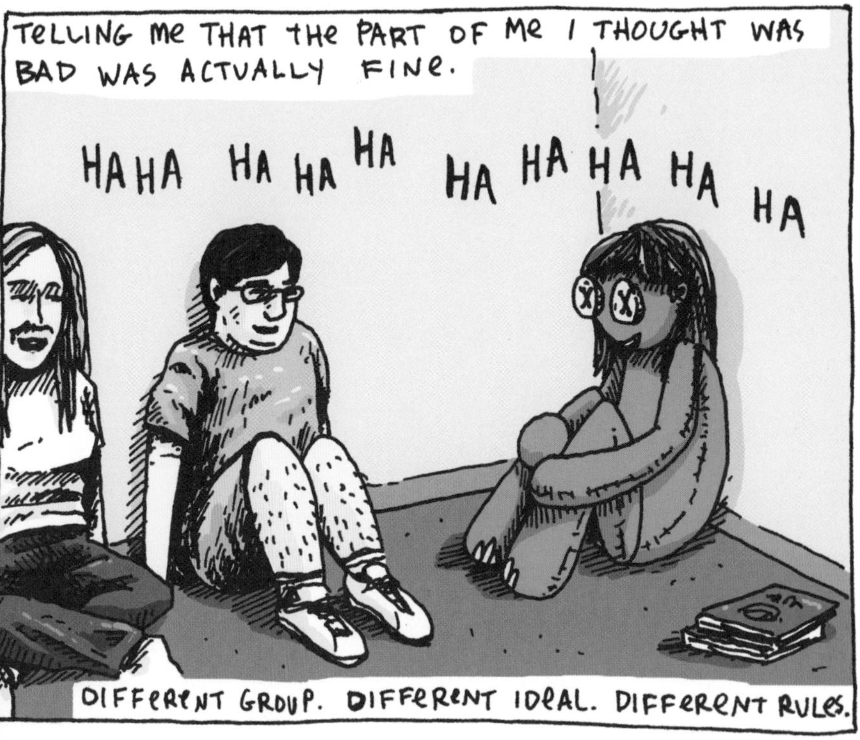
TELLING ME THAT THE PART OF ME I THOUGHT WAS BAD WAS ACTUALLY FINE.
HAHA HA HA HA HA HA HA HA HA HA
DIFFERENT GROUP. DIFFERENT IDEAL. DIFFERENT RULES.

CHAPTER SIX

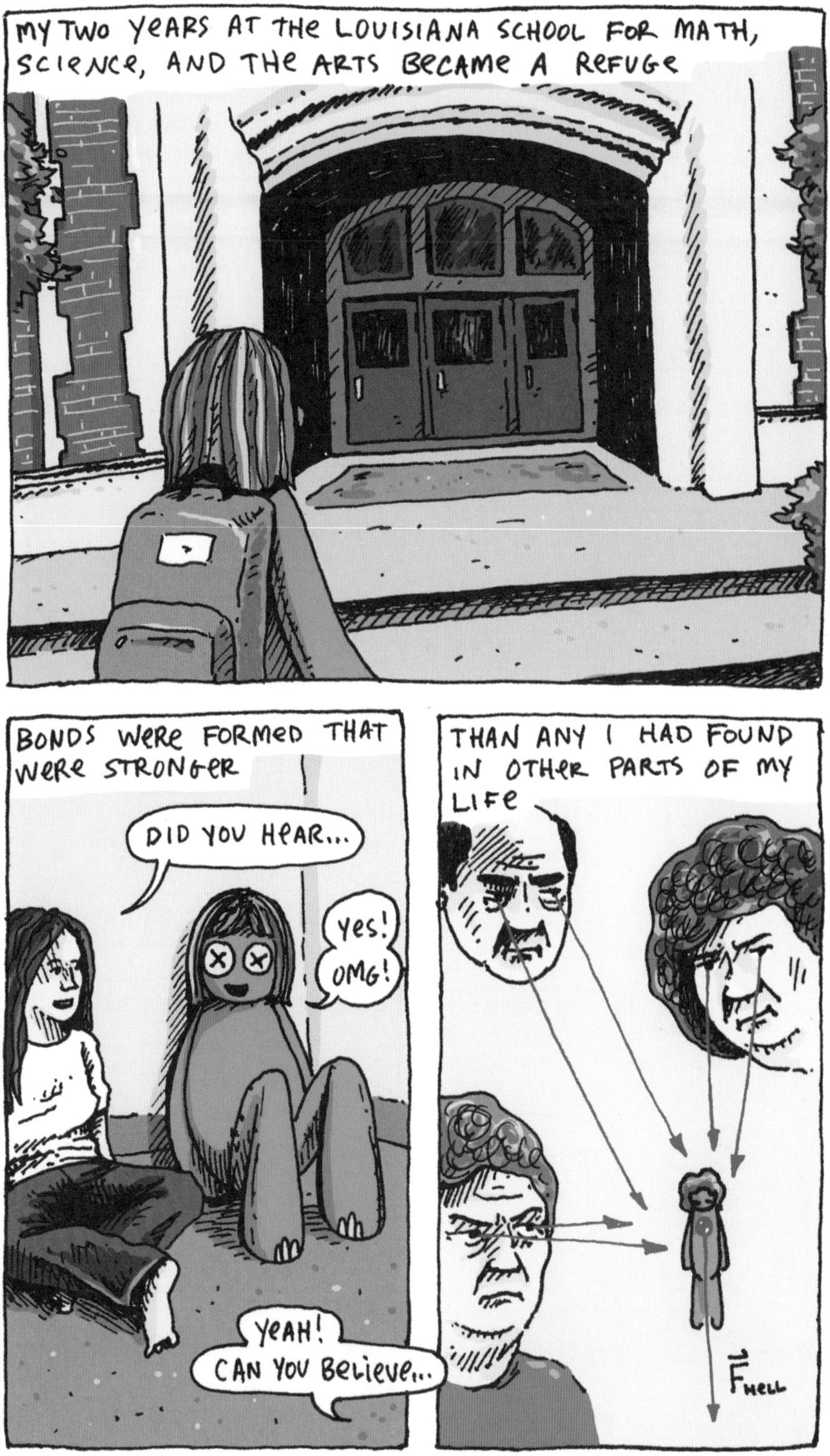
MY TWO YEARS AT THE LOUISIANA SCHOOL FOR MATH, SCIENCE, AND THE ARTS BECAME A REFUGE
BONDS WERE FORMED THAT WERE STRONGER
DID YOU HEAR...
YES! OMG!
YEAH! CAN YOU BELIEVE...
THAN ANY I HAD FOUND IN OTHER PARTS OF MY LIFE
F HELL

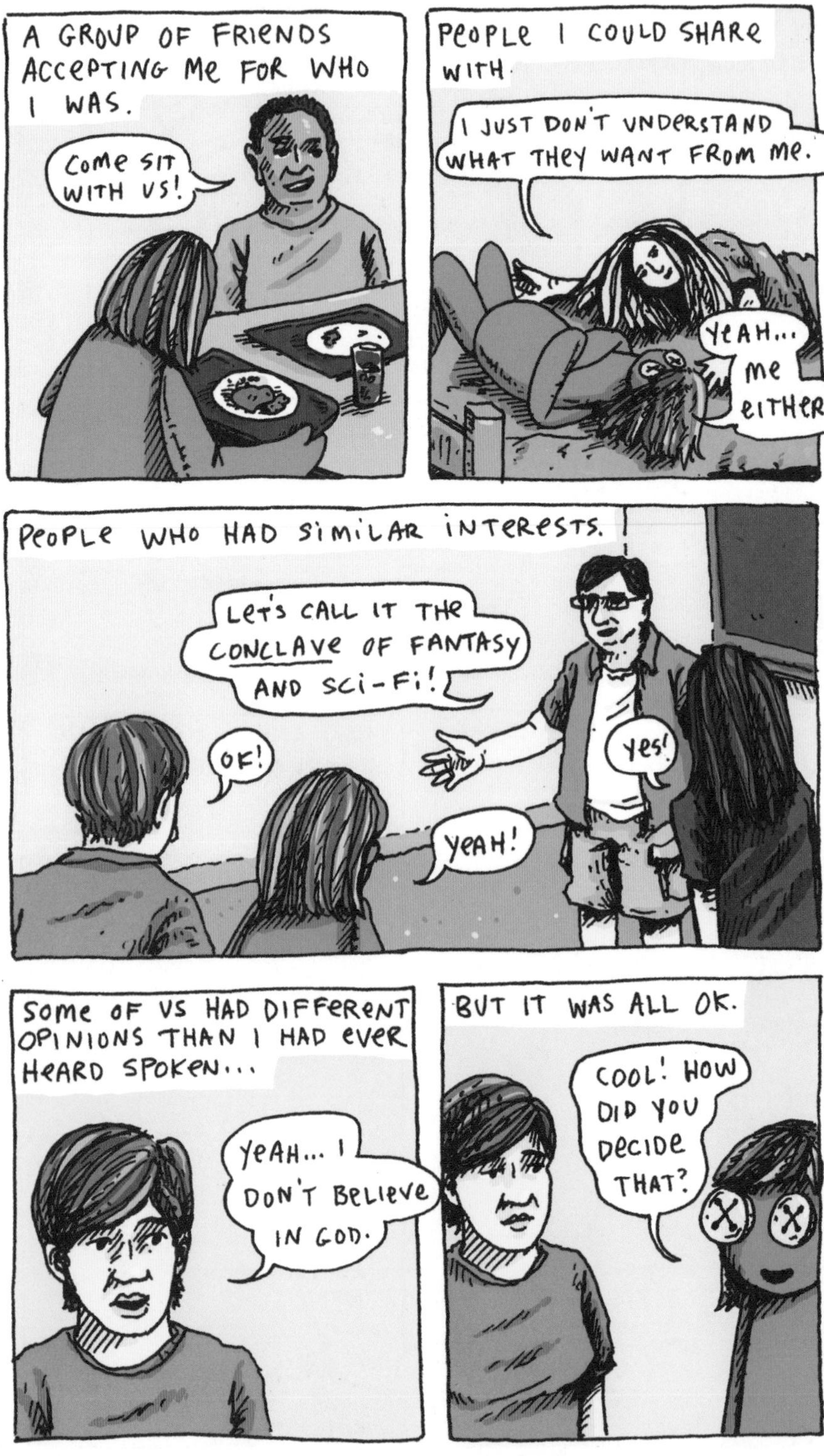
A GROUP OF FRIENDS ACCEPTING ME FOR WHO I WAS.
COME SIT WITH US!
PEOPLE I COULD SHARE WITH.
I JUST DON'T UNDERSTAND WHAT THEY WANT FROM ME.
YEAH... ME EITHER.
PEOPLE WHO HAD SIMILAR INTERESTS.
LET'S CALL IT THE CONCLAVE OF FANTASY AND SCI-FI!
OK!
YES!
YEAH!
SOME OF US HAD DIFFERENT OPINIONS THAN I HAD EVER HEARD SPOKEN...
YEAH... I DON'T BELIEVE IN GOD.
BUT IT WAS ALL OK.
COOL! HOW DID YOU DECIDE THAT?

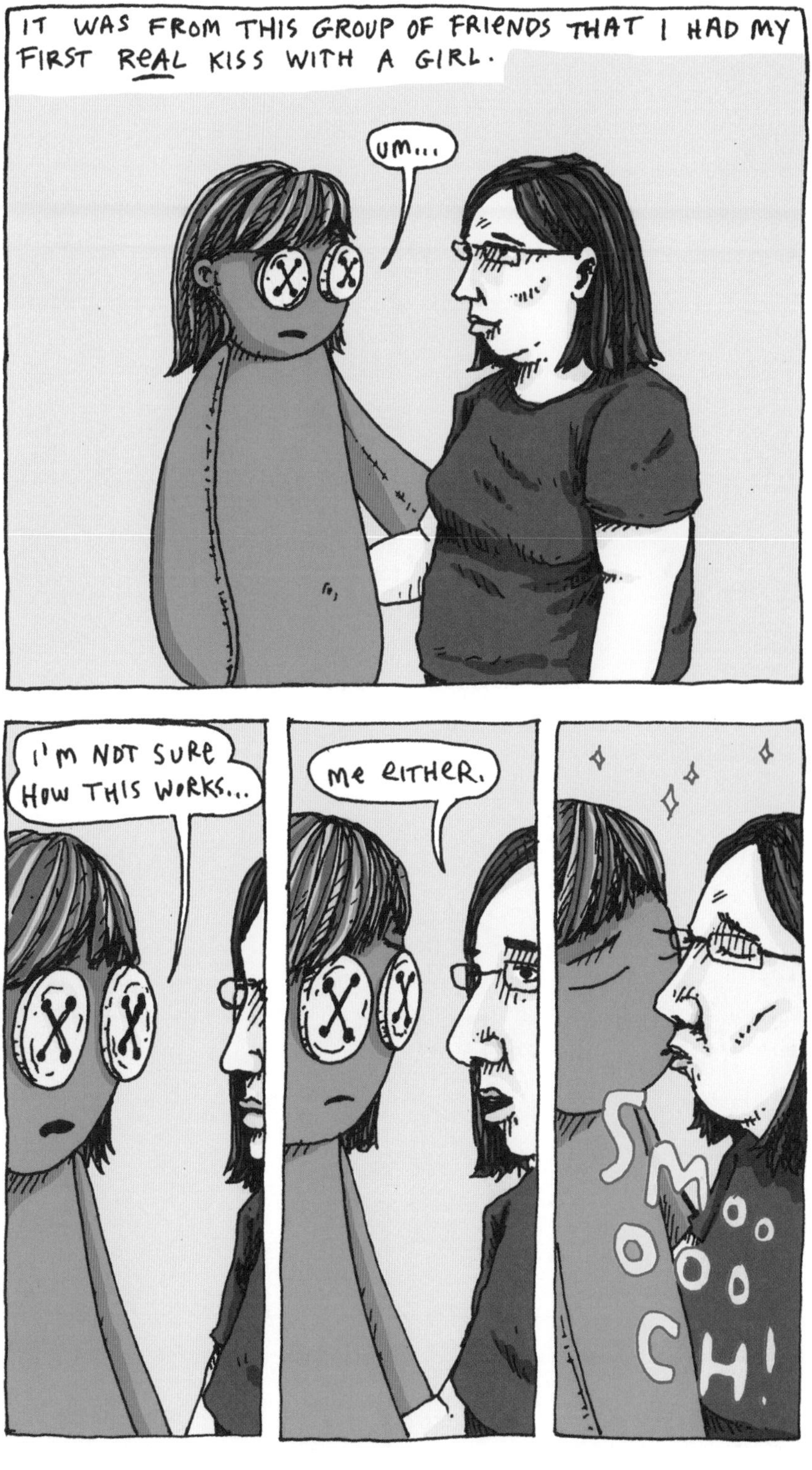
IT WAS FROM THIS GROUP OF FRIENDS THAT I HAD MY FIRST REAL KISS WITH A GIRL.
UM...
I'M NOT SURE HOW THIS WORKS...
ME EITHER.
SMOOOOOCH!

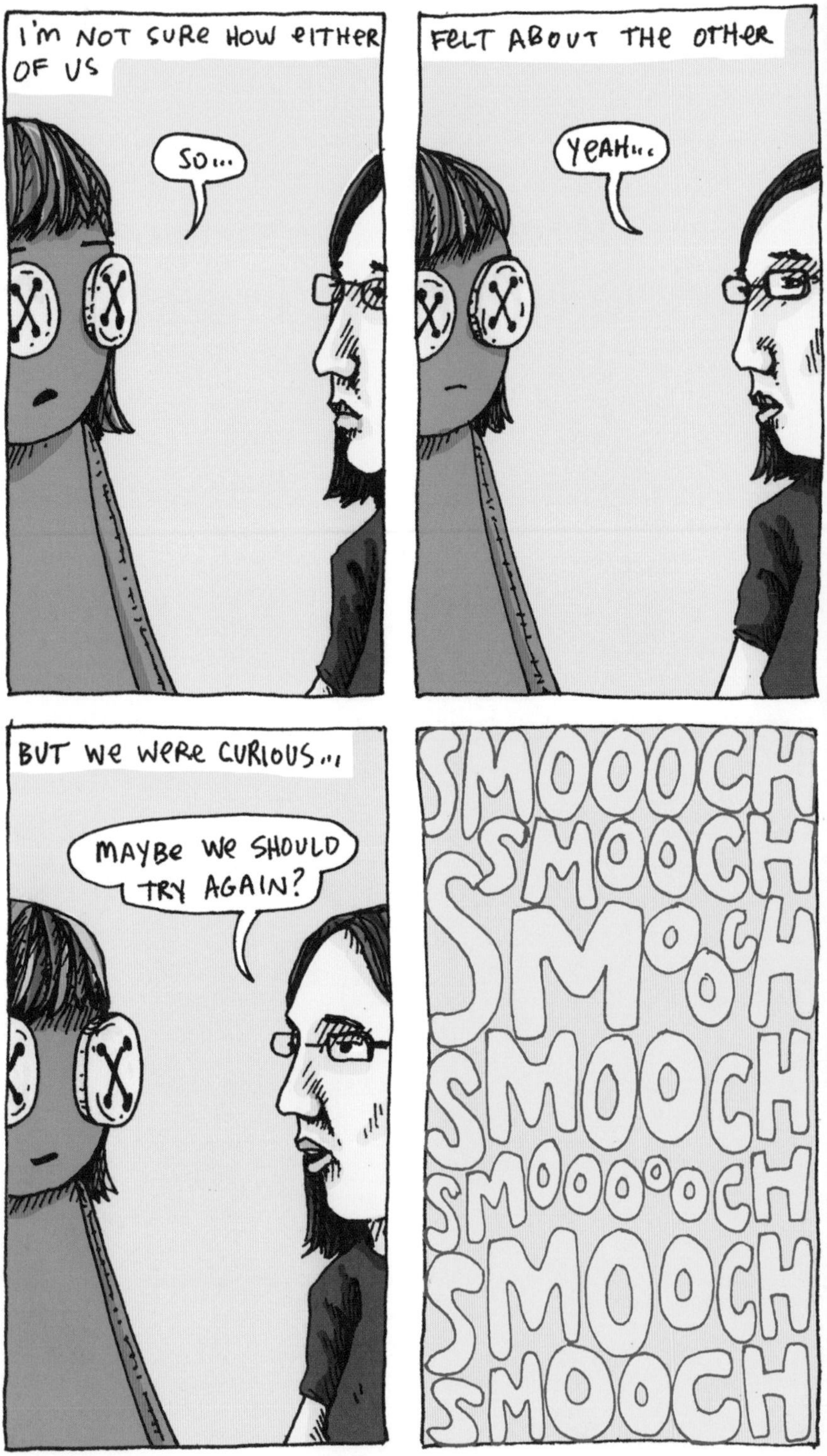
I'M NOT SURE HOW EITHER OF US
SO...
FELT ABOUT THE OTHER
YEAH...
BUT WE WERE CURIOUS...
MAYBE WE SHOULD TRY AGAIN?
SMOOOCH SMOOCH SMOOCH SMOOCH SMOOOOOCH SMOOCH SMOOCH

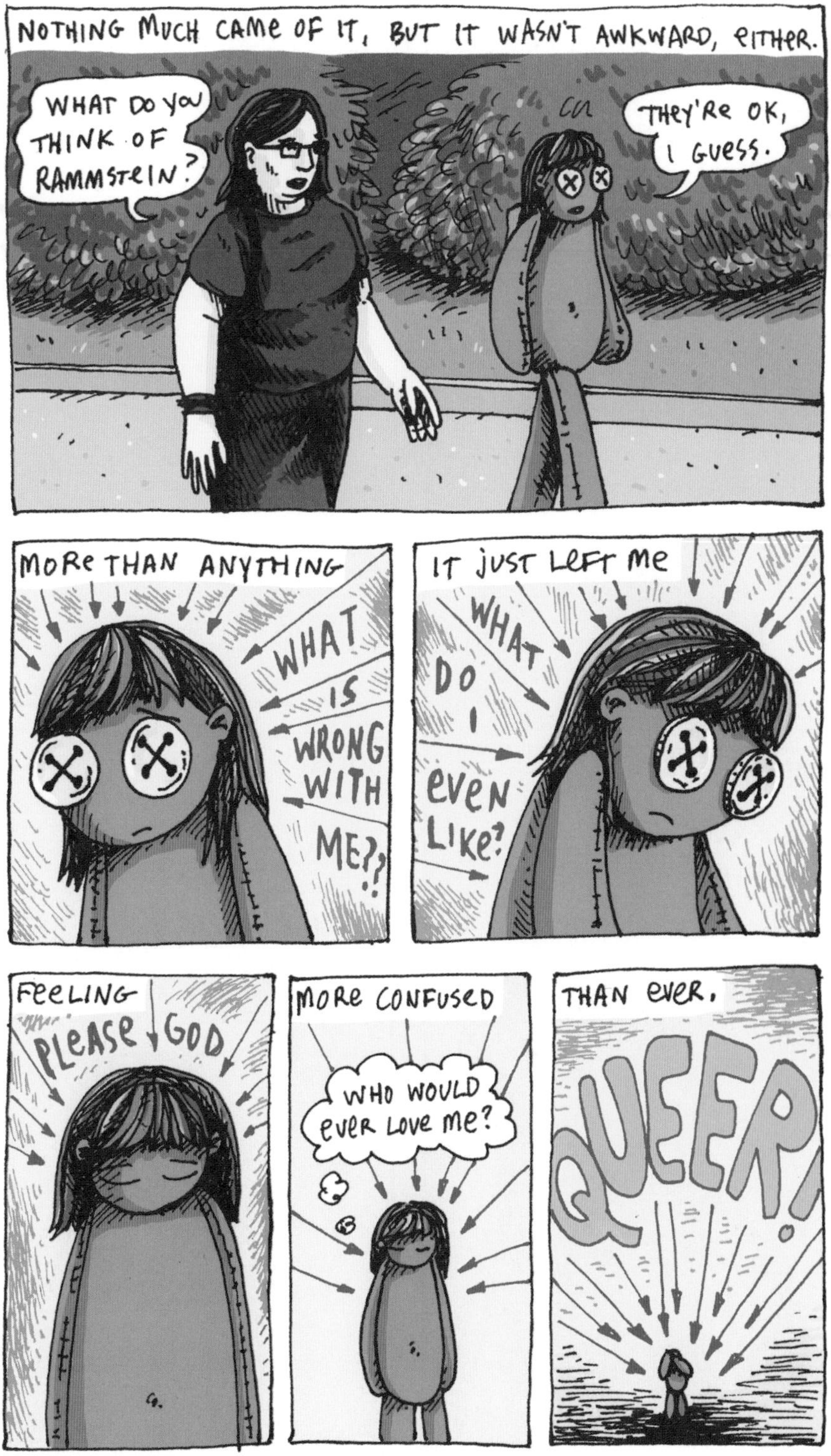
NOTHING MUCH CAME OF IT, BUT IT WASN'T AWKWARD, EITHER.
WHAT DO YOU THINK OF RAMMSTEIN?
THEY'RE OK, I GUESS.
MORE THAN ANYTHING
WHAT IS WRONG WITH ME?!?
IT JUST LEFT ME
WHAT DO I EVEN LIKE?
FEELING
PLEASE GOD
MORE CONFUSED
WHO WOULD EVER LOVE ME?
THAN EVER.
QUEER!

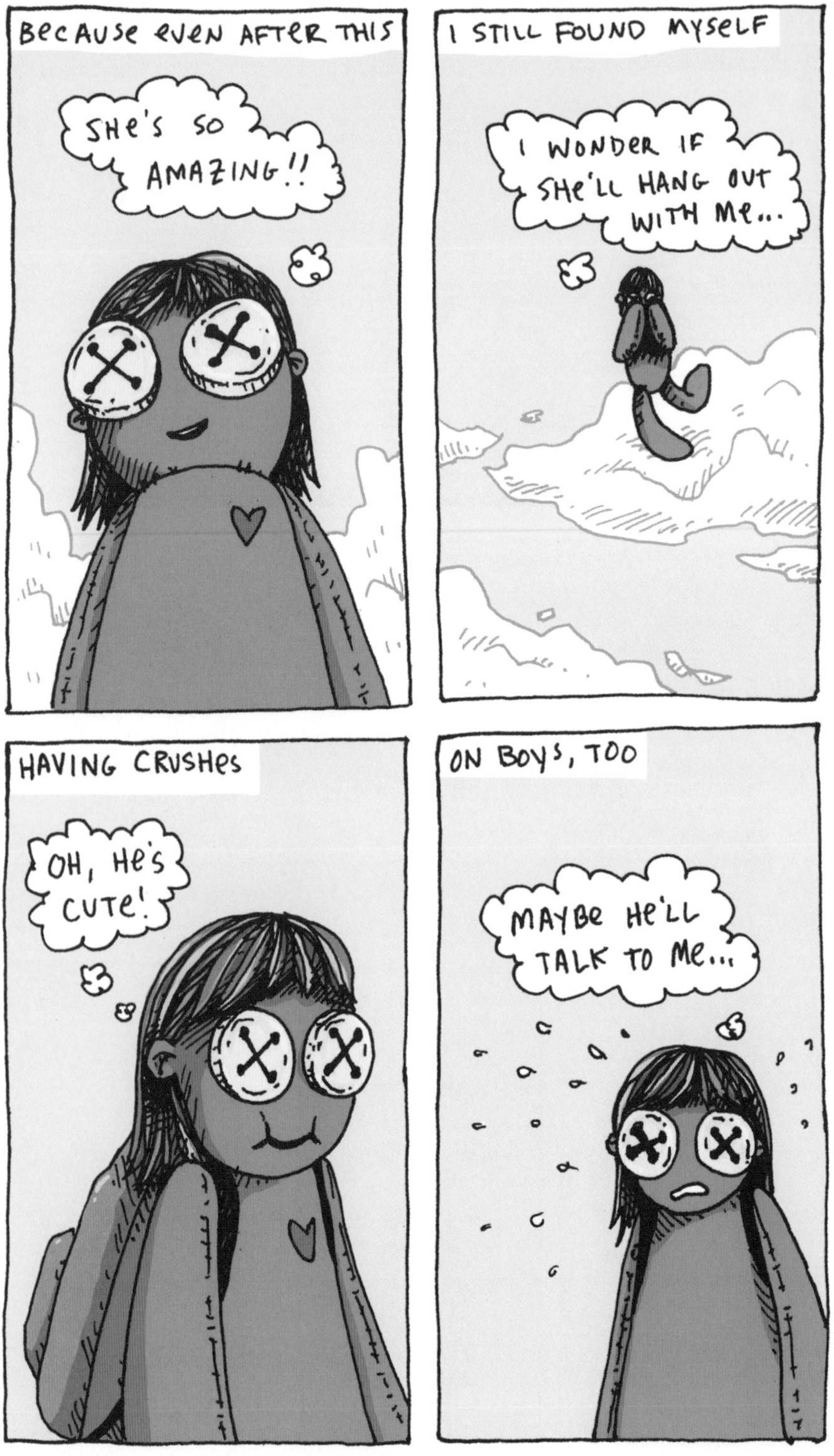
BECAUSE EVEN AFTER THIS
SHE'S SO AMAZING!!
I STILL FOUND MYSELF
I WONDER IF SHE'LL HANG OUT WITH ME...
HAVING CRUSHES
OH, HE'S CUTE!
ON BOYS, TOO
MAYBE HE'LL TALK TO ME...

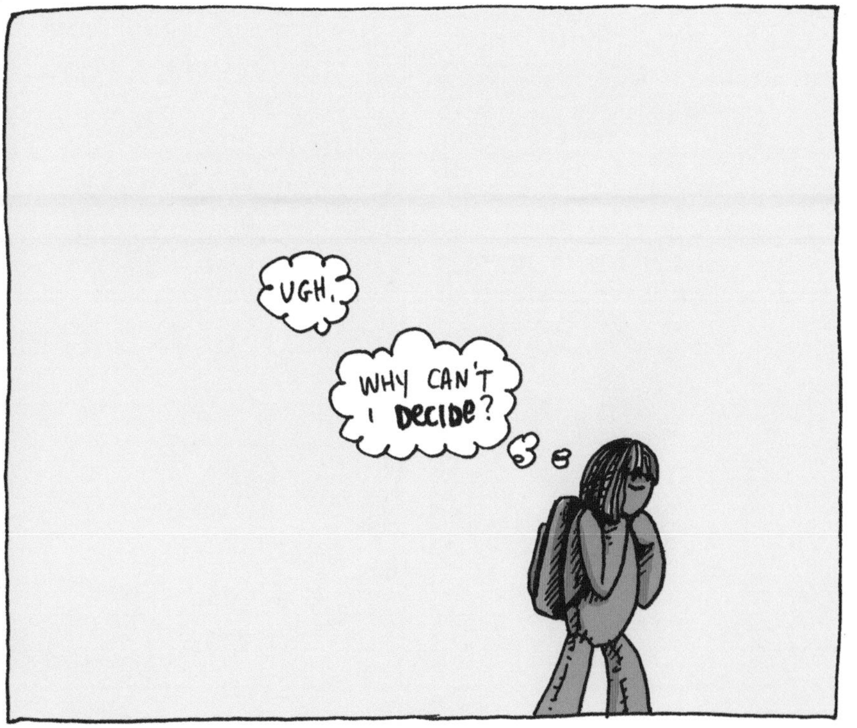
UGH.
WHY CAN'T I DECIDE?

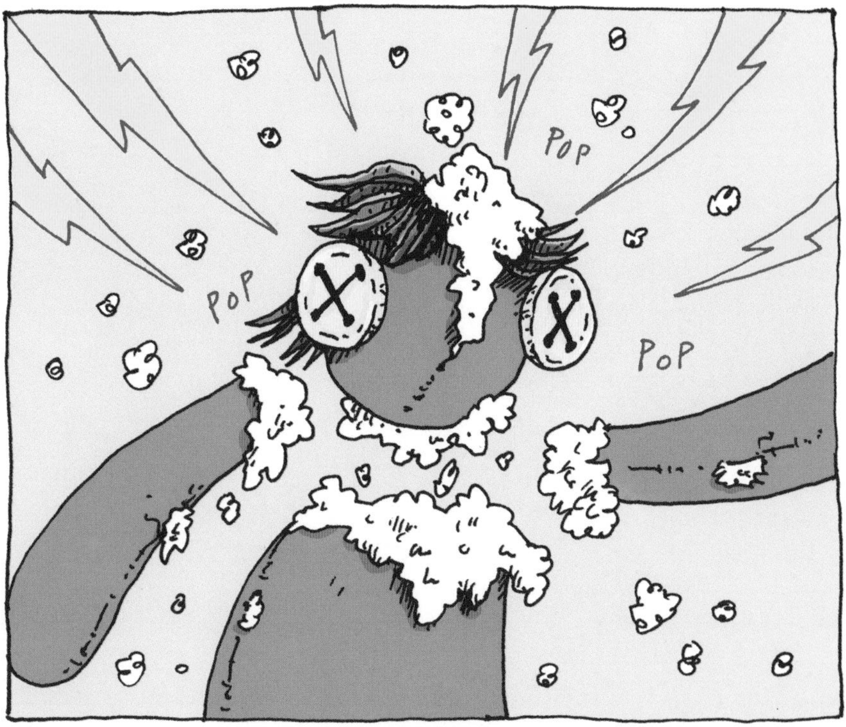
POP
POP
POP

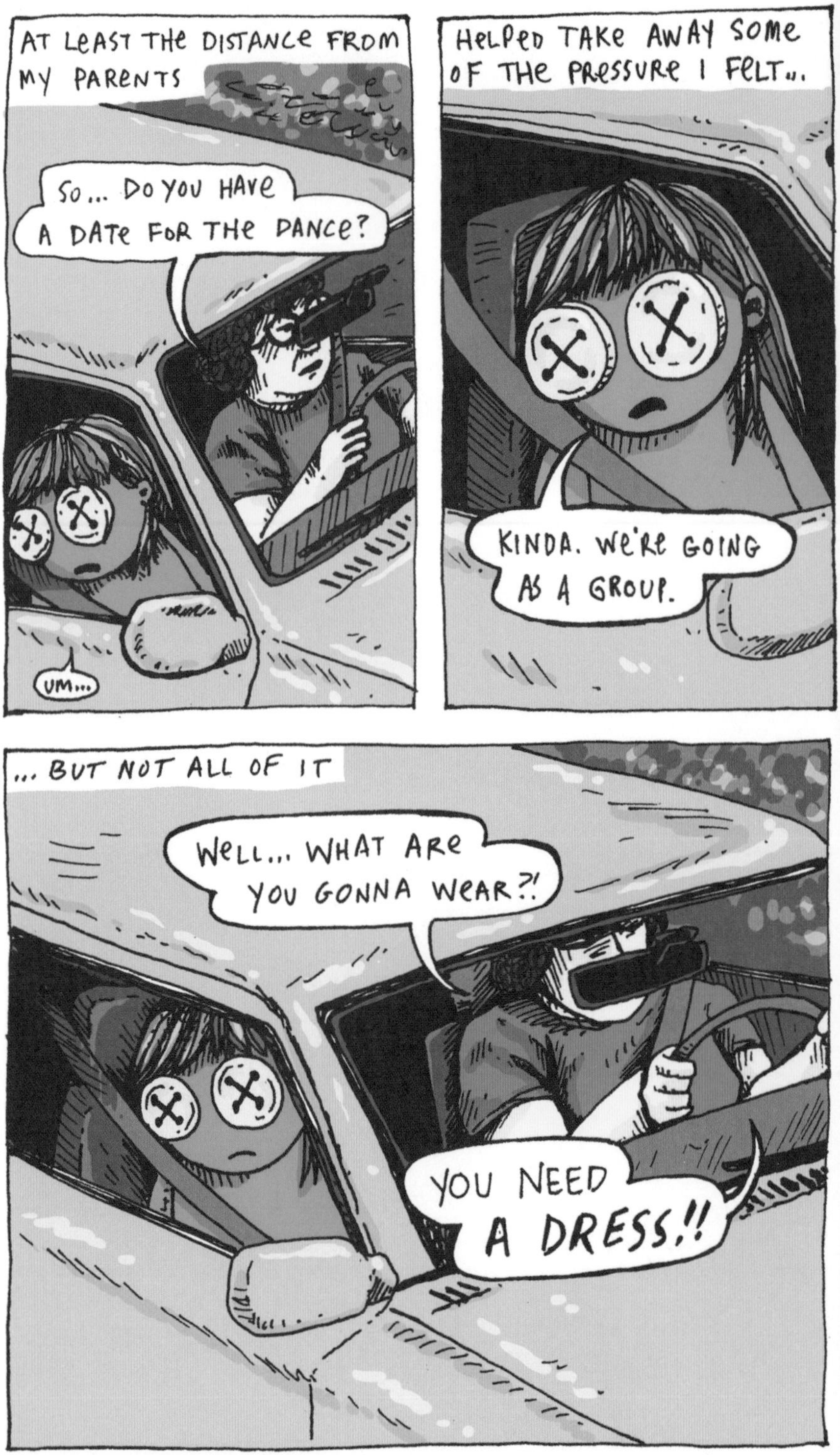
AT LEAST THE DISTANCE FROM MY PARENTS
SO... DO YOU HAVE A DATE FOR THE DANCE?
UM...
HELPED TAKE AWAY SOME OF THE PRESSURE I FELT...
KINDA. WE'RE GOING AS A GROUP.
... BUT NOT ALL OF IT
WELL... WHAT ARE YOU GONNA WEAR?!
YOU NEED A DRESS!!

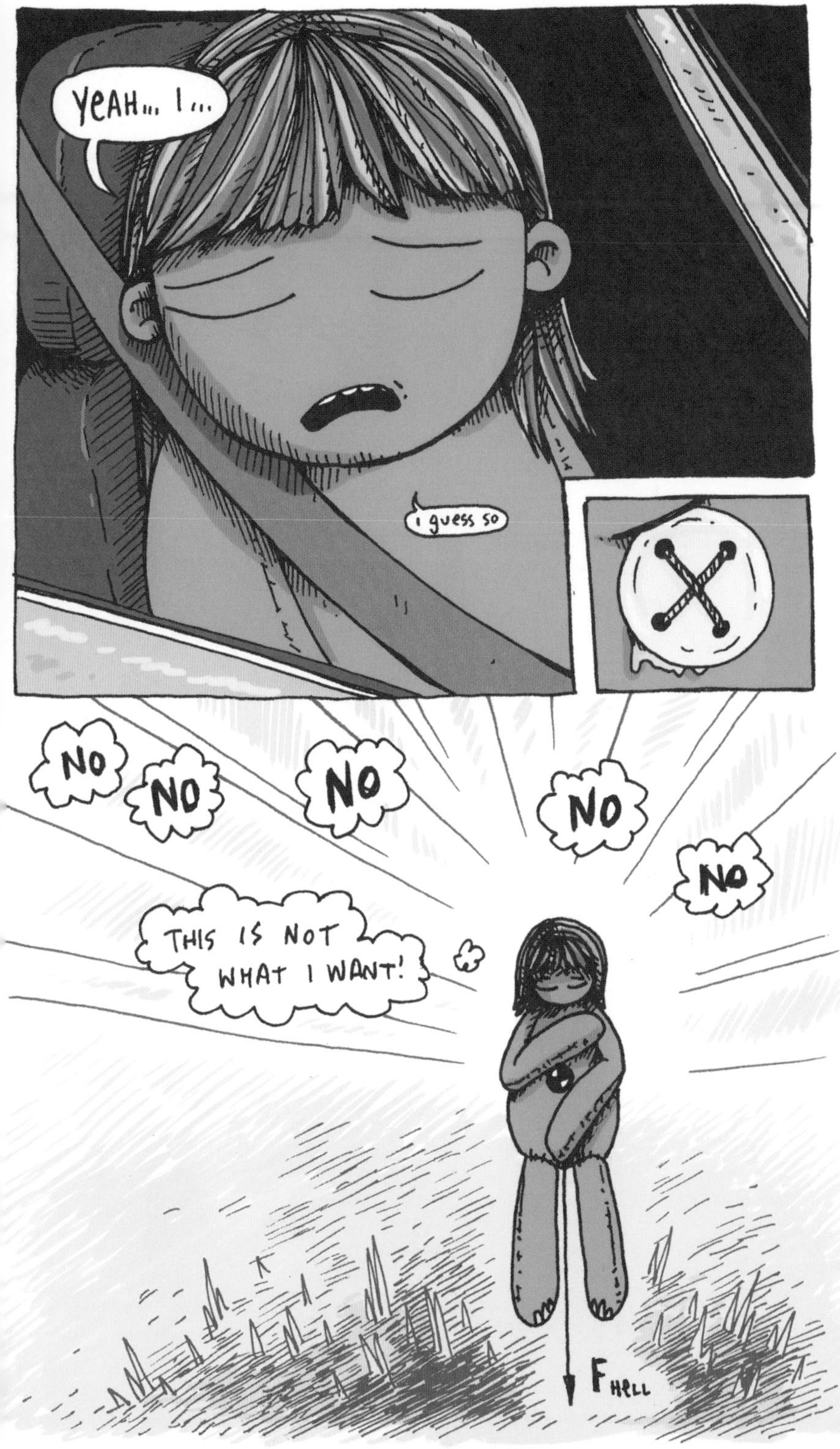
YEAH... I...
i guess so
NO
NO
NO
NO
NO
THIS IS NOT WHAT I WANT!
F HELL

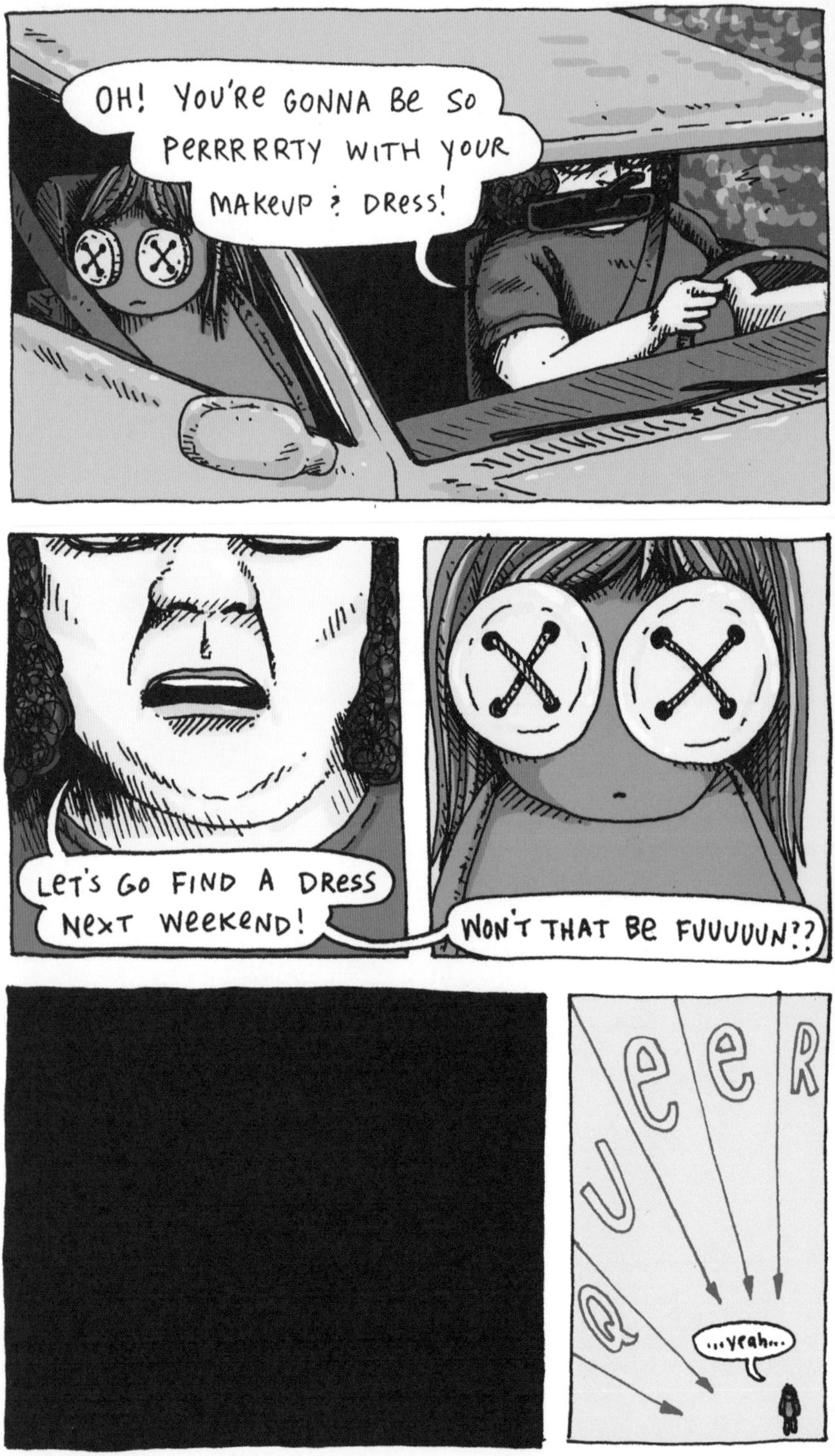
OH! YOU'RE GONNA BE SO PERRRRRTY WITH YOUR MAKEUP & DRESS!
LET'S GO FIND A DRESS NEXT WEEKEND!
WON'T THAT BE FUUUUUN??
QUEER
...yeah...

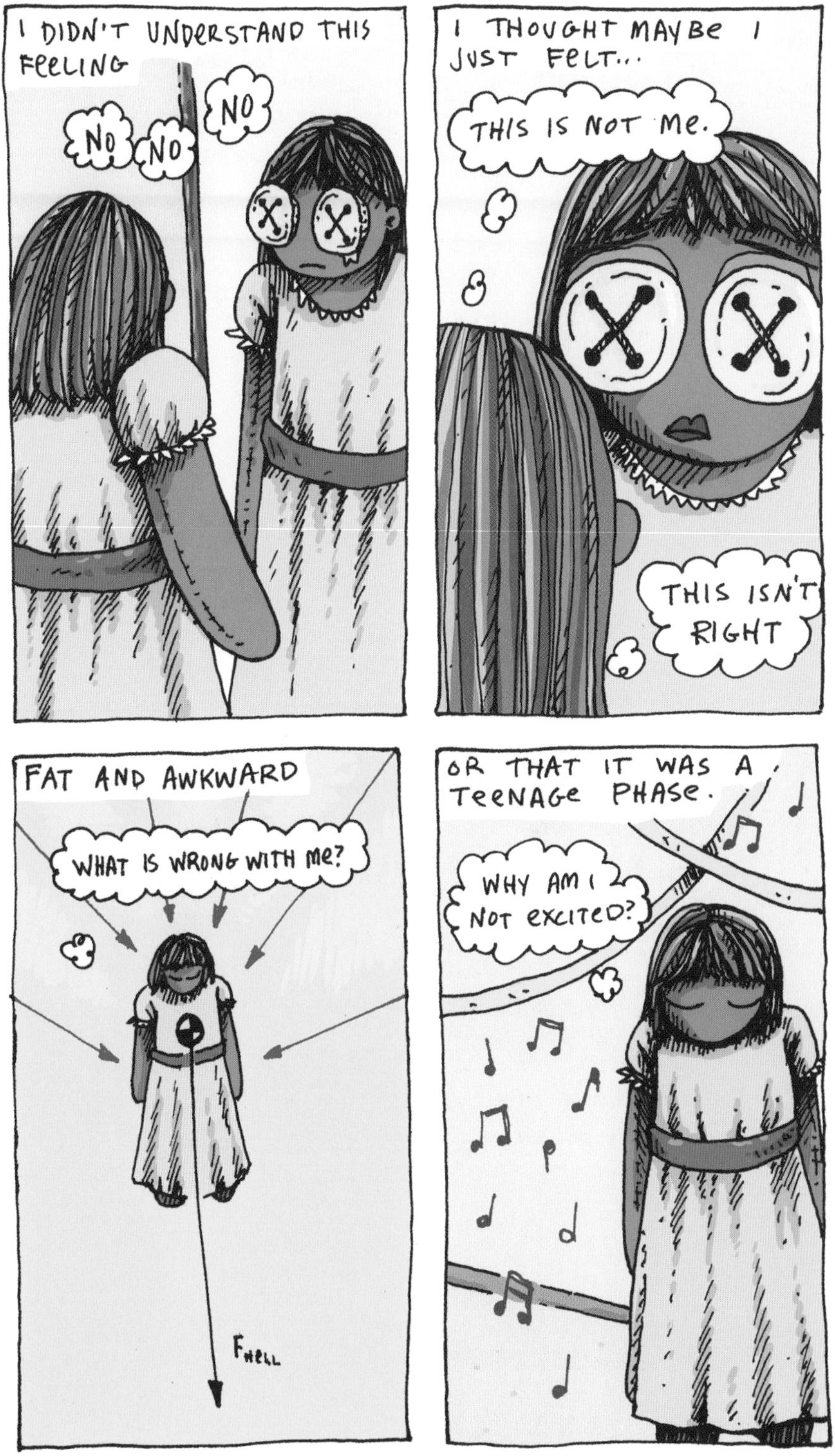
I DIDN'T UNDERSTAND THIS FEELING
NO
NO
NO
I THOUGHT MAYBE I JUST FELT...
THIS IS NOT ME.
THIS ISN'T RIGHT
FAT AND AWKWARD
WHAT IS WRONG WITH ME?
FWELL
OR THAT IT WAS A TEENAGE PHASE.
WHY AM I NOT EXCITED?

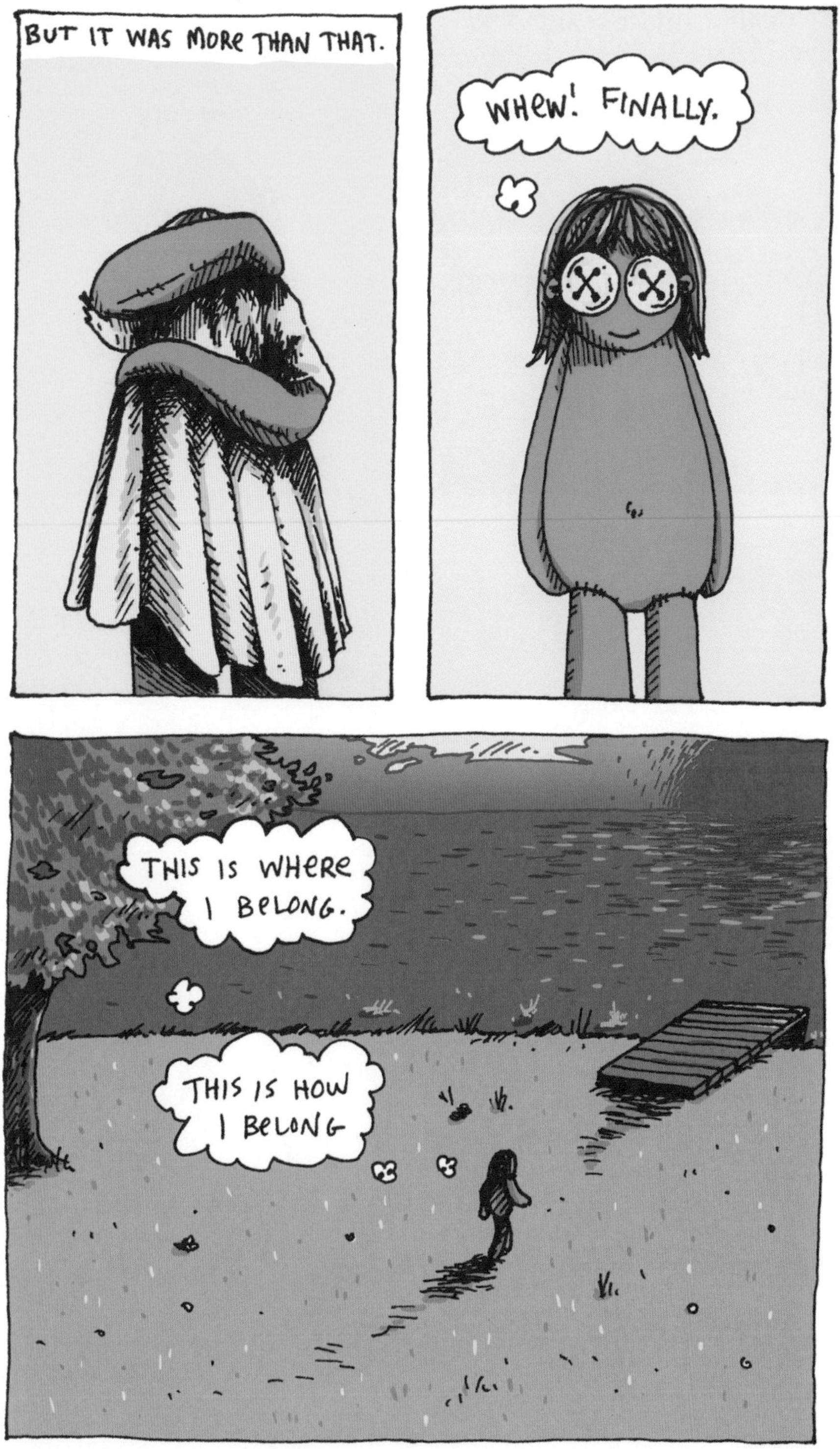
BUT IT WAS MORE THAN THAT.
WHEW! FINALLY.
THIS IS WHERE I BELONG.
THIS IS HOW I BELONG

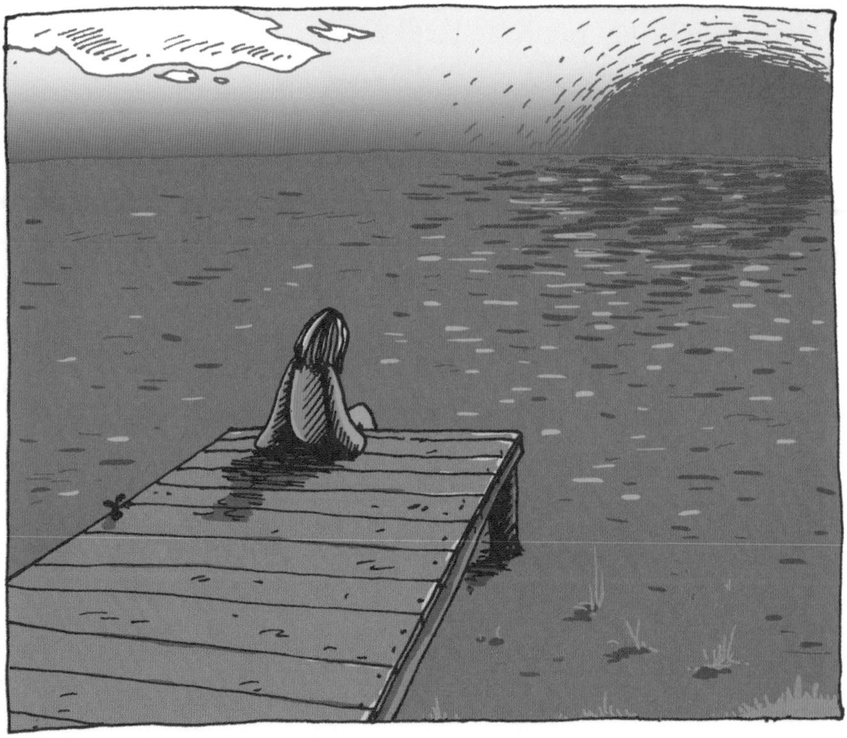

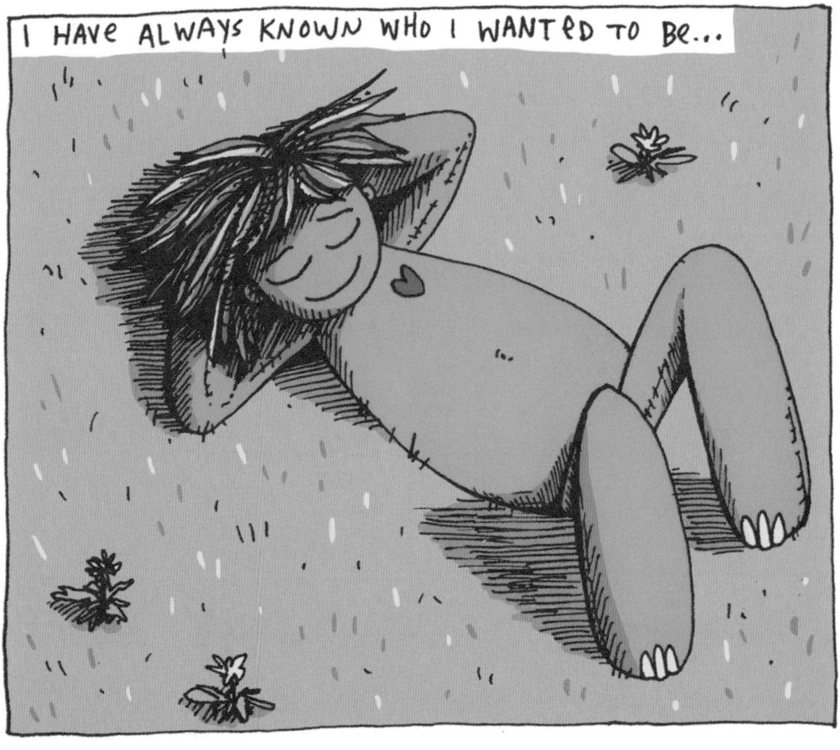
I HAVE ALWAYS KNOWN WHO I WANTED TO BE...

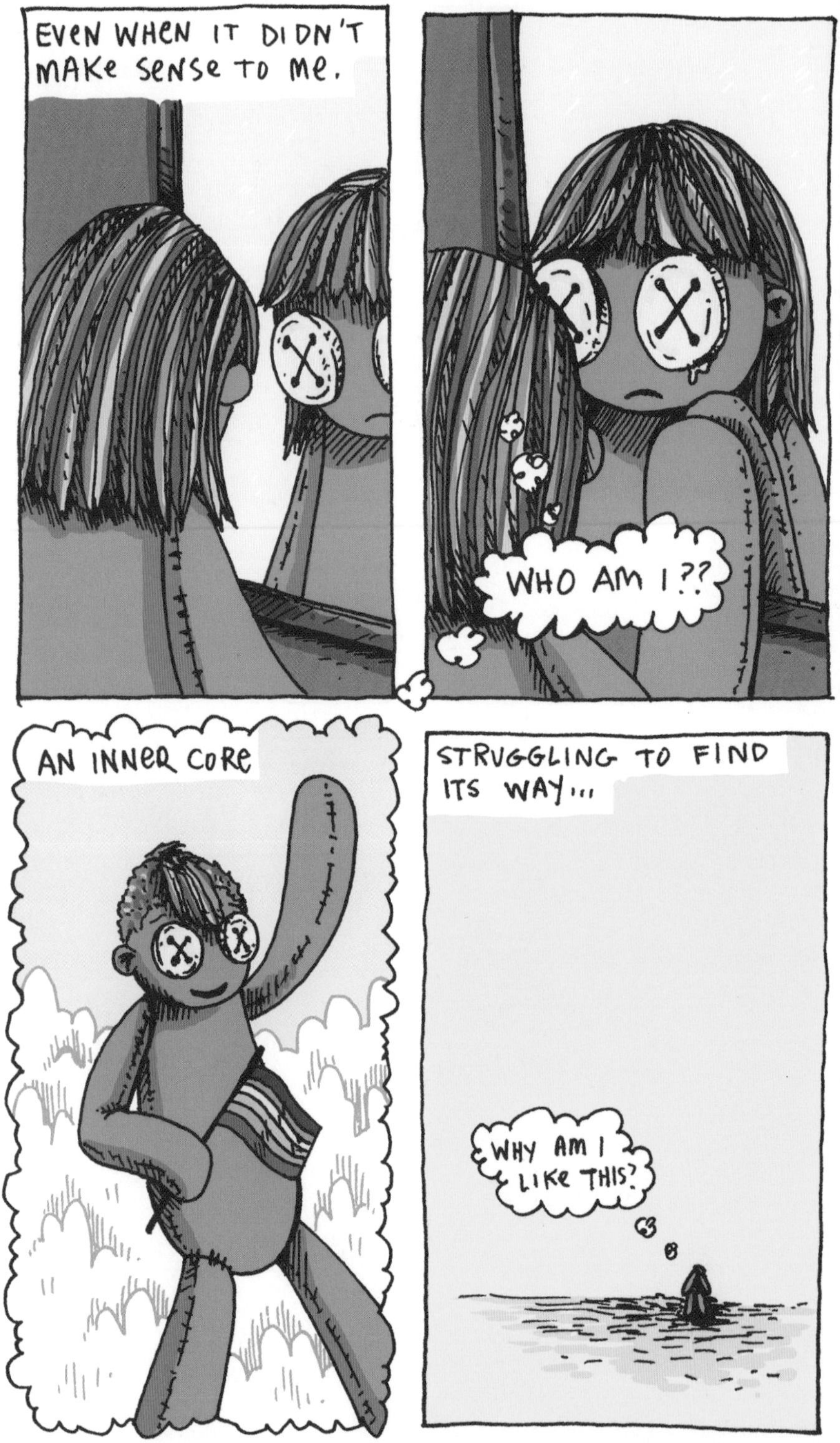
EVEN WHEN IT DIDN'T MAKE SENSE TO ME.
WHO AM I??
AN INNER CORE
STRUGGLING TO FIND ITS WAY...
WHY AM I LIKE THIS?

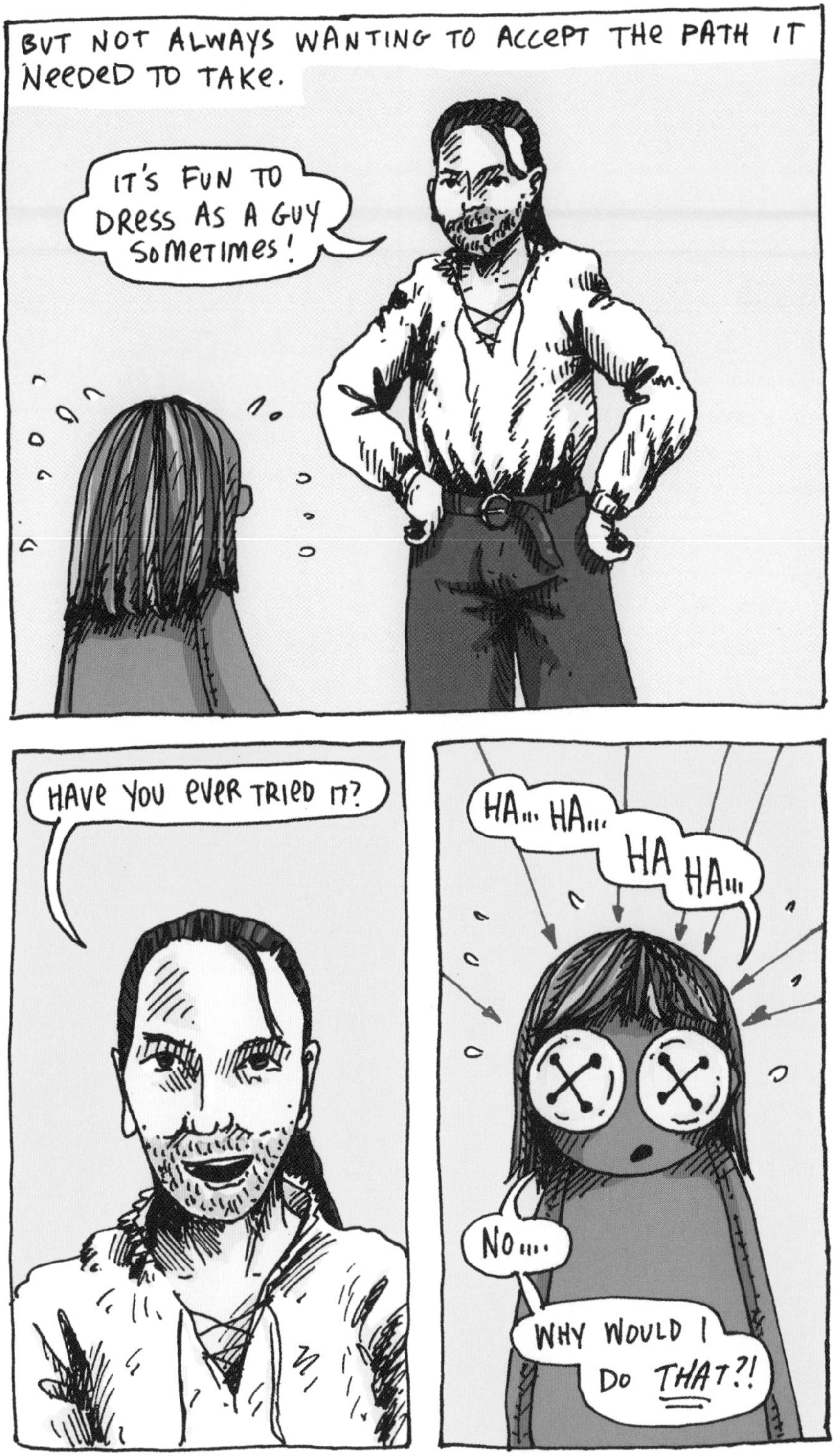
BUT NOT ALWAYS WANTING TO ACCEPT THE PATH IT NEEDED TO TAKE.
IT'S FUN TO DRESS AS A GUY SOMETIMES!
HAVE YOU EVER TRIED IT?
HA... HA... HA HA...
NO....
WHY WOULD I DO THAT?!

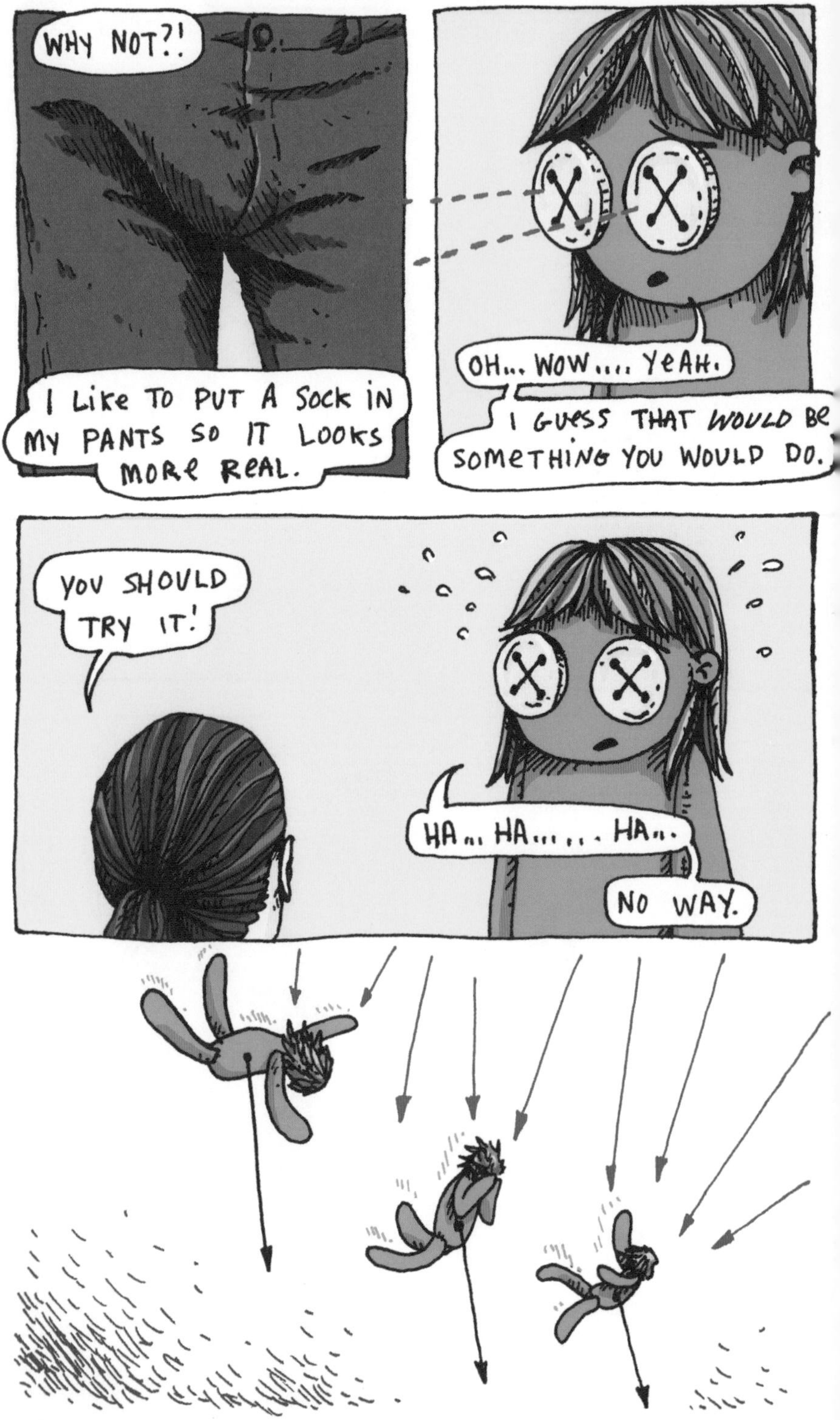
WHY NOT?!
I LIKE TO PUT A SOCK IN MY PANTS SO IT LOOKS MORE REAL.
OH... WOW.... YEAH.
I GUESS THAT WOULD BE SOMETHING YOU WOULD DO.
YOU SHOULD TRY IT!
HA... HA...... HA...
NO WAY.

THERE IT WAS AGAIN, THAT FEELING I DIDN'T UNDERSTAND

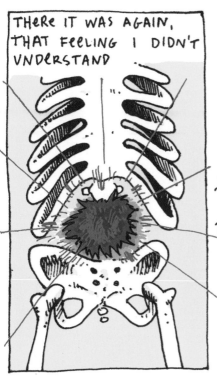

NOT KNOWING WHAT FELT WRONG

AND ALSO KNOWING THAT EVERYTHING WAS WRONG.

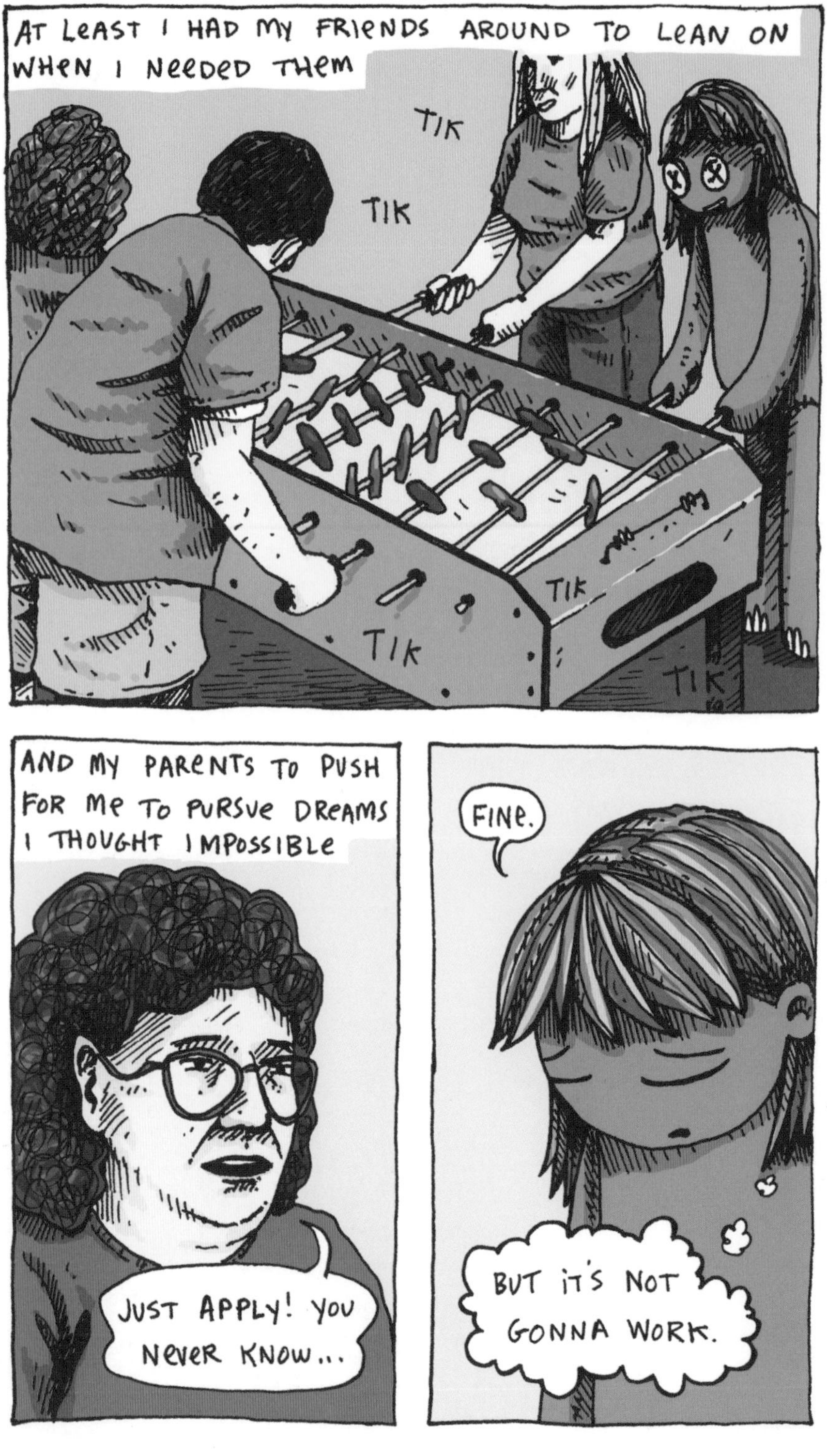
AT LEAST I HAD MY FRIENDS AROUND TO LEAN ON WHEN I NEEDED THEM
TIK
TIK
TIK
TIK
TIK
AND MY PARENTS TO PUSH FOR ME TO PURSUE DREAMS I THOUGHT IMPOSSIBLE
JUST APPLY! YOU NEVER KNOW...
FINE.
BUT IT'S NOT GONNA WORK.

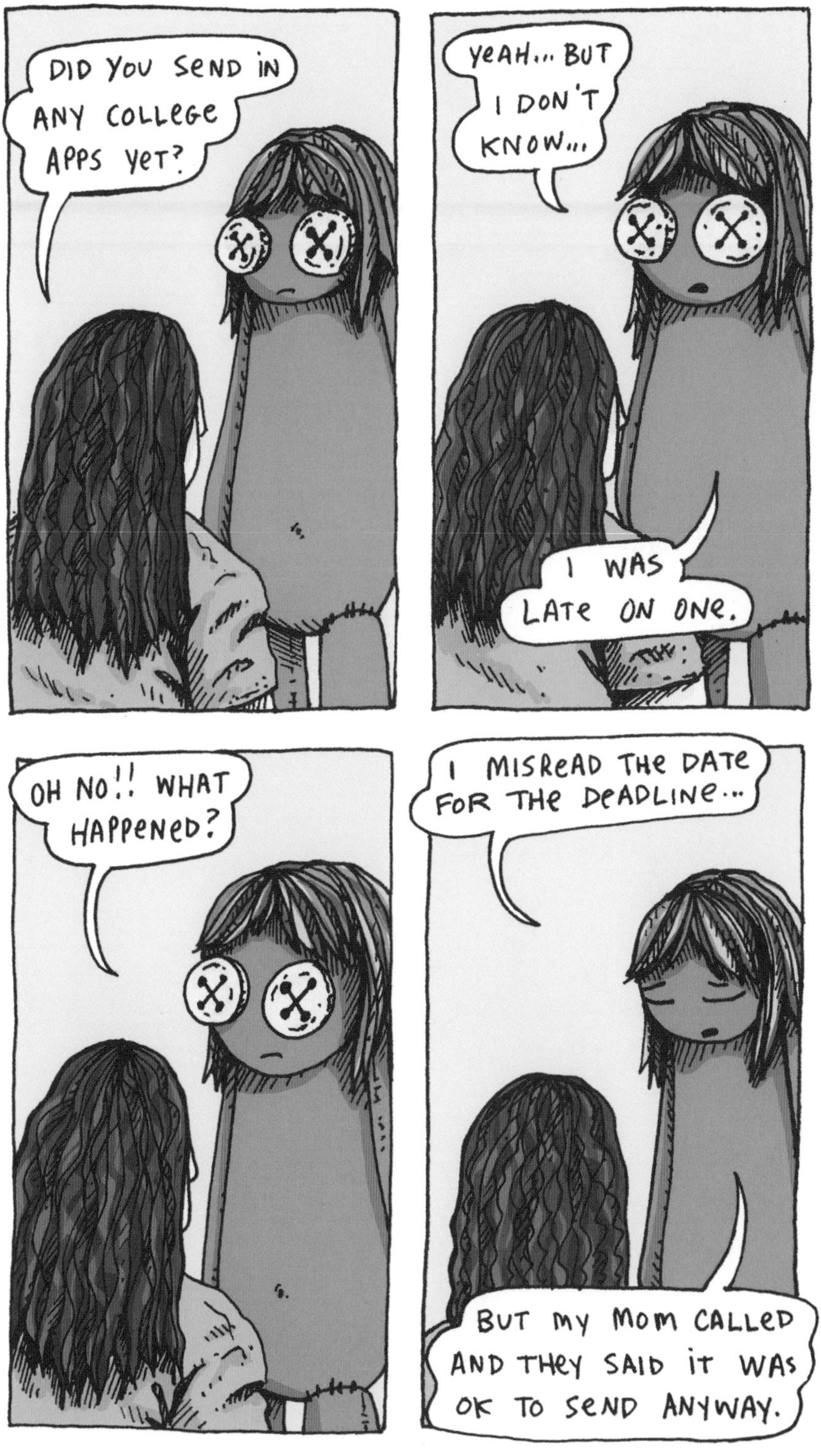
DID YOU SEND IN ANY COLLEGE APPS YET?
YEAH... BUT I DON'T KNOW...
I WAS LATE ON ONE.
OH NO!! WHAT HAPPENED?
I MISREAD THE DATE FOR THE DEADLINE...
BUT MY MOM CALLED AND THEY SAID IT WAS OK TO SEND ANYWAY.

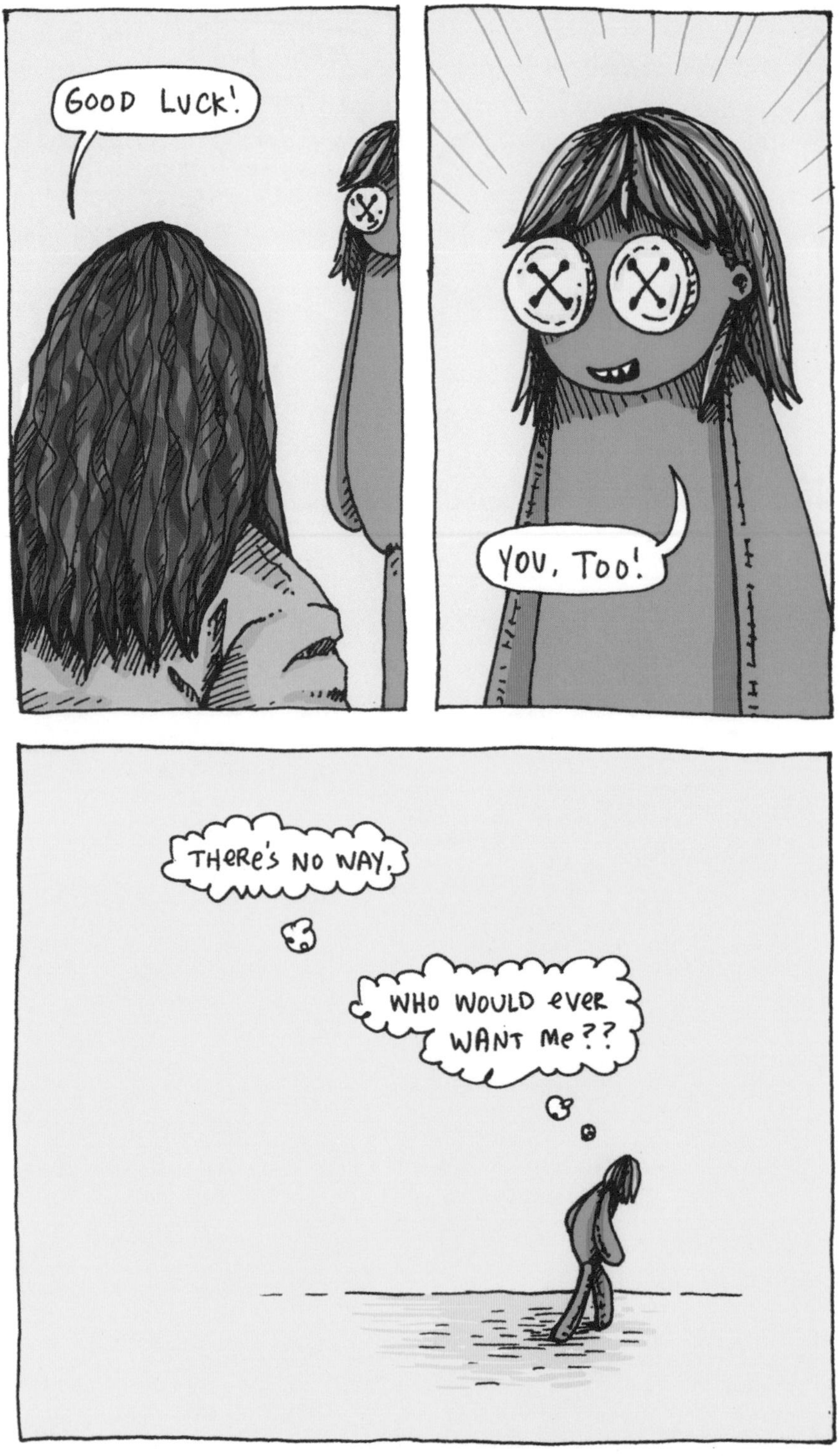
GOOD LUCK!
YOU, TOO!
THERE'S NO WAY.
WHO WOULD EVER WANT ME??

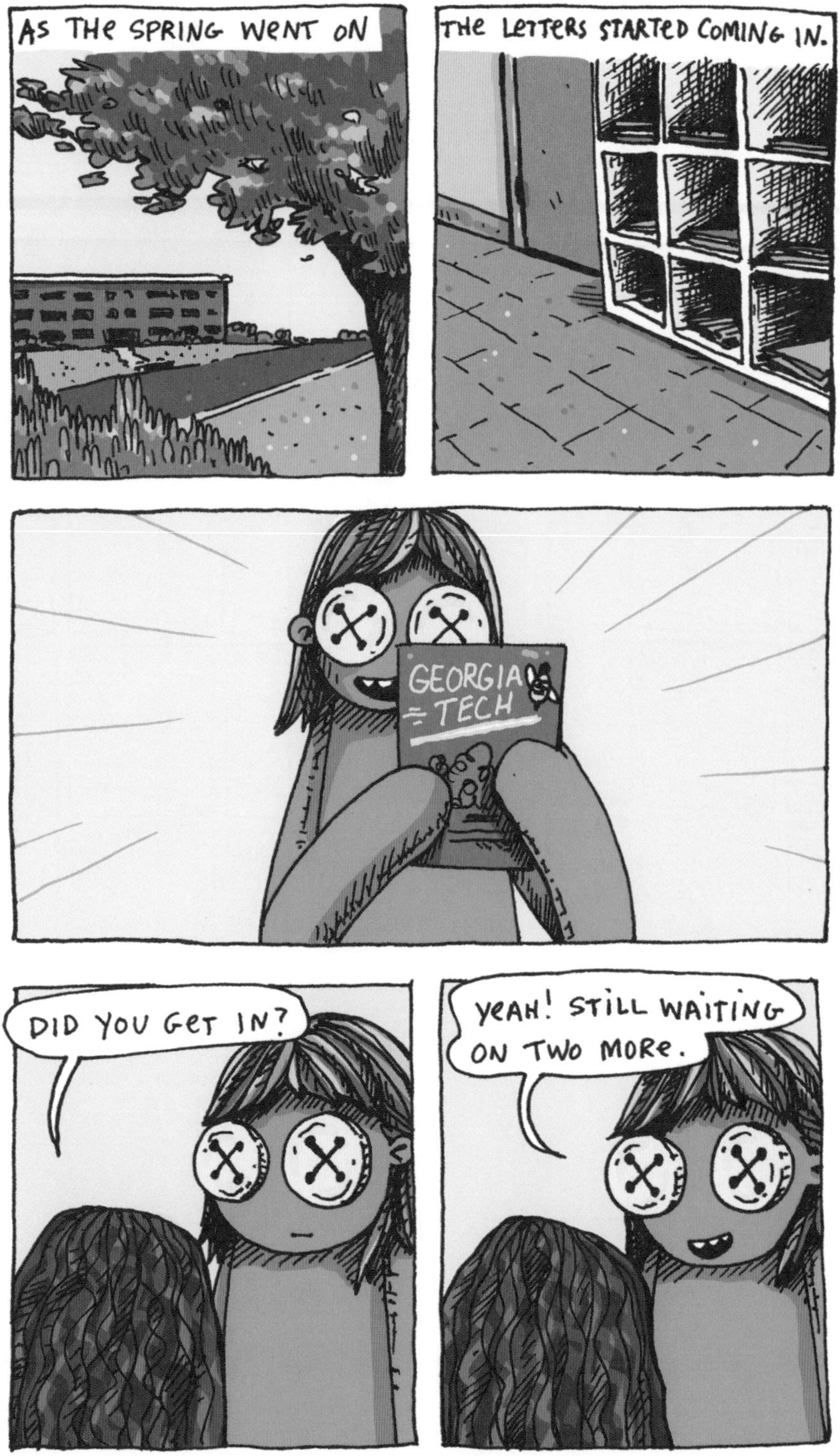
AS THE SPRING WENT ON
THE LETTERS STARTED COMING IN.
GEORGIA TECH
DID YOU GET IN?
YEAH! STILL WAITING ON TWO MORE.

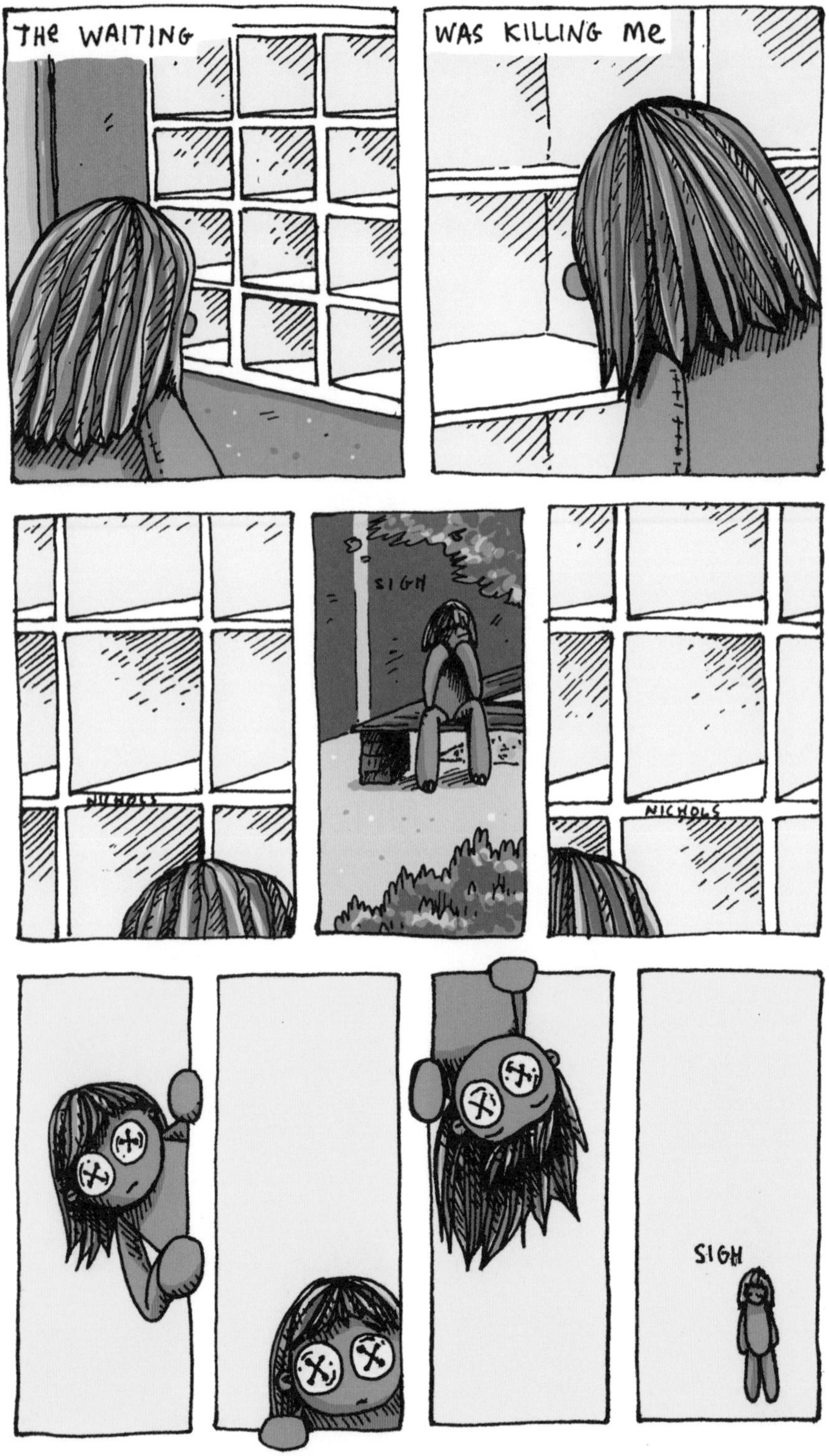
THE WAITING
WAS KILLING ME
NICHOLS
SIGH
NICHOLS
SIGH

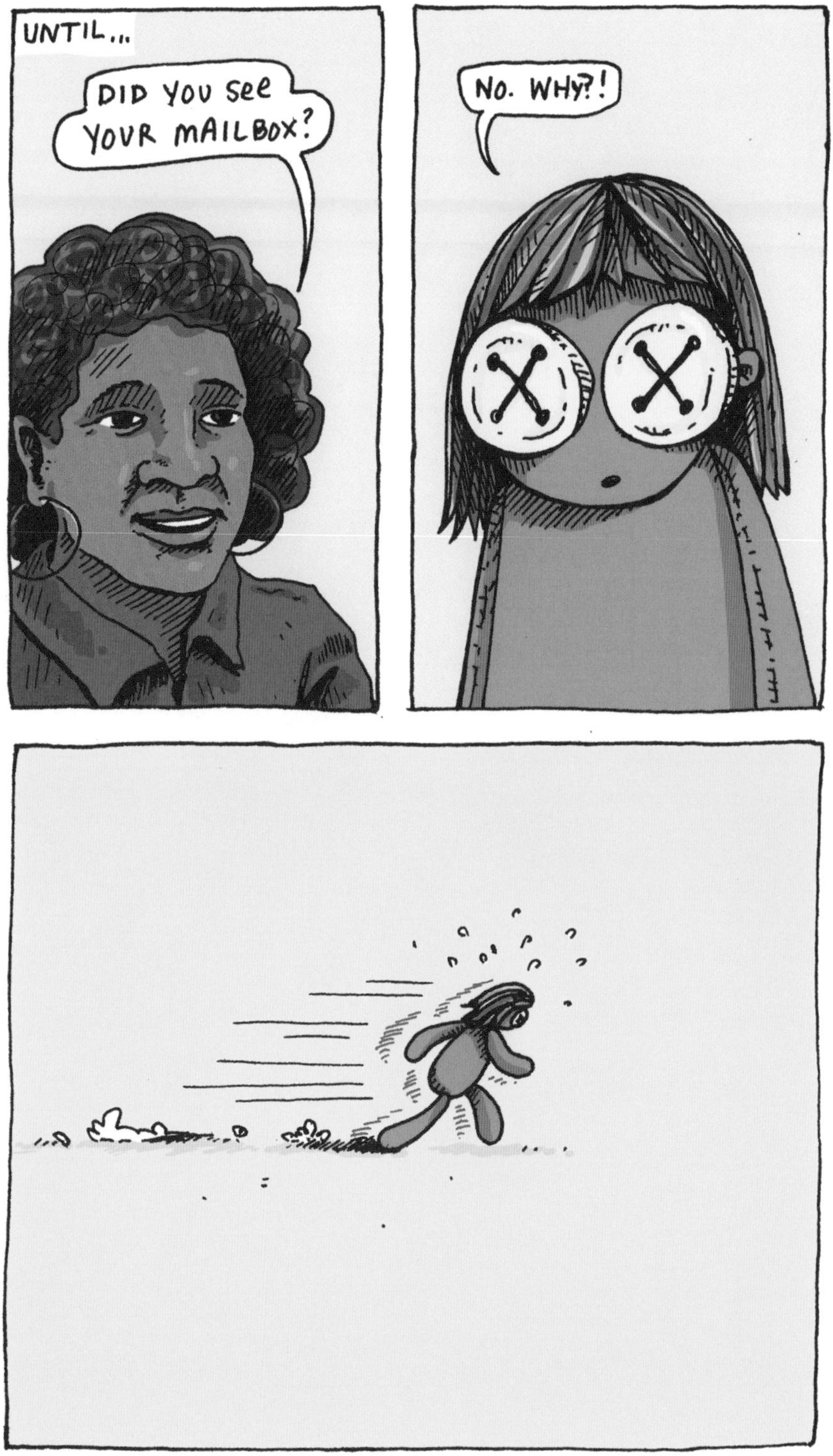
UNTIL...
DID YOU SEE YOUR MAILBOX?
NO. WHY?!

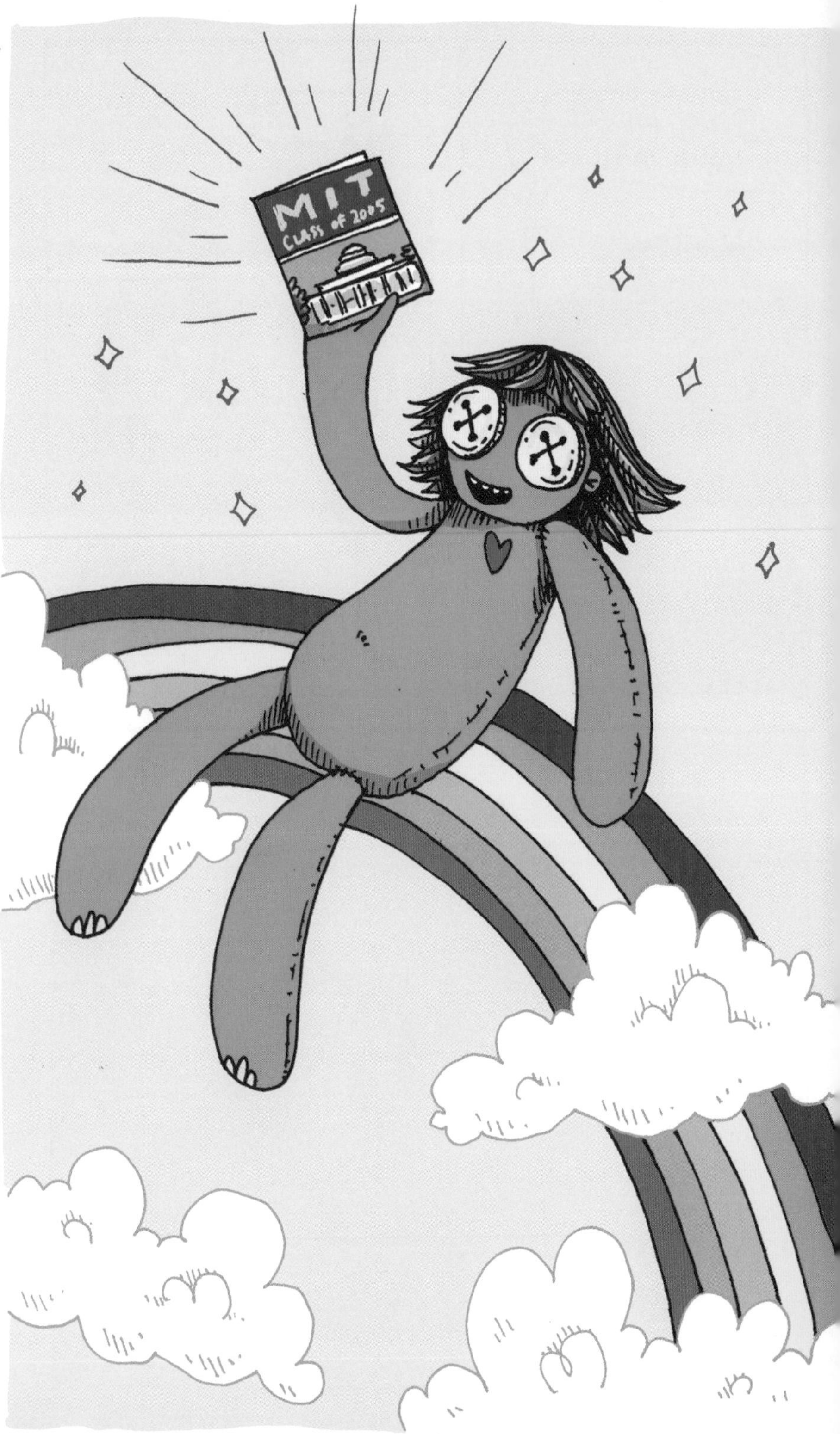
MIT
CLASS OF 2005

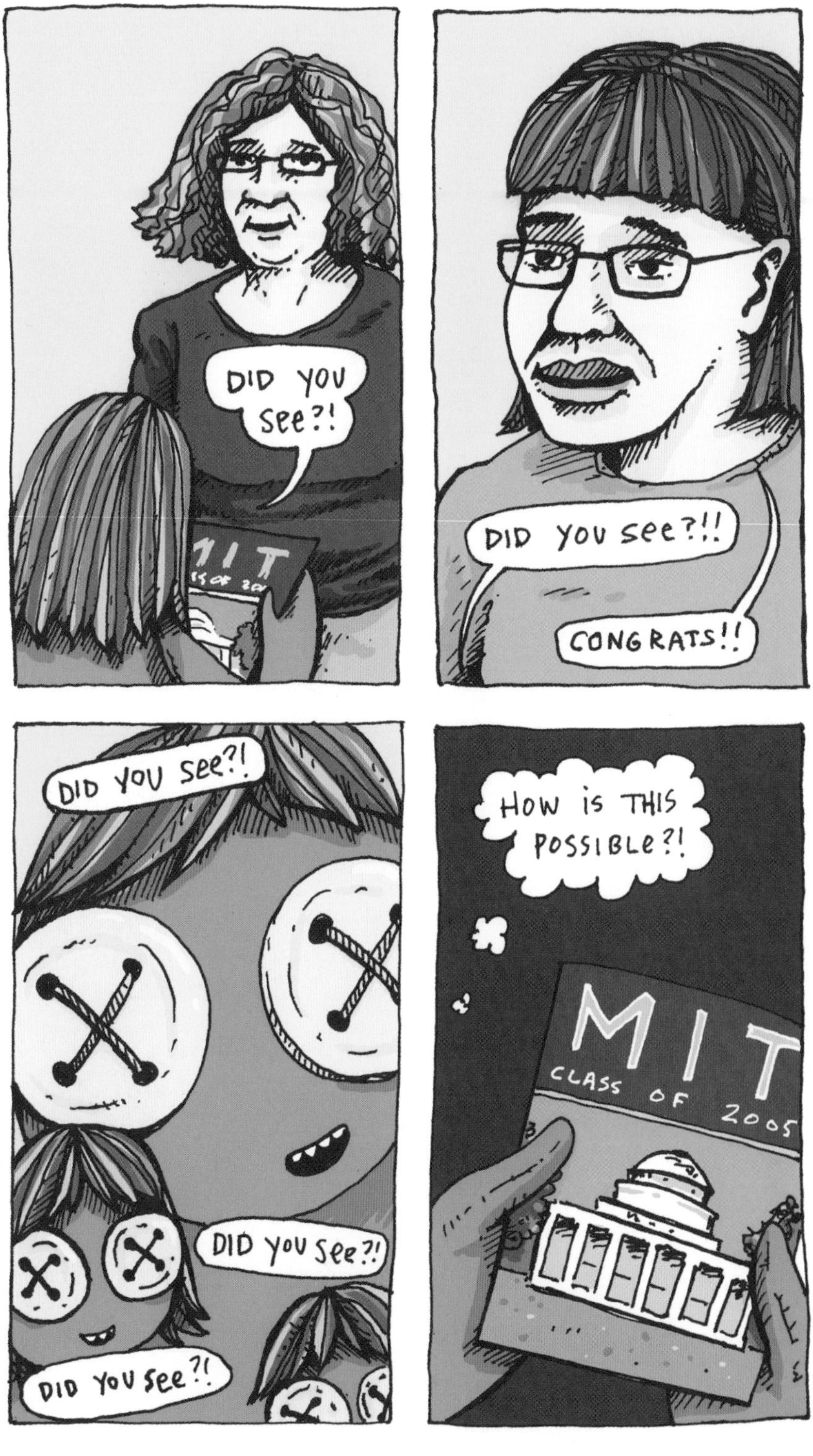
DID YOU SEE?!
MIT
DID YOU SEE?!!
CONGRATS!!
DID YOU SEE?!
DID YOU SEE?!
DID YOU SEE?!
HOW IS THIS POSSIBLE?!
MIT
CLASS OF 2005

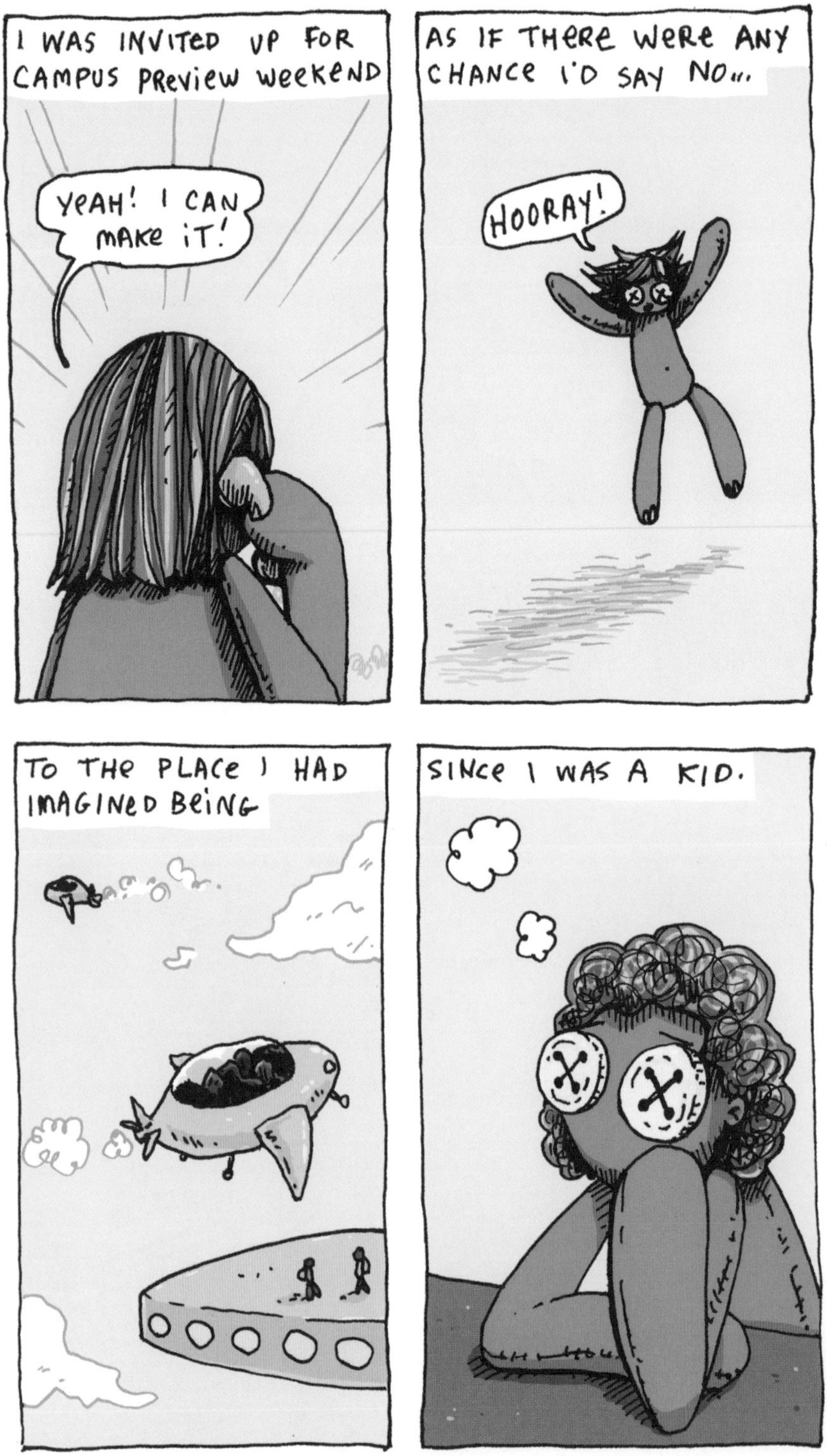
I WAS INVITED UP FOR CAMPUS PREVIEW WEEKEND
YEAH! I CAN MAKE IT!
AS IF THERE WERE ANY CHANCE I'D SAY NO...
HOORAY!
TO THE PLACE I HAD IMAGINED BEING
SINCE I WAS A KID.

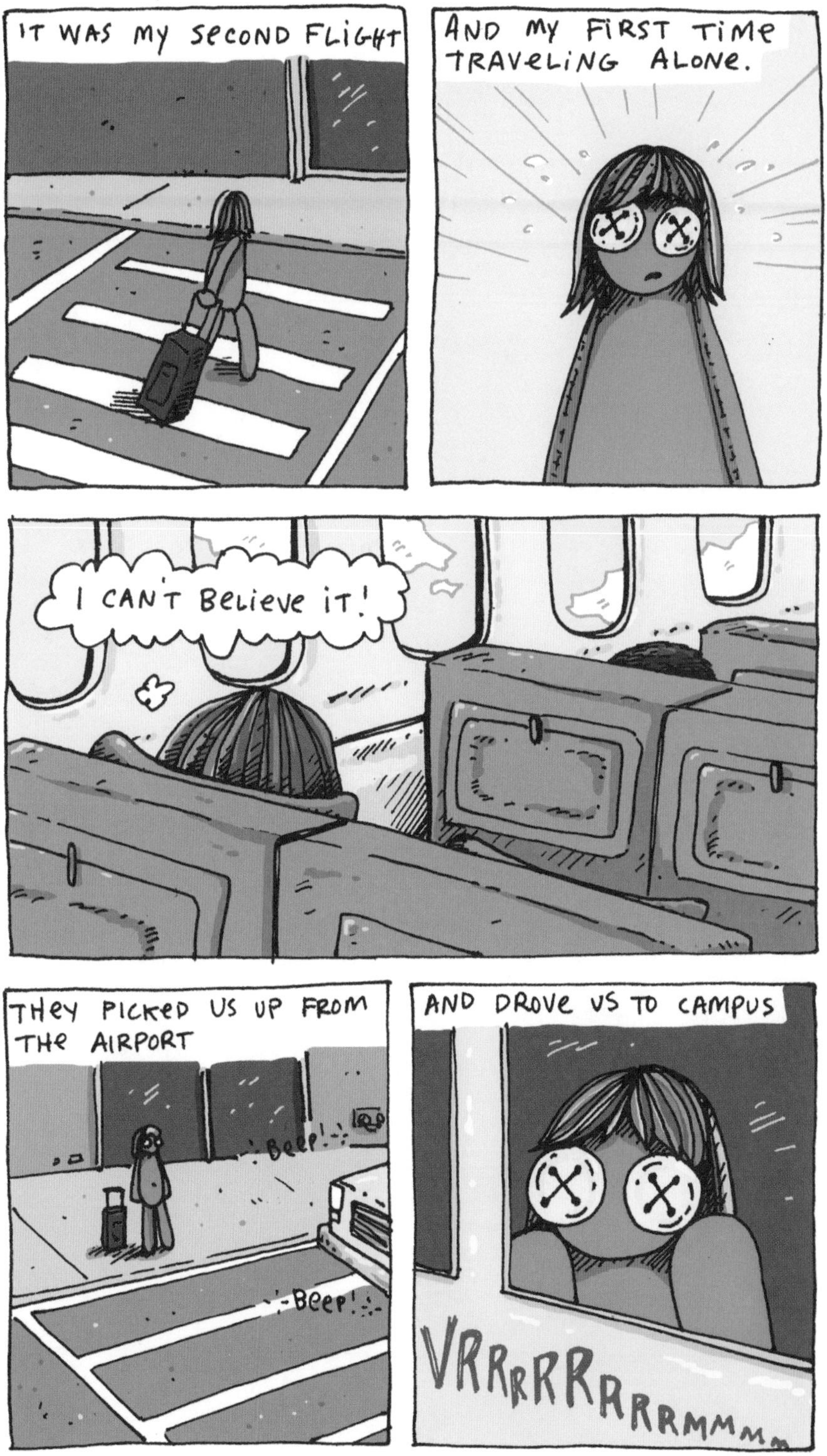
IT WAS MY SECOND FLIGHT
AND MY FIRST TIME TRAVELING ALONE.
I CAN'T BELIEVE IT!
THEY PICKED US UP FROM THE AIRPORT
BEEP!
BEEP!
AND DROVE US TO CAMPUS
VRRRRRRRRRMMMMM

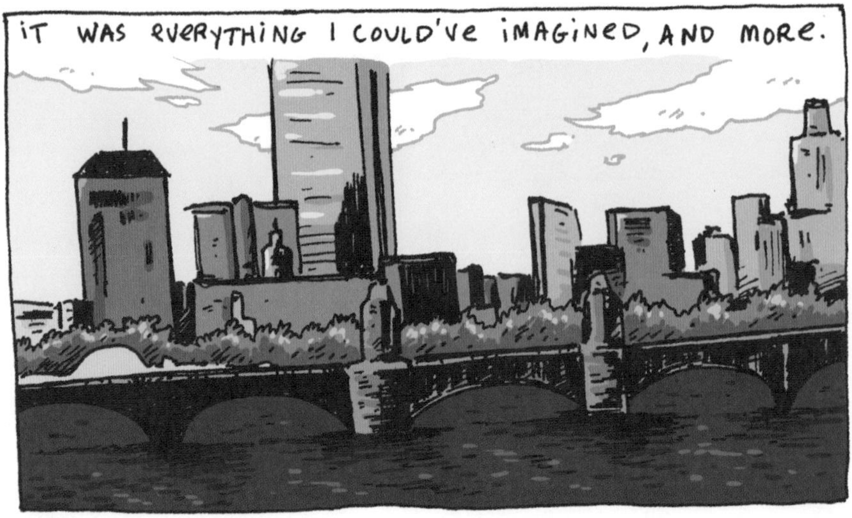
IT WAS EVERYTHING I COULD'VE IMAGINED, AND MORE.

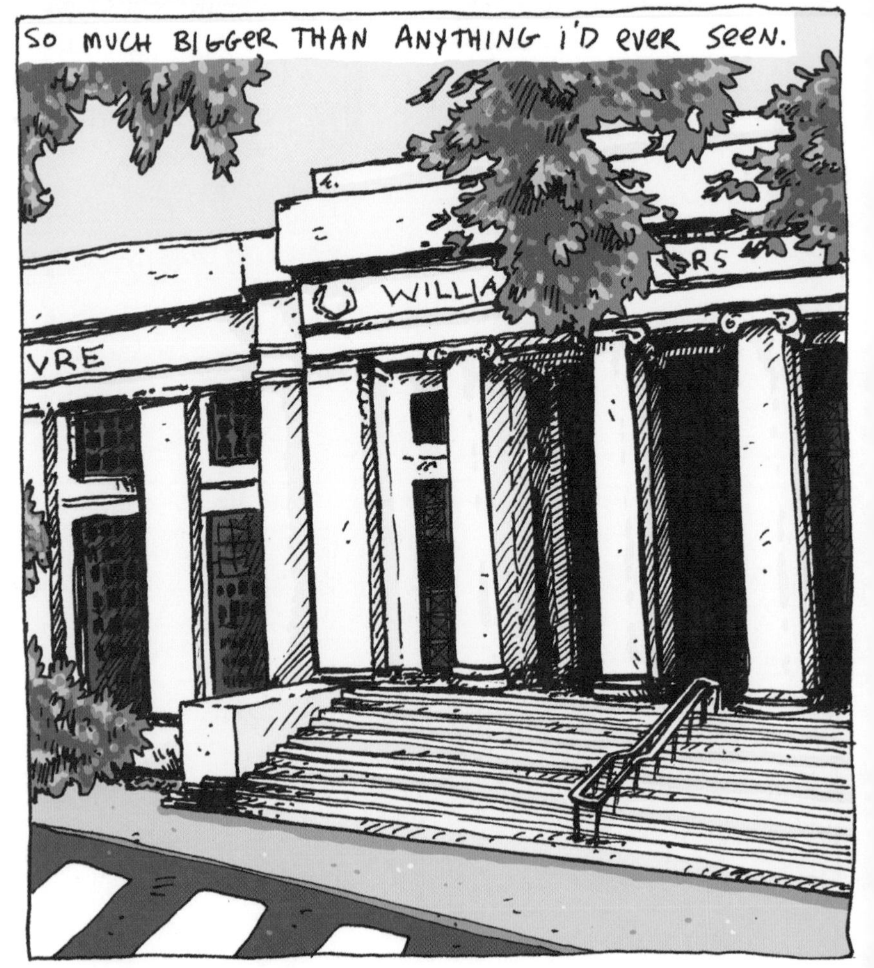
SO MUCH BIGGER THAN ANYTHING I'D EVER SEEN.
WILLIA
RS
VRE

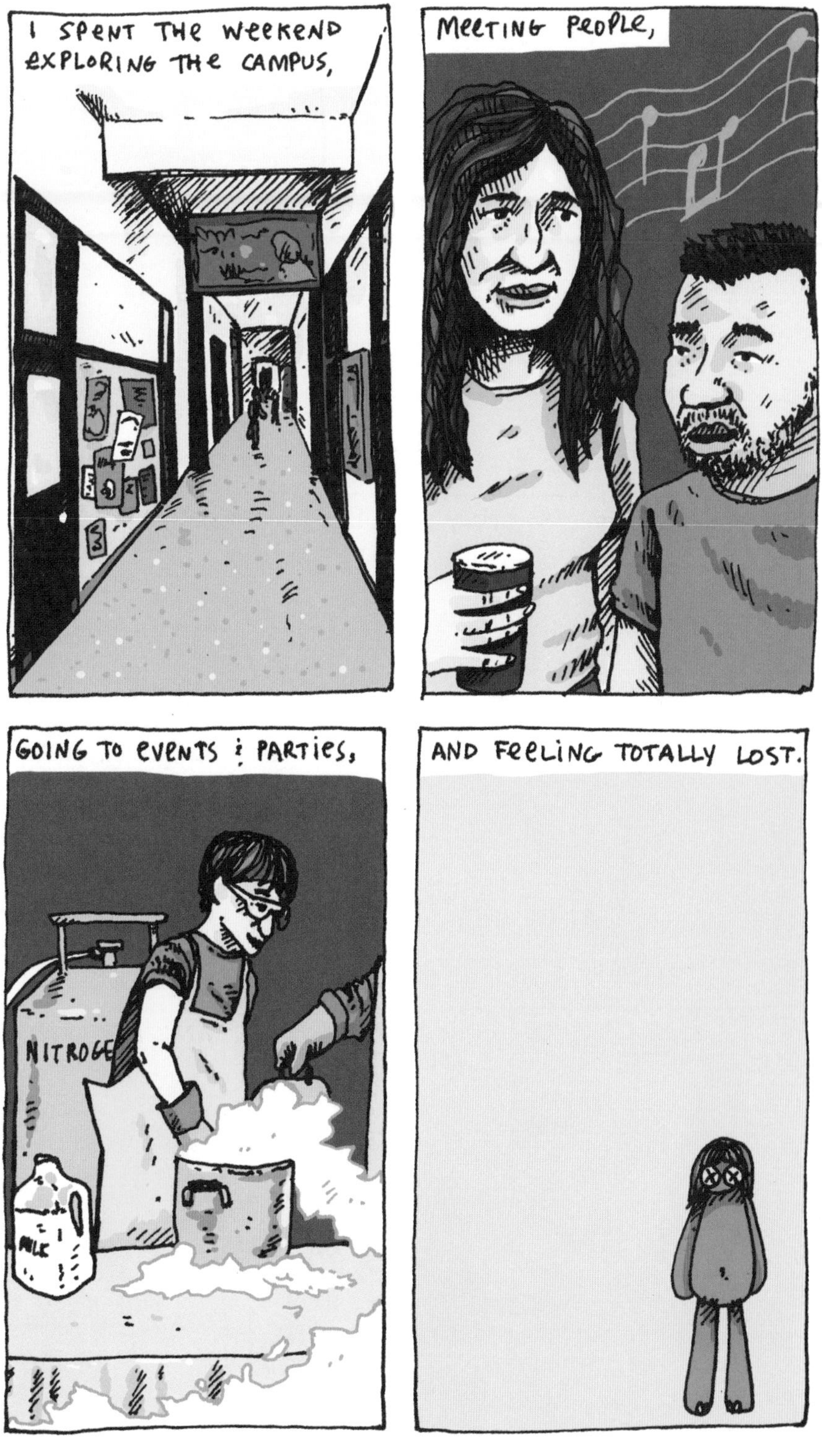
I SPENT THE WEEKEND EXPLORING THE CAMPUS,
MEETING PEOPLE,
GOING TO EVENTS & PARTIES,
NITROGE
MILK
AND FEELING TOTALLY LOST.

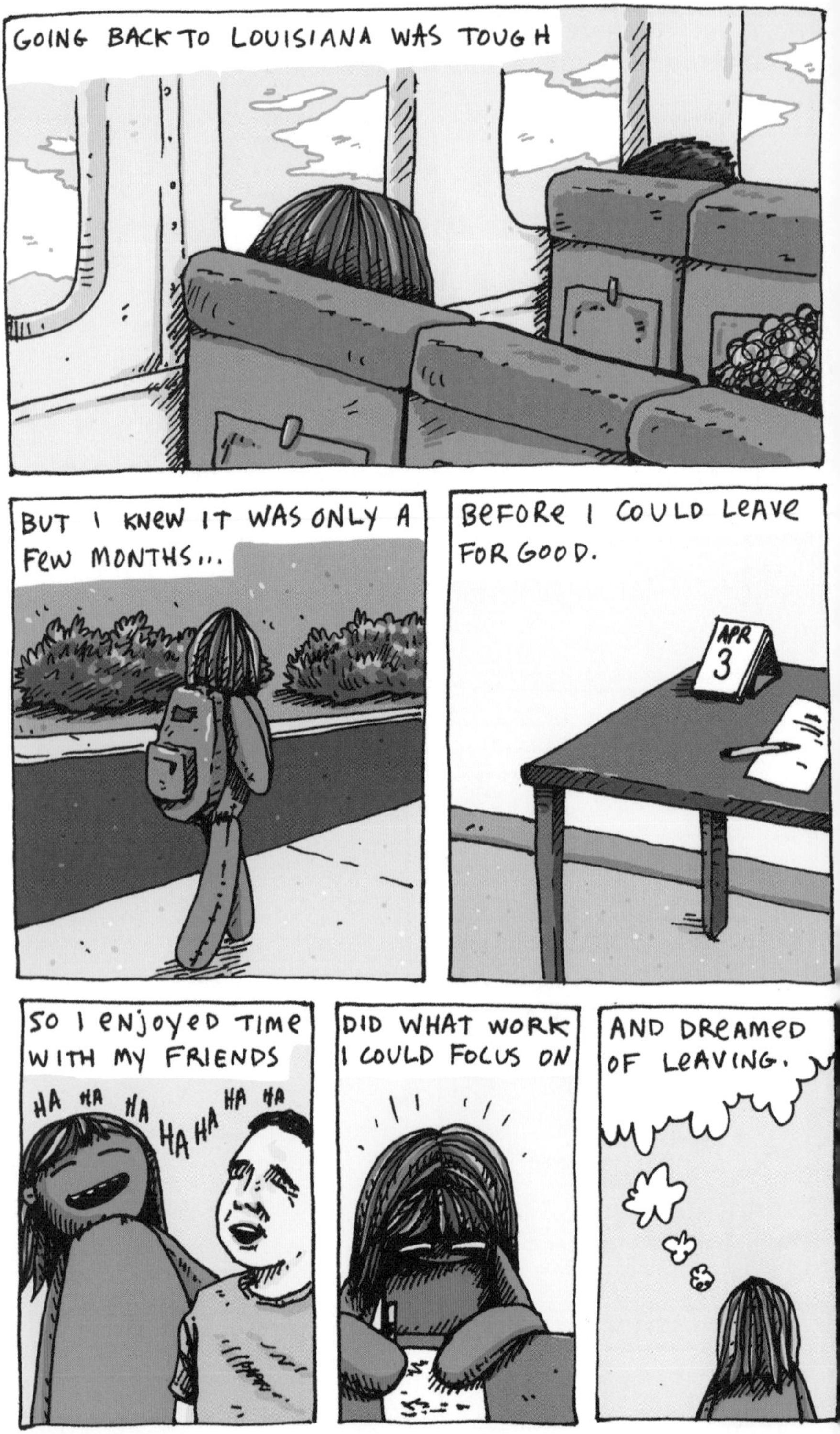
GOING BACK TO LOUISIANA WAS TOUGH
BUT I KNEW IT WAS ONLY A FEW MONTHS...
BEFORE I COULD LEAVE FOR GOOD.
APR 3
SO I ENJOYED TIME WITH MY FRIENDS
HA HA HA HA HA HA HA
DID WHAT WORK I COULD FOCUS ON
AND DREAMED OF LEAVING.

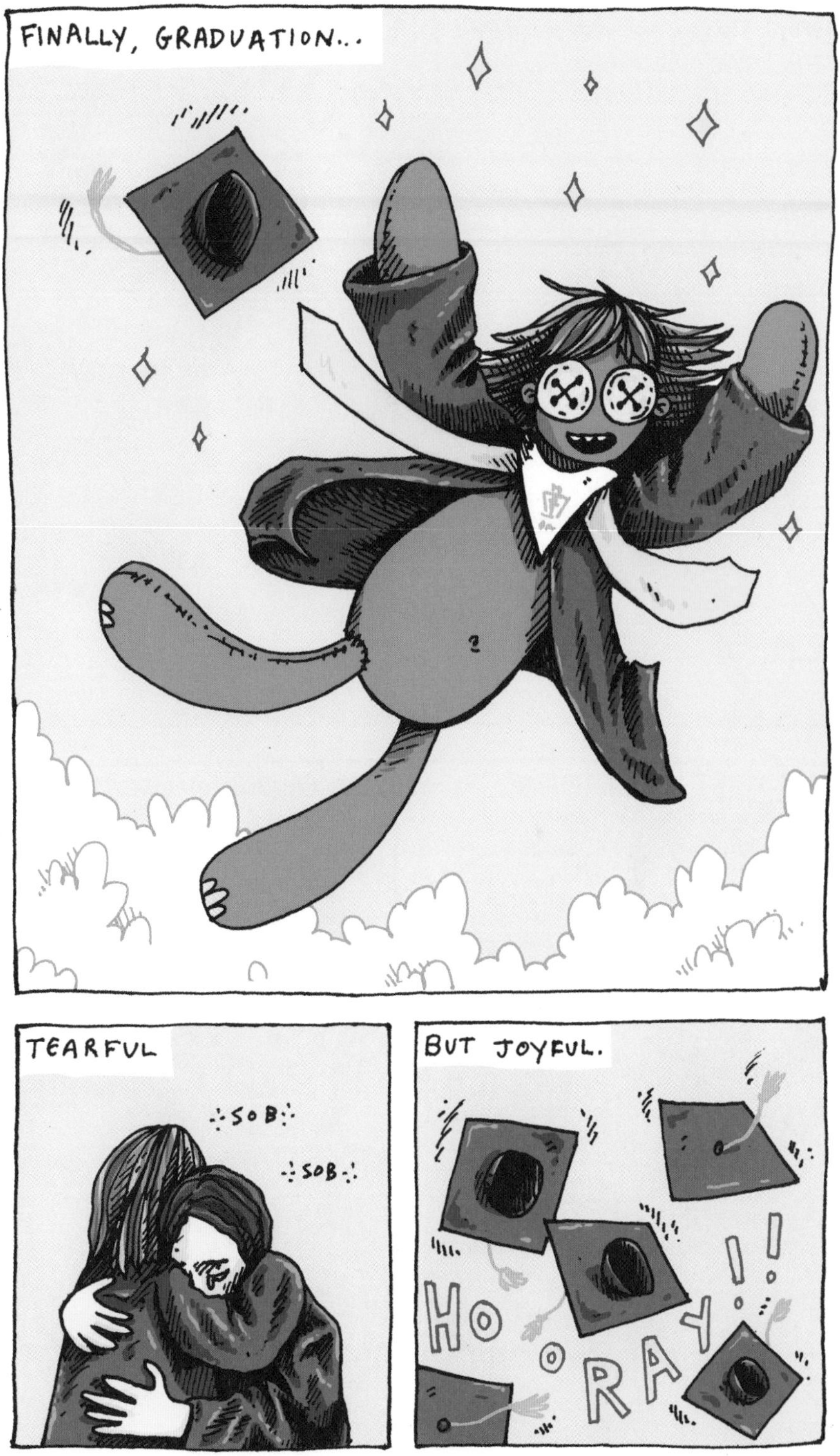
FINALLY, GRADUATION...
TEARFUL
SOB
SOB
BUT JOYFUL.
HOORAY!!

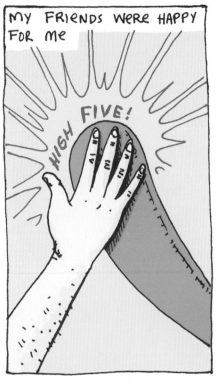

MY FRIENDS WERE HAPPY FOR ME

HIGH FIVE!

CONGRATS!

SO WERE MY FAMILY

GOOD JOB!

AND CHURCH MEMBERS.

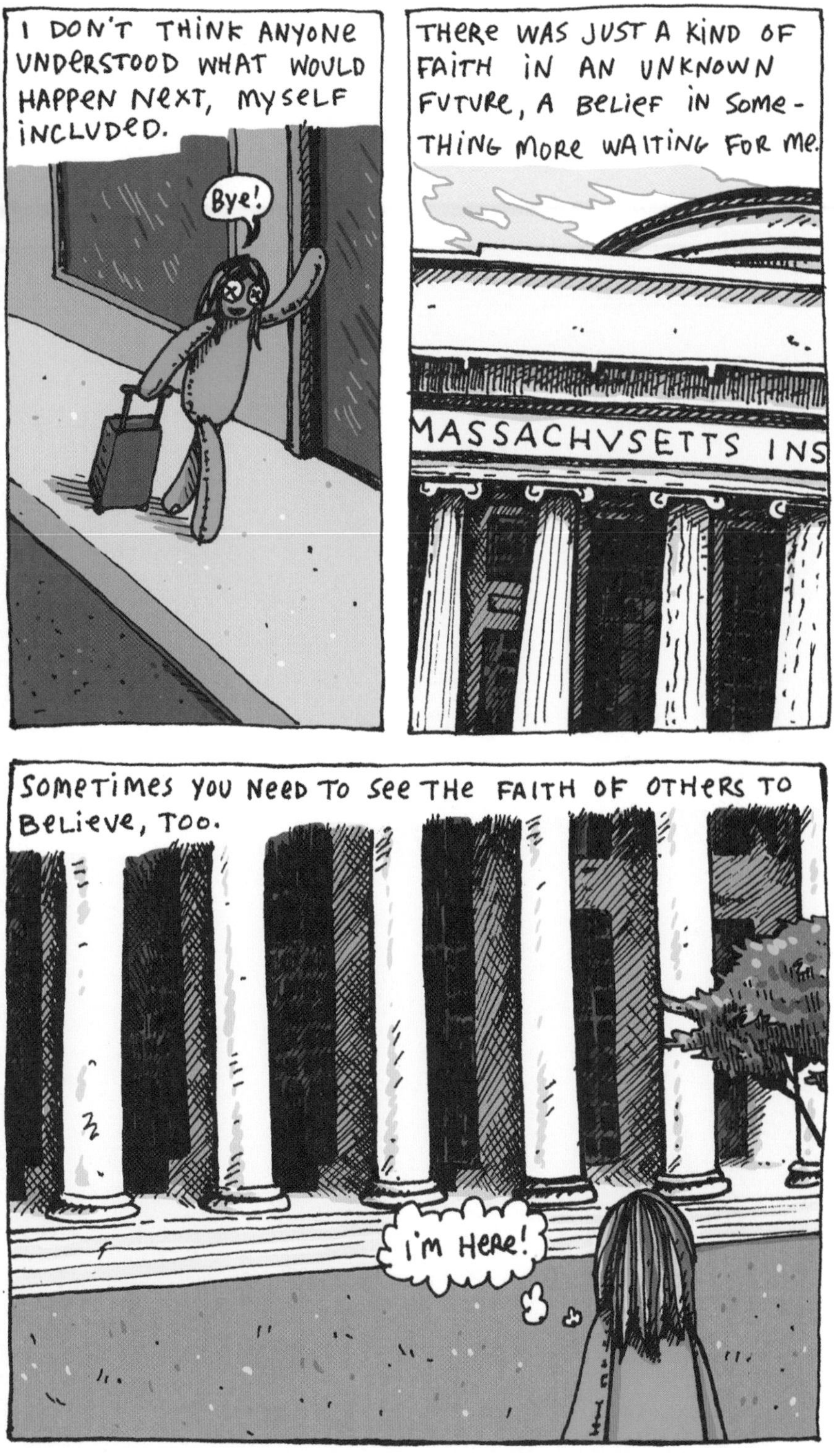
I DON'T THINK ANYONE UNDERSTOOD WHAT WOULD HAPPEN NEXT, MYSELF INCLUDED.
Bye!
THERE WAS JUST A KIND OF FAITH IN AN UNKNOWN FUTURE, A BELIEF IN SOME-THING MORE WAITING FOR ME.
MASSACHUSETTS INS
SOMETIMES YOU NEED TO SEE THE FAITH OF OTHERS TO BELIEVE, TOO.
I'M HERE!

CHAPTER SEVEN

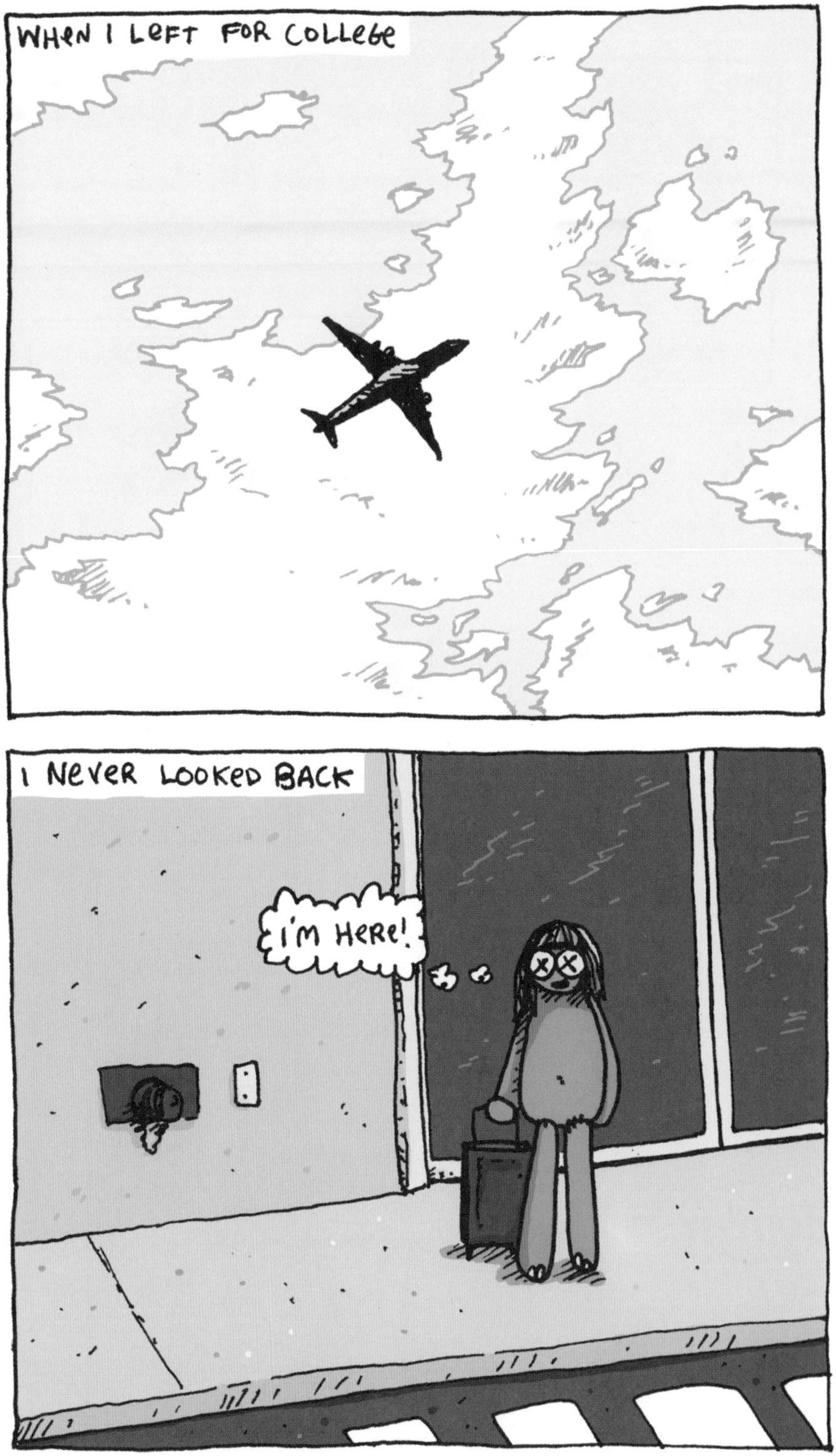
WHEN I LEFT FOR COLLEGE
I NEVER LOOKED BACK
I'M HERE!

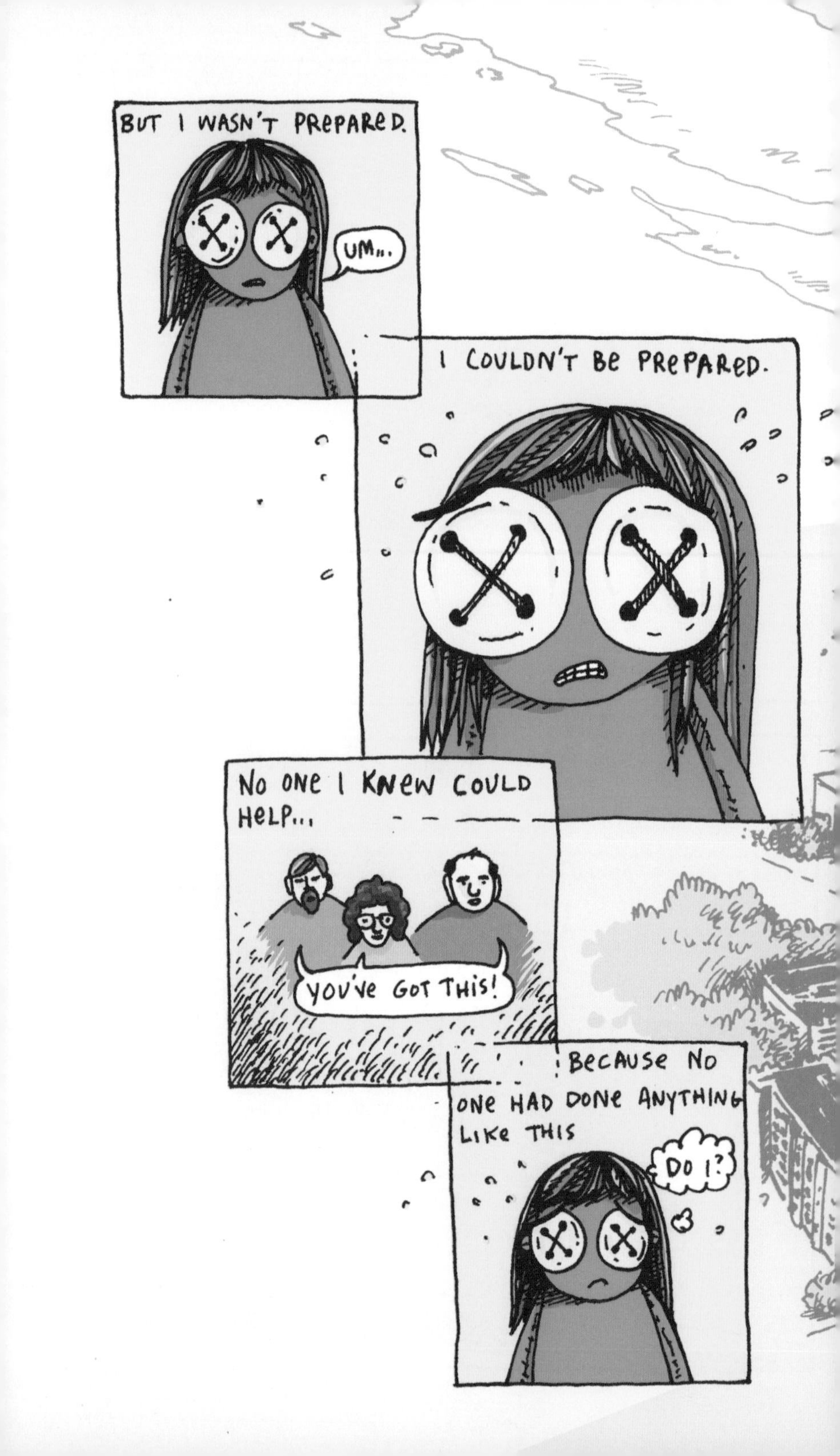

BUT I WASN'T PREPARED.
UM...
I COULDN'T BE PREPARED.
NO ONE I KNEW COULD HELP...
YOU'VE GOT THIS!
BECAUSE NO ONE HAD DONE ANYTHING LIKE THIS
DO I?

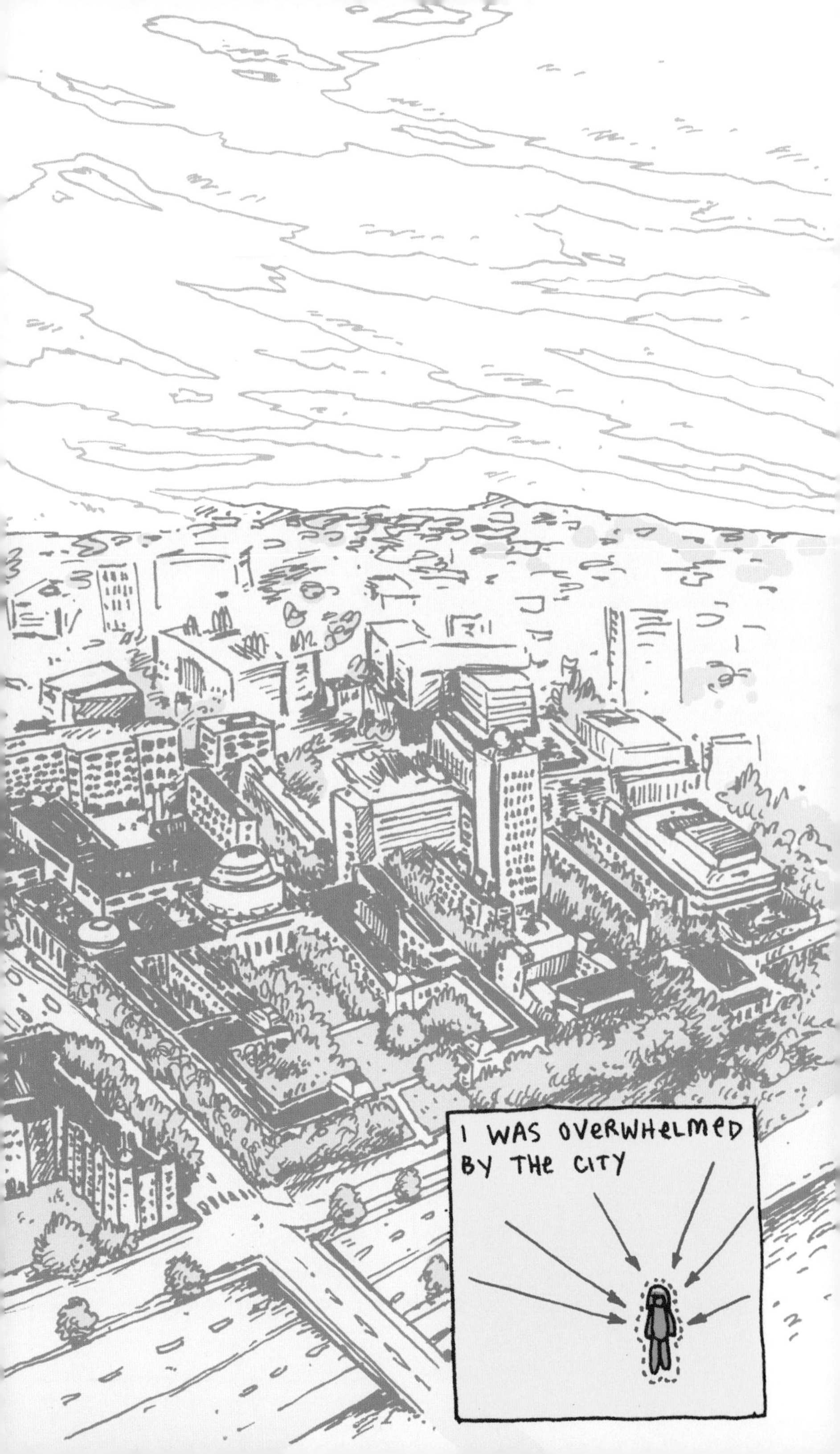
I WAS OVERWHELMED BY THE CITY

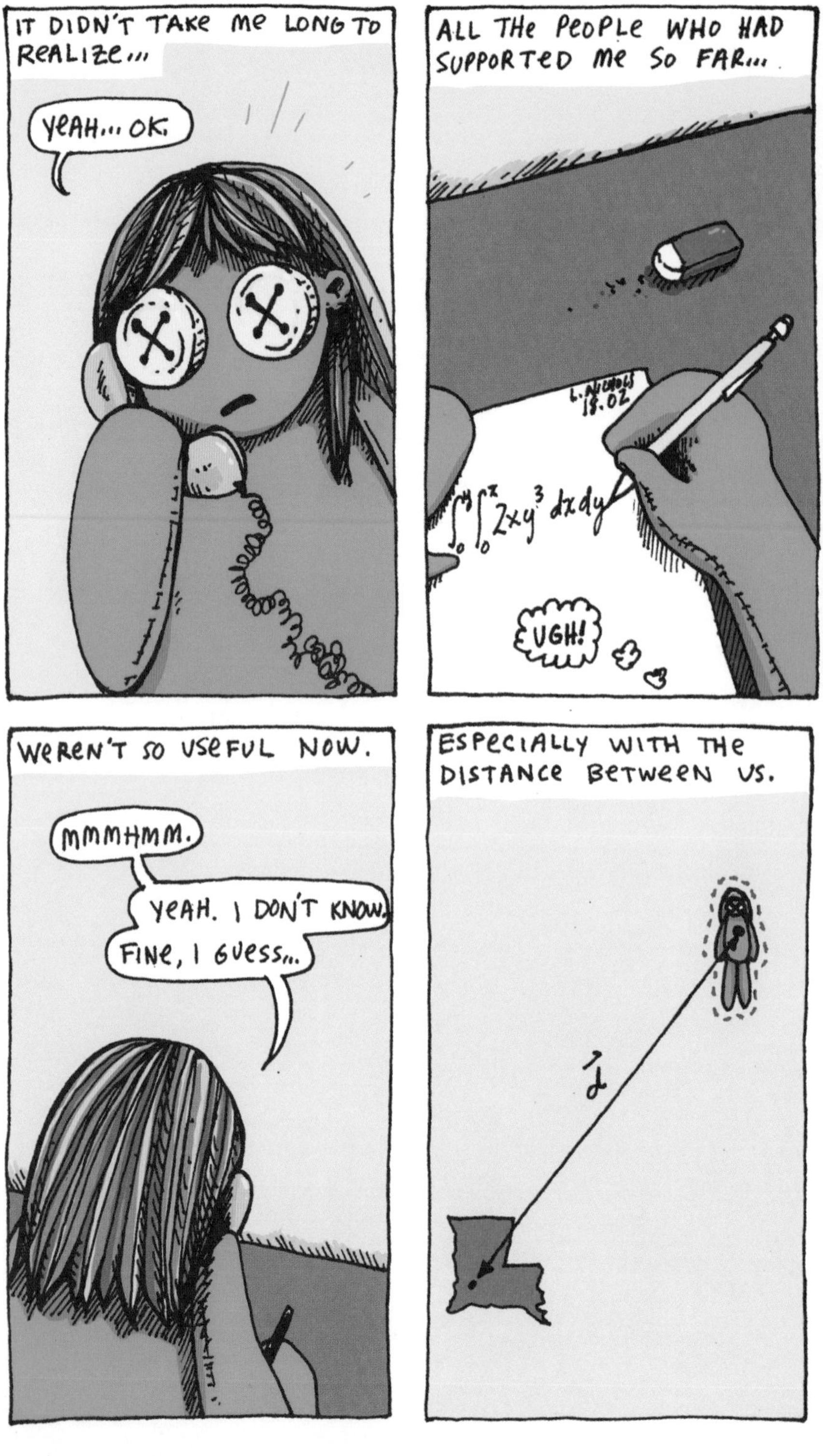
IT DIDN'T TAKE ME LONG TO REALIZE...
YEAH... OK.
ALL THE PEOPLE WHO HAD SUPPORTED ME SO FAR...
L. NICHOLS 18.02
UGH!
WEREN'T SO USEFUL NOW.
MMMHMM.
YEAH. I DON'T KNOW.
FINE, I GUESS...
ESPECIALLY WITH THE DISTANCE BETWEEN US.

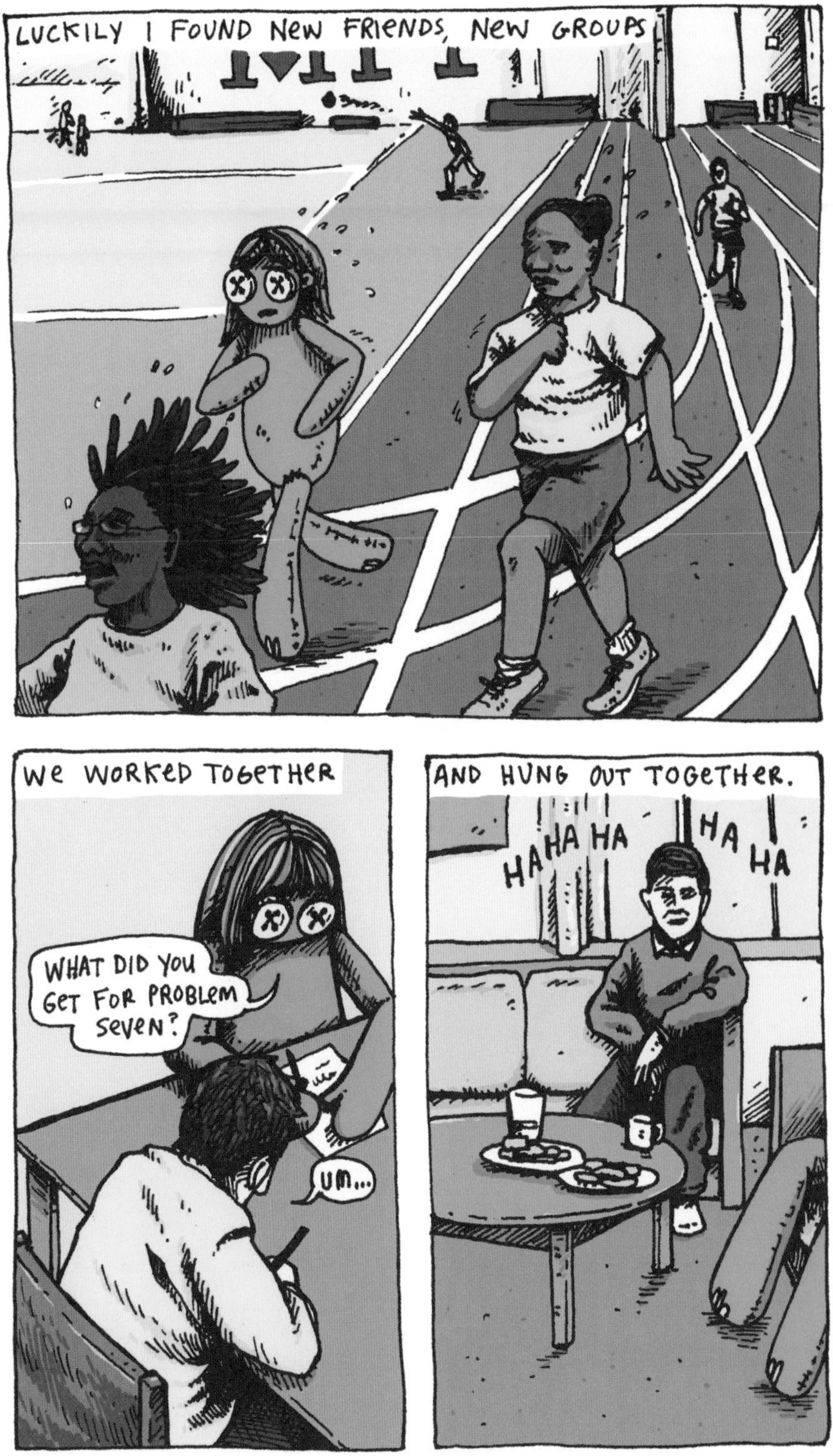
LUCKILY I FOUND NEW FRIENDS, NEW GROUPS
WE WORKED TOGETHER
WHAT DID YOU GET FOR PROBLEM SEVEN?
UM...
AND HUNG OUT TOGETHER.
HAHA HA
HA HA

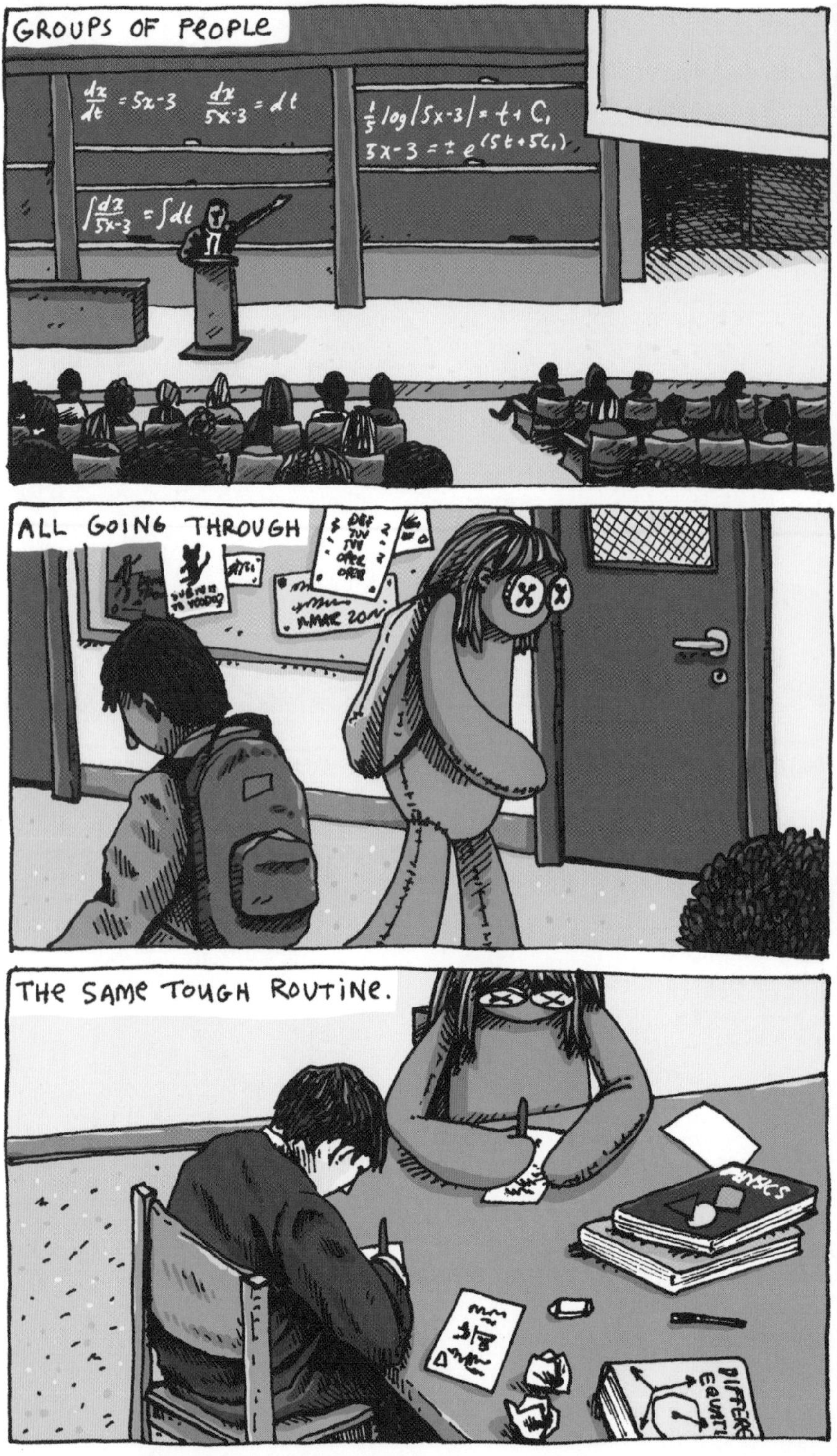
GROUPS OF PEOPLE
$\frac{dx}{dt} = 5x-3$ $\frac{dx}{5x-3} = dt$
$\int \frac{dx}{5x-3} = \int dt$
$\frac{1}{5} \log|5x-3| = t + C_1$
$5x-3 = \pm e^{(5t+5C_1)}$
ALL GOING THROUGH
THE SAME TOUGH ROUTINE.
PHYSICS

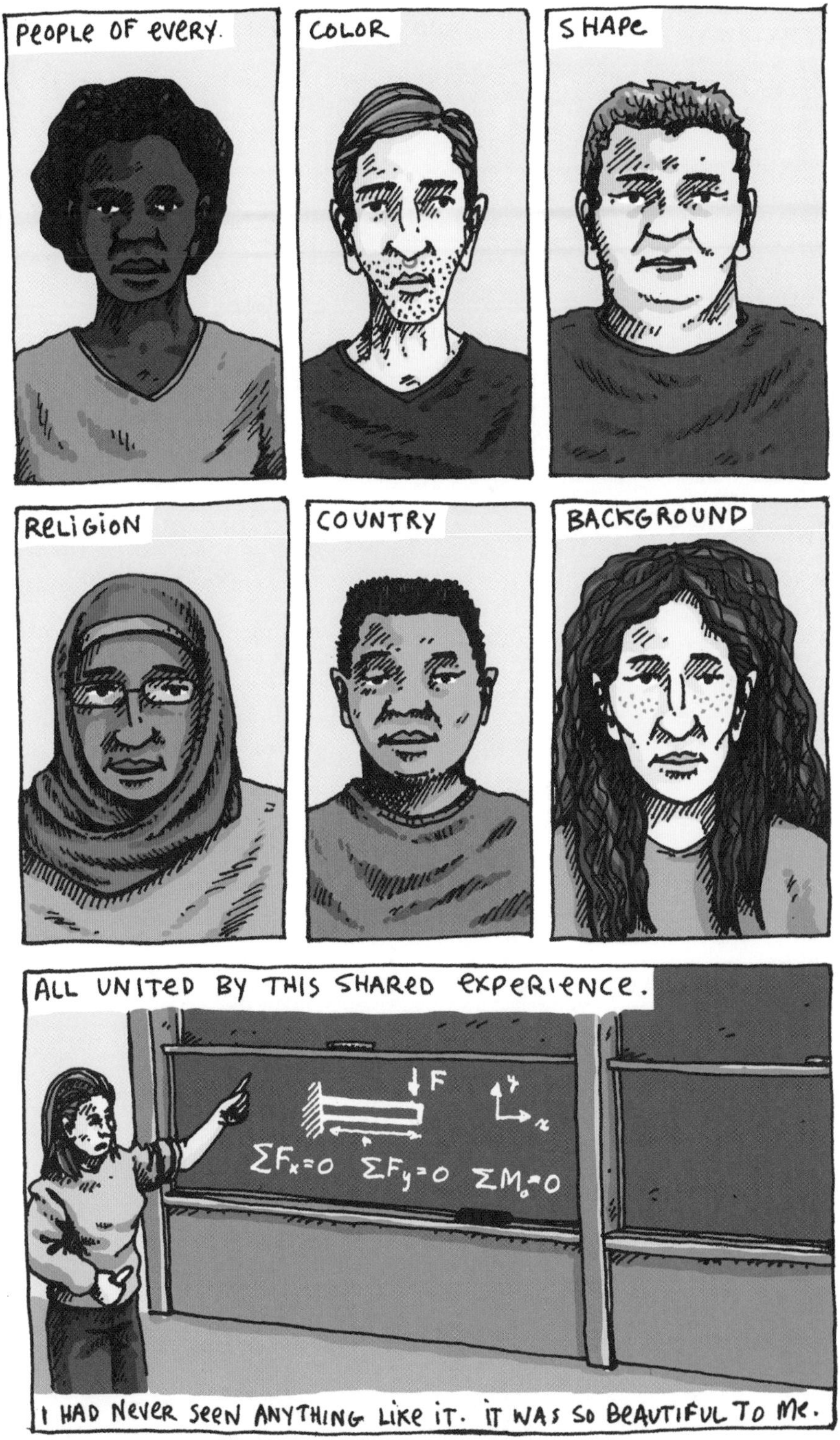
PEOPLE OF EVERY
COLOR
SHAPE
RELIGION
COUNTRY
BACKGROUND
ALL UNITED BY THIS SHARED EXPERIENCE.
F
y
x
ΣFx=0 ΣFy=0 ΣMo=0
I HAD NEVER SEEN ANYTHING LIKE IT. IT WAS SO BEAUTIFUL TO ME.

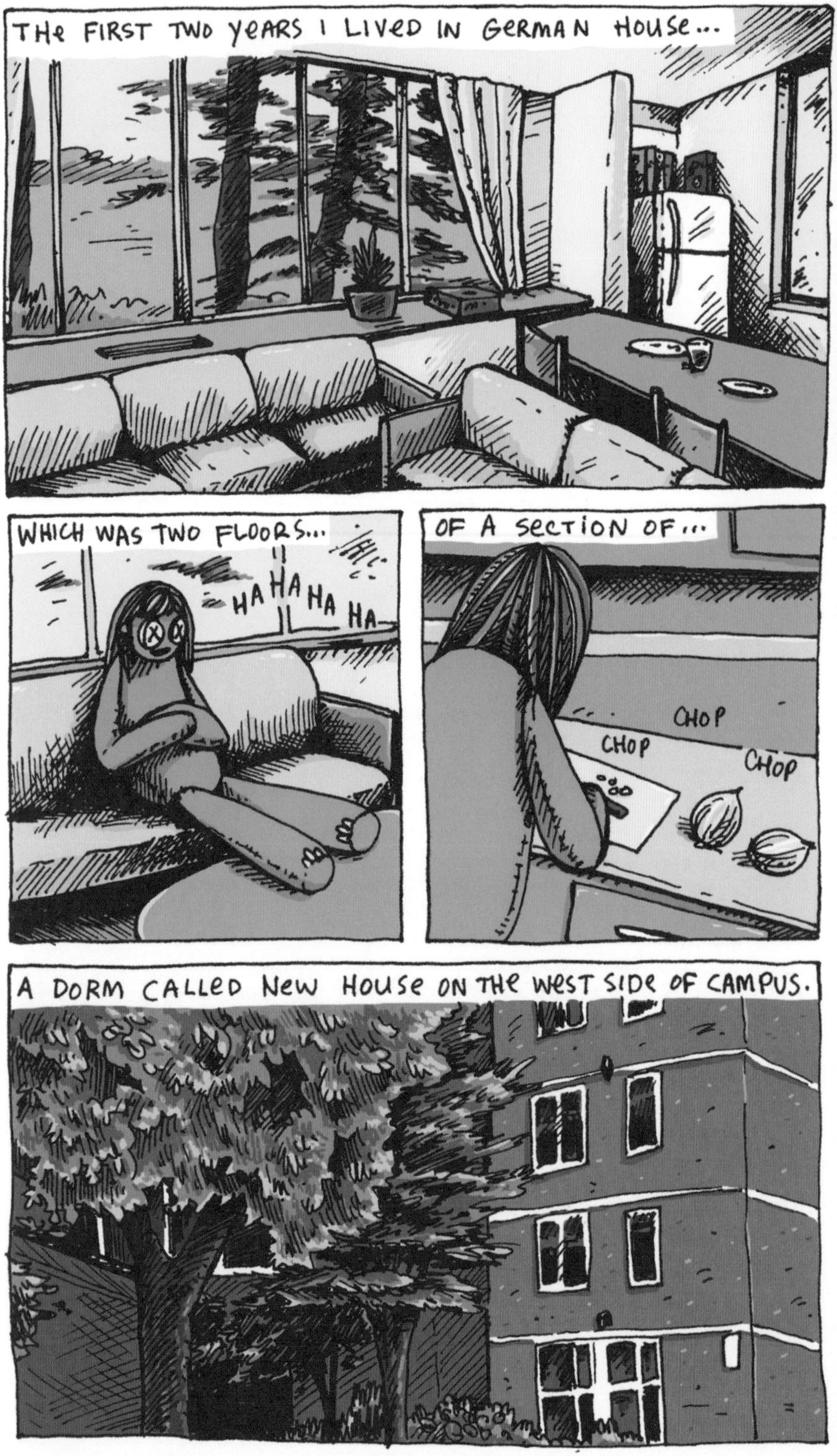
THE FIRST TWO YEARS I LIVED IN GERMAN HOUSE...
WHICH WAS TWO FLOORS...
HA HA HA HA HA
OF A SECTION OF...
CHOP
CHOP
CHOP
A DORM CALLED NEW HOUSE ON THE WEST SIDE OF CAMPUS.

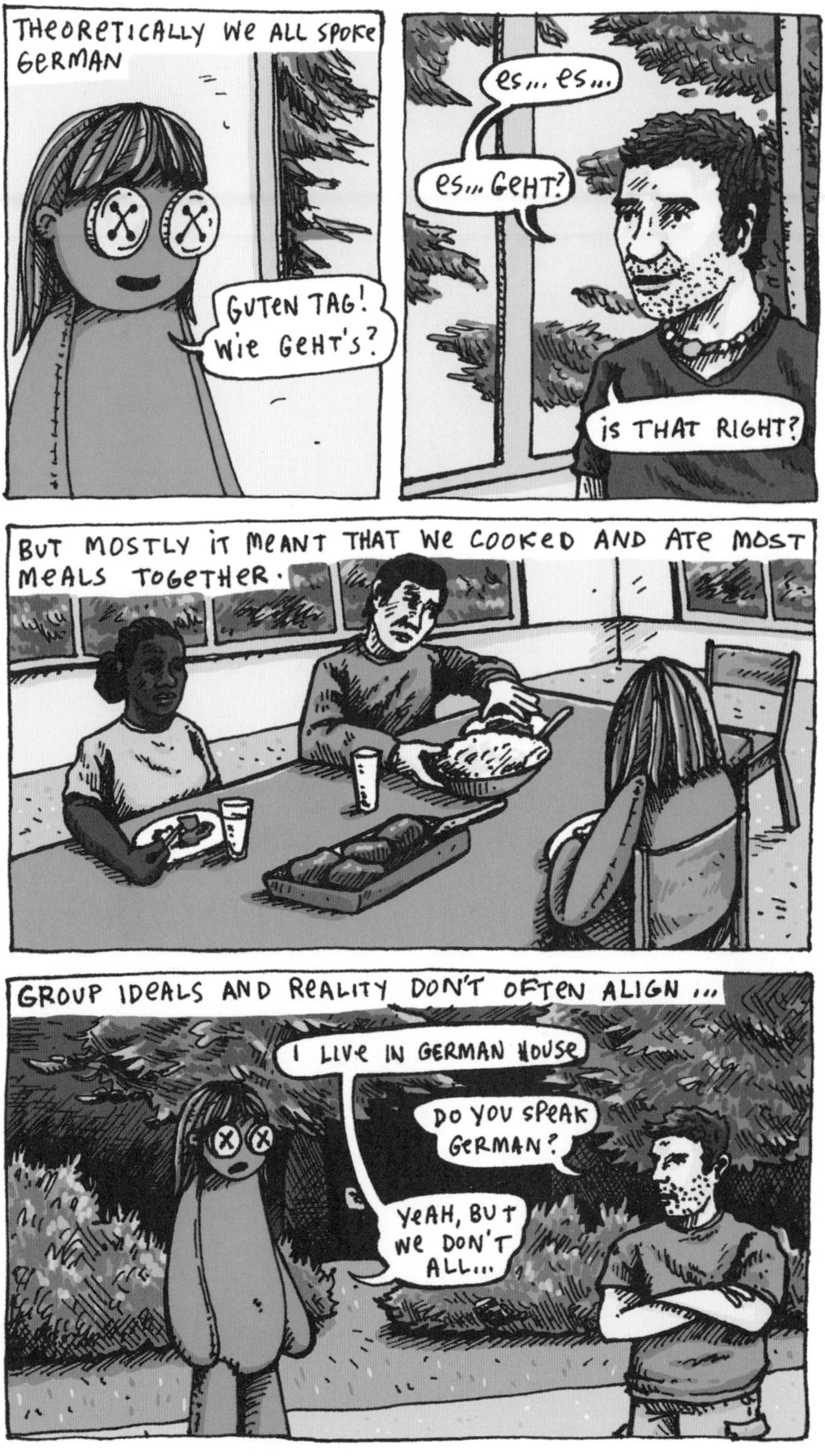
THEORETICALLY WE ALL SPOKE GERMAN
GUTEN TAG! WIE GEHT'S?
ES... ES...
ES... GEHT?
IS THAT RIGHT?
BUT MOSTLY IT MEANT THAT WE COOKED AND ATE MOST MEALS TOGETHER.
GROUP IDEALS AND REALITY DON'T OFTEN ALIGN ...
I LIVE IN GERMAN HOUSE
DO YOU SPEAK GERMAN?
YEAH, BUT WE DON'T ALL...

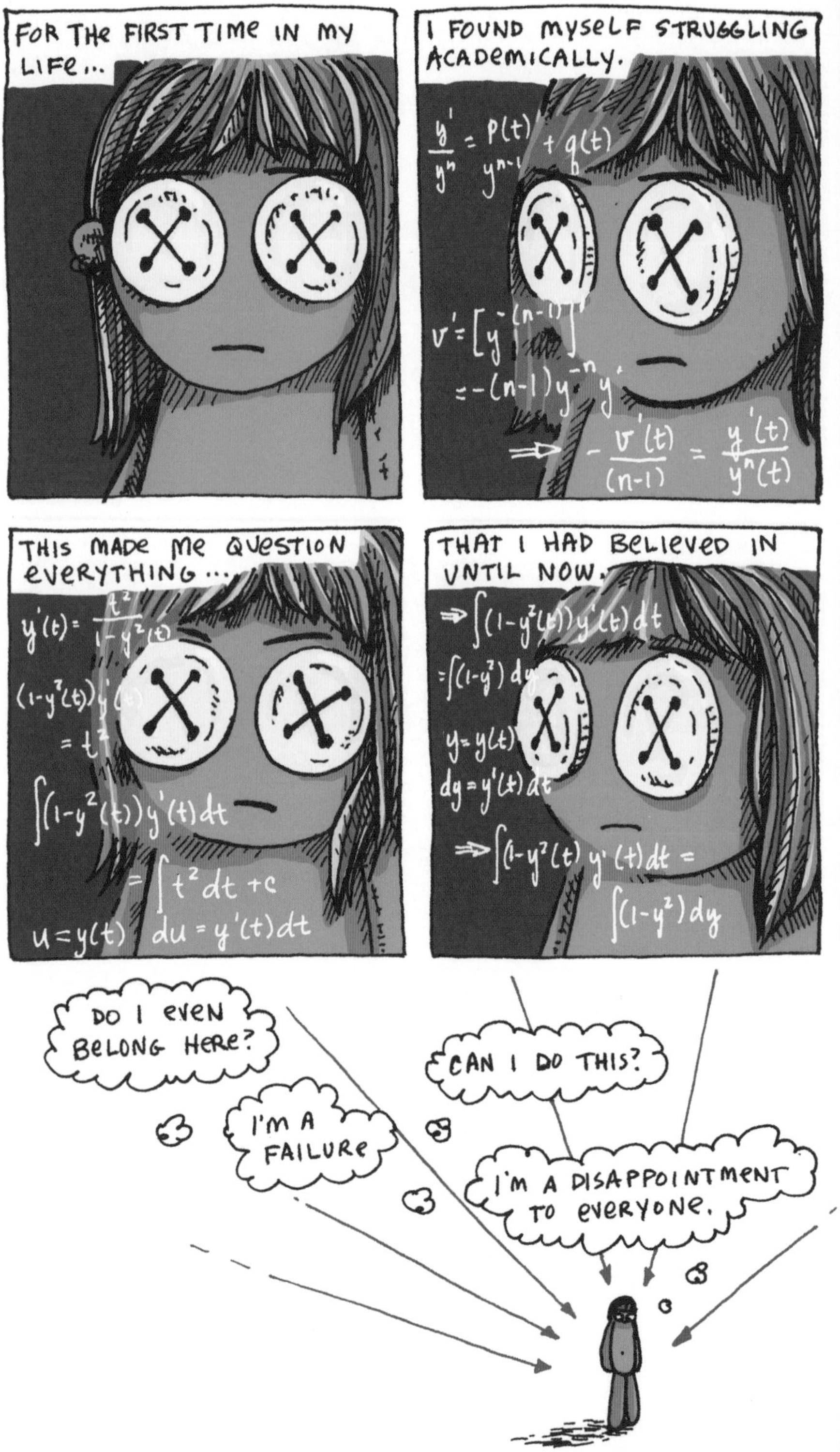
FOR THE FIRST TIME IN MY LIFE...
I FOUND MYSELF STRUGGLING ACADEMICALLY.
THIS MADE ME QUESTION EVERYTHING...
THAT I HAD BELIEVED IN UNTIL NOW.
DO I EVEN BELONG HERE?
CAN I DO THIS?
I'M A FAILURE
I'M A DISAPPOINTMENT TO EVERYONE.

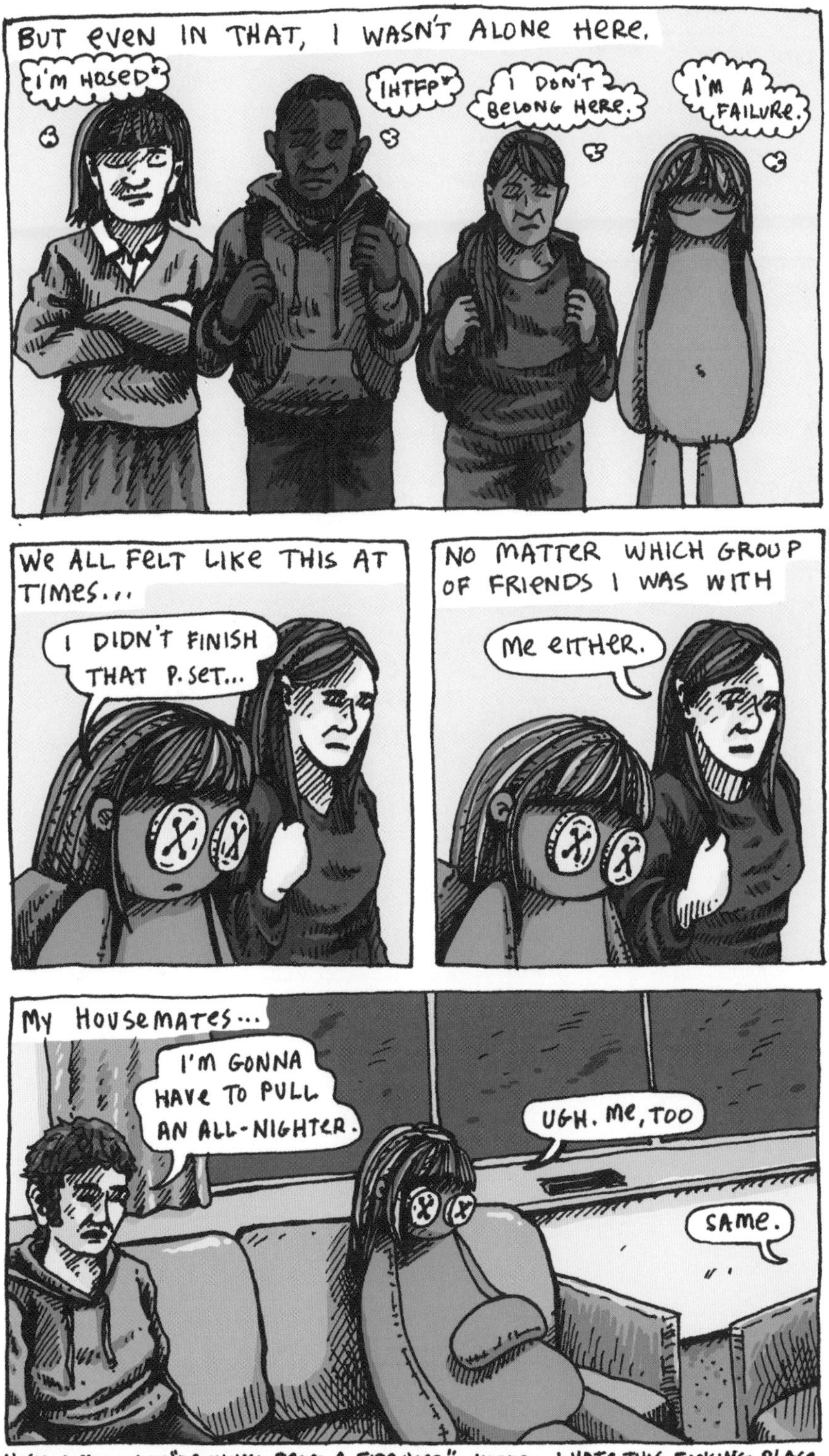
BUT EVEN IN THAT, I WASN'T ALONE HERE.
I'M HOSED*
IHTFP*
I DON'T BELONG HERE.
I'M A FAILURE.
WE ALL FELT LIKE THIS AT TIMES...
I DIDN'T FINISH THAT P. SET...
NO MATTER WHICH GROUP OF FRIENDS I WAS WITH
ME EITHER.
MY HOUSEMATES...
I'M GONNA HAVE TO PULL AN ALL-NIGHTER.
UGH. ME, TOO
SAME.

*HOSED → MIT IS LIKE "DRINKING FROM A FIRE HOSE." IHTFP = I HATE THIS FUCKING PLACE.

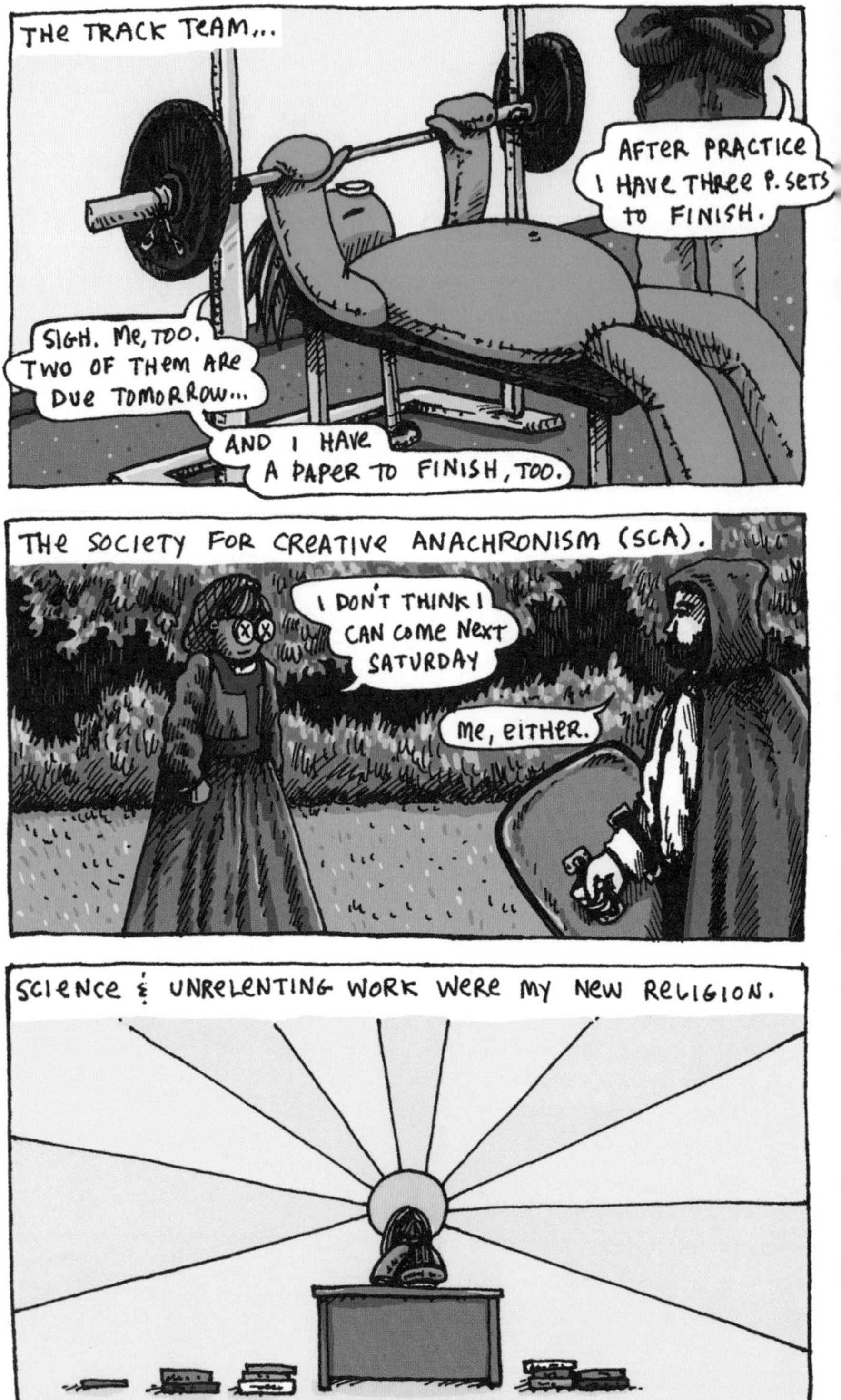
THE TRACK TEAM...
AFTER PRACTICE I HAVE THREE P. SETS TO FINISH.
SIGH. ME, TOO. TWO OF THEM ARE DUE TOMORROW...
AND I HAVE A PAPER TO FINISH, TOO.
THE SOCIETY FOR CREATIVE ANACHRONISM (SCA).
I DON'T THINK I CAN COME NEXT SATURDAY
ME, EITHER.
SCIENCE & UNRELENTING WORK WERE MY NEW RELIGION.

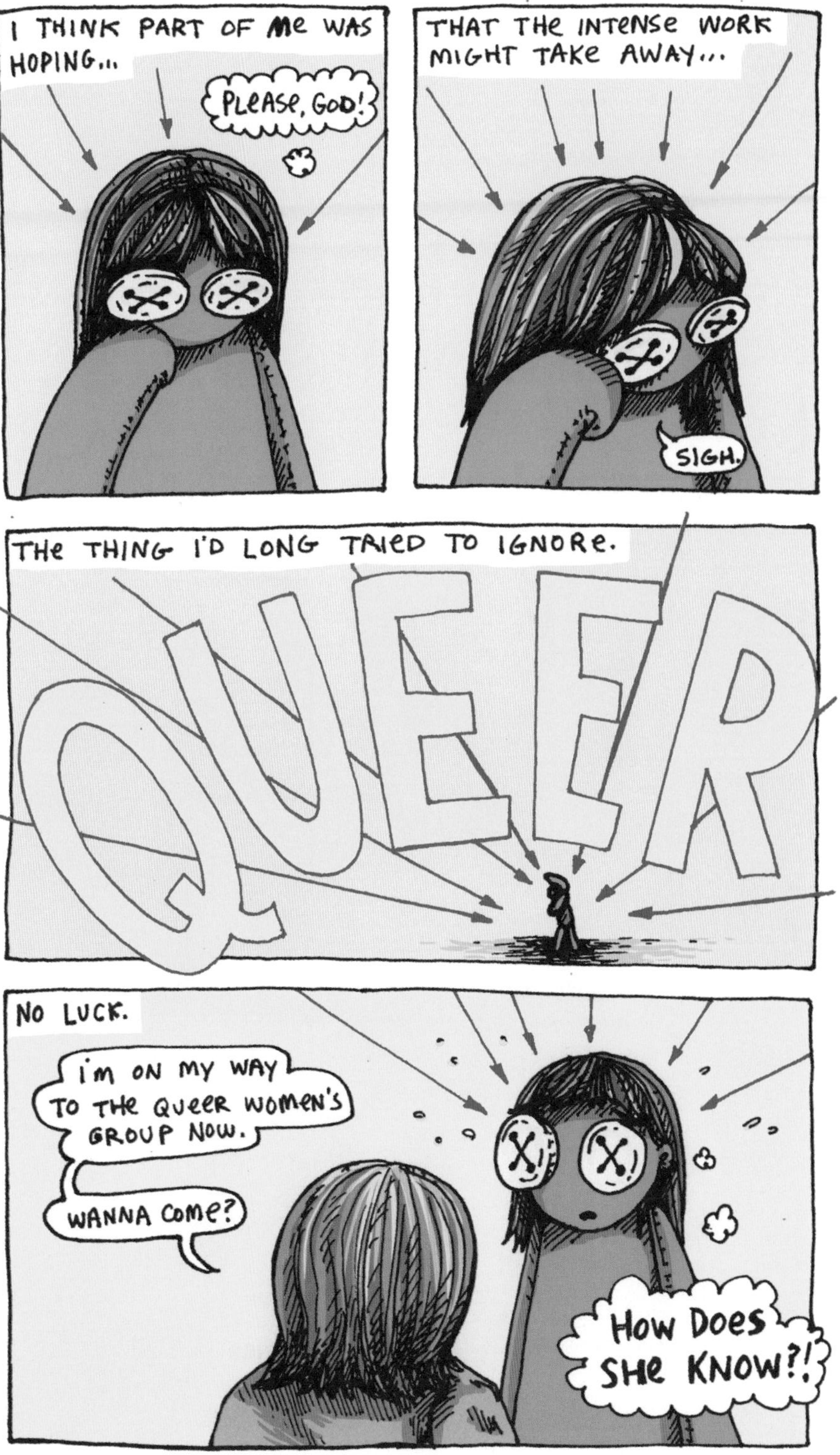
I THINK PART OF ME WAS HOPING...
PLEASE, GOD!
THAT THE INTENSE WORK MIGHT TAKE AWAY...
SIGH.
THE THING I'D LONG TRIED TO IGNORE.
QUEER
NO LUCK.
I'M ON MY WAY TO THE QUEER WOMEN'S GROUP NOW.
WANNA COME?
HOW DOES SHE KNOW?!

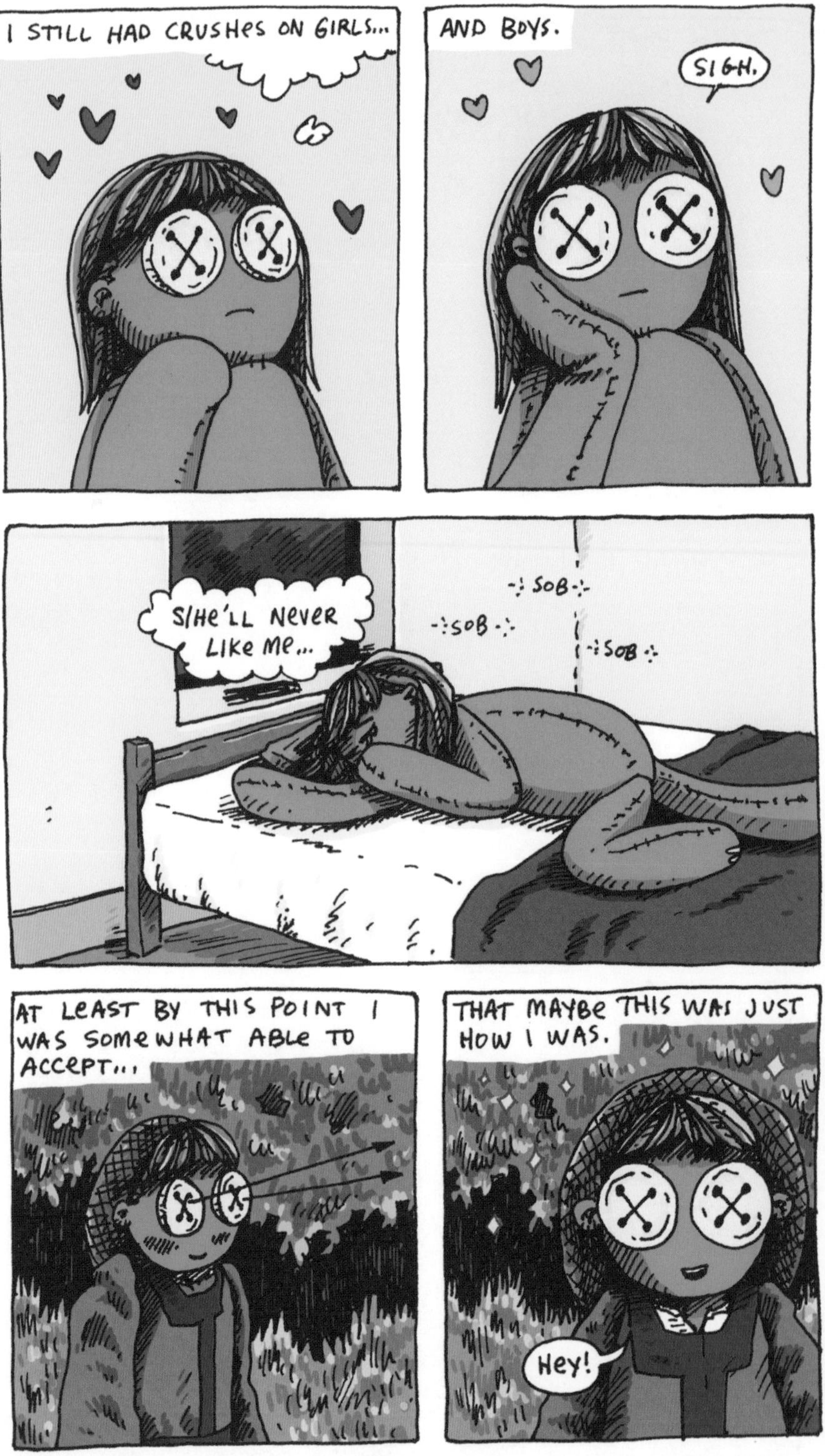
I STILL HAD CRUSHES ON GIRLS...
AND BOYS.
SIGH.
S/HE'LL NEVER LIKE ME...
SOB
SOB
SOB
AT LEAST BY THIS POINT I WAS SOMEWHAT ABLE TO ACCEPT...
THAT MAYBE THIS WAS JUST HOW I WAS.
HEY!

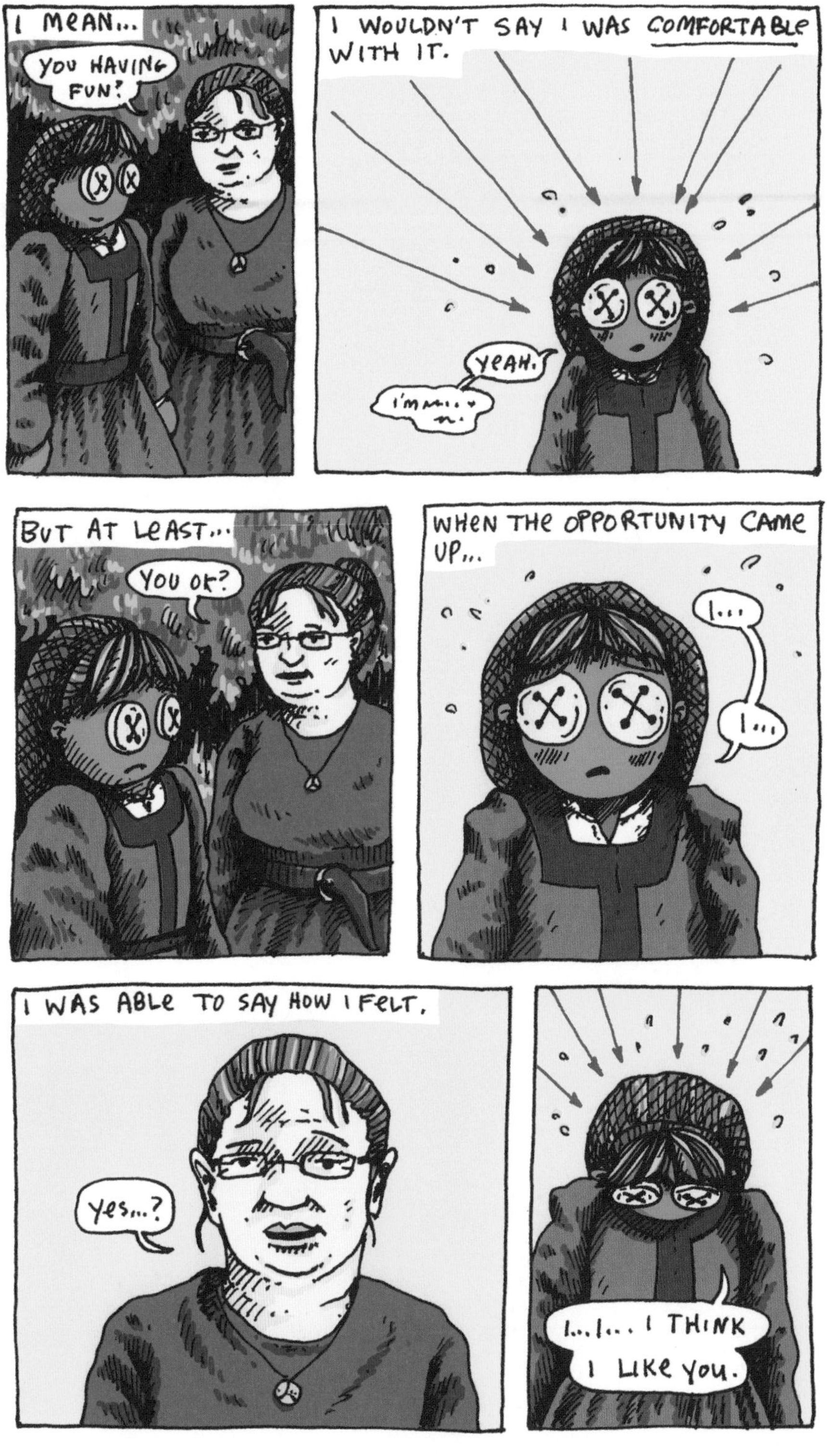
I MEAN...
YOU HAVING FUN?
I WOULDN'T SAY I WAS COMFORTABLE WITH IT.
YEAH.
BUT AT LEAST...
YOU OK?
WHEN THE OPPORTUNITY CAME UP...
I...
I...
I WAS ABLE TO SAY HOW I FELT.
YES...?
I...I... I THINK I LIKE YOU.

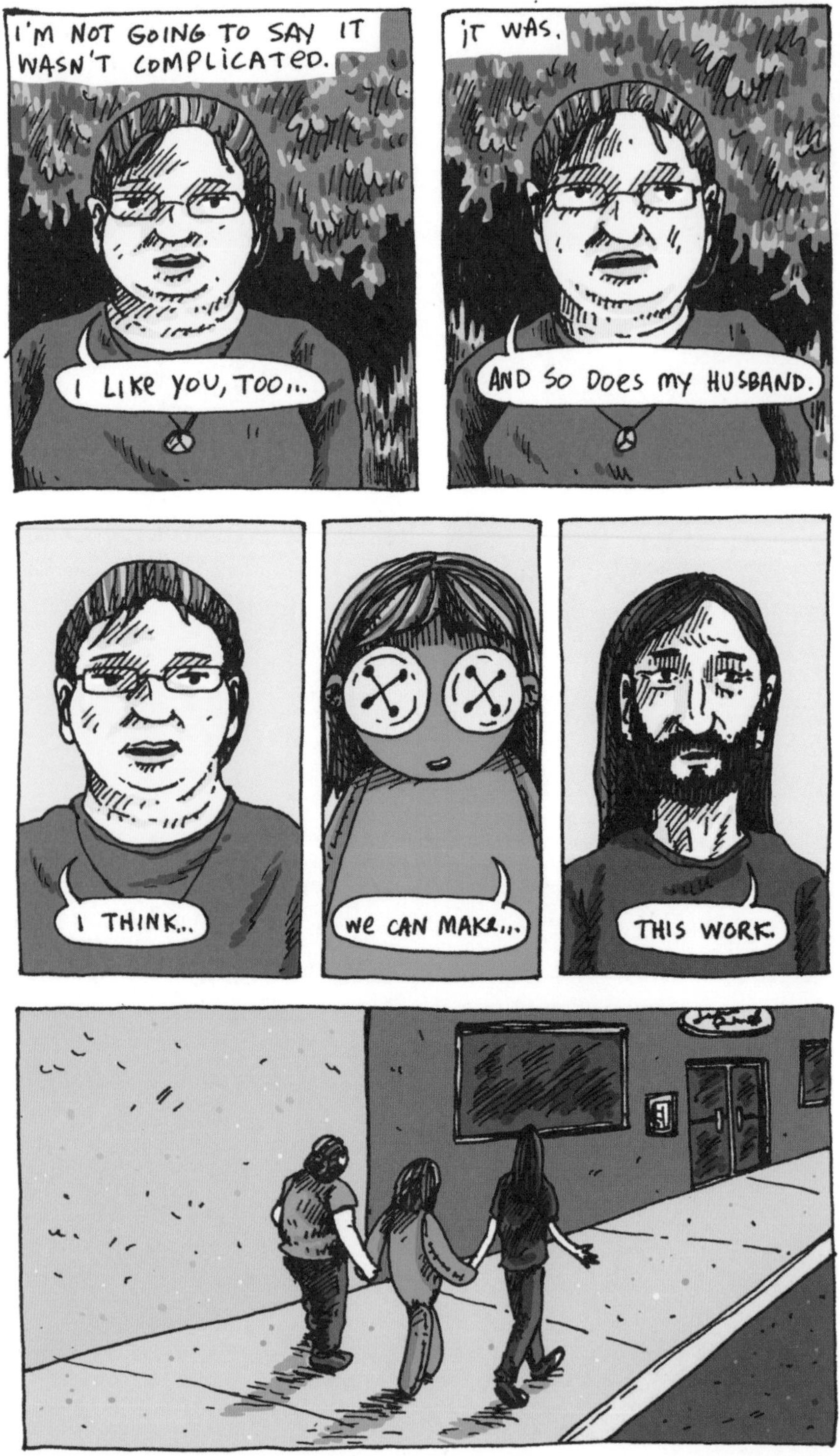
I'M NOT GOING TO SAY IT WASN'T COMPLICATED.
I LIKE YOU, TOO...
IT WAS.
AND SO DOES MY HUSBAND.
I THINK...
WE CAN MAKE...
THIS WORK.

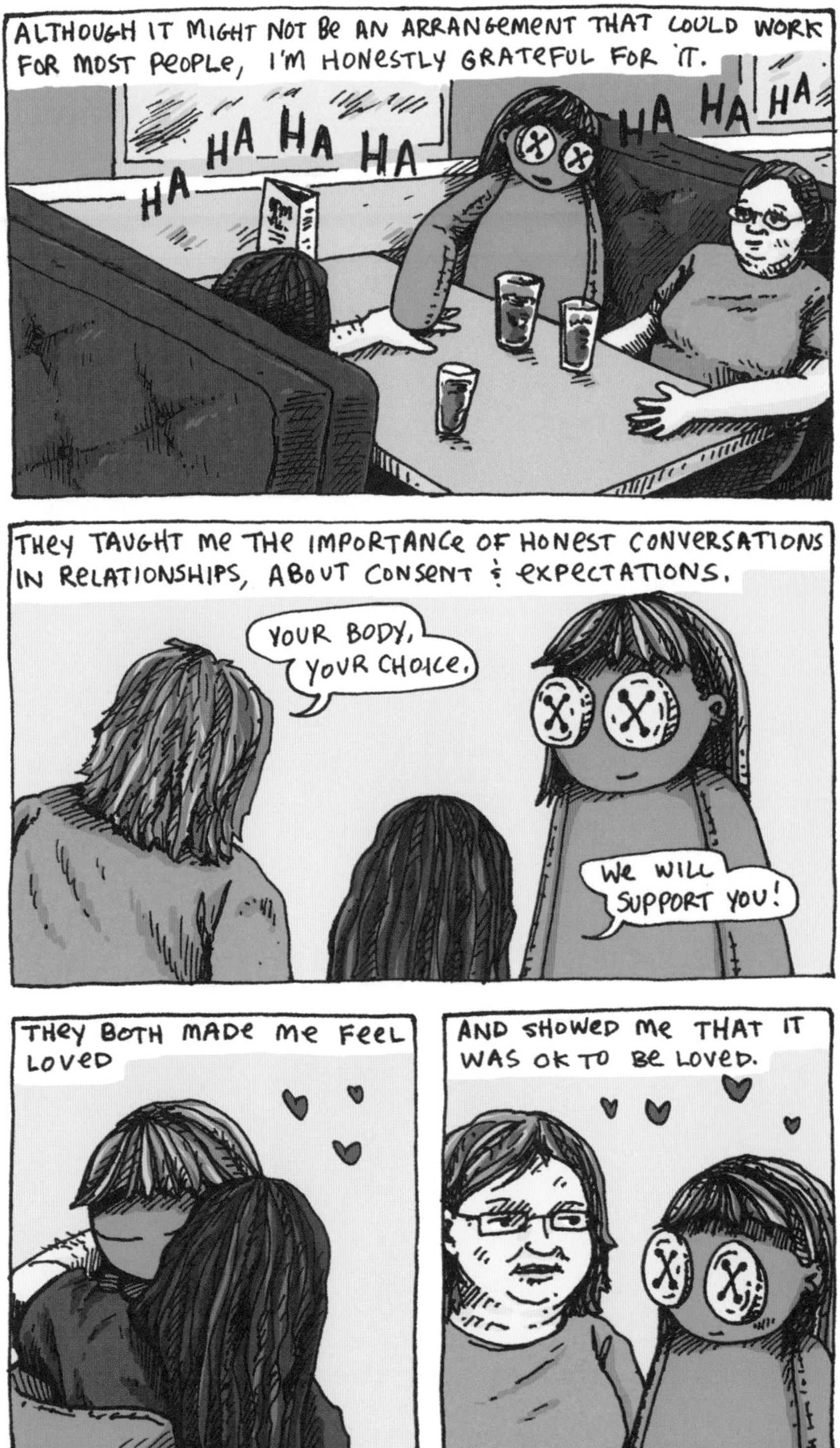
ALTHOUGH IT MIGHT NOT BE AN ARRANGEMENT THAT COULD WORK FOR MOST PEOPLE, I'M HONESTLY GRATEFUL FOR IT.
HA HA HA HA
HA HA HA
THEY TAUGHT ME THE IMPORTANCE OF HONEST CONVERSATIONS IN RELATIONSHIPS, ABOUT CONSENT & EXPECTATIONS.
YOUR BODY, YOUR CHOICE.
WE WILL SUPPORT YOU!
THEY BOTH MADE ME FEEL LOVED
AND SHOWED ME THAT IT WAS OK TO BE LOVED.

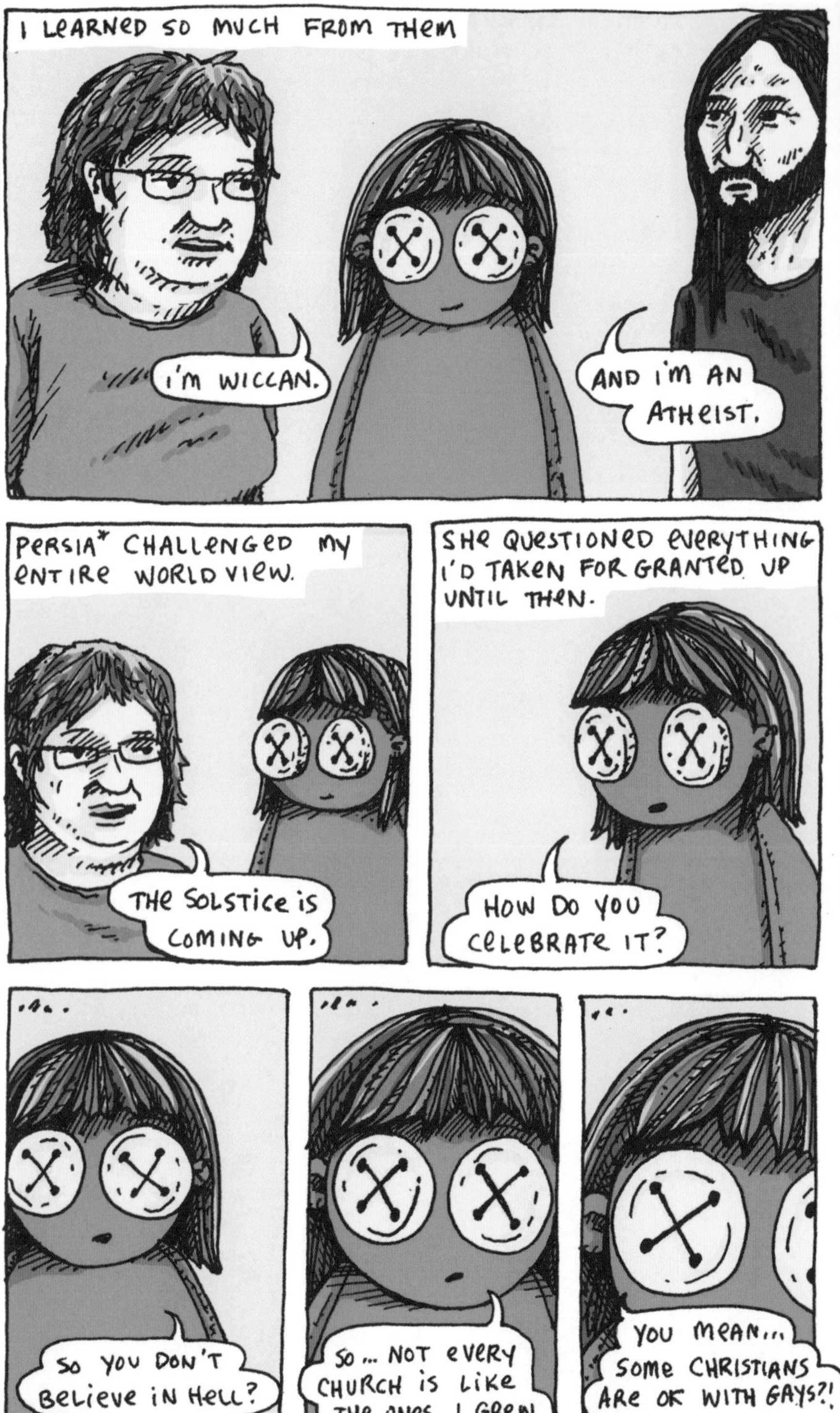
I LEARNED SO MUCH FROM THEM
I'M WICCAN.
AND I'M AN ATHEIST.
PERSIA* CHALLENGED MY ENTIRE WORLDVIEW.
THE SOLSTICE IS COMING UP.
SHE QUESTIONED EVERYTHING I'D TAKEN FOR GRANTED UP UNTIL THEN.
HOW DO YOU CELEBRATE IT?
SO YOU DON'T BELIEVE IN HELL?
SO... NOT EVERY CHURCH IS LIKE THE ONES I GREW UP WITH?
YOU MEAN... SOME CHRISTIANS ARE OK WITH GAYS?!
* NAME CHANGED.

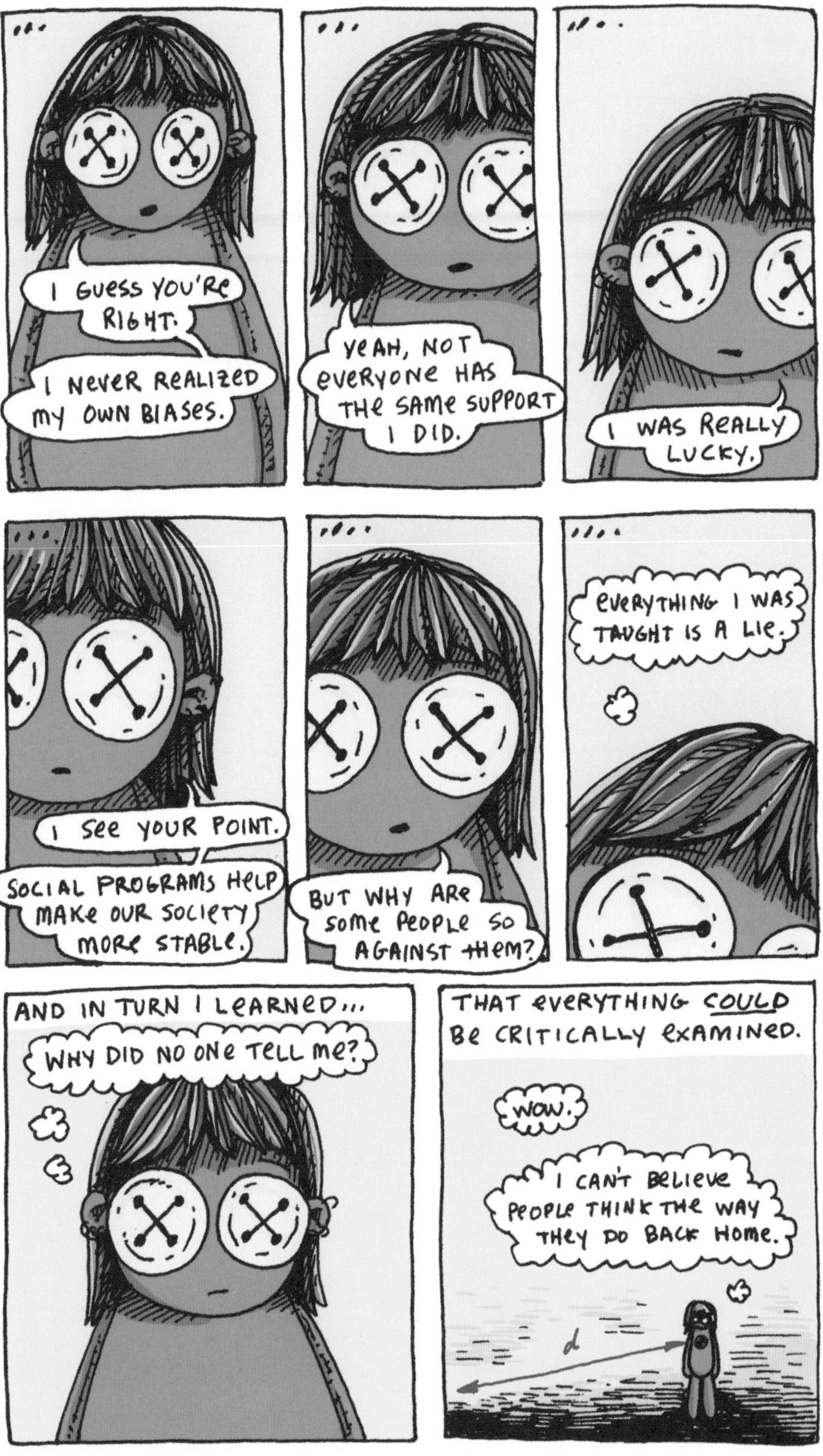
...
I GUESS YOU'RE RIGHT.
I NEVER REALIZED MY OWN BIASES.
...
YEAH, NOT EVERYONE HAS THE SAME SUPPORT I DID.
...
I WAS REALLY LUCKY.
...
I SEE YOUR POINT.
SOCIAL PROGRAMS HELP MAKE OUR SOCIETY MORE STABLE.
...
BUT WHY ARE SOME PEOPLE SO AGAINST THEM?
...
EVERYTHING I WAS TAUGHT IS A LIE.
AND IN TURN I LEARNED...
WHY DID NO ONE TELL ME?
THAT EVERYTHING COULD BE CRITICALLY EXAMINED.
WOW.
I CAN'T BELIEVE PEOPLE THINK THE WAY THEY DO BACK HOME.
d

EVENTUALLY I BROKE UP WITH THEM

YEAH... I DON'T THINK I CAN KEEP SEEING YOU.

I'VE JUST GOT TOO MUCH GOING ON.

IT'S OK. I UNDERSTAND.

MY ACADEMIC STRUGGLES HAD GROWN

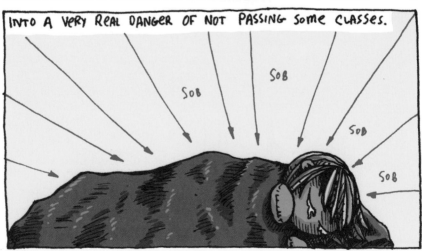

INTO A VERY REAL DANGER OF NOT PASSING SOME CLASSES.

SOB

SOB

SOB

SOB

SO I KNUCKLED DOWN

AND STUDIED FOR FINALS.

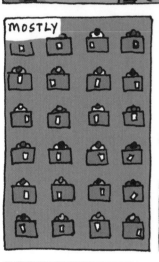

MOSTLY

THIS

WORKED...

I'VE GOT THIS!

EXCEPT FOR ONE CLASS

OH NO.

I GOT A.....D?!

UGH.

F FAIL

(AT MIT AS A FRESHMAN, D's ARE A FAILING GRADE)

I HAD NEVER FAILED BEFORE.

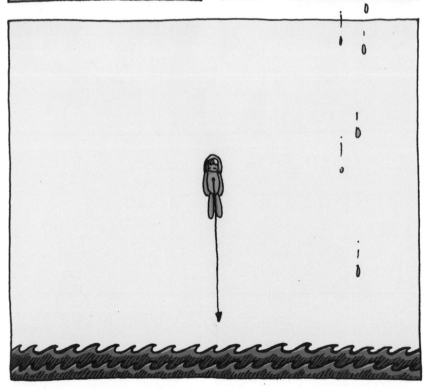

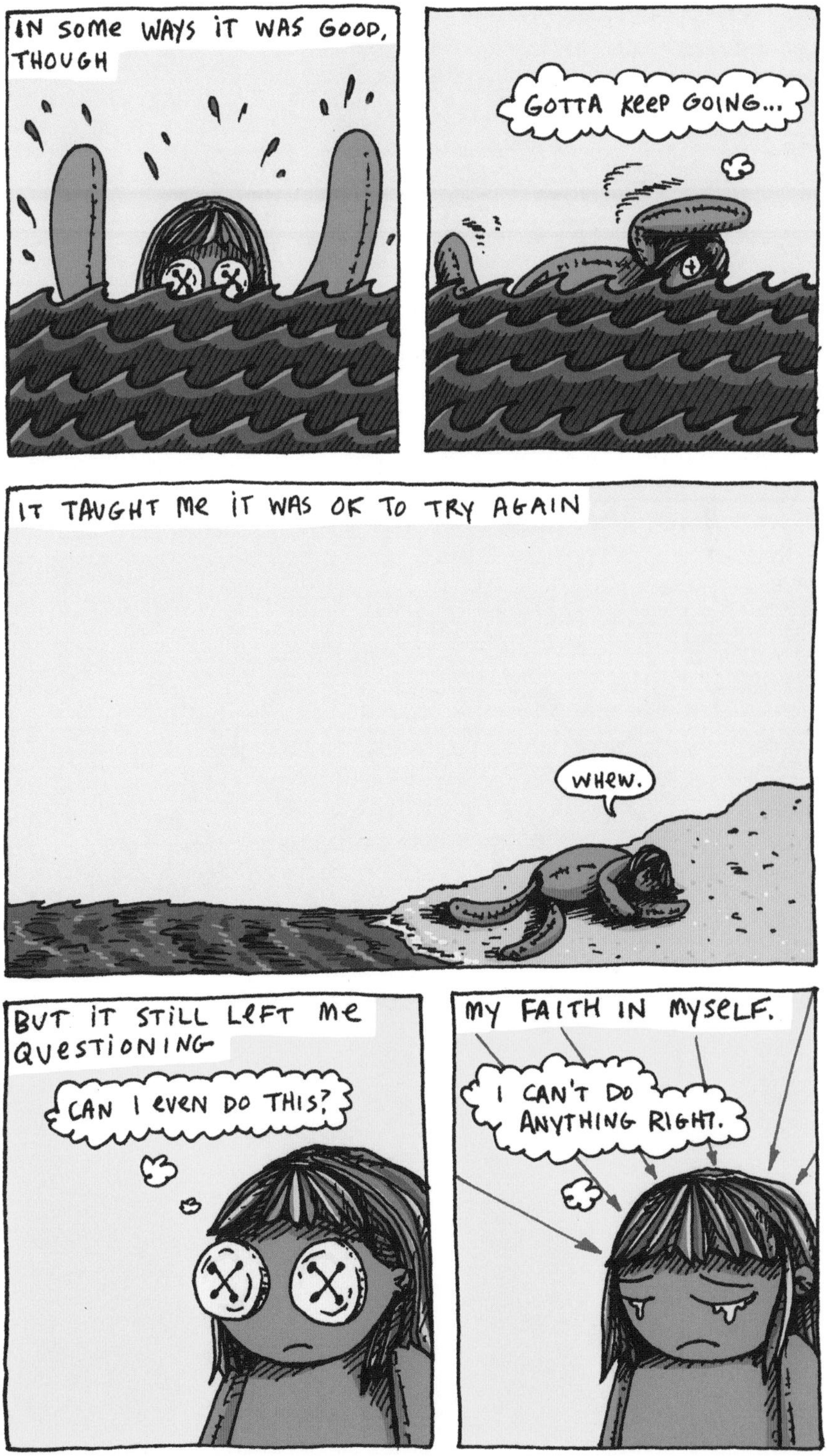
IN SOME WAYS IT WAS GOOD, THOUGH
GOTTA KEEP GOING...
IT TAUGHT ME IT WAS OK TO TRY AGAIN
WHEW.
BUT IT STILL LEFT ME QUESTIONING
CAN I EVEN DO THIS?
MY FAITH IN MYSELF.
I CAN'T DO ANYTHING RIGHT.

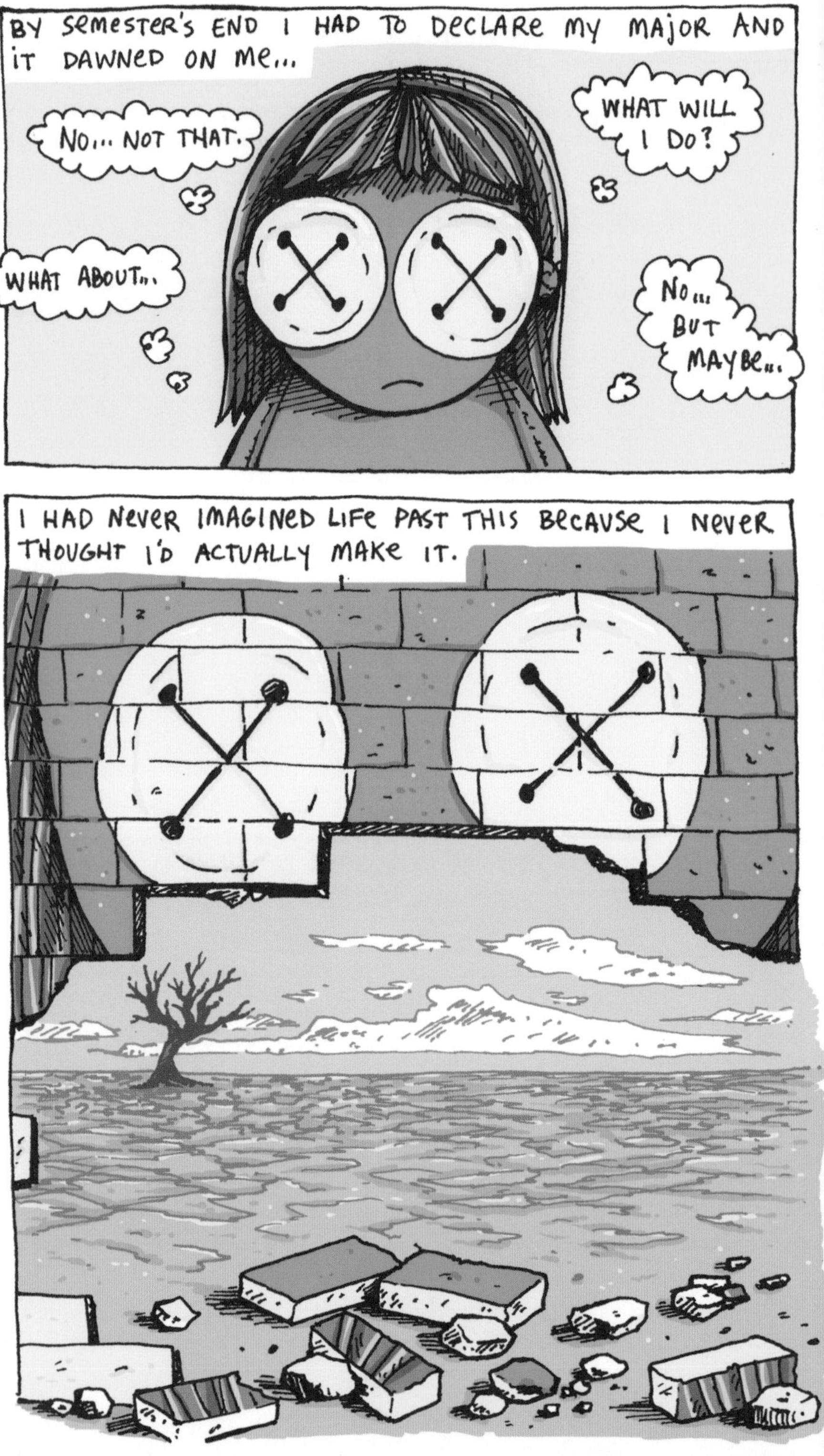
BY SEMESTER'S END I HAD TO DECLARE MY MAJOR AND IT DAWNED ON ME...
NO... NOT THAT.
WHAT WILL I DO?
WHAT ABOUT...
NO... BUT MAYBE...
I HAD NEVER IMAGINED LIFE PAST THIS BECAUSE I NEVER THOUGHT I'D ACTUALLY MAKE IT.

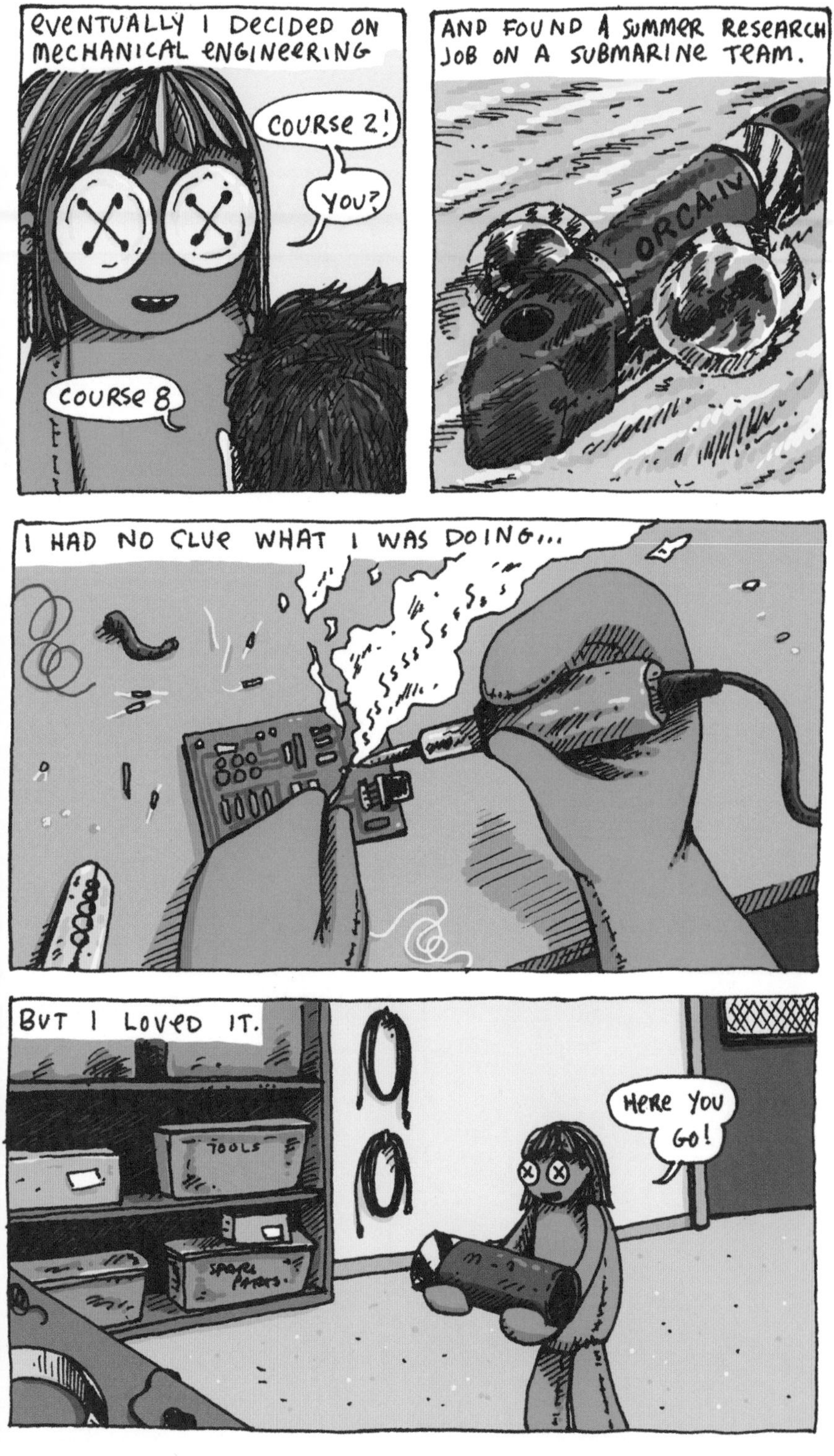
EVENTUALLY I DECIDED ON MECHANICAL ENGINEERING
COURSE 2!
YOU?
COURSE 8
AND FOUND A SUMMER RESEARCH JOB ON A SUBMARINE TEAM.
ORCA-IV
I HAD NO CLUE WHAT I WAS DOING...
SSSSSSSSS
BUT I LOVED IT.
TOOLS
SPARE PARTS.
HERE YOU GO!

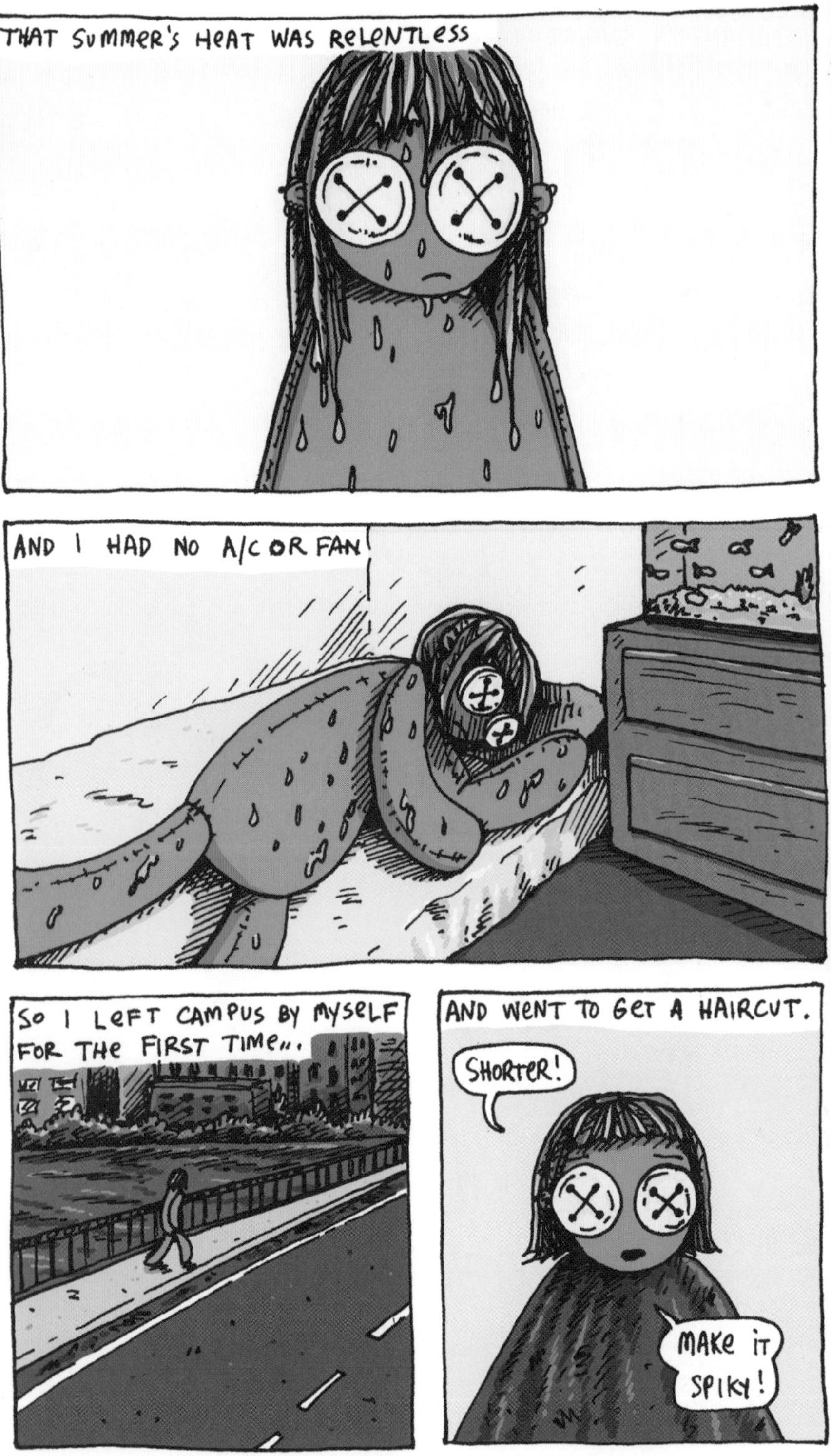
THAT SUMMER'S HEAT WAS RELENTLESS
AND I HAD NO A/C OR FAN
SO I LEFT CAMPUS BY MYSELF FOR THE FIRST TIME..
AND WENT TO GET A HAIRCUT.
SHORTER!
MAKE IT SPIKY!

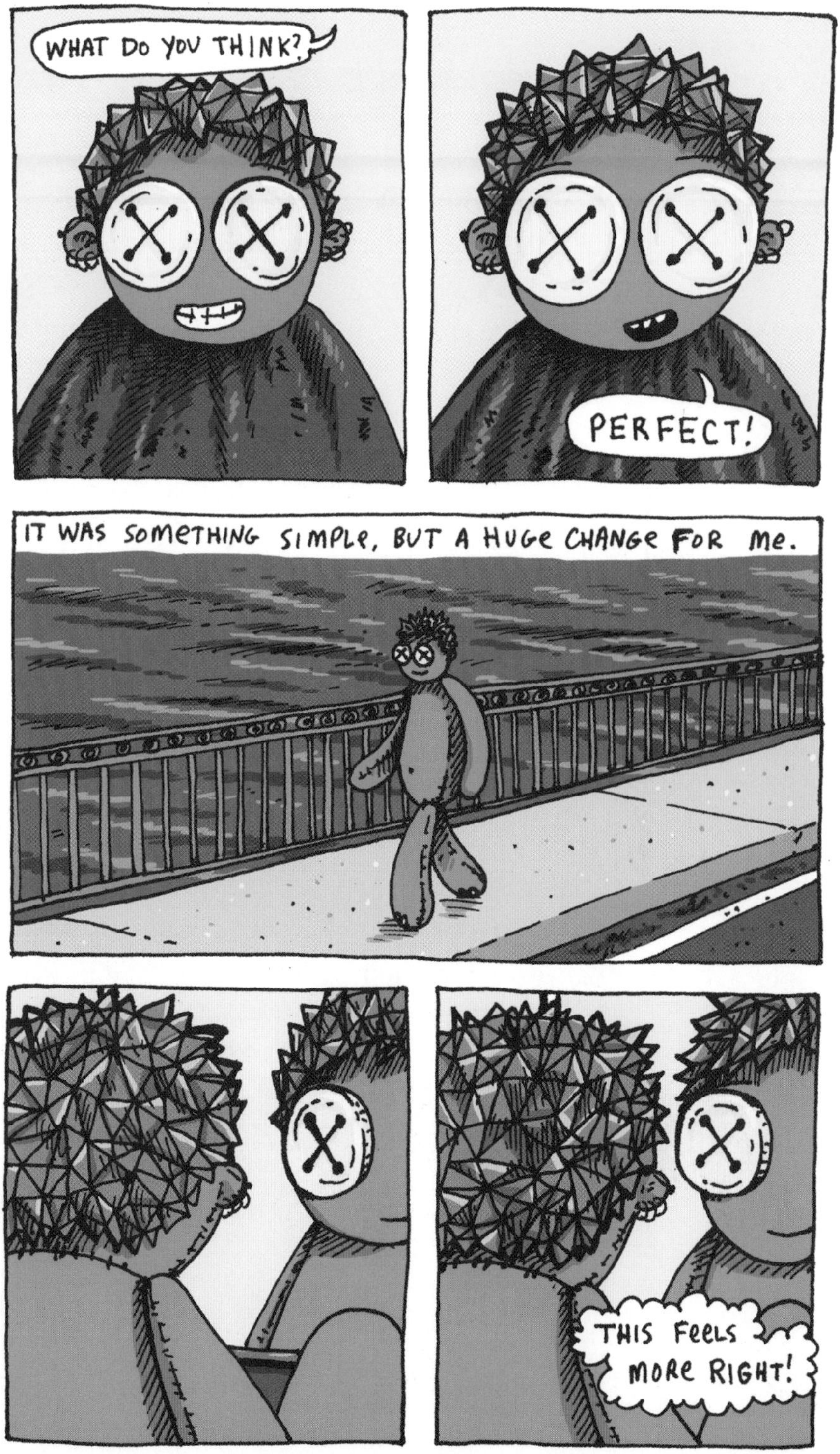
WHAT DO YOU THINK?
PERFECT!
IT WAS SOMETHING SIMPLE, BUT A HUGE CHANGE FOR ME.
THIS FEELS MORE RIGHT!

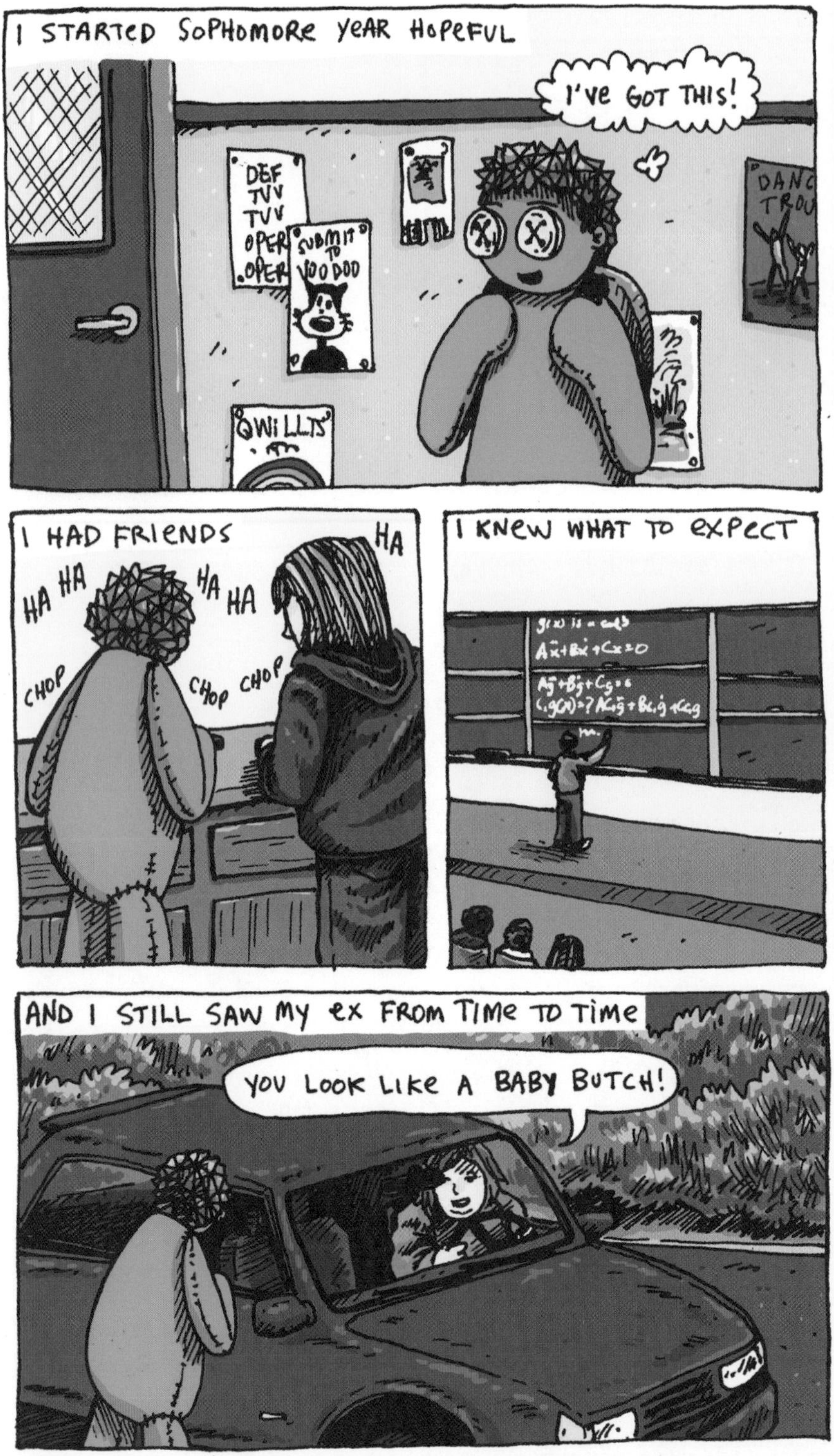
I STARTED SOPHOMORE YEAR HOPEFUL
I'VE GOT THIS!
SUBMIT TO VOODOO
I HAD FRIENDS
HA HA
HA HA
HA
CHOP
CHOP CHOP
I KNEW WHAT TO EXPECT
AND I STILL SAW MY EX FROM TIME TO TIME
YOU LOOK LIKE A BABY BUTCH!

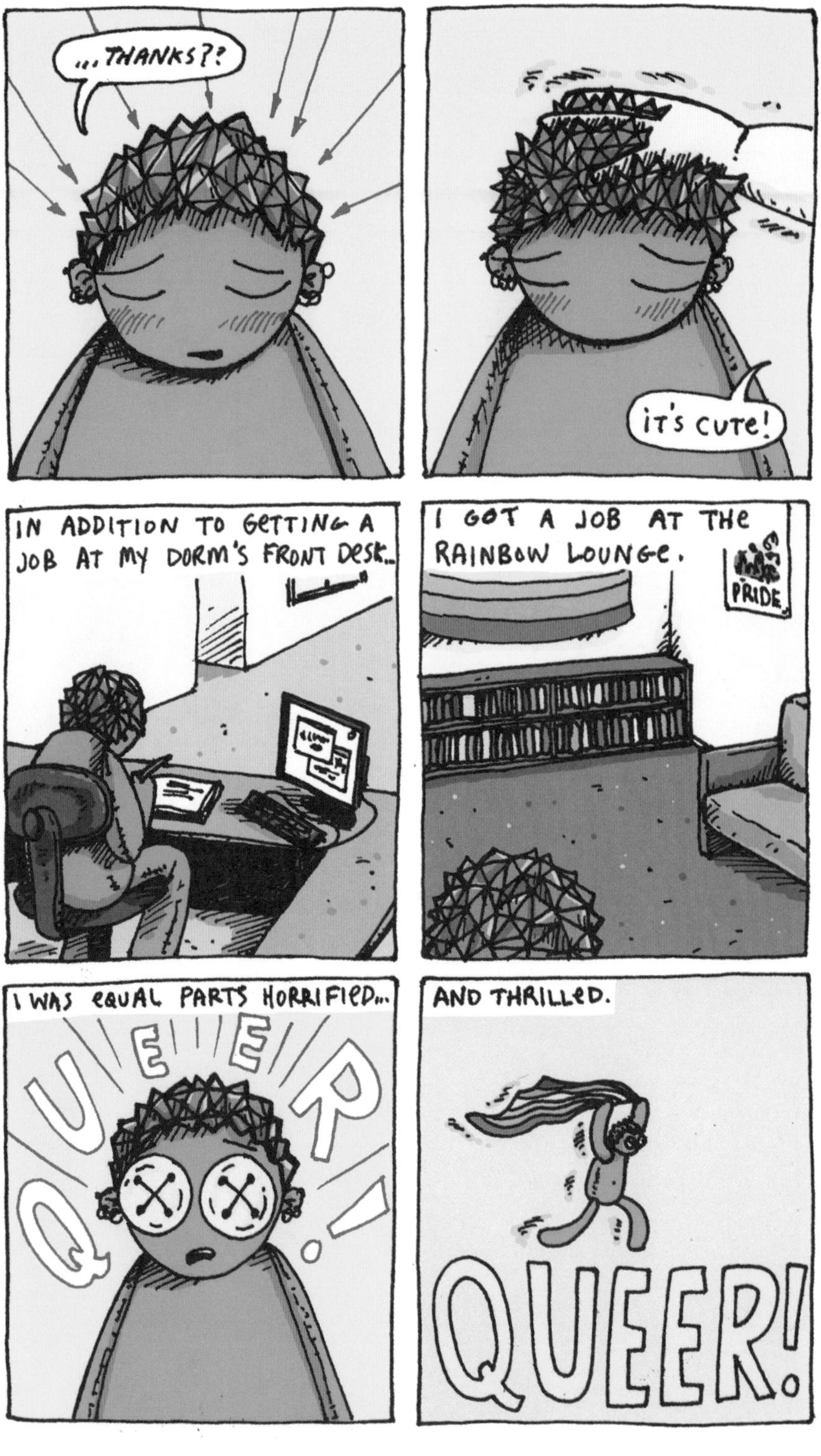
...THANKS?!?
IT'S CUTE!
IN ADDITION TO GETTING A JOB AT MY DORM'S FRONT DESK...
I GOT A JOB AT THE RAINBOW LOUNGE.
PRIDE
I WAS EQUAL PARTS HORRIFIED...
QUEER!
AND THRILLED.
QUEER!

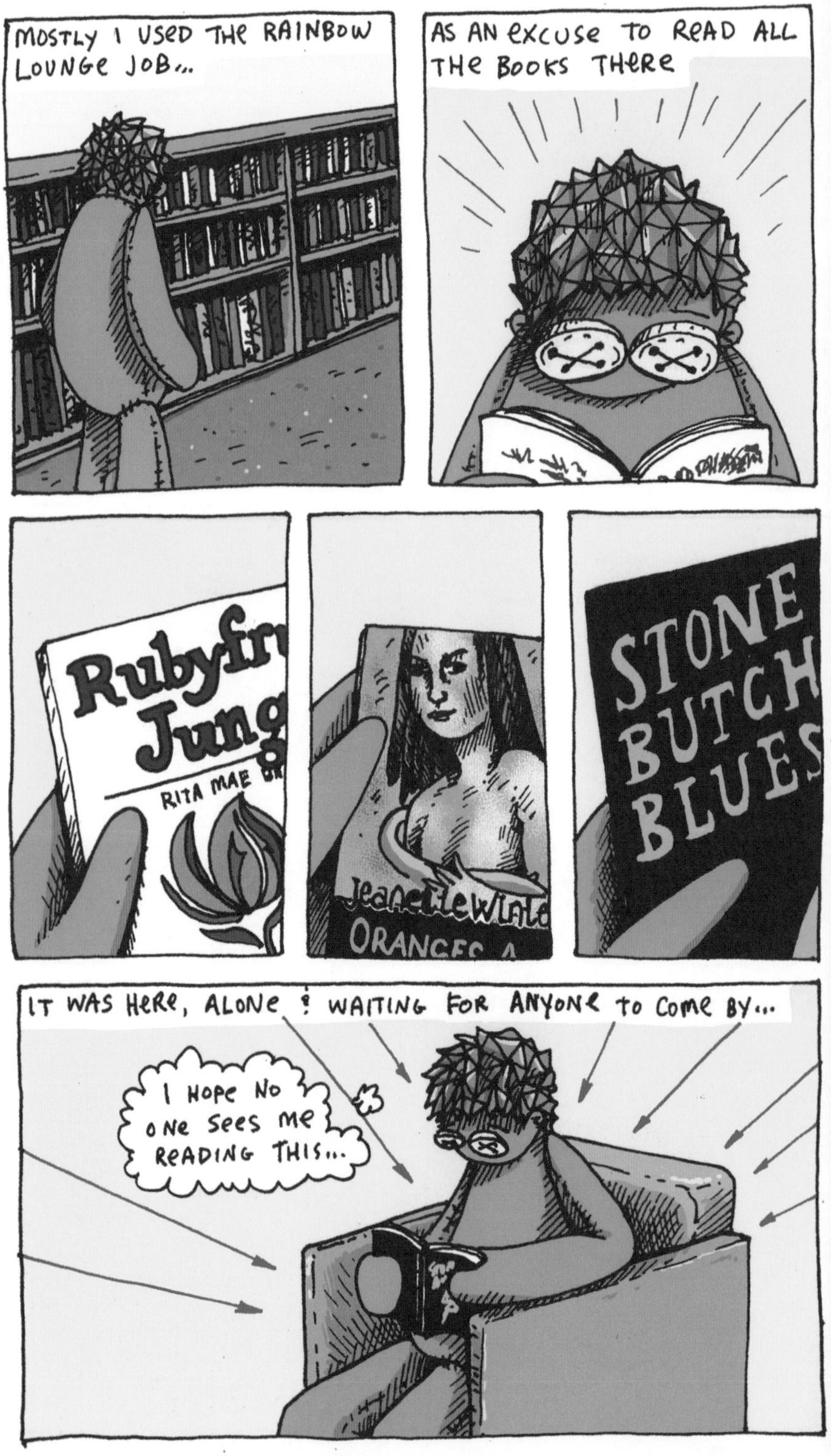
MOSTLY I USED THE RAINBOW LOUNGE JOB...
AS AN EXCUSE TO READ ALL THE BOOKS THERE
Rubyfru
Jung
RITA MAE
ORANGES A
STONE BUTCH BLUES
IT WAS HERE, ALONE & WAITING FOR ANYONE TO COME BY...
I HOPE NO ONE SEES ME READING THIS...

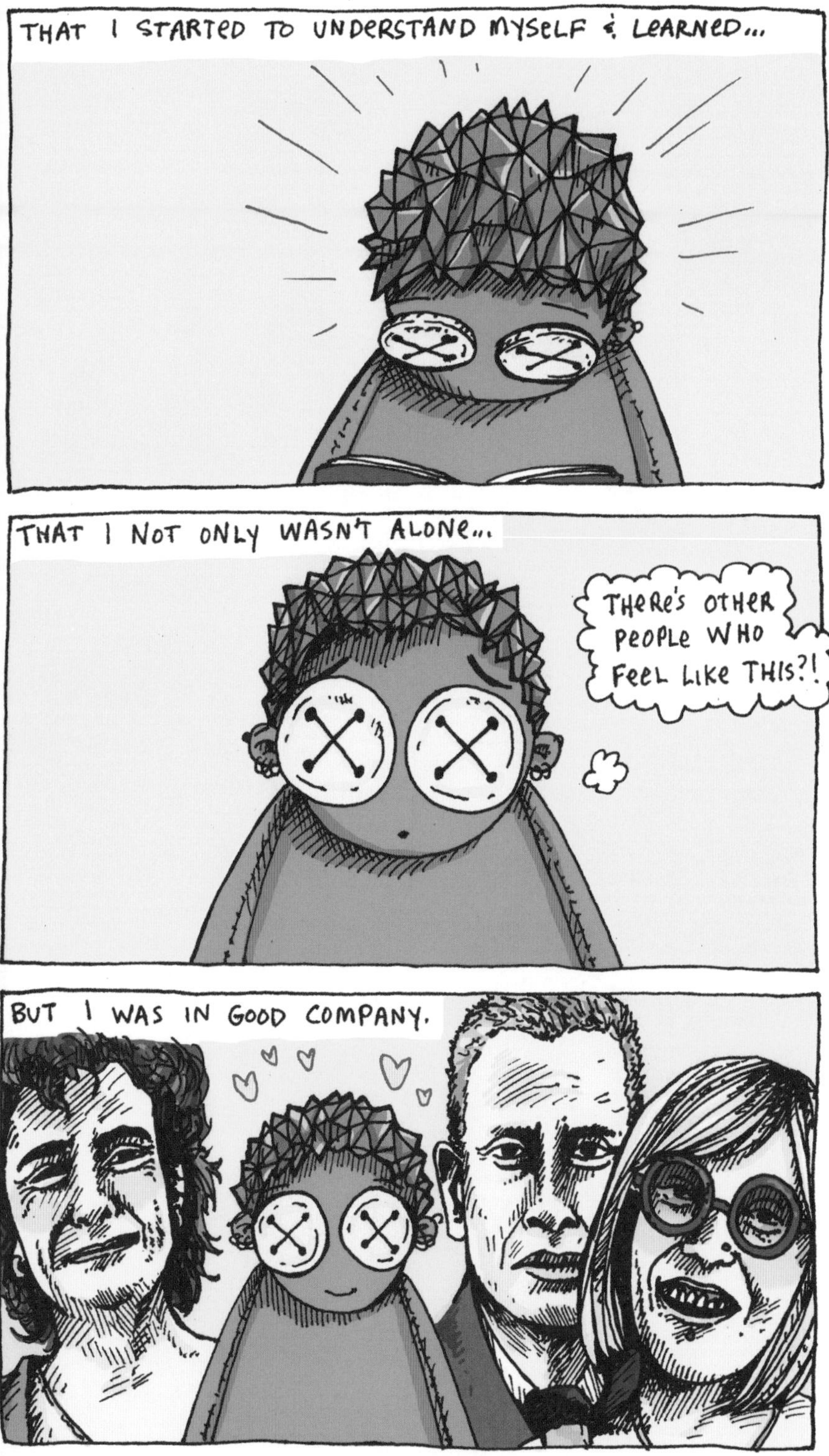
THAT I STARTED TO UNDERSTAND MYSELF & LEARNED...
THAT I NOT ONLY WASN'T ALONE...
THERE'S OTHER PEOPLE WHO FEEL LIKE THIS?!
BUT I WAS IN GOOD COMPANY.

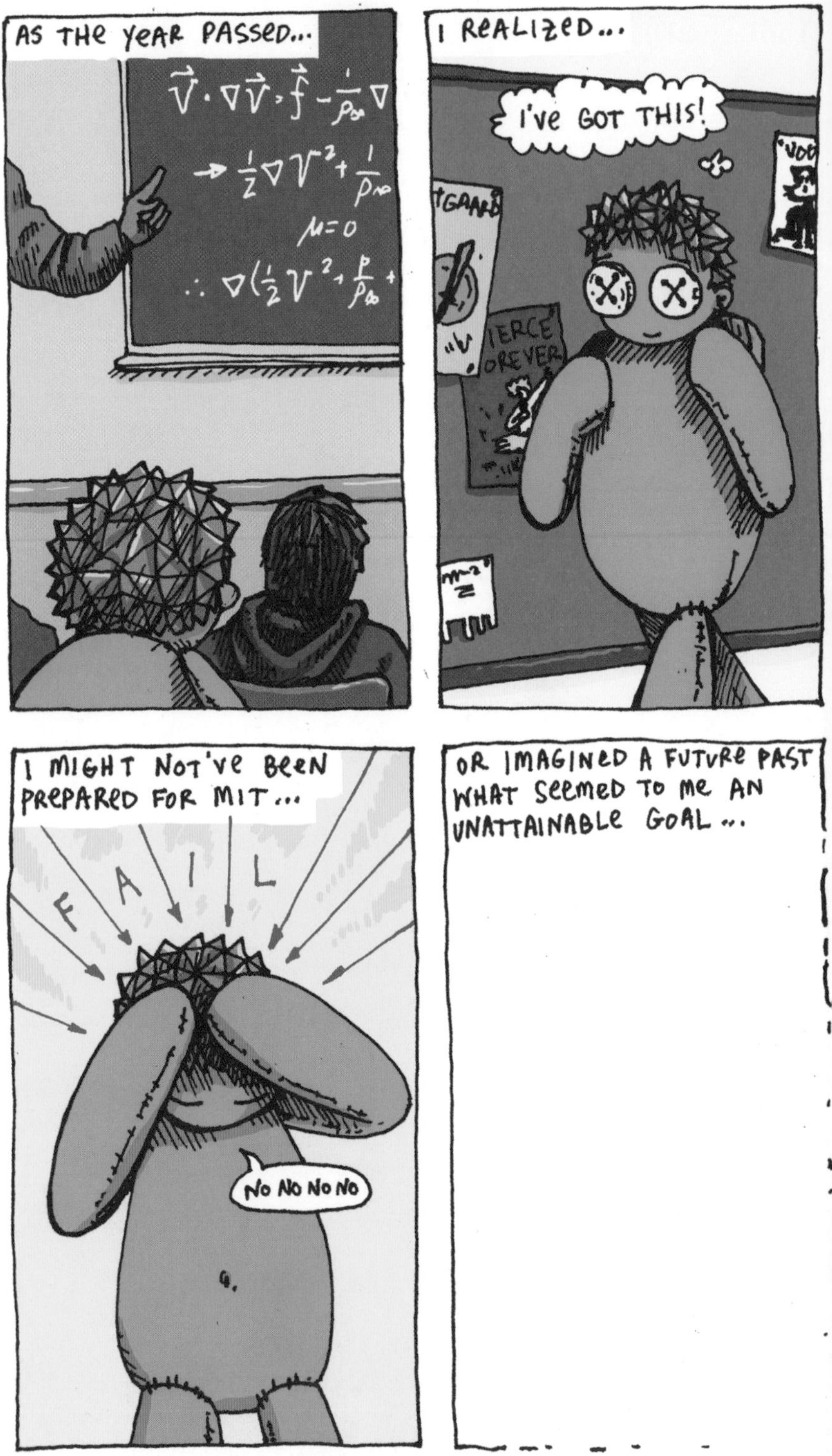
AS THE YEAR PASSED...
I REALIZED...
I'VE GOT THIS!
I MIGHT NOT'VE BEEN PREPARED FOR MIT...
F A I L
NO NO NO NO
OR IMAGINED A FUTURE PAST WHAT SEEMED TO ME AN UNATTAINABLE GOAL...

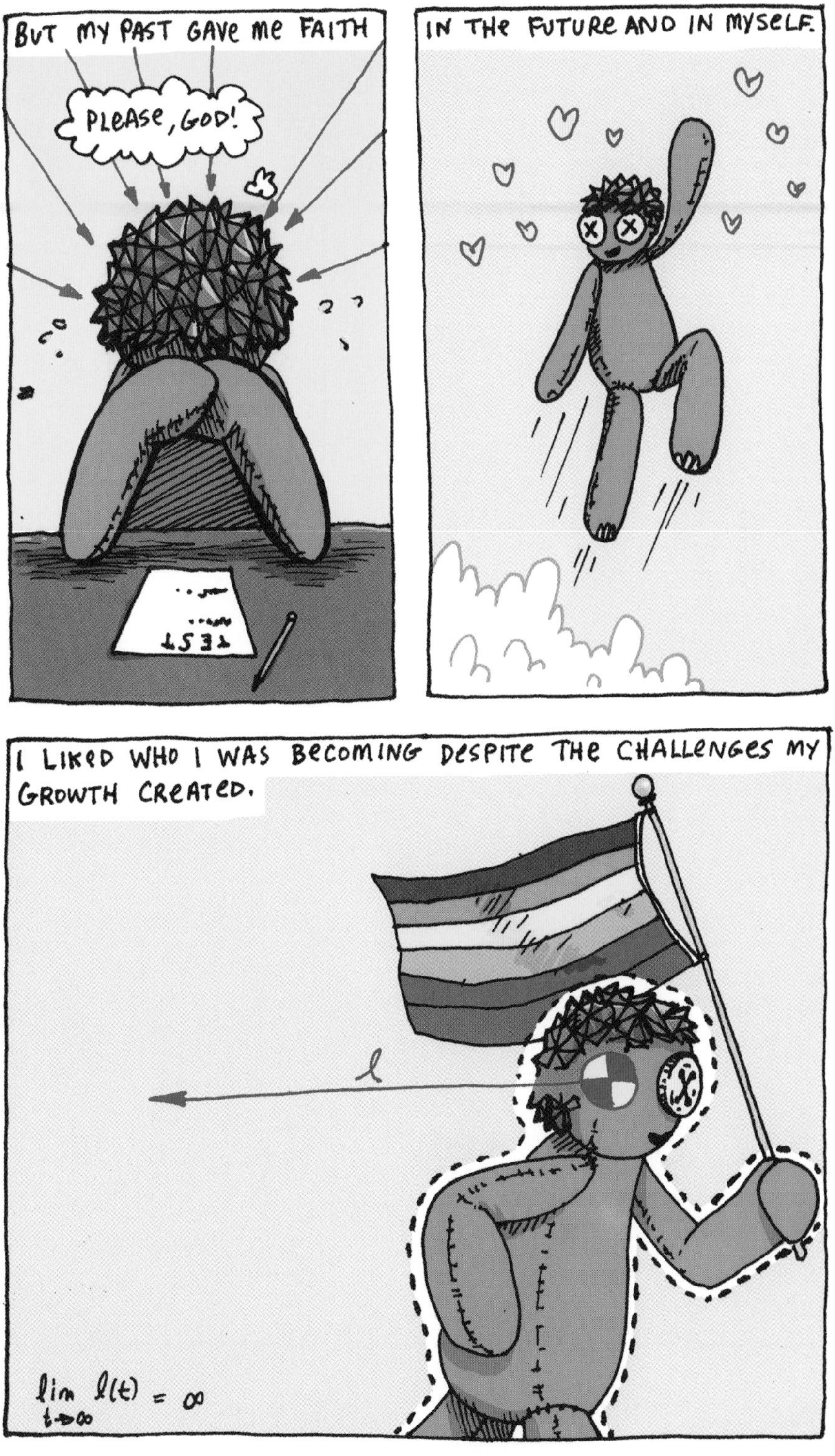
BUT MY PAST GAVE ME FAITH
PLEASE, GOD!
TEST
IN THE FUTURE AND IN MYSELF.
I LIKED WHO I WAS BECOMING DESPITE THE CHALLENGES MY GROWTH CREATED.
l
$\lim_{t \to \infty} l(t) = \infty$

CHAPTER EIGHT

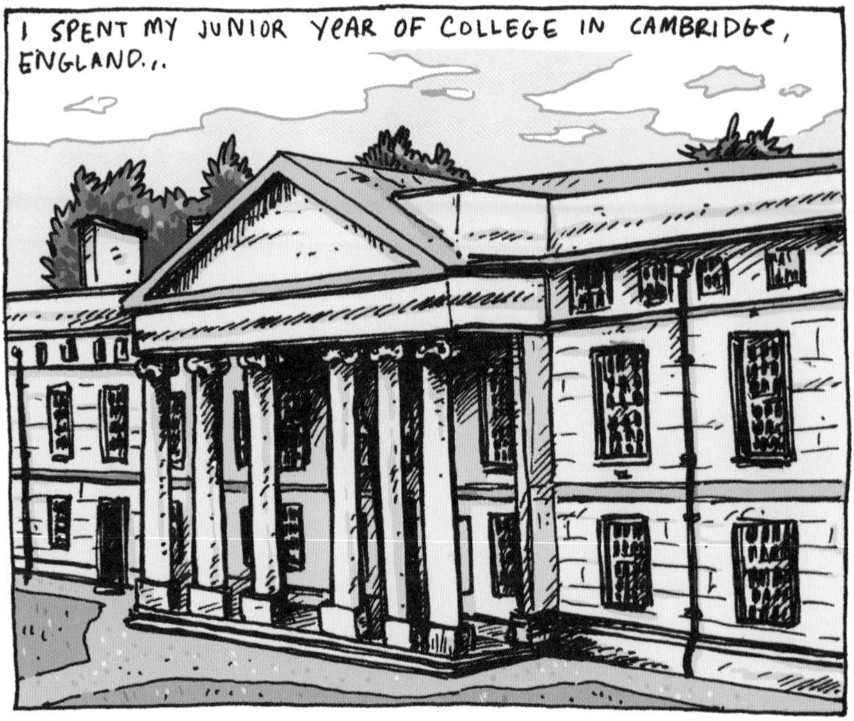
I SPENT MY JUNIOR YEAR OF COLLEGE IN CAMBRIDGE, ENGLAND...

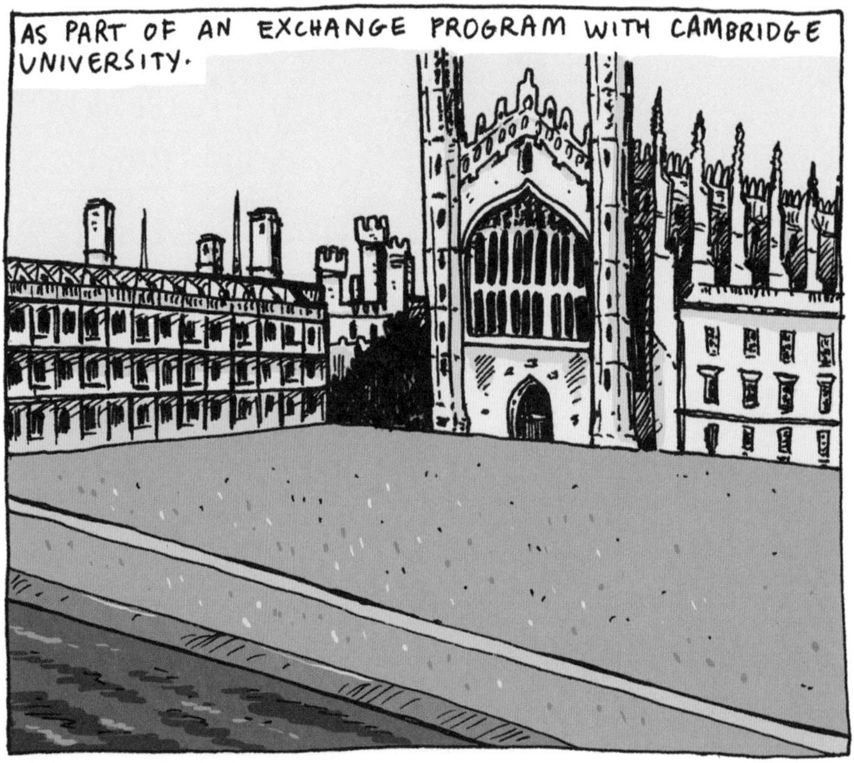
AS PART OF AN EXCHANGE PROGRAM WITH CAMBRIDGE UNIVERSITY.

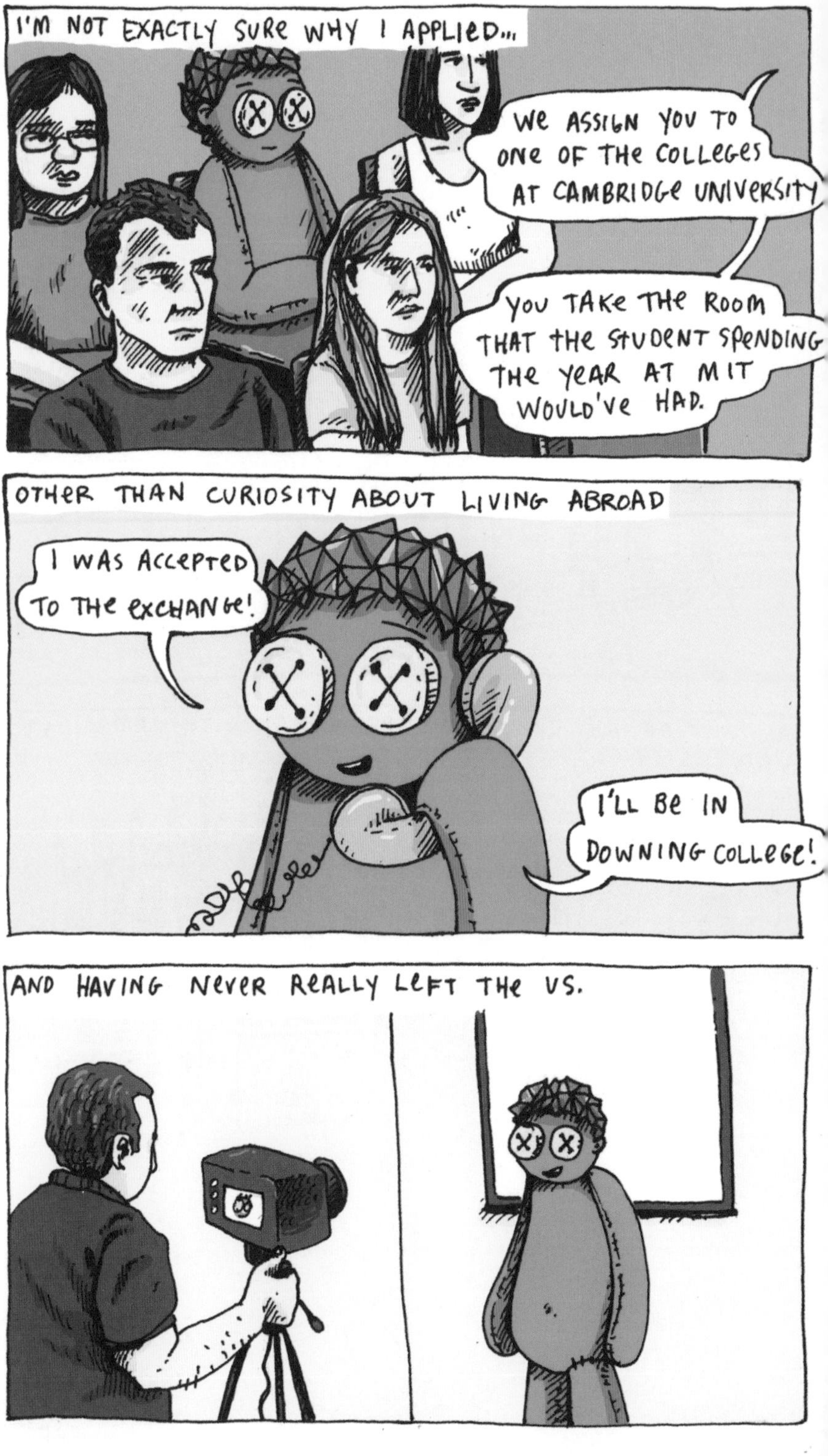
I'M NOT EXACTLY SURE WHY I APPLIED...
WE ASSIGN YOU TO ONE OF THE COLLEGES AT CAMBRIDGE UNIVERSITY
YOU TAKE THE ROOM THAT THE STUDENT SPENDING THE YEAR AT MIT WOULD'VE HAD.
OTHER THAN CURIOSITY ABOUT LIVING ABROAD
I WAS ACCEPTED TO THE EXCHANGE!
I'LL BE IN DOWNING COLLEGE!
AND HAVING NEVER REALLY LEFT THE US.

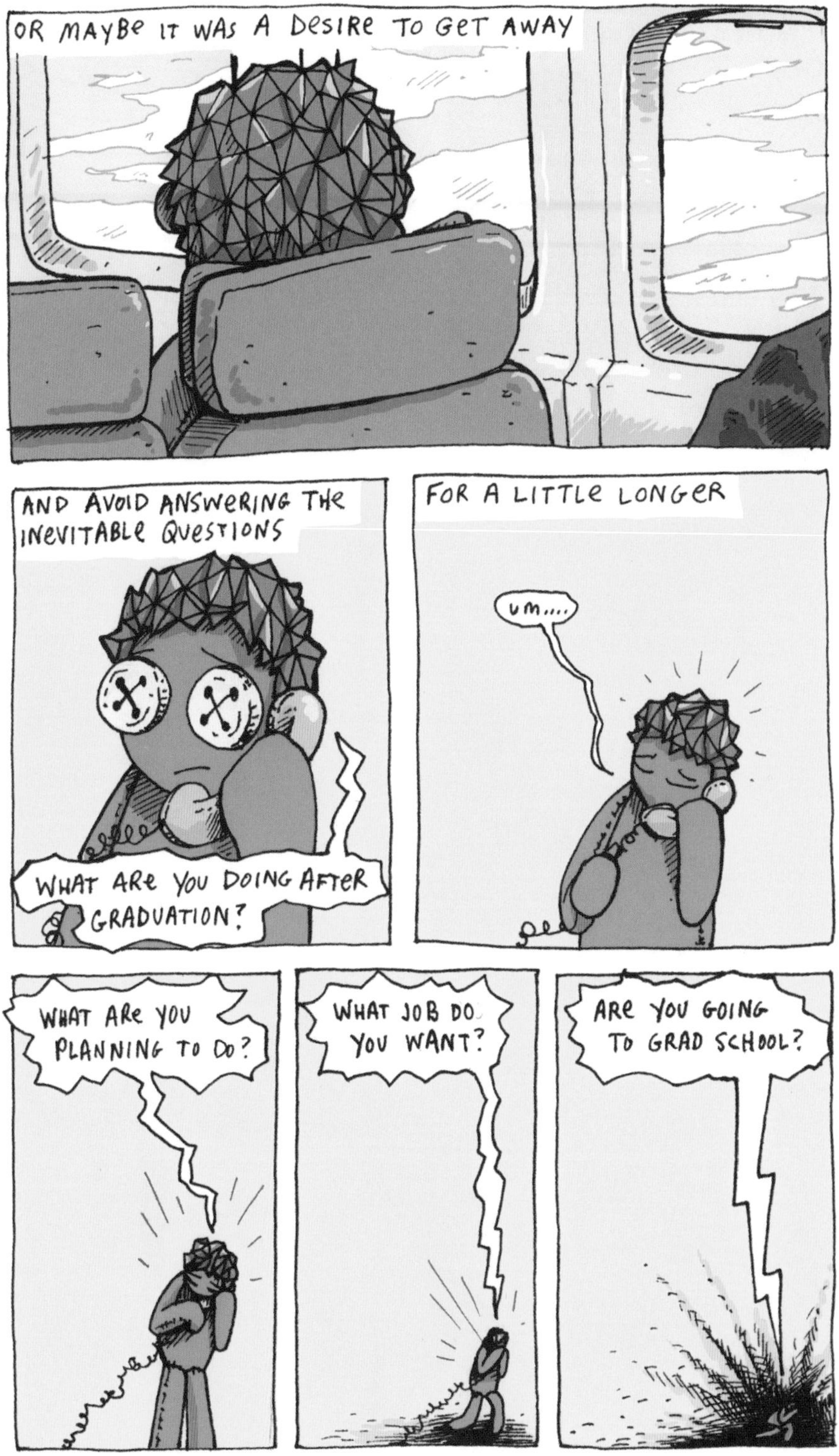
OR MAYBE IT WAS A DESIRE TO GET AWAY
AND AVOID ANSWERING THE INEVITABLE QUESTIONS
WHAT ARE YOU DOING AFTER GRADUATION?
FOR A LITTLE LONGER
UM....
WHAT ARE YOU PLANNING TO DO?
WHAT JOB DO YOU WANT?
ARE YOU GOING TO GRAD SCHOOL?

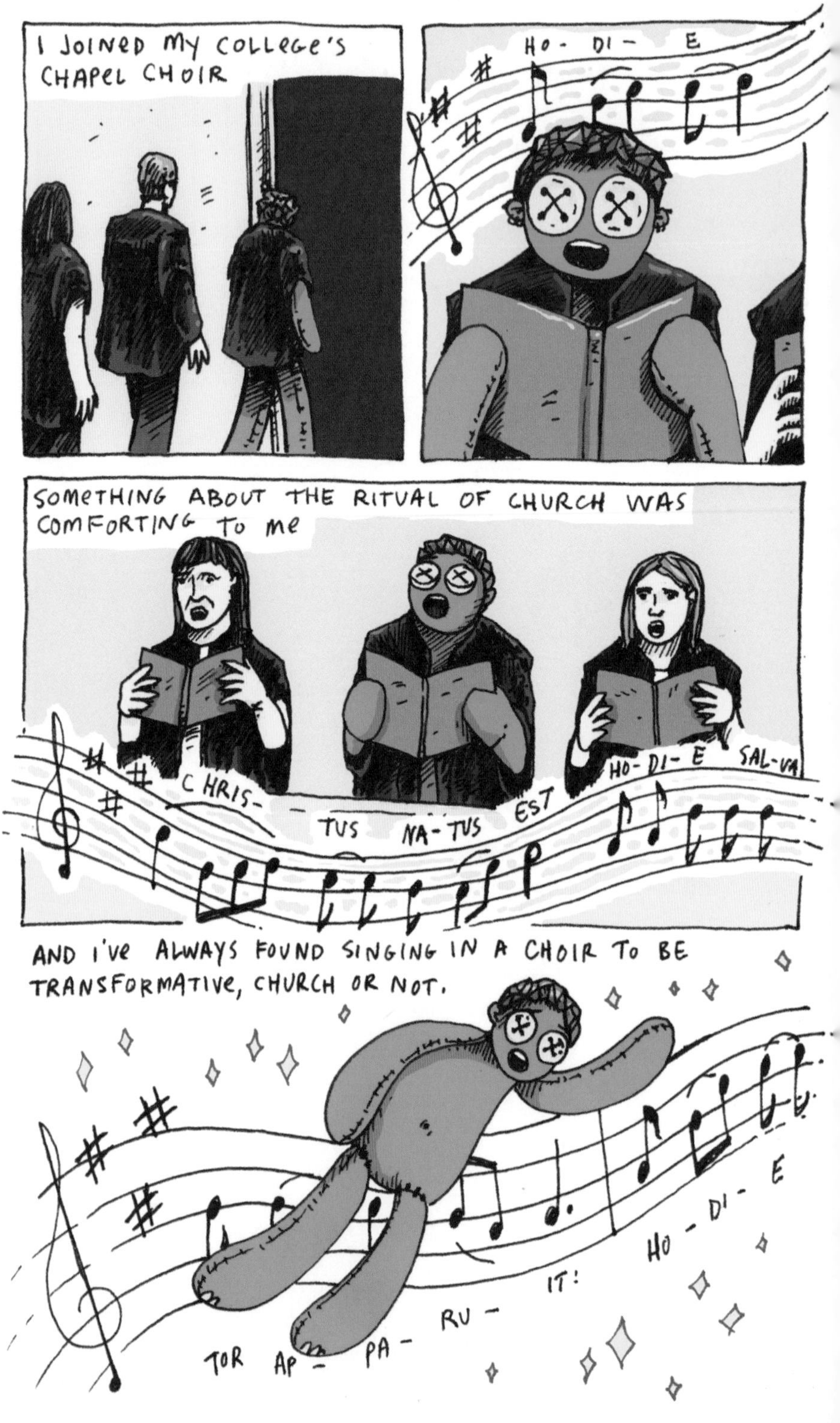
I JOINED MY COLLEGE'S CHAPEL CHOIR
HO- DI- E
SOMETHING ABOUT THE RITUAL OF CHURCH WAS COMFORTING TO ME
CHRIS- TUS NA- TUS EST HO- DI- E SAL- VA
AND I'VE ALWAYS FOUND SINGING IN A CHOIR TO BE TRANSFORMATIVE, CHURCH OR NOT.
TOR AP- PA- RU- IT! HO- DI- E

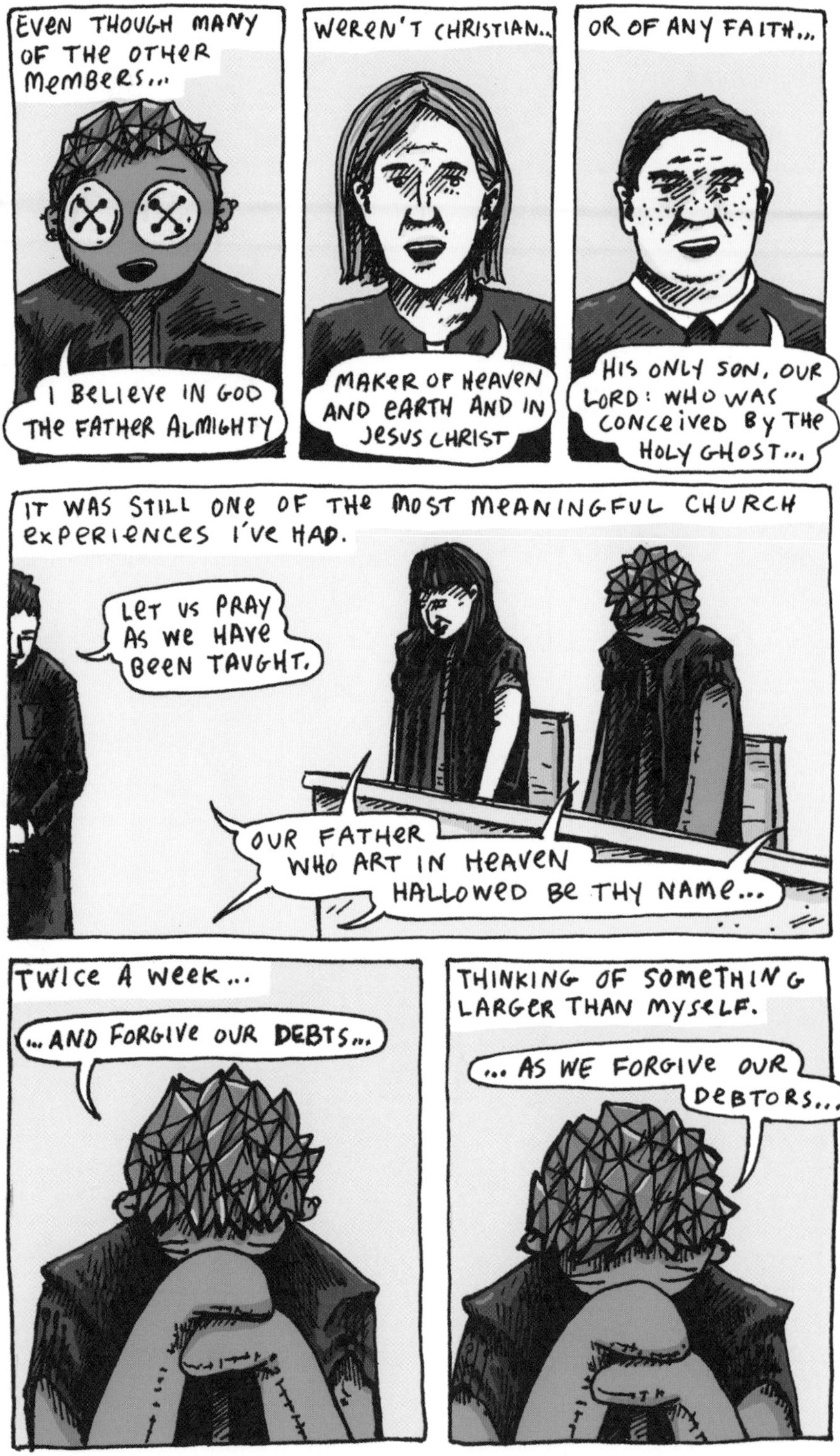
EVEN THOUGH MANY OF THE OTHER MEMBERS...
I BELIEVE IN GOD THE FATHER ALMIGHTY
WEREN'T CHRISTIAN...
MAKER OF HEAVEN AND EARTH AND IN JESUS CHRIST
OR OF ANY FAITH...
HIS ONLY SON, OUR LORD: WHO WAS CONCEIVED BY THE HOLY GHOST...
IT WAS STILL ONE OF THE MOST MEANINGFUL CHURCH EXPERIENCES I'VE HAD.
LET US PRAY AS WE HAVE BEEN TAUGHT.
OUR FATHER WHO ART IN HEAVEN HALLOWED BE THY NAME...
TWICE A WEEK...
...AND FORGIVE OUR DEBTS...
THINKING OF SOMETHING LARGER THAN MYSELF.
...AS WE FORGIVE OUR DEBTORS...

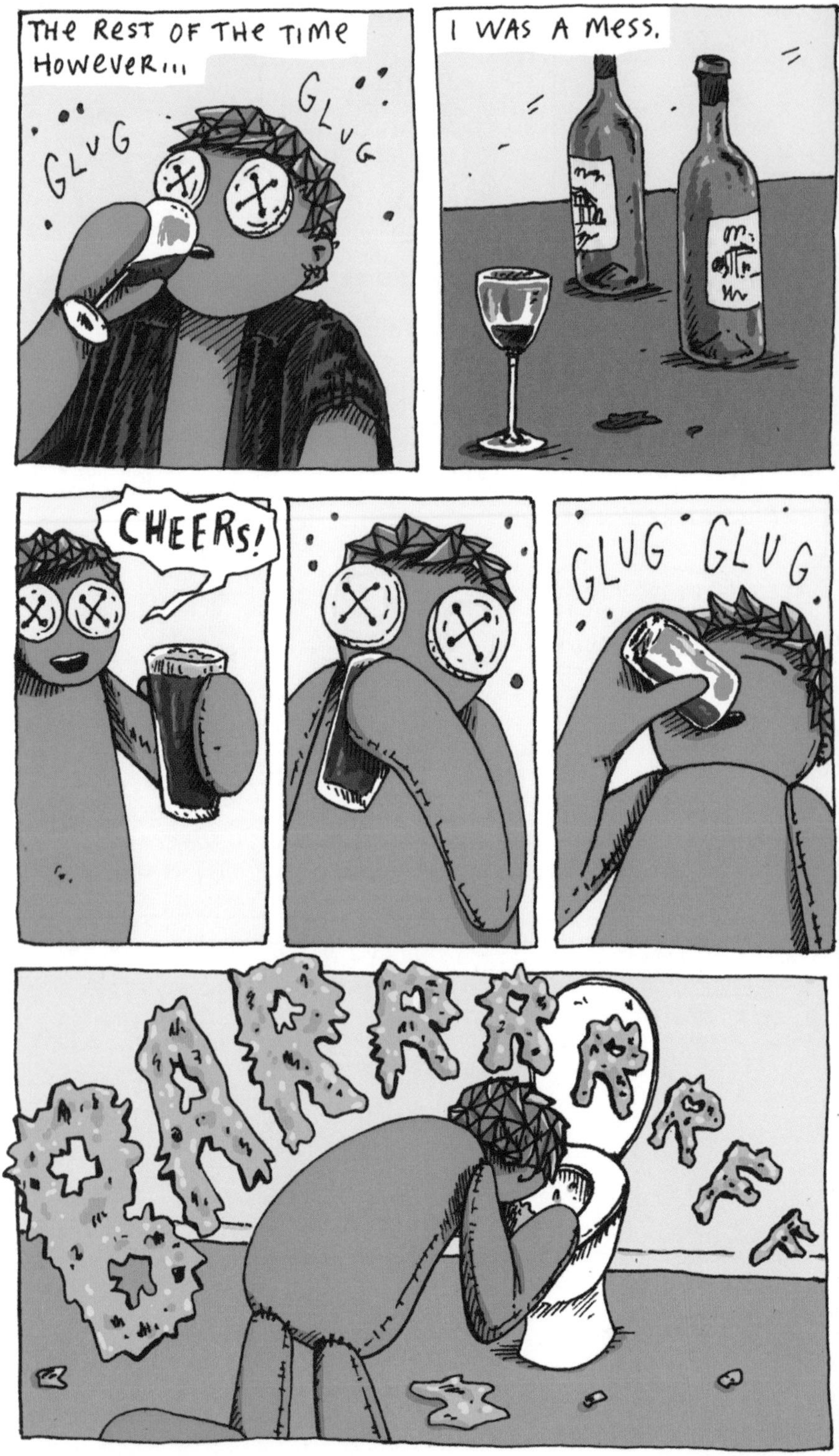
THE REST OF THE TIME HOWEVER...
GLUG
GLUG
I WAS A MESS.
CHEERS!
GLUG GLUG
OARRRRR

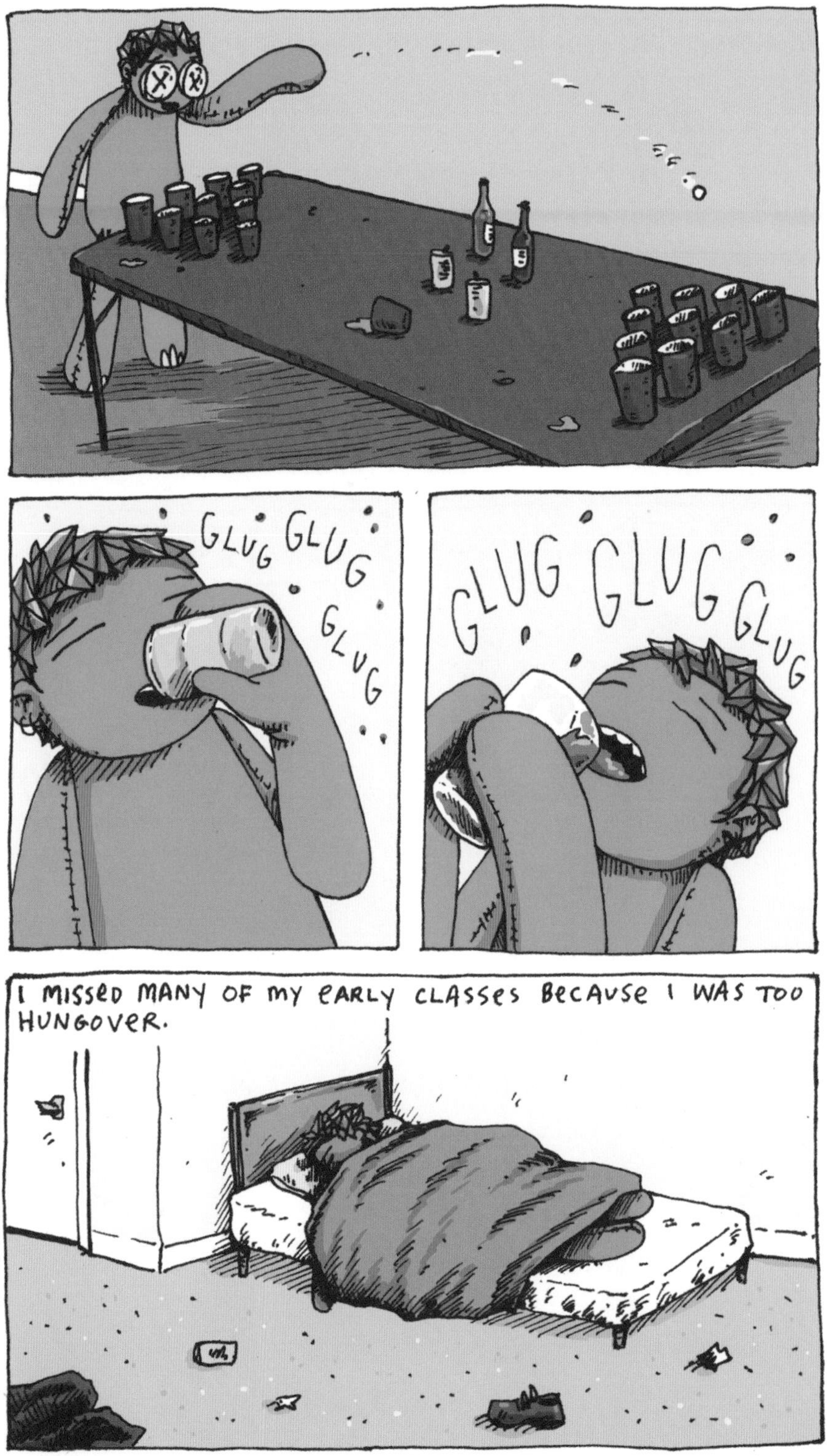
GLUG GLUG
GLUG
GLUG GLUG GLUG
I MISSED MANY OF MY EARLY CLASSES BECAUSE I WAS TOO HUNGOVER.

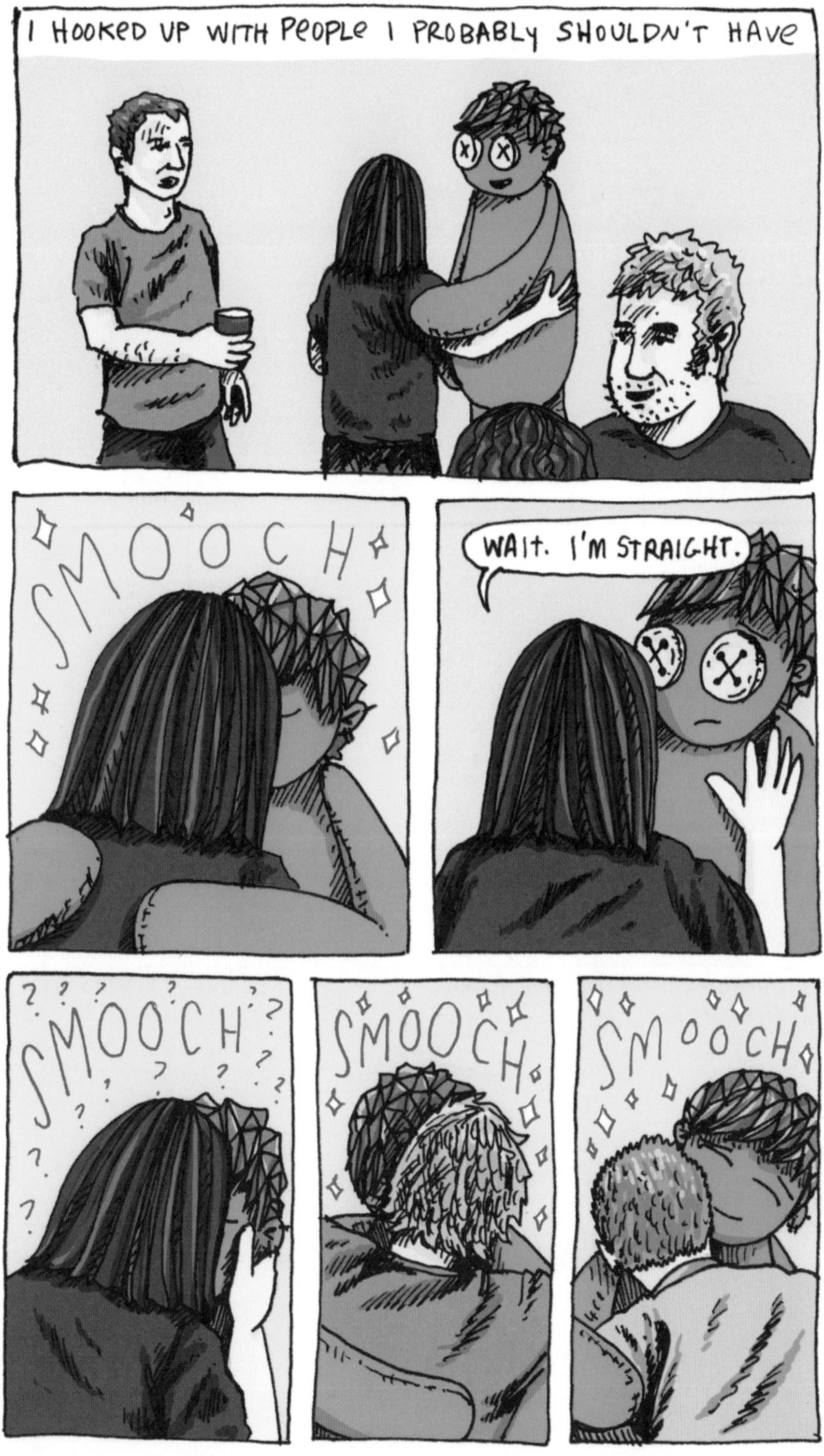
I HOOKED UP WITH PEOPLE I PROBABLY SHOULDN'T HAVE
SMOOCH
WAIT. I'M STRAIGHT.
SMOOCH
SMOOCH
SMOOCH

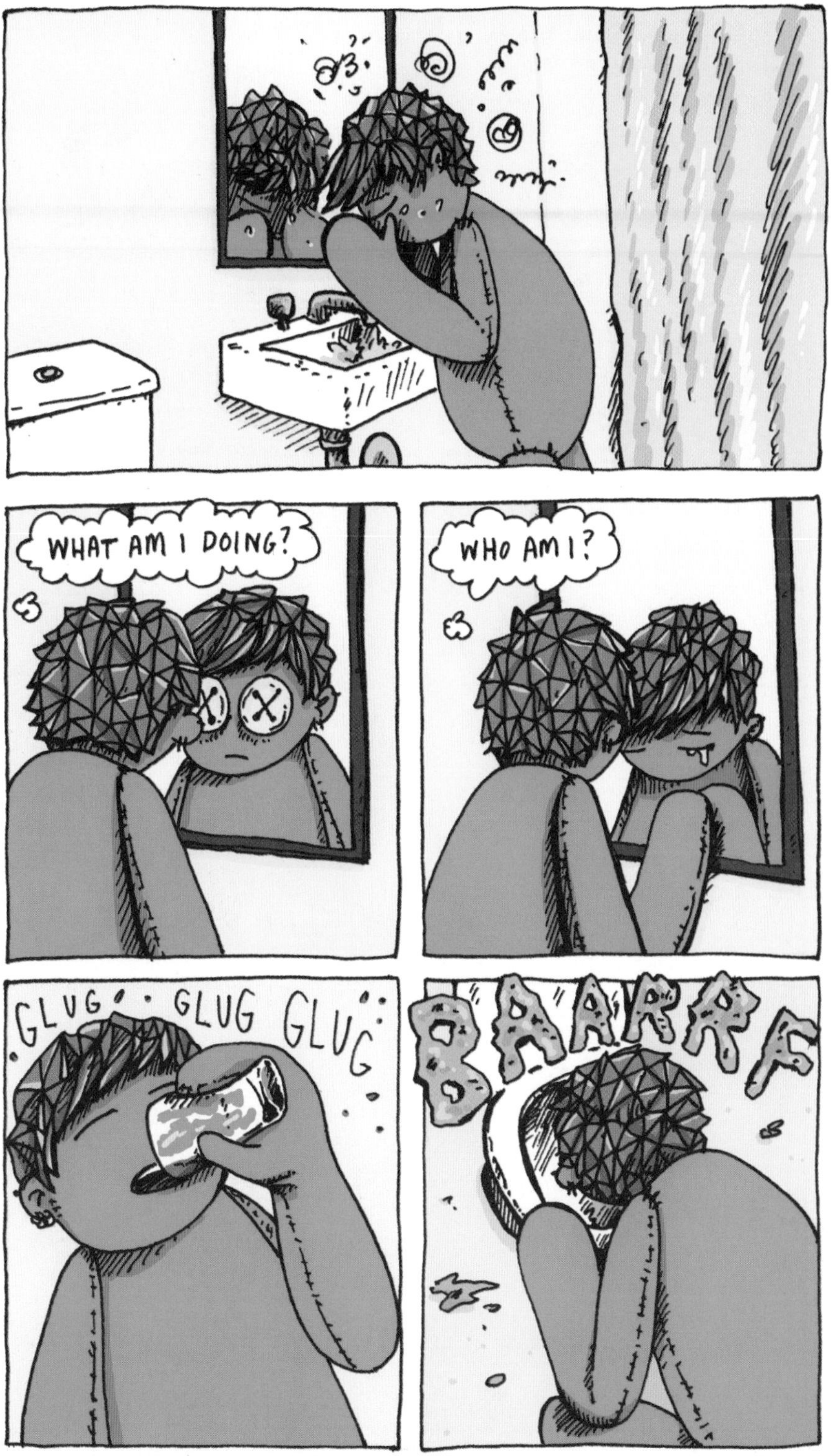
WHAT AM I DOING?
WHO AM I?
GLUG GLUG GLUG
BAARRF

OTHER THAN CHOIR THE ONLY THING THAT KEPT ME GROUNDED...

WAS DRAWING.

IT BECAME A WAY FOR ME TO SORT MY FEELINGS OUT.

IT WAS MY REFUGE.

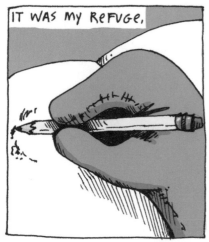

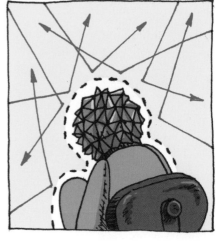

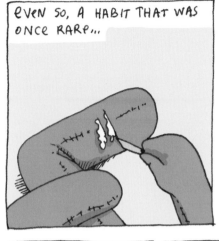

EVEN SO, A HABIT THAT WAS ONCE RARE...

BECAME COMMON.

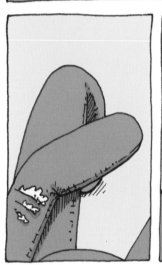

I DIDN'T UNDERSTAND

WHO AM I

CAN'T YOU SEE?!

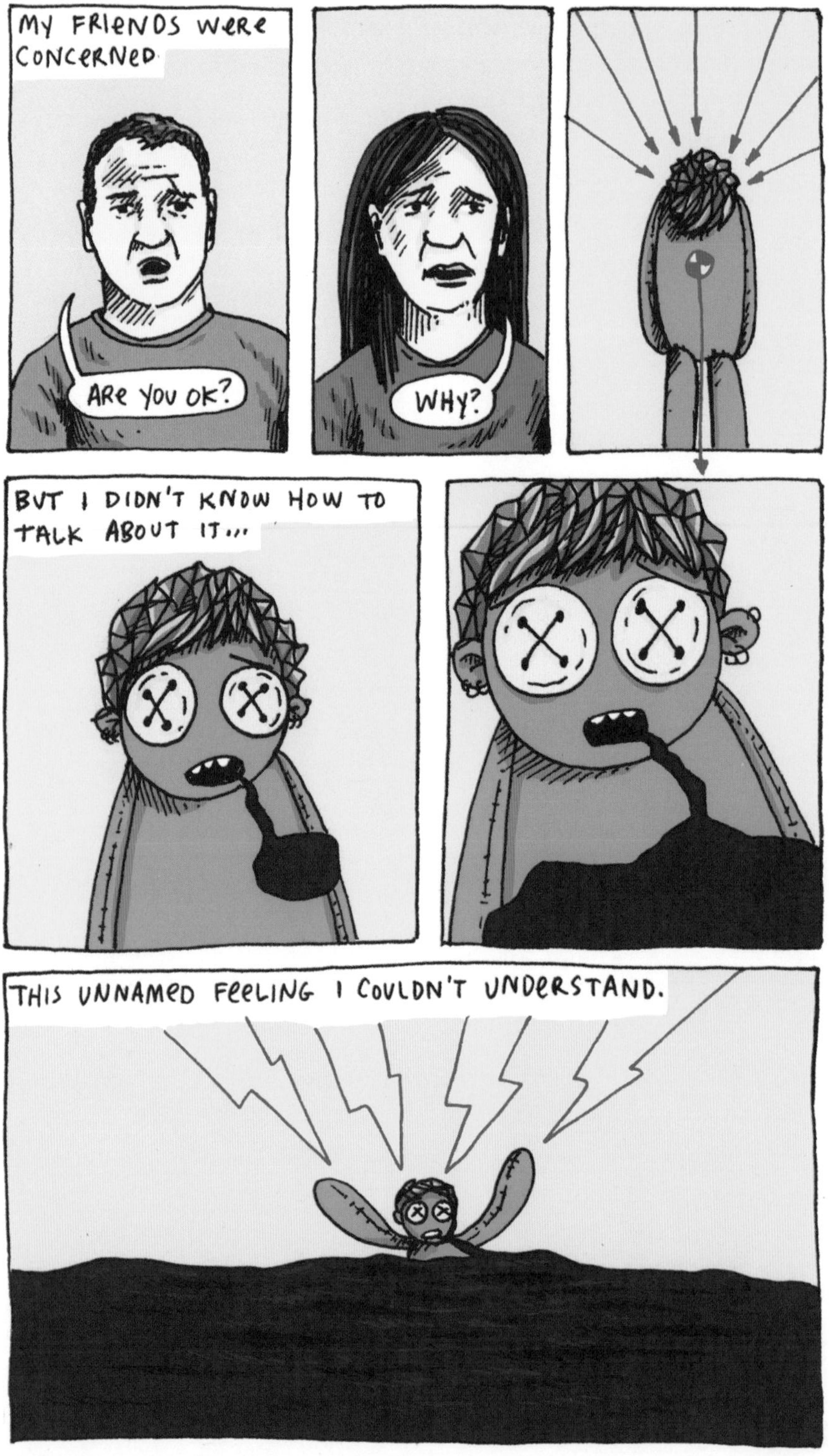
MY FRIENDS WERE CONCERNED
ARE YOU OK?
WHY?
BUT I DIDN'T KNOW HOW TO TALK ABOUT IT...
THIS UNNAMED FEELING I COULDN'T UNDERSTAND.

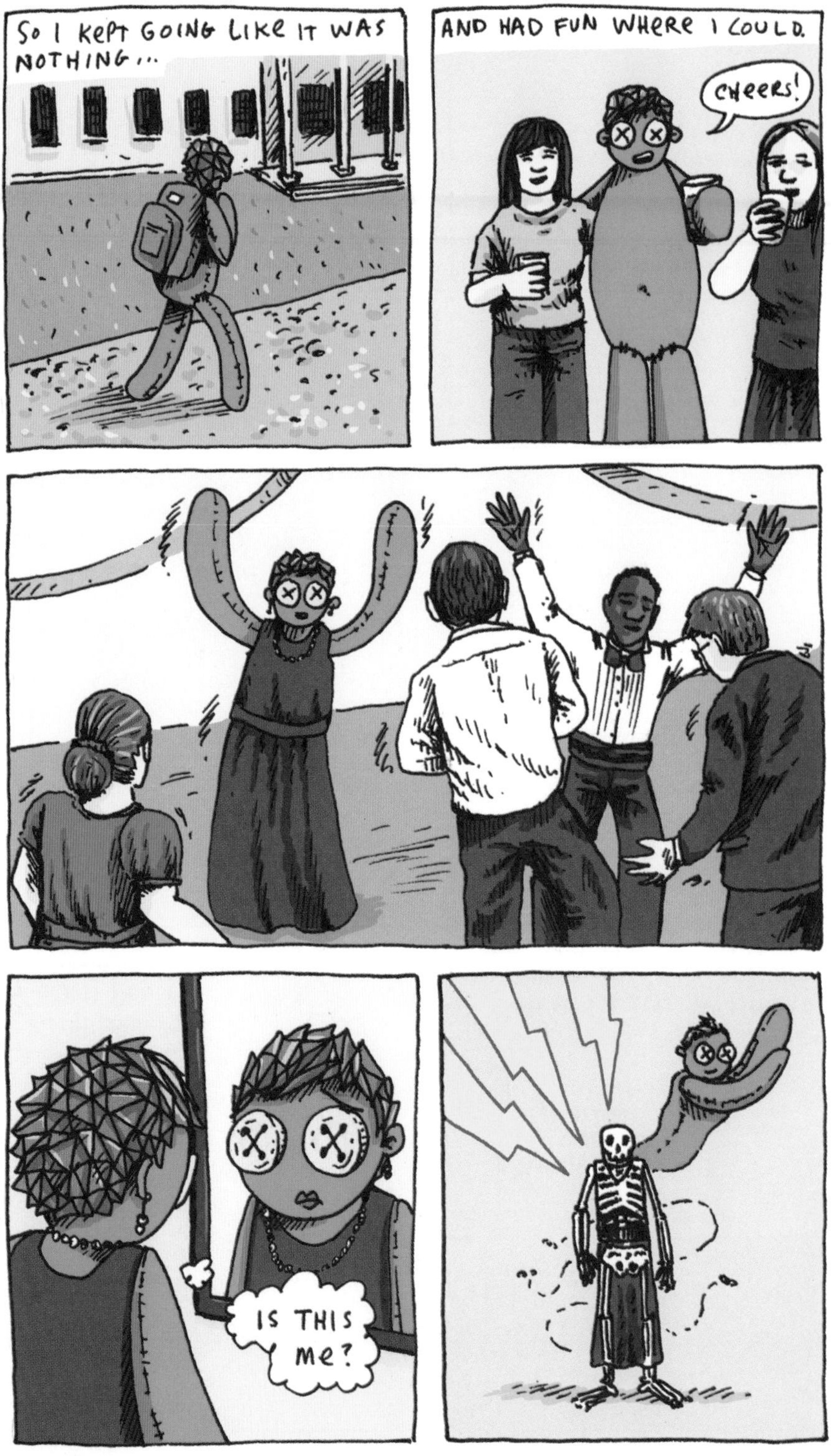
SO I KEPT GOING LIKE IT WAS NOTHING...
AND HAD FUN WHERE I COULD.
CHEERS!
IS THIS ME?

IT WASN'T AN EASY YEAR IN ENGLAND...

BUT I GREW A LOT & MADE FRIENDS ALONG THE WAY.

IT'S CHECKPOINT CHARLIE!

COOL!

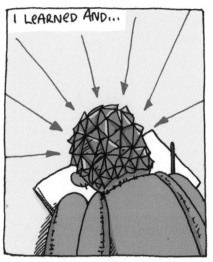

I LEARNED AND...

I CHANGED.

SNIP SNIP SNIP

PART OF THIS WAS DECIDING TO SWITCH DORMS WHEN I WENT BACK TO MIT.

CHOICE 1
EAST CAMPUS
CHOICE 2
SENIOR HOUSE

CLIK

I GOT INTO SENIOR HOUSE!

COOL! WE'LL BE NEIGHBORS!

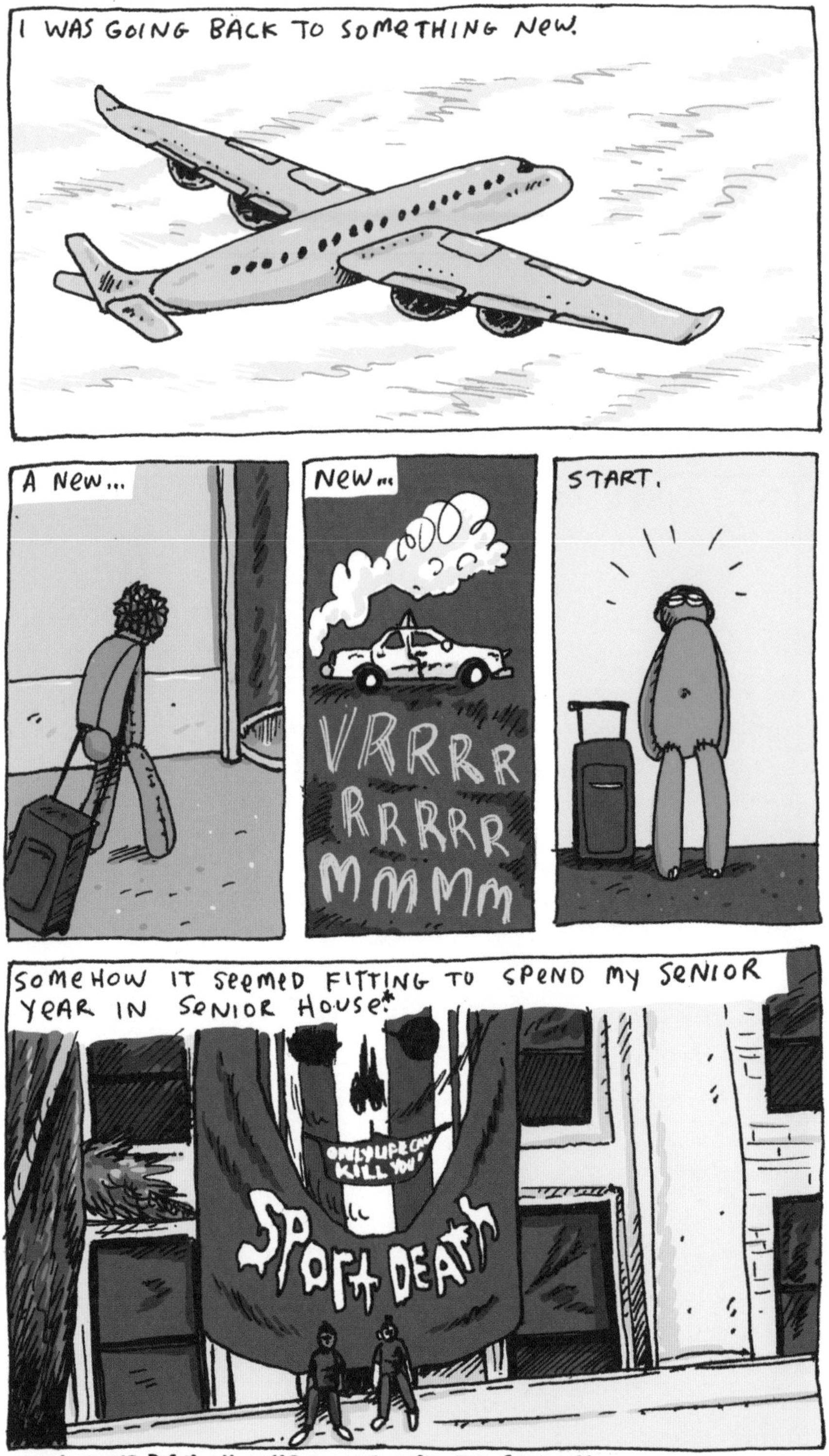
I WAS GOING BACK TO SOMETHING NEW.
A NEW...
NEW...
VRRRRR
RRRRR
MMMM
START.
SOMEHOW IT SEEMED FITTING TO SPEND MY SENIOR YEAR IN SENIOR HOUSE.*
ONLY LIFE CAN KILL YOU
SPORT DEATH

* THE OLDEST DORM ON CAMPUS – NOT JUST FOR SENIORS

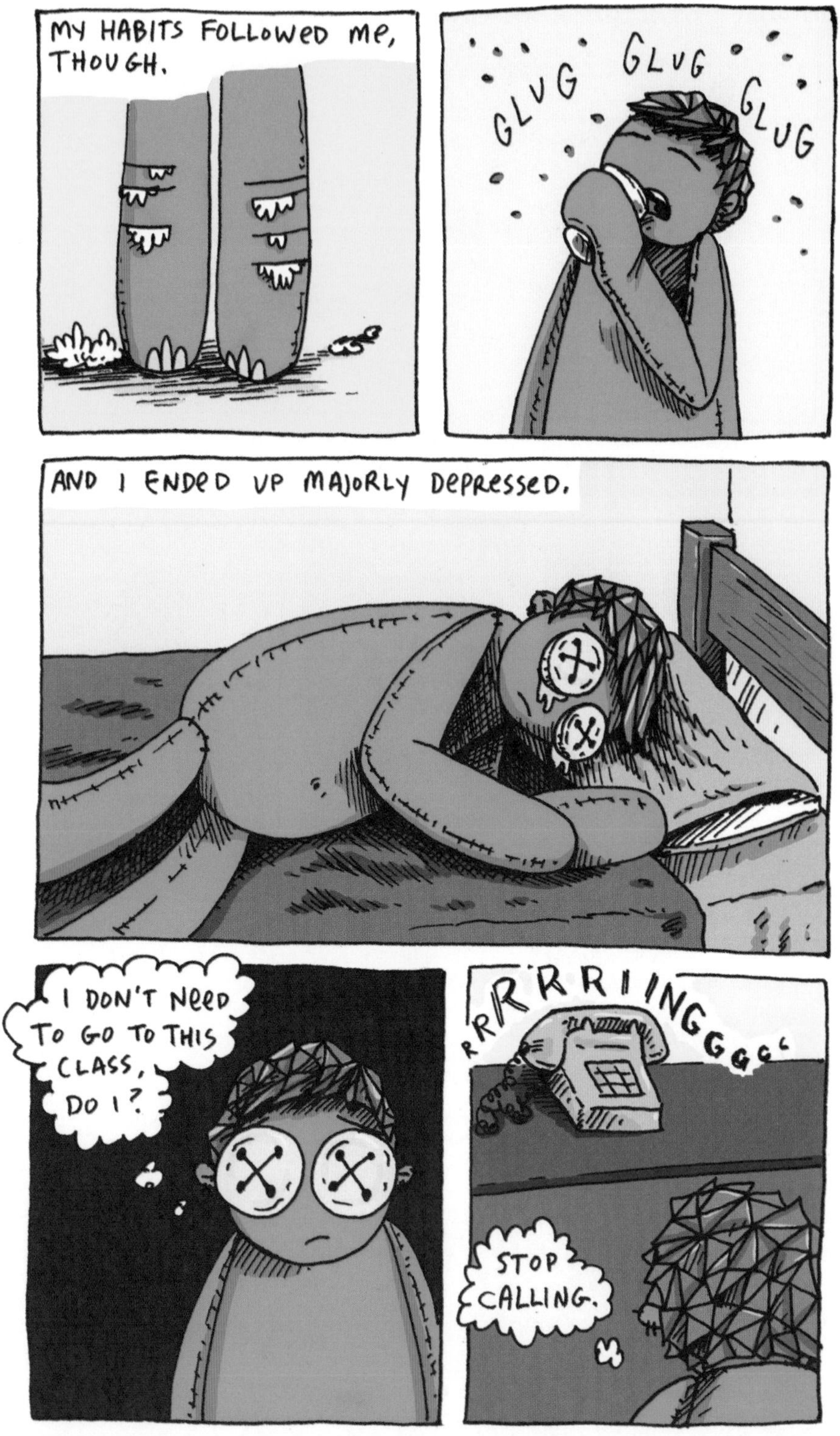
MY HABITS FOLLOWED ME, THOUGH.
GLUG GLUG GLUG
AND I ENDED UP MAJORLY DEPRESSED.
I DON'T NEED TO GO TO THIS CLASS, DO I?
RRRRRIIINGGGGG
STOP CALLING.

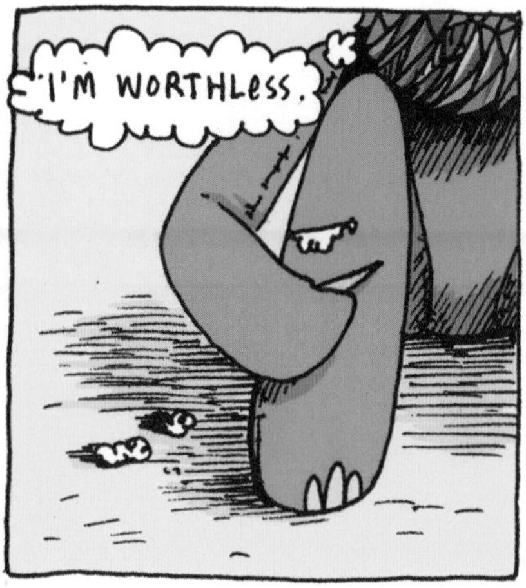
I'M WORTHLESS.

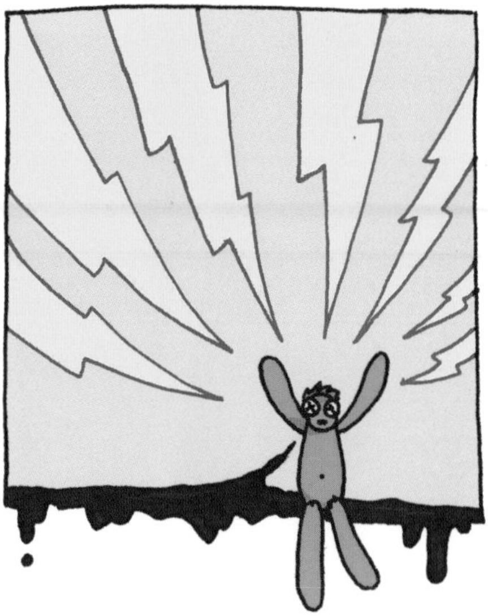

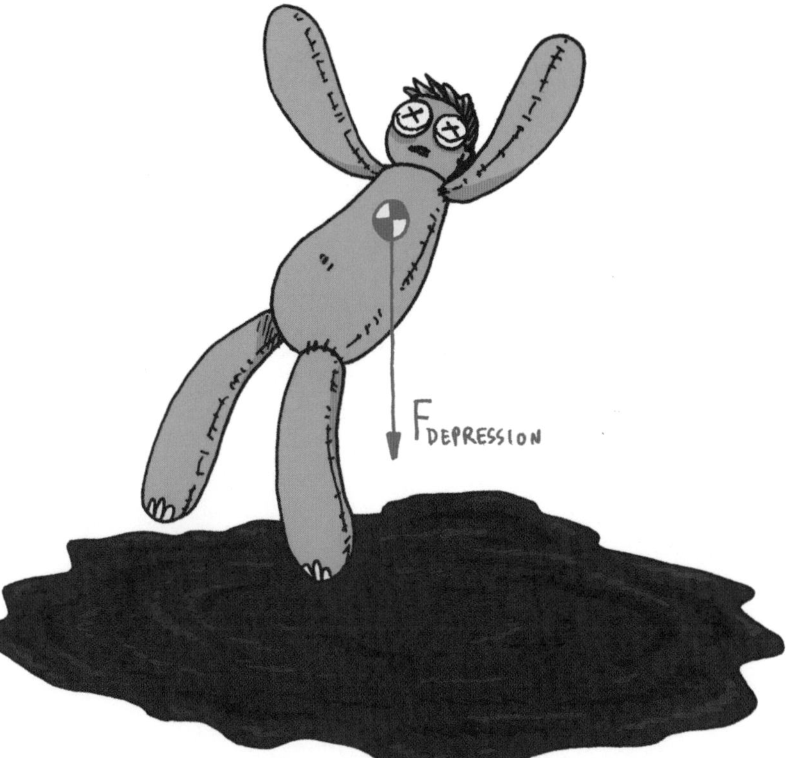
F DEPRESSION

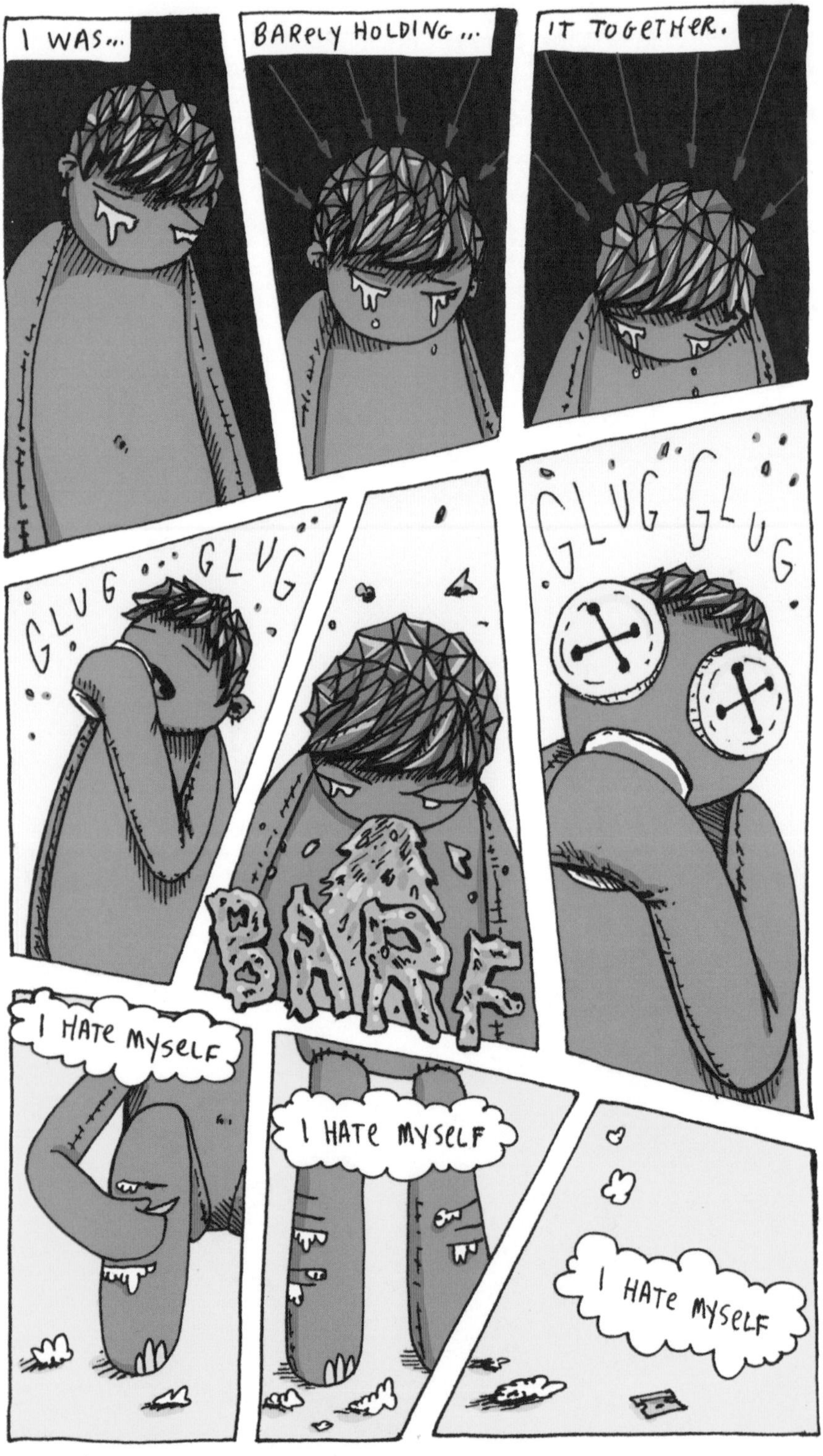
I WAS...
BARELY HOLDING...
IT TOGETHER.
GLUG... GLUG
BARF
GLUG GLUG
I HATE MYSELF
I HATE MYSELF
I HATE MYSELF

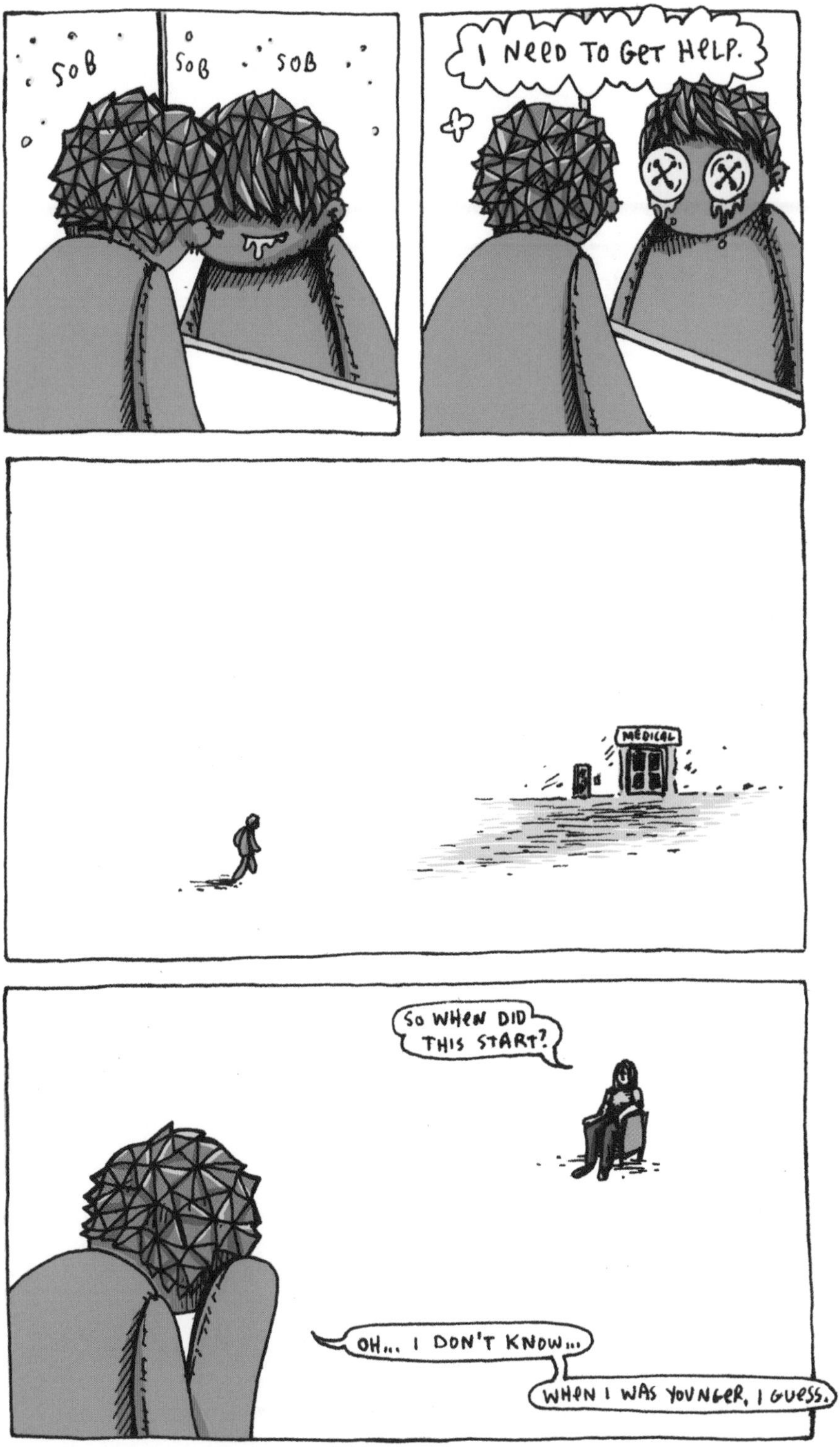
SOB
SOB
SOB
I NEED TO GET HELP.
MEDICAL
SO WHEN DID THIS START?
OH... I DON'T KNOW...
WHEN I WAS YOUNGER, I GUESS.

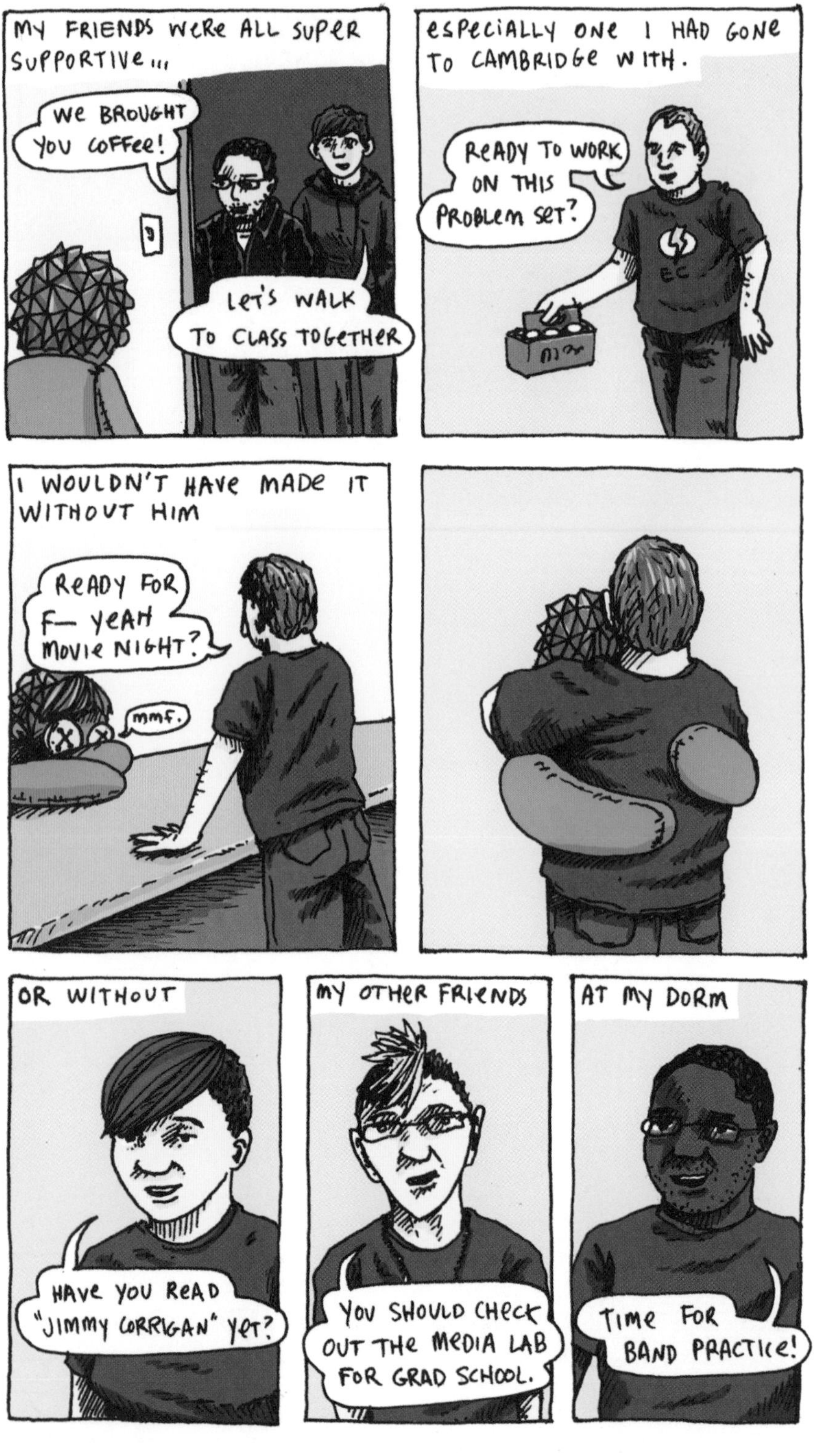
MY FRIENDS WERE ALL SUPER SUPPORTIVE...
WE BROUGHT YOU COFFEE!
LET'S WALK TO CLASS TOGETHER
ESPECIALLY ONE I HAD GONE TO CAMBRIDGE WITH.
READY TO WORK ON THIS PROBLEM SET?
EC
I WOULDN'T HAVE MADE IT WITHOUT HIM
READY FOR F— YEAH MOVIE NIGHT?
MMF.
OR WITHOUT
HAVE YOU READ "JIMMY CORRIGAN" YET?
MY OTHER FRIENDS
YOU SHOULD CHECK OUT THE MEDIA LAB FOR GRAD SCHOOL.
AT MY DORM
TIME FOR BAND PRACTICE!

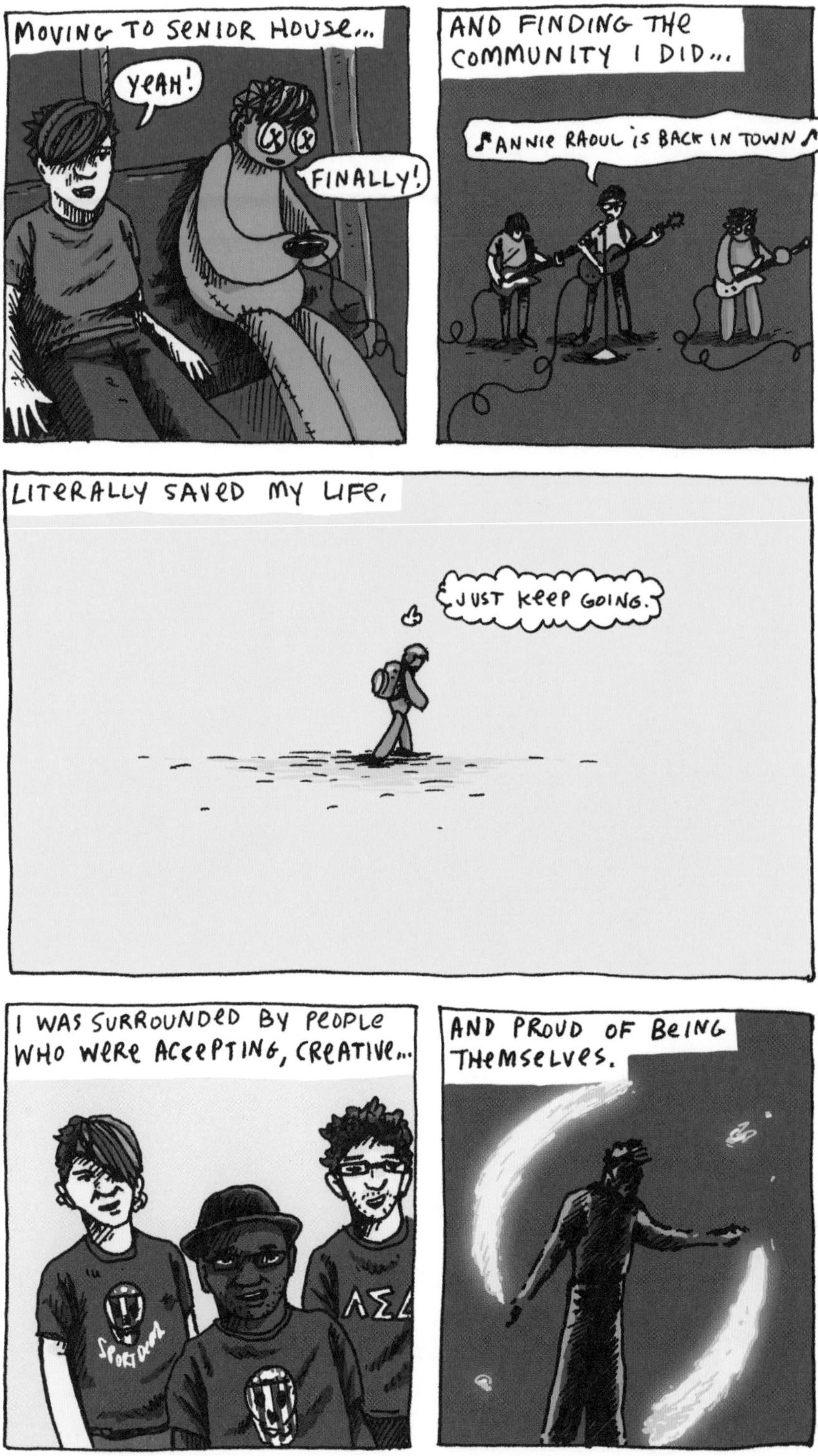
MOVING TO SENIOR HOUSE...
YEAH!
FINALLY!
AND FINDING THE COMMUNITY I DID...
♪ANNIE RAOUL IS BACK IN TOWN♪
LITERALLY SAVED MY LIFE.
JUST KEEP GOING.
I WAS SURROUNDED BY PEOPLE WHO WERE ACCEPTING, CREATIVE...
ΛΣΣ
AND PROUD OF BEING THEMSELVES.

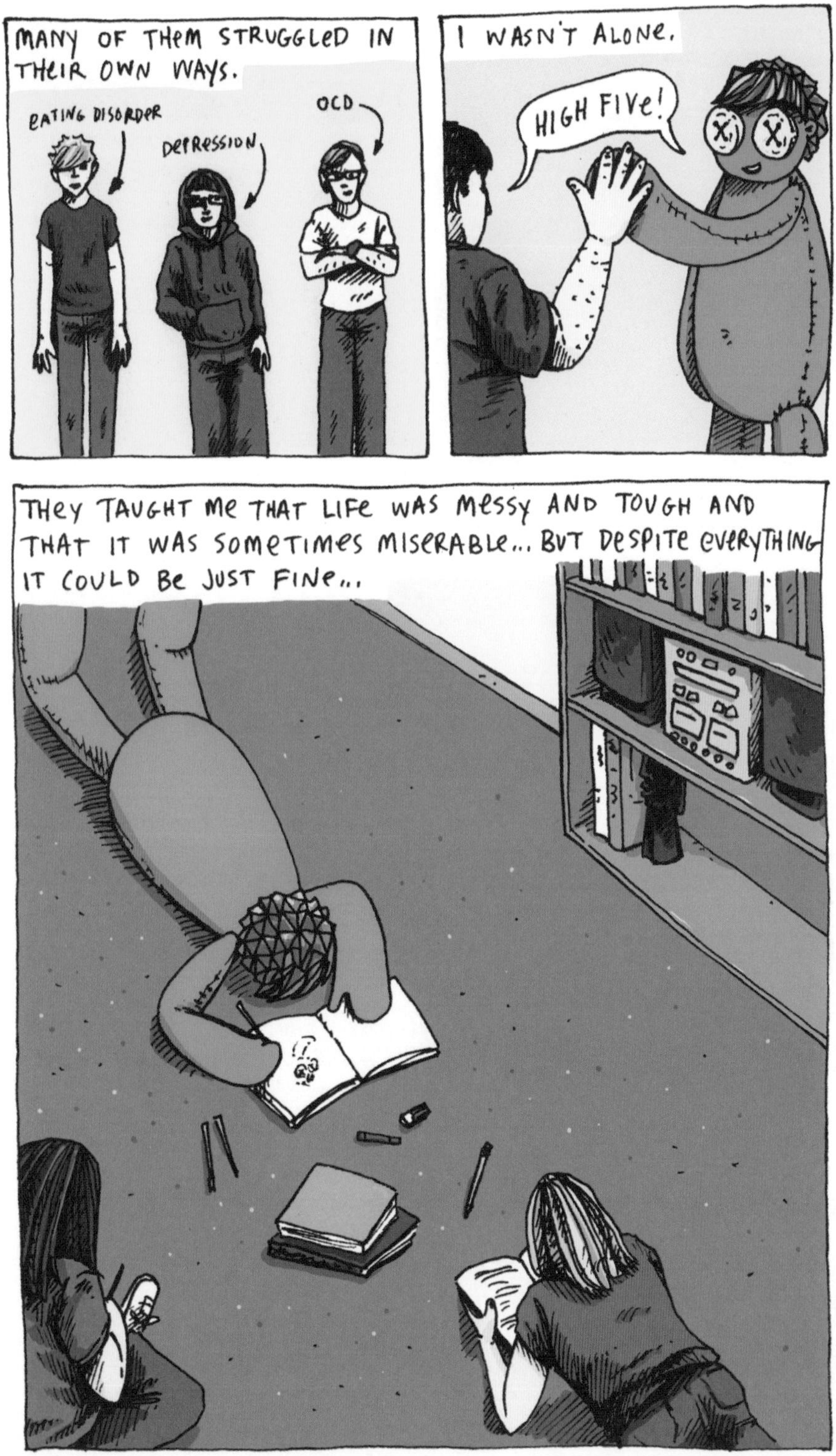
MANY OF THEM STRUGGLED IN THEIR OWN WAYS.
EATING DISORDER
DEPRESSION
OCD
I WASN'T ALONE.
HIGH FIVE!
THEY TAUGHT ME THAT LIFE WAS MESSY AND TOUGH AND THAT IT WAS SOMETIMES MISERABLE... BUT DESPITE EVERYTHING IT COULD BE JUST FINE...

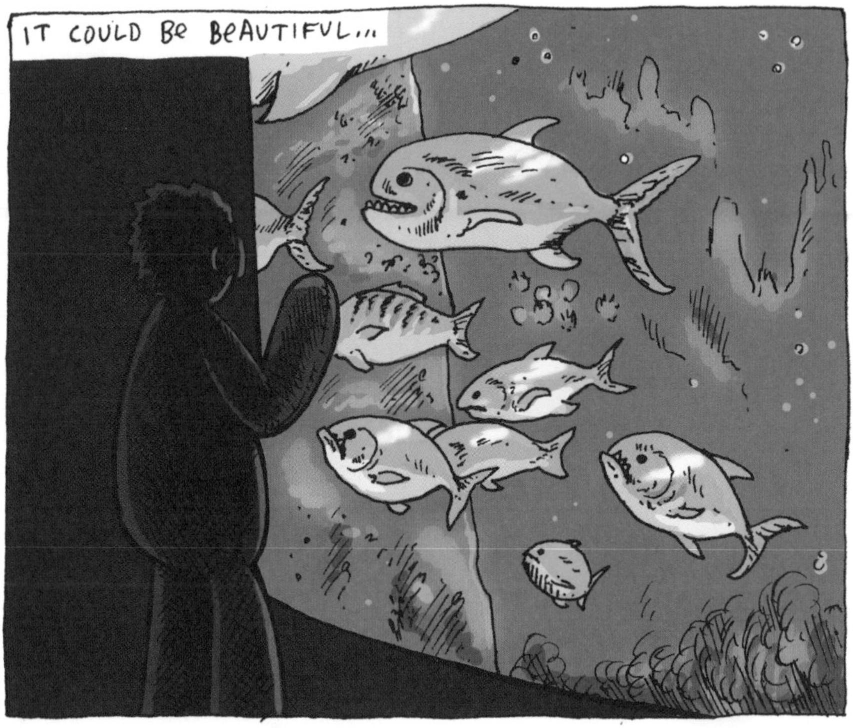
IT COULD BE BEAUTIFUL...

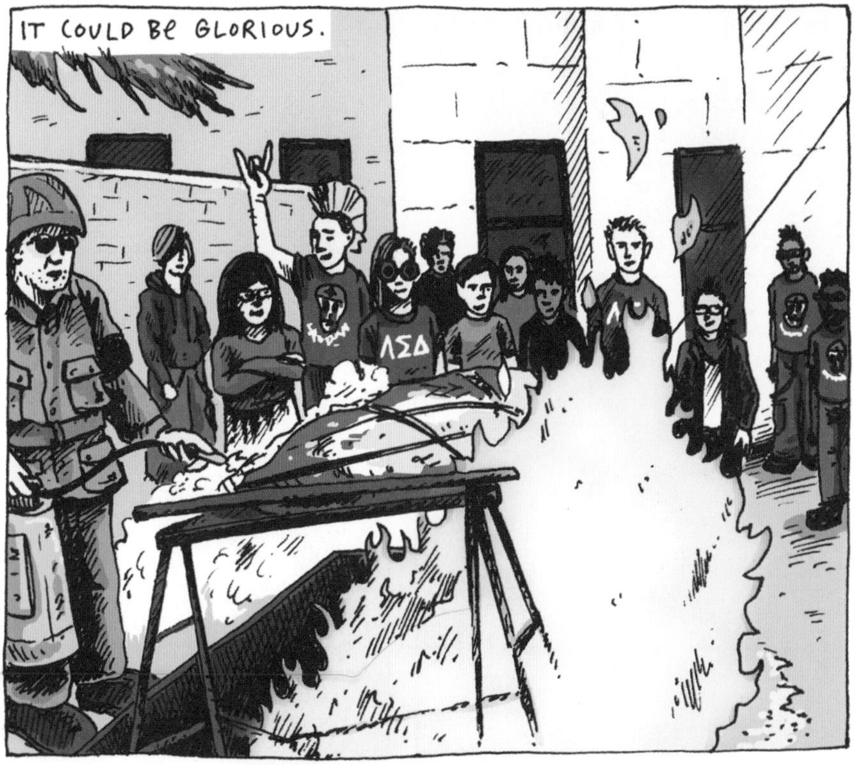
IT COULD BE GLORIOUS.
ΛΣΔ

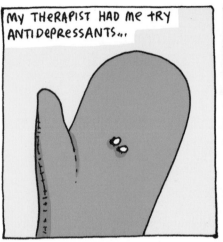

MY THERAPIST HAD ME TRY ANTIDEPRESSANTS...

WHICH HELPED SOME.

SHE ALSO HAD ME LEARN MINDFULNESS TECHNIQUES.

WHEN YOU FIND YOURSELF HARMING OR GOING THAT WAY, STOP AND COUNT BACKWARD FROM 10...

AND OBSERVE AROUND YOU.

DO YOU KNOW WHAT STARTS AN EPISODE?

WHAT STATE OF MIND ARE YOU IN?

I DON'T KNOW.

I JUST HURT... AND WANT TO HURT

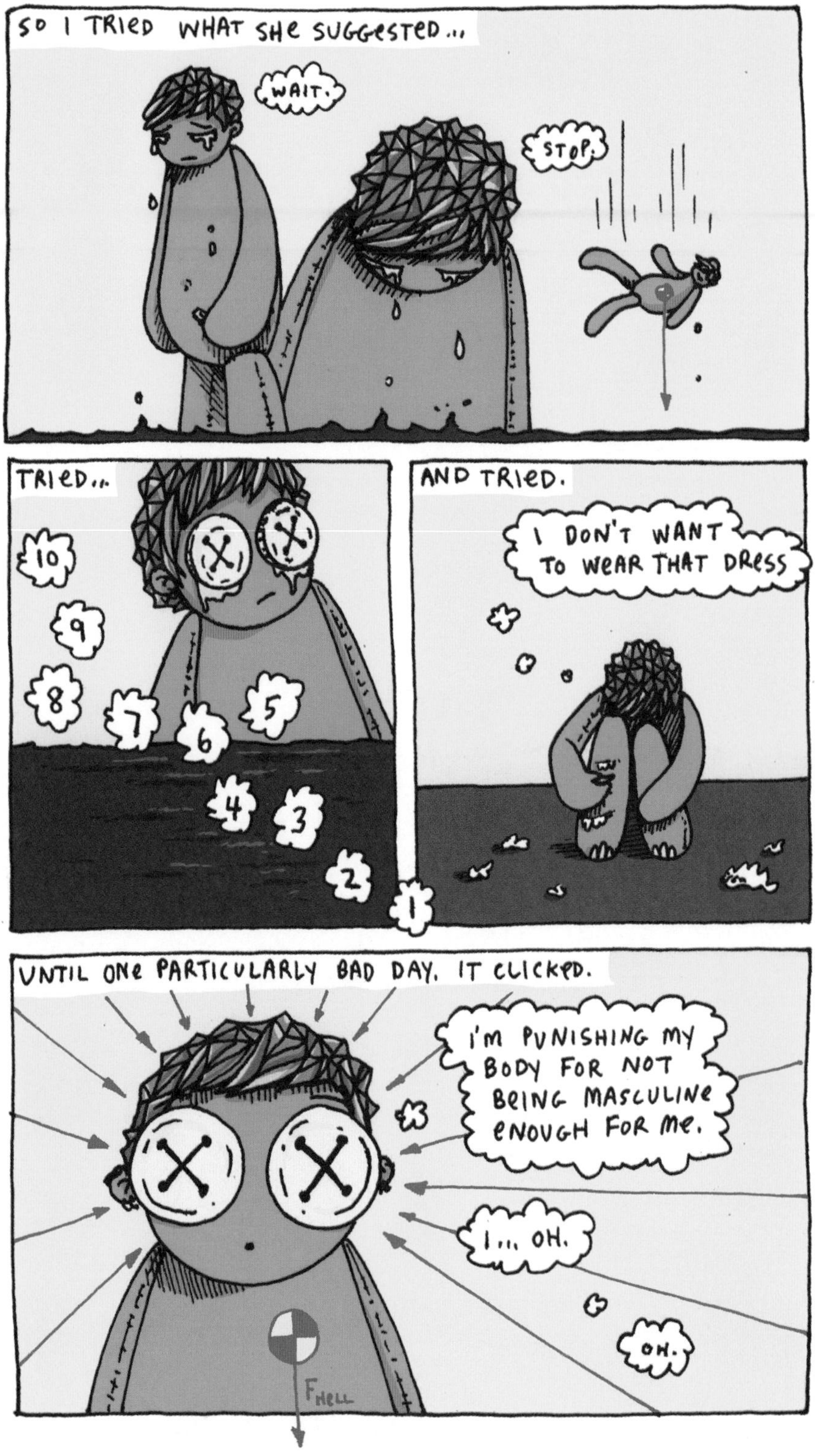
SO I TRIED WHAT SHE SUGGESTED...
WAIT.
STOP.
TRIED...
10
9
8
7
6
5
4
3
2
1
AND TRIED.
I DON'T WANT TO WEAR THAT DRESS
UNTIL ONE PARTICULARLY BAD DAY, IT CLICKED.
I'M PUNISHING MY BODY FOR NOT BEING MASCULINE ENOUGH FOR ME.
I... OH.
OH.

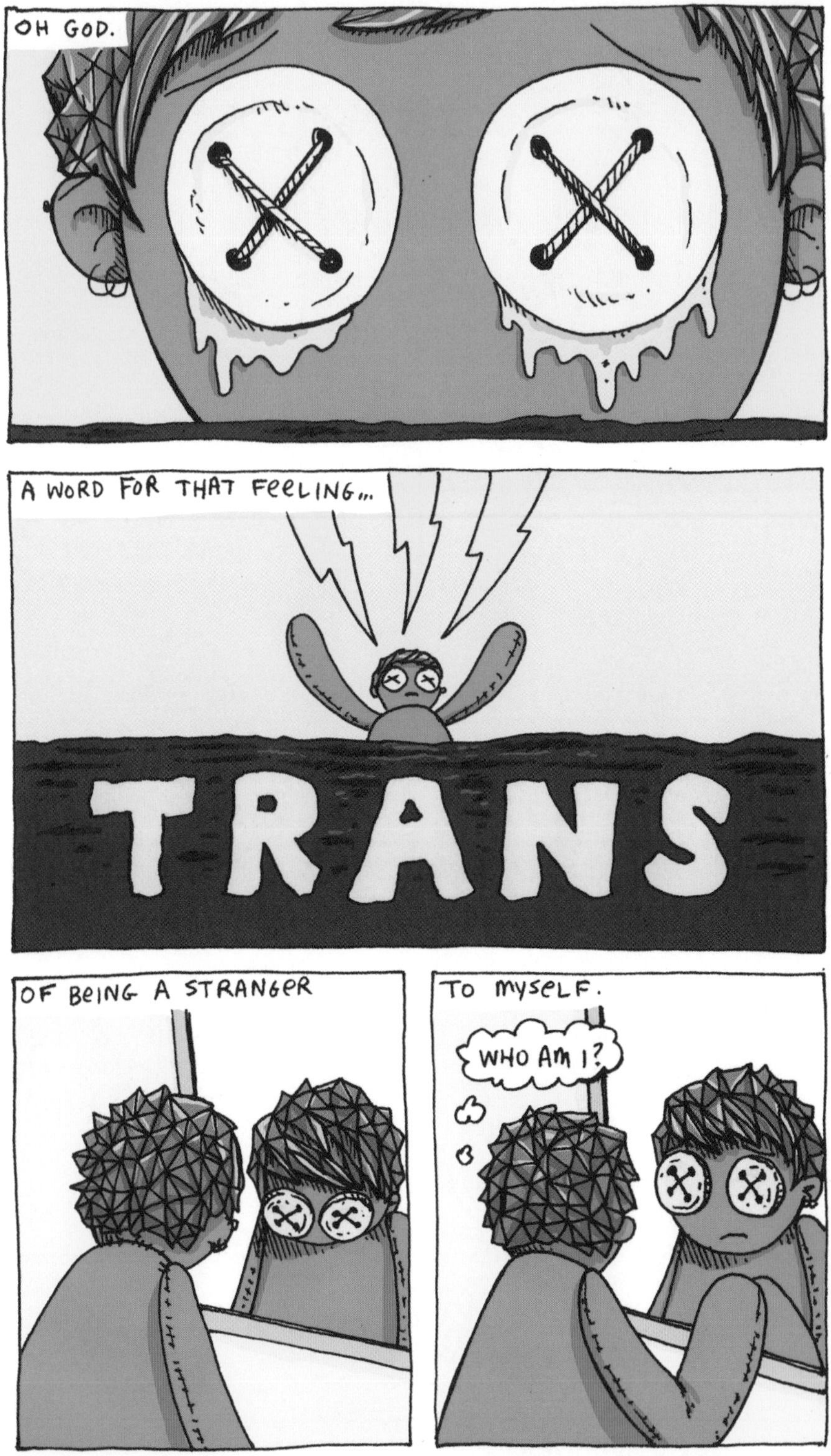
OH GOD.
A WORD FOR THAT FEELING...
TRANS
OF BEING A STRANGER
TO MYSELF.
WHO AM I?

I STARTED GOING TO A TRANS SUPPORT GROUP

...HI, I'M L. AND THE PRONOUNS I PREFER ARE HE/HIM.

AND DID MY BEST TO KEEP UP WITH SCHOOL WORK SO I COULD GRADUATE ON TIME.

ORESTEIA

I EVEN MANAGED TO

APPLY TO GRAD SCHOOL

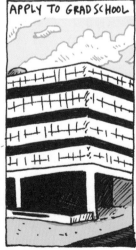

AND BE ACCEPTED!

NO WAY!

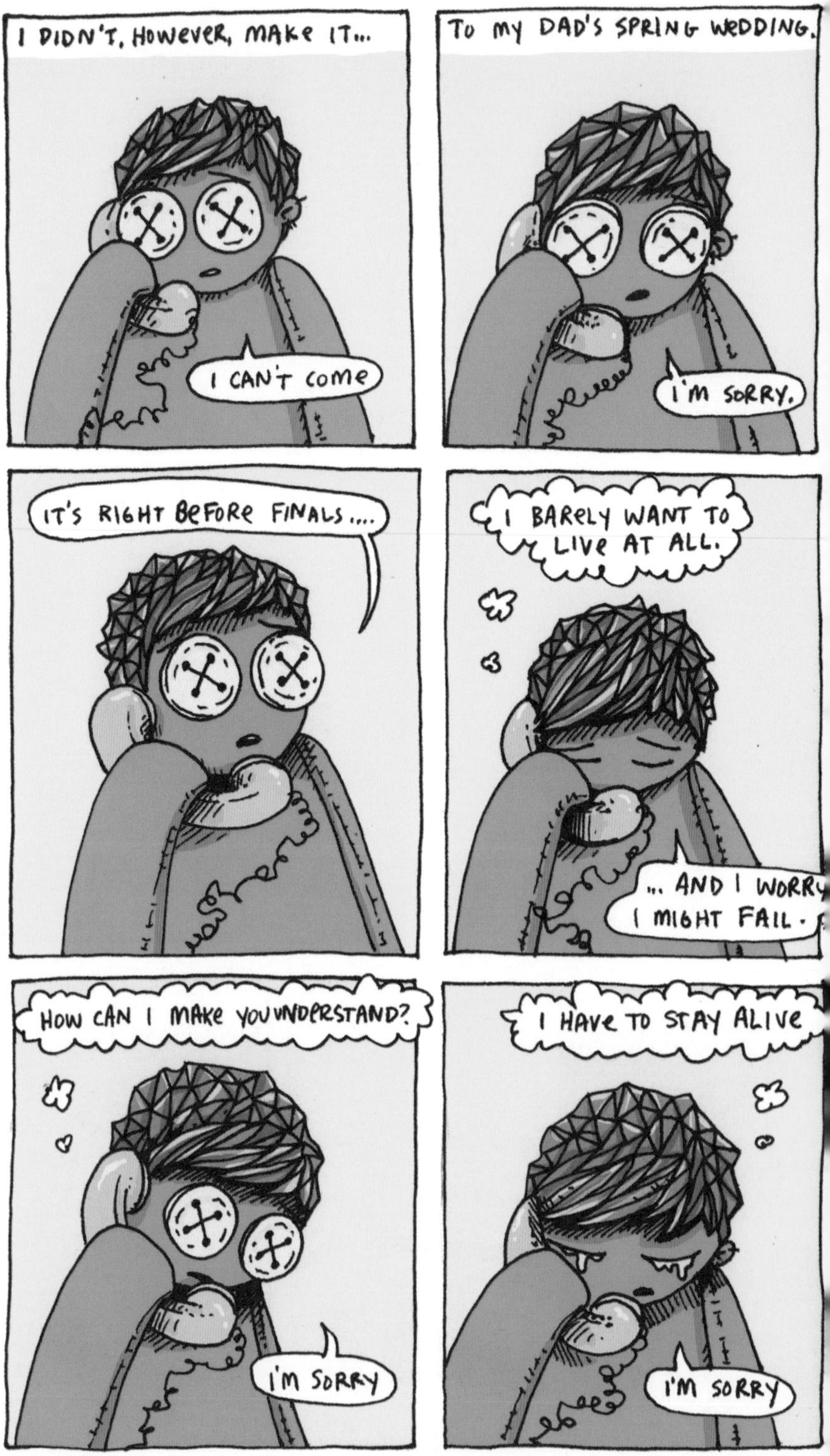
I DIDN'T, HOWEVER, MAKE IT...
I CAN'T COME
TO MY DAD'S SPRING WEDDING.
I'M SORRY.
IT'S RIGHT BEFORE FINALS.....
I BARELY WANT TO LIVE AT ALL.
... AND I WORRY I MIGHT FAIL.
HOW CAN I MAKE YOU UNDERSTAND?
I'M SORRY
I HAVE TO STAY ALIVE
I'M SORRY

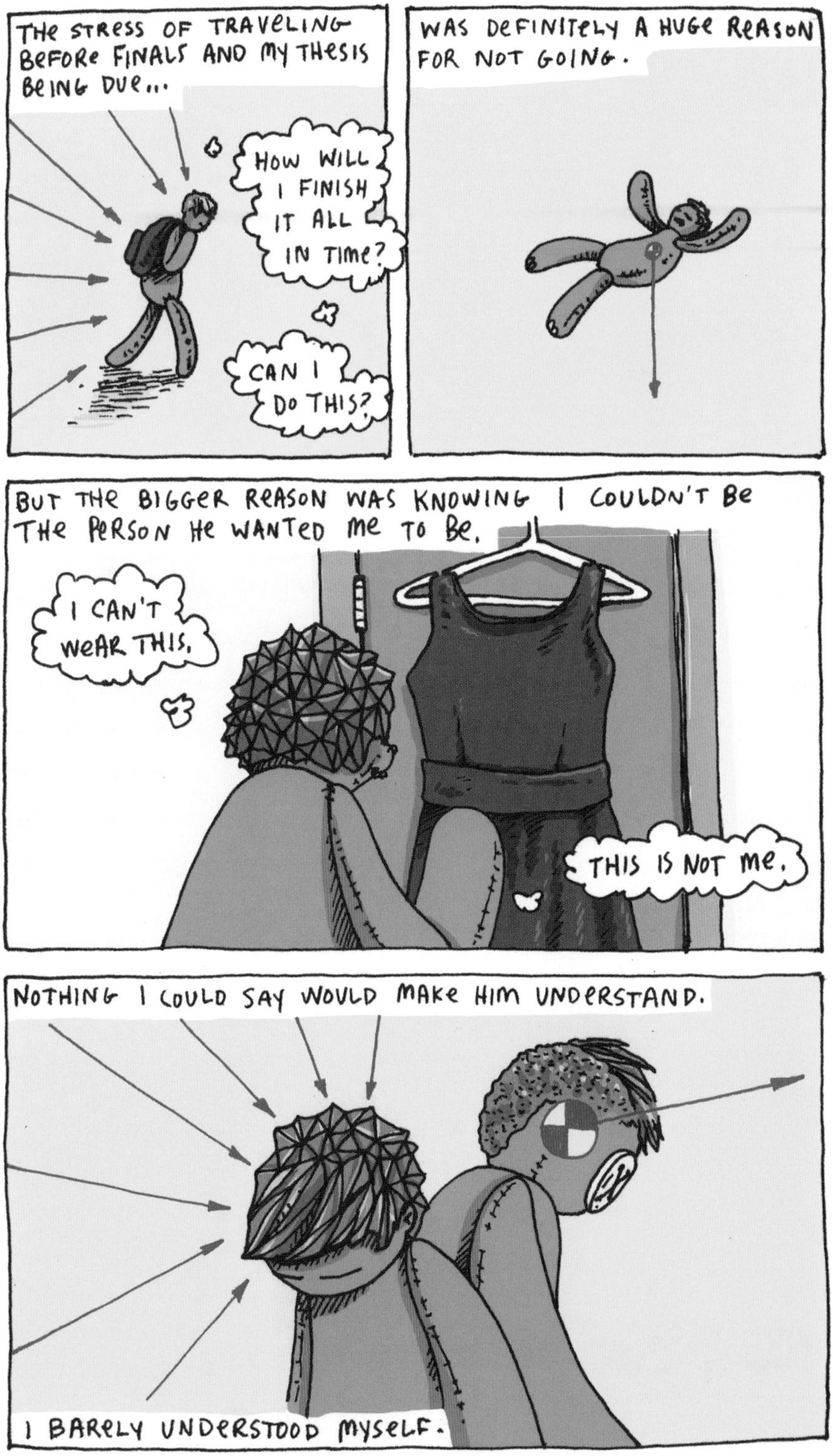
THE STRESS OF TRAVELING BEFORE FINALS AND MY THESIS BEING DUE...
HOW WILL I FINISH IT ALL IN TIME?
CAN I DO THIS?
WAS DEFINITELY A HUGE REASON FOR NOT GOING.
BUT THE BIGGER REASON WAS KNOWING I COULDN'T BE THE PERSON HE WANTED ME TO BE.
I CAN'T WEAR THIS.
THIS IS NOT ME.
NOTHING I COULD SAY WOULD MAKE HIM UNDERSTAND.
I BARELY UNDERSTOOD MYSELF.

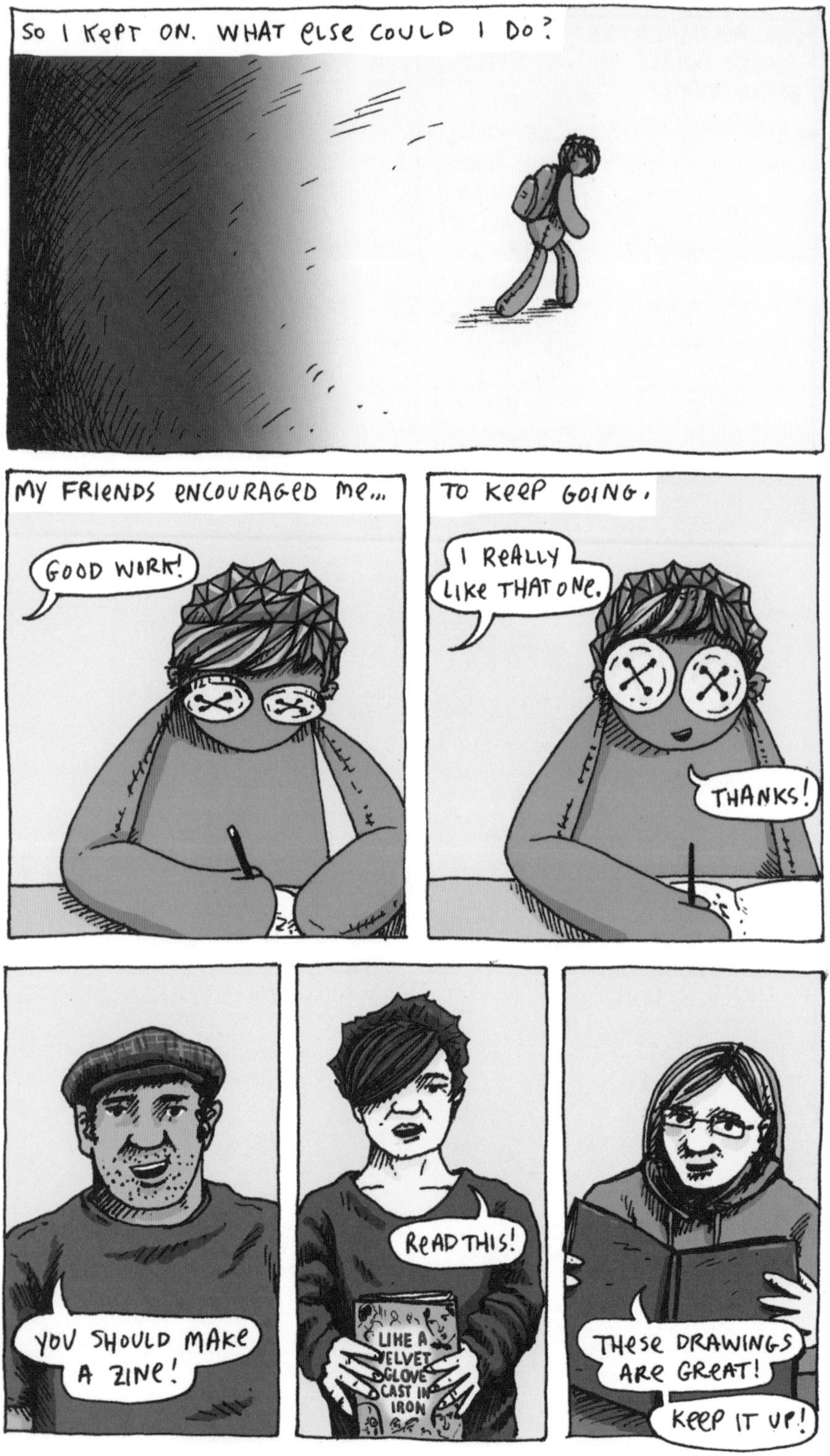

SO I KEPT ON. WHAT ELSE COULD I DO?
MY FRIENDS ENCOURAGED ME...
GOOD WORK!
TO KEEP GOING.
I REALLY LIKE THAT ONE.
THANKS!
YOU SHOULD MAKE A ZINE!
READ THIS!
LIKE A VELVET GLOVE CAST IN IRON
THESE DRAWINGS ARE GREAT!
KEEP IT UP!

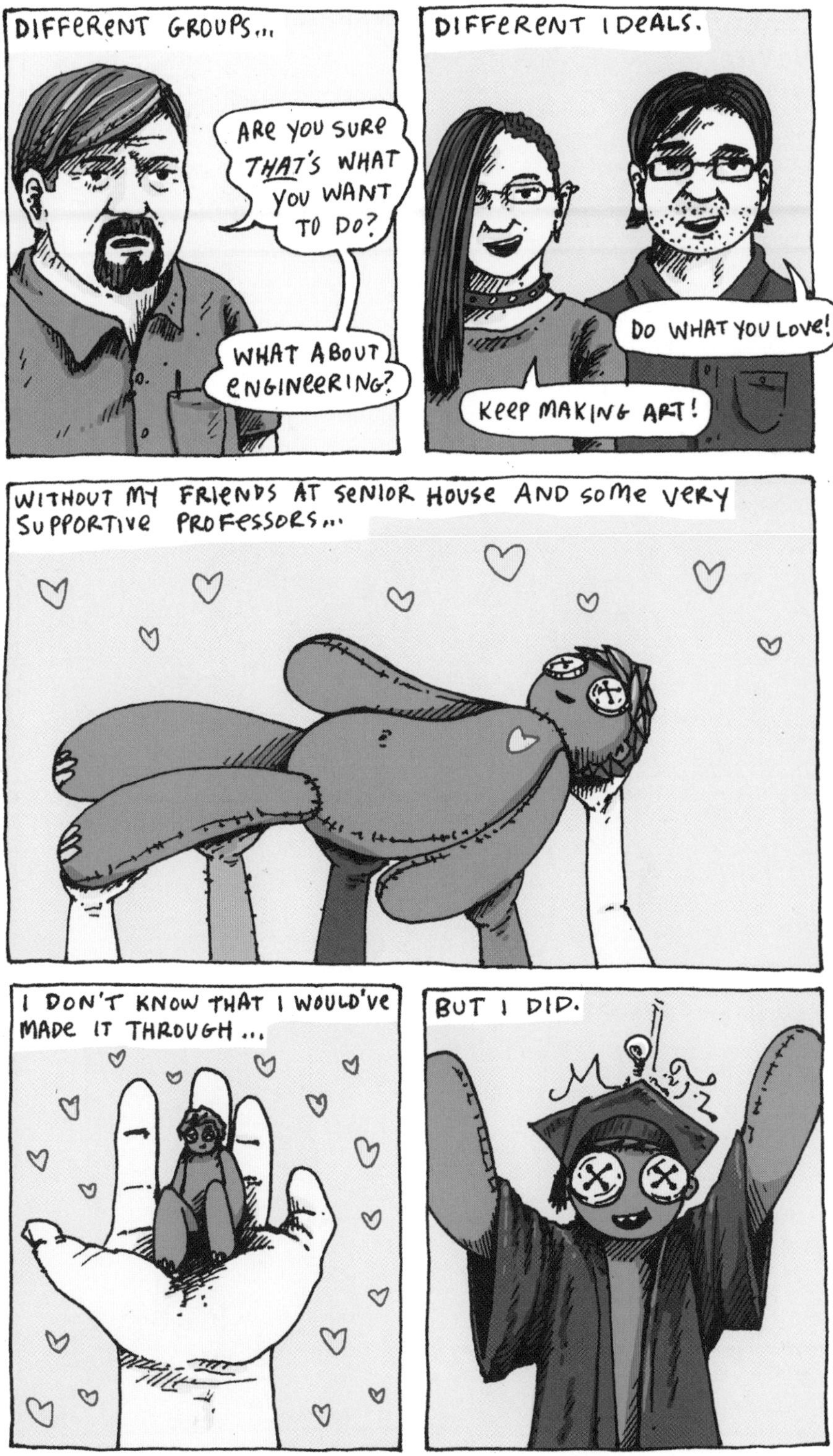
DIFFERENT GROUPS...
ARE YOU SURE THAT'S WHAT YOU WANT TO DO?
WHAT ABOUT ENGINEERING?
DIFFERENT IDEALS.
DO WHAT YOU LOVE!
KEEP MAKING ART!
WITHOUT MY FRIENDS AT SENIOR HOUSE AND SOME VERY SUPPORTIVE PROFESSORS...
I DON'T KNOW THAT I WOULD'VE MADE IT THROUGH...
BUT I DID.

SOMETIMES YOU CAN CHANGE BEFORE YOU EVEN CONSCIOUSLY NOTICE.

WAIT UP!

SOMETIMES THINGS CLICK INTO PLACE UNEXPECTEDLY

AND HABITS ABRUPTLY END.

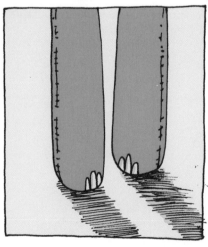

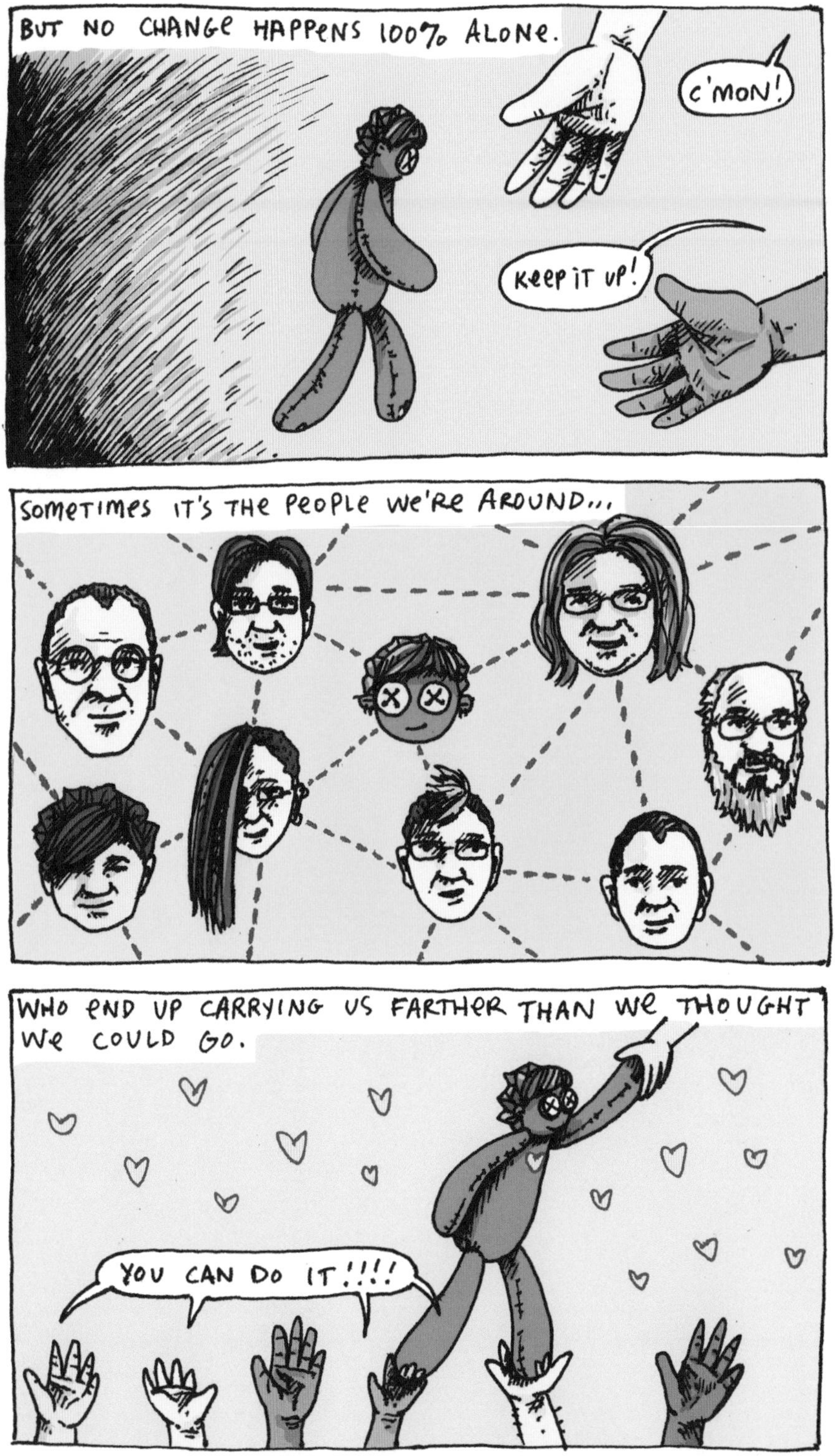
BUT NO CHANGE HAPPENS 100% ALONE.
C'MON!
KEEP IT UP!
SOMETIMES IT'S THE PEOPLE WE'RE AROUND...
WHO END UP CARRYING US FARTHER THAN WE THOUGHT WE COULD GO.
YOU CAN DO IT!!!!

CHAPTER NINE

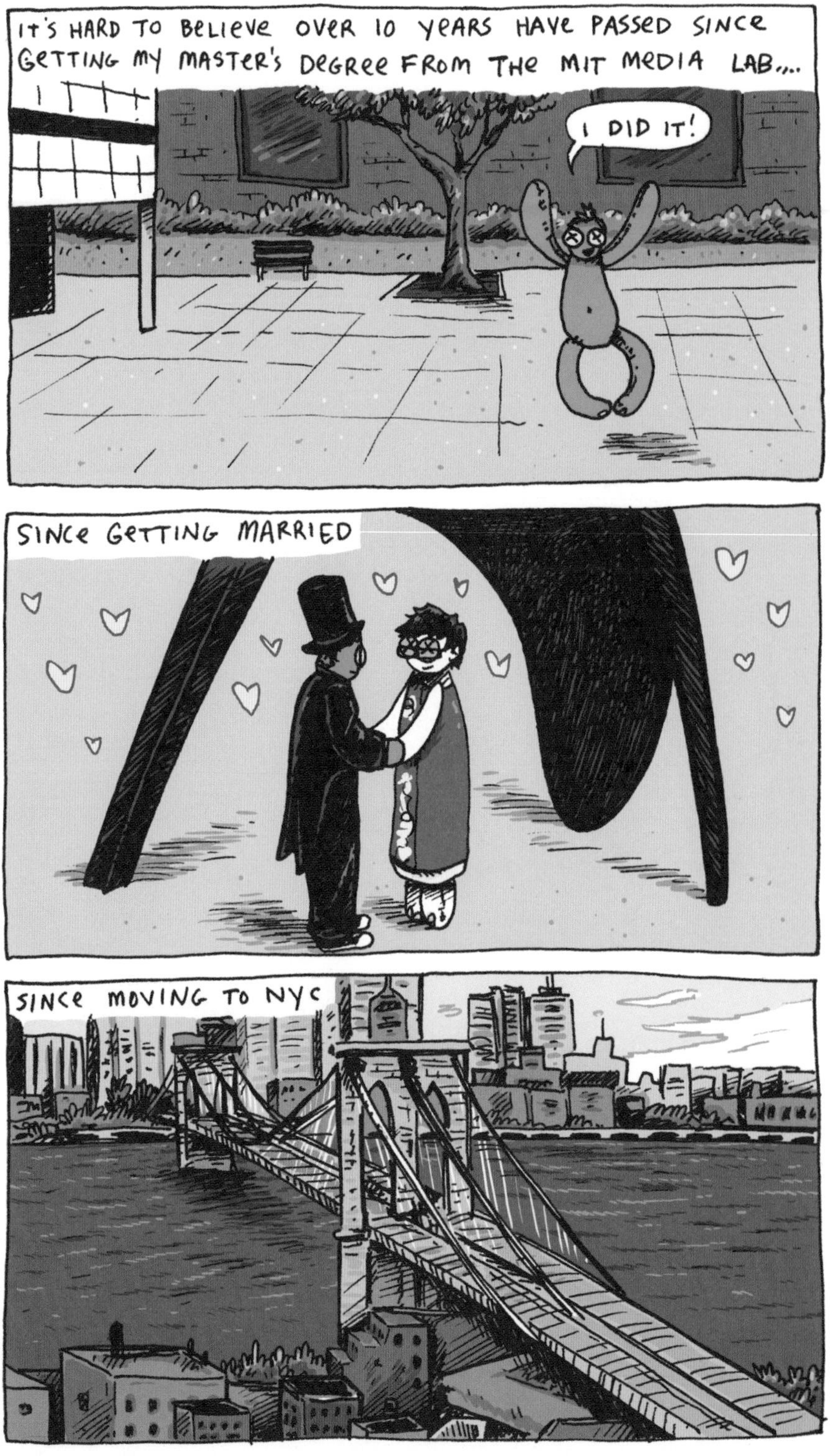
IT'S HARD TO BELIEVE OVER 10 YEARS HAVE PASSED SINCE GETTING MY MASTER'S DEGREE FROM THE MIT MEDIA LAB....
I DID IT!
SINCE GETTING MARRIED
SINCE MOVING TO NYC

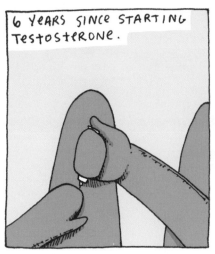

6 YEARS SINCE STARTING Testosterone.

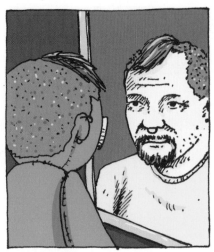

3 YEARS SINCE MY FIRST KID WAS BORN.

2 YEARS SINCE LEAVING NYC.

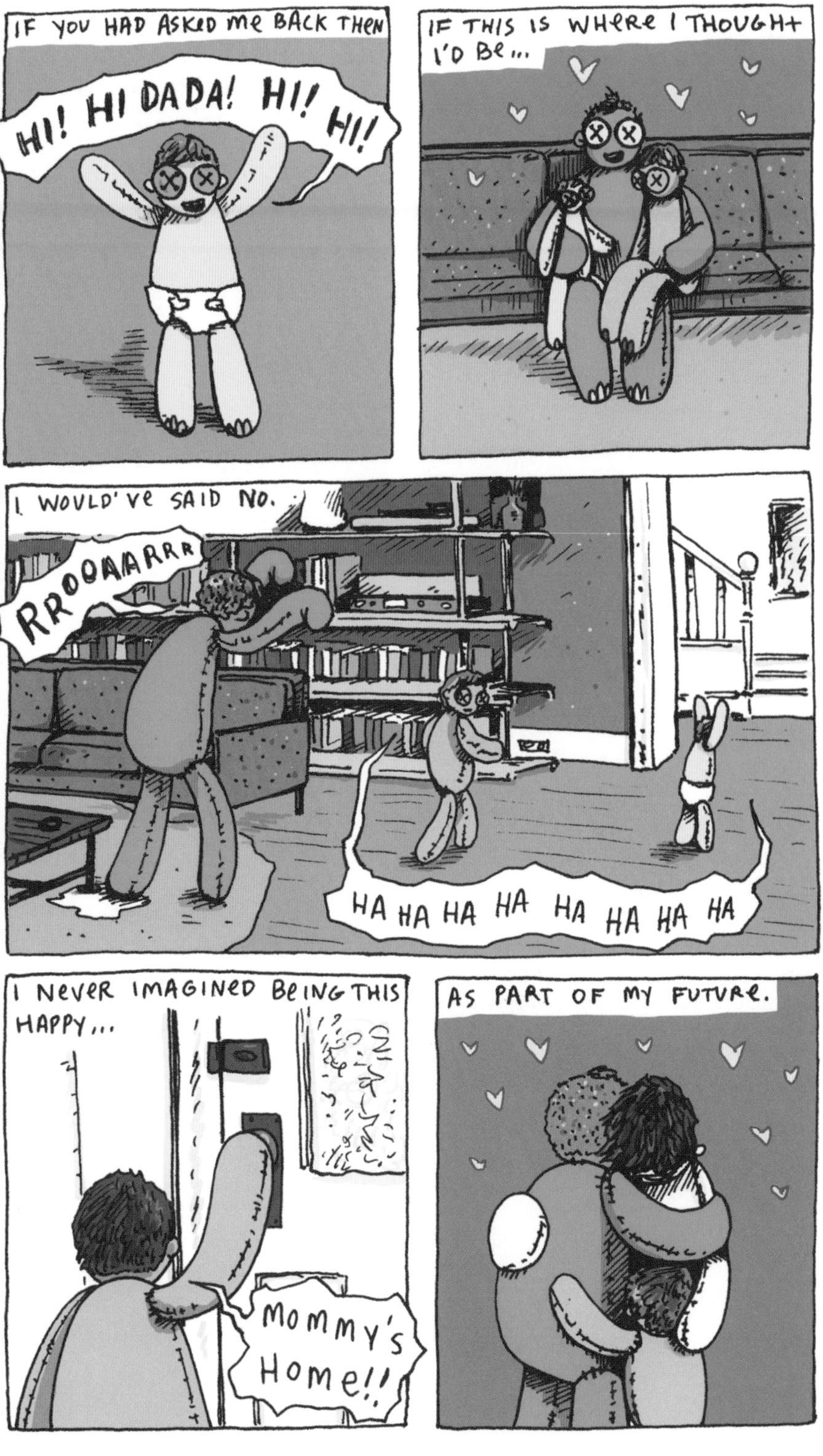
IF YOU HAD ASKED ME BACK THEN
HI! HI DADA! HI! HI!
IF THIS IS WHERE I THOUGHT I'D BE...
I WOULD'VE SAID NO.
RROOAARRR
HA HA HA HA HA HA HA HA
I NEVER IMAGINED BEING THIS HAPPY...
MOMMY'S HOME!!
AS PART OF MY FUTURE.

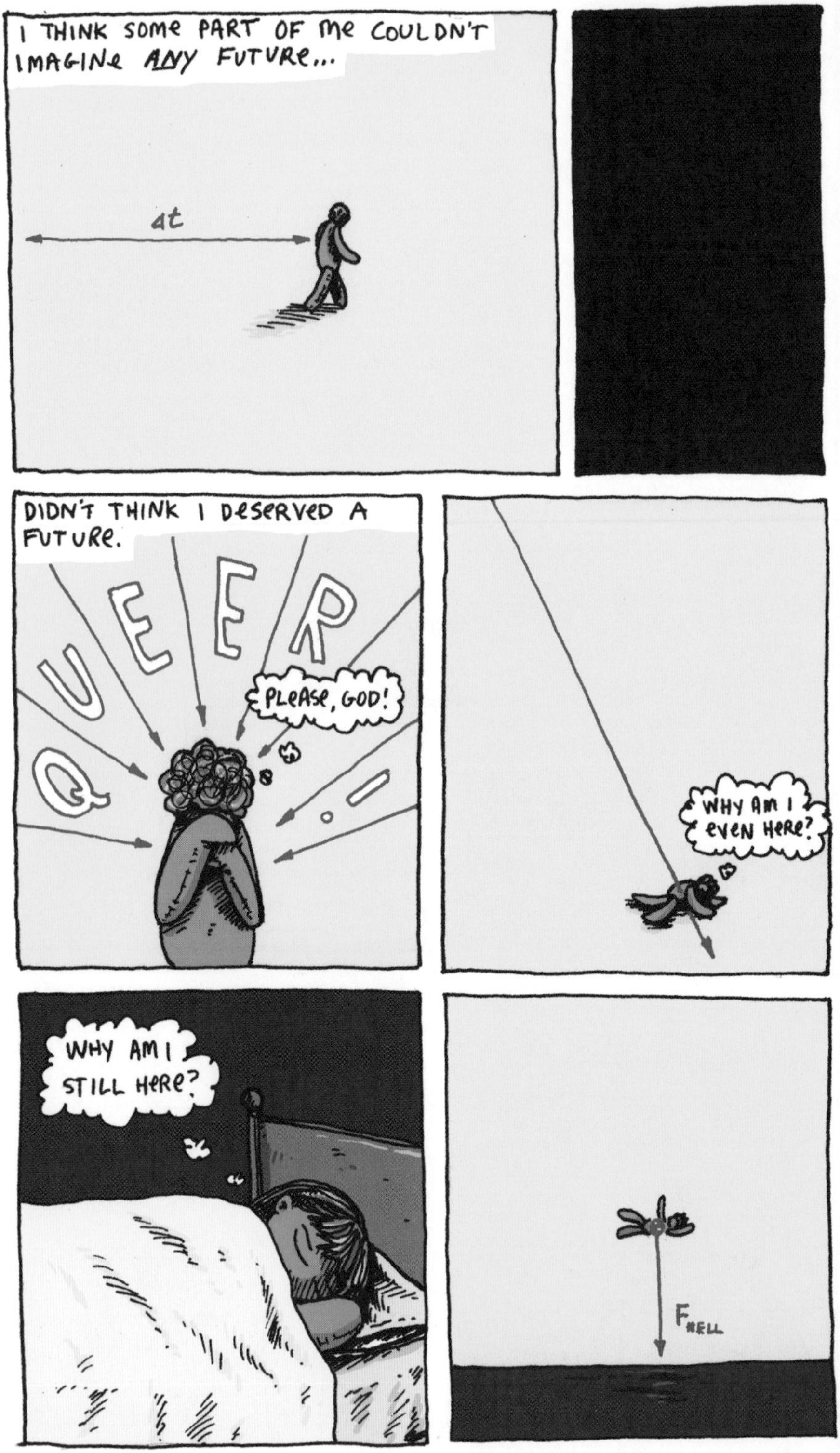
I THINK SOME PART OF ME COULDN'T IMAGINE ANY FUTURE...
at
DIDN'T THINK I DESERVED A FUTURE.
QUEER
PLEASE, GOD!
WHY AM I EVEN HERE?
WHY AM I STILL HERE?
F

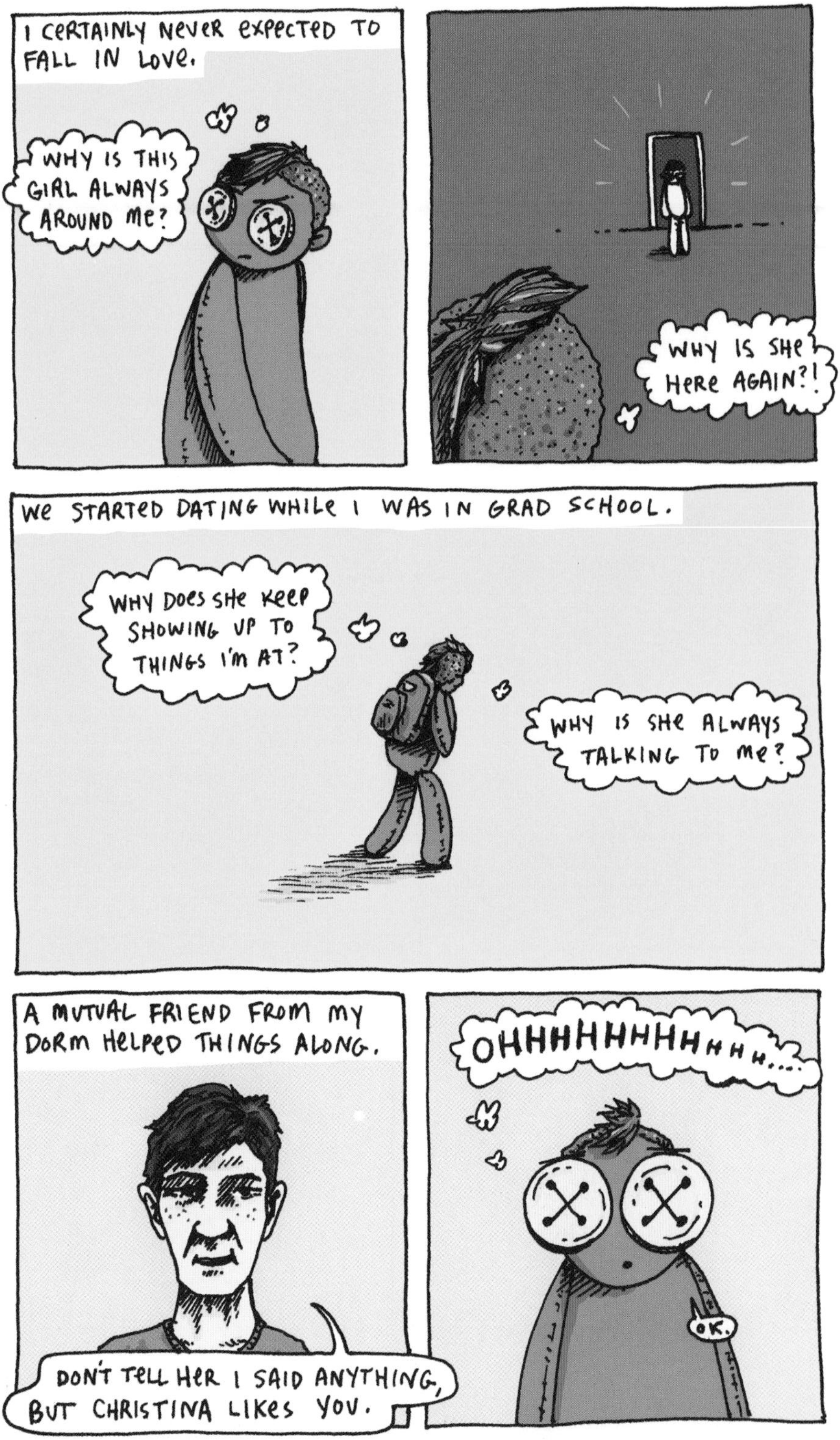
I CERTAINLY NEVER EXPECTED TO FALL IN LOVE.
WHY IS THIS GIRL ALWAYS AROUND ME?
WHY IS SHE HERE AGAIN?!
WE STARTED DATING WHILE I WAS IN GRAD SCHOOL.
WHY DOES SHE KEEP SHOWING UP TO THINGS I'M AT?
WHY IS SHE ALWAYS TALKING TO ME?
A MUTUAL FRIEND FROM MY DORM HELPED THINGS ALONG.
DON'T TELL HER I SAID ANYTHING, BUT CHRISTINA LIKES YOU.
OHHHHHHHHHHHH....
OK.

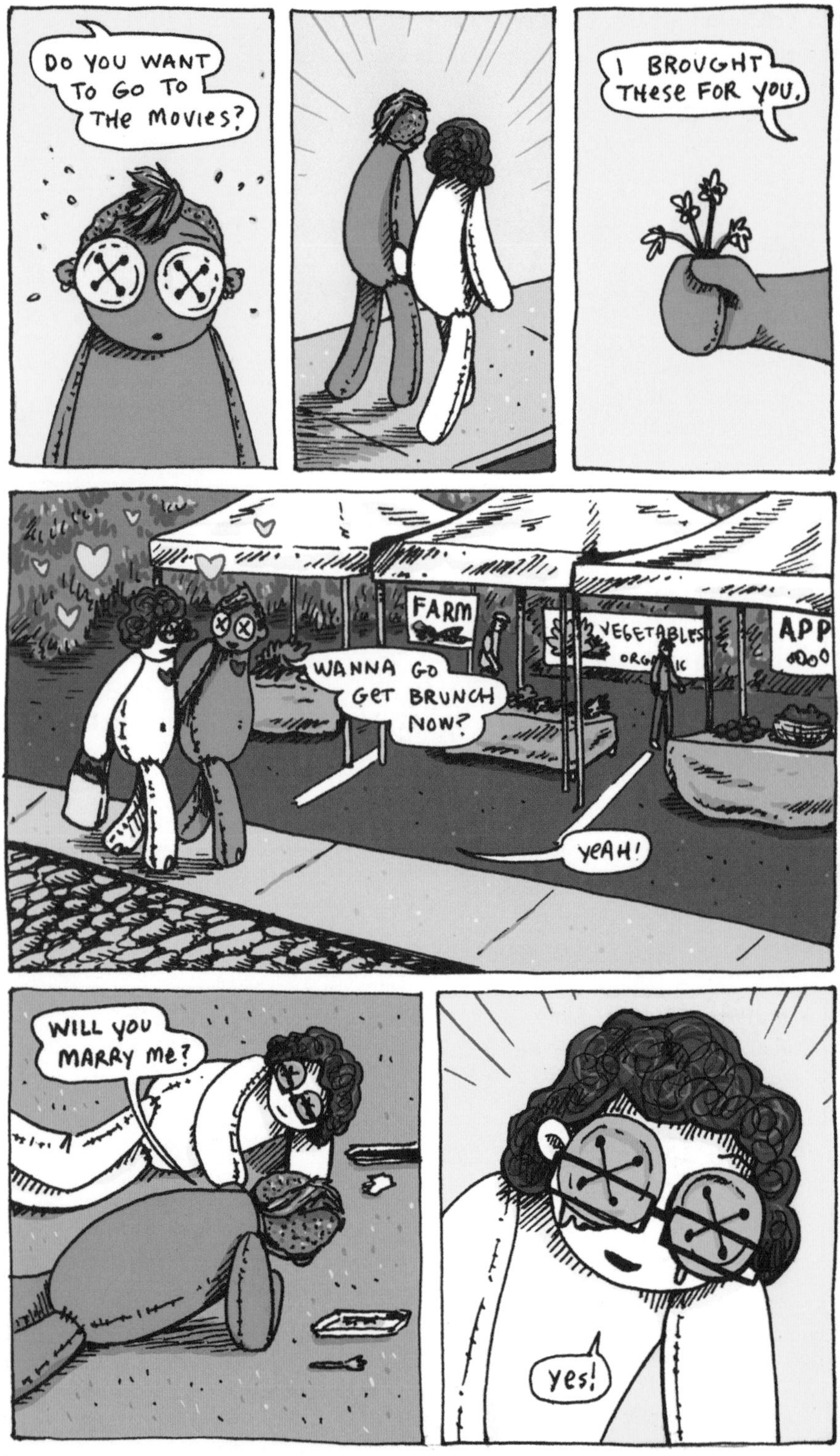
DO YOU WANT TO GO TO THE MOVIES?
I BROUGHT THESE FOR YOU.
FARM
VEGETABLES
ORG IC
APP
WANNA GO GET BRUNCH NOW?
YEAH!
WILL YOU MARRY ME?
YES!

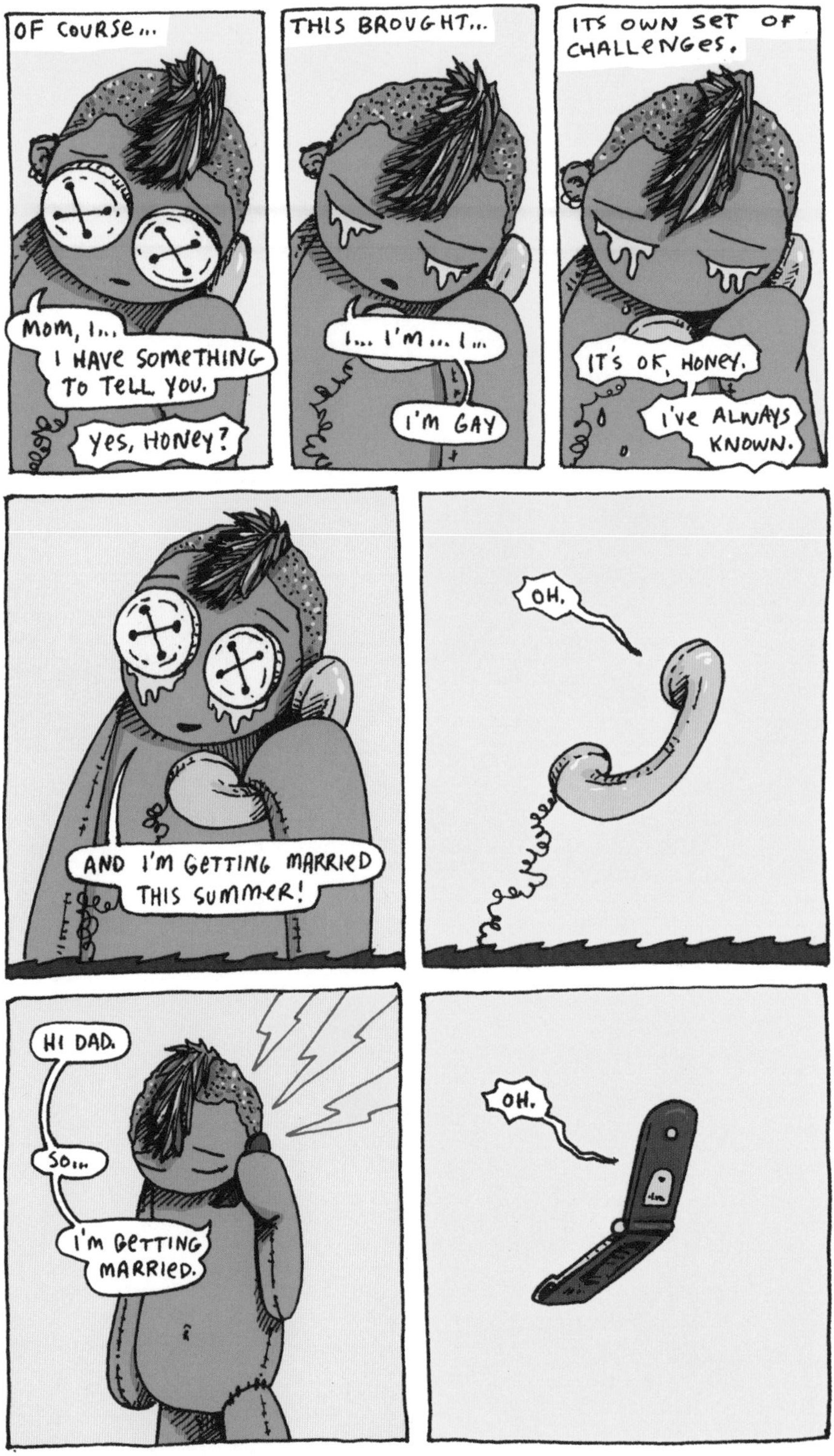
OF COURSE...
MOM, I...
I HAVE SOMETHING TO TELL YOU.
YES, HONEY?
THIS BROUGHT...
I... I'M... I...
I'M GAY
ITS OWN SET OF CHALLENGES.
IT'S OK, HONEY.
I'VE ALWAYS KNOWN.
AND I'M GETTING MARRIED THIS SUMMER!
OH.
HI DAD.
SO...
I'M GETTING MARRIED.
OH.

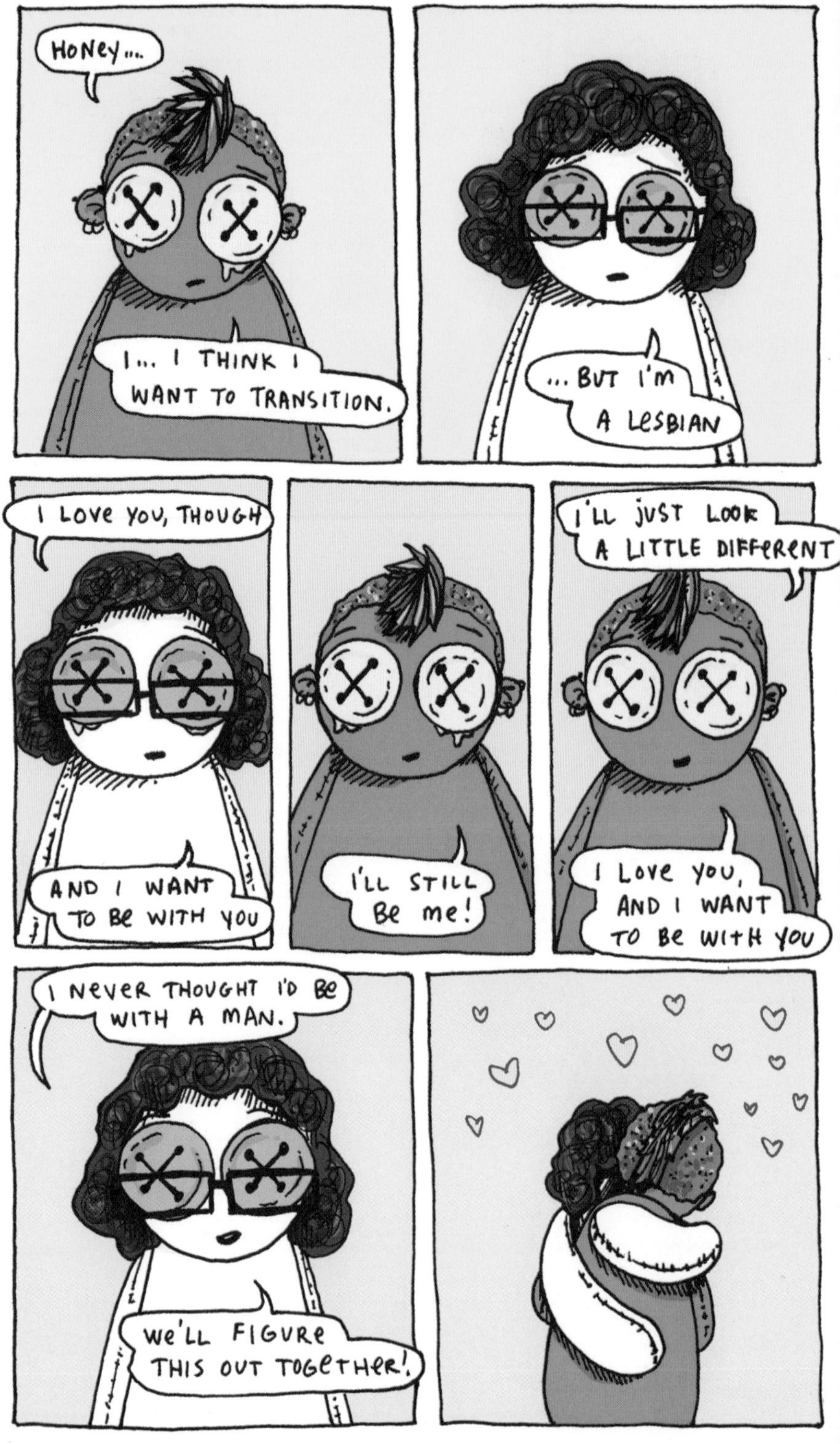
HONEY....
I... I THINK I WANT TO TRANSITION.
...BUT I'M A LESBIAN
I LOVE YOU, THOUGH
AND I WANT TO BE WITH YOU
I'LL STILL BE ME!
I'LL JUST LOOK A LITTLE DIFFERENT
I LOVE YOU, AND I WANT TO BE WITH YOU
I NEVER THOUGHT I'D BE WITH A MAN.
WE'LL FIGURE THIS OUT TOGETHER!

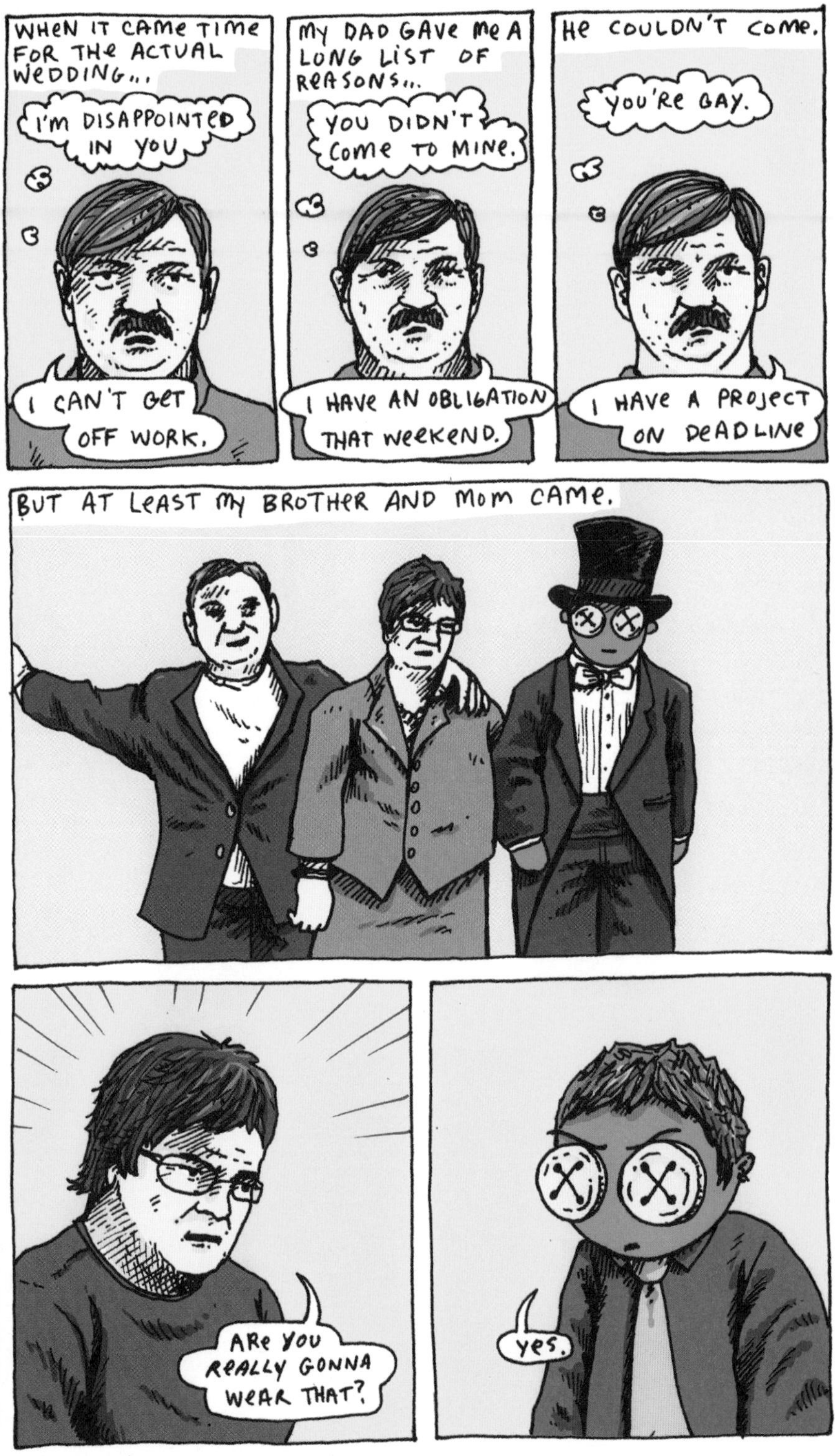
WHEN IT CAME TIME FOR THE ACTUAL WEDDING...
I'M DISAPPOINTED IN YOU
I CAN'T GET OFF WORK.
MY DAD GAVE ME A LONG LIST OF REASONS...
YOU DIDN'T COME TO MINE.
I HAVE AN OBLIGATION THAT WEEKEND.
HE COULDN'T COME.
YOU'RE GAY.
I HAVE A PROJECT ON DEADLINE
BUT AT LEAST MY BROTHER AND MOM CAME.
ARE YOU REALLY GONNA WEAR THAT?
YES.

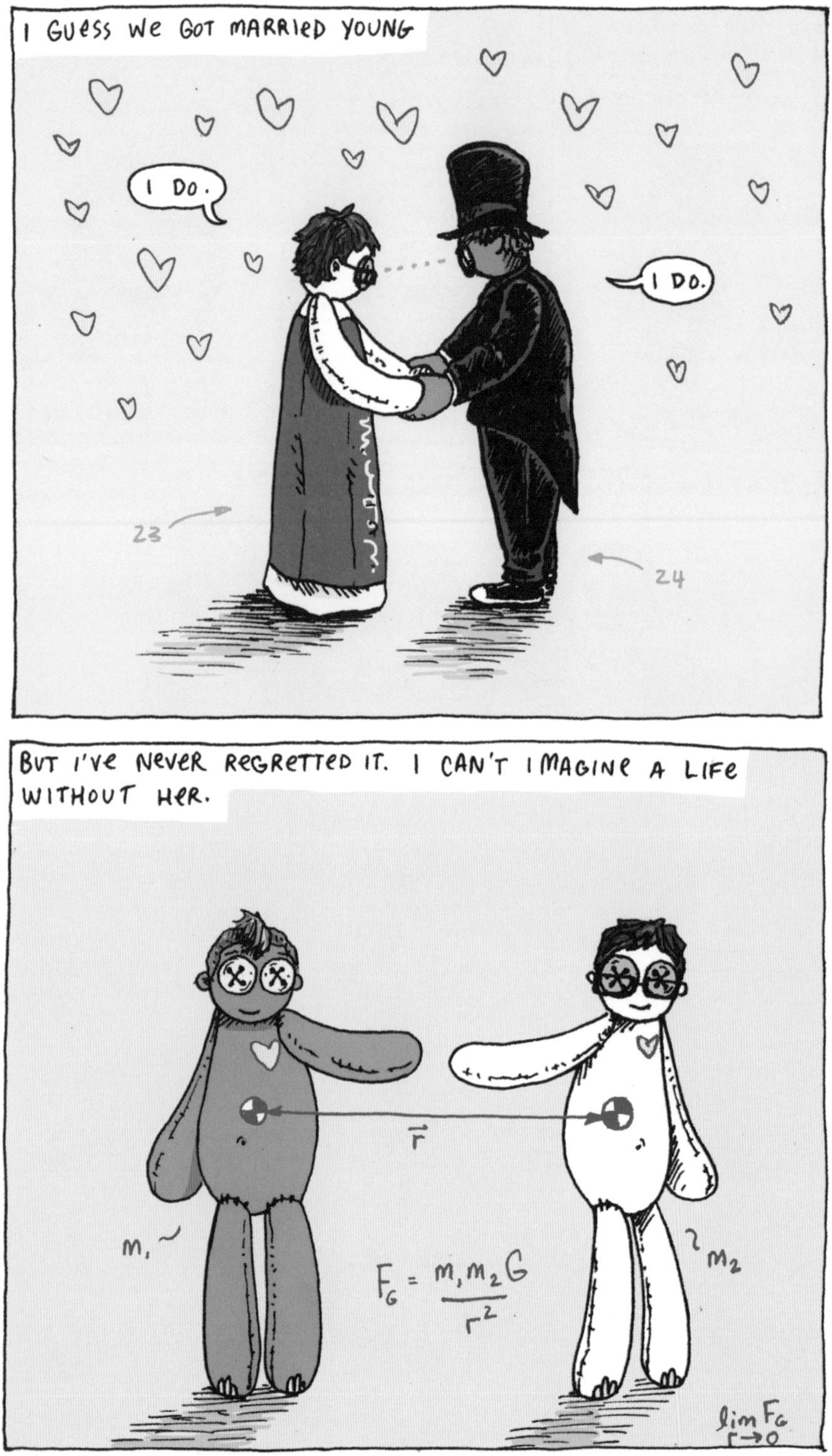

I GUESS WE GOT MARRIED YOUNG
I DO.
I DO.
23
24
BUT I'VE NEVER REGRETTED IT. I CAN'T IMAGINE A LIFE WITHOUT HER.
$\vec{r}$
m_1
m_2
$F_G = \frac{m_1 m_2 G}{r^2}$
$\lim_{r \to 0} F_G$

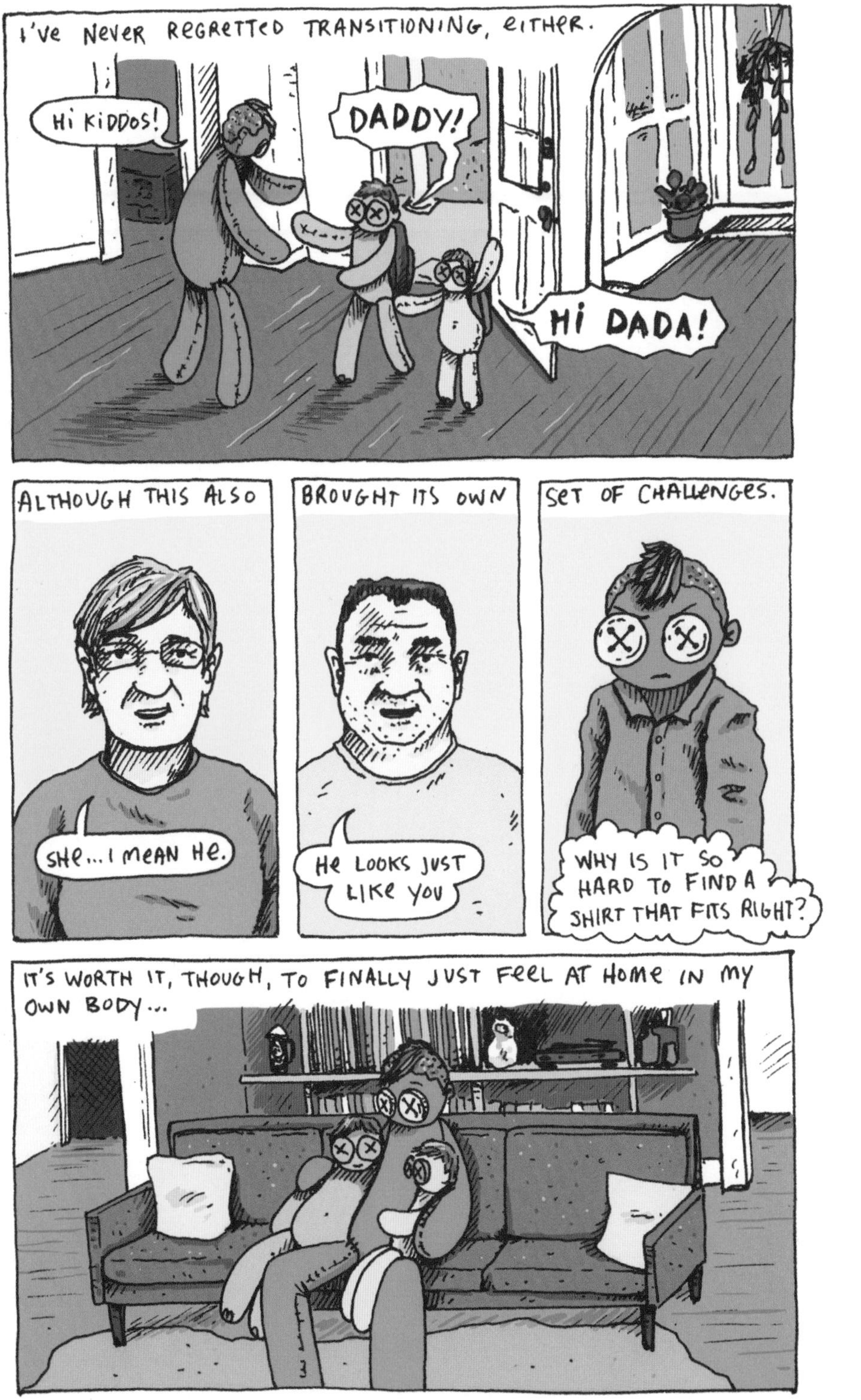
I've never regretted transitioning, either.
Hi kiddos!
DADDY!
Hi DADA!
Although this also
brought its own
set of challenges.
She... I mean he.
He looks just like you
Why is it so hard to find a shirt that fits right?
It's worth it, though, to finally just feel at home in my own body...

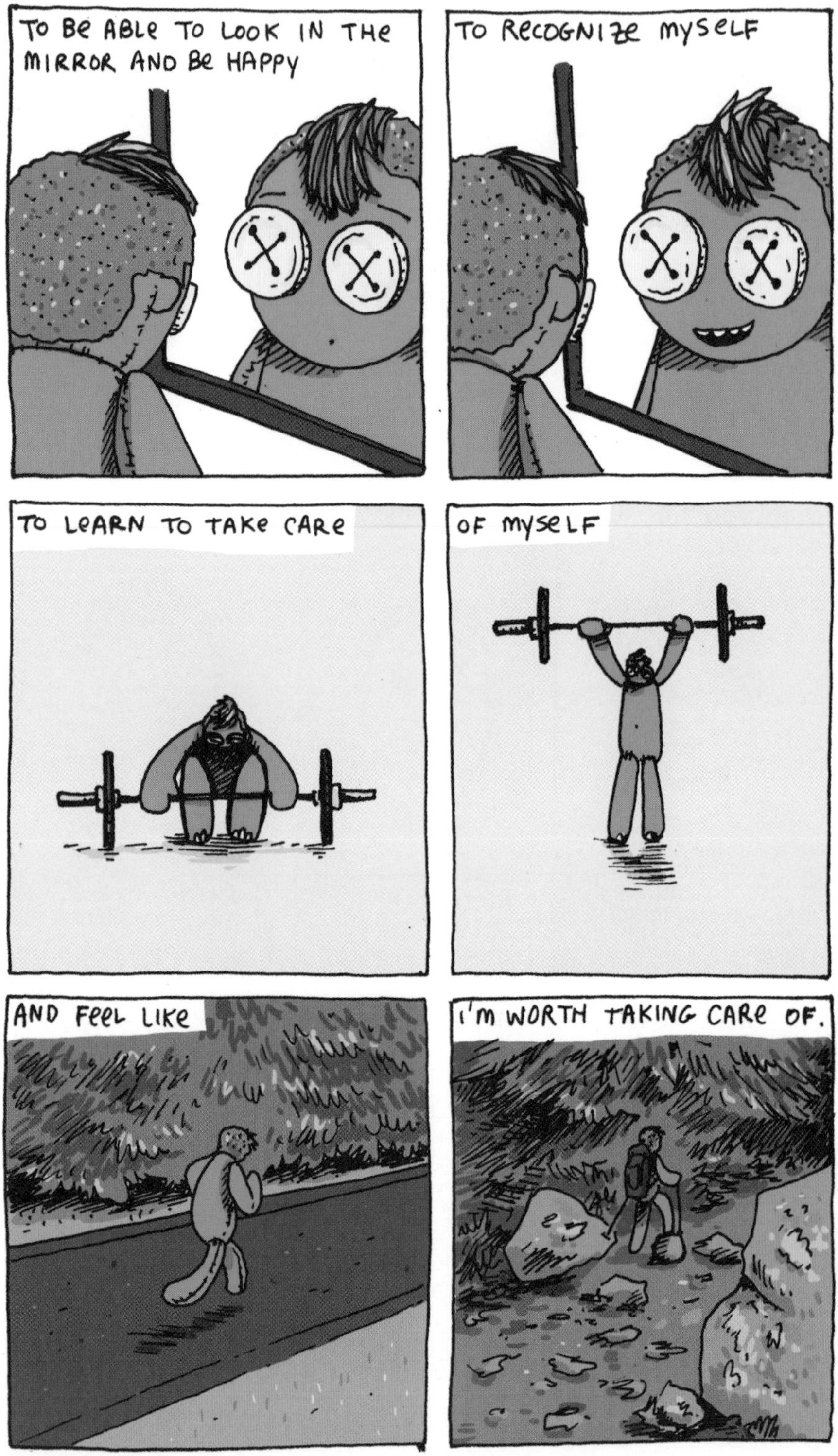
TO BE ABLE TO LOOK IN THE MIRROR AND BE HAPPY
TO RECOGNIZE MYSELF
TO LEARN TO TAKE CARE
OF MYSELF
AND FEEL LIKE
I'M WORTH TAKING CARE OF.

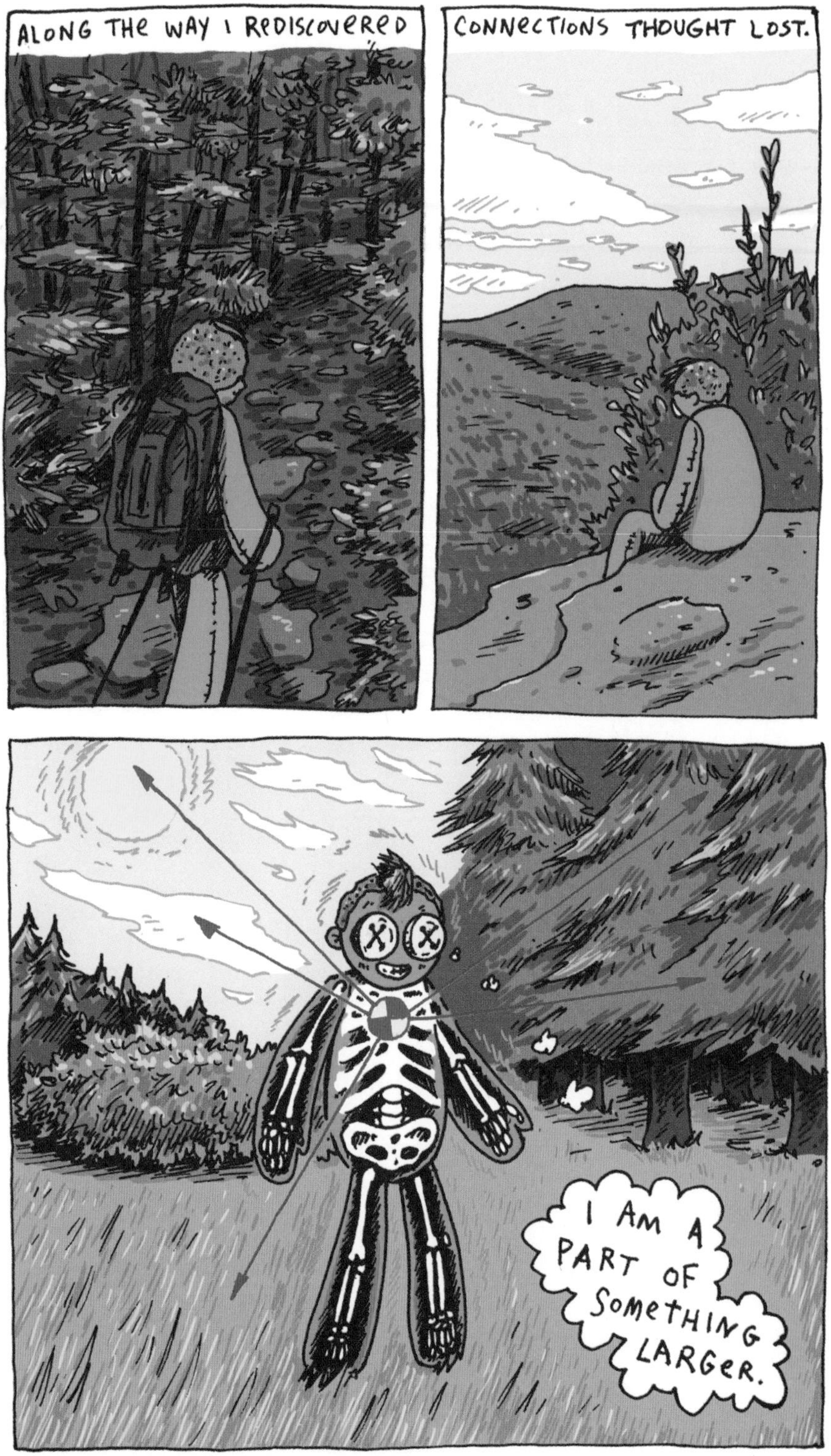
ALONG THE WAY I REDISCOVERED
CONNECTIONS THOUGHT LOST.
I AM A PART OF SOMETHING LARGER.

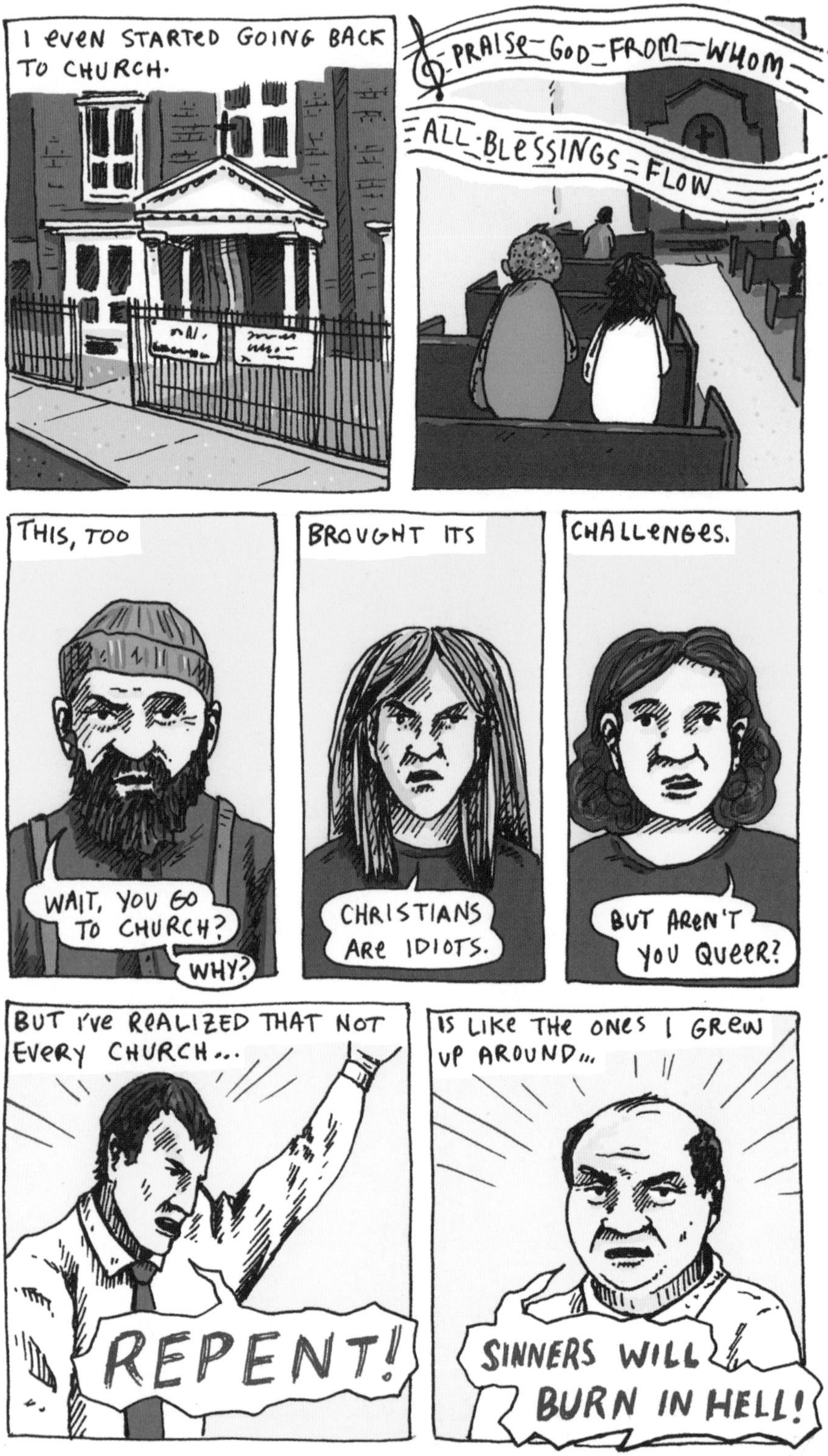
I EVEN STARTED GOING BACK TO CHURCH.
PRAISE GOD FROM WHOM
ALL BLESSINGS FLOW
THIS, TOO
WAIT, YOU GO TO CHURCH?
WHY?
BROUGHT ITS
CHRISTIANS ARE IDIOTS.
CHALLENGES.
BUT AREN'T YOU QUEER?
BUT I'VE REALIZED THAT NOT EVERY CHURCH...
REPENT!
IS LIKE THE ONES I GREW UP AROUND...
SINNERS WILL BURN IN HELL!

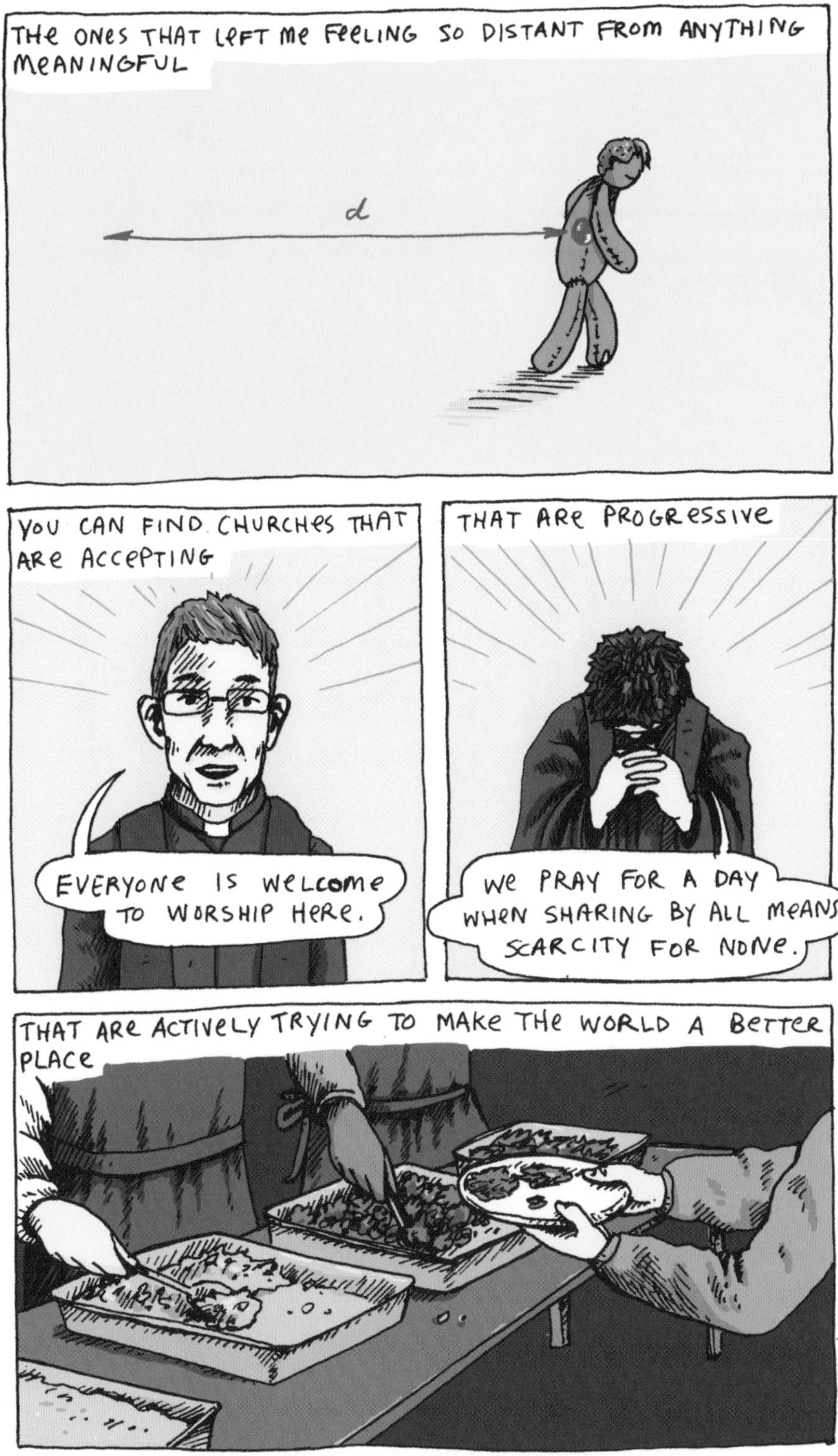
THE ONES THAT LEFT ME FEELING SO DISTANT FROM ANYTHING MEANINGFUL
d
YOU CAN FIND CHURCHES THAT ARE ACCEPTING
EVERYONE IS WELCOME TO WORSHIP HERE.
THAT ARE PROGRESSIVE
WE PRAY FOR A DAY WHEN SHARING BY ALL MEANS SCARCITY FOR NONE.
THAT ARE ACTIVELY TRYING TO MAKE THE WORLD A BETTER PLACE

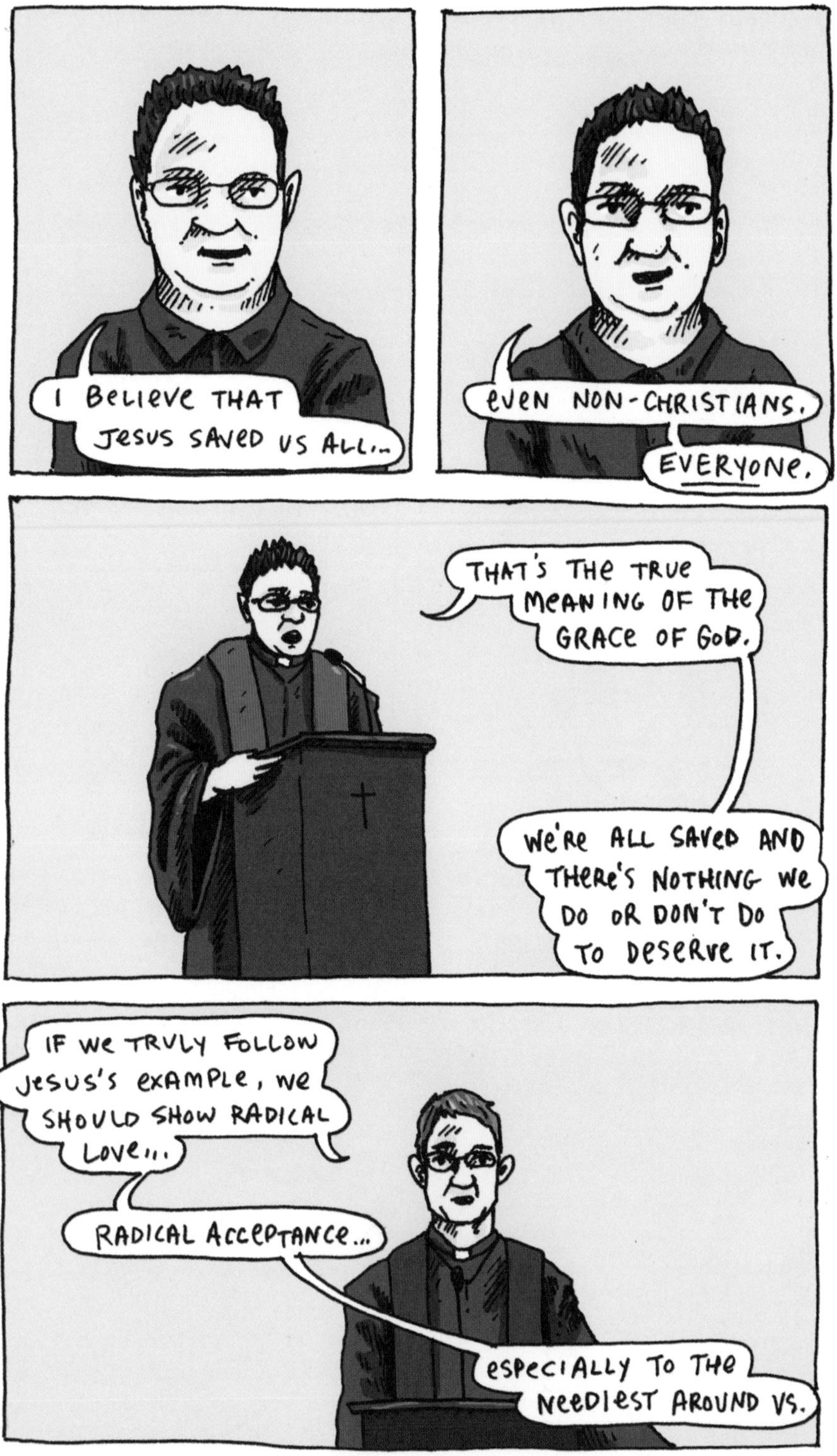
I BELIEVE THAT JESUS SAVED US ALL...
EVEN NON-CHRISTIANS.
EVERYONE.
THAT'S THE TRUE MEANING OF THE GRACE OF GOD.
WE'RE ALL SAVED AND THERE'S NOTHING WE DO OR DON'T DO TO DESERVE IT.
IF WE TRULY FOLLOW JESUS'S EXAMPLE, WE SHOULD SHOW RADICAL LOVE...
RADICAL ACCEPTANCE...
ESPECIALLY TO THE NEEDIEST AROUND US.

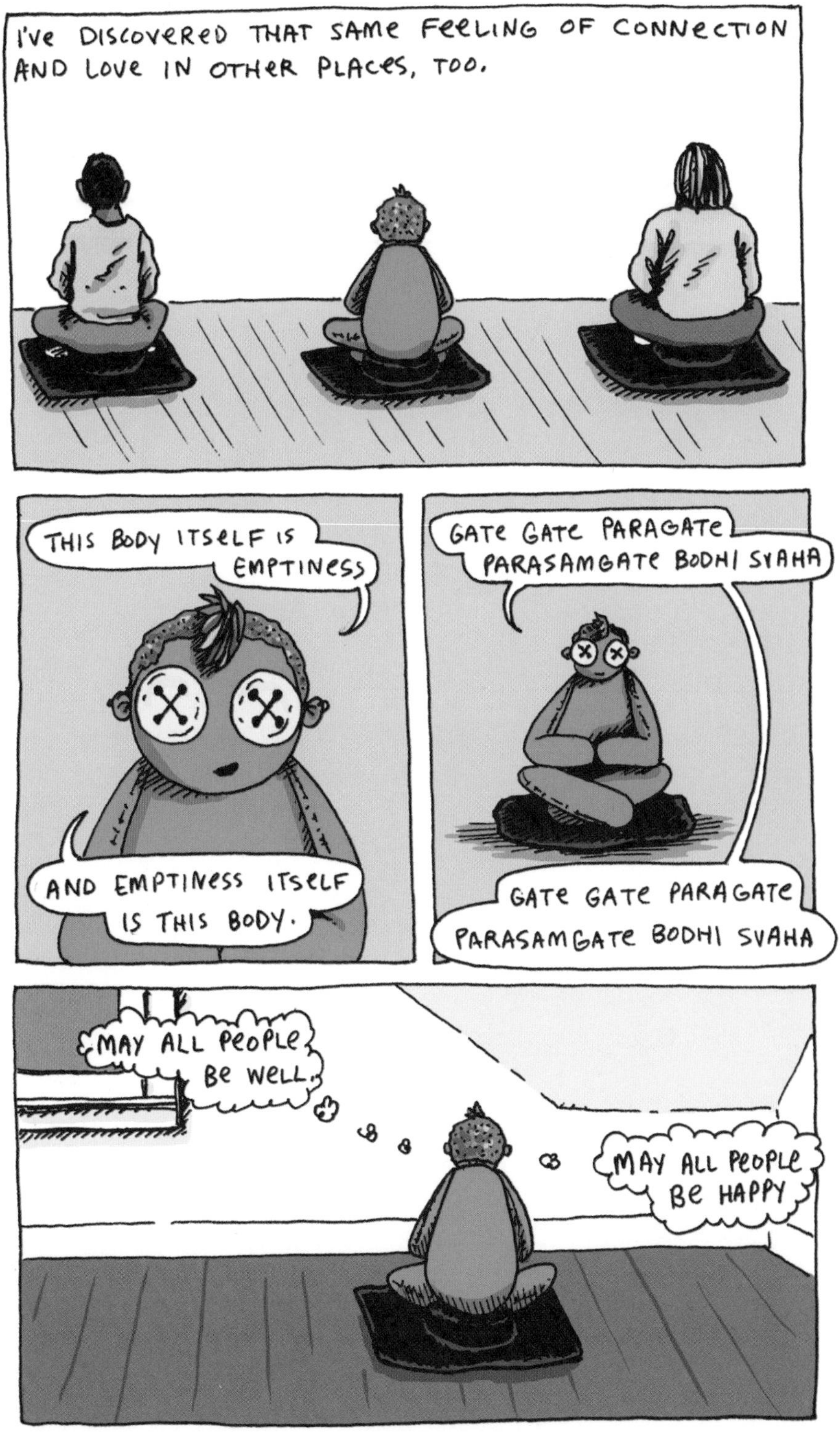
I'VE DISCOVERED THAT SAME FEELING OF CONNECTION AND LOVE IN OTHER PLACES, TOO.
THIS BODY ITSELF IS EMPTINESS
AND EMPTINESS ITSELF IS THIS BODY.
GATE GATE PARAGATE PARASAMGATE BODHI SVAHA
GATE GATE PARAGATE PARASAMGATE BODHI SVAHA
MAY ALL PEOPLE BE WELL.
MAY ALL PEOPLE BE HAPPY

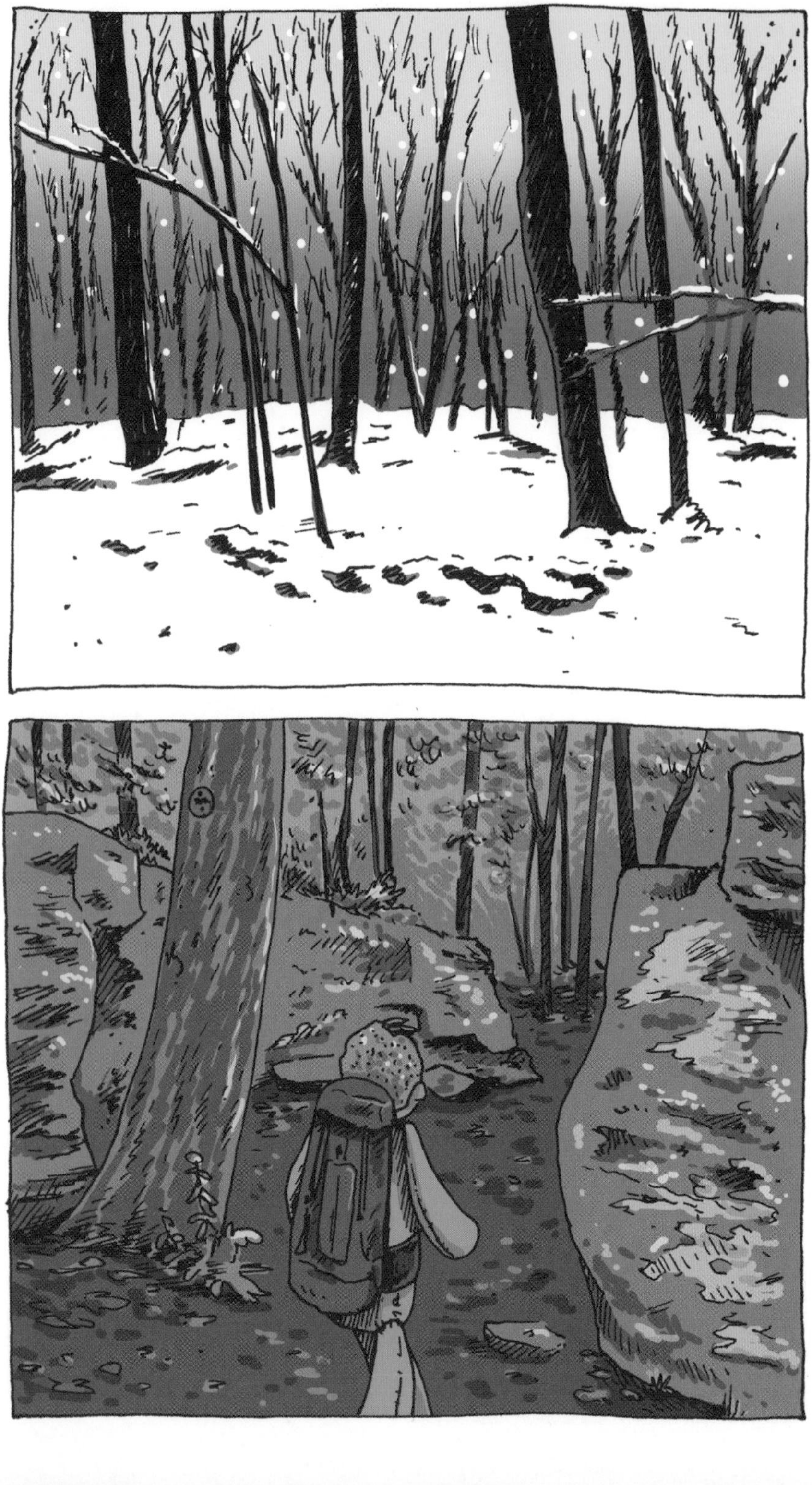

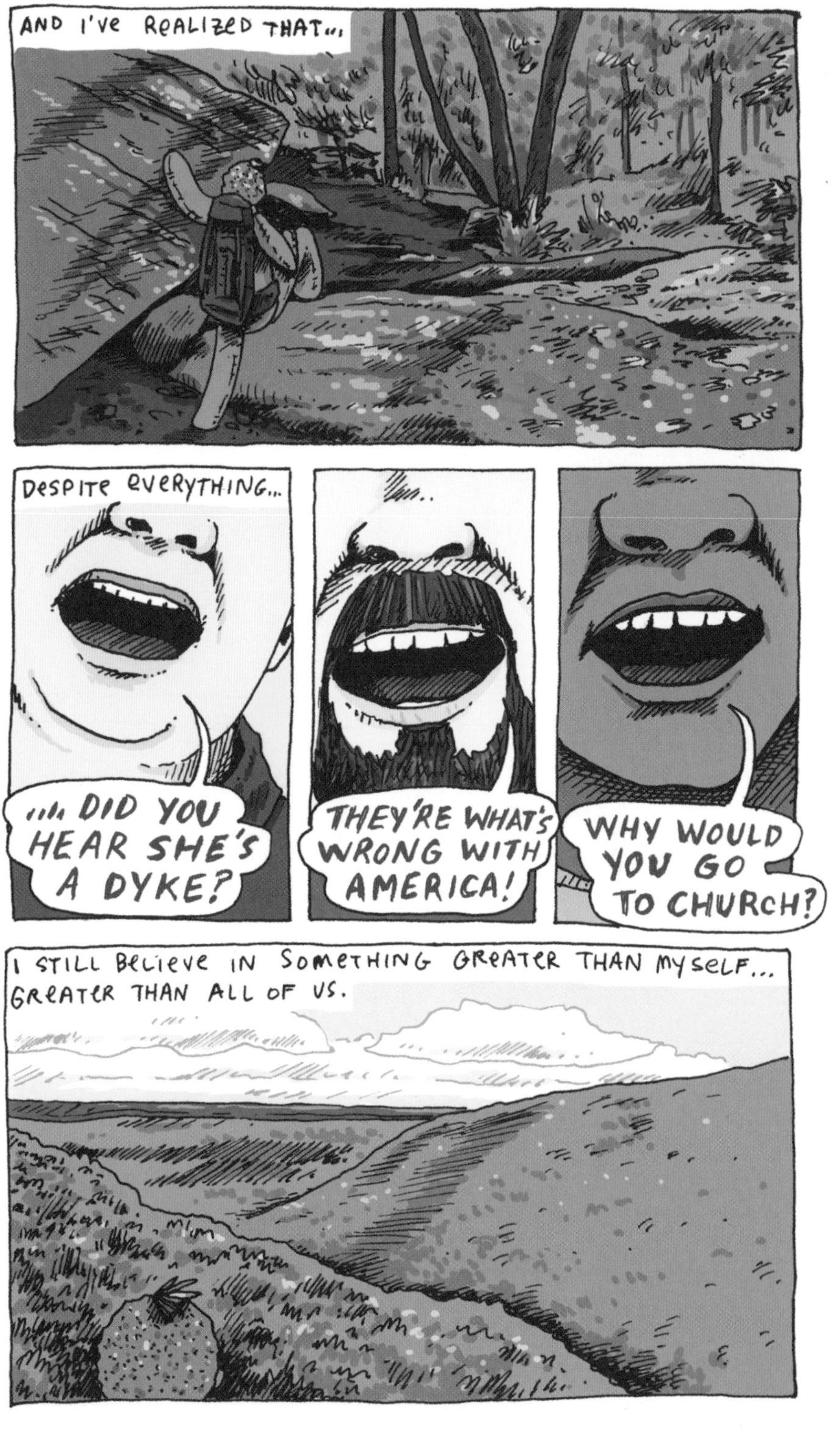
AND I'VE REALIZED THAT...
DESPITE EVERYTHING...
... DID YOU HEAR SHE'S A DYKE?
THEY'RE WHAT'S WRONG WITH AMERICA!
WHY WOULD YOU GO TO CHURCH?
I STILL BELIEVE IN SOMETHING GREATER THAN MYSELF...
GREATER THAN ALL OF US.

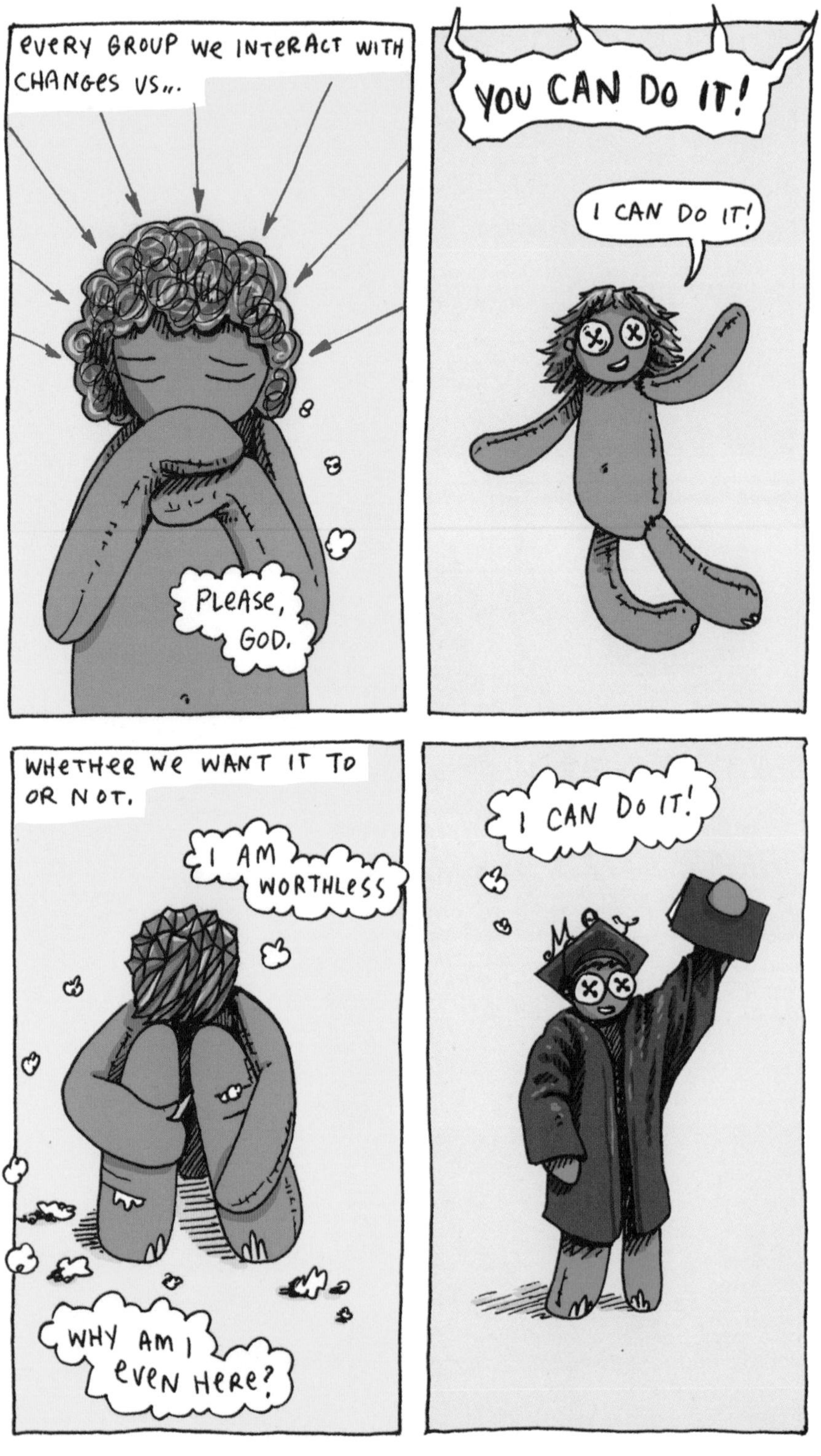
EVERY GROUP WE INTERACT WITH CHANGES US...
PLEASE, GOD.
YOU CAN DO IT!
I CAN DO IT!
WHETHER WE WANT IT TO OR NOT.
I AM WORTHLESS
WHY AM I EVEN HERE?
I CAN DO IT!

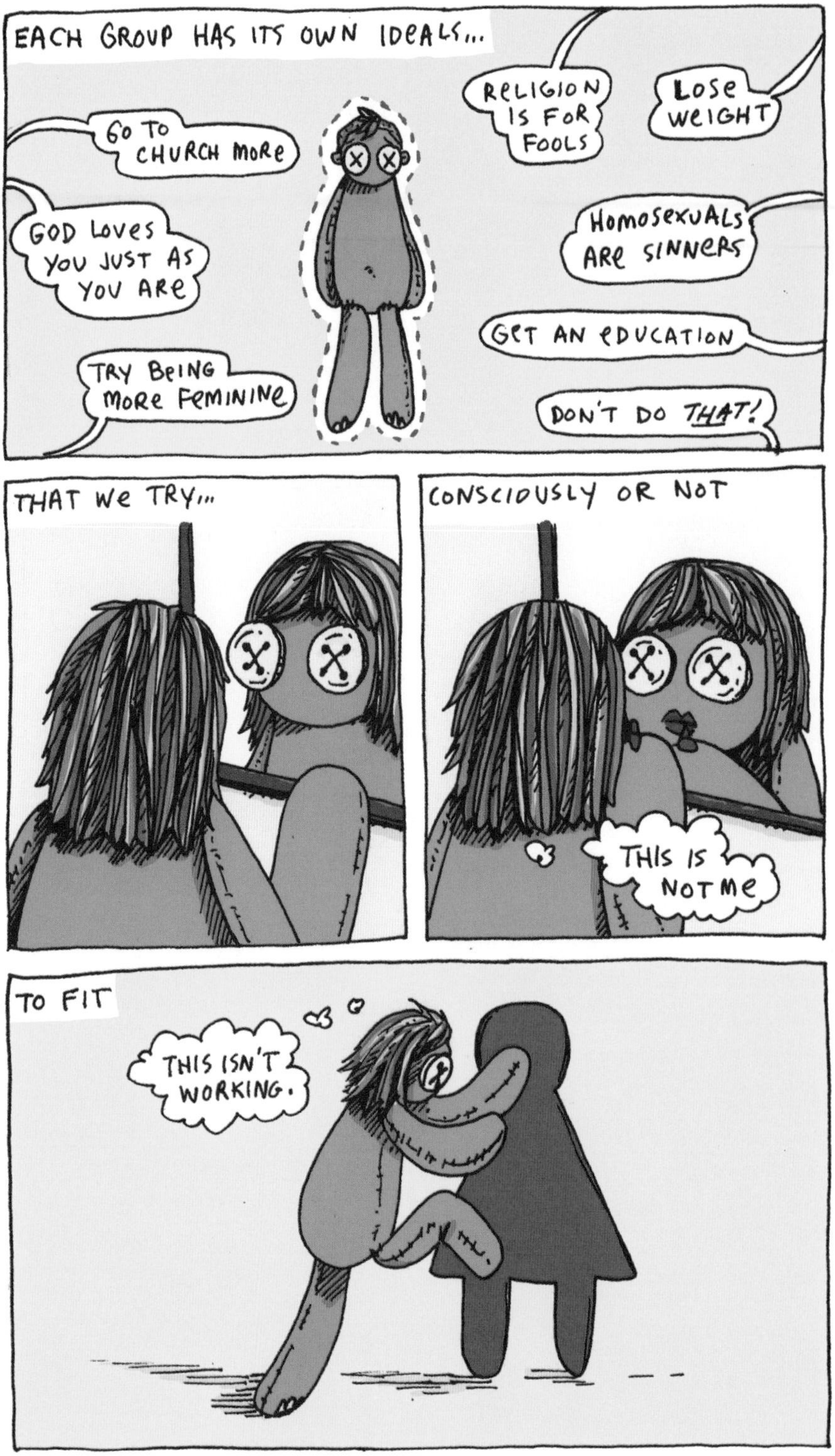
EACH GROUP HAS ITS OWN IDEALS...
GO TO CHURCH MORE
RELIGION IS FOR FOOLS
LOSE WEIGHT
GOD LOVES YOU JUST AS YOU ARE
HOMOSEXUALS ARE SINNERS
GET AN EDUCATION
TRY BEING MORE FEMININE
DON'T DO THAT!
THAT WE TRY...
CONSCIOUSLY OR NOT
THIS IS NOT ME
TO FIT
THIS ISN'T WORKING.

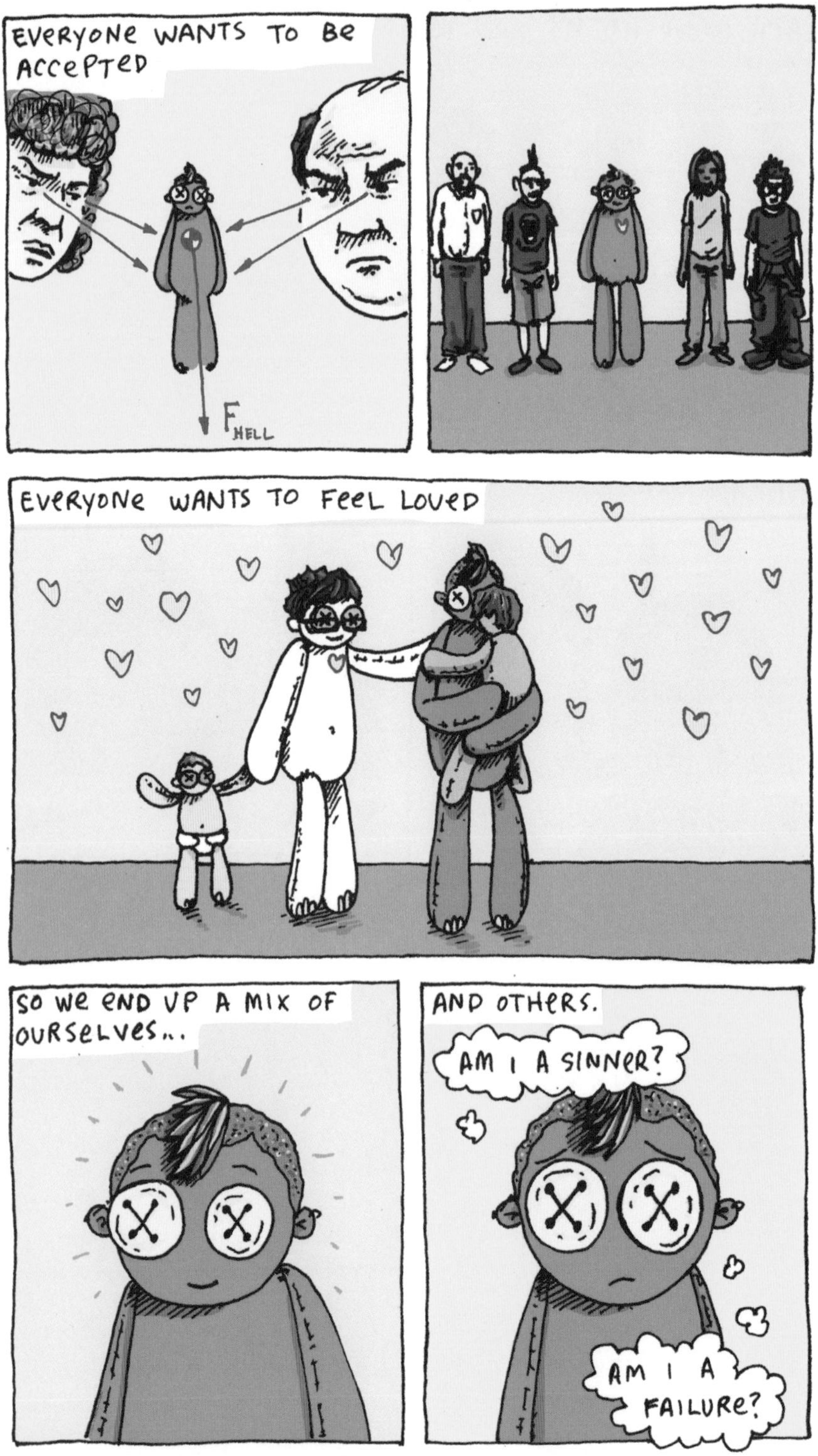
EVERYONE WANTS TO BE ACCEPTED
F HELL
EVERYONE WANTS TO FEEL LOVED
SO WE END UP A MIX OF OURSELVES...
AND OTHERS.
AM I A SINNER?
AM I A FAILURE?

SOME CHANGES LAST...

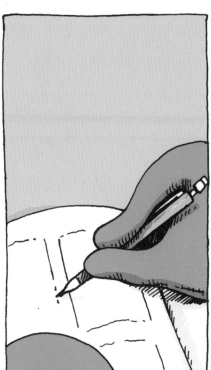

WHILE OTHERS FADE

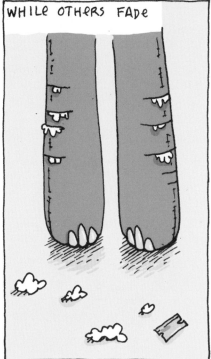

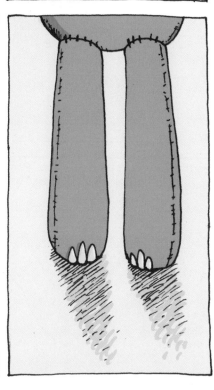

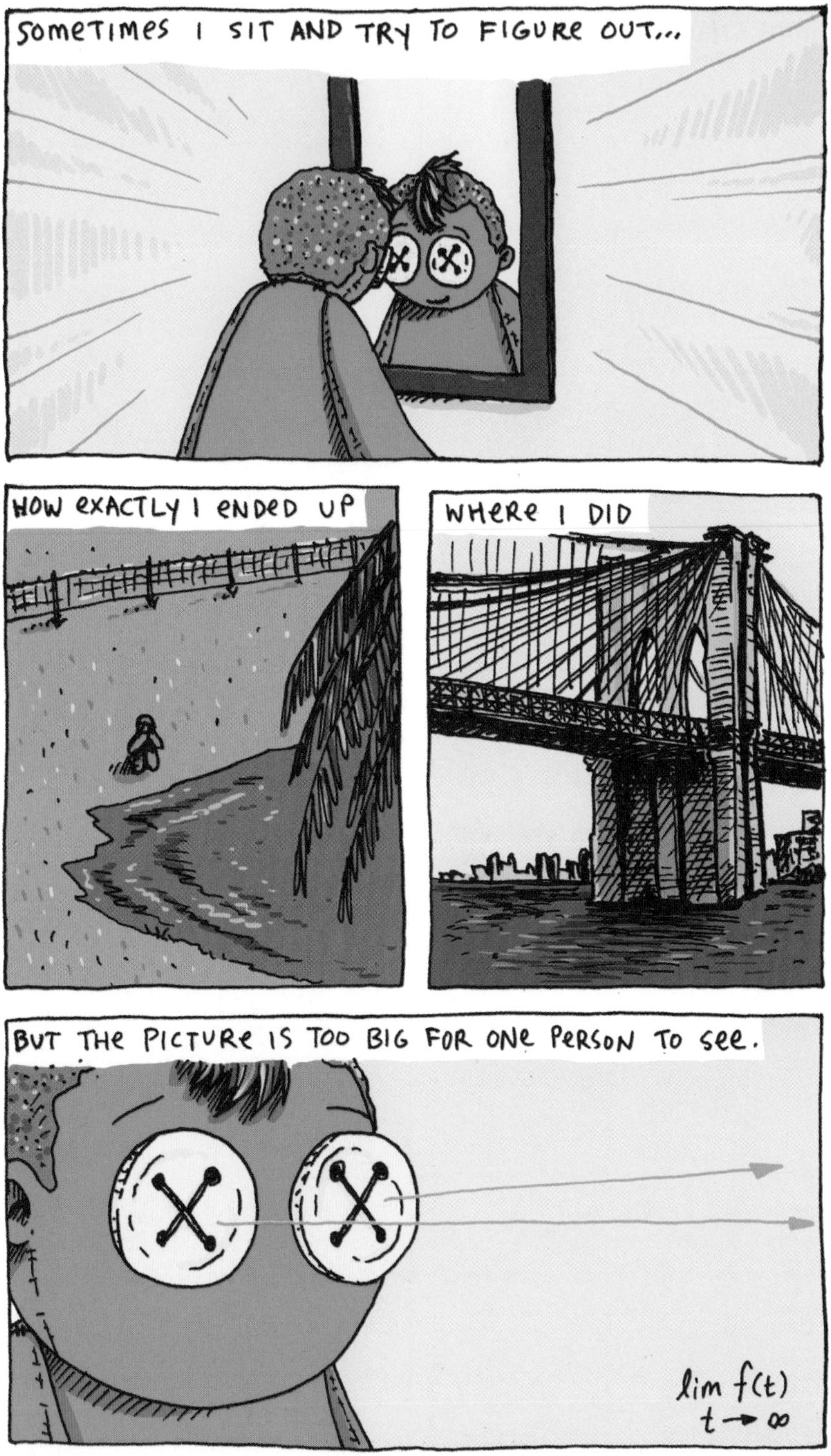
SOMETIMES I SIT AND TRY TO FIGURE OUT...
HOW EXACTLY I ENDED UP
WHERE I DID
BUT THE PICTURE IS TOO BIG FOR ONE PERSON TO SEE.
lim f(t)
t → ∞

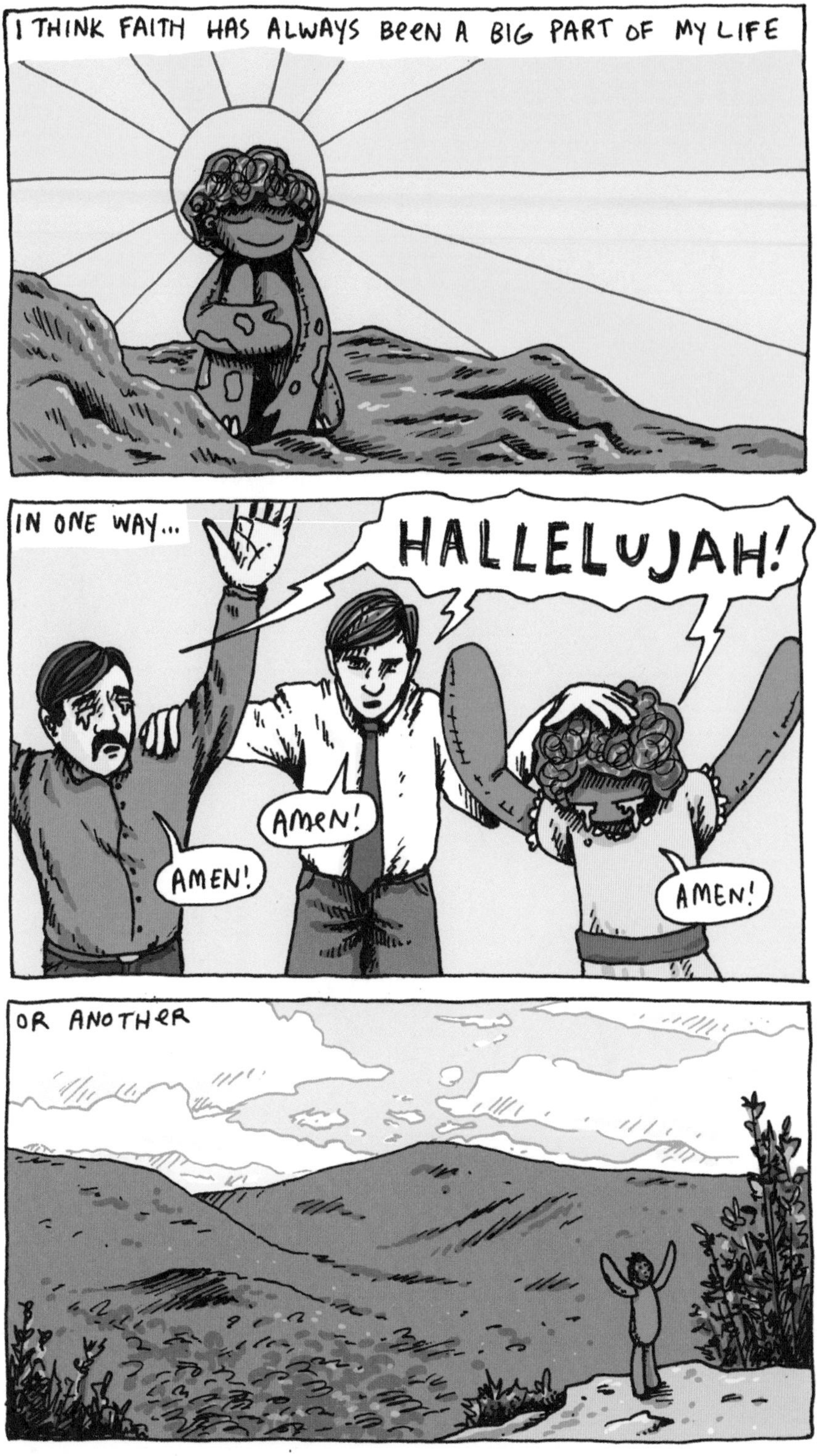
I THINK FAITH HAS ALWAYS BEEN A BIG PART OF MY LIFE
IN ONE WAY...
HALLELUJAH!
AMEN!
AMEN!
AMEN!
OR ANOTHER

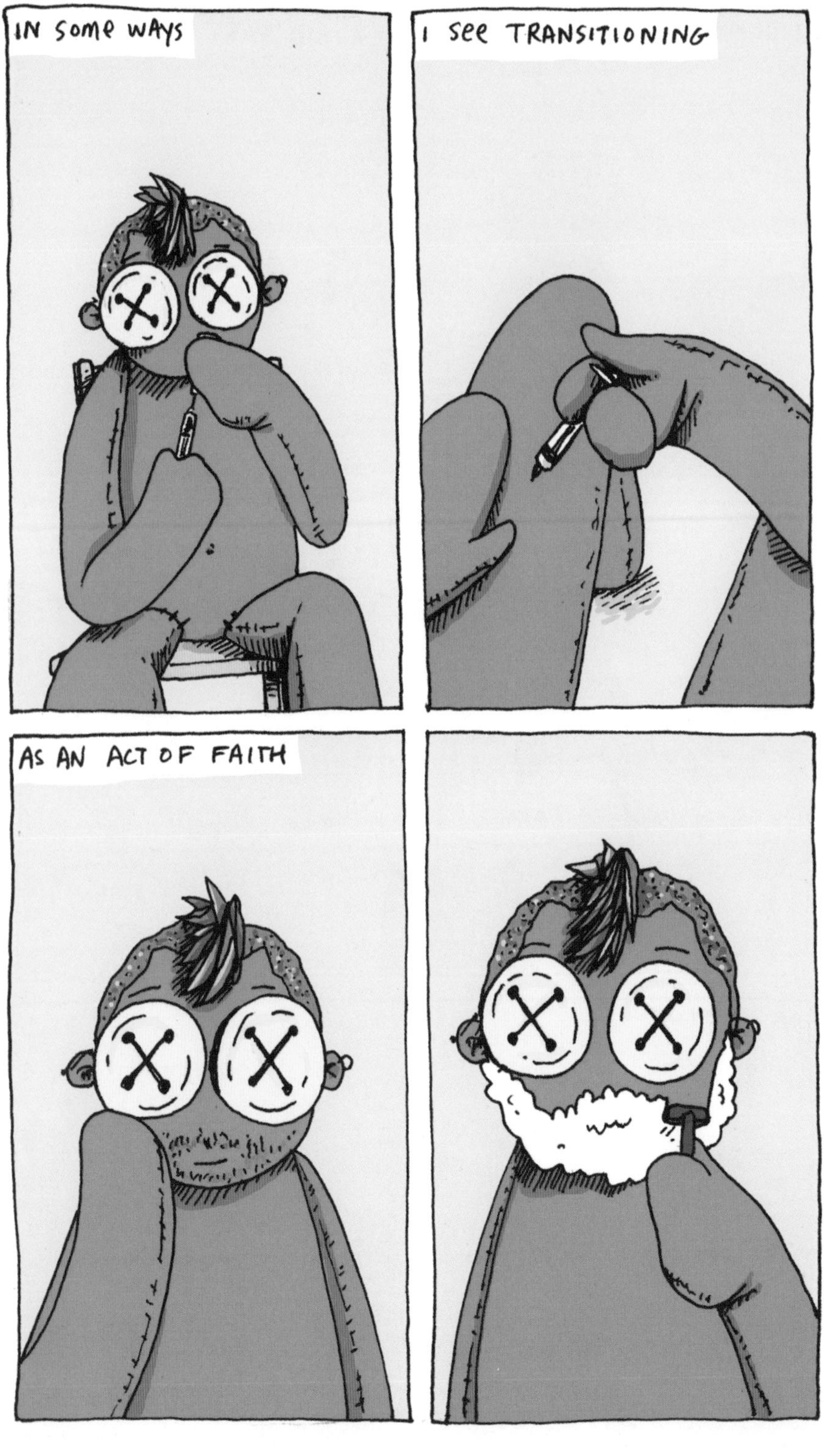
IN SOME WAYS
I SEE TRANSITIONING
AS AN ACT OF FAITH

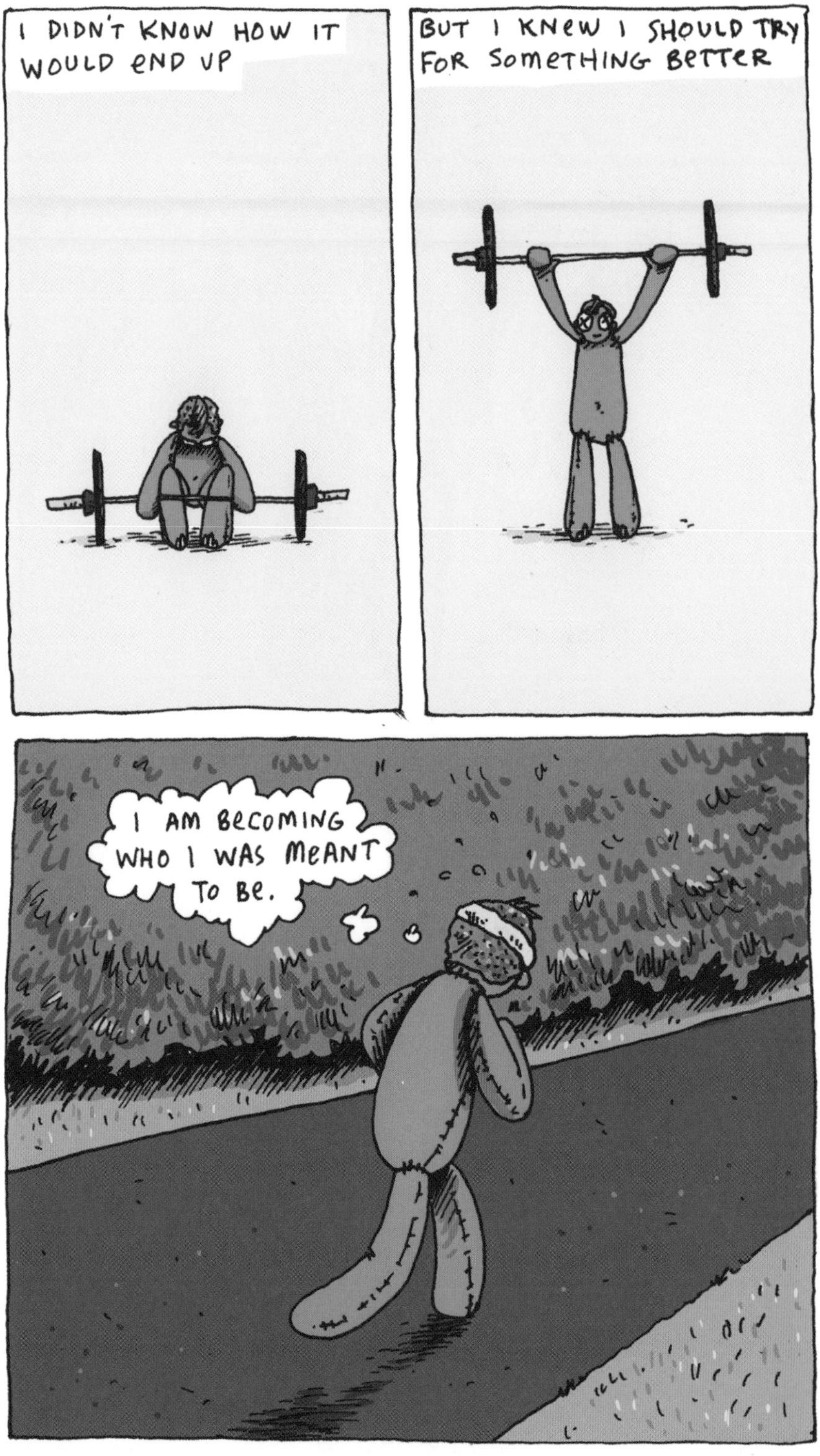
I DIDN'T KNOW HOW IT WOULD END UP
BUT I KNEW I SHOULD TRY FOR SOMETHING BETTER
I AM BECOMING WHO I WAS MEANT TO BE.

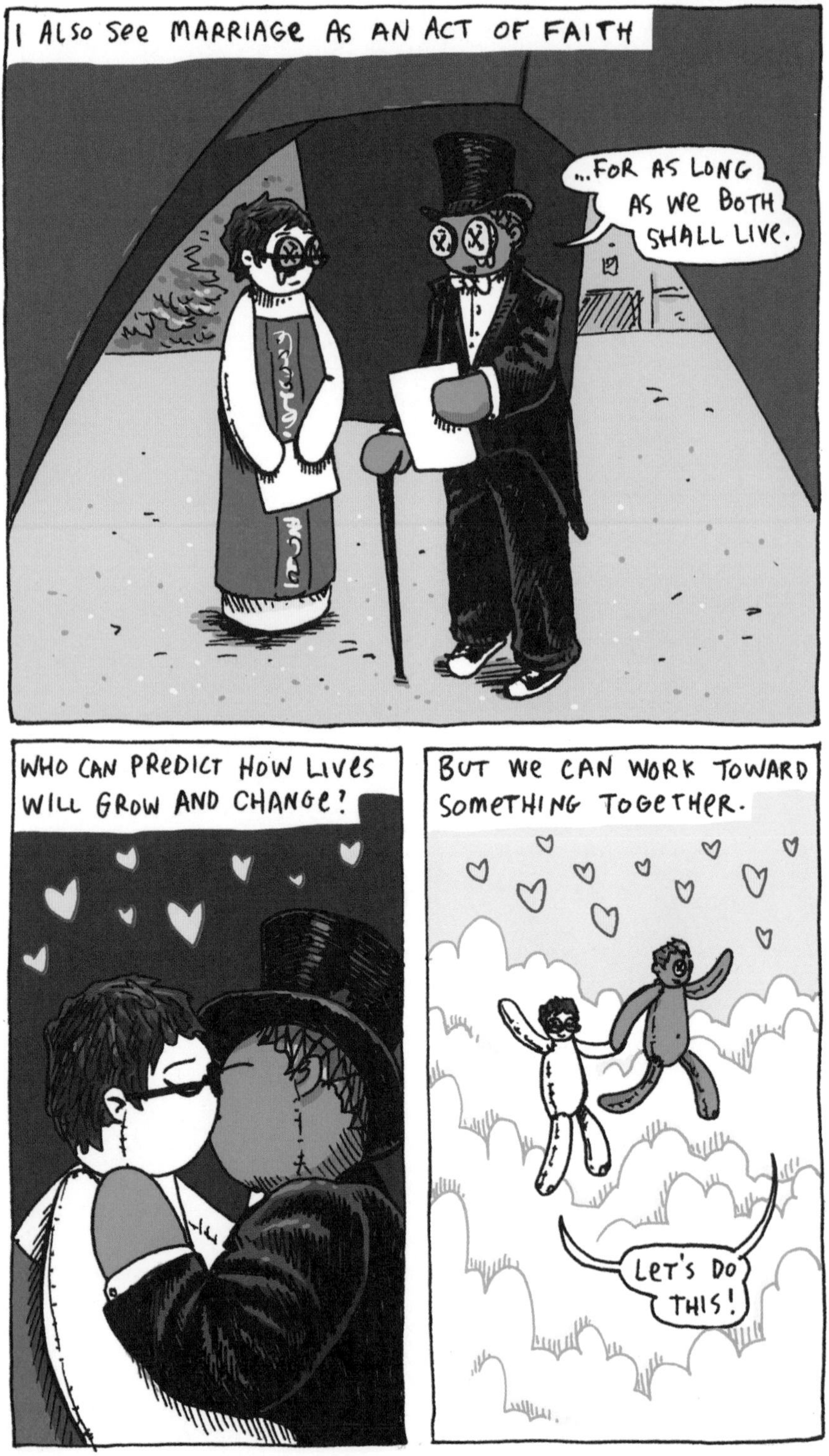
I ALSO SEE MARRIAGE AS AN ACT OF FAITH
...FOR AS LONG AS WE BOTH SHALL LIVE.
WHO CAN PREDICT HOW LIVES WILL GROW AND CHANGE?
BUT WE CAN WORK TOWARD SOMETHING TOGETHER.
LET'S DO THIS!

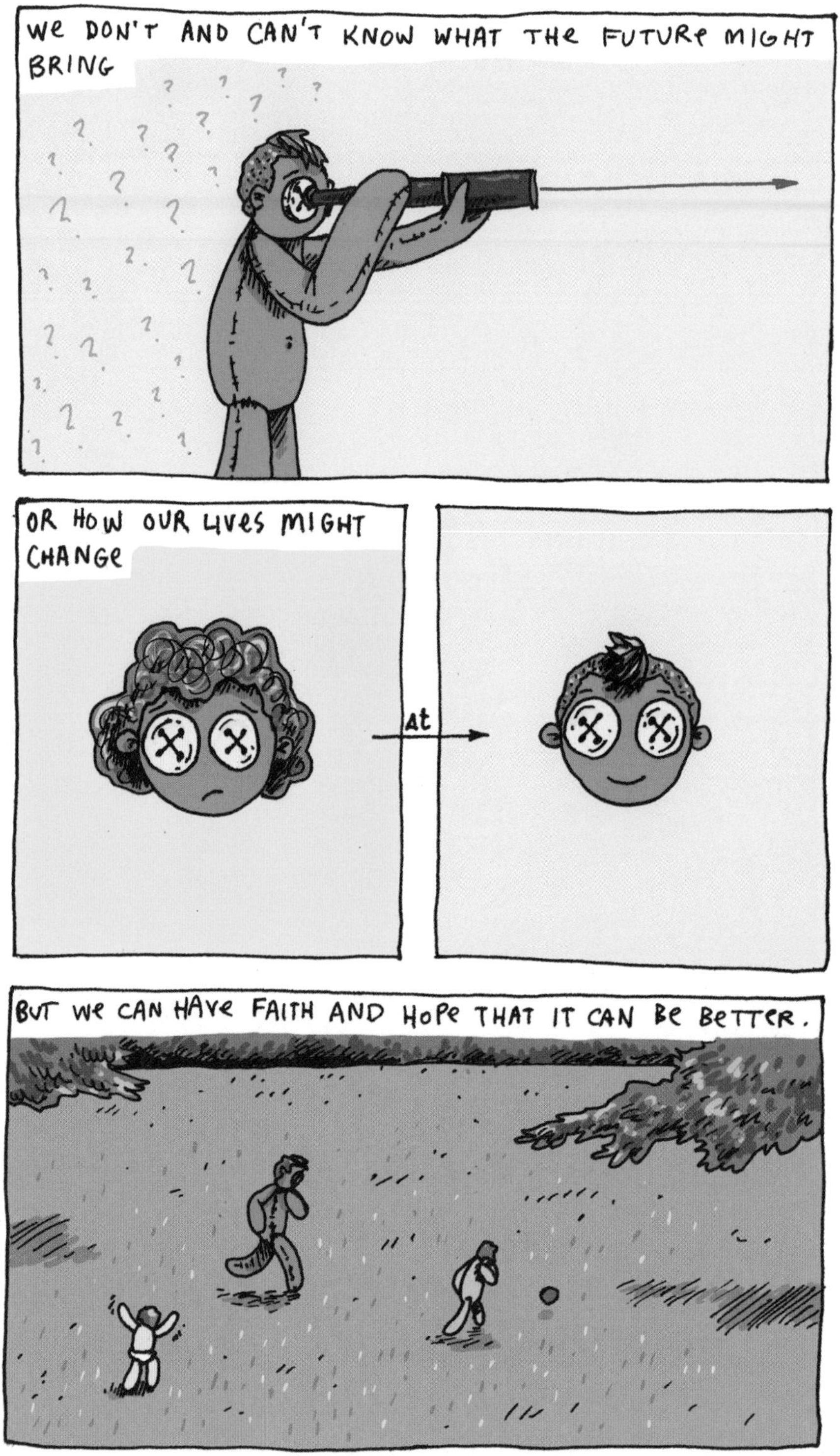
WE DON'T AND CAN'T KNOW WHAT THE FUTURE MIGHT BRING
OR HOW OUR LIVES MIGHT CHANGE
at
BUT WE CAN HAVE FAITH AND HOPE THAT IT CAN BE BETTER.

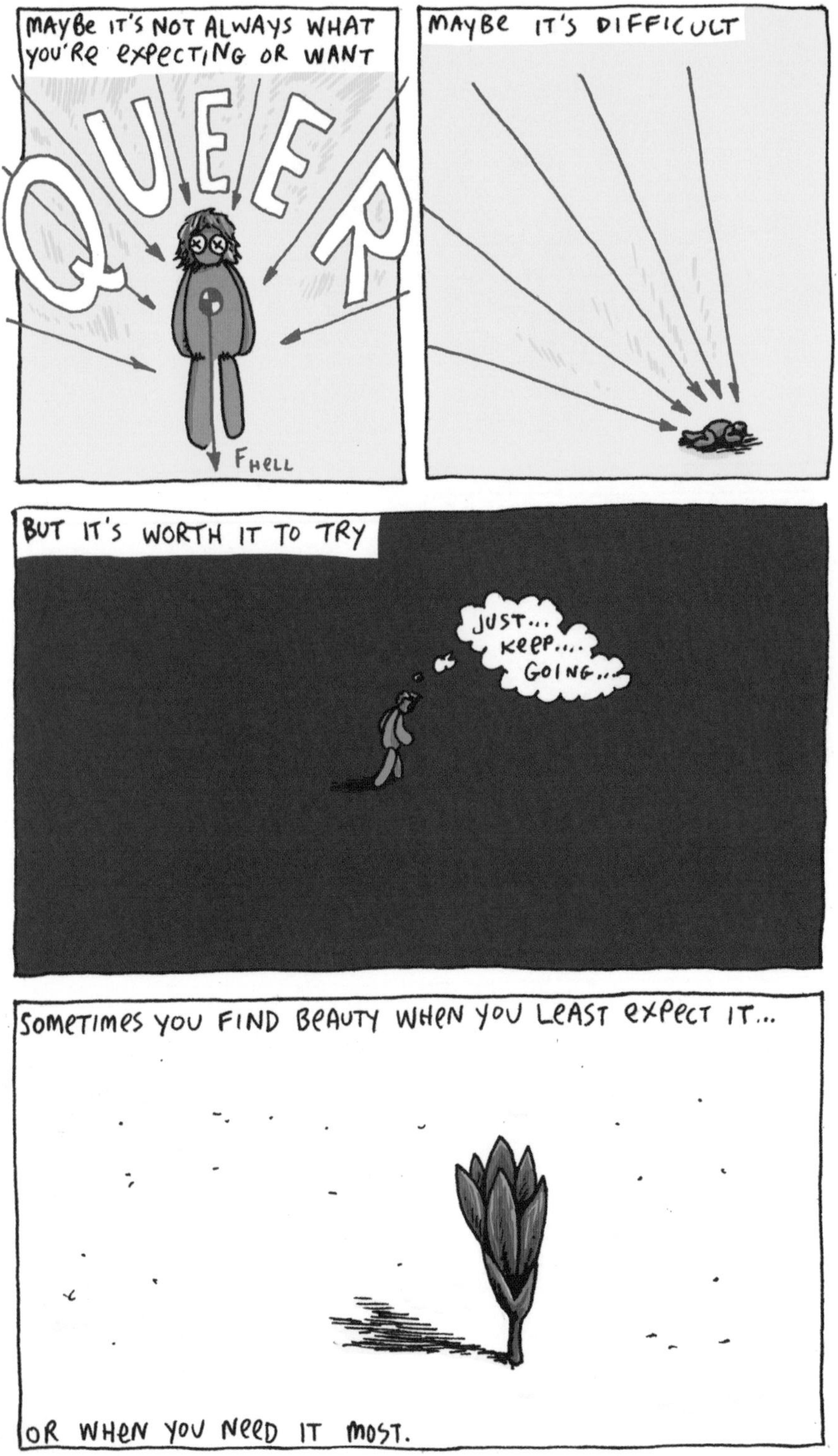
MAYBE IT'S NOT ALWAYS WHAT YOU'RE EXPECTING OR WANT
QUEER
FHELL
MAYBE IT'S DIFFICULT
BUT IT'S WORTH IT TO TRY
JUST... KEEP.... GOING...
SOMETIMES YOU FIND BEAUTY WHEN YOU LEAST EXPECT IT...
OR WHEN YOU NEED IT MOST.

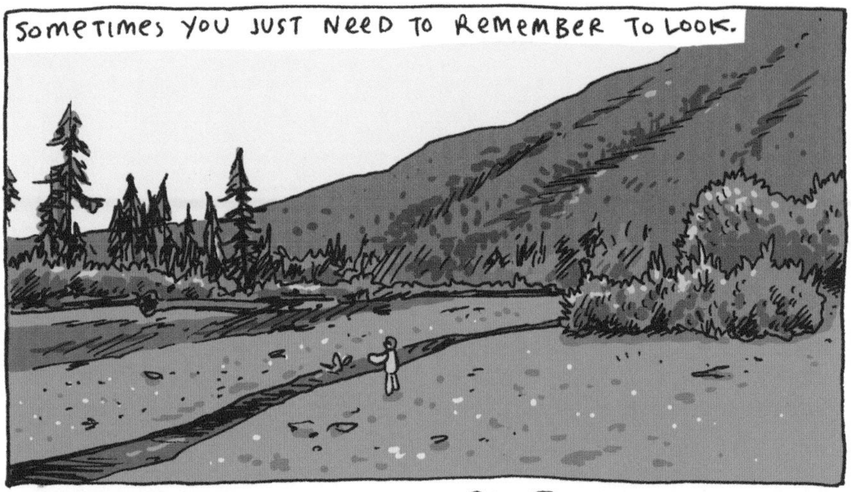
SOMETIMES YOU JUST NEED TO REMEMBER TO LOOK.

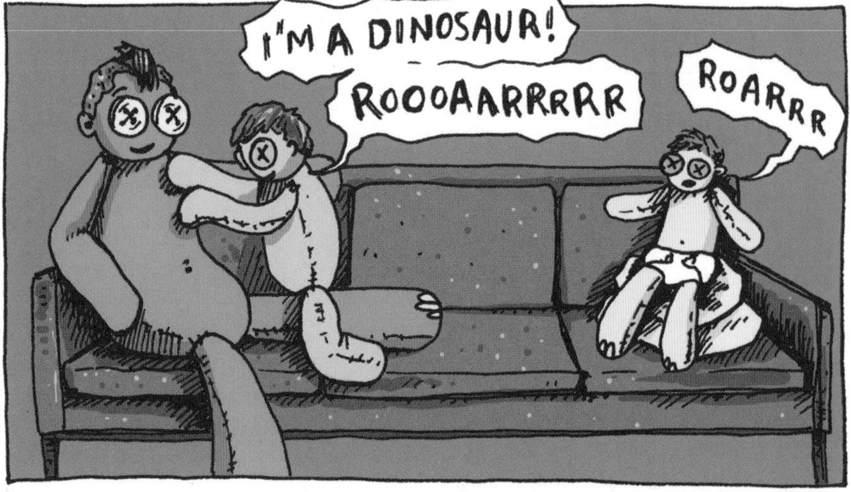
I'M A DINOSAUR!
ROOOAARRRRR
ROARRR

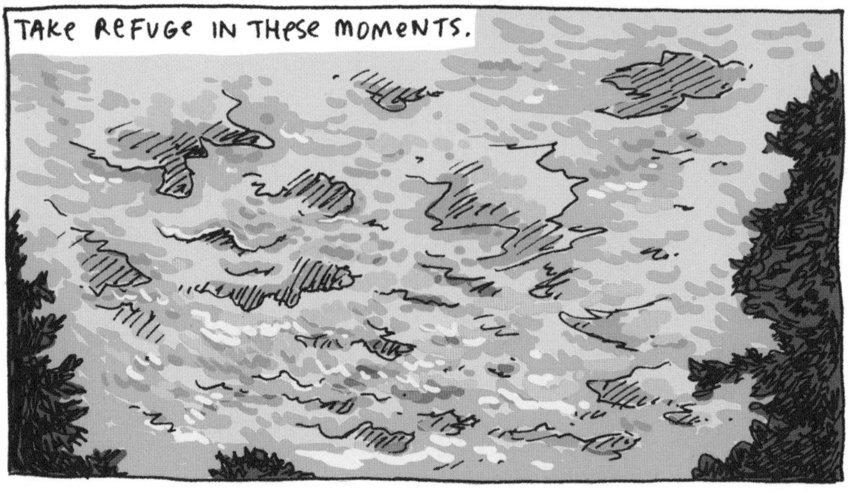
TAKE REFUGE IN THESE MOMENTS.

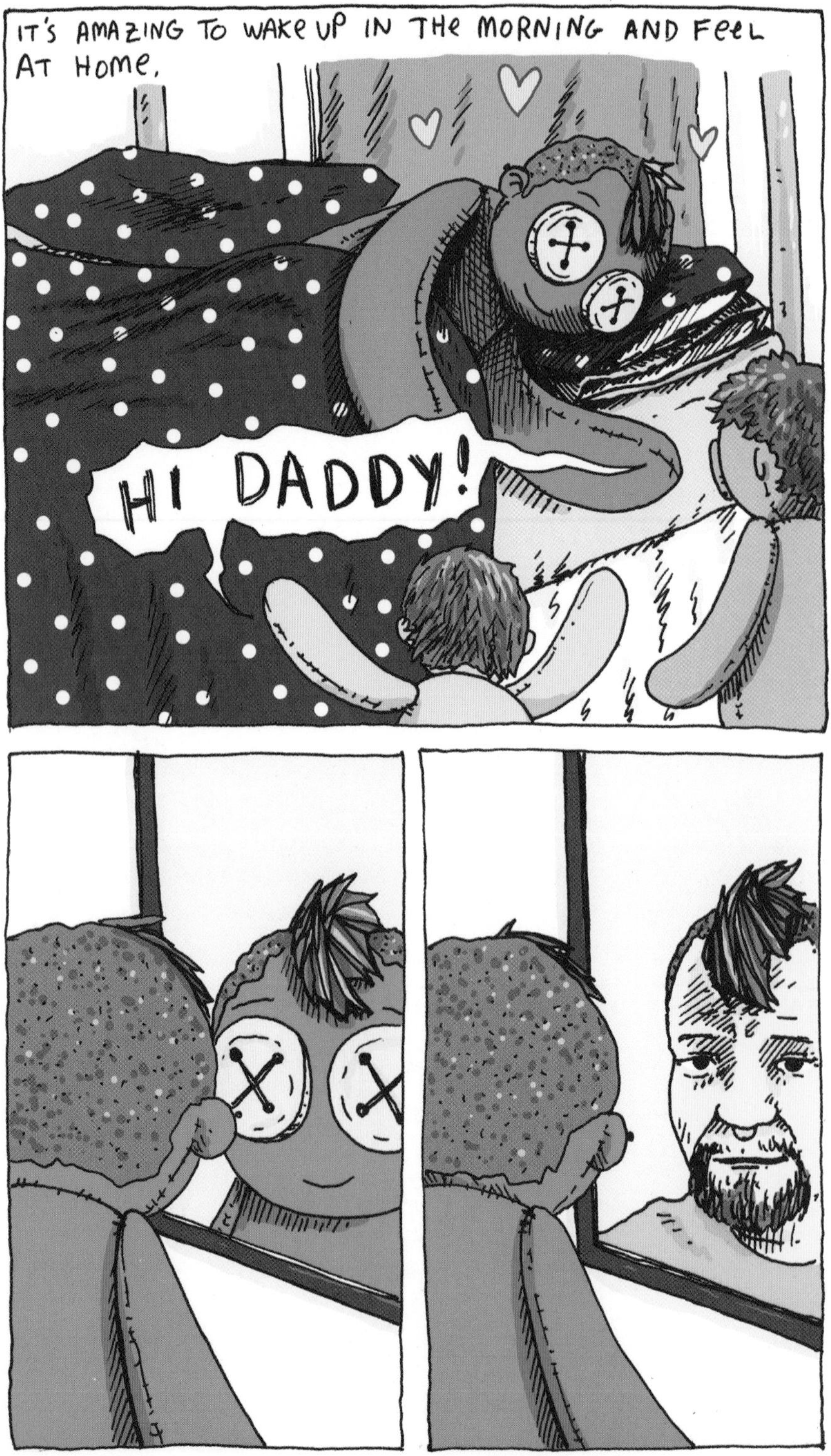
IT'S AMAZING TO WAKE UP IN THE MORNING AND FEEL AT HOME.
HI DADDY!

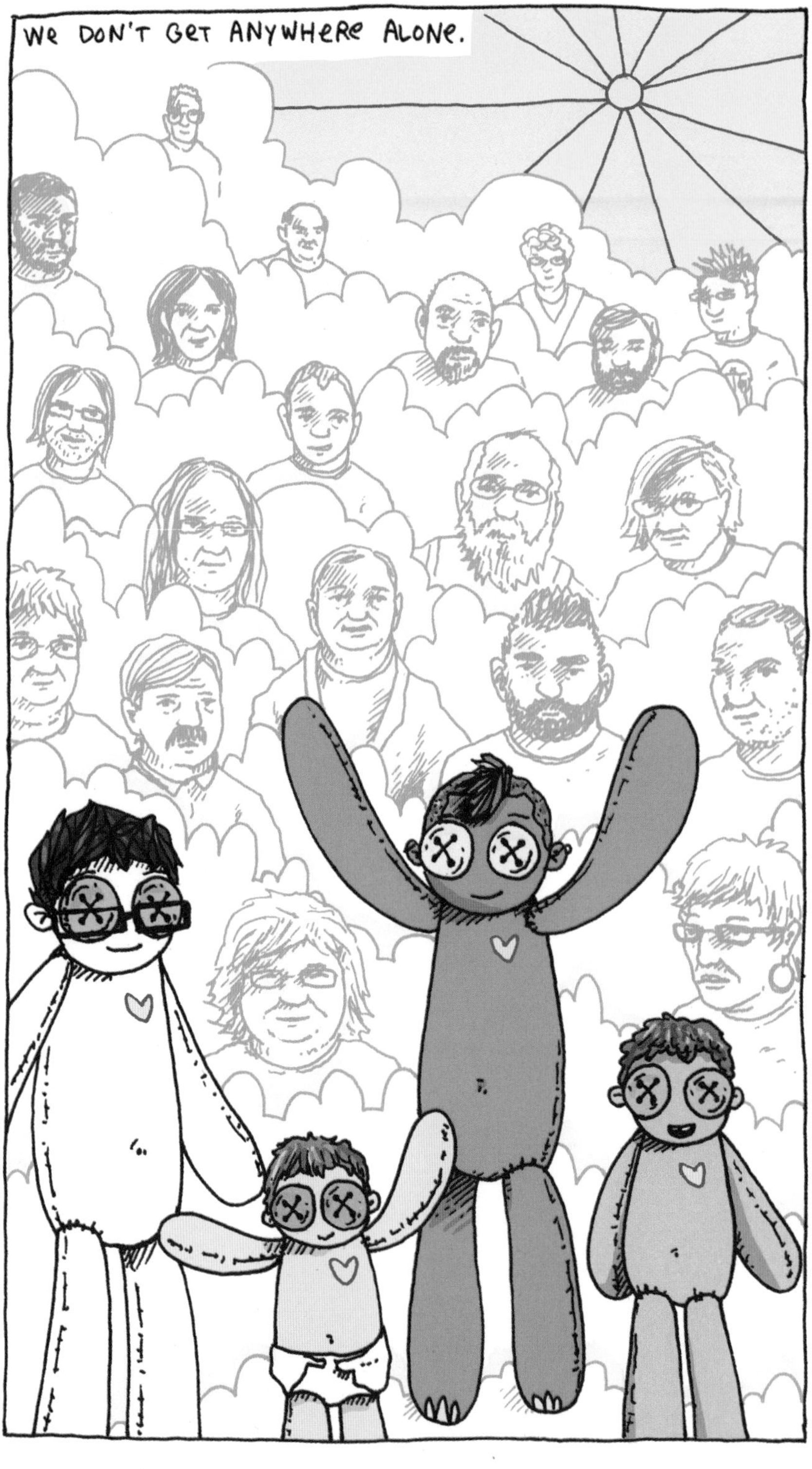
WE DON'T GET ANYWHERE ALONE.

THANKS TO —
CHRISTINA FOR EVERYTHING, ALWAYS,

LEON, KEVIN, ANNIE, BOX, AND ALL THE OTHER COMICS
PEOPLE WHO ENCOURAGED THIS PROJECT ALONG THE WAY.

ALL MY FRIENDS FROM EVERY FLOCK. HOPEFULLY YOU
KNOW WHO YOU ARE. I WOULD THANK YOU ALL
INDIVIDUALLY, BUT THERE'S NOT ENOUGH SPACE IN
ANY BOOK. I WOULDN'T BE HERE WITHOUT YOU.

31901064210059